Understanding
Politics

Ideas, Institutions, and Issues

ELEVENTH EDITION

THOMAS M. MAGSTADT, Ph.D.

The Johns Hopkins School
of Advanced International Studies (SAIS)

CENGAGE
Learning·

Australia • Brazil • Mexico • Singapore • United Kingdom • United States

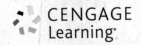
CENGAGE
Learning

Understanding Politics: Ideas, Institutions, and Issues, 11th Edition
Thomas M. Magstadt

Product Director: Suzanne Jeans

Product Manager: Carolyn Merrill

Content Developer: Michael B. Kopf

Content Coordinator: Eireann Aspell

Product Assistant: Abigail Hess

Media Developer: Laura Hildebrand

Marketing Director: Michelle Williams

Marketing Manager: Valerie Hartman

Marketing Development Manager:
   Courtney Wolstoncroft

Manufacturing Planner: Fola Orekoya

Senior Rights Acquisition Specialist:
   Jennifer Meyer Dare

Art and Design Direction, Production
   Management, and Composition: Cenveo®
   Publisher Services

Cover image and chapter-opening images
   used throughout the text courtesy of
   Matthias Kulka/Corbis.

For product information and technology assistance, contact us at
Cengage Learning Academic Resource Center, 1-800-423-0563

For permission to use material from this text or product,
submit all requests online at **www.cengage.com/permissions.**
Further permissions questions can be e-mailed to
permissionrequest@cengage.com.

Library of Congress Control Number: 2013946148

Student Edition:

ISBN-13: 978-1-285-45235-7

ISBN-10: 1-285-45235-6

Cengage Learning

200 First Stamford Place, 4th Floor
Stamford, CT 06902
USA

Cengage Learning is a leading provider of customized learning solutions with office locations around the globe, including Singapore, the United Kingdom, Australia, Mexico, Brazil and Japan. Locate your local office at **international.cengage.com/region.**

Cengage Learning products are represented in Canada by Nelson Education, Ltd.

For your course and learning solutions, visit **www.cengage.com.**

Purchase any of our products at your local college store or at our preferred online store **www.cengagebrain.com.**

Instructors: Please visit **login.cengage.com** and log in to access instructor-specific resources.

Printed in the United States of America
1 2 3 4 5 6 7 17 16 15 14 13

BRIEF CONTENTS

CONTENTS

Contents

We live in a global age. Events anywhere in the world affect people everywhere. Terrorist acts, wars, natural disasters, economic downturns, banking crises, and volatile stock markets are everyday occurrences. Seismic events in faraway places such as the Indian Ocean tsunami in December 2004 that killed more than 200,000 people in western Sumatra, and left an estimated 1.5 million people homeless, or the earthquake that hit the east coast of northern Japan in March 2011, causing a meltdown in the Fukushima Daiichi nuclear facility, may not affect our own lives directly. But if the global economy is disrupted, the indirect effects can be far reaching. The reverse is also true. The 9/11 terrorist attacks happened in the United States but led to costly wars in Afghanistan and Iraq.

Things change with blinding speed in this age of globalization. We now have smart weapons that make it possible to use unmanned aerial vehicles (UAVs), called "drones," armed with guns and bombs, one of the new developments explored in Chapter 15. Both the planes and the weapons are remote controlled, taking the risk out of "flying" combat missions. That's a big change in the art and science of war fighting.

The same technological revolution in the way we fight wars is also changing the way we make things—all kinds of things. For example, using a 3D laser printer it's now possible to produce everything from medical implants to high quality musical instruments, from racing-car parts to solid-state batteries and mechanical devices once made by hand or manufactured by workers on assembly lines.

Another big change is the rise of a global elite. There were more millionaires in the world than Australians in 2010—more than 24 million according to a "Global Wealth Report" by a major Swiss bank. And they control more than a third of total global assets worth nearly $70 trillion. This global trend toward greater economic inequality and concentration of wealth is also happening in the United States, and has been at least since the 1980s. According to *Forbes* magazine, the combined worth of the 400 richest Americans climbed 8% to $1.37 trillion in 2011.

The rise of a new global meritocracy is brain-power driven. In today's world, more than ever before, the wealth of nations and individuals is based on entrepreneurial science and engineering—that is, ideas converted into products for a global marketplace.

Technology is revolutionizing politics, as well as business, but the basic nature of the decision makers, the people who run things, remains unchanged. In Chapter 14 the role Facebook played in the Egyptian uprising in early 2011 is featured. But the struggle for power continues unabated; so, too, does the search for peace, order, and justice.

Paradoxically, the limits of power, even in its most concentrated forms, are everywhere apparent—from ancient places, such as Palestine and Iraq in the Middle East and Afghanistan in Central Asia; to Europe where the "euro crisis" threatens to undo a mighty supranational project six decades in the making;

to the United States of America with its relatively short history and even shorter memory. The cost of failed policies and corrupt, incompetent leadership is also apparent in our world—and in our nation's capital, Washington, D.C.

But when it comes to the quality of citizenship, the implications of recent advances in telecommunications, Internet access, and social networking are not so clear. It's easier than ever in our wired world to learn more about what's going on in the world, be more attuned to the news, and vote more intelligently than ever. Studies show, however, a *decline* in civic knowledge and education in the United States.

This double deficiency—both at the top and bottom of political society—is a kind of stealth crisis, one that, not unlike a stealth bomber, gives ample evidence of its existence but continues to go largely unnoticed. Meanwhile, there is no absence of injustice, intolerance, misguided idealism, zealotry, and human suffering—proof enough that the ever-more polluted and crowded planet we inhabit has not changed for the better, even though the West's fortunate few are far more secure and comfortable than the vast majority who live in the so-called developing regions of the globe.

Since *Understanding Politics* made its debut in 1984, nothing has shaken my conviction that politics matters. I still believe now, as I did then, that as citizens in a country that claims to be a model democracy, students need to acquire a working knowledge of the political and economic forces that shape our world. Ironically, as news and information have become more and more accessible—thanks in no small part to the Internet—interest in public affairs and a willingness to get involved have declined. Indeed, many Americans are not engaged in the political process except perhaps to vote.

The study of politics is a gateway to a broader and better understanding of human nature, society, and the world. This idea is what originally inspired the writing of *Understanding Politics*. It is also what has sustained my own interest through multiple revisions—that, plus a sense that the book was, is, and always will be essentially a work in progress.

A successful introduction to politics must balance two key objectives: (1) dispel anxieties associated with the attempt to understand political science, especially for the uninitiated; and (2) provide the intellectual stimulation necessary to challenge today's college students. This book is testimony to the fact that the science and philosophy of politics fall squarely within the liberal arts tradition. The phrase "science and philosophy of politics" points to one of the deepest cleavages within the discipline: analysts who approach politics from the standpoint of science often stress the importance of power, whereas those who view it through the wide-angle lens of philosophy often emphasize the importance of justice. But the distinction between power and justice—like that between science and philosophy—is too often exaggerated.

Moral and political questions are ultimately inseparable in the real world. That is, the exercise of power, in itself, is not what makes an action political; rather, what makes power *political* is the debate about its proper or improper uses and who benefits or suffers as a result. Thus, whenever questions of fairness are raised in the realm of public policy (for example, questions concerning abortion, capital punishment, or the use of force by police or the military), the essential ingredients of politics are present. Excessive attention to either the concept of power or that of morality is likely to confound our efforts in making sense of politics or, for that matter, in finding lasting solutions to the problems that afflict and divide us. Thus, it is always necessary to balance the equation, tempering political realism with a penchant for justice.

Similarly, the dichotomy so often drawn between facts and values is misleading. Rational judgments—in the sense of reasoned opinions about what is good and just—are sometimes more definitive (or less elusive) than facts. For example, the proposition that "genocide is evil" is true. (Its opposite— "genocide is good"—is morally indefensible.) It is a well-known fact that Adolf Hitler and the Nazis committed genocide. We can therefore say that Hitler was evil *as a matter of fact* and not "simply" because mass murder is abhorrent to our *personal* values.

Other value-laden propositions can be stated with a high degree of probability but not absolute certainty. For example, "If you want to reduce violent crime, first reduce poverty." Still other questions of this kind may be too difficult or too close to call—in the abortion controversy, for example, does the right of a woman to biological self-determination outweigh the right to life? It makes no sense to ignore the most important questions in life simply because the answers are not easy. Even when the right answers are unclear, it is often possible to recognize wrong answers—a moderating force in itself.

This book gives due attention to contemporary political issues without ignoring the more enduring questions that often underlie them. For example, a voter's dilemma as to who would make the best mayor, governor, or president raises deeper questions: What qualifications are necessary for public office? What is wrong with a system that all too often fails to produce distinguished— or distinctive—choices? Similarly, conflicts between nation-states or social groups raise philosophical as well as empirical questions about why human beings continue to fight and kill one another on a mass scale.

Although I have tried to minimize the use of names and dates, political ideas cannot be fruitfully discussed in a historical vacuum. The choice of examples throughout the text is dictated by a particular understanding of the relationship between politics and history. The consequences of certain events in the first half of the last century—World Wars I and II, the October Revolution in Lenin's Russia, the Holocaust in Hitler's Germany—are still present today. We too seldom think or talk about "living history"—about all the ways antecedents (decisions and actions in the past) influence the present and constrain the future.

Inevitably, some themes and events are discussed in more than one chapter: The world of politics is more like a seamless web than a chest of drawers. In politics, as in nature, a given event or phenomenon often has many meanings and is connected to other events and phenomena in ways that are not immediately apparent. Emphasizing the common threads among major political ideas, institutions, and issues helps beginning students make sense of seemingly unrelated bits and pieces of the political puzzle. Seeing how the various parts fit together is a necessary step toward understanding politics.

Understanding Politics employs a foundation-building approach to the study of politics and government. It begins by identifying political phenomena, such as war and terrorism, that students find interesting and then seeks to describe and explain them. In an effort to build on students' natural curiosity, I try to avoid much of the jargon and many of the technical or arcane disputes that too often characterize the more advanced literature in the field of political science.

Rather than probe the deepest recesses of a single discipline, the book unapologetically borrows insights from various disciplines, including history, economics, psychology, and sociology, as well as philosophy. It is intended to be a true liberal arts approach to the study of government and politics. The goal is ambitious: to challenge students to begin a lifelong learning process that alone can lead to a generation of citizens who are well informed, actively engaged, self-confident, and thoughtful and who have a capacity for indignation in the face of public hypocrisy, dishonesty, stupidity, or gross ineptitude.

Chapter 1, "Introduction: The Study of Politics," defines the basic concepts of politics and centers on how and why it is studied. This chapter lays the groundwork for the remainder of the text and stands alone as its introduction. Chapter 2, "The Idea of the Public Good: Ideologies and Isms," deals with basic belief systems, including ideologies of the Right and Left, such as communism and fascism, and "isms" of the Right and Left, such as liberalism and conservatism.

Part 1, "Comparative Political Systems: Models and Theories," analyzes utopian, democratic, and authoritarian forms of government, as well as political systems caught in the difficult transition from authoritarian to democratic institutions. This part, which comprises Chapters 3 through 6, looks at different kinds of political regimes in a theoretical light.

Part 2, "Established and Emerging Democracies," consists of three chapters that examine parliamentary democracies (Chapter 7), transitional states (Chapter 8), and developing countries (Chapter 9). Virtually all governments in today's world either aspire to some form of democracy or claim to be "democratic." This amazing fact is itself irrefutable evidence of the power of an idea. Though often abused, the idea of democracy has fired the imaginations of people everywhere for more than two centuries. In an age when bad news is written in blood and body counts are more likely to refer to innocent civilians than armed combatants, we would do well to remember that democratic ideals have never before been so warmly embraced or so widely (if imperfectly) institutionalized.

In Part 3, "Politics by Civil Means: Citizens, Leaders, and Policies," four chapters (10 through 13) focus on the political process and public policy. The United States is featured in this section, which examines citizenship and political socialization, political participation (including opinion polling and voting behavior), political organization (parties and interest groups), political leadership, political ideologies (or divergent "approaches to the public good"), and contemporary public policy issues.

Part 4, "Politics by Violent Means: Revolution, War, and Terrorism," examines conflict as a special and universal problem in politics. It divides the problem into three categories: revolution, terrorism, and war (corresponding to Chapters 14, 15, and 16, respectively). Viewed from the aftermath of 9/11, when the president of the United States declared international terrorism to be the preeminent threat in the world and blurred the distinction between counter-terrorist policy and all-out war, Part 4 is guaranteed to stimulate the curiosity of students and provoke spirited class discussions. Invading and occupying a country (Iraq) that had nothing to do with the 9/11 attacks, did not possess "weapons of mass destruction," and did not pose a threat to the United States was a curious response to the problem posed by the existence of a malevolent terrorist network (al Qaeda) harbored by a fundamentalist regime (the Taliban) in a land (Afghanistan) virtually impossible to subdue by conquest and notoriously impervious to outside influence. Indeed, this response affords ample opportunity for contemplation about the motives, causes, and consequences of war at the beginning of a new millennium.

Finally, Part 5, "Politics without Government," introduces students to key concepts in the study of international relations, describes key patterns, and discusses perennial problems. Chapter 17 examines the basic principles and concepts in international relations and the evolving structure and context of world politics, as well as draws attention to a number of global issues. Chapter 18 looks at international law and organizations and the search for world order—a fitting note on which to end the course.

In this new edition—the eleventh—I have retained the pedagogical features that characterized the previous ten editions. Thus, each chapter begins with an outline and ends with a summary, Internet links, and review questions. With this edition, however, the glossary is posted online (www.cengage.com/login) as well as included at the end of the book. As in the past, the notes precede the index at the back of the book. In addition, the text contains a wide variety of photos, figures, maps, tables, and features, many of which have been revised or replaced with updated materials.

NEW IN THE ELEVENTH EDITION

The eleventh edition includes three kinds of features, which have been reworked and updated wherever necessary. "Maps That Matter" are devoted to political geography. Some past events and achievements of enduring political importance are highlighted in "Landmarks in History." Finally, "Politics and Ideas" give students a bird's-eye view of perennial questions and key issues in political theory and philosophy.

As always, major developments in the United States and on the world stage have intervened since the last edition went to press. This edition covers the 2012 presidential campaign and the reelection of the country's first African American president; the battle of the budget and acrimonious partisan politics surrounding the so-called fiscal cliff; the use of the filibuster to block votes in the U.S. Senate; and the deep divisions in U.S. society over such issues as gun control, income inequality, immigration, abortion, health care, tax fairness, gay rights, and gender equality. The new edition also expands on the previous discussion of the role of state regulation—and the limits of deregulation—in market economies, an issue that has resurfaced with a vengeance in the United States in recent years due, in large part, to the banking crisis of 2008, the Great Recession it set in motion, and the multi-billion-dollar federal bailout of "too big to fail" financial institutions and corporations.

Readers can expect to find broad coverage of recent developments beyond the United States as well. Coverage of the "euro crisis" is expanded and updated. There is also much new material covering the 2012 election of Socialist François Hollande as France's new president; the 2012–2013 changing of the guard in China; the Fukushima Daiichi nuclear disaster in Japan (and subsequent leadership change); the bloody civil war in Syria, and the continuing turmoil in the Middle East and North Africa. The "agenda" samplers for the four liberal democracies featured in Chapter 7 (Great Britain, France, Germany, and Japan) reflect developments through 2012 and the first half of 2013. The material covering India and Israel, two of the world's most challenged representative democracies, is updated but, sadly, the existential circumstances—the predicaments and realities they face—have not changed for either country (and are not likely to change anytime in the expectable future).

There are other revisions, text enhancements, and new features too numerous to mention. I personally selected much of the art work appearing in this edition—a lot of work, but worth the effort and fun to boot. Many of the photographers featured in these pages are amateurs with a good camera, a great eye, and a generous spirit.

Supplements for Students and Instructors

Online PowerLecture with Cognero® for Magstadt's *Understanding Politics, 11th Edition*
ISBN-13: 978-1-285-77571-5

This PowerLecture is an all-in-one online multimedia resource for class preparation, presentation, and testing. Accessible through Cengage.com/login with your faculty account, you will find available for download: book-specific Microsoft® PowerPoint® presentations; a Test Bank in both Microsoft® Word® and Cognero® formats; an Instructor Manual; Microsoft® PowerPoint® Image Slides; and a JPEG Image Library.

The Test Bank, offered in Microsoft® Word® and Cognero® formats, contains multiple-choice and essay questions for each chapter. Cognero® is a flexible, online system that allows you to author, edit, and manage test bank content for *Understanding Politics, 11th Edition*. Create multiple test versions instantly and deliver through your LMS from your classroom, or wherever you may be, with no special installs or downloads required.

The Instructor's Manual contains for each chapter: an outline and summary; critical thinking questions; in-class activities; lecture launching suggestions; a list of key terms with definitions; and suggested readings and Web resources.

The Microsoft® PowerPoint® presentations are ready-to-use, visual outlines of each chapter. These presentations are easily customized for your lectures and offered along with chapter-specific Microsoft® PowerPoint® Image Slides and JPEG Image Libraries. Access your Online PowerLecture at www.cengage.com/login.

Free Companion Web Site for Magstadt's *Understanding Politics, 11th Edition*
ISBN-13: 978-1-285-45241-8

This free companion website for *Understanding Politics, 11th Edition* is accessible through cengagebrain.com allows access to chapter specific interactive learning tools including flashcards, quizzes, glossaries, and more.

CourseReader 0-30: Introduction to Political Science
PAC ISBN: 978-1-133-23216-2
IAC ISBN: 978-1-111-47997-8

CourseReader: Introduction to Political Science allows you to create your reader, your way, in just minutes. This affordable, fully customizable online reader provides access to thousands of permissions-cleared readings, articles, primary sources, and audio and video selections from the regularly-updated Gale research library database. This easy-to-use solution allows you to search for and select just the material you want for your courses. Each selection opens with a descriptive introduction to provide context, and concludes with critical-thinking and multiple-choice questions to reinforce key points. CourseReader is loaded with convenient tools like highlighting, printing, note-taking, and downloadable PDFs and MP3 audio files for each reading. CourseReader is the perfect complement to any Political Science course. It can be bundled with your current textbook, sold alone, or integrated into your learning management system. CourseReader 0-30 allows access to up to 30 selections in the reader. Please contact your Cengage sales representative for details.

I also encourage readers to visit my WorldViewWest website at www.worldviewwest.com and to direct any comments or questions to tmagstadt@cs.com.

ACKNOWLEDGMENTS

Through eleven editions and more than two decades, many individuals associated with several different publishing houses and universities have helped make this book a success. Among the scholars and teachers who reviewed the work for previous editions in manuscript, offering helpful criticisms and suggestions, were Donald G. Baker, Southampton College, Long Island University; Peter Longo, University of Nebraska at Kearney; Iraj Paydar, Bellevue Community College; Ruth Ann Strickland, Appalachian State University; Sean K. Anderson, Idaho State University; Daniel Aseltine, Chaffey College; Thomas A. Kolsky, Montgomery County Community College; Linda Valenty, California Polytechnic State University—San Luis Obispo; Andrei Korobkov, Middle Tennessee University; Ethan Fishman, University of South Alabama; Mack Murray, Seattle Community College; Lawrence Okere, University of Arkansas; Keith Milks, Nash Community College; Frank Bean, Garden City Community College; Jean-Gabriel Jolivet, South-western College; Jose Lopez-Gonzalez, Towson University; and Naomi Robertson, Macon State College.

For the current edition, that vital role fell to reviewers: Lynn Maurer, Southern Illinois University at Edwardsville; Steven Majstorovic, University of Wisconsin at Eau Claire; Shari MacLachlan, Palm Beach State College;

Henry Patterson, Lorain County Community College; Henry Steck, SUNY-Cortland; and Bruce Frassinelli, Lehigh Carbon Community College.

I also wish to express my appreciation to editors Carolyn Merrill, Anita Devine, and Tom Finn who were all instrumental in getting the eleventh edition out in a timely fashion. Finally, as always, I owe a huge debt of gratitude to my family and friends, especially Mary Jo (who died in 1990), Becky, Michael, David, Amy, Alexa, Barbara, and the Coffee Boys of Westwood Hills—Hugh Brown, Glion Curtis, Grant Mallet, Howard Martin, Stan Nelson, Gary Ripple, Harris Rayl, and, last but not least, G. Ross Stephens.

ABOUT THE AUTHOR

Thomas M. Magstadt earned his doctorate at The Johns Hopkins University School of Advanced International Studies (SAIS). He has taught at several colleges and universities, including the Graduate School of International Management, Augustana College (Sioux Falls), the University of Nebraska at Kearney, the Air War College, and the University of Missouri–Kansas City. He has also chaired two political science departments, worked as an intelligence analyst, served as director of the Midwest Conference on World Affairs, and lectured as a Fulbright scholar in the Czech Republic. In addition to publishing articles in newspapers, magazines, and professional journals, Dr. Magstadt is the author of *An Empire If You Can Keep It* (Washington, DC: Congressional Quarterly Press, 2004); *Nations and Governments: Comparative Politics in Regional Perspective,* fifth edition (Belmont, CA: Wadsworth, Cengage Learning, 2005); *Contemporary European Politics* (Belmont, CA: Wadsworth, Cengage Learning, 2007); *The European Union on the World Stage: Sovereignty, Soft Power, and the Search for Consensus* (publication pending) and is creator of WorldViewWest, a website devoted to world affairs located at www.worldviewwest.com. He lectured on the European Union at the University of Kansas from 2007 to 2010.

In the second half of 2012 two things dominated the political news in the United States: (1) a close and crucial presidential election and (2) a divided government. The latter involved one chamber of Congress controlled by Republicans and the other controlled by Democrats, and pitted the legislative branch of the federal government against the executive branch. The spectacle of the world's only superpower paralyzed by extreme partisanship and teetering on the brink of a "fiscal cliff" loomed like a portent of something dark and ominous. There were even rumors of a coming end-of-the-world apocalypse—December 21, 2012, to be exact, the final day of the old Mayan calendar.

This politically charged atmosphere, and the pervasive sense of an impending crisis, was nothing new. In 2008, two events had dominated the news in the United States and around the world. First, a financial meltdown and plummeting stock market wiped out fortunes and rocked the global economy to its very foundations. Second, in the midst of this maelstrom, Barack Obama became the first African American elected to the nation's highest office. Obama had energized millions, many of whom were first-time voters.

In spite of the deepening recession, there was a new sense of hope, if not optimism. There was also a new sense of urgency about dealing with the nation's troubled economy and a host of other problems that President Obama inherited from his predecessor, including how to extricate the United States from protracted and costly wars in Iraq and Afghanistan. By 2012 hope had faded and optimism was in short supply; the emotions closest to the surface—the ones politicians are so quick to exploit—were anger and disappointment.

In 2009, President Obama moved to revive the U.S. economy, which had fallen into the deepest recession since the Great Depression of the 1930s. The economic stimulus package he pushed through Congress, where Democrats enjoyed a solid majority in both the House and Senate, was widely viewed by the mass media and the public as a Wall Street "bailout"—a massive multibillion dollar gift to the very financial institutions that had caused the problem. It was also criticized as a "jobless recovery" as unemployment rose to nearly 10% and youth unemployment (16- to 19-year-olds) rose about 25% in 2010. Nearly half of young people aged 16 to 24 did not have jobs, the highest since World War II.

Obama also spearheaded a controversial health care reform that satisfied few, confused everyone, and angered many voters on both sides of the acrimonious debate. His decision to order a "surge" in Afghanistan, committing 30,000 more U.S. troops to an unpopular and unwinnable war, did not turn the tide or improve his standing in the opinion polls.

The public discontent eagerly exploited by conservative media personalities and the amorphous "Tea Party" movement resulted in a crushing defeat for the Democrats in the 2010 midterm elections, when Republicans regained control of the House and cut deeply into the Democrats' majority in the Senate (for details, see Part 3, especially Chapters 11 and 13).

Such dramatic events as a stock market crash or pivotal elections that can change the course of a nation's history have one thing in common: they are intensely political. Politics is everywhere, even when it's less obvious. To see it, we often have to read between the lines or go behind the scenes. And we have to think for ourselves.

For any democracy to succeed in the long run it is vital that citizens pay attention, place a high value on political literacy, and demonstrate it by voting intelligently. The other way, revolution (see Chapter 14), is a drastic measure and a last resort—one the American colonists chose in 1776 and the Confederate South chose in 1860.

We too often take citizenship and freedom for granted. At a minimum, being a good citizen requires us to have a basic understanding of the ideas, institutions, and issues that constitute the stuff of politics.

WHY STUDY POLITICS?

A basic understanding of politics is a vital part of any citizen's education. To realize the full benefits, make a sincere effort to learn and, above all, keep an open mind.

Self-Interest

Because personal happiness depends in no small degree on what government does or does not do, we all have a considerable stake in understanding how government works (or why it is not working). To college students, for example, federal work-study programs, state subsidies to public education, low-interest loans, federal grants, and court decisions designed to protect (or not protect) students' rights are political matters of great significance. Through the study of politics, we become more aware of our dependence on the political system and better equipped to determine when to favor and when to oppose change. At the same time, such study helps reveal the limits of politics and our ability to bring about positive change. It is sobering to consider that each of us is only one person in a nation of millions (and a world of billions), most of whom have opinions and prejudices no less firmly held than are our own.

The Public Interest

What could be more vital to the public interest than the moral character and conduct of the citizenry? Civil society is defined by and reflected in the kinds of everyday decisions and choices made by ordinary people leading ordinary lives. At the same time, people are greatly influenced by civil society and the prevailing culture and climate of politics. People with very similar capabilities and desires can develop quite different moral standards, depending on the circumstances. Politics plays a vital role in shaping these circumstances, and it is fair to say that the public interest hangs in the balance.

BASIC CONCEPTS OF POLITICS

Politics has been variously defined as "the art of the possible," as the study of "who gets what, when, and how," as the "authoritative allocation of values," and in countless other ways. A simple definition of politics is surprisingly elusive, but most of us know it when we see it. Like other disciplines, political science has a lexicon and language all its own. We start our language lesson with three words that carry a great deal of political freight: *power, order,* and *justice.*

politics
The process by which a community selects rulers and empowers them to make decisions, take action to attain common goals, and reconcile conflicts within the community.

Power

power
The capacity to influence or control the behavior of persons and institutions, whether by persuasion or coercion.

Power is the currency of all politics. Without power, no government can make and enforce laws, provide security, regulate the economy, conduct foreign policy, or wage war. There are many kinds of power. In this book, we are interested in *political* power. The means of coercion play an important role in politics, but political power cannot be equated with force. Indeed, the sources of power are many and varied. A large population, a booming economy, a cohesive society, and wise leadership—all are examples of quite different power sources.

We often define power in terms of national wealth or military spending. We once called the most formidable states Great Powers; now we call them "superpowers." Power defined in this way is tangible and measurable. Critics of this classical view make a useful distinction between "hard power" and "soft power." Hard power refers to the means and instruments of brute force or coercion, primarily military and economic clout. Soft power is "attractive" rather than coercive: the essence of soft power is "the important ability to get others to want what you want."[1]

Power is never equally distributed. Yet the need to concentrate power in the hands of a few inevitably raises three big questions: Who wields power? In whose interests? And to what ends?

The most basic question of all is "Who rules?" Sometimes we have only to look at a nation's constitution and observe the workings of its government to find the answer. But it may be difficult to determine who really rules when the government is cloaked in secrecy or when, as is often the case, informal patterns of power are very different from the textbook diagrams.

authority
Command of the obedience of society's members by a government.

legitimacy
The exercise of political power in a community in a way that is voluntarily accepted by the members of that community.

legitimate authority
The legal and moral right of a government to rule over a specific population and control a specific territory; the term *legitimacy* usually implies a widely recognized claim of governmental authority and voluntary acceptance on the part of the population(s) directly affected.

The terms *power* and *authority* are often confused and even used interchangeably. In reality, they denote two distinct dimensions of politics. According to Mao Zedong, the late Chinese Communist leader, "Political power flows from the barrel of a gun." Political power is clearly associated with the means of coercion (the regular police, secret police, and the army), but power can also flow from wealth, personal charisma, ideology, religion, and many other sources, including the moral standing of a particular individual or group in society.

Authority flows not only (or even mainly) from the barrel of a gun but also from the *norms* society accepts and even cherishes. These norms are moral, spiritual, and legal codes of behavior or good conduct. Thus, authority implies **legitimacy**—a condition in which power is exercised by common consensus through established institutions. Note this definition does not mean, nor is it meant to imply, that democracy is the only legitimate form of government possible. Any government that enjoys the consent of the governed is legitimate—including a monarchy, military dictatorship, or theocracy.

The acid test of **legitimate authority** is not whether people have the right to vote or to strike or dissent openly, but how much *value* people attach to these rights. If a majority of the people are content with the existing political order just as it is (with or without voting rights), the legitimacy of the ruler(s) is simply not in question. But, as history amply demonstrates, it is possible to seize power and to rule without a popular mandate or public approval, without moral, spiritual, or legal justification—in other words, without true (legitimate) authority. Power seizures occurred in Mauritania and Guinea in 2008; more than a dozen contemporary rulers, mostly in Africa, came to power in this manner. Adolf Hitler's failed "Beer Hall Putsch" in 1923 is a famous example of an attempted power seizure. Although such attempts often fail, they are evidence of political instability—as the case of Weimar Germany illustrates.

Claiming authority is useless without the means to enforce it. The right to rule—a condition that minimizes the need for repression—hinges in large part on legitimacy or popularity.

Legitimacy and popularity go hand in hand. Illegitimate rulers are unpopular rulers. Such rulers are faced with a choice: relinquish power or repress opposition. Whether repression works depends, in turn, on the answer to three questions. First, how widespread and determined is the opposition? Second, does the government have adequate financial resources and coercive capabilities to defeat its opponents and deter future challenges? Third, does the government have the will to use all means necessary to defeat the rebellion?

If the opposition is broadly based and the government waivers for whatever reason, repression is likely to fail. Regimes changed in Russia in 1917 and 1992 following failed attempts to crush the opposition. Two other examples include Cuba in 1958, where Fidel Castro led a successful revolution, and Iran in 1978, where a mass uprising led to the overthrow of the Shah. A similar pattern was evident in many East European states in 1989, when repressive communist regimes collapsed like so many falling dominoes.

If people respect the ruler(s) and play by the rules without being forced to do so (or threatened with the consequences), the task of maintaining order and stability in society is going to be much easier. It stands to reason that people who feel exploited and oppressed make poorly motivated workers. The perverse work ethic of Soviet-style dictatorships, where it was frequently said, "We pretend to work and they pretend to pay us," helps explain the decline and fall of communism in the Soviet Union and Eastern Europe, dramatized by the spontaneous tearing down of the Berlin Wall in 1989.

Order

Order exists on several levels. First, it denotes structures, rules, rituals, procedures, and practices that make up the political system embedded in every **society**. What exactly is society? In essence, society is an aggregation of individuals who share a common identity. Usually that identity is at least partially defined by geography because people who live in close proximity often know each other, enjoy shared experiences, speak the same language, and have similar values and interests. The process of instilling a sense of common purpose or creating a single political allegiance among diverse groups of people is complex and works better from the bottom up than from the top down. The breakup of the Soviet Union and Yugoslavia in the early 1990s, after more than seven decades as multinational states, suggests new communities are often fragile and tend to fall apart quickly if there are not strong cultural and psychological bonds under the political structures.

order
In a political context, an existing or desired arrangement of institutions based on certain principles, such as liberty, equality, prosperity, and security. Also often associated with the rule of law (as in the phrase "law and order") and with conservative values such as stability, obedience, and respect for legitimate authority.

society
An aggregation of individuals who share a common identity. Usually that identity is at least partially defined by geography because people who live in close proximity often know one another, enjoy shared experiences, speak the same language, and have similar values and interests.

social contract
A concept in political theory most often associated with Thomas Hobbes, Jean-Jacques Rousseau, and John Locke. The social contract is an implicit agreement among individuals to form a civil society and to accept certain moral and political obligations essential to its preservation.

government
The persons and institutions that make and enforce rules or laws for the larger community.

republic
A form of government in which sovereignty resides in the people of that country, rather than with the rulers. The vast majority of republics today are democratic or representative republics, meaning that sovereign power is exercised by elected representatives who are responsible to the citizenry.

The idea that individuals become a cohesive community through an unwritten **social contract** has been fundamental to Western political thought since the seventeenth century. Basic to social contract theory is the notion that the right to rule is based on the consent of the governed. Civil liberties in this type of community are a matter of natural law and natural rights—that is, they do not depend on written laws but rather are inherent in Nature. Nature with a capital N is a set of self-evident truths that, in the eyes of social contract theorists, can be known through a combination of reason and observation. A corollary of this theory is that whenever government turns oppressive, when it arbitrarily takes away such natural rights as life, liberty, and (perhaps) property, the people have a right to revolt (see Chapter 14).

Government is a human invention by which societies are ruled and binding rules are made. Given the rich variety of governments in the world, how might we categorize them all? Traditionally we've distinguished between **republics**, in which sovereignty ultimately resides in the people, and governments such as monarchies or tyrannies, in which sovereignty rests with the rulers. Today, almost all republics are democratic (or representative) republics, meaning political systems wherein elected representatives responsible to the people exercise sovereign power.[2]

Some political scientists draw a simple distinction between democracies, which hold free elections, and dictatorships, which do not. Others emphasize political economy, distinguishing between governments enmeshed in capitalist or market-based systems and governments based on socialist or state-regulated systems. Finally, governments in developing countries face different kinds of challenges than do governments in developed countries. Not surprisingly, more economically developed countries often have markedly more well-established political institutions—including political parties, regular elections, civil and criminal courts—than most less-developed countries, and more stable political systems.

In the modern world, the **state** is the sole repository of **sovereignty**. A sovereign state is a community with well-defined territorial boundaries administered by a single government capable of making and enforcing laws. In addition it typically claims a monopoly on the legitimate use of force; raises armies for the defense of its territory and population; levies and collects taxes; regulates trade and commerce; establishes courts, judges, and magistrates to settle disputes and punish lawbreakers; and sends envoys (ambassadors) to represent its interests abroad, negotiate treaties, and gather useful information. Entities that share *some* but not all of the characteristics of states include fiefdoms and chiefdoms, bands and tribes, universal international organizations (such as the United Nations), and regional supranational organizations (such as the European Union).

In the language of politics, "state" usually means **country**. France, for instance, may be called either a state or a country. (In certain federal systems of government, a state is an administrative subdivision, such as New York, Florida, Texas, or California in the United States; however, such states within a state are not sovereign.)

The term *nation* is also a synonym for *state* or *country*. Thus, the only way to know for certain whether *state* means part of a country (for example, the United States) or a whole country (say, France or China) is to consider the context. By the same token, context is the key to understanding what we mean by the word *nation*.

A **nation** is made up of a distinct group of people who share a common background, including geographic location, history, racial or ethnic characteristics, religion, language, culture, or belief in common political ideas. Geography heads this list because members of a nation typically exhibit a strong collective sense of belonging associated with a particular territory for which they are willing to fight and die if necessary.

Countries with relatively homogeneous populations (with great similarity among members) were most common in old Europe, but this once-defining characteristic of European nation-states is no longer true. The recent influx of newcomers from former colonial areas—in particular the Muslim majority countries of North Africa, the Arab world, and South Asia, and post–Cold War east-west population movements in Europe—has brought the issue of immigration to the forefront of politics in France, Germany, the United Kingdom, Spain, Italy, the Netherlands, Belgium, and even the Scandinavian countries. Belgium provides a rare example of a European state that was divided culturally and linguistically (French-speaking Walloons and Dutch-speaking Flemish) from the start.

India, Russia, and Nigeria are three highly diverse states. India's constitution officially recognizes no fewer than eighteen native tongues! The actual number spoken is far larger. As a nation of immigrants, the United States is also very diverse, but the process of assimilation eventually brings the children of newcomers, if not the newcomers themselves, into the mainstream.[3]

The **nation-state** is a state encompassing a single nation in which the overwhelming majority of the people form a dominant in-group who share common cultural, ethnic, and linguistic characteristics and all others are part of a distinct out-group or minority. This concept is rooted in a specific time and place—that is, in modern Western Europe. (See "Landmarks in History" for the story of the first nation-state.) The concept of the nation-state fits less comfortably in other regions of the world, where the political boundaries of sovereign states—many of which were European colonies before World War II—often do not coincide with ethnic or cultural geography. In some instances, ethnic, religious, or tribal groups that were bitter traditional enemies were thrown together in new "states," resulting in societies prone to great instability or even civil war.

Decolonization after World War II gave rise to many polyglot states in which various ethnic or tribal groups were not assimilated into the new social order. Many decades later, the all-important task of **nation-building** in these new states is still far from finished. Thus, in 1967, Nigeria plunged into a vicious civil war when one large ethnic group, the Igbo, tried unsuccessfully to secede and form an independent state called Biafra. In 1994, Rwanda witnessed one of the bloodiest massacres in modern times when the numerically superior Hutus slaughtered hundreds of thousands of Tutsis, including women and children. In early 2008, tribal violence in Kenya's Rift Valley and beyond claimed the lives

state
In its sovereign form, an independent political-administrative unit that successfully claims the allegiance of a given population, exercises a monopoly on the legitimate use of coercive force, and controls the territory inhabited by its citizens or subjects; in its other common form, a state is the major political-administrative subdivision of a federal system and, as such, is not sovereign but rather depends on the central authority (sometimes called the "national government") for resource allocations (tax transfers and grants), defense (military protection and emergency relief), and regulation of economic relations with other federal subdivisions (nonsovereign states) and external entities (sovereign states).

sovereignty
A government's capacity to assert supreme power successfully in a political state.

THE PEACE OF WESTPHALIA (1648): The Origins of the Modern Nation-State System

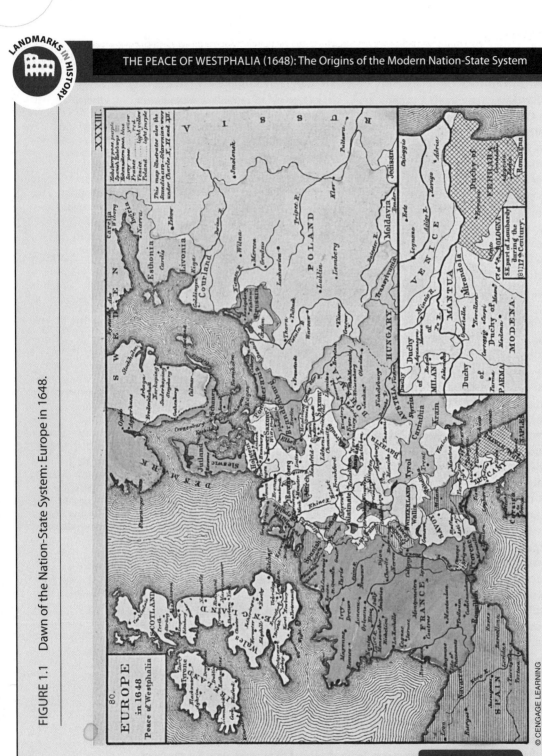

FIGURE 1.1   Dawn of the Nation-State System: Europe in 1648.

(Continued)

Most historians believe the Peace of Westphalia marks the beginning of the modern European state system. The main actors in forging the peace, which ended the Thirty Years' War in 1648, were Sweden and France as the challengers, Spain and the dying Holy Roman Empire as the defenders of the status quo, and the newly independent Netherlands.

At first glance, the map of Europe in the mid-seventeenth century does not look much like it does today. However, on closer inspection we see the outlines of modern Europe emerge (see Map 1.1)—visual proof that the treaty laid the foundations of the nation-state as we see it in Europe today.

The emergence of the nation-state system transformed Europe from a continent of territorial empires to one based on relatively compact geographic units that share a single dominant language and culture. This pattern was unprecedented, and it would shape both European and world history in the centuries to come.

France under Napoleon attempted to establish a new continental empire at the beginning of the nineteenth century but ultimately failed. Two other empires—Austria-Hungary and Russia—remained, but they were eclipsed by a rising new nation-state at the end of the nineteenth century and perished in World War I. After World War I, only the newly constituted Soviet empire existed in Europe. After World War II, what remained of Europe's overseas colonial empires also disintegrated. Today, the entire world, with few exceptions, is carved up into nation-states—the legacy of a treaty that, for better or worse, set the stage for a new world order.

of hundreds of innocent people following the outcome of a presidential election that many believed was rigged.

In India, where Hindus and Muslims frequently clash and sporadic violence breaks out among militant Sikhs in Punjab and where hundreds of languages and dialects are spoken, characterizing the country as a nation-state misses the point altogether. In Sri Lanka (formerly Ceylon), Hindu Tamils have long waged a terrorist guerrilla war against the majority Singhalese, who are Buddhist.

Even in the Slavic-speaking parts of Europe, age-old ethnic rivalries have caused the breakup of preexisting states. The Soviet Union, Yugoslavia, and Czechoslovakia are all multinational states that self-destructed in the 1990s.

Finally, **stateless nations,** such as the Palestinians and Kurds, share a sense of common identity but have no homeland. The existence of these nations without states has created highly volatile situations, most notably in the Middle East.

Justice

We willingly accept the rule of the few over the many only if the public interest—or common good—is significantly advanced in the process. The concept of **justice** is no less fundamental than power in politics, and it is essential to a stable order. Is power exercised fairly, in the interest of the ruled, or merely for the sake of the rulers? For more than 2,000 years, political observers have maintained the distinction between the public-spirited exercise of political

country
As a political term, it refers loosely to a sovereign state and is roughly equivalent to "nation" or "nation-state"; *country* is often used as a term of endearment—for example, in the phrase "my country 'tis of thee, sweet land of liberty" in the patriotic song every U.S. child learns in elementary school; *country* has an emotional dimension not present in the word *state*.

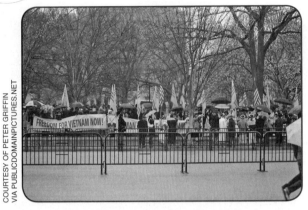

Citizens unhappy about government policies at home or abroad can express themselves in any number of ways, including demonstrations and marches. Here on a rainy day in Washington citizens are protesting in Lafayette Park across the street from the White House.

power on one hand and self-interested rule on the other. This distinction attests to the importance of justice in political life.

Not all states and regimes allow questions of justice to be raised; in fact, throughout history, most have not. Even today, some governments brutally and systematically repress political dissent, because they fear the consequences.

Often, criticism of *how* a government rules implicitly or explicitly raises questions about its moral or legal *right* to rule. One of the most important measures of liberty is the right to question whether the government is acting justly.

Questions about whether a particular ruler is legitimate or a given policy is desirable stem from human nature itself. The Greek philosopher Aristotle (384–322 BCE) observed that human beings alone use reason and language "to declare what is advantageous and what is just and unjust." Therefore, "it is the peculiarity of man, in comparison with the rest of the animal world, that he alone possess a perception of good and evil, of the just and unjust."[4]

The same human faculties that make moral judgment possible also make **political literacy**—the ability to think and speak intelligently about politics— necessary. In other words, moral judgment and political literacy are two sides of the same coin.

THE PROBLEM OF DIRTY HANDS

Based on everyday observation, it's easy to get the impression that politics and morality operate in separate realms of human experience, that power always corrupts, and that anyone who thinks differently is hopelessly naïve. Political theorists have long recognized and debated whether it is possible to exercise power and still remain true to one's principles. It's called the problem of "dirty hands."

In politics, anything is possible, including the unthinkable. When morality is set aside, justice is placed entirely at the mercy of raw power.

The rise and fall of Nazi Germany (1933–1945) under Adolf Hitler illustrates the tremendous impact a regime can have on the moral character of its citizens. At the core of Nazi ideology was a doctrine of racial supremacy. Hitler ranted about the superiority of the so-called Aryan race. The purity of the German nation was supposedly threatened with adulteration by inferior races, or *untermenschen*. Policies based on this maniacal worldview resulted in the systematic murder of millions of innocent men, women, and children. Approximately 6 million Jews and millions of others, including Poles, Gypsies, homosexuals, and people with disabilities, were killed in cold blood.

nation
Often interchangeable with *state* or *country*; in common usage, denotes a specific people with a distinct language and culture or a major ethnic group—for example, the French, Dutch, Chinese, and Japanese people each constitute a nation as well as a state, hence the term nation-state. Not all nations are fortunate enough to have a state of their own; modern examples include the Kurds (Turkey, Iraq, and Iran), Palestinians (West Bank and Gaza, Lebanon, Jordan), Pashtuns (Afghanistan), and Uighurs and Tibetans (China).

During the Nazi era, the German nation appears, at first glance, to have become little more than an extension of Hitler's will—in other words, the awesome moral responsibility for the Holocaust somehow rested on the shoulders of one man, Adolf Hitler. But some dispute this interpretation. For example, according to Irving Kristol,

> When one studies the case of The Nazi there comes a sickening emptiness of the stomach and a sense of bafflement. Can this be all? The disparity between the crime and the criminal is too monstrous.
>
> We expect to find evil men, paragons of wickedness, slobbering, maniacal brutes; we are prepared to trace the lineaments of The Nazi on the face of every individual Nazi in order to define triumphantly the essential features of his character. But the Nazi leaders were not diabolists, they did not worship evil. For—greatest of ironies—the Nazis, like Adam and Eve before the fall, knew not of good and evil, and it is this cast of moral indifference that makes them appear so petty and colorless and superficial.[5]

One such person, according to political theorist Hannah Arendt, was Adolf Eichmann, a Nazi functionary who administered much of the extermination

MUSEO DEL HOLOCAUSTO/REUTERS/LANDOV

Nazi mass murderer Adolf Eichmann. An ordinary man? Pictured here is the Red Cross identity document Adolf Eichmann used to enter Argentina under the fake name Ricardo Klement in 1950.

IDEAS AND POLITICS

SCHINDLER'S LIST

Not all Germans, or Europeans, were as indifferent or self-serving in the face of evil as was Eichmann. A notable, if atypical, exception was Oskar Schindler,* whose renown has increased enormously due to the movie *Schindler's List*. Schindler was a German businessman who belonged to the Nazi Party. He at first exploited labor but then used his business and political connections to save the lives of his Jewish workers.

No doubt most of us would identify more with the Christian rescuers or with Schindler than with Eichmann, but the disturbing fact remains that far more Germans (including tens of thousands of Hitler Youth), mesmerized by Hitler's message

of hate, behaved more like Eichmann than like Schindler.

Eichmann claimed to have no obsessive hatred toward Jews (although, obviously, he was not sufficiently skeptical or mentally independent to resist the widespread anti-Semitism that existed in Germany at that time). In short, Eichmann was morally indifferent. Justice was simply not an issue. In Kristol's words, he "knew not of good and evil."

*An attempt to examine Schindler and the courageous acts of other righteous Christians is set forth in Eva Fogelman, *Conscience and Courage: Rescuers of Jews During the Holocaust* (New York: Doubleday, 1994). Also see Samuel P. Oliner and Pearl M. Oliner, *The Altruistic Personality: Rescuers of Jews in Nazi Europe* (New York: Free Press, 1988).

nation-state
A geographically defined community administered by a government.

nation-building
The process of forming a common identity based on the notion of belonging to a political community separate and distinct from all others; often the concept of "nation" is based on common ethnolinguistic roots.

stateless nation
People (or nations) scattered over the territory of several states or dispersed widely and who have no autonomous, independent, or sovereign governing body of their own; examples of stateless nations include the Kurds, Palestinians, and Tibetans (see also *nation*).

justice
Fairness; the distribution of rewards and burdens in society in accordance with what is deserved.

political literacy
The ability to think and speak intelligently about politics.

methodology
The way scientists and scholars set about exploring, explaining, proving, or disproving propositions in different academic disciplines. The precise methods vary according to the discipline and the object, event, process, or phenomenon under investigation.

program. In Arendt's view, Eichmann was not a particularly unusual man.[6] He had a strong desire to get ahead, to be a success in life. He took special pride in his ability to do a job efficiently. Although not particularly thoughtful or reflective, he was intelligent. Arendt also describes Eichmann as somewhat insecure, but not noticeably more so than many "normal" people (see "Ideas and Politics").

HOW TO STUDY POLITICS

Aristotle is the father of political science.[7] He not only wrote about politics and ethics, but he also described different political systems and suggested a scheme for classifying and evaluating them. For Aristotle, political science simply meant political investigation; thus, a political scientist was one who sought, through systematic inquiry, to understand the truth about politics. In this sense, Aristotle's approach to studying politics more than 2,000 years ago has much in common with what political scientists do today. Yet the discipline has changed a great deal since Aristotle's time.

There is no consensus on how best to study politics. Political scientists can and do choose among different approaches, ask different kinds of questions, and address different audiences. This fact is often a source of some dismay within the discipline, but it is hardly surprising and probably unavoidable given the vast universe of human activity the study of politics encompasses. Let us explore why and how contemporary political scientists study politics.

For What Purposes?

Some of the most important questions in politics are "should" and "ought" questions, the kind scientists seeking objective truth tend to avoid. These are the great *normative* political questions that resonate throughout human history: When is war justified? Do people have a right to revolt? Is the right to life absolute? Does everyone have a right to liberty? Is state repression ever justified? Is official secrecy justified? What about censorship? Do citizens have a right to privacy?

Some issues lend themselves to empirical analysis more than others. Studying elections can reveal flaws in the voting process—skewed voting districts or impediments to voter registration, for example—and lead to appropriate changes or reforms, such as redistricting or switching from written ballots to voting machines. Opinion polls help leaders gauge the mood of the public and better understand the effect of government policies (see Chapter 11). The answers to many basic issues in politics, however, can only be discovered through intelligent thought—reason, logic, and philosophical discourse.

By What Methods?

Should political science strive to predict or forecast events? Is the study of politics a science akin to physics or chemistry? Answers to such questions lie in the realm of **methodology**. There are many ways to classify political scientists. We will focus on one basic distinction—that between *positivism* and *normativism*.

Positivism emphasizes empirical research (which relies on observation) and couches problems in terms of variables we can measure. **Behaviorism** is an offshoot of positivism that focuses mainly on the study of political behavior. Behaviorists use quantitative analysis to challenge the conventional wisdom—for example, what motivates voters or why a given election turned out the way it did. Following the facts—statistical data—wherever they may lead is the hallmark of the so-called hard sciences. The results of empirical research can cast long-standing "truths" into serious doubt or exposes "facts" as fallacies.

Normativism is based on the idea closely associated with the German political philosopher Immanuel Kant that the "ought" and the "is" are inseparable from each other and that the "ought" cannot be derived from the "is." Sticking strictly to the facts, a trademark of positivism, thus raises a serious problem for the adherents of normative theory, who are interested not only in describing actions and consequences but also in prescribing policies and remedies. Seen in this light, values are at the core of political analysis. In studying Congress, for example, value-based political science might ask: Did special interests unduly influence health care reform in 2009–2010? Or with respect to U.S. foreign policy: Was the invasion of Iraq in 2003 necessary?

Scholars and policy analysts seeking answers to such questions often resort to philosophy, history, constitutional law, court cases, treaties, declassified documents, and expert opinion. For example, in explaining why the Constitution adopted in 1787 did not abolish slavery, scholars often skip over the question as to whether or why slavery is wrong. Instead, they examine the writings and speeches of the founding fathers, the economic interests they represented, the social class to which they all belonged, and the like. The reason they (we) don't dwell on the moral question is that everyone knows slavery is wrong. Slavery is an extreme case, but many political issues are at least as much about values as about facts.

In truth, it is not always easy to distinguish between a fact and a value. Moreover, in politics, values *are* facts. We all bring certain values to everything we do. At the same time, however, we can never get at the truth if we don't place a high value on facts. For example, if an influential segment of the population believes that abortion is a sin, that is a *value* based on a religious belief. We can argue all day long whether that view is right or wrong, but there is no escaping the *fact* that this belief exists and that politicians, government officials, and judges will have no choice but to deal with it. Moreover, whatever legislation or jurisdiction is brought to bear on this question will have consequences for society as a whole. This is but one simple example among many illustrating the sense in which facts and values are entangled in the political life of every society, always have been, and always will be.

The Study of Human Behavior Behavioral scientists are wary of value judgments, preferring instead to concentrate on facts. They employ the scientific method familiar to investigators in such fields as biology, physics, and chemistry, asking questions answerable only by carefully assembling a research design, gathering data, and using the tools of statistical analysis to test hypotheses.

positivism
A philosophy of science, originated by Auguste Comte, that stresses observable, scientific facts as the sole basis of proof and truth; a skeptical view of ideas or beliefs based on religion or metaphysics.

behaviorism
An approach to the study of politics that emphasizes fact-based evaluations of action.

normativism
An approach to the study of politics that is based on examining fundamental and enduring questions.

Behaviorists develop mathematical models to try and explain voting behavior, coalition-building, decision making, even the causes of war.

In a December 1996 journal article ("Partisan Effects of Voter Turnout in Senatorial and Gubernatorial Elections") researchers asked: Is it really true, as is widely believed, that high voter turnout favors Democrats? [8] The prevailing belief that Democrats benefit from high voter turnout assumes: (1) people with lower socioeconomic status (SES) vote less often than people with higher SES; (2) as voter turnout rises, more people on the lower end of the SES ladder vote; and (3) lower-end voters are likely to vote for the party they trust to advance working-class interests—namely, the Democratic Party. This belief is reinforced whenever low voter turnout coincides with Republican victories. It also explains why most Democrats favored (and Republicans opposed) the 1993 National Voter Registration Act—popularly known as the Motor Voter Bill—which eased voter registration procedures.

The researchers examined 1,842 state elections going all the way back to 1928: 983 for senator and 859 for governor. Applying a mathematical test, the researchers concluded that from 1928 to 1964, high voter turnout aided the Democratic Party, as generally believed, but after 1964 there was no such correlation either in senatorial or gubernatorial races.

Why? Although this question was beyond the scope of the study, its findings were consistent with another complex theory of voting behavior. The rise in the number of independents since 1964 (and the resulting decline in party identification and partisan voting) made it difficult to calculate which party would benefit from a large voter turnout in any given race. By the mid-1990s, nearly one-third of all voters identified themselves as independents, while ticket splitting (not voting for *only* Republicans or *only* Democrats—a so-called straight ticket) and swing voting (see Chapter 11) became common. In the 2010 midterm elections, Republicans were the beneficiaries of a huge swing vote.

Behaviorists, like other research scientists, are typically content to take small steps on the road to knowledge. Each step points the way to future studies.

Studying human behavior can be as frustrating as it is fascinating. There are almost always multiple explanations for human behavior, and it is often difficult to isolate a single cause or distinguish it from a mere

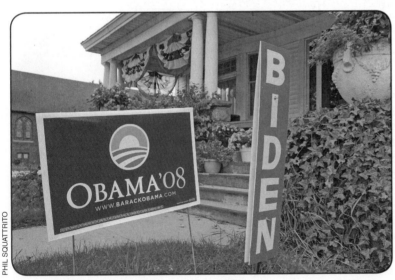

PHIL SQUATTRITO

Political scientists analyze patterns and trends in voting behavior to learn more about who votes, how different segments of the population vote, and why people vote the way they do. Political strategists use this information to help clients (candidates for office) win elections. Think about it: If you were running for the state legislature or Congress, what would you want to know about voters in your district?

statistical correlation. For instance, several studies indicate that criminals tend to be less intelligent than law-abiding citizens. But is low intelligence a cause of crime? What about social factors such as poverty, drug or alcohol addiction, or a history of being abused as a child? What about free will? Many reject the idea that society—rather than the criminal—is somehow responsible for the crime.

Political scientists often disagree not only about how to study politics but also about which questions to ask. Behaviorists typically prefer to examine specific and narrowly defined questions, answering them by applying quantitative techniques—sophisticated statistical methods such as regression analysis and analysis of variance.

Many broader questions of politics, especially those raising issues of justice, lie beyond the scope of this sort of investigation. Questions such as "What is justice?" or "What is the role of the state in society?" require us to makes moral choices and value judgments. Even if we cannot resolve such questions scientifically, they are worth asking. Confining the study of politics *only* to the kinds of questions we can subject to quantitative analysis risks turning political science into an academic game of Trivial Pursuit.

Given the complexity of human behavior, it is not surprising that experts argue over methodology or how to do science. Although the lively debate sparked by the behavioral revolution has cooled, it divided the discipline for several decades and is likely to continue to do so for years to come.

The Political (Science) Puzzle

Thus, political science, like politics, means different things to different people. The subject matter of politics is so wide ranging that it is difficult to study without being broken down into more manageable pieces. Like physicians, political scientists often divide into specialties and subfields—some specialize in *political theory*, whereas others focus on *U.S. government and politics, comparative politics, international relations, political economy, public administration,* or *public policy.*

Political Theory The origins of what we now call political science are to be found in Greek philosophy and date back to Socrates and Plato (c. 400 BCE). The Socratic method of teaching and seeking Truth was to ask a series of pithy questions—What is the good life? Is there a natural right to liberty?—while questioning every answer in order to expose logical fallacies.

Political theory seeks answers to such questions through reason, logic, and experience. Famous names in the history of political thought include Aristotle, Thomas Hobbes, John Locke, Jean-Jacques Rousseau, and John Stuart Mill, among others. These thinkers ranged far and wide but met at the intersection of politics and ethics.

Because people on opposite sides of the political fence believe that they are right and the other guys are wrong, understanding politics requires us, at a minimum, to be open-minded and familiarize ourselves with arguments pro and con.[9] Knowledge of costs and moral consequences in politics is essential to a clear sense of purpose and coherent policy.

rational choice
The role of reason over emotion in human behavior. Political behavior, in this view, follows logical and even predictable patterns so long as we understand the key role of self-interest.

political realism
The philosophy that power is the key variable in all political relationships and should be used pragmatically and prudently to advance the national interest; policies are judged good or bad on the basis of their effect on national interests, not on their level of morality.

political culture
The moral values, beliefs, and myths by which people live and for which they are willing to die.

Are we humans rational by nature or are we driven by passions such as love, hate, anger, and prejudice? Advocates of **rational choice** theory emphasize the role of reason over emotion in human behavior. Political behavior, arguably, follows logical and even predictable patterns. The key to understanding politics is self-interest. This approach, which forms the basis for a theory of international relations known as **political realism** (see Chapter 17), holds that individuals and states alike act according to the iron logic of self-interest.

Other political scientists argue that rational choice theory is an oversimplification because states and groups are composed of human beings with disparate interests, perceptions, and beliefs. The key is not self-interest pure and simple, but culture and shared values. In this view, we cannot explain political behavior by reference to logic and rationality alone. Instead, the behavior of individuals and of groups is a product of specific influences that vary from place to place—in other words, political behavior is a product of **political culture**.

Of course, it is not necessary to adhere dogmatically to one theory or the other. Both contain important insights and we can perhaps best see them as complementary rather than conflicting.

U.S. Government and Politics Understanding our own political institutions is vitally important. When we speak of U.S. government, our frame of reference changes depending on whether we mean national, state, or local politics. Similarly, when we study political behavior in the United States, it makes a big difference whether we are focusing on individual behavior or the behavior of groups such as interest groups, ethnic groups, age cohorts, and the like. Teaching and learning about one's own government is, in effect, an exercise in civic education.

Citizens in a democracy need to know how the government works, what rights they are guaranteed by the Constitution, and how to decide what to believe. We need to remember that the United States is home to the oldest written constitution, a behemoth economy, and the most potent military capability of all time. Prestige, power, and wealth have political and moral consequences; namely, an obligation to act responsibly as citizens of both a powerful country and an interdependent world.

Comparative Politics Comparative politics seeks to contrast and evaluate governments and political systems. Comparing forms of government, stages of economic development, domestic and foreign policies, and political traditions enables political scientists to formulate meaningful generalizations. Some comparativists specialize in a particular region of the world or a particular nation. Others focus on a particular issue or political phenomenon, such as terrorism, political instability, or voting behavior.

All political systems share certain characteristics. Figure 1.2 depicts one famous model, developed by political scientist David Easton in 1965. This model suggests that all political systems function within the context of political cultures, which consist of traditions, values, and common knowledge. It assumes citizens have expectations of and place demands on the political system, but they also support the system in various ways: They may participate in government, vote, or simply obey the laws of the state. The demands they make

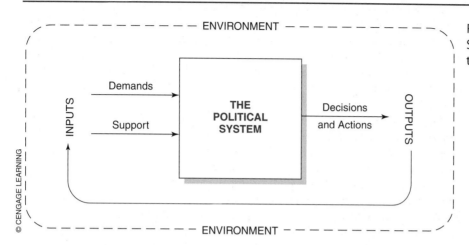

FIGURE 1.2 A Simplified Model of the Political System.

© CENGAGE LEARNING

and supports they provide in turn influence the government's decisions, edicts, laws, and orders.

Countries, of course, differ in countless ways. Some political scientists see the differences among countries as being more significant than the similarities, and they differentiate among political systems in various ways. This book distinguishes among democratic, authoritarian, and totalitarian states. Typologies change over time, reflecting new trends and seismic shifts in world politics or the global economy. For example, after the fall of communism, the distinction between established liberal democracies and "transitional states" gained currency (see Chapter 8). It also became fashionable to distinguish between viable states and so-called failed states (see Chapter 9).

International Relations Specialists in international relations analyze how nations interact. Why do nations sometimes live in peace and harmony but go to war at other times? The advent of the nuclear age, of course, brought new urgency to the study of international relations, but the threat of an all-out nuclear war now appears far less menacing than other threats, including international terrorism, global warming, energy security, and, most recently, the economic meltdown.

Although war and peace are ever-present problems in international relations, they are by no means the only ones. The role of morality in foreign policy continues to be a matter of lively debate. Political realists argue that considerations of national interest have always been paramount in international politics and always will be.[10] Others argue that enlightened self-interest can lead to world peace and an end to the cycle of war. Realists often dismiss such ideas as too idealistic in a dog-eat-dog world. Idealists counter that realists are too fatalistic and that war is not inevitable but rather a self-fulfilling prophecy. Still others say the distinction between the national interest and international morality is exaggerated; that democracies, for example, derive mutual benefit from protecting each other and that in so doing they also promote world peace.[11]

Public Administration Public administration is all about how governments organize and operate, about how bureaucracies work and interact with citizens and one another. In federal systems, intergovernmental relations is a major focus of study. Students of public administration examine budgets, procedures, and processes in an attempt to improve efficiency and reduce waste and duplication. One perennial question deals with bureaucratic behavior: How and why do bureaucracies develop vested interests and special relationships (such as between the Pentagon and defense contractors, or the Department of Commerce and trade associations) quite apart from the laws and policies they are established to implement?

Political scientists who study public administration frequently concentrate on case studies, paying attention to whether governmental power is exercised in a manner consistent with the public interest. In this sense, public administration shares the concerns of political science as a whole.

THE POWER OF IDEAS

In politics, money talks—or so people say. Listening to the news, it's easy to get the impression that Congress is up for sale. As a summer intern in the United States Senate many years ago, one of the first things I was told is, "Son, in Washington it isn't what you know but who you know."

Often we start out life being idealistic and then quickly run up against reality. For young students of politics, it's easy to fall into a trap, to lurch from one extreme to the other. If money is all that matters, justice is an illusion, ideas are irrelevant, and things can never change. But is it true? Are the cynics the smart ones?

One view, recently showcased in the prominent journal *The Economist*, holds that intelligence, not money, is what really matters. Smart people are the inventors, innovators, and entrepreneurs who make things happen: "The strongest force shaping politics is not blood or money but ideas." Big movements in world history are propelled by big ideas and "the people who influence government the most are often those who generate compelling ideas."[12] If true, ideas *do* matter and justice is possible.

In a world operating on free market principles, this argument goes, intelligence is the great equalizer. The children of the poor can—and often do—have greater native intelligence than rich kids. Thus, a college dropout can have a bright idea, launch a social network called Facebook on the Internet, and become a billionaire in his mid-twenties. Years earlier, another college dropout with an idea started a computer software company called Microsoft and soon reached the top of the *Fortune* 400 list of the world's richest individuals. Bill Gates III remained at the top of that list in 2011.

But entrepreneurs like Mark Zuckerberg and Bill Gates operate in the realm of business, not politics. Do ideas have the same impact in the realm of politics in today's world? Do smart people get elected to high office in the same way as they climb the corporate ladder to become CEO's and join the ranks of the superrich? That is one of the fundamental questions this book will challenge you to answer.

And one word of caution. Don't expect to find easy answers. And don't expect the answers to be revealed suddenly in a burst of divine light. The role of education is to ask the right questions. The key to a life well lived is to search for the right answers—wherever that might take you.

SUMMARY

Understanding politics is a matter of self-interest. By exploring politics, we gain a better appreciation of what is—and what is not—in the public interest.

This chapter focuses on three fundamental concepts: power, order, and justice. It also explores the interrelationships between power and order, order and justice, and justice and power.

Political power can be defined as the capacity to maintain order in society. Whenever governments promulgate new laws or sign treaties or go to war they are exercising political power. Whenever we pay our taxes, put money in a parking meter, or remove our shoes prior to boarding an airplane we, in effect, bow to the power of government.

When governments exercise power they often do it in the name of order. Power and authority are closely related: authority is the official exercise of power. If we accept the rules and the rulers who make and enforce them, then government also enjoys legitimacy.

Questions of justice are often embedded in political disputes. If the public interest is not advanced by a given policy or if society no longer accepts the authority of the government as legitimate, the resulting discontent can lead to political instability and even rebellion or revolution.

Political science seeks to discover the basic principles and processes at work in political life. Classical political theory points to moral and philosophical truths, political realism stresses the role of self-interest and rational action, and behaviorism attempts to find scientific answers through empirical research and data analysis. Most political scientists specialize in one or more subfields such as political theory, U.S. government and politics, comparative politics, international relations, political economy, public administration, or public policy.

Politics matters. This simple truth was tragically illustrated by the rise of Nazism in Germany.

KEY TERMS

politics   3
power   4
authority   4
legitimacy   4
legitimate authority   4
order   5
society   5
social contract   6
government   6

republics   6
state   6
sovereignty   6
country   6
nation   7
nation-state   7
nation-building   7
stateless nations   9
justice   9

political literacy   10
methodology   12
positivism   13
behaviorism   13
normativism   13
rational choice   16
political realism   16
political culture   16

REVIEW QUESTIONS

1. On what three fundamental concepts is the study of politics based?
2. How does one identify a political problem? Are some conflicts more political than others? Explain.
3. How do political scientists differ from one another?
4. In what ways can individuals benefit from the study of politics and government?

CHAPTER 2

The Idea of the Public Good

Ideologies and Isms

Political Ends and Means
Ideologies and the Public Good

Ideologies and Politics in the
United States

THINK ABOUT IT

What is the public good?

What are three kinds of ideologies?

What are five core values?

Who and what did the terms liberalism *and* conservatism *originally represent? What are the philosophical differences between conservative ideas and classical liberal thought?*

How have the labels "liberal" and "conservative" changed? What do they mean in contemporary American politics?

I n Lewis Carroll's classic tale *Alice in Wonderland,* Alice loses her way in a dense forest and encounters the Cheshire Cat who is sitting on a tree branch. "Would you tell me, please, which way I ought to go from here?" asks Alice. "That depends a good deal on where you want to get to," replies the Cat. "I don't much care where," says Alice. "Then it doesn't matter which way you go," muses the Cat.

Like Alice lost in the forest, we too occasionally find ourselves adrift. Governments and societies are no different. Political leadership can be woefully deficient or hopelessly divided as to what course of action is best in a crisis or what to do about the economy or the environment or health care or a new threat to national security. Intelligent decisions, as Alice's encounter with the Cheshire Cat illustrates, can take place only after we have set clear aims and goals. Before politics can effectively convert mass energy (society) into collective effort (government), which is the essence of public policy, we need a consensus on where we want to go or what we want to be as a society a year from now or perhaps ten years up the road. Otherwise, our leaders, like the rest of us, cannot possibly know how to get there. This is the reason it is so essential for citizens in a democracy to be politically literate. There are plenty of people eager to tell us *what* to think, but in this text you will learn *how* to think about politics.

POLITICAL ENDS AND MEANS

public good
The shared beliefs of a political community as to what goals government ought to attain (for example, to achieve the fullest possible measure of security, prosperity, equality, liberty, or justice for all citizens).

In politics, ends and means are inextricably intertwined. Implicit in debates over public policy is a belief in the idea of the **public good**, that it is the government's role to identify and pursue aims of benefit to society as a whole rather than to a favored few. But the focus of policy debates is often explicitly about means rather than ends. For example, politicians may disagree over whether a tax cut at a particular time will help promote the common good (prosperity) by encouraging saving and investment, balancing the national budget, reducing the rate of inflation, and so on. Although they disagree about the best monetary and fiscal strategies, both sides would agree that economic growth and stability is a proper aim of government.

In political systems with no curbs on executive authority, where the leader has unlimited power, government may have little to do with the public interest.[1] In constitutional democracies, by contrast, the public good is associated with core values such as security, prosperity, equality, liberty, and justice (see Chapter 13). These goals are the navigational guides for keeping the ship of state on course. Arguments about whether to tack this way or that, given the prevailing political currents and crosswinds, are the essence of public policy debates.

IDEOLOGIES AND THE PUBLIC GOOD

The concept of Left and Right originated in the European parliamentary practice of seating parties that favor social and political change to the left of the presiding officer; those opposing change (or favoring a return to a previous form of government), to the right. "You are where you sit," in other words.

Today people may have only vague ideas about government or how it works or what it is actually doing at any given time.[2] Even so, many lean one way or another, toward conservative or liberal views. When people go beyond merely leaning and adopt a rigid, closed system of political ideas, however, they cross a line and enter the realm of **ideology**. Ideologies act as filters that true believers (or adherents) use to interpret events, explain human behavior, and justify political action.

The use of labels—or "isms" as they are often called—is a kind of shorthand that, ideally, facilitates political thought and debate, rather than becoming a way to discredit one's political opponents. One note of caution: these labels do not have precisely the same meaning everywhere. Thus, what is considered "liberal" in the United Kingdom might be considered "conservative" in the United States (Figure 2.1).

Conservatives in the United States traditionally favor a strong national defense, deregulation of business and industry, and tax cuts on capital gains (income from stocks, real estate, and other investments) and inheritances. They often staunchly oppose social spending ("welfare") on the grounds that giveaway programs reward sloth and indolence. Prior to the Reagan Revolution of the 1980s, Republicans championed balanced budgets and limited government. In 2012–2013, Tea Party Republicans in Congress joined the fight for deficit reduction, but insisted that it be done without raising taxes on the wealthy.

By contrast, liberals tend to favor public assistance programs, cuts in military spending, a progressive tax system (one that levies higher taxes on higher incomes), and government regulation in such areas as the food and drug industry, occupational safety and health, housing, transportation, and energy. In 2012–2013, Democrats demanded that spending cuts be offset with targeted tax increases, in particular on individual earnings in excess of $400,000 and capital gains.

Compared to Europe's parliamentary democracies, the political spectrum in the United States is shifted to the right. Ideas and policies widely viewed as "socialist" in the United States—national health care, for example—are mainstream in European countries, and any attempts to tamper with social programs

ideology
Any set of fixed, predictable ideas held by politicians and citizens on how to serve the public good.

FIGURE 2.1   FOCUS
Conservative or Liberal?

	U.S. Conservatives*	British Liberals§
Constitutionalism	Yes	Yes
Religious tolerance	Yes	Yes
Market economy	Yes	Yes
Protectionism	No	No
Pacifism	No	No

© CENGAGE LEARNING

* Values historically associated with the Republican Party in the United States, though not necessarily with the policies of any given administration or president

§ Values historically associated with the Whig Party in the United Kingdom, often called classical liberalism are likely to provoke a public outcry, as the anti-austerity protests that swept across Europe (notably, Greece, Spain, Ireland, Italy, and France) between 2010 and 2012 attest. Liberals in the United States look a lot like conservatives in Europe. As anyone who watches Fox News knows, the word "liberal" is frequently associated with leftist views in the United States (and President Obama's policy initiatives are routinely labeled "socialist"). Liberal meant something quite different in the United Kingdom, where it originated, and it still denotes a desire to maximize individual liberty as the first principle of good government.

Leftists in Europe often belong to socialist parties, but there is no viable Socialist Party in the United States. In the May 2012 presidential election, for example, voters in France handed Socialist Party leader, François Hollande a sweeping victory, giving the Socialists an absolute majority of 300 seats in the National Assembly. (What if that were to happen in the United States? You can't imagine it? That's because it can't happen here, which begs the question: Why?)

We'll learn more about European politics in general, and France in particular, in Chapter 7; for now, think of Socialists winning elections as a measure of the vast differences in the way Americans and Europeans define the public good.

In this chapter, we group ideologies under three headings: antigovernment ideologies, right-wing ideologies, and left-wing ideologies. Left and Right are very broad categories, however, and there are many shades of gray. Only when the political system becomes severely polarized, as it did, for example, in Germany between the two world wars, are people forced to choose between black and white.

In the two-party system of the United States, the choice is limited to red (Republican) and blue (Democrat). After September 11, 2001, the political climate became more polarized and partisan, as reflected in the charged rhetoric of media figures like Rush Limbaugh, Glenn Beck, and Sean Hannity on the right and of Keith Olbermann and Rachel Maddow on the left. In 2010–2012, the most extreme partisanship since World War II gave rise to government paralysis and gridlock in Congress, which in turn exacerbated political polarization and gave birth to the Tea Party movement. History provides sobering examples of what can happen when a government is dysfunctional, wealth is extremely concentrated, and people become disillusioned.

Antigovernment Ideologies

Opposition to government *in principle* is **anarchism**. The Russian revolutionary Mikhail Bakunin (1814–1876), who reveled in the "joy of destruction" and called for violent uprisings by society's beggars and criminals, is often considered the father of modern anarchism. A close relative of anarchism is **nihilism**, which glorifies destruction as an end in itself, rather than as a means to overthrow the existing system or rebuild society. In Russia during the last half of the nineteenth century, anarchists helped precipitate the discontent that led to the 1905 Revolution, sometimes called a dress rehearsal for the 1917 October Revolution.

Ideologies of the Right

Monarchism is at the opposite end of the political spectrum. Until the twentieth century, monarchy was the prevalent form of government throughout the

anarchism
A system that opposes in principle the existence of any form of government, often through violence and lawlessness.

nihilism
A philosophy that holds that the total destruction of all existing social and political institutions is a desirable end in itself.

monarchism
A system based on the belief that political power should be concentrated in one person (for example, a king) who rules by decree.

world. Whether they were called kings or emperors, czars or sultans, or sheiks or shahs, monarchs once ruled the world. Aristotle regarded monarchy—rule by a wise king—as the best form of government (although he recognized that wise kings, as opposed to tyrants, were very rare).

However archaic it may look to modern eyes, monarchism is not dead. Jordan, Kuwait, Morocco, Saudi Arabia, and the oil-rich Persian Gulf mini-states, as well as Bhutan, Brunei, and Swaziland, are still monarchies. Jordan and Morocco are limited monarchies; in both countries, the chief executive rules for life by virtue of royal birth rather than by merit, mandate, or popular election. Most other countries that still pay lip service to monarchism are, in fact, *constitutional* monarchies in which the king or queen is a figurehead. The United Kingdom is the example we know best in the United States, but Belgium, the Netherlands, Spain, Denmark, Norway, and Sweden all have monarchs as titular rulers.

After World War I, **fascism** supplanted monarchism as the principal ideology of the extreme Right. In Germany, National Socialism—more commonly known as **Nazism**—was a particularly virulent form of this ideology (see Chapter 6). Predicated on the "superiority" of one race or nation and demanding abject obedience to authority, fascism exerted a powerful influence in Europe and South America from the 1920s to the 1940s. The prime examples in history are the Axis powers (Germany, Italy, and Japan) in World War II, but other instances of authoritarian regimes bearing a close resemblance to fascism—including Spain (Francisco Franco), Portugal (Oliveira Salazar), and Hungary (Miklos Horthy)—existed in this period as well.

Argentina under Juan Perón (1946–1955) closely resembled the fascist model after World War II, as did military dictatorships in Brazil, Paraguay, and several other Latin American countries. However, Perón never engaged in the kind of violence and mass repression associated with General Augusto Pinochet in Chile (1974–1990) or General Rafael Jorge Videla in Argentina (1976–1981). More recent examples include Kim Jong-Il of North Korea (who died in December 2011), Hosni Mubarak of Egypt (overthrown in the 2011 Egyptian Revolution), Muammar Qaddafi of Libya (also overthrown in 2011 as part of the wider "Arab Spring"), Omar al-Bashir of Sudan, and Bashar al-Assad of Syria (see Chapter 5).

Fascism enjoyed mass support in many countries largely because of its appeal to nationalism, ethnicity, and (in the case of Nazi Germany) race. Other ideological roots of fascism can be found in romanticism, xenophobia, populism, and even a form of hierarchical socialism.

One of the distinguishing features of many extreme right-wing ideologies is a blatant appeal to popular prejudices and hatred.[3] Such an appeal often strikes a responsive chord when large numbers of people, who are part of the racial or ethnic majority, have either not shared fully in the benefits of society or have individually and collectively suffered severe financial reversals. In turbulent times, people are prone to follow a demagogue, to believe in conspiracy theories, and to seek scapegoats, such as a racial, ethnic, or religious minority group; an opposing political party; a foreign country; and the like. Xenophobia and antipathy to foreigners, immigrants, and even tourists have been on the rise in

fascism
A totalitarian political system that is headed by a popular charismatic leader and in which a single political party and carefully controlled violence form the bases of complete social and political control. Fascism differs from communism in that the economic structure, although controlled by the state, is privately owned.

Nazism
Officially called National Socialism, Nazism is a form of fascism based on extreme nationalism, militarism, and racism; the ideology associated with Adolf Hitler and the Holocaust.

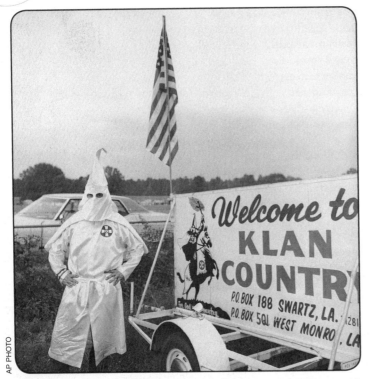

AP PHOTO

Hate groups like the Ku Klux Klan feed on ignorance, prejudice, and fear and often use racial or religious differences to create a scapegoat. As human beings, we want simple answers, quick fixes, and someone to blame when things go wrong.

many European countries (including France, Germany, the Netherlands, and the United Kingdom) and in the United States since the 1990s. Remnants of the American Nazi Party and the Ku Klux Klan (KKK) have lingered as well.

Belief in racial superiority supplies an underlying rationale for a whole range of radical policies dealing with immigration (foreigners must be kept out), civil rights (African Americans, Jews, and other minorities are genetically inferior and do not deserve the same constitutional protections as whites), and foreign policy (threats to white America must be met with deadly force). At the far-right extreme, these groups are organized along paramilitary lines, engage in various survivalist practices, and preach violence. Although the KKK has largely faded from view, it still has die-hard followers, including some in law enforcement. In February 2009, the Nebraska Supreme Court upheld the firing of State Highway Patrol trooper Robert Henderson for his ties to the KKK. The KKK's long history of violence toward African Americans—symbolized by the white sheets worn by its members and the crosses set ablaze at rallies—has made it synonymous with bigotry and racial intolerance.

The Religious Right The religious right in the United States emerged as an important nationwide political force in 1980. The election as president of a conservative Republican, Ronald Reagan, both coincided with and accelerated efforts to create a new right-wing political coalition in the United States. The coalition that emerged combined the modern political techniques of mass mailings, extensive political fundraising, and the repeated use of the mass media (especially television) with a call for the restoration of traditional values, including an end to abortion, the reinstatement of prayer in public schools, a campaign against pornography, the recognition of the family as the basis of U.S. life, and a drive to oppose communism relentlessly on every front.

This movement contained a core of fundamentalist or evangelical Christians, called the New Right, who saw politics as an outgrowth of their core religious values. Beginning in the 1980s, television evangelists such as the late Jerry Falwell (who spearheaded a movement called the Moral Majority) and Pat Robertson (who ran unsuccessfully for president in 1988) gained a mass following. The far right suffered a setback in 1992 when Pat Buchanan's presidential bid also fizzled.

The election of George W. Bush, who openly courted the fundamentalist Christian vote, was widely viewed as victory for the religious right. Roman Catholics and Southern Baptists, along with other evangelical groups, joined forces in a new kind of coalition against what many regular churchgoers saw as an alarming upsurge in immorality and sinful behavior, including abortion, gay marriage, and the teaching of evolution in public schools. The last issue, along with stem cell research, pitted religion against science.

The Christian Coalition, another conservative group, has roots in the Pentecostal church. Boasting as many as one million members, the Christian Coalition produces and distributes a kind of morality scorecard, evaluating political candidates' positions on key issues from the perspective of religious dogma. Its members focus on getting elected to local school boards in order to advocate for patriotism (as opposed to multiculturalism), religion, and a return to the basics in education.

The Christian Coalition's success raised two serious questions. First, was the Christian Coalition best understood as a well-meaning effort by decent citizens to participate in the political arena or as a dangerously divisive blurring by religious bigots of the separation between church and state? Second, was it an interest group or a political party?

Evangelical Christians who embrace a strict interpretation of the Bible often vote on the basis of moral issues such as opposition to abortion and gay marriage rather than on economic issues such as income inequality, tax reform, or job creation.

The 2006 midterm elections and the 2008 election both pointed to the possibility that the political potency of the religious right in U.S. politics was declining. Some critics have suggested revoking the tax-exempt status of religious establishments that cross the line and transform themselves into political movements.[4] But the strength of religious fundamentalists, particularly in the South and Midwest, combined with an antiquated scheme of representation that gives small, sparsely populated states disproportionate voting power in Congress, makes it likely that religion will continue to play a huge role in American politics at all levels in the years to come.

Capitalism The dominant ideology in the United States, Europe, and Asia today is **capitalism**. Even in Communist China, where Maoism remains the official ideology, capitalism is the engine driving the amazing revitalization of the economy since the death of Mao Zedong in 1976. The collapse of communism and its explicit rejection of private property, the profit motive, and social inequality was a triumphant moment for proponents of free enterprise and the free-market economy. Indeed, the Cold War was in no small measure an ideological contest between the United States and the Soviet Union over this very issue.

capitalism
An economic system in which individuals own the means of production and can legally amass unlimited personal wealth. Capitalist theory holds that governments should not impose any unnecessary restrictions on economic activity and that the laws of supply and demand can best regulate the economy. In a capitalist system, the private sector (mainly business and consumers), rather than government, makes most of the key decisions about production, employment, savings, investment, and the like; the opposite of a centrally planned economy such as existed in the Soviet Union under Stalin and Stalin's successors.

In the contemporary world, capitalism is the ideology of mainline conservatives; at the same time, however, it is a basic feature of classical liberalism. In the United States, it is the Republican Party that most enthusiastically embraces capitalism, although few Democrats in Congress ever dare to denounce big business. However disappointing or frustrating this fact may be to some rank-and-file voters, it is not difficult to discern the reasons for it. Capitalism is the ideology of big business, as well as of powerful Washington lobbies, including the U.S. Chamber of Commerce and the National Association of Manufacturers. It also provides the moral and philosophical justification for the often ruthless practices of multinational corporations (MNCs), such as Walmart, Microsoft, McDonald's, and Wall Street financiers, practices that would otherwise appear to be based on nothing more high-minded than the idea that "greed is good." (The U.S. actor Michael Douglas won an Academy Award for his performance in *Wall Street*, a 1987 film in which his "Master of the Universe" character spoke those very words.)

What is capitalism? It means different things to different people. It can refer to an economic theory based on the principles found in Adam Smith's *Wealth of Nations* (discussed later in this chapter). Or it can mean an ideology that elevates the virtues of freedom and independence, individualism and initiative, invention and innovation, risk-taking and reward for success. We can also view it as an elaborate myth system used to justify the class privileges of a wealthy elite and the exploitation of the workers who produce society's wealth. The latter interpretation, of course, derives most notably from the writings of Karl Marx (see "Ideologies of the Left" section in this chapter).

As an economic theory, capitalism stresses the role of market forces—mainly supply and demand—in regulating economic activity; determining prices, values, and costs; and allocating scarce resources. In theory it opposes government interference, and in practice it opposes government regulation. It applauds the notion that, in the words of President Calvin Coolidge, "the business of America is business." Capitalism's proponents, however, often *assume* we have a free market operating solely on the principles of supply and demand; they seldom consider whether it really exists. In fact, the free market is a myth, useful for public relations or propaganda but not for understanding how modern economies actually work. No modern economy can function without all sorts of rules and regulations. The question is not whether rules are necessary, but rather who makes the rules and in whose interests. The key to the success of a market economy is competition, not deregulation.

As an ideology, capitalism opposes high taxes (especially on business), social welfare, and government giveaways. Conservatives tend to believe wealth is a sign of success and a reward for virtue. Rich people deserve to be rich. Poverty is the fault of poor people themselves, who are lazy, indolent, and irresponsible. Relieving poverty is the job of charity and the church, not government. Capitalists also tend (or pretend) to believe in the trickle-down theory: if the most enterprising members of society are permitted to succeed and to reinvest wealth, rather than handing it all over to the tax collector, the economy will grow, prosperity will trickle down to the lower levels, and everybody will be better off.

Critics of capitalism argue that the free market is a fiction and that big business only pretends to support deregulation and the increased competition it fosters. Meanwhile, giant corporations routinely seek tax favors, subsidies, and regulatory concessions and fight antitrust legislation at every turn. Revelations of large-scale fraud and corruption in recent years, symbolized by such fallen corporate outlaws as Enron and WorldCom, had badly stained the image of U.S. business even before the financial meltdown in the fall of 2008. But then came the failure of major investment firms including Lehman Brothers, Wachovia, and Merrill Lynch in 2008, followed by bailouts of banks, automakers, and insurance giant AIG, which were teetering on the brink of bankruptcy.

One measure of how far the corporate sector had fallen in the public esteem: the insurance giant AIG (American International Group) saw its stock plunge from a 52-week high of $52.25 to a low of $0.38 in February 2009. Sensational front-page stories of fraud, misfeasance, and self-aggrandizement associated with such prominent financiers as Bernie Madoff, Robert Allen Stanford, and Jamie Dimon—CEO of JPMorgan Chase & Company blamed for a $2 billion trading loss in 2012—further undermined public trust in business, banks, and Wall Street. Prominent pundits with national audiences—writers like Bill Moyers, Matt Taibbi, Paul Krugman, Joseph Stiglitz, William Black— kept these stories from fading and furnished a steady stream of evidence about collusion between Washington and Wall Street, corruption in Congress, and crime in the suites.

Proponents of **libertarianism** generally agree with the axiom, "That government is best, which governs least." Like classical liberals, libertarians stress the value of individual liberty; but an obsession with fighting all forms of government regulation—even measures aimed at public safety or income security for the elderly—often leads them to embrace policies at odds with logic or common sense. Thus, for example, to quote libertarian Senator Rand Paul (son of 2012 presidential candidate Ron Paul), "a free society will abide unofficial, private discrimination, even when that means allowing hate-filled groups to exclude people based on the color of their skin." Paul also opposed gun control, called for the United States to withdraw from the United Nations Human Rights Commission, and advocated abolishing the Federal Reserve System.

Ideologies of the Left

Left-wing ideologies propose a view of human beings living together harmoniously without great disparities in wealth or social classes. In contrast to capitalism, public goods take priority over private possessions. If equality is the end, state control is the means—control of everything from banking, transportation, and heavy industry to the mass media, education, and health care.

Socialism is fundamentally opposed to capitalism, which contends that private ownership and enterprise in the context of a competitive free-market economy is the best and only way to bring about prosperity. Socialism is "an ideology that rejects individualism, private ownership, and private profits in favor of a system based on economic collectivism, governmental, societal, or industrial-group ownership of the means of production and distribution of goods, and social responsibility."[5]

libertarianism
The belief that the state is a necessary evil best kept small and weak relative to society; libertarians typically value individual liberty above social services and security.

socialism
A public philosophy favoring social welfare and general prosperity over individual self-reliance and private wealth.

communism
An ideology based on radical equality; the antithesis of capitalism.

Marxism
An ideology based on the writings of Karl Marx (1818–1883), who theorized that the future belonged to a rising underclass of urban-industrial workers he called "the proletariat."

dialectical materialism
Karl Marx's theory of historical progression, according to which economic classes struggle with one another, producing an evolving series of economic systems that will lead, ultimately, to a classless society.

bourgeoisie
In Marxist ideology, the capitalist class.

proletariat
In Marxist theory, a member of the working class.

surplus value
Excessive profits created through workers' labor and pocketed by the capitalist or owning class.

law of capitalist accumulation
According to Karl Marx, the invariable rule that stronger capitalists, motivated solely by greed, will gradually eliminate weaker competitors and gain increasing control of the market.

monopoly capitalism
The last stage before the downfall of the whole capitalist system.

Communism is sometimes used interchangeably with **Marxism,** named after its founder Karl Marx (1818–1883). Marx and his associate Friedrich Engels (1820–1895) envisioned a radical transformation of society attainable only by open class conflict aimed at the overthrow of "monopoly capitalism."

Marx and Engels opened the famous *Communist Manifesto* (1848) with the bold assertion, "All history is the history of class struggle." All societies, Marx contended, evolve through the same historical stages, each of which represents a dominant economic pattern (the thesis) that contains the seeds of a new and conflicting pattern (the antithesis). Out of the inexorable clash between thesis and antithesis—a process Marx called **dialectical materialism**—comes a synthesis, or new stage in socioeconomic development. Thus, the Industrial Revolution was the capitalist stage of history, which succeeded the feudal stage when the **bourgeoisie** (urban artisans and merchants) wrested political and economic power from the feudal landlords. The laws of history—or dialectic—which made the rise of capitalism inevitable, also make "class struggle" between capitalists (or owning class) and the proletariat (working class) inevitable—and guarantee the outcome.

Marxist theory holds that the main feature of the modern industrial era is the emergence of two antagonistic classes—wealthy capitalists, who own the means of production, and impoverished workers, the **proletariat,** who are paid subsistence wages. The difference between those wages and the value of the products created through the workers' labor is **surplus value,** or excessive profits, which the capitalists pocket. In this way, owners systematically exploit the workers and unwittingly lay the groundwork for a proletarian revolution.

How? According to Marx's **law of capitalist accumulation,** the rule is get big or get out. Bigger is always better. Small companies lose out or are gobbled up by big ones. In today's world of mergers and hostile takeovers, Marx appears nothing less than prescient here. Eventually, the most successful competitors in this dog-eat-dog contest force all the others out, thus ushering in the era of **monopoly capitalism,** the last stage before the downfall of the whole capitalist system.

The widening gap between rich and poor is the capitalist system's undoing. As human labor is replaced by more cost-effective machine labor, unemployment grows, purchasing power dwindles, and domestic markets shrink. The result is a built-in tendency toward business recession and depression. It all sounded eerily familiar in the midst of the 2008–2009 global recession.

Countless human beings become surplus labor—jobless, penniless, and hopeless. According to the **law of pauperization,** this result is inescapable. For orthodox Marxists, the "crisis of capitalism" and the resulting proletarian revolution are equally inevitable. Because capitalists will not relinquish their power, privilege, or property without a struggle, the overthrow of capitalism can occur only through violent revolution.

The belief that violent mass action is necessary to bring about radical change was central to the theories of Marx's follower Vladimir Lenin (1870–1924), the founder of the Communist Party of the Soviet Union and the foremost leader of the Russian Revolution of 1917. Lenin argued that parliamentary democracy and "bourgeois legality" were mere superstructures designed to mask the underlying reality of capitalist exploitation. As a result, these revolutionaries disdained the kind of representative institutions prevalent in the United States and Western Europe.

With the fall of communism in the Soviet Union and Eastern Europe, **Marxism-Leninism** has lost a great deal of its luster (see "Ideas and Politics"). Even so, the doctrine retains some appeal among the poor and downtrodden, primarily because of its crusading spirit and its promise of deliverance from the injustices of "monopoly capitalism."[6] After World War II, communism spearheaded or sponsored "national wars of liberation" aimed at the overthrow of

IDEAS AND POLITICS

FORGET COMMUNISM, SOCIALISM IS HERE TO STAY

FIGURE 2.2   The leaders of three Latin American democracies (shaded here) have expressed Marxist ideas and adopted anticapitalist rhetoric and policies. Cuba (also shaded) has been a nondemocratic Marxist state since the late 1950s.

In contrast to what happened in many European democracies, Marxism has never gained a toehold in the United States. Yet, in many other parts of the world, Marxist parties have flourished at one time or another. In Castro's Cuba, most of Asia, and parts of sub-Saharan Africa, Communist or Socialist parties long dominated the political scene, and "national wars of liberation" were often spearheaded by self-avowed Marxists.

In many other countries, most notably in Western Europe, nonruling communist parties achieved democratic respectability. The communist parties of France and Italy, to cite two important examples, are legally recognized parties that regularly participate in national elections. Socialist parties are mainstream political parties throughout Europe.

In the 1970s, communist party leaders in Italy and Spain led a movement called Eurocommunism. They renounced violent revolution and sought to change society from within by winning elections.

In recent times, Marxist parties have declined but by no means disappeared. After the "Plural Left" coalition won the French parliamentary elections in May 1997, three Communists were appointed to the cabinet of Socialist Prime Minister Lionel Jospin. In recent years, the elected leaders of Venezuela, Bolivia, and Nicaragua have all expressed sympathy with Marxist ideas and have embraced socialist policies. And China, now boasting the world's second largest economy, is still a communist one-party state. In addition, four other countries continue to be Communist ruled: Cuba, Laos, North Korea, and Vietnam.

© CENGAGE LEARNING

law of pauperization
In Karl Marx's view, the rule that capitalism has a built-in tendency toward recession and unemployment, and thus workers inevitably become surplus labor.

Marxism-Leninism
In the history of the Russian Revolution, Lenin's anticapitalist rationale for the overthrow of the czar (absolute monarch) and the establishment of a new political order based on communist principles set forth in the writings of Karl Marx.

Democratic Socialism
A form of government based on popular elections, public ownership and control of the main sectors of the economy, and broad welfare programs in health and education to benefit citizens.

gradualism
The belief that major changes in society should take place slowly, through reform, rather than suddenly, through revolution.

welfare state
A state whose government is concerned with providing for the social welfare of its citizens and does so usually with specific public policies, such as health insurance, minimum wages, and housing subsidies.

existing governments, especially in the Third World. Since the collapse of communism in Europe, however, the revolutionary role played by the Soviet state and Marxist ideology on the world stage has given way to Islamism—not Islam, the religion, but Islamism, an anti-Western ideological offshoot that seeks to restore the moral purity of Islamic societies (see Chapter 15).

Democratic Socialism, the other main branch of socialist ideology, embraces collectivist ends, but it is committed to democratic means. Unlike orthodox Marxists, democratic socialists believe in **gradualism,** or reform, rather than revolution, but they hold to the view that social justice cannot be achieved without substantial economic equality. They also tend to favor a greatly expanded role for government and a tightly regulated economy. Socialist parties typically advocate nationalization of key parts of the economy—transportation, communications, public utilities, banking and finance, insurance, and such basic industries as automobile manufacturing, iron and steel processing, mining, and energy. The modern-day **welfare state,** wherein government assumes broad responsibility for the health, education, and welfare of its citizens, is the brainchild of European social democracy.

The goal of the welfare state is to alleviate poverty and inequality through large-scale income redistribution. Essentially a cradle-to-grave system, the welfare state model features free or subsidized university education and medical care, generous public assistance (family allowances), pension plans, and a variety of other social services. To finance these programs and services, socialists advocate high taxes on corporations and the wealthy, including steeply progressive income taxes and stiff inheritance taxes designed to close the gap between rich and poor.

Democratic Socialism has had a major impact in Western Europe. The United Kingdom and the Scandinavian countries provide the classic examples. The welfare state became the norm in Europe after World War II, but the aftermath of the 2008 global financial meltdown puts its viability to a severe test. Many EU governments, including Greece, Ireland, Portugal, and Spain, were running huge budget deficits in 2010. Greece, in particular, teetered on the brink of bankruptcy between 2010 and 2012. Indeed, the EU was forced to bail out the governments of Greece, Ireland, and Portugal with massive infusions of euros to prevent them from defaulting and potentially causing the collapse of the euro zone itself. The chronic deficits that led to the euro crisis of 2010–2012 were—and still are—in no small measure a result of generous welfare-state benefits, including health care and pensions, in place in these countries. Attempts to economize through austerity measures (spending cuts and tax increases) met with mass protests in 2012, especially in Greece and Spain.

Unlike France, Spain, and other European countries, the United States does not have a strong socialist party nor has "socialism" ever lost the stigma Americans typically attach to it. In 1932, with the Great Depression in full swing, Socialist Party candidate Norman Thomas polled nearly 900,000 votes, but even that result amounted to only about 2% of the total votes cast!

Nonetheless, many entrenched social programs in the United States resemble measures associated with the welfare state. Examples include Social Security, Medicare, farm subsidies, family assistance, unemployment compensation, and federally subsidized housing. Compared with most Europeans, U.S. citizens pay less in taxes but also get far less in social benefits—except for high-level government employees, the professional military class, and, of course, members of Congress, who enjoy cradle-to-grave benefits that would make even the most ardent socialist blush.

IDEOLOGIES AND POLITICS IN THE UNITED STATES

U.S. politics is essentially a tug-of-war between **liberals** and **conservatives**. These two terms often generate more heat than light, but it is difficult to sort the central issues in U.S. politics without reference to the "liberals" and "conservatives."

The Uses and Abuses of Labels

The political ideas virtually everyone in the United States embraces evolved from a 300-year-old liberal tradition in Western political thought that sees the safeguarding of individual rights as the central aim and purpose of government. Liberals and conservatives alike champion freedom and human rights, but they argue about which rights are fundamental. Liberals tend to favor narrowing the gap between rich and poor, whereas conservatives stress the virtues of free enterprise and tend toward a minimalist definition of equality (for example, equal rights = the right to vote, equal opportunity = the right to basic education, and the like). In general, liberals typically define *equality* broadly in social, political, and economic terms; conservatives tend to confine *equality* to the political realm.

Several factors blur the distinction between liberalism and conservatism in the United States. First, although there are plenty of impassioned liberals and conservatives eager to sound off on television talk shows, in practice voters tend to be more pragmatic than dogmatic. Voters want results, not rhetoric. Second, although politicians often make bold campaign promises, few are willing to go out on a limb by proposing any change that's likely to be controversial (for example, campaign finance reform, health care reform, or bank nationalization). Third, liberals and conservatives sometimes come down on the same side, but for different reasons. For example, conservatives are opposed to pornography on religious and moral grounds; many liberals, on the other hand, favor a ban on "dirty" books because pornography, they say, exploits and degrades women.

Common Themes

Liberalism and conservatism are both rooted in principles found in the political philosophy of John Locke[7] and enshrined in the Declaration of Independence: that all human beings are created equal; that they are endowed with certain unalienable rights, including the rights of life, liberty, and the pursuit of happiness (Jefferson's expansion of Locke's "right to property"); that government exists to protect these rights; and that governmental legitimacy derives from the consent of the governed, rather than from royal birth or divine right.

When government becomes alienated from the society it exists to serve, the people have the right to alter or abolish it. Indeed, the purposes of government

liberal
A political philosophy that emphasizes individualism, equality, and civil rights above other values (see also *conservative*).

conservative
A political philosophy that emphasizes prosperity, security, and tradition above other values (see also *liberal*).

are clearly spelled out in the preamble to the U.S. Constitution: to "establish Justice, insure domestic Tranquility, provide for the common defence, promote the general Welfare, and secure the Blessings of Liberty." As we are about to discover, however, these stirring words are also an invitation to debate.

Conservatives: Economic Rights and Free Enterprise

In stressing economic rights and private property, modern-day conservatives echo and expand on arguments first propounded by political philosophers in the seventeenth and eighteenth centuries. The dawning of the Age of Democracy brought doom to Europe's monarchies and unleashed the economic potential of a nascent middle class and thereby set the stage for the Industrial Revolution.

commercial republic
This concept, found in the Federalist Papers, is most closely identified with Alexander Hamilton, who championed the idea of a democracy based on economic vitality, capitalistic principles, and private enterprise free of undue state regulation.

John Locke (1632–1704) Locke contributed greatly to the idea of the **commercial republic,** a concept that forms the core of modern conservatism. Locke is famous as an early champion of property rights. For Locke, protecting private property is one of the main purposes of government. Locke thus helped lay the foundations for free enterprise and the modern market economy, including such basic concepts as legal liability and contractual obligation.

Many earlier philosophers, from Aristotle to Thomas Aquinas (1224–1274), cautioned against excessive concern for worldly possessions. Locke, in contrast, imagined a society in which invention and innovation are rewarded, the instinct to acquire goods is encouraged, and money serves as the universal medium of exchange. Where wealth can be accumulated, reinvested, and expanded, Locke reasoned, society will prosper; and a prosperous society is a happy one.

Baron de Montesquieu (1689–1755) Although Locke developed the general theory of the commercial republic, the French political philosopher Baron de Montesquieu, in his famous *The Spirit of the Laws* (1748), identified a number of specific advantages of business and commerce. In Montesquieu's view, nations that trade extensively with other nations are likely to be predisposed toward peace because war disrupts international commerce. Montesquieu asserted that commerce would open new avenues for individual self-advancement; that focusing on wealth creation would combat religious fanaticism; and that a culture of commerce would elevate individual morality. A commercial democracy, Montesquieu believed, would foster certain modest bourgeois virtues, including "frugality, economy, moderation, labor, prudence, tranquility, order, and rule."[8]

Adam Smith (1723–1790) Following in the footsteps of Locke and Montesquieu, Adam Smith set forth the operating principles of the market economy. Known to many as the "worldly philosopher," Smith is the preeminent theorist of modern capitalism. In his famous treatise, *An Inquiry into the Nature and Causes of the Wealth of Nations* (1776), Smith explored the dynamics of a commercial society free of regulations or interference from the state. Like Locke, Smith observed that self-interest plays a pivotal role in human relations:

> It is not from the benevolence of the butcher, the brewer, or the baker that we expect our dinner, but from their regard to their own self-interest. We address ourselves, not to their humanity but to their self-love, and never talk to them of our own necessities but of their advantages.[9]

Smith famously theorized about the "invisible hand" of the marketplace, expressed in the *law of supply and demand*. This law, he argued, determines market value. Where supply is large and demand is small, the market value (or price) of the item in question will be driven down until only the most efficient producers remain. Conversely, where demand is great and supply is low, the market value of a given item will be driven up. Eventually, prices will decline as competition intensifies, again leaving only the most efficient producers in a position to retain or expand their share of the market. In this way, the market automatically seeks supply-and-demand equilibrium.

Smith believed self-interest and market forces would combine to sustain economic competition, which in turn would keep prices close to the actual cost of production. If prices did rise too much, producers would be undercut by eager competitors. In this view, self-interest and market conditions make prices self-adjusting: high prices provide an incentive for increased competition, and low prices lead to increased demand and hence increased production. Finally, Smith's free-enterprise theory holds that individuals voluntarily enter precisely those professions and occupations that society considers most valuable because the monetary rewards are irresistible, even if the work itself is not particularly glamorous.[10]

Taken as a whole, these concepts define what has come to be known as **laissez faire capitalism,** or the idea that the marketplace, unfettered by central state planning, is the best regulator of the economy.* Smith argued for the existence of a **natural harmony of interests**: what is good for the happiness of the individual is also good for society, and vice versa, because people will unintentionally serve society's needs as they pursue their own self-interests *without government intervention.*

Modern Conservatism Conservatives are generally opposed to big government and heavy taxes, especially on business and wealth. Conservative political parties and politicians typically appeal to commercial interests and corporate industry, as well as to voters for whom traditional family and religious values are paramount. Critics fault conservatives for opposing state regulation even at the cost of consumer safety, environmental protection, or minority rights.

Conservatives argue that the quest for individual affluence brings with it certain collective benefits, including a shared belief in the work ethic, a love of order and stability, and a healthy self-restraint on the part of government. These collective "goods" are most likely to result, they argue, from a political system that ensures the best possible conditions for the pursuit of personal gain.

Two of the most prominent conservative thinkers in the post–World War II period were Friedrich Hayek (1899–1992) and Milton Friedman (1912–2006). Hayek, a leading member of the Austrian School of Economics, won the Nobel Prize in Economics (with Gunnar Myrdal) in 1974. His book *The Road to*

laissez faire capitalism
An ideology that views the marketplace, unfettered by state interference, as the best regulator of the economic life of a society.

natural harmony of interests
According to Adam Smith, what is good for the happiness of the individual is also good for society, and vice versa, because people will unintentionally serve society's needs as they pursue their own self-interests without government intervention.

---

*Although the French term *laissez faire*—literally "let do" or "let be"—is often associated with Adam Smith's philosophy, Smith did not actually use the term. The first known use of this term in an English-language publication appeared in a book titled the *Principles of Trade* (1774) written by George Whatley and Benjamin Franklin.

Serfdom (1944) inspired a generation of Western free-market economists, and Hayek became an iconic figure for libertarians in the United States.

Friedman was the main architect behind the restoration of classical liberalism as the official economic orthodoxy in the United States (under Ronald Reagan), the United Kingdom (under Margaret Thatcher), Germany (under Helmut Kohl), and beyond. According to *The Economist*, Friedman "was the most influential economist of the second half of the twentieth century...possibly of all of it."[11] In his most famous work, *Capitalism and Freedom* (1962), Friedman argued forcefully that the secret to political and social freedom is to place strict limits on the role of government in the economy. In other words, capitalism is the key to democracy. In this view, it is desirable to minimize government by assigning to the public sector only those few functions that the private sector cannot do on its own—namely, to enforce contracts, spur competition, regulate interest rates and the money supply, and protect "the irresponsible, whether madman or child."

Liberals: Civil Rights and Social Justice

Liberals tend to hold civil rights most dear. They are often vigorous defenders of individuals or groups they see as victims of past discrimination, including racial minorities, women, and the poor. Rightly or wrongly, liberals are often associated with certain social groups and occupations such as blue-collar workers, minorities, gays and lesbians, feminists, intellectuals, and college professors. In general, liberals favor governmental action to promote greater equality in society. At the same time, however, they oppose curbs on freedom of expression, as well as on efforts to "legislate morality."

In the classical liberal view, respect for the dignity of the individual is a seminal value. In his treatise *On Liberty* (1859), John Stuart Mill eloquently stated the case for individualism:

> He who lets the world, or his own portion of it, choose his plan of life for him, has no need of any other faculty than the ape-like one of imitation. He who chooses his plan for himself, employs all his faculties. He must use observation to see, reasoning and judgment to foresee, activity to gather materials for decision, discrimination to decide, and when he has decided, firmness and self-control to hold to his deliberate decision....Human nature is not a machine to be built after a model, and set to do exactly the work prescribed for it, but a tree, which requires to grow and develop on all sides, according to the tendency of the inward forces which make it a living thing.[12]

Mill was at pains to protect individuality from the stifling conformity of mass opinion. Democracy by its very nature, Mill argued, is ill-equipped to protect individuality, as it is based on the principle of majority rule. Thus, following Mill, liberals point out that defenders of majority rule often confuse quantity (the number of people holding a particular view) with quality (the logic and evidence for or against it) and equate numerical superiority with political truth. In a political culture that idealizes the majority, dissenters are often frowned on or even persecuted.

John Stuart Mill (1806–1873). English philosopher and political economist.

Liberals value individualism as the wellspring of creativity, dynamism, and invention in society, the source of social progress. Protecting dissent and minority rights allows a broad range of ideas to be disseminated; keeps government honest; and sets up a symbiotic relationship between the individual and society, one that benefits both.

Differences Essential and Exaggerated

Liberals and conservatives often hold contrasting views on human nature. Liberals typically accent the goodness in human beings. Even though they do not deny human vices or the presence of crime in society, they tend to view antisocial behavior as society's fault. Thus, liberals believe that to reduce crime, society must alleviate the conditions of poverty, racism, and despair. Human beings are innocent at birth and "go bad" in response to circumstances over which they have no control. If you are raised in a violent, drug-infested, inner-city neighborhood with inadequate police protection, you are far more likely to turn to a life of crime than if you are raised in a comfortable and safe middle-class neighborhood in the suburbs.

Conservatives take a dimmer view of human nature. They argue that human beings are not naturally virtuous; that coercion, deterrence, and punishment are necessary to keep people in line; that individuals differ in motivation, ability, moral character, and luck; and that it is not the role of government to minimize or moderate these differences. Consequently, conservatives are seldom troubled by great disparities in wealth or privilege. By the same token, they are generally less inclined to attribute antisocial behavior to poverty or social injustice. There will always be some "bad apples" in society, conservatives argue, and the only solution to crime is punishment. Liberals, on the other hand, maintain that alleviating poverty and injustice is the best way to reduce crime and that punishment without rehabilitation is a dead end.

Is change good or bad? Liberals generally take a progressive view of history, believing the average person is better off now than a generation ago or a century or two ago. They adopt a forward-looking optimism about the long-term possibilities for peace and harmony. As they see it, change is often a good thing.

Conservatives, by contrast, look to the past for guidance in meeting the challenges of the present. They are far less inclined than liberals to equate change with progress. They view society as a fragile organism held together by shared beliefs and common values. Custom and convention, established institutions (family, church, and state), and deeply ingrained moral reflexes are the keys to a steady state and stable social order. Like society itself, traditions should never be changed (or exchanged) too rapidly. As Edmund Burke put it, "change in order to conserve."

The differences between liberals and conservatives, though not insignificant, can be (and often are) exaggerated. Liberals and conservatives share a fundamental belief in the dignity of the individual, freedom of speech, the press, and religion, equality of opportunity, and other important values. In recent years, however, conservativism in U.S. politics has become associated with extreme right-wing groups and voting blocs such as the Tea Party movement, religious fundamentalists, and anti-immigration "nativists."

war on terror
After 9/11, President George W. Bush declared a worldwide "war on terrorism" aimed at defeating international terrorist organizations, destroying terrorist training camps, and bringing terrorists themselves to justice.

Here's what famed political commentator Fareed Zakaria, dismayed at the trends toward conservative radicalism in the United States, wrote in *Time* magazine in June 2011:

> From Aristotle to Edmund Burke, the greatest conservative thinkers have said that to change societies, one must understand them, accept them as they are and help them evolve.
> Watching this election campaign, one wonders what has happened to that tradition. Conservatives now espouse ideas drawn from abstract principles with little regard to the realities of America's present or past.[13]

The "Values Divide" and the War on Terror

The tension between liberals and conservatives escalated into what came to be called a "culture war" or "values divide" in the 1980s.[14] In the 1990s, then Speaker of the House Newt Gingrich launched the "Contract with America"—a conservative agenda aimed at preventing tax increases and balancing the federal budget, as well as a series of congressional reforms. In 2001, a new divide was opened after the September 11 attacks. The ensuing "**war on terror**" was framed within a **neoconservative** worldview and carried out by a president intent upon making homeland security and a crusade against international terrorism the twin pillars of U.S. policy.

Deep divisions over emotionally charged social issues of a moral nature, such as abortion, gay marriage, and stem cell research, also contributed to the polarization of the U.S. body politic in the first decades of the new century. For many conservatives, morality is unambiguous and grounded in religion, whereas liberals tend to believe that morality is personal. Thus, many liberals oppose prayer in schools, favor broad legal and social rights for gays and lesbians, and are pro-choice on abortion. Most conservatives, on the other hand, argue that banning school prayer, allowing gay marriage, and legalizing abortion are morally wrong. Liberals counter that policies denying individual choice violate what is morally right.[15] For liberals, tolerance of diversity is a moral imperative; for conservatives, giving legal sanction to abortion and LGBT (Lesbian, Gay, Bisexual, and Transgender) marriage is itself immoral.

Lost in the din of angry voices was the inaudible voice of reason and the spirit of mutual tolerance. Lost, too, was a willingness to ask fundamental questions: What does the First Amendment separation of church and state mean? Does it work only in one direction—

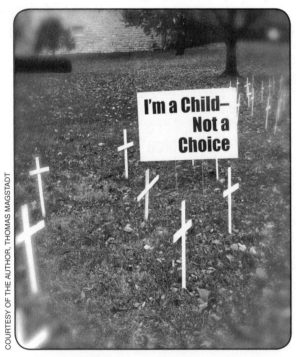

Anti-abortion sign among crosses set on imaginary burial plots of unborn babies on the grounds of a Roman Catholic Church in the politically charged days leading up to the 2012 presidential election.

to protect religion from interference by the state? Or does it also protect the state and its political processes—above all, elections—from interference by tax-exempt (and thus, in effect, subsidized) religious organizations?

Conservatives have traditionally placed little trust in government, believing that less is more. Where tax-funded public programs are necessary, state and local governments are closer to the people and therefore better suited than the federal government to administer them. However, both major political parties have had a hand in the ever-expanding role of the federal government.

A somewhat harsh view of human nature predisposes conservatives to be tougher than liberals in dealing with perceived threats to personal safety, public order, and homeland security. Bush's military response to the 9/11 attacks, which at first greatly boosted his popularity ratings, was in keeping with this stance.

Liberals insist that the rights of the accused be protected even if it means some criminals will escape punishment. The war on terror gave rise to a new controversy over these rights when the Bush administration refused to classify captured alleged terrorists as criminals or prisoners of war, preferring instead to create a new category of detainee—illegal enemy combatants. As such, the government said, these people were entitled to none of the legal protections provided in the U.S. Constitution or under international law.

Conservatives typically do not share liberals' concern for protecting provocative speech, especially when they perceive the speakers as "radicals." Thus, in the war on terror, liberals expressed alarm at provisions of the Patriot Act that allow for increased surveillance powers, warrantless searches and seizures, and, in general, invasions of personal privacy long held to be barred by the Fourth Amendment. Section 215 of the act gives FBI agents pursuing an antiterrorism investigation broad power to demand personal information and private records from citizens. The law also contains a gag rule prohibiting public comment on Section 215 orders. Not surprisingly, libertarians have joined liberals in objecting to what they see as a blatant violation of the Bill of Rights (especially the First and Fourth Amendments).

Although Section 215 was set to expire in December 2009, President Obama backed its reauthorization. The Obama administration caused a furor in November 2010 when it authorized the Transportation Security Administration (TSA) to conduct full body scans of airline passengers—including pat downs.

President Obama vowed to pursue a very different (and more liberal) view in both foreign and domestic policy than his predecessor. But Obama's critics lament that he has failed to keep his promises—to close the Guantanamo prison (the notorious "Gitmo"), for example, or to renounce the practice of "extraordinary rendition," whereby suspected terrorists were grabbed anywhere in the world and taken to secret detention centers to be harshly interrogated and even waterboarded (a form of torture).

In foreign affairs, liberals tend to favor reduced defense spending, whereas conservatives are more apt to follow the adage, "Fear God and keep your powder dry." But, again, this generalization breaks down on close examination. Indeed, the so-called Blue Dog Democrats in Congress (Democrats who identify themselves as either moderate or conservative) are no less opposed to cuts in defense spending than most Republicans.

neoconservative
In the United States, a term associated with the ideology of top advisors and Cabinet members during the presidency of George W. Bush; neoconservatives advocate a strong national defense, decisive military action in the face of threats or provocations, pro-Israeli policy in the Middle East, and a minimum of government interference in the economy. In general, neoconservatives are opposed to federal regulation of business and banking.

Choosing Sides versus Making Choices

Politics is often called a game, as in the "game of politics" or the "political game." In games, we typically choose sides; we cheer for our team and celebrate when we win. Most games have clear winners and losers. Ties are possible in European football (soccer) but not in most other sports.

Politics also has winners and losers—for example, in elections. But outcomes are not so simple or clear-cut. Winning an election means bearing the burdens of government, as well as gaining power. When the winners abuse that power or use it for personal gain or make bad decisions with disastrous consequences, the whole country is the loser; and trust in government is damaged. Thus, choosing sides is a necessity, but it is not the same thing as making wise choices. One sides with conservatives and still votes for a Democrat, or vice versa. The character and qualifications of candidates are, arguably, more important than whether the candidate is a Republican or a Democrat.

Many voters in the United States prefer not to be identified as members of either major party. Independents tend to choose sides one election at a time. Roughly 30% of the U.S. electorate classify themselves as independent in opinion polls.[16] They are the major reason getting the "swing vote" has become crucial to winning elections in recent times. Independents tend to choose which candidate or party to support on the basis of issues, like the state of the economy, taxes, or health care reform, rather than on ideology. In politics, unfortunately, common sense is often uncommon—the exception rather than the rule.

We can easily fall into the trap of believing there are two (and only two) sides to every argument—one right and the other wrong. But the more adamant or partisan each side becomes, the more likely that the truth will elude both, that it will be found somewhere in the gulf between the two extremes. Why? Because politics, like life itself, is too complicated to be reduced to pat answers, populist slogans, or simple solutions.

SUMMARY

Governments seek to attain certain social and economic goals in accordance with some concept of the public good. How vigorously, diligently, or honestly they pursue these goals depends on a number of variables, including the ideology they claim to embrace. An ideology is a logically consistent set of propositions about the public good.

We can classify ideologies as antigovernment (anarchism, libertarianism), right-wing (monarchism, fascism), or left-wing (revolutionary communism, Democratic Socialism, radical egalitarianism). U.S. politics is dominated by two relatively moderate tendencies that are both offshoots of classical liberalism, which stresses individual rights and limited government. It is surprisingly difficult to differentiate clearly between these two viewpoints, principally because so-called liberals and conservatives in the United States often share fundamental values and assumptions. Conservatives stress economic rights; liberals emphasize civil rights. Conservatives are often associated with money and business, on the one hand, and with religious fundamentalism, on the other; liberals are often associated with labor, minorities, gays and lesbians, feminists, intellectuals, and college professors. However, these stereotypes can be misleading: not everybody in the business world is conservative, and not all college professors are liberal.

Liberals look to the future, believing progress will ensure a better life for all; conservatives look to the past for guidance in dealing with problems. Liberals believe in the essential decency and potential goodness of human beings; conservatives take a less charitable view. These differences are reflected in the divergent public policy aims of the two ideological groups.

KEY TERMS

public good   22
ideology   23
anarchism   24
nihilism   24
monarchism   24
fascism   25
Nazism   25
capitalism   27
libertarianism   29
Socialism   29
communism   30
Marxism   30
dialectical materialism   30

bourgeoisie   30
proletariat   30
surplus value   30
law of capitalist
    accumulation   30
monopoly
    capitalism   30
law of
    pauperization   30
Marxism-Leninism   31
Democratic
    Socialism   32
gradualism   32

welfare state   32
liberals   33
conservatives   33
commercial
    republic   34
laissez faire
    capitalism   35
natural harmony of
    interests   35
war on terror   38
neoconservative   38

REVIEW QUESTIONS

1. Constitutional governments might define the public good in terms of attaining certain goals. What are these goals?
2. In what sense does the performance of a government depend essentially on its success in promoting the public good?
3. What is ideology? Is it a scientific term that is easily applied to a political analysis? Why or why not?
4. In twentieth-century Europe, communism and Democratic Socialism vied for popular approval. What are the main points of agreement and disagreement between these two ideological camps?
5. How can we distinguish between a liberal and a conservative in the United States? What fundamental assumptions separate these two ideologies?

CHAPTER 3

Utopias
Model States

THINK ABOUT IT

What is a utopia?

What are the names of four utopian thinkers, and why are they worth studying?

Why is thinking about the ideal state a good exercise?

Why is striving to achieve perfection in the political arena a bad idea?

What constitutes the public good and the good society?[1] To make meaningful comparisons between or among political systems, we first have to clarify what the public good *is* and *is not*. Ideas about utopia found in the writings of philosophers, theologians, and novelists give us a glimpse of the possibilities, of what the best society the imagination can conjure might look like. Imagining the best society leads inevitably to politics: What kind of a government would such a society have? Would a perfect society have any *need* for government? If politics is all about settling differences without violence, perhaps a society without conflict would be altogether *apolitical*.

The study of utopia raises questions about the limits of politics, about the very possibility of rising above politics. Perhaps there is wisdom in the adage that says "the best is the enemy of the good." History tells us that striving for too much can be as bad as—or, in extreme cases, far worse than—settling for too little.

The word *utopia* comes from the title of a book written by Sir Thomas More (1478–1535), the lord chancellor of England under King Henry VIII and an influential humanist. More coined the word from the Greek terms *ou topos*, meaning "no place," and *eutopos*, "a place where all is well." Hence, we might say that a **utopia** is a nonexistent place where people dwell in perfect health, harmony, and happiness.

The literature of Western political philosophy contains a number of elaborate utopian blueprints, each of which represents some thinker's best attempt at imagining the best political order. Thinking about a utopian society leads inexorably toward a critical examination of one's own society and gives us criteria for judging how well we measure up to the ideal. What it often fails to do is tell us how to get there or what dangers and sacrifices we might encounter along the way.

The American people are famous for taking a practical, no-nonsense, problem-solving approach to life. Starry-eyed idealism is for others. And yet, there have in fact been utopian experiments attempted in the United States. In 1826, for example, British industrialist Robert Owen attempted just such an experiment at New Harmony, Indiana. The experiment lasted only two years. Owen's son offered this colorful description of New Harmony society that hints at one reason it failed: "a heterogeneous collection of radicals …honest latitudinarians, and lazy theorists, with a sprinkling of unprincipled sharpers thrown in." [2]

Our exploration of famous utopias begins with Plato's *Republic,* which we contrast with three later versions of utopia: Sir Francis Bacon's *New Atlantis,* Karl Marx's "classless society," and B. F. Skinner's *Walden Two.* Each author finds answers in a different place. For Plato, the answer lies in the realm of philosophy; for Bacon, in science; for Marx, in economics; and for Skinner, in psychology.

There are many other noteworthy examples of utopian literature, including More's *Utopia* (1516) and U.S. writer Edward Bellamy's *Looking Backward, 2000–1887* (1888). There is also a fascinating body of literature on dystopia— well-intended political experiments that went terribly wrong. The purpose of these works, which we review at the end of the chapter, is to demonstrate the danger of trying to build a perfect order in an imperfect world.

utopia
Any visionary system embodying perfect political and social order.

PLATO'S *REPUBLIC*: PHILOSOPHY IS THE ANSWER

Plato's *Republic* takes the form of a long dialogue between Socrates (c. 470–399 BCE) and several imaginary participants. Socrates, considered the first Western political philosopher, held that "the unexamined life is a life not worth living," an idea that has become a cornerstone of Western civilization. As portrayed by Plato (c. 428–348 BCE), Socrates's most brilliant student, Socratic philosophy—the notion that there is no higher purpose than the fearless pursuit of Truth—represents a fundamental alternative to the earlier works of Homer, who praised the virtues of courage and honor, and the later teachings of Jesus, who proclaimed belief in God and moral behavior in accordance with God's word to be the basis of the most exalted life.

Socrates lived for the sake of knowledge unadulterated by power, prejudice, politics, or religion; and in the end he died for it. The rulers of Athens mistrusted Socrates's relentless search for answers to penetrating philosophical questions. Eventually he was accused and convicted of undermining belief in the established gods and corrupting Athenian youth. His execution (by a self-administered drink of hemlock) stands as a poignant reminder of the tension between intellectual freedom and the political order.

In *The Republic*, Socrates begins with an inquiry into the meaning of justice and then proceeds to a discussion of the best political order, one in which there can be no tension between justice and power, philosophers and rulers.[3] There would be no reason for rulers to fear the teachings of philosophers, no need to choose between loyalty to the state and devotion to the truth.

The Perfect Polity

As Plato tells the story, a skeptical listener challenges Socrates to explain why it is better to be just than unjust. Is it not true, he asks, that the successful man who gains power and possessions from unjust actions is much happier than the just man who, like Socrates, has neither power nor possessions?[4]

Socrates first proposes that political life arises from the fact that no individual can be self-sufficient. He goes on to describe a very simple society with no government and no scarcity, whose farmers, shoemakers, and other artisans produce just enough for the perpetuation of a plain and placid way of life. In this society, which seeks to satisfy basic human needs (food, drink, and shelter), each person has a job, a special function essential to maintain the society and keep the economy going.

Prosperity feeds the ambitions and desires of the people for luxuries and more space. The *polis* (city-state) needs to expand to satisfy these demands and to defend itself from attack, and for these tasks, soldiers are necessary. The soldiers, who form the second class in the republic, are initially called guardians.

The education of the guardians encompasses the entire range of human activities, including the aesthetic, intellectual, moral, and physical aspects of life. Because the real aim of education is to teach the truth, censorship is necessary. Ideas that are deemed untrue or dangerous cannot be permitted. Strict discipline is maintained, and everything is held in common, including personal

ANCIENT GREECE: BIRTHPLACE OF JUSTICE

FIGURE 3.1   The Beginnings of Historic Greece, 700–600 BCE.

Ancient Greece was home to Socrates and Plato and the birthplace of political philosophy, thanks in no small part to these two great thinkers. It was the Greeks who invented political philosophy and who placed justice at the very heart of political thought and practice.

Political philosophy is the study of fundamental questions about the state, government, politics, law, and, above all, justice. Indeed, justice is the common thread running through virtually all public policy issues today, but it is often implicit rather than openly acknowledged, despite the fact that we often closely associate justice and liberty. The U.S. Pledge of Allegiance, for example, speaks of "liberty and justice for all."

Of course, justice means different things to different people, depending on the culture and context in which it is used. In the Western tradition, its meaning often depends on whether we use it in a broad or narrow sense. Broadly speaking, justice is essentially a matter of distribution (who gets what, when, and how). In the narrower sense, it is about punishment for breaking the law and about rules of truth and evidence that determine judgments in the law. Today, justice is often couched in the language of political economy (property rights, taxation, contracts, fair trade practices, capital markets, and the like). Although "justice" has been adapted to fit the needs and values of modern society, the concept has been central to Western political thought since at least the time of the ancient Greeks, nearly two and a half millennia ago.

property and spouses. The public good takes precedence over private goods; society supersedes the individual.

At age twenty, some students are designated auxiliaries and assigned the role of defending the city. They will be the republic's soldiers. The others, who retain the name of guardian, continue in school. At the end of a prolonged period of study, a guardian, by understanding the truth of things, can become a philosopher and thus a potential ruler, as only philosophers—those superior in wisdom—hold the highest offices. In the perfect polity, **philosopher-kings** alone are fit to govern.

Plato's republic is a class society. The three classes—farmers and artisans, warrior-auxiliaries, and philosopher-guardians—each excel in one of three virtues essential to the ideal city-state: moderation (workers and artisans), courage (warrior-auxiliaries), and wisdom (philosophers). Only the latter understand the true meaning of justice, the mother of all virtues.

Arguably, so long as each class does its job well (growing food and making things, defending the city, or ruling), the result is justice for all. According to one commentator, "all of Western man's aspirations to justice and the good life are given expression and fulfillment in Socrates' proposals."[5] This is a society based on merit, rather than on pedigree, where everyone's talents can find expression, and where the pursuit of the good life does not depend on personal wealth. It is a society where justice is the watchword and wise men rule for the common good.[6]

To ensure that public servants place the public interest above private interests, family relationships are banned among the soldier and guardian classes.

A eugenics program provides for state control of human sexual relations and ensures the continued existence of exceptional individuals. The guardian class propagates only through carefully orchestrated "marriage festivals" planned for the sole purpose of collective (and selective) breeding. Nothing is left to chance.

By now you are probably thinking that Socrates's idea of utopia is not a place where you would want to live. Socrates would probably not be surprised. After all, if Socrates was right, only a very few among us can ever understand the true meaning of justice. Which raises the question: How can the ruled be persuaded that the rulers know best? Socrates's surprising answer: tell a big lie.

The Noble Lie

To convince the lower class of its proper status, the philosopher-kings are in charge of perpetuating the noble lie—an official myth or ideology—on which the just city depends. The myth is clearly designed to get citizens to see each other as members of a single family (what today we call a nation) and to ensure popular acceptance of the class system essential to the republic's existence. It goes as follows.

Everyone is taught at an early age that all memories of past experiences are only dreams, that they have actually been beneath the earth, where they were fashioned and trained. When they were ready, mother earth sent them to the surface. But first, while still in her womb, where they gestated, they were given souls fashioned of gold

philosopher-king
Wise philosopher who governs Plato's ideal city in *The Republic*.

STEPHEN BISGROVE /ALAMY

One of the greatest philosophers of ancient Greece, Plato believed ideal state authority should rest in the hands of the philosopher-king: "Until philosophers are kings, . . . cities will never have rest from their evils." Look up the word "mimesis" in the dictionary or Google it. Then think about it. . . .

(in the case of philosophers), silver (auxiliaries), or iron and bronze (farmers and artisans).

But in building his theoretical construct, Socrates uncovers serious difficulties. His model is highly impractical, if not impossible. It comes at too dear a price—the abolition of families, the establishment of censorship, and, of course, the big lie underpinning the legitimacy of the regime. Another difficulty arises from the fact that the ideal rulers, philosopher-kings, do not desire to rule— precisely what qualifies them to exercise supreme power! For Socrates, those who lust for power are not fit to rule; philosophers thirst after knowledge, not power, which is why they are best suited to be kings.

Although *The Republic* may not be an actionable blueprint for a political regime, it is valuable for its insights into the nature of justice, the roots of tyranny, and the key role of education in civil society. It is also interesting as a didactic tool and for the methodology Socrates employs. First he builds a utopia, then he tears it down by exposing the practical impediments to its implementation. In sum, *The Republic* is best understood as a philosophical exercise, not as a prescription. Socrates's excursion into utopia is an attempt to advance political thought, not to guide political action.

FRANCIS BACON'S *NEW ATLANTIS*: SCIENCE IS THE ANSWER

The idea that a utopia is possible first gained currency in the seventeenth century. In *The New Atlantis* published in 1627, Francis Bacon describes the imaginary voyage of travelers who discover an island called Bensalem. The travelers have suffered greatly during their long sojourn in the Pacific, and they need food and rest. At first the islanders warn them not to land, but after some negotiations, the travelers are allowed to disembark. Their negative first impressions fade as they come to see the island as it really is: a blissfully happy place.

Bacon merely sketched most of the practical details of day-to-day life in Bensalem. Although its envoys have made secret expeditions to Europe to learn about advances in science, the island is otherwise completely cut off from other societies, eliminating the need for self-defense. It is also economically self-sufficient, endowed with abundant natural resources.

Bensalem is a Christian society, but one that emphasizes religious freedom. Members of various religious faiths hold important positions, and toleration is the norm. The foundation of Bensalem society is the family, and marriage and moral behavior are celebrated. An ancient ruler named Solamona, renowned for his benevolence and wisdom, promulgated laws so perfect that some 2,000 years later they still require no revision.

Bensalem is also a progressive society. Its best minds are assembled at a great college, appropriately called Solomon's House. There, through experimentation and observation, they apply the rules of science to the discovery of "knowledge of causes, and secret motions of things; and the enlarging of the bounds of human empire, to the

Francis Bacon (1561–1626)—English philosopher, scientist, essayist, and statesman—promulgated the idea that science is the key to humanity's comfortable self-preservation: "Nature to be commanded must be obeyed."

effecting of all things possible." In contrast to Plato's Republic, Bensalem pursues knowledge not simply for its own sake, but also for the conquest of nature. Greater material comfort, better health, and a more secure and prosperous way of life make up the great legacy of the academy's laboratories, experimental lakes, medicine shops, and observatories. In Bensalem, science can and should be used for "the relief of man's estate."

In many respects, Bacon's seventeenth-century vision seems prophetic. Through science, for example, life expectancy on the island increases dramatically as whole strains of illness are eradicated. New types of fruits and flowers are produced, some with curative powers. Medical treatment undergoes a technological revolution. The Bensalemites' love of learning and science leads to remarkable discoveries that unlock some of nature's darkest secrets—for example, they can predict impending natural disasters.

Scholars debate Bacon's true intentions in *The New Atlantis*, but few dismiss him as a pie-in-the-sky dreamer. One noted authority sees him as the "first really modern utopian" because Bacon's ideal society was based on science, rather than on religion or superstition.[7] Although his book was not meant to be a precise outline of the future, Bacon envisioned a time and place in which science and social progress, which in his mind go hand in hand, would proceed unimpeded. Bacon's vision of a technological utopia was not a protest against existing society so much as a key to the future and an invitation to imagine a world where science is set free to bring about the radical improvement of the human condition.

classless society
In Marxist political theory, the ideal society in which wealth is equally distributed according to the principle "from each according to his ability, to each according to his needs."

KARL MARX'S CLASSLESS SOCIETY: ECONOMICS IS THE ANSWER

Karl Marx—German philosopher, economist, and revolutionary— believed a just world could be achieved only through the evolution of humanity from a capitalist to a socialist economy and society: "The history of all hitherto existing society is the history of class struggle."

Karl Marx (1818–1883) was also a utopian thinker, but in a different way from Plato or Bacon. Marx's predecessors began with elaborate descriptions of their paradises; and when they engaged in social criticism, it was usually implicit. Marx, by contrast, began with an explicit criticism of existing society and sketched only the broadest outlines of his utopia.

As the originator of "scientific socialism," Marx based his historical analysis on rigorous empirical observation, rather than on abstract reasoning. Nevertheless, the utopian element in Marxism is evident. Unlike earlier utopians, Marx believed his ideal society was not only possible, but also inevitable. Class struggle is the means; the **classless society** is the inevitable end.

Why inevitable? Because, Marx says, human history is a product of irresistible forces. Thus, one socioeconomic system—set of class relations—gives rise to an opposing class system, and out of the struggle between the two comes a new system, a synthesis of the two. This thesis-antithesis-synthesis process is the essence of Marx's theory of dialectical materialism.

The Centrality of Economics

The harsh working conditions and widespread suffering associated with capitalism in the mid-nineteenth century provoked Marx's attack on economic inequality. The wealthy commercial and industrial elites—the bourgeois capitalist class—opposed reforms aimed at improving the living conditions of the impoverished working class—the proletariat. Marx's *Das Kapital* is punctuated with vivid descriptions of employment practices that aroused his anger, such as the following:

> Mary Anne Walkley had worked without intermission for 26½ hours, with 60 other girls, 30 in one room that only afforded ⅓ of the cubic feet of air required for them.... Mary Anne Walkley fell ill on the Friday [and] died on Sunday.... The doctor, Mr. Keys, called too late to the death-bed, duly bore witness before the coroner's jury that "Mary Anne Walkley had died from long hours of work in an overcrowded work-room."[8]

To Marx, the death of Mary Anne Walkley was no mere accident. The machinery of capitalism was remorseless: Mary Anne Walkley was just one of many children who would not live to adulthood.

Marx believed economics, or the production and distribution of material necessities, was the ultimate determinant of human life and that human societies rose and fell according to the inexorable interplay of economic forces. He believed Mary Anne Walkley's harsh life and premature death were dictated by the profit-driven economics of the mid-nineteenth century. But the internal progressive logic of capitalism made it equally inevitable, according to Marx, that the superstructures of power built on greed and exploitation would collapse in a great social upheaval led by the impoverished and alienated proletariat.

The Road to Paradise

Marx referred to the first stage in the revolution that would overthrow capitalism as the **dictatorship of the proletariat.** During this time, the guiding principle would be, "From each according to his abilities, to each according to his needs." Private ownership of property would be abolished. Measures would be put into effect that set the stage for a classless society—including a very progressive income tax, abolition of the right of inheritance, state ownership of banks and communications and transportation systems, introduction of universal (and free) education, abolition of child labor, the "extension of factories and instruments of production owned by the State," and, finally, "the bringing into cultivation of waste-lands, and the improvement of the soil generally in accordance with a common plan."[9]

Eventually, the state and government as we know it would vanish. In the absence of social classes, class antagonisms would disappear according to Marx's collaborator Friedrich Engels, the role of the state as the arbiter and regulator of social relations would become unnecessary, and "the government of persons [would be] replaced by the administration of things and by the direction of the processes of production." In the end, "The State is not 'abolished,' it withers away."[10]

The Classless Society

The natural demise of government, Marx prophesied, would usher in a new and final stage—the classless society. Under capitalism, Marx wrote, "everyone has a definite, circumscribed sphere of activity which is put upon him and from which he cannot escape. He is hunter, fisherman or shepherd, or a 'critical critic,'

dictatorship of the proletariat
In Marxist theory, the political stage immediately following the workers' revolution, during which the Communist Party controls the state and defends it against a capitalist resurgence or counterrevolution; the dictatorship of the proletariat leads into pure communism and the classless society.

and must remain so if he does not want to lose his means of subsistence."[11] Conversely, under communism,

> [when] each one does not have a circumscribed sphere of activity but can train himself in any branch he chooses, society by regulating the common production makes it possible for me to…hunt in the morning, to fish in the afternoon, to carry on cattle-breeding in the evening, also to criticize the food—just as I please—without becoming either hunter, fisherman, shepherd or critic.[12]

Marx believed that human beings come into the world with a clean slate, and what is subsequently written on that slate is determined by society, rather than by genetic inheritance. Along with individual self-fulfillment, social bliss would blossom in the new order, which would be populated by "loyal, wise, and incorruptible friends, devoted to one another with an absolutely unselfish benevolence."[13] One student of Marxist utopianism observed that its description of communist society shares with most other utopian works a "single ethical core," characterized by "cooperative rather than competitive labor, purposeful achievement for societal ends rather than self-indulgence or private hedonism, and an ethic of social responsibility for each member rather than of struggle for survival of the fittest."[14]

The **withering away of the state** so central to Marxist ideology was thus based on a belief in the natural harmony of interests: Eliminate private property and the division of labor, and you eliminate social inequality. Eliminate social inequality, and you eliminate the cause of armed conflict. Obviously, no class struggle is possible when classes no longer exist. Finally, eliminate armed conflict, and you eliminate the need for the state. After all, past societies were nothing more than human contrivances for the perpetuation of class dominance. With the disappearance of social classes, according to Marx, government as we have known it will simply atrophy as a result of its own obsolescence.

The picture of the future that Marx and Engels presented to the world was indeed captivating—and thoroughly utopian:

> Crime would disappear, the span of life would increase, brotherhood and cooperation would inculcate a new morality, [and] scientific progress would grow by leaps and bounds.
>
> Above all, with socialism spreading throughout the world, the greatest blight of humankind, war, and its twin brother, nationalism, would have no place. International brotherhood would follow.…With the socialist revolution humanity will complete its "prehistoric" stage and enter for the first time into what might be called its own history.…After the revolution a united classless society will be able for the first time to decide which way to go and what to do with its resources and capabilities. For the first time we shall make our own history! It is a "leap from slavery into freedom; from darkness into light."[15]

B. F. SKINNER'S *WALDEN TWO*: PSYCHOLOGY IS THE ANSWER

Psychologist B. F. Skinner (1904–1990) was perhaps the most influential contemporary writer on **behavioral psychology**. Skinner believed that all human behavior is environmentally determined, a mere response to external stimuli.

---

withering away of the state
A Marxist category of analysis describing what happens after capitalism is overthrown, private property and social classes are abolished, and the need for coercive state power supposedly disappears.

behavioral psychology
A school of psychological thought that holds that the way people (and animals) act is determined by the stimuli they receive from the environment and from other persons and that human or animal behavior can be manipulated by carefully structuring the environment to provide positive stimuli for desired behavior and negative stimuli for unwanted behavior.

His experiments, designed to control animal behavior (including the training of pigeons to play Ping-Pong), and his theories about the relationship of human freedom to behavior modification have been the object of both acclaim and alarm. In his fictional work *Walden Two* (1948), Skinner outlined his notion of a modern utopian society. He actually believed it possible to create the society described in *Walden Two* with the tools made available by the new science of human behavior.

The Good Life

As described in *Walden Two*, Skinner's imagined utopia is a world within a world. Its fictional founder, psychologist T. E. Frazier, has managed to obtain "for taxes" a tract of land that previously contained seven or eight rundown farms, conveniently self-enclosed, symbolizing its self-sufficiency.

A pioneer in the field of behavioral psychology, U.S. psychologist B. F. Skinner described a utopian society fashioned by the modification of human behavior: "We simply arrange a world in which serious conflicts occur as seldom as possible."

Although concerned about the problem of creating a good society, Frazier disdains philosophy. Difficult questions such as "What constitutes the good life?" he dismisses as irrelevant. "We all know what's good, until we stop to think about it," he declares.[16] For Frazier, the basic ingredients of the good life are obvious: good health, an absolute minimum of unpleasant labor, a chance to exercise your talents and abilities, and true leisure (that is, freedom from the economic and social pressures that, in Frazier's view, render the so-called leisure class the least relaxed of people). These goals are realized in *Walden Two*'s pleasant atmosphere of noncompetitive social harmony.

The Science of Behavioral Engineering

Frazier summed his view about how to produce individual happiness and group harmony in this way:

> I can't give you a rational justification for any of it. I can't reduce it to any principle of "the greatest good." This is the Good Life. We know it. It's a fact, not a theory....We don't puzzle our little minds over the outcome of Love versus Duty. We simply arrange a world in which serious conflicts occur as seldom as possible or, with a little luck, not at all.[17]

The key word here is "arrange." The *kind* of world to be arranged is of only passing interest to Frazier; what commands his attention is the question of *how to do* the arranging. He is concerned not with ends, but with means, not with philosophy, but with scientific experimentation. He is the quintessential methodologist.

Because political action has not helped build a better world, "other measures" are required. What other measures? A revolution in the science of behavior modification:

> Considering how long society has been at it, you'd expect a better job. But the campaigns have been badly planned and the victory has never been secure. The behavior of the individual has been shaped according to revelations of "good conduct," never as the result of experimental study. But why

not experiment? The questions are simple enough. What's the best behavior for the individual so far as the group is concerned? And how can the individual be induced to behave in that way? Why not explore these questions in a scientific spirit?[18]

The Walden Two experiment represents this kind of scientific exploration. Initially, Frazier develops an experimental code of good behavior. Everyone is expected to adhere to it under the supervision of certain behavioral scientists (such as Frazier) called managers. Positive reinforcement, rather than punishment, helps instill behavioral patterns; and a system of finely tuned frustrations and annoyances eliminates the destructive emotions of anger, fear, and lust. For example, to engender self-restraint, Frazier has the schoolteachers hang lollipops, which they are not to lick, around the children's necks. Such **behavioral engineering** will prove successful, Frazier asserts, not because it physically controls outward behavior, but because the conscious manipulation of stimuli effectively influences "the *inclination* to behave—the motives, the desires, the wishes."[19]

Children are placed in a scientifically controlled environment from infancy. They are raised in nurseries and never live with their parents. (Nor do their parents live with one another.) Private property is abolished, all eat together in common dining halls, and boys and girls marry and have children at fifteen or sixteen.

behavioral engineering
The carefully programmed use of rewards and punishments to instill desired patterns of behavior in an individual or an animal.

The Behavioral Scientist as God

Much that is familiar in the outside world is notably absent at Walden Two. Although its residents feel free, there is no freedom in this community. The idea of freedom is illusory, Frazier argues, because all behavior is conditioned. History is viewed "only as entertainment"; schoolchildren do not even study this "spurious science." Religion is not forbidden, but, like government in Marx's utopia, it has withered away through social obsolescence ("Psychologists are our priests," Frazier asserts). Moral codes of right and wrong have given way to "experimental ethics." Politics has no value: "You can't make progress toward the Good Life by political action! Not under any current form of government! You must operate upon another level entirely."[20]

Life at Walden Two has, in fact, been organized to create the most propitious circumstances for the managers' experiments in behavior modification. Although Frazier justifies this on the basis of increased human happiness, we are left with the gnawing sense that something significant is missing—some sort of check on the power of the behavioral engineers who run the community. Power will not corrupt the managers, we are told, for they "are part of a noncompetitive culture in which a thirst for power is a curiosity."[21] They do not use force (nobody does at Walden Two), and the offices they hold are not permanent. These reassurances have a hollow ring, however. Clearly, the love of power—an obsessive need to control others—is not absent from Frazier's own soul. As the founder of Walden Two, he appears to view himself as a kind of messiah who has discovered the secret to a whole new way of life: "I look upon my work and, behold, it is good."[22] Frazier is the ultimate "control freak": a mere mortal who would be God.

UTOPIA REVISITED

Think about it: injustice, conflict, jealousies, rivalries, and individual frustrations—all are absent in these utopias. No deep-seated tensions divide individuals; no great antagonisms exist between society and the state. Each utopia, however, is inspired by a different vision and is ordered according to a different plan.

In *The Republic*, Plato explored the limits of human perfection; he sought not only to depict his idea of the best political order, but also to make clear the problems in attempting to bring it about. Bacon wrote *The New Atlantis* to show not the limits of human achievement but the possibilities that a society wholly predicated on modern science might achieve. His is a hopeful work that promises tangible improvement in human welfare. For Marx, the path to utopia is class struggle and revolution. For Skinner, behavior modification is the solution.

To create a completely happy and harmonious world, a writer must postulate a breakthrough in the way society is constituted. As we have seen, Plato saw philosophy as the key. His republic could not exist until or unless the wisest philosophers ruled (an unlikely prospect at best). Bacon believed the scientific method, rather than logic and deduction, would blaze the trail to a better world. For Marx, philosophy and science were overshadowed by economics; public (collective) common ownership of the means of production, he believed, was the only way to achieve a peaceful and plentiful world. Finally, Skinner viewed the scientific manipulation of human behavior as the key to social and personal fulfillment.

With the advent of modern science and technology, some political thinkers began to take more seriously the practical possibility of achieving utopia. For thinkers like Bacon, Marx, and Skinner, the good life was a real possibility, not a pipe dream.

Utopias are futuristic blueprints for society. Underlying them are certain shared assumptions about human beings and what is best for them. Let's examine these assumptions.

Utopia and Human Nature

Even if an ideal state could be brought into existence, it would be ephemeral. Why? Simple logic, for one thing: If utopia is the best form of government possible, any change is to be resisted at all costs. But the world is constantly changing. So how can any society on earth remain static and still survive? The former Soviet Union, for

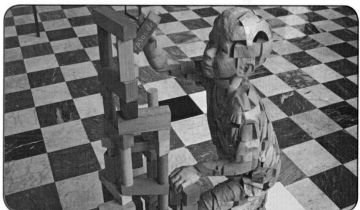

If advances in behavioral science make it possible in theory to reprogram the human mind, who is to say that advances in genetic science will not make it possible one day soon to create the perfect mind in the perfect human body, one free of birth defects, weaknesses, and inherited traits deemed undesirable by society? If so, would the result be a true "master race"? Or would it be a nightmare? What do you think?

example, failed to adapt to a rapidly changing world; the People's Republic of China did not. Both started out as revolutionary states with the goal of creating the kind of classless society Marx envisaged. Although neither succeeded in building a utopia (far from it), one has ceased to exist; the other is challenging the United States for world leadership.

Another big obstacle is human nature. Vices such as dishonesty, lust, greed, malice, and caprice are too common; virtues such as honor, fidelity, kindness, charity, and tolerance are too rare. Not surprisingly, utopian thinkers have often sought ways to reengineer the human makeup through **eugenics** or compulsory education or the abolition of private property. Utopian thinkers often blame institutions that protect, sanction, and perpetuate inequalities, and conclude that the only way to rid society of great disparities in wealth is to abolish established institutions. In many utopias, communal activities, common residences, and public meals replace private property ownership, and cooperation is valued above competition.

Josiah Warren, one participant in the New Harmony Society, mentioned at the beginning of this chapter, reflected on the failure of Robert Owen's utopian project, "We had assured ourselves of our unanimous devotedness to the cause and expected unanimity of thought and action: but instead …we met diversity of opinions…entirely beyond anything we had just left behind us in common society." He added:

> We found more antagonisms than we had been accustomed to in common life. If we had demanded or even expected infinite diversity, disunion and disintegration we should have found ourselves in harmony with the facts and with each other on one point at least. We differed, we contended and ran ourselves into confusion: our legislative proceedings were just like all others, excepting that we did not come to blows or pistols; because Mr. Owen had shown us that all our thoughts, feelings and actions were the inevitable effects of the causes that produce them; and that it would be just as rational to punish the fruit of a tree for being what it is, as to punish each other for being what we are.[23]

eugenics
The science of controlling the hereditary traits in a species, usually by selective mating, in an attempt to improve the species.

Utopia and the Rejection of Politics

If utopians are correct that environment can influence individuals so profoundly, then malleable humans are capable not only of moral perfection, but also of moral corruption. Any flaw in the construction of a utopia—even a moral principle the great majority embrace—can therefore turn a dream into a nightmare. Thus, for example, Michael Young's 1958 book, *The Rise of the Meritocracy*, debunks the ideal of a social order based on pure merit.* Set in 2034 and written from the perspective of an academic social critic analyzing the development of post-aristocratic British society, this work (in which Young coined the term "meritocracy") was interpreted as a paean to the best and the brightest. In fact, says its author, it was "a satire meant to be a warning

*See also Christopher Hayes, *The Twilight of the Elites: America After Meritocracy* (New York: Crown Publishers, 2012). Hayes dates the "corruption and incompetence" of the meritocracy in politics, government, business, banking, and education, among other professions, to the 1960s and 70s.

(which needless to say has not been heeded) against what might happen" if "those who are judged to have merit of a particular kind harden into a new social class without room in it for others."

In almost every utopia (for example, Marx's dictatorship of the proletariat), political power is centralized, giving the state powerful tools with which to reshape and control society. By themselves these tools are neutral; everything depends on how they are used—wisely or foolishly, efficiently or wastefully, for good or for ill. Utopian thinkers tend to assume power will always be used benignly. But in the absence of checks and balances, there is scant reason to believe it will be—and tons of evidence to the contrary.

Utopian thinkers typically display relatively little interest in politics, in the actual workings of government, or, for that matter, in reconciling opposing views. Truth and justice are treated as self-evident, and there is one—and only one—solution to all the problems that beset society. The solution is not to be found in politics, but in the transcendence of politics.

DYSTOPIA: FROM DREAM TO NIGHTMARE

It is significant that the nightmare books of our age have not been about new Draculas and Frankensteins but about what may be termed dystopias—inverted utopias, in which an imagined megalithic government brings human life to an exquisite pitch of misery.

—Anthony Burgess

The dangers of unchecked political power, and the more general theme of utopia-turned-nightmare, are vividly developed in such well-known works as George Orwell's *1984* (1949) and Aldous Huxley's *Brave New World* (1932). Such classic works, along with more recent literary utopias such as Margaret Atwood's *The Handmaid's Tale*, P. D. James's *Children of Men*, Cormac McCarthy's Pulitzer Prize–winning *The Road*, and Lois Lowry's *The Giver*, provide graphic descriptions of a **dystopia,** or a society whose creators set out to build a perfect political order only to discover that, having promised the impossible, they could remain in power only by coercion and by maintaining a ruthless monopoly over the means of communication.

dystopia
A society whose creators set out to build the perfect political order only to discover that they cannot remain in power except through coercion and by maintaining a ruthless monopoly over the means of communication.

A Right to Be Frightened

In 1962, British author Anthony Burgess published a novel with an odd-sounding title: *A Clockwork Orange. Clockwork* received little notice until 1971 when Stanley Kubrick's film adaptation of the book hit movie theaters around the world and it became an overnight sensation. The story is about a juvenile delinquent named Alex who is clever, predatory, and, oddly enough, a music lover (Beethoven, not the Beatles). His crimes of violence include robbery, vandalism, and rape.

Alex is arrested and imprisoned but the Home Office (the British equivalent of the Ministry of the Interior) decides to use "a form of aversion therapy guaranteed, in a mere two weeks, to eliminate criminal propensities forever."[24] Alex welcomes the opportunity to be "cured" of his violent tendencies, and he is confident the treatment won't tame his aggressive libido. He is given injections that induce extreme nausea and at the same time is made to watch films about violence. Soon even thinking about a violent act makes him violently ill. The sight of a desirable woman nauseates him.

But the films also used symphonic music as "emotional heighteners" and now he cannot even stand to listen to Beethoven. Hearing a recording of the Ninth Symphony causes Alex to attempt suicide. We leave the story there. You will have to read the book or watch the movie to find out how it ends.

Burgess published a soul-searching commentary on this famous work in 1973.[25] In it he alluded to Huxley's *Brave New World* and Orwell's *1984*. He noted, "B. F. Skinner's book *Beyond Freedom and Dignity* came out at the very time that *A Clockwork Orange* first appeared on the screen, ready to demonstrate the advantages of what we may call beneficent brainwashing." Skinner was an advocate of positive reinforcement as a way to inculcate habits conducive to peace and harmony in society. "It is...conditioning of the wrong sort that turns the hero of *A Clockwork Orange* into a vomiting paragon of non-aggression," Burgess notes. He concedes that a good deal of conformity is necessary for a society to work, "But when patterns of conformity are imposed by the state, then one has a right to be frightened."[26]

Orwell's World

In *1984*, the totalitarian rulers (personified by a shadowy figure called Big Brother) retain power by manipulating not only the people's actions and forms of behavior, but also their sources and methods of thought. Thus, the Ministry of Truth is established for the sole purpose of systematically lying to the citizenry; a new language ("Newspeak") is invented to purge all words, ideas, and expressions considered dangerous by the government; and a contradictory kind of logic ("double-think") is introduced to make the minds of the citizenry receptive to the opportunistic zigzags of official propaganda.

According to the official ideology, the purpose behind state terror, strict censorship, and constant surveillance is to prevent enemies of the revolution from stopping the march toward full communism—a worker's paradise in which everyone will be happy, secure, prosperous, and equal. In theory, the masses are finally put in control of their own destiny; in practice, they become a new class of slaves whose fate is in the hands of the most ruthless tyrant(s) imaginable.

Utopia and Terrorism

In Chapter 16, we explore the nature of terrorism and its impact on domestic and international politics in the contemporary world. Acts of terror are often associated with religious or ideological zeal, especially when they include the ultimate sacrifice, as in the case of suicide bombers. At least one scholar sees a close connection between the utopian quest for social justice and the Islamist glorification of martyrs.[27]

We might well wonder what could possibly motivate another human being to carry out a mission that is at once barbaric and self-destructive, like the September 11, 2001, attacks on the World Trade Center and the Pentagon, the horrific commuter train bombings in Madrid in March 2004, or the London subway bombings of July 2005. Indeed, terrorist attacks against civilians continue on a daily basis in Iraq and all too frequently in other parts of the world. Such acts are shocking and difficult to understand. What motivates a group of people to plan, prepare, and finally execute a mass murder based on a joint suicide pact?

There is no simple answer. It is quite likely that some terrorists are motivated by a perverted idea of the possible, a misguided sense of what could be if only the imagined source of all evil were annihilated.[28] The identity of the targeted "evil" is almost incidental. Extremists who imagine a time when, for example, Islamic societies were pure and unadulterated—a time before Western ideas, values, music, money, and military occupation corrupted the faithful— can too easily find a justification for killing innocent people in the name of a higher purpose. It is a disturbing fact that in modern history a longing for utopia, a place on earth where happiness knows no limits, is often associated with violence that knows no limits either.

SUMMARY

In the sixteenth century, Sir Thomas More coined the term *utopia* to signify an imaginary society of perfect harmony and happiness. More's *Utopia* was a subtle attack on the ills of English society under Henry VIII. The first important attempt to define the "perfect" political order, however, had been made by Plato in *The Republic*.

Four works stand out as representative of utopian thought in the history of Western political philosophy. In *The Republic*, Plato sought the just society through philosophical inquiry. In the seventeenth century, Francis Bacon's *New Atlantis* demonstrated how the human condition could be elevated through modern science. Karl Marx later propounded the view that only through the radical reorganization of economic relationships within society could true justice and an end to human misery be achieved. The ultimate aim of Marx's theory of social transformation is the creation of a classless society. Finally, in B. F. Skinner's *Walden Two*, a prime example of a contemporary utopian scheme, behavioral psychology holds the key to utopia. The form and content of the just society were of less concern to Skinner than the methods for bringing such a society into existence.

Thoughts of utopia have been inspired by idealism and impatience with social injustices. However, its presumed desirability conflicts with its practical possibility. The principal obstacle to utopian society is the unpredictability and selfishness of human nature, which utopian thinkers commonly have sought to control through eugenics programs, compulsory education, and the abolition of private property.

Utopian visionaries often blame politics for the failure to improve society. As a result, in many utopian blueprints, the role of politics in bringing about desired change is either greatly reduced or eliminated entirely. This leaves most utopian schemes open to criticism, for they could easily become blueprints for totalitarianism. Such blueprints often take shape in writings about dystopias— utopias that turn into nightmares.

KEY TERMS

utopia   45
philosopher-kings   48
classless society   50
dictatorship of the
  proletariat   51

withering away of the
  state   52
behavioral
  psychology   52

behavioral
  engineering   54
eugenics   56
dystopia   57

REVIEW QUESTIONS

1. What is the origin of the term *utopia*? What does the word mean?
2. How have utopian writers differed about the practicality of utopia?
3. Utopian writers often make certain basic assumptions about human nature and society. What are they? Which, if any, do you agree with and why?
4. What can the study of utopian thought teach us about politics in the contemporary world?
5. In the twentieth century, totalitarianism greatly influenced certain novelists who produced chilling stories that turn utopia upside down. Describe one fictional dystopia about which you have read. What, in the novelist's view, brought it into being?

CHAPTER 4

Constitutional Democracy
Models of Representation

THINK ABOUT IT

What is liberal democracy?

What are four models of American democracy?

What is the "tyranny of the majority" and how can it be avoided?

Why are the rule of law and due process fundamental to constitutional government?

Constitutional democracy is a form of government based on representation. In common usage, the term *democracy* is applied loosely—often too loosely to have any real meaning. Any government that does not operate openly and according to clearly established rules does not qualify as democratic. We tend to focus on the rules that govern the governed (laws and regulations), but what is even more important is what rules govern the government—a constitution that functions as the supreme law, the law above ordinary statutory law. That distinction is vitally important as a protection against tyranny; without it, corrupt or misguided legislators could simply change the form of government by a simple majority vote.

Democracies almost invariably rest on constitutional foundations and typically feature elections, representative assemblies (legislatures), an independent judiciary, a free press, and various other institutional constraints on executive power. Cultivating a political culture that places the constitution on a pedestal is a key factor stable democracies share in common.

LIBERAL DEMOCRACY: MODELS AND THEORIES

Democracy means different things to different people. One scholar has identified nine different models of democracy—four "classical" forms and five "contemporary" ones."[1] One of the oldest models is **direct democracy**, which in ancient Greece encompassed a small city-state (Athens) wherein citizens (all those entitled to vote) participated directly in political deliberations and the decision-making process. Another classical model is the **republic**, a form of limited democracy more suitable to a large state and pioneered by the Romans in ancient times.

Governance in the Roman republic required elections and two representative bodies (a senate and an assembly), but it was not very democratic by today's standards. The modern form of republican government is **constitutional democracy**, which stresses political equality and individual liberties. A modern democracy, by definition, is a competitive marketplace of ideas and interests.

Political scientist Richard Katz has developed a useful "typology of liberal democratic theories."[2] Katz's typology asks two key questions. First, is a given society by nature stable or volatile? For a variety of historical, cultural, and demographic reasons, some societies are—or appear to be—more governable than others. Second, do the elites or the masses pose the greatest danger to democracy? Two famous figures in U.S. history, a British philosopher, and three twentieth-century scholars all came up with different theories of democracy corresponding to these two basic questions. Jeremy Bentham and Joseph Schumpeter viewed society as a single undifferentiated mass of individuals, rather than as a collection of groups, classes, or factions. The others saw society as divided or segmented (differentiated), although they differed on exactly how and what this differentiation means.

James Madison and Robert Dahl stated that society is pluralistic, containing many groups, but stressed that individuals belong to more than one group.

direct democracy
A form of government in which political decisions are made directly by citizens, rather than by their representatives.

republic
A form of government in which sovereignty resides in the people of that country, rather than with the rulers. The vast majority of republics today are democratic or representative republics, meaning that sovereign power is exercised by elected representatives who are responsible to the citizenry.

constitutional democracy
A system of limited government, based on majority rule, in which political power is scattered among many factions and interest groups and governmental actions and institutions must conform to rules defined by a constitution.

This overlapping membership creates *crosscutting cleavages*. In other words, individuals identify simultaneously with various groups and organizations, such as town, city, suburb, neighborhood, school, church, or synagogue. But John Calhoun saw society as segmented, rather than fragmented. Arendt Lijphart, a renowned political scientist, is famous for his theory of *consociationalism*, which describes ways democracies can resolve conflicts through power sharing. For theorists like Calhoun and Lijphart, overlapping affinities, interests, and loyalties will not break down the barriers that divide society on the basis of income, race, gender, regions, and the like without deliberate action and wise leadership.

The political implications of these different conceptions of society become clearer when we ask the second question: What is the greatest danger to democracy? For Bentham, who advocated "the greatest good for the greatest number," the economic and social elites threaten democracy, whereas for Schumpeter, the masses clamoring for socialism or a welfare state are the problem. In Schumpeter's view, democracy cannot endure without capitalism to spur economic growth. But because the masses see capitalism as the chief cause of inequality and democracy is based on majority rule, Schumpeter was pessimistic about the future of liberal-democratic government.

For the other four theorists, *pluralism* is more important than class distinctions, but they differ in terms of who and what pose the greatest threat to democracy. Madison and Calhoun saw the elites as the main danger, whereas Dahl and Lijphart identified the masses as the greatest threat.

Who is right? Clearly, it is a difficult question, and perhaps that's the key insight: It points to the conclusion that there are no simple answers, that there is some truth in each of these theories. The type of liberal democracy we choose depends on a larger political theory that takes account of human nature and makes a judgment about the main threat(s) to freedom—democracy's defining value. Next we take a closer look at republics and constitutions.

REPUBLICS AND CONSTITUTIONS

Countries as diverse as France, Poland, India, South Africa, Brazil, and Mexico are all examples of constitutional democracies in action. Official names, such as the German Federal Republic or the Republic of South Korea, reflect the fact that the essence of modern democracy is representation. For this reason, nothing is more vital to the life of republics than regular elections based on the right to vote and the secret ballot. We take this right for granted, but it is a freedom that didn't exist anywhere else in the world when the United States came into being. Today more people enjoy the right to vote in more places than at any other time in history. But to cite one exception among many, it is a right 1.3 billion people in the People's Republic of China—a country with the largest population and second most powerful economy in the world—do not enjoy to this day.

Of course, even where the people have basic rights guaranteed by a constitution, they cannot simply do anything they wish. Every constitutional democracy worthy of the name imposes limitations on **majority rule** and protects minority rights.

majority rule
The principle that any candidate or program that receives at least half of all votes plus one prevails.

By the same token, those in power cannot do whatever they wish either, thanks to **checks and balances** in the constitution defining the basic organization and operation of the government, assigning powers to each branch (executive, legislative, and judiciary), and setting limits to the exercise of those powers.

Most contemporary democracies have written constitutions, but they differ greatly in age and length, as well as content. Some, like those of the United States and France, are models of brevity. Others, including those of India and Kenya, are lengthy and detailed. India's constitution differentiates governmental powers into federal (97), state (66), and concurrent (47). Kenya's constitution allocates authority between the central and regional governments in elaborate detail, covering such subjects as animal disease control, the regulation of barbers and hairdressers, and houses occupied by disorderly residents.

The United Kingdom, the "mother of all parliaments," does not have a formal written constitution. Instead, the British constitution is inscribed in the minds and hearts of the British people. It is a deeply ingrained consensual social contract consisting of custom and convention and certain bedrock principles found in historic documents, royal decrees, acts of Parliament, and judicial precedent.

Constitutional democracies must satisfy three competing, and sometimes conflicting, requirements. First, because such governments are democratic, they must be *responsive* to the people. Second, because they are governed in accordance with established rules and procedures, they are *limited* in the goals they can pursue and the means by which they can pursue them. Finally, like all governments, constitutional democracies cannot succeed or long survive unless they are *effective* in maintaining law and order, managing complex economies, and protecting the civilian population against external threats, such as incursions and invasions by foreign armies, as well as violent crime, natural disasters, and terrorism.

BOTTOMS UP: THE IDEA OF AMERICA

The United States is the birthplace of the first modern theory of representative democracy actually put into practice. Far from perfect at its inception (perpetuating slavery, for example), it nonetheless was a daring departure from the past and a bold attempt to reshape the future, which it did. The success of a political system based on a balance between "bottom-up" and "top-down" power is a defining moment in the history of the modern world (see "Landmarks in History").

The *idea* of America is a product of the eighteenth-century Enlightenment that, in turn, grew out of the Italian Renaissance of the late fifteenth century. The political views of the American Founders, including George Washington, Benjamin Franklin, John Adams, Thomas Jefferson, James Madison, and Alexander Hamilton, drew heavily on the contributions of famous thinkers who lived and wrote during that earlier time—Niccolò Machiavelli, Thomas Hobbes, Jean-Jacques Rousseau, John Locke, and Baron de Montesquieu, among others.

These modern political thinkers all agreed on at least one point: that the purpose of government is not, as Aristotle had claimed, to nurture virtue but

PHILADELPHIA: Birthplace of Liberty

FIGURE 4.1 Map of Colonial America. Philadelphia, Boston, and New York were the three major cities. Washington, D.C., did not come into being until after the U.S. Constitution was adopted in 1788.

LIBRARY OF CONGRESS

On July 4, 1776, the Continental Congress, which met in Philadelphia, Pennsylvania, adopted the Declaration of Independence—an audacious act of defiance against the king of England that was certain to provoke war with the world's preeminent naval power.

The Declaration, which begins with the ringing words, "We hold these truths to be self-evident, that all men are created equal," followed a long struggle between the colonists and the colonizers over issues such as the power to tax, regulate trade and commerce, and

(Continued)

(CONTINUED)

quarter troops. At the root of all these disputes, however, was a thirst for liberty, a burning desire to escape unjust and arbitrary rule. Other grievances included "imposing Taxes on us without our Consent [and] depriving us in many cases, of the benefits of Trial by Jury."

Today schoolchildren still recite the Declaration, and once learned, the key words are seldom forgotten. People, it asserts, have "unalienable Rights" (derived from the "Creator"). These rights are "Life, Liberty and the pursuit of Happiness." The "just powers" of governments derive "from the consent of the governed." This revolutionary manifesto—a stirring call to arms by any measure—came at a time when absolute monarchies ruled all Europe. It preceded the French Revolution by thirteen years. Its creation was the act that led to the modern world's first, and oldest, constitutional democracy.

rather to combat vice. An unflattering view of human nature led these thinkers to stress the pursuit of realistic goals—liberty or security, for example, which is attainable, rather than virtue, which is not.

"America" has been synonymous with liberty in the minds of people all over the world. Arguably, it is the idea itself more than the reality that for many decades gave the United States vast reserves of "soft power" (the ability to get others to want what we want). But the unpopular and protracted Vietnam War eroded that soft power, as did the costly and controversial war in Iraq.

FOUR MODELS OF AMERICAN DEMOCRACY

The principle of majority rule is basic to constitutional democracy. Free elections decide who rules. Citizens play an important role in government—choosing who will hold high office and, therefore, who will make the laws, formulate the policies, and administer the programs on which well-ordered civil societies depend.

Alexander Hamilton (1757–1804). One of the principal authors of the Federalist Papers, published serially in two prominent newspapers in 1787–1788, and still the most authoritative source for the interpretation of the U.S. Constitution. An unrelenting advocate of a strong federal government and an assertive executive branch, Hamilton was the first U.S. Secretary of the Treasury and chief architect of the U.S. system of taxation, the plan for funding the national debt, and the first National Bank. Hamilton died at age 49 from a gunshot wound inflicted by his archenemy, Aaron Burr, in a duel. He is pictured on the U.S. ten dollar bill.

Alexander Hamilton: Federalism

Constitutional democracies cannot ignore the opinions and beliefs of the majority. However, a popular government is not necessarily a viable one. In the words of Alexander Hamilton (1757–1804), "a government ought to contain in itself every power requisite to the full accomplishment of the objects committed to its care,…free from every other control, but a regard to the public good and to the sense of the people."[3]

What good is democracy if the government cannot protect its citizens, promote prosperity, and provide essential services such as education, law enforcement, water treatment, and firefighting? In Hamilton's view, checks and balances, however necessary in a democracy, ought not be carried so far as to impede or impair

the government's ability to act energetically. Madison noted that one of the "very important" difficulties encountered at the Constitutional Convention was "combining the requisite stability and energy in Government, with the inviolable attention due to liberty, and to the Republican form."[4]

Hamilton the indomitable Federalist argued the most passionately—and fought the most fiercely—for a strong central government. With good reason, George Washington turned to Hamilton, the United States' first secretary of the treasury, to put the fledging national government's finances in order and to create a tax system, a federal budget, a central bank, the Customs Service, and the Coast Guard. A brilliant administrator with a penchant for micromanaging everything he touched, Hamilton endeavored to construct a strong central government, one that would be financially solvent, stable, and competent to act without constantly having to secure agreement among the separate states or seek the lowest common denominator among them.

In a real sense, the U.S. Constitution stands as a monument to Hamilton's vision. The president as chief executive is given the power to conduct the nation's foreign affairs, veto legislation, and appoint judges (with the approval of the Senate). The Congress has the power "to make all Laws which shall be necessary and proper"—a formulation that underscores the Founders' determination to avoid the kind of political paralysis that had thrown the colonies into a crisis under the ill-fated Articles of Confederation. And under the so-called **Supremacy Clause** (Article VI, Paragraph 2), all treaties are entrenched as the "supreme Law of the Land; and the Judges in every State shall be bound thereby, any Thing in the Constitution or Laws of any State to the contrary notwithstanding."

Stability and continuity are essential to the success of any government. Established procedures for changing leaders by regularized methods (elections and appointments) are vitally important and represent one of the principal advantages of democracy over modern dictatorships.

History and tradition, along with symbolism and ritual, reinforce the sense of continuity in governments. Citing the need for continuity, Madison opposed Thomas Jefferson's proposal for recurring constitutional conventions, on the grounds that because "every appeal to the people would carry an implication of some defect in the government, frequent appeals would, in a great measure, deprive the government of that veneration which time bestows on everything, and without which perhaps the wisest and freest governments would not possess the requisite stability" and that even "the most rational government will not find it a superfluous advantage to have the prejudices of the community on its side."[5]

Hamilton and other delegates at Philadelphia sought to create a powerful and unified executive branch capable of resisting both the encroachments of Congress and the centrifugal pull of the states. They understood that the absence of a hereditary monarch, regular elections, and the possibility of impeachment are all effective checks on executive power.[6]

For better or worse, Congress is well equipped to resist an overreaching chief executive. Even a popular president can be impeded or even impeached when the opposition party controls Congress. Thus, for example, President Richard Nixon's attempt to use the IRS and the FBI to intimidate his opponents in 1972

Supremacy Clause
Article VI, Section 2, of the Constitution, which declares that acts of Congress are "the Supreme law of the Land…binding on the Judges in every State."

backfired and led to his forced resignation. More recently, when Republicans won control of the House of Representatives in the 2010 midterm elections, they blocked virtually all legislation proposed to implement President Obama's policies, causing what many observers described as a "gridlocked" federal government.

The American Founders deliberately set the stage for a contest. The document they adopted at Philadelphia left plenty of room for interpretation, maneuver, and debate. Its ambiguity is a source of both frustration and strength. Where the line between capabilities and constraints is drawn depends on a mix of history, political culture, and circumstances.

Thomas Jefferson: Anti-Federalism

The validity of democracy is far from self-evident. As Socrates pointed out some twenty-five centuries ago, faced with big decisions on important matters, people turn to experts. Why, then, if we want good government, would we trust ordinary citizens who, after all, tend to be apathetic and ill informed to make wise decisions? If you asked your physician whether or not to undergo an operation, "you would be appalled if he explained that his policy in such cases was to poll a random sampling of passersby and act in accordance with the will of the majority."[7] Yet that is what democracies do all the time, often with dire consequences.

Thomas Jefferson (1743–1826) had more faith in "We the People" than Socrates did or, for that matter, than did many of the other Founders, including Hamilton and John Adams. For Jefferson, the author of the Declaration of Independence, majority rule was the only way to run a democracy. Unlike James Madison and others at Philadelphia, Jefferson did not see the principle of majority rule as a danger to the stability of a future government. Indeed, it was Jefferson who, in 1787, wrote in defense of Shays' Rebellion: "The tree of liberty must be refreshed from time to time with the blood of patriots and tyrants."

Jefferson and Madison embraced quite different views of human nature. Jefferson believed in the basic goodness of the people, that presented with clear alternatives the majority would normally make a rational choice. Alexis de Tocqueville (1805–1859) offered a cogent defense of majority rule in his classic two-volume study, *Democracy in America* (1835): "The moral authority of the majority is partly based upon the notion that there is more intelligence and more wisdom in a great number of men collected together than in a single individual." "The moral power of the majority," Tocqueville wrote, "is founded upon yet another principle, which is, that the interests of the many are to be preferred to those of the few."[8] Moreover, Tocqueville noted, the possibility that today's minority can become tomorrow's majority gives the principle of majority rule a universal appeal.[9]

The political principle of majority rule, therefore, finds support both in the ideal of equality and in self-interest. However, achieving it is not as easy, nor always as highly prized, as we might think. In the United States, where the two-party system is well entrenched, elections typically produce a clear majority in both state and national legislatures. They also produce the *appearance* of a clear majority in most presidential elections. But as we discovered in the

2000 presidential election, when Al Gore won the popular vote but lost the election to George W. Bush, the candidate who gets the most votes is not automatically assured of getting elected. The **winner-takes-all system** awards all the electoral votes in a given state to the candidate who gets the most votes, even if nobody gets a clear majority.

Unlike the United States, most democracies around the world are based on the British system. Parliamentary democracies typically have multiple political parties competing for votes in national elections. Multiparty systems often do not produce a clear majority in the parliament. The upshot is usually a coalition government consisting of two or more parties. The advantage of this system is that voters have more choices; the disadvantage is that no single party has a clear mandate and the very *possibility* of majority rule is called into question. No single party in a coalition government can hew to its own platform and ignore the wishes of its partners in the coalition. In these circumstances, the result is likely to be a government that reflects the lowest common denominator, rather than the will of the people—and a disenchanted electorate.

Even in the United Kingdom, the world's foremost *two-party* parliamentary system, majority rule is problematic. British elections nearly always produce a clear majority in Parliament (see Chapter 7), but the winning party seldom garners more than 45% of the popular votes (and often significantly less). The reason is that the **plurality vote system**—which the British invented—is still in use there (as it is in the United States).

The distinction between majority and plurality voting raises a theoretical problem. If a candidate or government is chosen on the basis of a plurality, rather than a majority, it means more voters did *not* vote for that candidate or government than did vote—possibly many more. But critics of American or British democracy can easily take a wrong turn. More often than not, the reason the majority does not rule is not that the minority has usurped power, but that *there is no clear majority*. Thus, to talk about the myth of the majority is not to denigrate majority rule, but rather to recognize the difficulty of putting it into practice.

The fact that the majority is often elusive raises a problem for democratic theory; the fact that it is often tyrannical raises a problem for democratic practice. Clearly, establishing government by majority rule is easier said than done. We turn next to this problem and how another great democratic theorist proposed to solve it.

James Madison: Balanced Government

Students are often surprised to learn many delegates to the Philadelphia Convention in 1787 did not fully share Jefferson's faith in the people. James Madison (1751–1836) stressed the natural tendency of society to fragment into factions based on self-interest, sectionalism, sectarian divisions, and the like. In Madison's view, Jefferson was naïve if he truly believed that nature predisposes human beings to live together in peace and harmony.

Both Madison and Hamilton expected individuals to act selfishly in politics, just as they do in personal matters, unless constrained by political arrangements designed for that purpose. The fairly clear distinctions that already existed

winner-takes-all system
Electoral system in which the candidate receiving the most votes wins.

plurality vote system
A system in which candidates who get the largest number of votes win, whether or not they garner a majority of the votes cast; in a majority vote system, if no candidate gets more than half the votes cast, a runoff election is held to determine the winner.

James Madison (1751–1836). Fourth President of the United States (1809–1817). Author of many of the Federalist Papers, including several that many constitutional scholars consider seminal, Madison is often called the "Father of the Constitution" in recognition of his leading role in drafting that document. Madison is also credited with authorship of the Bill of Rights. An ally of Jefferson against the Federalists, Madison opposed various centralizing measures favored by Hamilton and John Adams. As president, Madison led the country into the War of 1812 against Britain. Perhaps more adept as a theoretician than as a practitioner of politics, Madison, as chief executive, changed his position on several key issues, favoring creation of a second National Bank (he had opposed the first), a strong military, and a high tariff to protect so-called infant industries.

between economic and social classes during the colonial period underscored Madison's fear of creating politically paralyzing or polarizing factionalism. How could a democratic government be structured to ensure that the public interest would not be sacrificed to the selfish interests of factions?

The Madisonian solution was to ensure factions pursuing selfish ends would encounter as many hurdles as possible. It was this idea that won the day in Philadelphia. The **separation of powers** is one key; the other is **federalism**. For followers of Madison and Hamilton, good government requires a system of checks and balances, which in turn requires the right architecture.

The Architecture of Liberty If people are not by nature virtuous and rulers are people, how can any system of rule *not* degenerate into tyranny? Here, in a nutshell, is the universal problem of politics. The Founders tried to solve this puzzle by developing what they called the "new science of politics," an ingenious arrangement of political institutions designed to permit a large measure of liberty while guarding against the arbitrary exercise of power by compartmentalizing the functions of government, thus preventing the concentration of power.

In *The Federalist*, Hamilton argued that the new U.S. Constitution would prevent "the extremes of tyranny and anarchy" that had plagued previous republics. He admonished his readers not to dwell on past examples: "The science of politics, like most other sciences, has received great improvement. The efficacy of various principles is now well understood, which were either not known at all, or imperfectly known to the ancients." Hamilton catalogued the structural improvements built into the Constitution by the pioneers of this new science:

The regular distribution of power into distinct departments; the introduction of legislative balances and checks; the institution of courts composed of judges, holding their offices during good behaviour; the representation of the people in the legislature by deputies of their own election—these are either wholly new discoveries or have made their principal progress toward perfection in modern times. They are means, and powerful means, by which the excellences of republican government may be retained and its imperfections lessened or avoided.[10]

Because, as Madison noted, "enlightened statesmen will not always be at the helm," it was necessary to create and enshrine durable institutions capable of checking the ambitions of those in power.[11] Elections provide one such check, but "experience has taught mankind the necessity of auxiliary precautions."[12] The chief precaution was to set up a permanent rivalry within the government: "The great security against a gradual concentration of the several powers in the same department, consists in giving to those who administer each department the necessary constitutional means and personal motives to resist encroachments of the others." In short, "Ambition must be made to counteract ambition."[13]

Checks and Balances In pursuit of this goal, the Founders attempted to make each branch of government largely independent of the other branches. Thus, the powers of each respective branch derive from specific provisions of the Constitution—Article I for the legislature, Article II for the executive, Article III for the judiciary. Each branch is given constitutional authority to perform certain prescribed tasks, and each is equipped with the tools to resist any illegitimate expansion of power by the other branches. These tools—called checks and balances—range from the mundane (the president's veto power) to the extraordinary (impeachment proceedings brought by Congress against a president). Together they make up the "necessary constitutional means" available to members of one branch of government for use against the encroachments of another.

As the authors of the Federalist Papers put it, "The interest of the [individual] must be connected with the constitutional rights of the place."[14] Protecting the powers and prerogatives vested in one branch would be motive enough to preserve the integrity of the whole tripartite system. Thus, Congress brought impeachment charges against President Nixon in 1974, alleging he had flouted the Constitution. (Nixon's abuse of power, including his role in the Watergate affair, was the main thrust of the case against him.)

Nearly a quarter of a century later, President Clinton was impeached after he resisted efforts by the Republican Congress to investigate his conduct in office. His opponents also charged that he lied to a grand jury. But Congress spurned public calls for impeachment of President Bush in 2006–2008 over the Iraq War and other issues related to the "war on terror."

Most of the Founders were clearly motivated by a mix of idealism and realism. According to Hamilton, "Men are ambitious, vindictive, and rapacious."[15] Madison concurred, although less bluntly:

> It may be a reflection on human nature, that such devices [as checks and balances] should be necessary to control the abuses of government. But what is government itself, but the greatest of all reflections on human nature? If men were angels, no government would be necessary. If angels were to govern men, neither external nor internal controls on government would be necessary.[16]

Ideally, politicians would discover they could best serve their personal interests (getting reelected) by promoting the public interest. If not, however, Madison's system, like Adam Smith's theory of the "invisible hand" in the marketplace, came equipped with an automatic adjustment mechanism. Thus, it was not on the lofty plane of morality or religion that the new science of politics found its justification, but instead on the firmer ground of institutionalized self-interest.

John C. Calhoun: Brokered Government

John C. Calhoun (1782–1850) was a younger contemporary of the Founders. In the first half of the nineteenth century, he was a leading political figure in the South and served as vice president of the United States from 1825 until 1832, when he resigned over policy differences with President Andrew Jackson.

Contemporary political scientists often refer to Calhoun as the first prominent exponent of a pluralist model of democracy. In the 1820s, Calhoun championed a theory of **brokered democracy** based on the assumption of selfish

separation of powers
The organization of government into distinct areas of legislative, executive, and judicial functions, each responsible to different constituencies and possessing its own powers and responsibilities; the system of dividing the governmental powers among three branches and giving each branch a unique role to play while making all three interdependent.

federalism
A system of limited government based on the division of authority between the central government and smaller regional governments.

brokered democracy
This theory holds that the interests of major groups cannot be steamrolled by the majority without jeopardizing democracy and that legislators and decision makers should act as brokers in writing laws and devising policies that are acceptable to all major groups in society.

motives in politics and what was, in his view, a universal tendency to interpret reality, and even *morality*, in self-serving ways—to put private interests *ahead* of the public interest.

Calhoun sought to tame this tendency through a mechanism he called the **concurrent majority**. In his model of U.S. democracy, there were (and are) many different economic, social, and sectional interests the government must mediate between and among. In a democracy, he reasoned, if one interest prevails over all the others because it has a majority of the votes on a given issue at a given time, neither justice nor the long-term survival of the system can be assured.

In his *Disquisition on Government*, Calhoun made an impassioned argument for protecting the interests of minorities against a steamrolling majority. The way to do so was to abandon the principle of majority rule in favor of government by concurrent majority. Thus, the decision-making model he advocated was one of *compromise* and *consensus* among all major competing interests on important policy questions of the day. If compromise failed and consensus could not be reached, the status quo would prevail indefinitely. In effect, Calhoun argued the case for protecting pluralism at all costs, granting a kind of veto power to minority groups.

Calhoun is a prime example of his own theory in action. As it turns out, he was not only a champion of concurrent majority decision making, but also the leading voice in the famous **nullification** controversy that divided the nation in the decades preceding the Civil War. Proponents of nullification, mainly southerners, held that a state could nullify acts of the Congress within its own borders—if Congress attempted to abolish slavery, for example, the southern states had the right to ignore it. This concept also came to be called "interposition" because it meant a state could interpose its own authority (or sovereignty) to void an act of Congress. Calhoun was, in effect, using the principle of minority rights *against* an oppressed racial minority, slaves.

For Calhoun and his southern cohort, "minority rights" and states' rights were inseparable. The tension between Federalists (favoring a strong national government) and Anti-Federalists (favoring states' rights) had been one of the major themes of the nation's founding and continued to be up to the Civil War.

In fact, the notion of **dual federalism** (near and dear to Calhoun's heart) prevailed between 1835 and 1860. Under dual federalism, the power of the national government was limited to its enumerated powers, southern states claimed sovereign powers, and the all-important question of what would happen or who would prevail in a contest of wills between two "sovereign" governments (national versus state) remained unresolved. The upshot was, of course, the Civil War.

Federalism was at the heart of the fight between the North and South. The Union victory over the Confederacy was a triumph for the concept of a single sovereign seat of government, but it did not resolve the tension between federal authority and the states' rights. An attenuated form of dual federalism survived at least until the Depression Era of the 1930s, when President Franklin Delano Roosevelt launched what political scientists often call "cooperative federalism"—a series of federally funded programs that, in time, redefined the relationship between the national government and the states. From that time to

---

concurrent majority
John Calhoun's theory of democracy, which holds that the main function of government is to mediate between and among the different economic, social, and sectional interests in U.S. society.

nullification
According to this controversial idea, a state can nullify acts of the U.S. Congress within its own borders; John Calhoun and other states' rights advocates put forward this doctrine prior to the Civil War.

dual federalism
Under this system, which prevailed in the United States between 1835 and 1860, the power of the national government was limited to enumerated powers; during this period, the southern states claimed sovereign powers.

the present, the federal government's power has expanded, and the states have taken a back seat. We turn next to a more detailed look at federalism.

Back to Basics: Federalism and the Separation of Powers

Federalism In theory, one way to limit constitutional government is through a division of powers, called federalism. In practice, however, it does not necessarily work that way. Modern examples of federal republics are the United States, Germany, Canada, India, Brazil, Mexico, and Nigeria. After World War II, federalism in Germany, for example, meant the states played a strong role in governing the country and truly did act as a check on central power (see "Ideas and Politics"). In the defunct Soviet Union, by contrast, federalism was a façade that allowed a tightly controlled and highly centralized dictatorship to pretend it was democratic.

Federalism in practice features a division of power between the national government and regional subdivisions. These subdivisions are often called *states*, not to be confused with sovereign states or nation-states.

The United States has a constitutional division of power between national and state governments. Article I, Section 8, of the Constitution, for instance, delineates many areas in which Congress is empowered to legislate. At the same time, the Tenth Amendment provides that all powers not granted to the national government are reserved for the states.

Originally under the U.S. Constitution, states were empowered to maintain internal peace and order, provide for education, and safeguard the people's health, safety, and welfare—through the government's *police powers*. These powers were once exercised almost exclusively by the states. However, the role

IDEAS AND POLITICS

FEDERALISM IN POSTWAR GERMANY

The link between federalism and liberty is particularly striking in the case of Germany. Democracy in Germany was reborn after World War II, when the nation was exhausted by war, defeated, and occupied by foreign armies. The Allied powers, led by the United States, were determined to prevent a new German state from again launching a campaign of military aggression in Europe. The best way to do that, they reasoned, was to inoculate Germany against the virus of dictatorship. The "vaccine" they decided to use was democratic federalism.

How could federalism possibly prevent the rise of a new Hitler? The key is the decentralized structure of Germany's government. The German states (called *Länder*) play an important role in governance on *both* the state and national levels. Delegates appointed by the sixteen state governments make up the upper house of the German parliament, the *Bundesrat*. The upper house has veto power over legislation directly affecting the states, including new taxes. In addition, most of the governmental bureaucracy in Germany falls under the control of the *Länder*. Ironically, Germany's federal system, which was created under close U.S. supervision, is a better example of how federalism is supposed to work than the U.S. system, which once functioned as an effective counterweight to the national (or central) government but no longer does.

of the national (or federal) government has grown enormously since the 1930s, when FDR launched a massive set of federal programs called the New Deal to create jobs and stimulate the economy in the midst of the Great Depression.

President Richard Nixon (1968–1973) tried to reverse this process with a policy called the *new federalism*, which was aimed at making government "more effective as well as more efficient." The two main elements of this policy were the use of so-called block grants to the states and general revenue sharing.

Both Ronald Reagan (1980–1988), a Republican, and Bill Clinton (1992–2000), a Democrat, paid lip service to *devolution* (transferring power back to the states), but did little to match words with deeds. President George W. Bush extended the federal government's law-enforcement and surveillance powers even as he reined in regulation of business and banking by various federal agencies created for that purpose.

Upon taking the oath of office, President Obama moved to reactivate departments and agencies charged with regulating energy and protecting the environment, but some critics on the left reproached him for making too many concessions to mining interests, big oil, builders of natural gas pipelines, and the like. Likewise, his failure to push for stricter regulation of the banking industry in the wake of the 2008 financial crisis also drew sharp criticism in the liberal media (to learn more, Google William Black or Matt Taibbi with keywords such as "bailout" or "financial fraud").

President Obama also imitated his predecessor in other ways: for example, using executive privilege in the summer of 2012 in an effort to thwart a Congressional investigation into a federal cross-border gun-tracking fiasco in Mexico called Operation Fast and Furious, despite a campaign promise to bring greater transparency to government. By the same token, Obama did not hesitate to exercise vast executive war powers during his first term, personally selecting targets for drone strikes and terrorist assassinations in Afghanistan and Pakistan from a "kill list," continuing the practice of "rendition" (capturing terrorist suspects abroad and handing them over to another government to be interrogated and tortured), detaining suspected terrorists without trial, and, of course, declining to close the notorious Guantanamo Bay military prison known as "Gitmo" (again despite a campaign promise to do so).

Why Federalism? The rationale for a division of power is to keep government as close to the people as possible. Thus, some delegates at the Philadelphia Convention argued that a federal system would create a first line of defense against a potentially tyrannical central government. Thus, the states were given equal representation in the newly created Senate, a key role in electing the president (the Electoral College), and an important role in amending the Constitution. Also, as noted earlier, the **reserved powers** provision in the Bill of Rights (the Tenth Amendment) was intended to protect and preserve states' rights.

The struggle to defend or extend states' rights is associated with major historic figures in the United States, including Thomas Jefferson, John Randolph, and John C. Calhoun. But Jefferson Davis, the institution of slavery, and the Civil War are also part of this story. A century later, southern segregationists like Strom Thurmond, George Wallace, and Lester Maddox unsuccessfully led

reserved powers
The reserved powers arise from the Tenth Amendment, which provides that powers not delegated to the federal government, "nor prohibited by it to the States, are reserved to the States respectively, or to the people."

the fight for states' rights against federal action to bring about desegregation in the South.

Federalism in the United States today is far weaker than it was originally. Great controversies once flared over the question of whether a state (for example, Virginia and Kentucky in 1798–1799 or South Carolina in the 1830s) or a region (the South in 1860) could resort to states' rights federalism to justify dissent from specific policies undertaken by the national government. When questions of interest or principle—the Alien and Sedition Acts of 1798, the tariff in the 1830s, slavery in the 1860s—divided the nation, political battles were often fought over the Supremacy Clause (Article VI) or the Tenth Amendment, over the constitutionality of national legislation or what level of government— national or state—had the right to decide.

Issues the Supremacy Clause could not settle, the Civil War did. Although there have been some notable clashes since then, especially in the South over school desegregation in the late 1950s and early 1960s, the federal government is now clearly in the driver's seat, with the states often competing for federal dollars in pursuit of policies hammered out at the federal level.[17]

In the 1990s, however, there was renewed competition between these two levels of government. For example, state governments experimented with educational reforms (charter schools, school vouchers, new ways to bring religion into the classroom) and a variety of anticrime measures (mandatory sentencing, three-strikes laws, victims' compensation). Some states also sought to roll back affirmative action.

After 2001, as the Bush administration rushed to deregulate business, California and some other states fought with the federal government over the right to enact tougher environmental standards than those mandated by Washington. In May 2009, the Obama administration announced that automakers and fourteen states led by California had agreed to a new national standard that by 2016 will match California's in reducing the CO_2 emissions from new vehicles by 30%. In taking this action and pledging to review and revamp federal environmental policies, Obama handed the states a rare intergovernmental victory.

These examples illustrate the sense in which federalism is *competitive,* as well as cooperative. Nonetheless, the federal government towers over the states by virtue of its vast powers to tax and borrow and spend, as well as its status under the Supremacy Clause.

The debate over federalism is ongoing. The Tea Party movement and libertarians who believe with Jefferson, "the government that governs least, governs best"—a view most recently championed by 2012 presidential candidate Ron Paul—argue that the pendulum has swung way too far toward centralization of power in Washington, D.C. Civil rights advocates counter by pointing to the pivotal role of the federal government in promoting racial and gender equality. (We examine the recent history of civil rights and the push for racial equality in Chapter 13.)

Federalism and Liberty Federalism helps protect civil and political liberties by limiting the scope of national government.[18] Nonetheless, the post-9/11

USA Patriot Act
A post-9/11 expansion of federal law-enforcement powers that greatly expands the powers of the executive branch to conduct domestic surveillance including warrantless wiretaps against U.S. citizens.

power of the purse
Under the U.S. Constitution, the provision that gives the Congress the exclusive right to impose taxes and the final word on government spending.

unitary system
A form of government in which most or all power to make and enforce laws resides in the central government; opposite of a federal system.

expansion of federal law-enforcement powers under the provisions of the **USA Patriot Act** raised questions about the proper balance between liberty and security in the twenty-first century. As a main pillar underpinning the ponderous policy architecture of the War on Terror, the Patriot Act greatly enlarged the powers of the executive branch to conduct domestic surveillance including warrantless wiretaps against U.S. citizens.

In contrast to a unitary system of government (see "Ideas and Politics"), the aim of a federal system is political-administrative decentralization. By "multiplying and simplifying the governments accessible" to ordinary citizens, "creating local organized structures capable of resisting centralized authority or mitigating its excesses," and enabling "government to be adapted to local needs and circumstances," decentralization allows "experimentation in the way problems are met." In short, federalism "is a vital safeguard to liberty and a way to educate an energetic and competent citizenry."[19]

Do we still have the necessary degree of decentralization, that "vital safeguard to liberty"? For better or worse, the post-9/11 trend, growing out of the actions and decisions of two presidents and involving both major political parties, has been toward more centralization of power in Washington, not less. This point leads naturally back to one of the perennial questions facing democracy—namely, how to reconcile individual rights and majority rule. We revisit that question in the following section.

The Separation of Powers The U.S. Constitution assigns specific tasks to each branch of government. Congress, for example, is given the **power of the purse.** The president proposes a budget and attempts to influence congressional

THE UNITARY ALTERNATIVE

Most governments in the world today are not federal systems. A far more common form of government is the **unitary system**, such as that found in the United Kingdom. It is called *unitary* because there is only one primary unit of government, the central government, which often turns over many affairs to local governments but is not required to do so. Notably absent from these systems is an intermediate level of government between the center and local political-administrative units.

Some unitary systems, for example those in France and Italy, have guarded the powers and prerogatives of the national government against encroachment by local magistrates, mayors, and politicians more jealously than have the British. In France, *prefects*—officials

appointed by the central government—mediate between the central government in Paris and the local departments. Until the socialist government of François Mitterrand instituted reforms in the early 1980s, the prefects had vast powers of *tutelage* over local governments. The French system of public administration was so centralized and tightly controlled that schoolchildren all over France studied the same subject at the same time every day.

Imagine the national government mandating such a system in the United States! Given the diversity of schools, curricula, accreditation requirements, and academic standards from state to state and school district to school district, do you think people would stand for it?

appropriations, but Congress always has the final word on governmental spending. This arrangement has not been widely copied by other liberal democracies, which typically give the executive branch the upper hand in setting the budget (expenditures), while giving the legislature the primary role on the revenue side (taxation).

In the U.S. model, power and authority are shared in a few areas. Overlapping responsibilities, for instance, characterize the government's **war powers.** Congress funds the armed forces (although the Constitution limits appropriations to two years) and declares war. However, the Constitution makes the president the commander in chief of the armed forces. Therefore, any significant military undertaking, declared or undeclared, requires the cooperation of both branches. Countries with similar institutions generally replicate this pattern, although the idea of civilian control over the military is nowhere more firmly established in principle or practice than in the United States. Even today, the possibility of a military takeover (a so-called coup d'état) in times of crisis remains a danger to civilian rule in some countries.

Members of the three branches in the U.S. government serve different terms of office and different constituencies. Under the Constitution, as amended, the president must stand for election every four years and is limited to two terms of office. The president and the vice president are the only two government officials in the United States who can receive a mandate from the entire national electorate (see "Ideas and Politics").

Members of the U.S. House of Representatives serve local constituencies in districts drawn by state legislatures (in most cases) and are elected for two-year terms. Senators represent states as a whole and serve six-year terms in office. The president, with the advice and consent of the Senate, appoints Supreme Court justices and all other federal judges. The Founders believed this method

war powers
The U.S. Constitution gives the Congress the power to raise and support armies, to provide and maintain a navy, to make rules regulating the armed forces, and to declare war; it makes the president the commander in chief of the armed forces.

presidential democracy
A democratic form of government in which the chief executive is chosen by separate election, serves a fixed term, and has powers carefully separated from those of the other branches of government.

PRESIDENTIAL DEMOCRACY

The U.S. government is often called a **presidential democracy** because the chief executive is elected in balloting separate from the vote for members of Congress. A presidential system is characterized by a separation of powers in which the legislative, executive, and judicial branches of the national government are each responsible to different constituencies for the exercise of their respective powers and responsibilities.

The government is formally organized along functional lines. Because all governments need to formulate, execute, and interpret laws, it is logical to create a legislature to perform the first of these functions (rule making), an executive to carry out the second

(rule implementation), and a judiciary to oversee the third (rule interpretation).

The logic of this arrangement knows no political or geographic boundaries. Today it is reflected in the composition of many democracies in all regions of the world. Presidential democracies are especially common in Latin America, but in various forms they are also scattered in such far-flung places as Russia, France, Yugoslavia, Nigeria, South Africa, Indonesia, and the Philippines.

The major alternative to presidential democracy is parliamentary democracy, which is especially common in Europe and which we discuss at length in Chapter 7.

of selection was more likely to result in fair and impartial justice than requiring judges to stand for election.

The presidential term of office varies from country to country. Presidents in Russia and Brazil, for example, are elected to four-year terms and can run for a second consecutive term, as in the United States. The president of Mexico is elected to a six-year term but cannot run for reelection. Until recently, France's president was elected to a renewable seven-year term; this was reduced to five years in 2000.

TOCQUEVILLE: THE TYRANNY OF THE MAJORITY

Imagine this Wild West scenario: A drifter falsely accused of the cold-blooded murder of a local citizen is jailed, pending trial by a judge and jury. An angry mob clamors for instant justice, but against this throng stand two solitary figures—a crotchety old deputy and the brave sheriff. The inevitable show-down takes place in the street in front of the sheriff's office. Led by the mayor and town council members (one of whom is the actual murderer), a lynch mob demands "the killer" be handed over immediately. Clearly, majority rule is at war with impartial justice. In the end, only heroic action by the sheriff saves the innocent man from being dragged off and hanged from the nearest tree.

When democratic government turns into mob rule, it becomes what Alexis de Tocqueville called the **tyranny of the majority**.[20] For this reason, political thinkers through the ages have often rejected democracy, fearing a majority based on one dominant class, religion, or political persuasion would trample the rights of minorities. The American Founders were conscious of this danger and sought to combat it by structural and procedural prescriptions written into the Constitution (see "Ideas and Politics").

tyranny of the majority
The condition arising when a dominant group uses its control of the government to abuse the rights of minority groups.

bicameralism
Division of the legislature into two houses.

IDEAS AND POLITICS

MINORITY RIGHTS

The Founders of the U.S. political system were troubled by the possibility that the majority would trample the rights of the minority. A **bicameral** legislative branch was designed to prevent large and powerful states from steamrolling smaller and weaker ones. The presidential veto, the independence of the courts, and federalism were also intended as safeguards against the excesses inherent in majority rule.

Many of the world's federal systems are presidential. In most cases, presidents have veto power over legislation, but a determined and united legislature can override a veto. Courts are typically set up to be independent, but there is never any guarantee that judges will be impartial.

In most presidential systems, chief executives can veto legislation. But presidents with the power to reject discriminatory laws also have the power to ignore laws aimed at protecting victims of discrimination. Institutional arrangements designed to curtail arbitrary rule and safeguard minority rights are necessary for democracy to work, but there is no substitute for a politically engaged citizenry and a vigilant electorate.

FIGURE 4.2   Map of Turkey. The Kurds predominate on both sides of Turkey's borders with Syria, Iraq, and Iran.

The United States witnessed acts resembling mob rule in the fall of 2001 during the panic that followed the terrorist attacks in New York and Washington, D.C. When the perpetrators were identified as Muslim extremists, many citizens, horrified by the enormity of the crime, turned against Arab and Muslim minorities living in the United States.

Examples of popular tyranny in democratic countries are not uncommon. In Germany, for example, a sizable Turkish minority has never been granted equal rights. In the Czech Republic (and elsewhere in Eastern Europe), the Czech majority discriminate against the Roma. In Israel, the Arab minority (that is, Arab-Palestinians who are Israeli citizens, rather than residents of the West Bank and Gaza) do not enjoy full political and social equality with the Jewish majority. In Turkey, the rights of the Kurdish minority have often fallen victim to the fears and prejudices of the Turkish majority (see Figure 4.2).

The French Revolution was the first revolt of the masses in modern history, but certainly not the last. In the period between the World War I and World War II, mass movements played an important role in bringing totalitarian regimes to power in Russia, Germany, and Italy—and crushing the seeds and seedlings of democracy.

JOHN LOCKE: THE RULE OF LAW

The idea that nations ought to be governed by impartial, binding laws is not new. Aristotle embraced the **rule of law** because the law represents "reason free from all passion."[21] Therefore, a government of laws is superior to one of individuals, even though individuals (officials, judges, the police) interpret and enforce the laws.

rule of law
The concept that the power and discretion of government and its officials ought to be restrained by a supreme set of neutral rules that prevent arbitrary and unfair action by government; also called *constitutionalism*.

constitutionalism
The concept that the power and discretion of government and its officials ought to be restrained by a supreme set of neutral rules that prevent arbitrary and unfair action by government; also called the *rule of law*.

Magna Carta
A list of political concessions granted in 1215 by King John to his barons that became the basis for the rule of law in England.

More than 2,000 years later, English philosopher John Locke (1632–1704) defended the rule of law on the basis of its close relationship to individual freedom. Locke believed freedom could not exist without written law and that good government must follow certain precepts (for instance, taxes should not be levied without the consent of the people).

To Locke, these rules constitute "laws" of the highest order because they embody what civil society is all about. They are laws above the law that place limitations on lawmakers. From Locke's concept of a higher law, the idea of **constitutionalism** evolved. As Locke noted (and as the inscription above the entrance to the Department of Justice building in Washington, D.C., reads), "Wherever Law ends, Tyranny begins."[22]

Locke was part of a proud English tradition that had long sought to establish limits on government. Rebellious barons forced King John to sign the famous **Magna Carta** in 1215. Originally, this document made concessions only to the feudal nobility, but it later became the foundation of British liberties. Containing some sixty-three clauses, it foreshadowed a system that replaced absolute monarchy with a power-sharing arrangement involving the Crown, aristocracy, and parliament. It obligated the king to seek the advice and consent of royal vassals on important policy matters, including taxation. Equally important was Clause 39, which guaranteed the accused an impartial trial and protection against arbitrary imprisonment and punishment. To that end it stated, "No free man shall be taken or imprisoned, or disposed, or outlawed, or banished, or in any way destroyed…except by the legal judgment of his peers or by the law of the land."

Several landmarks in establishing the rule of law in Britain were achieved during the seventeenth century, in Locke's time. The Petition of Right (1628) further advanced the idea of due process of law while limiting the monarch's power of taxation. In addition, abolishing the dreaded Star Chamber in 1641 did away with a court that used torture to gain confessions and imposed punishment on subjects at the request of the Crown. Finally, the Habeas Corpus Act (1679) limited government's power to imprison people arbitrarily. It imposed substantial penalties on judges who failed to issue timely writs of *habeas corpus*, which demonstrated the accused had been legally detained and properly charged with a crime.

Also originating in the seventeenth century was a judicial precedent that came to have enormous influence in the United States. Renowned English jurist Sir Edward Coke's (1552–1634) opinion in Dr. Bonham's case (1610) asserted that English common law, including the Magna Carta, was the standard to which ordinary acts of Parliament, as well as the British Crown, should be made to conform.[23]

CONSTITUTIONALISM AND DUE PROCESS

Britain's democratic institutions evolved over many centuries. In the United States, it happened very differently—a constitution was hammered out over a period of four months in 1787 at a convention in Philadelphia. The U.S. Constitution and Bill of Rights (the latter of which was largely derived from

English common law) became the standards against which popularly enacted laws would be judged.

Constitutionalism enshrines proper procedure. For instance, the Constitution as interpreted by the U.S. Supreme Court prohibits the president of the United States, even during wartime, from seizing or nationalizing industries, such as steel mills, without congressional approval.[24] Similarly, the concept of **due process**—prescribed procedural rules—dictates that a citizen accused of a crime shall be provided with an attorney, allowed to confront witnesses, informed of the charges brought against him or her, and so on. For the same reason, administrative agencies are compelled by law to provide public notice to those who might be adversely affected by a pending decision. In each instance, the rationale behind the idea of due process is the same: In any game, fairness requires that all the players play by the same rule and that the referee(s) not show favorites. If the winner of an election cheats and gets caught, the cheater is removed from office and can even face jail time. In fact, that was precisely the situation in 1974 when President Nixon was forced to resign (or face certain impeachment) following revelations about his role in the Watergate scandal.

Some critics argue that the principle of due process is taken to extremes in the United States. For example, if the suspect confesses to the crime without being informed that she has a right to remain silent, the confession will be inadmissible in court. In virtually every other liberal democracy in the world, including the United Kingdom, France, Canada, and Australia, to cite but a few examples, a confession is a confession as long as it is not extracted by torture or trickery. Conversely, critics at home and abroad condemn the United States for holding many suspected terrorists at "Gitmo" indefinitely without the right to habeas corpus, and using harsh, inhumane interrogation methods. What do you think?

It is not enough to proclaim the rule of law—words are important, but deeds are imperative if justice is to be done. After the Civil War, the Fourteenth Amendment explicitly guaranteed **equal protection** of the laws to all citizens, including former slaves living in the Deep South. But African Americans continued to be victims of discrimination for many years thereafter. By the same token, women did not gain the right to vote until 1920 and enjoyed few opportunities outside the confines of home and family until fairly recently.

In the United States, government is restricted as to how it can make laws or punish citizens accused of breaking laws. In practice, however, exactly how or where to draw the line between the state and society, between the public and the private, and between authority and liberty is often unclear. Citizens are free to express themselves, but this right is not absolute. Thus, freedom of speech does not give anyone the right to make obscene phone calls, to send death threats through the mail, or to incite a riot.

REMODELING DEMOCRACY: HAVE IT YOUR WAY

Political scientists frequently use models to illustrate or clarify a particular theory or to show a range of possibilities. The fact that so many countries became laboratories for democratic experimentation in the 1990s gave rise to renewed

due process
A guarantee of fair legal procedure; it is found in the Fifth and Fourteenth Amendments of the U.S. Constitution.

equal protection
The doctrine enshrined in the Fourteenth Amendment that holds that the prohibitions placed on the federal government and the protections afforded American citizens under the Bill of Rights also apply to the states.

academic interest in democracy and provided a great variety of "specimens" to study. One upshot was the appearance of a new body of theories and models of democracy.

We give the most attention in this text to three existing models of democracy: the U.S. presidential model, the British parliamentary model, and the French half-and-half, or hybrid, model that combines features of the U.S. and British systems (see Chapter 7). All three are representative democracies and differ primarily in structural and procedural matters—in the way representatives are elected, the relationship between the executive and legislative branches, the role of political parties, and the way the national leader comes to power.

Another way of thinking about democracies is to focus on the role people and participation play under different models. After all, democracy is, by definition, a form of rule by the people. William Hudson, for example, identified four distinct theories of citizen participation and developed a model of democracy for each (Figure 4.3).[25]

The main function of government in Hudson's **protective democracy** is to safeguard liberty rather than national security. Citizens may play a passive political role in this model, but they make up for it by playing an extremely active role in economics. The government is the guardian or protector of the free market, but not its master. According to Hudson, this theory holds that "democracy exists so that free competitive individuals may have and enjoy a maximum of freedom to pursue material wealth."[26] The limits on government are ensured through the elements so familiar to students of the U.S. Constitution, including the separation of powers, federalism, bicameralism, and the Bill of Rights.

In Hudson's **developmental democracy**, the government's focus is on the development of virtuous citizens, not modern economies or political systems. This model views democracy as a kind of school for civic education and socialization. It sees indirect or representative democracy as a way to train citizens in those habits and virtues essential to progress, stability, and prosperity. Their broad participation through voting and expressing opinions is thus essential to making them *feel* closer to government and to help them gain a

---

protective democracy
A self-contradictory governing model put in place in the United States after the 9/11 terrorist attacks; a government that places national security above liberty and justifies curtailment of constitutional rights in times of crisis or war; an oxymoron.

developmental democracy
A model of democracy that emphasizes the development of virtuous citizens; postulates that one essential role of representative government is to serve as a school for civic education to create a politically literate electorate.

FIGURE 4.3
Hudson's Typology of Democracy. Note that although all four models are democratic, the emphasis is different in each one. Does it matter?

Protective democracy = individual liberties + property rights

Pluralist democracy = self-interest + coalescence + oligarchy

Developmental democracy = teaching citizenship through civic activity

Participatory democracy = politically active citizens + multiple opportunities better understanding of the public good, even if they are not active decision makers in it. The paternalistic element is perhaps what most distinguishes it from Hudson's other models.

The **pluralist democracy** model is the one most people recognize immediately. It features vigorous competition among various interests in a society where diversity is the norm. Hudson's model of pluralism, however, emphasizes its tendency to evolve into a hierarchical order dominated by economic elites. This tendency occurs naturally in a society where individuals are free to form associations or interest groups, because the success of organizations depends on group cohesion, common purpose, and strong leadership. Thus, pluralistic democracy is inherently oligarchic. In a society that places a high priority on business, entrepreneurship, and the amassing of personal wealth, the natural result is social and economic inequality.

The final model—**participatory democracy**—is the most straightforward of the four and the closest to a practicable model of direct democracy. In theory, direct democracy means citizens themselves, not elected representatives, decide all major questions of public life. This model could perhaps work in a community or small city-state of a few hundred or even a few thousand citizens at most. It cannot easily work in a large modern state encompassing much territory, many towns and cities, and millions of inhabitants who may or may not even speak the same language.

Nonetheless, participatory democracy is based on the conviction that apathy is a conditioned response, not a trait inherent in human nature. Deprived of opportunities to participate in meaningful ways, people will naturally tune out or get turned off. The key to a vibrant citizenry—and therefore to a healthy democracy—is active participation on a large scale across a wide spectrum of issues. Participatory democracy goes farther, arguing not only that citizens *would* participate actively in politics given the chance, but also that they *should* participate—that is, that they have a right to do so.

Hudson's models of democracy, like all others, are just that—models. They do not represent actual democracies, nor are they necessarily the best way to characterize or categorize different types of democracy. But they do point to basic political questions that confront all contemporary democracies, which was precisely Hudson's intention in developing these models in the first place. The models become the basis for his book analyzing "eight challenges to America's future," namely, restoring the separation of powers, restraining the "imperial judiciary," combating "radical individualism," promoting citizen participation, reforming the "trivialized" election process, curbing the "privileged position" of business, addressing problems of inequality, and, finally, making the "national security state" more transparent and less threatening to its own citizens.

Moving from theory to policy, as Hudson does, is, by its very nature, controversial. In matters of politics, scholars disagree on what the problems are, as well as on how to deal with them. Students may ask, if experts (including college professors) cannot agree on the questions facing democracy, much less on the answers, what is the point of theorizing about democracy? The short answer is that even if it does not provide clear-cut solutions, theory helps us think

pluralist democracy
A model of democracy that stresses vigorous competition among various interests in a free society; akin to the idea of market forces and the role of free enterprise in classic economic theory.

participatory democracy
A model of democracy that seeks to expand citizen participation in government to the maximum possible degree; emphasizes universal suffrage, transparency in government, and opportunities for direct action; includes elements of direct democracy.

about political problems, identify different policy options, and anticipate their consequences. The study of politics is a *social* science, and there is seldom agreement on the vital issues facing society. The existence of different viewpoints is a trademark of constitutional democracy.

We turn, finally, to the future of democracy, and pose two questions. Are existing models of democracy still viable, or is a new one tailored to globalization and the new world order necessary and possible? Is democracy in America broken, as many close observers and a growing number of disillusioned citizens now believe?

THE FUTURE OF DEMOCRACY

Wherever people have access to computers, they are connected to the outside world. The physical distances that separate us are no longer the great barriers they once were to the spread of popular culture, capital, consumer goods, services, and ideas. Given (1) the transforming nature of the new information technologies, (2) an ever-expanding global economy undergoing a tectonic shift in the distribution of wealth from North America and Europe to Asia, and (3) the challenges posed by the new model of authoritarian capitalism propelling a rapidly rising People's Republic of China to prominence, is it possible that democracy as we know it is obsolete?

Cosmopolitan Democracy

cosmopolitan democracy
A model of democracy that sees the individual as part of a world order and not merely (or even primarily) as a citizen of a particular nation-state; often summarized in the slogan, "Think globally, act locally."

Some scholars do believe we need a new model of democracy suitable to an age of globalization. Political scientist David Held has developed a model he calls **cosmopolitan democracy** that attempts to go beyond existing models.

The word *cosmopolitan* in this context denotes a sense of belonging to the world rather than to a particular nation or state. A cosmopolitan individual is, by definition, a frequent traveler who is comfortable abroad, values cultural diversity, and respects the rights of others to live and worship as they choose. Cosmopolitans find the nation-state too confining; they blame nationalism and tribalism for the prejudice and patriotic fervor that divides the world into "us" and "them" and instead foresee a strengthening sense of community without borders.

SEIU HEALTHCARE 775NW

An immigration reform rally in Seattle, Washington, on April 10, 2010. The Washington Immigration Reform Coalition (WIRC) for America, an umbrella group of about sixty organizations, organized this national day of protest to urge Congress to pass a Comprehensive Immigration Reform Bill.

Proponents of cosmopolitan democracy favor the extension of citizenship rights and responsibilities across supranational associations like the European Union (EU). In this way, "people would come…to enjoy multiple citizenships— political membership in the diverse political communities which significantly affect them." They would not only be citizens of a state, but also fully empowered members of "the wider regional and global networks" that are shaping the world we all live in.[27]

But it is unclear what it would mean to be governed by the rules and institutions of cosmopolitan democracy or how such a political system would work in practice. Nor is it likely that national leaders or the citizenry anywhere will embrace the idea. In all probability, age-old loyalties, institutions, and ways of thinking will prove highly resistant to any fundamental change.

Democracy in America: Broke and Broken Beyond Repair?

Nobody knows exactly what globalization and the spread of information, particularly via the Internet, will mean for the future of democracy, but clearly the transformations taking place will change our economic and political institutions. In Europe, for example, the EU now encompasses twenty-seven member-states and constitutes the largest single economy in the world. Many obstacles still stand in the way of a full-fledged political union, but economic integration, a common currency (the euro), qualified majority voting in the European Council, and a directly elected European Parliament have already brought about significant changes in the way Europeans are governed.[28]

Growing economic interdependence among the world's countries is creating an ever-increasing flow of goods, services, labor, and capital across borders and oceans. The most powerful countries in the world, including the United States, exercise less internal control over their fiscal and monetary policies, tariffs, and other trade policies than they once did. Even in the area of immigration and naturalization, long considered a litmus test of state sovereignty, governments are finding it difficult to police international borders and prevent "illegals" from gaining entry.

One thing has not changed despite all the turbulence: the world is still closely watching what happens in Washington. What it sees these days is a system that is not working very well, that many experts are saying is not only broke (a comment on the mounting multitrillion-dollar public and private debt), but also broken. The evidence they cite ranges from gridlock in Congress to the role of money in elections to a panoply of policy fiascos—botched health care reform, tax cuts for the rich, a jobless recovery, chronic federal and state budget deficits, a sagging real estate market, and the "endless" war in Afghanistan, to cite but a few signs of what many see as an increasingly dysfunctional system. Even the Wikileaks disclosure of classified U.S. documents on its website in the fall of 2010 was widely viewed as Washington's fault for failing to manage and control the way classified documents are handled within the U.S. government.

Although it is possible, as some critics suggest, that we are witnessing the decline of the United States as a world power, it is not necessarily so. The problems are real and the machinery of government appears incapable of finding or following through on solutions. The question is not whether American democracy is working—it clearly is not —but whether the system is broken beyond repair, whether it is still capable of adapting to a changing world environment. Meanwhile, the rest of the world continues to look to Washington for leadership in meeting the challenges of pollution and global warming, population and urban overcrowding, energy security and conservation, nuclear proliferation and international terrorism, and the list goes on.

The rise of democracy in its many permutations has been a hallmark of the modern era. The number and variety of democracies multiplied during the course of the twentieth century, a process that greatly accelerated in the 1980s (in Latin America) and 1990s (Eastern Europe). Even so, it is too soon to declare victory for constitutional democracy, the open society, or free-market capitalism.

SUMMARY

In constitutional democracies, governments derive authority from the consent of the governed. Popular election, in theory, ensures that all viewpoints and interests will be represented. Such representation is the defining principle of a republic. Constitutions are designed to place limitations on what governments can and cannot do.

There is no one universally accepted model or theory of liberal democracy. The type of liberal democracy we choose implies a particular view of the basic nature of human society and the main threat(s) to peace and stability.

The idea of America is synonymous with representative democracy in the minds of people all over the world. For inspiration, the Founders drew upon the writings of political thinkers who lived and wrote from the time of the Renaissance to the Enlightenment and who were themselves inspired by classical political philosophy, particularly the writings of Plato and Aristotle from the time of ancient Greece. "The architecture of liberty" grew out of the new science of politics developed by the Founders. That new science was designed to prevent tyranny by compartmentalizing the functions of government (separation of powers) and ensuring that each of the compartments (branches) would have the means to defend itself against encroachment by the others (checks and balances).

We trace three distinct models of American democracy to the ideas of Thomas Jefferson (majority rule), James Madison (balanced government), and John C. Calhoun (brokered government). A fourth model of strong central government is associated with Alexander Hamilton. These early leaders disagreed about how much democracy was too much. Jefferson, for example, favored broad individual liberties and narrow limits on government, whereas Hamilton and others emphasized the need for an energetic national government. Madison falls somewhere between Jefferson and Hamilton. He recognized the danger of governmental paralysis, as well as the need for "energy," but he argued that the best way to achieve freedom and stability was by encouraging a vigorous pluralism, or competition among rival interests. Calhoun was a proponent of states' rights—his views contrasted most sharply with Hamilton's and were closer to Jefferson's.

The concept of popular control through majority rule is central to the creation of a responsive government and holds that the wisdom and interests of the majority are preferable to those of the minority. However, constitutional democracies also place limits on the powers of the government. Protection of individual rights, the rule of law (constitutionalism), and federalism are the principal strategies used to prevent tyranny of the majority. The chapter closes with a look at four contemporary models of democracy and looks into the future of democracy in the light of globalization. A cosmopolitan model of democracy that has practical appeal is yet to be found, but there is no question that technology and globalizing forces have an impact on governments of all types, including democracies.

KEY TERMS

direct democracy 62
republic 62
constitutional
   democracy 62
majority rule 63
checks and
   balances 64
Supremacy Clause 67
winner-takes-all
   system 69
plurality vote
   system 69
separation of
   powers 71
federalism 71
brokered
   democracy 71

concurrent
   majority 72
nullification 72
dual federalism 72
reserved powers 74
USA Patriot Act 76
power of the purse 76
unitary system 76
presidential
   democracy 77
war powers 77
tyranny of the
   majority 78
bicameralism 78
rule of law 79

constitutionalism 80
Magna Carta 80
due process 81
equal protection 81
protective
   democracy 82
developmental
   democracy 82
pluralist
   democracy 83
participatory
   democracy 83
cosmopolitan
   democracy 84

REVIEW QUESTIONS

1. Describe the model of democracy you prefer, and differentiate it from the others. Why did you choose the one you did?
2. What is a republic? Do you think republics are or are not *real* democracies? Explain.
3. Name at least three classical models of American democracy, and explain how they differ from one another.
4. What is federalism? What advantages does this form of government offer?
5. Why did Alexis de Tocqueville (among others) express certain reservations about majority rule?
6. Discuss John Locke's contribution to democratic theory. Can you locate Locke's influence in the U.S. Constitution? If so, where is it?

7. For the theorists involved in the debate over the U.S. Constitution, what was the philosophy behind the "new science of politics"?
8. Recapitulate William Hudson's typology of democracy, and relate it to the models of democracy discussed at the beginning of the chapter.
9. Define *cosmopolitan democracy*, and explain the political context of theoretical attempts to come up with a new, universal model of democracy.

CHAPTER 5

The Authoritarian Model

Myth and Reality

THINK ABOUT IT

What are the virtues of authoritarianism?

What are the vices of authoritarian rulers?

What are two present-day examples of authoritarian rule?

What are five myths about authoritarianism?

Why does the United States sometimes prop up dictatorships and sometimes seek to overthrow them?

Perfection, of a kind, was what he was after,
And the poetry he invented was easy to understand;
He knew human folly like the back of his hand,
And was greatly interested in armies and fleets;
When he laughed, respectable senators burst with laughter,
And when he cried the little children died in the streets.

—W. H. Auden, "Epitaph on a Tyrant"

History and logic point to disturbing fact: Dictatorship is more natural than democracy. But natural is not *always* better, especially in the realm of politics, where "nature"—especially *human* nature—is often the problem. The perennial challenge of politics is to temper the violent, antisocial side of human nature—greed, pride, deceit, lust, jealousy, and vengeance—with the kinder, gentler side associated with humility, empathy, honesty, civility, and a sense of fairness.

One way to compare political and economic systems objectively (that is, using common criteria, rules of evidence, and methods of data collection) is to ask whether some regimes are better than others at fostering the type of character traits most compatible with social harmony, happiness, and progress. Are people happier living under freely elected ("democratic") governments than under authoritarian ones? Are they nicer to each other? If you think the answers to questions like these are obvious, think again. Surveys show that people in New Zealand (a constitutional monarchy) are happier than people in Greece or Spain (both democracies), but were people in Greece and Spain in 2012 happier than people in Oman or Bhutan (both monarchies)? Indeed, rather than rely on statistical indicators based on Gross National Product (GNP), Bhutan seeks to measure Gross National Happiness using these four categories: sustainable development, cultural values, natural environment, and good governance.

Until relatively recently, authoritarian states greatly outnumbered democracies in the world. Indeed, democracies with a few notable exceptions (Australia, New Zealand, India, and Japan) were prevalent only in Western Europe and North America prior to the 1980s and 1990s when military dictatorships in Latin America and communist regimes in Eastern Europe gave way to multiparty civilian rule.

Authoritarian states come in various shapes and sizes. They can be traditional (monarchies and theocracies) or modern. Modern one-party authoritarian states often assume the form of military juntas (the "j" is pronounced like the "h" in hoop) or civilian dictatorships. At the other end of the spectrum are monarchies found mainly in the Arab Middle East. Examples include Morocco, Saudi Arabia, Jordan, Kuwait, Oman, Bahrain, Qatar, and the United Arab Emirates. In Iran after the fall of Shah Reza Pahlavi in 1979 a rigid and repressive anti-Western **theocracy** replaced a pro-U.S. modern dictatorship.

Whatever precise shape and form they assume, authoritarian states share certain telltale traits. Self-appointed rulers typically run the show, and all political

authoritarian state
Wherever supreme political power is concentrated in one person (dictatorship) or a small group of persons (oligarchy), individual rights are subordinate to the wishes of the state, and all means necessary are used to repress dissent and crush opposition.

theocracy
A state like present-day Iran in which religious leaders monopolize political power, legitimate authority derives from a common belief in one god, and there is no separation of church and state.

power—in practice and often in principle—resides in one or several persons. In contrast to totalitarian rulers who typically use a utopian ideology to justify harsh or brutal acts of state repression, the most successful authoritarian rulers tend to be pragmatic, spurning ideological or religious dogmas, censoring the press, jailing dissidents, and, above all, encouraging trade, investment, and economic development.

Typically, authoritarian rulers do not try to control every aspect of society and the economy. Politically, they do what they think is necessary to keep themselves in power. Authoritarian regimes continue to be the main alternative to constitutional democracy. As such, they warrant closer examination.

THE VIRTUES OF AUTHORITARIAN STATES

Virtues? Authoritarian regimes have had a great deal more success over a lot longer period than democracies. Other than for a few relatively brief historical periods—classical Greece and Rome, medieval and Renaissance Italy, and the contemporary age—monarchy as a political system has had few serious challengers (though many individual monarchs have been less fortunate). Even during the more "enlightened" eras, monarchy was the most prevalent form of government. In the golden age of the Greek city-state system, for example, the principal alternative to monarchy was another form of authoritarianism, oligarchy. Republics were rare.

Why? What are the advantages of authoritarian rule? First, unlike democratic systems based on constitutions and the rule of law, a dictatorship is relatively simple and efficient. There is less need to develop complex structures, procedures, and rules.

Second, dictatorships can act quickly. There is no need to bargain or compromise or cajole. Individuals loyal to the regime typically staff the bureaucracy. Recruitment is based on patronage and nepotism rather than on merit.

Third, neither special interest groups nor public opinion can block or blunt state action. Any serious opposition is suppressed; critics are silenced, jailed, exiled, or executed.

Fourth, a strong leader can collect taxes, build infrastructure (canals, roads, bridges), raise armies, and rally the nation for defensive purposes like self-preservation or offensive ones like expansion. Abraham Lincoln, one of our most admired and revered presidents, exercised dictatorial powers during the Civil War.

Fifth, unlike democracies, dictatorships often remain politically stable for a long time, even in the face of economic failure. In Cuba, for example, a dictatorship has survived for over half a century despite hardships and poverty due in no small part to strenuous U.S. efforts to isolate and overthrow Fidel Castro.

In contrast, democracies depend on economic prosperity and a robust middle class. Countries that can afford the luxury of schools and other social infrastructure essential to an informed citizenry are generally better candidates for democracy than are poor, less-developed countries, where people are caught up in a daily struggle for survival.

THE VICES OF AUTHORITARIAN RULERS

As Lord Acton (1834–1902) famously observed, "Power corrupts; absolute power corrupts absolutely." Power is intoxicating and addictive—a first drink often gives rise to an unquenchable thirst or (different metaphor, same idea) a ravenous hunger. Moreover, the appetite grows with the eating. Indeed, the tendency to use power as a means of gaining more power is well documented and all too human. There is thus a universal tendency in human relations toward concentration of power.

In authoritarian states, a single ruler or a ruling elite controls the government. The single-head form of government is called an **autocracy**, whereas the elite-group form is known as an **oligarchy**, sometimes referred to as a **junta** or ruling clique. Authoritarian rulers are the sole repositories of power and authority. In this type of regime tenure in office depends less on elections, which are typically rigged to produce the desired outcome, and more on a combination of myth and might. Meanwhile, the people are often told that obedience to authority is a moral, sacred, or patriotic duty; on the other hand, the rulers stand ready to use brute force whenever rebellion rears its head.

Authoritarianism and dictatorship go hand in hand. The dictators who came to power after World War II have nearly all died or been deposed (see "Landmarks in History"). Muammar el-Qaddafi of Libya was one exception until the start of 2011 when, facing heavy rebel opposition and having lost any claim to legitimate authority, his days in power appeared to be numbered; Fidel Castro of Cuba, now old and infirm, handed power to his younger brother Raúl in 2008 but remained First Secretary of the Communist Party. Dictators in Syria and Nigeria died in the late 1990s.

In sub-Saharan Africa, the Congo remains in a prolonged state of turmoil after decades of rule by a thieving dictator named Mobutu. Nigeria's civilian government is plagued by corruption on all levels, threatened by internal ethnic and religious conflicts, and highly dependent on the military for security and stability. In the Middle East, Bashar al-Assad, son of Syria's former ruler, has shown himself to be a brutal dictator in his own right, one who does not hesitate to use lethal force to put down popular antigovernment protests, killing thousands of civilians in the process, including thirty-two children in a single shelling attack (on the city of Houla) in May 2012.

Until its turn toward democracy in the 1980s, Latin America had a long tradition of military rule. Indeed, after World War II, military dictatorships were common in most regions of the world, including Asia, the Middle East and North Africa (the so-called Arab world), and sub-Saharan Africa. Thus, for example, prior to the Egyptian Revolution of 2011–2012, Egypt's presidents (of which there were only *three* over a sixty-year period) came to power by first rising

autocracy
Unchecked political power exercised by a single ruler.

oligarchy
A form of authoritarian government in which a small group of powerful individuals wields absolute power.

junta
A ruling oligarchy, especially one made up of military officers.

HULTON ARCHIVE/GETTY IMAGES

Known to history simply as Lord Acton (1834–1902), Baron John Emerich Edward Dahlberg-Acton was a distinguished British aristocrat and historian. He greatly admired the American federal structure, which he believed to be the ideal guarantor of individual liberty; and as an ardent supporter of states' rights, he sympathized with the Confederacy in the American Civil War. Never one to engage in hero worship, Acton admonished that "Great men are almost always bad men."

LANDMARKS IN HISTORY

FALLEN TYRANTS OF THE POSTWAR ERA: A Roll Call

Ruler	Country	Tenure	How Removed
Rafael Trujillo	Dominican Republic	1930–1961	Assassinated
François "Papa Doc" Duvalier	Haiti	1957–1971	Died in office
Idi Amin	Uganda	1971–1979	Ousted (fled)
Jean-Bedel Bokassa	Central African Republic	1965–1979	Ousted (fled)
Reza Pahlavi	Iran	1941–1979	Ousted (fled)
Augusto Pinochet	Chile	1973–1979	Lost election (fled)
Anastasio Somoza	Nicaragua	1967–1979	Ousted (fled)
Jean-Claude "Baby Doc" Duvalier	Haiti	1971–1986	Ousted (fled)
Ferdinand Marcos	Philippines	1972–1986	Ousted (fled)
Alfredo Stroessner	Paraguay	1954–1989	Ousted (exiled)
Mobutu Sese Seko	The Congo (Zaire)	1965–1997	Ousted (fled)
Slobodan Milosevic	Serbia (former Yugoslavia)	1989–1997	Resigned
Saddam Hussein	Iraq	1979–2003	Executed
Hosni Mubarak	Egypt	1981–2011	Ousted (fled)
Muammar Qaddafi	Libya	1969–2011	Ousted (fled; caught; killed)
Kim Jong-Il	North Korea	1994–2011	Died in office

to a senior officer rank in the army (see "Ideas and Politics"). Where the military dominates the political system, it often rules as an *institution* rather than through a single individual. A ruling committee, or junta, consisting of generals headed by a "president" who is also a general, is the usual pattern. The military frequently claims legitimacy on the grounds that civilian leaders are corrupt and venal, or that only the military can maintain order and stability.

Senior military officers continue to play an important governing role even in many Latin American countries where popularly elected civilian presidents now govern. In sub-Saharan Africa, hopeful signs two decades ago that civilian rule was the wave of the future soon faded, as violence, disease, and poverty—and official corruption on a scale rarely matched and seemingly impossible to eradicate—continue to plague many societies.

Authoritarian rulers generally do not respect individual rights when they interfere with the power or policy goals of the state. The interests of the state stand above the interests of society or the welfare of the rank-and-file citizenry. Yet there are important differences among authoritarian rulers. They vary in the extent to which they impose conformity and suppress intellectual and artistic freedom. The amount of force, repression, and violence they employ also

SCHINDLER'S LIST

Until the beginning of 2011, Egypt's leader, Hosni Mubarak, ruled as an elected president, but for all practical purposes he was a dictator. Mubarak, who followed in the footsteps of three previous military dictators ("president" was a euphemism in the context of Egyptian politics), came to power following the assassination of President Anwar al-Sadat in 1981.

Egypt is an Islamic society but has had a secular state since 1952 when a colonel named Gamal Abdel Nasser and the Free Officers staged a coup against the monarch, King Farouk. Nasser ruled as personal dictator from 1956 until his death in 1970. Soon after assuming the presidency, Nasser nationalized the Suez Canal, an act that led to war with the United Kingdom, France, and Israel (the Suez Crisis of 1956).

Anwar Sadat, another general, succeeded Nasser and ruled Egypt for nearly a decade before he met his untimely demise. Mubarak, his successor, was reelected by plebiscites (direct popular votes) in 1987, 1993, and 1999. As popular elections, these exercises were a farce because Mubarak ran unopposed until 2005. But that election, too, was rigged, as the security apparatus, official state media, and ballot boxes remained firmly under Mubarak's control (his main rival who dared to contest the outcome was arrested and imprisoned).

Reporters Without Borders ranked the Egyptian media 133rd of 168 countries in the year immediately preceding Mubarak's overthrow. According to the Human Development Index, which uses various economic and social standards and measures of comparison, Egypt ranked 111th of 177 countries.

Egypt lacks the oil reserves that have made not a few other Arab states rich, and its economy relies heavily on agriculture and on a massive annual foreign aid package from the United States. Many Egyptians blamed Mubarak for the extreme social and economic inequality that enabled a few wealthy Egyptians to live in luxury while the vast majority remained mired in poverty. Many also resented Mubarak's submissive stance toward the United States and his refusal to confront Israel—policies that contrast sharply with his strong-arm tactics in dealing with domestic opponents.

Mubarak's stunning overthrow in January 2011 left the generals in charge. After a turbulent sixteen-month transition, the country's military rulers finally allowed something bearing a resemblance to free elections to take place in May 2012, but not all would-be popular candidates were on the ballot. Then, after the votes were cast, the outcome was not announced for a week; meanwhile, the generals had dissolved the parliament and issued a new provisional constitution granting the military sweeping powers.

Mohammed Morsi was eventually declared the winner. Morsi is a member of the Muslim Brotherhood, a militant Islamic group with a long history in opposition and a large popular following in Egypt. Morsi is the country's first Islamist, as well as its first civilian, president—a major break from Nasser's model of a modern military and resolutely secular regime. Even so, he pointedly pledged to be "a president for all Egyptians."

If history is any guide, Egypt will probably continue to be a democracy in name only. But there is a possibility that things will be different this time. The revolts in Egypt, Tunisia, Libya, and elsewhere in the Middle East were led by young people who constitute the majority of the population in all of these countries. They are the best educated, most technologically sophisticated, and have the highest unemployment rate—and they are less constrained than previous generations by religion and tradition.

During the tumultuous Arab Spring of 2011, some observers maintained that Egypt and the Arab World would never be the same. Perhaps. But will the Middle East of the future be more stable and less conflict-prone than in the past?* What do you think?

*In the wake of the Egyptian presidential election, for example, one serious news source declared, "the Middle East is in frightening turmoil." See "Egypt in peril," *The Economist*, June 23, 2012, p. 13.

FIGURE 5.1   Types of Authoritarian Governments.

Authoritarian governments are characterized by a concentration of power and an intolerance of political opposition.

Autocratic and oligarchic governments differ in the number of rulers in control.

Benevolent and dictatorial regimes differ in that they have different ends for which political power is exercised.

Autocratic (kings, caliphs, etc.)

Oligarchic (military juntas, cliques, etc.)

Benevolent

Dictatorial

Benevolent

Dictatorial

Hard-core

Clear rules, uniformly applied

Arbitrary rules, strictly enforced

Clear rules, uniformly applied

Hard and soft dictatorships differ in the methods they use to govern.

© CENGAGE LEARNING

varies greatly. Some rulers use coercion sparingly, whereas others, appropriately labeled tyrants, display an enthusiasm for cracking down on dissenters.

Finally, although all tyrants are dictators, not all dictators are tyrants (Figure 5.1). Some like the Josip Broz Tito (1892–1980) in the former Yugoslavia and Anwar al-Sadat (1918–1981) in Egypt pursue higher aims even at great personal and political risk. Ambitious national programs undertaken to industrialize, reform, or modernize the economy point to the possibility of a benevolent dictatorship. This has been demonstrated by Lee Kuan Yew, the no-nonsense political boss of Singapore for three decades (1959–1990), and Jigme Khesar Namgyel Wangchuk, a hereditary monarch who rules the tiny Himalayan kingdom of Bhutan under a constitution that places the people's "happiness" at its core.

But even benevolent dictators have limited tolerance for political opposition and often deal harshly with "trouble-makers." Dictators sometimes show surprising self-restraint so long as detractors and dissidents remain isolated, do not try to create an organized opposition or conspire to start a revolution, and pose no real threat to the regime. Some pathological tyrants are merciless toward opponents, whether real or imagined: Cambodia ("Kampuchea") under

Jubilant demonstrators in Tahrir Square in Egypt during the Arab Spring in January of 2011.

Pol Pot, Iraq under Saddam Hussein, and North Korea under Kim Jong-Il are three examples of what happens when dictators recognize no moral limits to the exercise of power.

Nonhereditary (or modern) autocratic rulers also use repression at times to maintain law and order (as do democracies), but they typically stage elections, pay lip service to constitutional norms, and show a degree of tolerance toward religious beliefs and cultural differences (think: Mubarak's Egypt). The inherent flaw in all dictatorships is that self-restraint never comes with any guarantees and rarely survives a serious challenge to the regime's existence. Arbitrary rules strictly enforced—that is the immutable law and the very essence of authoritarianism.

CHARACTERISTICS OF AUTHORITARIAN STATES

Authoritarian rulers frequently come to power by force or violence, using the element of surprise to overthrow the government in a **coup d'état**. Until quite recently, such power seizures were common in Asia, Latin America, the Middle East, and sub-Saharan Africa.

Maintaining a power monopoly is the main aim of authoritarian states. The army and the police are the principal instruments of coercion, hence the

coup d'état
The attempted seizure of government power by an alternate power group (often the military) that seeks to gain control of vital government institutions without any fundamental alteration in the form of government or society.

high incidence of military rule. Many civilian rulers of authoritarian states start out as military strongmen as was the case in Egypt, where three of the last four leaders—Nasser, Sadat, and Mubarak—were military commanders before becoming president.

To frustrate actual or potential political opposition, authoritarian rulers often impose strict press censorship, outlaw opposition parties, and exert firm control over the legal system, which is manipulated to prosecute (and sometimes persecute) political opponents. Monopoly control of the mass media and the courts gives absolute rulers a potent propaganda tool and the means to suppress dissent in the face of official corruption and often egregious human rights violations, whereas repression is typically justified in the name of order and stability.

Until recently, authoritarian states with few exceptions were typically slow to modernize and characterized by gross social inequality, rural poverty, and a host of related problems—official corruption on a grand scale, comparatively high illiteracy and high infant mortality rates, and low life expectancy. Authoritarianism "does not attempt to get rid of or to transform all other groups or classes in the state, it simply reduces them to subservience."[1] Indirect state control of the "commanding heights" (heavy industry, banking, energy, railroads, foreign trade) is far more common than outright state ownership of the means of production—a stark contrast with Stalinist *totalitarian* regimes during the Cold War (see Chapter 6).

Unlike totalitarian regimes, most dictatorships are indifferent to the way people live or what they do, as long as they stay away from politics. To be sure, dictators rarely make the lives of the people better—often, exactly the opposite. One recent case in point: Zimbabwe's President Robert Mugabe.

Though authoritarian rulers rarely do what is best for the people, they often do prevent the worst by maintaining law and order.[2] In Iraq, the bloody breakdown in civil society following the U.S.-led invasion in 2003 underscored this point, as did the violent breakup of Yugoslavia in the 1990s.

THE POLITICS OF AUTHORITARIANISM

Aristotle argued that all authoritarian forms of rule, despite important differences among them, are a perversion of good government. In his view, "Those constitutions which consider the common interest are *right* constitutions, judged by the standard of absolute justice," whereas "those constitutions which consider only the personal interests of the rulers are all wrong constitutions, or *perversions* of the right forms. Such perverted forms are despotic."[3]

This perversion of ends usually entails a like perversion of means. Despots (cruel dictators) often justify self-serving policies on the grounds that harsh measures are necessary to preserve order or protect the nation from its enemies. Or they may use brute force simply to mask or prevent criticism of their own failed policies. Throughout history, authoritarian rulers and regimes have been notorious for ruthlessly persecuting political opponents. Raising questions regarding who should rule or how is tantamount to treason. In short, where despotism thrives, politics does not.

AUTHORITARIANISM IN PRACTICE: A TALE OF TWO STATES

Despite a promising trend toward constitutional rule in the 1990s, much of Asia and sub-Saharan Africa continue to be ruled by authoritarian regimes. In this section we focus on two examples of authoritarian rule: China and Iran.

China since Mao has undergone a remarkable transformation from having a stalled Stalinist economy to becoming the most dynamic major economy in the world (see Figure 5.2). Iran is a large country (population 79 million) in Southwest Asia at the crossroads between continents and major countries—Russia, China, and India to the north and east, and the Arab states, Israel, Africa, and Europe to the south and west. Politically, Iran is a pariah state—a repressive theocracy with nuclear ambitions widely viewed in the West as a state-sponsor of international terrorism.

China: Police-State Capitalism

In little more than three decades, the People's Republic of China (PRC) has transformed itself from an isolated totalitarian state with a dysfunctional command economy into the world's leading model of authoritarian capitalism. Today China is a global power with a dynamic economy achieving high growth rates year after year for more than two decades. China's economic miracle is the result of a cheap and abundant labor supply, pragmatic policies, skillful diplomacy aimed at opening Western consumer markets to Chinese exports, and special economic zones (SEZs) to attract foreign investment and create jobs for a rapidly expanding urban population. The SEZs combine liberal foreign-ownership policies with generous tax incentives.[4]

Measured in GDP per capita and despite having the second biggest national economy in the world, China remains a poor country compared to neighboring states such as Japan, South Korea, Taiwan, and Singapore. At present, the United States and the European Union, China's two principal trading partners, have bigger economies and far exceed China in per capita GDP. But an official U.S. intelligence assessment in December 2012 predicted that China will overtake the United States as the lead economic power before 2030.

Although the PRC has shed its legacy of Maoist totalitarian rule, China continues to be a monolithic police state. The path to power for Mao's Chinese Communist Party differed sharply from that of Lenin's Bolsheviks. Because Mao's victory followed a protracted guerrilla war against the Japanese and the Chinese Nationalist government of Chiang Kai-shek, the army played a much greater role in Mao's theory and practice of revolution than in Lenin's. When the Chinese Communists came to power in 1949, the army and the party were fused into a single organization.

Acting as a virtual government, the army was charged not only with fighting but also with administration, including maintenance of law and order, construction and public works, management of the economy, and education and indoctrination. In effect, the army became the nucleus of the new revolutionary government, the People's Republic of China (PRC).

FIGURE 5.2 The People's Republic of China. Note that many of China's greatest cities are in the east; note where Taiwan is located; note also the close proximity of Japan to the Korean Peninsula.

The PRC was closely allied with the Soviet Union at first, but the era of friendship and cooperation between two communist behemoths lasted less than a decade. Mao's revolutionary quest and his bizarre penchant for self-destructive ideological purity found expression in the Great Leap Forward in 1957–1958. Less than a decade later, Mao's utopian obsession led to his decision to launch the Great Proletarian Cultural Revolution designed to smash the party-state bureaucracy. The Cultural Revolution destroyed what remained of the PRC's bureaucratic and managerial classes, as well as its infrastructure and industry. With the economy utterly ruined and the society in turmoil, China's people were destitute and devoid of hope—until Mao's last act.

Changing of the Guard Mao Zedong died in 1976. For China's long-suffering masses, it was the best thing that ever happened—a watershed in modern Chinese history. According to one China scholar, "Mao's death marked the end of an era; what was not clear was who would lead China and in what direction in the era to come."[5]

After two years of halting reforms, the nation's post-Mao leadership under the direction of Deng Xiaoping (who had twice been purged by Mao for his alleged lack of revolutionary zeal) abandoned ideological fervor in favor of a sober, businesslike pragmatism symbolized by such slogans as "practice is the sole criterion of truth" and "seek truth from facts." Economic development replaced class struggle, and a welcome mat replaced the "no trespassing" sign that had impeded China's trade relations with the West for nearly three decades.

CHUNG SUNG-JUN/ISTOCKPHOTO.COM

In November 2012, President Xi Jinping was elevated to the role of Secretary General, the highest position in the Communist Party of China. In March 2013 Xi was named to succeed Hu Jintao as president of the People's Republic of China.

Politburo
A small clique that formed the supreme decision-making body in the former Soviet Union. Some Politburo members also belonged to the Secretariat and were ministers of key government departments.

Banished were the mass campaigns, crash programs, hero worship, and ideological fanaticism that had been the hall-marks of Maoism. Expanding trade, especially with the industrial democracies, became a principal aim of Beijing's diplomacy. Deng's economic reforms (notably, the SEZs mentioned previously) were gradually implemented between 1978 and 1982, as he carefully and patiently consolidated his power within the ruling **Politburo**—the Kremlin's supreme decision-making body. By the fall of 1982, the reform-minded Deng was in full command.

Deng remained China's paramount ruler until his death, at the age of 92, in early 1997. His successors—first Jiang Zemin, and since 2003 Hu Jintao—continued Deng's pragmatic political and economic policies. Together with Prime Minister Wen Jiaobao, Hu guided China's rise to a position of unprecedented economic and political ascendancy in the new global economy. In a country currently second only to the United States as an economic and military power, and where only a very few top leaders make all key policy decisions, the changing of the guard is a matter of vital importance—not only for China, but also for the United States and the world.

In November 2012 the all-important Eighteenth National Party Congress elected a new Central Committee and chose the next generation of leaders; former Vice President Xi Jinping succeeded Hu as China's supreme leader—as such, Xi is General Secretary of the Communist Party of China, the President of the People's Republic of China, and the Chairman of the Central Military Commission. In economic policy, Xi appears to share the worldview and pragmatic approach of his predecessors. Time will tell whether he will loosen the Communist Party's iron grip on political power. If not, how will he manage the late-stage transition from an insular state walled off from the world to a global power open to the ever-expanding universe of information technology (IT), trade, and tourism? Think about it.

The Two Faces of China   China after Mao has shown two faces to the world: one turned outward and smiling, the other inward and frowning—upon dissent, that is. The external world sees the face of a reliable business partner; the face it shows its own people is stern and intimidating. Of late, however, China watchers in the West detect a disturbing policy shift in Beijing's dealings with the outside world. In the words of Richard Armitage, a key foreign policy official in the George W. Bush administration, "The smiling diplomacy is over." The fact that China's military spending rose at least fourfold in little more than a decade lends credence to this early warning.[6] (But keep in mind the United States spends four-and-a-half times as much on weapons and war every year—nearly as much as the rest of the world combined—and remains the world's largest arms producer, consumer, and exporter.)

China's Communist Party continues to maintain a monopoly on political power. Party members constitute a ruling elite that enjoys special privileges. The emergence of a class of *nouveau riche* entrepreneurs and a burgeoning middle class are changing the face of Chinese society, though with little impact on

China's all-powerful party-state system thus far. High party ranking remains a prerequisite to membership in China's political class.

Before 1978, Maoism—a radical peasant-based brand of communism that glorified revolution as a form of moral purification—was the official ideology of China. After 1978, Deng's pragmatic view prevailed—that economic growth, and not class struggle, ought to be the main measure of success for both the party and the state. In Deng's own words, "It matters not if a cat is black or white, as long as it catches mice." No longer would the party invoke Marxist ideology to justify its programs or policies or to legitimize the party's rule.[7]

A Communist Party that distances itself from communism is not only a novelty but also an anomaly, one that raises a key question: How long can China's leadership continue to restrict freedom of expression and the open exchange of ideas in the Information Age? China's engagement in the global economy has necessitated opening Chinese society to outsiders. Even so, while the world now has far greater access to Mainland China than during the Maoist era, the political process remains off limits and shrouded in secrecy. Meanwhile, economic growth is slowing, the influx from poor rural areas to the cities continues unabated, and urban pollution and congestion worsen, aggravating otherwise difficult conditions and causing social stress to rise.

Market-Oriented Reforms   In the post-Mao era, Beijing looked to the West for loans and direct foreign investment, thus violating a long-standing ideological taboo. The approach worked wonders; Western capital began pouring into the country in the 1980s and continued fueling China's modernization drive thereafter.

At the same time, agriculture was decollectivized. Under this system, the state makes contracts with individual households to purchase specified products; farmers can also sell produce in private markets. Not surprisingly, these reprivatizing, farm-friendly reforms have proven remarkably effective in boosting agricultural output.

In industry and commerce, too, China has moved toward a greater reliance on market forces. One statistic is remarkably revealing. In 1978, there were no privately owned businesses in China; by 1995, approximately one-third of all businesses were privately owned (Figure 5.3). Subsequently, the number of state-owned and state-controlled enterprises fell sharply between 1995 and 2001, while urban jobs in the state sector drop from three-fifths to less than one-third of total urban employment.[8]

The results of China's agricultural and industrial revolution have been impressive. After decades of induced turmoil under Mao, China's economy has revived. In fact, China has been one of the world's fastest-growing economies during the past two decades. In 2010, China's economy surpassed Japan's in size, making it the biggest in Asia, and the third biggest economy in the world, behind only the European Union (the biggest), and the United States (ranked number two).

For all its recent success, China is still relatively poor in terms of per capita wealth. In 2010, although China's total GDP was slightly larger than that of Japan, Japan's per capita income was four times that of China ($34,850

FIGURE 5.3   An Emerging Private Sector. Private ownership of business in China increased dramatically after Mao Zedong's death in 1976.

*Partly government owned

SOURCE: *Originally published in* Newsweek, *March 3, 1997, vol. 89, no. 9, p. 27. The research is attributed to The Heritage Foundation and IMF, conducted by Anna Kuchment and Dante Chinni. Reprinted by permission of The Heritage Foundation and the IMF.*

versus $8,390 at purchasing power parity). Nonetheless, China achieved "the most astonishing economic transformation in human history," according to *The Economist*. "In a country that is home to one-fifth of humanity some 200 million people have been lifted out of poverty."[9]

Exports continue to be a major source of China's economic dynamism. By 2003, China's trade surplus with the United States had surpassed Japan's. The overall U.S. trade deficit with China alone accounted for about one-fourth of the total. This imbalance had jumped from $124 billion in 2003 to $266 billion in 2008, and China was garnering the largest trade surpluses in the history of the modern world. Critics charge that China's currency (the renminbi) is undervalued, making its goods cheaper, and thus more competitive, in foreign markets than they should be.

Beijing has resisted international pressure to revalue its currency. Because its economy is extremely export-dependent, China has been eager to counteract any falloff in global demand—despite the fact that China has reported record trade surpluses in recent years. In 2011, China ran up a record $282 billion trade surplus with the United States. The U.S.-China trade deficit hit an all-time monthly record of $29.4 billion in October 2012 and set a new single-year record.

China's huge trade surpluses have resulted in vast state holdings of foreign reserves totaling more than $3 trillion in 2012. China has invested most of its vast foreign-exchange reserves through several large **sovereign wealth funds** in U.S. Treasury bonds and T-Bills, in the process becoming the U.S. government's second-biggest creditor (behind Japan). As a consequence, the United States and China are now economic codependents: the United States provides the major market for China's exports; and China, in turn, flush with foreign reserves, finances a major part of Washington's massive budget deficits.

But to coin a phrase from a Johnny Mercer song and 2003 movie, "something's gotta give." How long can the United States continue outsourcing and losing jobs to China? How long will U.S. consumers be willing and/or able to buy China's exports? Perhaps China can go on producing without consuming more and the United States can go on consuming without producing more indefinitely. Perhaps not.

Beijing faces other economic challenges as well. Glaring income disparities exist for the first time since the communist takeover in 1949. The coastal provinces of the east—Shanghai is a particularly striking example—are growing much faster than the rural provinces of central and western China and produce two to four times the income, according to official statistics. Costs of this rapid development include appalling air pollution in China's teeming cities, rivers that run thick with silt, industrial waste and sewage, and scenes of great natural beauty lost forever to dams and reservoirs for hydroelectric power generation (see "Maps That Matter").

In sum, market-friendly reforms have produced a vibrant economy, rising incomes, and a new class of millionaires, but at the price of growing social inequality and severe damage to the environment. When China formally joined the WTO in 2001, *The Economist* asserted, "China's accession to the WTO…will be its biggest step since Communist rule began more than 50 years ago toward the integration of its economic system with that of the capitalist West."[10] More than decade later the West was still waiting for the other shoe to drop.

Expanded Personal Freedoms?   Despite severe restrictions on political dissent, China today is a more liberal society than it was during Mao's erratic totalitarian rule. People are permitted to exhibit greater individuality and enjoy greater personal freedom to decide where to live and work, when to marry, what fads in fashion and music to follow, and the like. This relaxation of police-state control and enforcement of strict conformity, however, stops short of civil rights and guarantees common in the West. To cite one example, since 1978 urban couples in China with certain exceptions are limited by law to having only one child. Also, artists and writers live under the constant threat of arbitrary arrest and imprisonment if they offend the censors.

sovereign wealth funds
A state-owned investment fund made up of financial assets such as stocks, bonds, precious metals, and property; such funds invest globally. China, for example, has invested huge sums in the United States via its sovereign wealth fund.

MAPS THAT MATTER

FIGURE 5.4   Deaths from Urban Air Pollution.

SOURCE: World Health Organization http://www.who.int/heli/risks/urban/en/uapmap.1.pdf

Deaths attributable to urban air pollution, 2004

UAP deaths/1 million population

- 0–50
- 50–150
- 150–250
- 250–400
- >400
- Data not available
- Not applicable

(Continued)

(CONTINUED)

The Chinese economy is on a collision course with the environment, argues writer David J. Lynch:

> Over the past two decades, China's economy has grown at an average annual rate of more than 9%. But the economic cost of environmental harm, measured in public health, worker absenteeism, and remediation efforts, is becoming prohibitively high. "This miracle will end soon because the environment can no longer keep pace," Pan Yue, deputy director of China's State Environmental Protection Administration, told the German magazine *Der Spiegel*.
>
> Environmental injury costs China 8% to 15% of its annual gross domestic product, Pan said. In the north, encroaching deserts are prompting human migrations that swell overburdened cities. In the south, factories have closed periodically for lack of water, according to [Elizabeth] Economy [of the Council on Foreign Relations], who wrote a book last year on China's environmental woes. The World Bank estimates such shutdowns cost $14 billion annually in lost output.

Since this article appeared, scientific evidence has mounted of global warming caused by excess carbon emissions released into the atmosphere. The international community has become increasingly alarmed about warnings that Earth is reaching a fateful tipping point—the moment when it will become impossible to reverse climate changes, and polar icecaps and glaciers will melt at an accelerating pace with disastrous consequences for the ecosystem. Meanwhile, in 2009 China and India—the two most populous countries in the world—were both continuing to build dozens of new carbon-emitting coal-fired power plants each year to supply electricity for construction, transport, and industry.

SOURCE: From David J. Lynch, "Pollution Poisons China's Progress," *USA Today*, July 4, 2005 (electronic edition). For an in-depth analysis of this problem, see Elizabeth Economy, "The Great Leap Backward: The Costs of China's Environmental Crisis," *Foreign Affairs*, vol. 86, no. 5, September/ October 2007, pp. 38–59; see also, Carin Zissis and Jayshree Bajorie, "China's Environmental Crisis," *Foreign Affairs*, updated August 4, 2008, accessed online at http://www.cfr.org/publication/12608/.

Political and Religious Repression Despite liberalization in the economic and social spheres, political and religious persecution persist. Not long after the death of Mao Zedong in 1978, a phenomenon known as the **Democracy Wall** captured world attention. On a wall in the heart of Beijing, opinions and views at variance with the official line—including blunt criticisms of the existing system and leaders—were displayed with the government's tacit approval. But a government crackdown in 1979, complete with arrests and show trials, put an end to Beijing's brief dalliance with free speech. A decade later, the **Tiananmen Square massacre** came to epitomize the Chinese government's persistent hostility to human rights (see "Landmarks in History").

Tiananmen Square continues to symbolize China's persecution of critics and dissidents. Political prisoners in China can expect harsh treatment. Perhaps the most famous Chinese political dissident in recent times is Liu Xiaobo, winner of the 2010 Nobel Peace Prize. When the prize was announced, Beijing's reaction was swift and furious. The Chinese state media imposed a blackout of the

Democracy Wall
A wall located near the Forbidden City in the heart of Beijing; on this wall thousands of people wrote criticisms and complaints against the regime in the winter of 1978–79. It was a rare opportunity for public dissent that ended in a government crackdown.

Tiananmen Square massacre
In 1989, unarmed civilian workers and students marched in Tiananmen Square in Beijing to demand democratic freedom and government reforms. Army troops responded with force, killing 1,500 demonstrators and wounding another 10,000.

ceremony in Oslo, and the country's draconian system of Internet censorship—the so-called Great Firewall of China—blocked news reports about the Nobel Prize. China warned that the award would harm relations with Norway, pressured other countries not to attend the event, and summoned Oslo's ambassador to Beijing to make a formal protest. Not only was Liu Xiaobo in prison when the honor was bestowed, but his entire family was also placed under house arrest.

Another famous Chinese dissident is Ai Weiwei, a painter and political activist who has openly criticized the Chinese government for failing to respect and protect human rights. Following his arrest at Beijing airport in April 2011, he was jailed for more than two months without being charged, although officials hinted at allegations of tax evasion. He was later released, but he is not allowed to leave the country. In a widely publicized interview in April 2012, Ai said he considers himself "quite free" but warned against expecting big changes so long as artists are considered enemies. Even so, he noted, the Internet now provides artists and intellectuals access to the world.

For the most part, the government controls religion by licensing and monitoring churches, monasteries, mosques, and other religious institutions. Beijing has been particularly ruthless in Tibet, according to Human Rights Watch and many other nongovernmental organizations (NGOs), where it has closed Buddhist monasteries and jailed and executed worshippers. After Tibet's religious leader, the Dalai Lama, escaped into exile in northern India in 1959, China brutally suppressed the national uprising in Lhasa, the capital.

New Social Disorders   China suffers some of the same problems affecting Western democracy. Corruption is widespread. With the blurring of the line between the public and private spheres, and with vast amounts of money circulating through China's burgeoning economy, business and politics have become tainted by routine acts of bribery, nepotism, and "unofficial favoritism."

LANDMARKS IN HISTORY

THE TRAGEDY OF TIANANMEN SQUARE

In May 1989, students and workers staged a mass march in Beijing to protest party privilege, official corruption, and the failure to democratize. The protest grew as throngs of demonstrators camped in Tiananmen Square, making speeches and shouting slogans. The rest of the world watched in rapt attention as the drama unfolded before Western television cameras. The fact that Mikhail Gorbachev, the father of "reform Communism," visited Beijing that same month for the first Sino-Soviet summit in three decades only added to the sense of high drama. When unrest spread throughout the country, Beijing declared martial law, but to no avail.

Army troops entered the Chinese capital with tanks and armor on June 3; it soon became apparent that the show of force was not a bluff. The crackdown that ensued brought the democracy movement to a bloody end as hundreds, possibly thousands, of protesters were killed or injured and many more arrested. Security forces later rounded up thousands of dissenters, and at least thirty-one were tried and executed. The atrocities against unarmed civilians in the Tiananmen Square massacre proved that China was still, at its core, a repressive state.

Protests are common and sometimes violent. In a village near Guangzhou in Guangdong Province, for example, one notice promised a handsome reward (10,000 yuan or $1,600) for turning in "criminals" involved in big riots that broke out after security guards beat up a street hawker. In a country where the press is tightly controlled by the state, such anecdotal evidence is often the only way to gauge what is actually happening outside of the capital and a few other major cities. Theft and robbery are also serious problems, as are drug-related crimes and prostitution—all represent the dark underside of China's economic expansion.[11]

The New China: Rival or Partner?   China is now a global power with a nuclear arsenal at its disposal. With the world's largest population, it has no difficulty finding conscripts for its armed forces, which total some 3 million troops. Since the late 1970s, China has sought to modernize its military capabilities. Today, it has the fastest-rising arms expenditures of any major world power. China also continues testing nuclear weapons and selling high-tech armaments on the international market. (But the United States is still by far the largest arms supplier to the world.)

Some analysts express alarm at what they see as China's massive arms buildup—its growing arsenal of cruise and ballistic missiles, its new and improved submarine fleet, its antiship ballistic missile program, and its electronic and cyberwarfare capabilities.[12] A view currently held at high levels in Washington is that China's advances in cyberspace and antisatellite warfare "could threaten America's primary way to project power" in the Pacific and protect "our forward air bases and carrier groups."[13]

Others caution against overreacting. They point out correctly that the United States is still far ahead in quantity and quality across the full range of state of the art weapons, and annual U.S. defense spending is five or six times more than that of China. Even as a percent of GDP, China devotes less than half as much to military spending as the United States.

In Asia, India's reluctance to forgo its nuclear weapons programs can be traced, in part, to its distrust not only of Pakistan but also of China. Japan is wary of China's military buildup, as is Russia. Bitter memories of the 1979 border war are still alive in Vietnam, and the Philippines, long a staunch U.S. ally in the western Pacific, have an unresolved dispute with the PRC over potentially oil-rich islands in the South China Sea.

And then there is a long-standing dispute over Taiwan: Beijing considers Taiwan a breakaway province of China, but the United States continues to back Taiwan's independence. Periodic Chinese naval exercises have reinforced this point, although Taiwan has continued to hold firm, buttressed by the U.S. Navy. But the meaning of China's emergence as a global power is far from certain.

In 2012 a long-time dispute between Japan and China over uninhabited islands in the East China Sea caused a near-rupture in relations. One consequence: the value of Japanese exports to China. A worse fear was that war would break out. In mid-January 2013, China sent a civilian surveillance plane to fly near the islands. That action provoked Japan and soon escalated to the point where both Tokyo and Beijing ordered fighter jets into the area of the disputed islands. According to one newspaper story at the time, "What began as a seemingly minor dispute is quickly turning into a gathering storm."[14]

In sum, China has replaced Russia as America's main rival, but that's where the similarity ends. China remains "inscrutable" to the rest of the world but no longer inaccessible. China continues its authoritarian ways in the realm of politics, but it has adapted with remarkable agility to the new global economy, opening its internal markets to foreign trade and investment and demonstrating remarkable flexibility and pragmatism in all things economic. Finally, China faces huge challenges at home and presents huge challenges to the rest of the world.

Iran: Petropariah in the Persian Gulf

As a political system, Iran is an oxymoron—a modern theocracy. The words "modern" and "theocracy" are a contradiction in terms, but Iran proves that in politics everything is possible. As an authoritarian state, Iran is in a class by itself—unique and isolated both in the Islamic world and in the larger global system.

Historically, at the peak of Persian civilization during the period of the Sassanid Dynasty (AD 224–661), Persia was a mighty empire encompassing all of today's Iran, Afghanistan, Iraq, Syria, the Caucasus (Armenia, Georgia, Azerbaijan, and Dagestan), southwestern Central Asia, part of Turkey, certain coastal parts of the Arabian Peninsula, the Persian Gulf area, southwestern Pakistan, and even stretched into India.

Iran is an Islamic state, but Persians are not Arabs. The language of Persia is Farsi, not Arabic. The dominant form of Islam in Iran is Shi'a, whereas most Arabs are Sunni. From the early 1950s until 1979 an absolute monarch called the Shah (from the Persian word *Shahansha* meaning "king of kings") ruled the country with troops and truncheons.

Shah Mohammad Reza Pahlavi was a ruthless secular ruler committed to modernization and economic development. He was also a very close friend of the United States. Under the Shah, Iran provided the United States with a trusted ally in one of the most important strategic areas of the world, the Persian Gulf.

In 1979 the hated Shah was overthrown in a popular uprising now commonly known as the Iranian Revolution and inspired by the Ayatollah Khomeini, a charismatic religious leader. The revolution put paid to the monarchy and put Khomeini in the driver's seat.

Khomeini set about creating the modern world's first and only theocracy—a government run by religious leaders and based on a strict interpretation of the Koran. Thereafter, Islamic law became the law of the land. Ultimate authority fell to a "supreme legal guide," the ayatollah, responsible only to God. Religious leaders serve in the Majlis (parliament) and play an active role in the political life of the nation. The Council of Guardians acts as a high court, using the Koran, not the constitution, as the ultimate arbiter. Many of Iran's 80,000 clerics became local political agents of the Islamic Republican Party (IRP).

The first years of Ayatollah Khomeini's rule were chaotic. Following the seizure of the U.S. embassy in Tehran in November 1979, 52 U.S. citizens were held hostage until January 1981. To many Iranians, the long history of collusion between the United States and the Shah justified a jihad against the United States (the "great Satan"). Nonetheless, the incident left Iran diplomatically isolated.

Internally, Khomeini launched a reign of terror; thousands of enemies of the Islamic state—intellectuals, former officials, military officers, and political figures—were arrested, tried, and executed. A series of bombings killed some Khomeini confederates, including the newly elected president (Khomeini had dismissed the first president). In retaliation, Khomeini crushed his political opponents.

In the midst of this instability, Iraq had invaded Iran. The bloody war of attrition that followed led to appalling carnage and suffering, drained the economies of both countries, disrupted oil supply lines, and for seven years held the entire region under the threat of a wider war. When the fighting stopped in 1988, there was no winner or loser.

Within a year of the war's end, the ayatollah died, leaving a bitter legacy. He had inspired Iran to shed Western influences, but the price was a pariah state, a perpetrator of terrorism abroad and human rights violations at home.

Iran's success in rebuilding its petroleum industries and armed forces after its prolonged war with Iraq, its refusal to condemn acts of aggression and international terrorism, and its success in developing sophisticated military capabilities to match Israel's, including nuclear weapons and medium-range missiles, all contributed to a renewed sense of alarm in the West (and, of course, Israel) from the early 1990s to the present.

Despite Barack Obama's campaign rhetoric about seeking an accommodation with Iran, diplomatic and trade relations between Tehran and Washington remained frozen during Obama's first term. Iran refused to bow to international pressures in 2010 and instead continued to operate its nuclear facilities and develop "dual-use" nuclear technology (having both peaceful and military applications). In November 2011, the International Atomic Energy Agency (IAEA) issued a report saying it had "serious concerns regarding possible military dimensions to Iran's nuclear program...[point to the conclusion] that Iran has carried out activities relevant to the development of a nuclear explosive device."[15]

AUTHORITARIANISM IN THEORY: MYTH VERSUS REALITY

The stigma often attached to authoritarianism has given rise to various popular misconceptions. This section focuses on six common assumptions that, on closer examination, are half-truths at best—a blend of fact and myth.

Myth 1: Authoritarianism Is a Sign of the Times

Authoritarianism is neither abnormal nor unique to the modern era. Indeed, at least until the second half of the twentieth century, it was the norm. At the time of the American Revolution, *democracy* was abnormal and widely viewed as a kind of aberration.

In *The Politics*, Aristotle provided an impressive catalog of the political tactics designed to render individuals incapable of concerted political action.

Niccolò Machiavelli (1469–1527). Renaissance Italy's most famous political philosopher, Machiavelli is also one of its most controversial characters. He approached the study of politics as a scientist determined to record what he observes, not what others want to believe. The political arena was his laboratory. He was a remorseless realist. In *The Prince*, he offered shocking advice to rulers not to let moral inhibitions weaken them in the face of political necessity. But what is often forgotten or overlooked is that he also counseled prudence: "no prince has ever benefited from making himself hated."

Persons thought to represent a political threat were eliminated. Autocratic rulers isolated individuals from one another by banning common meals, cultural societies, and other communal activities. Secret police spied on citizens, used informants to weed out dissents, and deliberately sowed seeds of mutual mistrust between friends and neighbors. Poverty, heavy taxes, and hard work monopolized the subjects' time and attention.* War was a yet another means of control, keeping "subjects constantly occupied and continually in need of a leader."[16]

Niccolò Machiavelli (1469–1527) expanded and updated Aristotle's impressive list of autocratic methods in a famous book, *The Prince* (1532). A virtual instructor's manual for dictators, *The Prince* is shockingly "Machiavellian"—in common usage, a pejorative term connoting cruelty, cunning, and everything commonly associated with "dirty politics." Those who would rule, Machiavelli contended, must practice "how not to be good." Rulers are advised to place expediency above morality, but to take pains to appear honest and upright.

Princes cannot operate according to the same moral code as subjects. Thus, deceit becomes a virtue and always keeping promises becomes a vice. It is good to be both feared and loved, but better to be feared; to cultivate the appearance of generosity but to give away mainly what belongs to others; to punish severely because anything less makes the ruler look weak and indecisive; to dole out benefits little by little, so as to constantly remind those on the receiving end of the prince's benevolence.

It is hardly surprising that the word *Machiavellian* has come to be associated with ruthless, immoral acts. Yet Machiavelli did not invent the methods he prescribed. He simply translated a set of practices prevalent in the dog-eat-dog city-state system of sixteenth-century Italy into a general theory of politics.

Myth 2: Authoritarian Rulers Are Always Tyrannical

Aristotle distinguished between two different forms of authoritarianism. One form, by far the most common of the two, relies on cruelty and repression—crude methods of political control. The purpose of such policies is to intimidate the population, thus inoculating the ruler(s) against a mass revolt.

A second kind of authoritarian ruler displays concern for the common good and avoids ostentation, gives no sign of any impropriety, honors worthy citizens, erects public monuments, and so on. Such a "half-good" autocrat would clearly be preferable to a "no-good" one.

Some autocratic rulers imprison, torture, and even murder real or imagined political enemies; others govern with a minimum of force. Some run the

---

*As an example, Aristotle cited the construction of the Egyptian pyramids. Recent archeological evidence, however, suggests the pyramid builders were paid laborers, not slaves. Perhaps, but talk about a hard life!

economy into the ground; others give economic development the highest priority. In Iran, for example, the Shah Reza Pahlavi modernized Iran's military, economy, and society, but he also had his political opponents imprisoned, tortured, and sometimes executed.

Myth 3: Authoritarian Rulers Are Never Legitimate

In the United States, we agree with John Locke that legitimacy arises from the consent of the governed. But consent is not the only measure of legitimacy—in fact, for long periods in history popular will was not even recognized as a criterion of legitimacy.

Instead, from the late Middle Ages through the eighteenth century, the prevalent form of government in Europe was monarchy, based on divine right conferred by religious belief or royal birth conferred by heredity. In Imperial China, the dynastic principle was one source of the emperor's legitimacy, but religion also played a major role; the Chinese emperor ruled under the "mandate of Heaven."

Many contemporary dictatorships have relied on a somewhat more informal and personal source of legitimacy—the popular appeal of a **charismatic leader**. Often charismatic rule is grounded in the personal magnetism, oratorical skills, or legendary feats of a national hero who has led the country to victory in war or revolution. Post–World War II examples include Egypt's Nasser (1956–1970), Indonesia's Sukarno (1945–1967), and Libya's Qaddafi (1969–2011). Many postcolonial Third World dictators came to power as "liberators" who led the struggle for independence and emerged as objects of hero worship.

Divine sanction, tradition, and charisma, then, are the historical pillars of autocratic rule. More often than not, these wellsprings of legitimacy have effectively sold the idea that the rulers have a *right* to rule without consulting the people. Having the right to rule does not mean the same thing as ruling rightly, of course. And unfortunately, dictators and tyrants have too often used this "right" to commit serious wrongs.

But legitimacy, like beauty, is in the eyes of the beholder. If the people embrace an autocrat or dictator, no matter how brutal, evil, or corrupt he or she might be, that is what counts. What outsiders might think of a ruler like Cuba's Fidel Castro or Venezuela's recently deceased Hugo Chávez is irrelevant.

Myth 4: Authoritarian Rulers Are Always Unpopular

Given a choice, people would choose to live in a democracy rather than a dictatorship, right? How then do we account for popular dictators?

First, difficult as it is for westerners to understand, some dictators are loved as well as feared. In the aftermath of war or revolution, for example, autocratic rulers can and sometimes do guide a country through a difficult period of reconstruction. Stability and order set the stage for economic growth and prosperity. Former President Lee Kuan Yew of Singapore is one example in recent times; two historical examples are Catherine the Great of Russia and Frederick the Great of Prussia.

Personal charisma is another source of popularity. The prototype of the charismatic "man on horseback" was Napoléon Bonaparte (1769–1821).

charismatic leader
A political leader who gains legitimacy largely through the adoration of the populace deriving from past heroic feats (real or imagined), personality traits, oratorical skills, and the like.

Napoléon seized power in a France convulsed by revolution and led it in a series of spectacularly successful military campaigns, nearly conquering the entire European continent. At the height of his military success, Napoléon enjoyed almost universal popularity in France.

Hitler, too, enjoyed broad support among the German rank and file. As one writer pointed out:

> It is sometimes assumed that one who rules with the support of the majority cannot be a tyrant; yet both Napoléon and Hitler, two of the greatest tyrants of all time, may well have had majority support through a great part of their reigns. Napoléon, in many of his aggressive campaigns, probably had majority support among the French, but his actions...were nonetheless tyrannical for that. Hitler, for all we know, might have had at least tacit support of the majority of the German people in his campaign against the Jews; his action was nonetheless tyrannical for that...A tyrant...may in many of his measures have popular support, but...his power will not depend upon it.[17]

Good people will not necessarily stand in the way of bad rulers. As the great Russian writer Fyodor Dostoyevsky (1821–1881) observed, in an age of equality, the masses desire security above all else, and they will gladly accept despotism in order to escape the burdens that accompany the benefits of freedom.[18] The truth is that despotic government is often more popular than we care to believe.

Myth 5: Authoritarianism Has No Redeeming Qualities

Even the worst tyrants can bring order out of political chaos and material progress out of economic stagnation. Thus, in the 1930s, Hitler directed a massive military buildup that jump-started Germany's economy. Apologists for Benito Mussolini (1883–1945), Italy's fascist dictator in World War II, have noted that at least he made the trains run on time. Stalin industrialized Soviet Russia and thus set the stage for its rise to superpower status after World War II. Such public policy successes by no means justify the excesses of these tyrants, but they do help explain their domestic popularity.

Perhaps the most impressive example of an autocratic regime that succeeded in creating sustained social and economic progress comes not from Europe but from China. Baron de Montesquieu, Adam Smith, and Karl Marx were all moved to comment on the classical Chinese system of government.[19] The vast network of dikes, irrigation ditches, and waterways that crisscrossed the immense Chinese realm is particularly noteworthy. This hydraulic system represented a signal achievement, exceeding in scale and scope any public works ever undertaken in the West in premodern times. What kind of civilization could build public works on such a stupendous scale?

One modern scholar, Karl Wittfogel, theorized that the Chinese system, which he labeled "oriental despotism," owed its distinctive features to the challenges of sustaining a huge population in a harsh and demanding environment.[20] Rice has long been a staple in China, and rice cultivation requires large amounts of water under controlled conditions. Thus, to solve the perennial food problem, Chinese civilization first had to solve the perennial water problem. This meant building sophisticated flood control, irrigation, and drainage works. The result was a system of *permanent agriculture* that enabled Chinese peasants to cultivate the same land for centuries without stripping the soil of its nutrients.

Constructing such a system necessitated a strong central government. A project as ambitious as the transformation of the natural environment in the ancient world could not have been attempted without political continuity and stability, social cohesion, scientific planning, resource mobilization, labor conscription, and bureaucratic coordination on a truly extraordinary scale. Thus, the technology and logistics of China's system of permanent agriculture gave rise to a vast bureaucracy and justified a thoroughgoing, imperial dictatorship.

Private property ownership was rare and vast public works projects were designed and implemented by a centralized bureaucracy dedicated to efficient administration. Admission to the bureaucratic class was based on a series of examinations. At the apex of the power pyramid sat the emperor, who ruled under the mandate of Heaven and whose power was absolute.

What about the Chinese people under this highly centralized form of government? The rank-and-file traded labor for food and were treated as subjects, not citizens. The masses had duties in relation to the state, but no rights. On the positive side, Imperial China lasted longer than any other system of government the world has ever known (from about 900 to 1800). As the saying goes, nothing succeeds like success.

Imperial China presents us with a paradox. On one hand, it stands as an example of a ruling order more despotic than most traditional forms of Western authoritarianism.[21] On the other hand, its economic and technical achievements, along with its art, language, and literature, were extremely impressive by any standard. Significant material advances accompanied China's early economic development. Although the emperors and scholar-officials were neither liberal nor politically enlightened, their system of hydraulic despotism resulted in a sufficient supply of food to support a large and growing population for centuries—though not without occasional famines.

Today, China continues to be governed under a centralized, authoritarian system, but despite having the world's largest population (1.3 billion), it boasts one of the world's fastest growing economies (see Chapter 8). On the other hand, China was in continual turmoil and plunged into an economic abyss for a quarter of a century after World War II under Chairman Mao, demonstrating the perils of a dictatorship devoid of checks and balances (see Chapter 6).

Still, we often apply tougher standards to dictatorships than to democracies. No form of government comes with a guarantee, including democracy.

Myth 6: Authoritarianism Is the Worst Possible Form of Government

Totalitarian states (the focus of the next chapter) go well beyond traditional autocracies in trampling on human rights—rounding up enemies, using slave labor, and carrying out acts of mass murder. One of the grim lessons of the last century is that the worst possible government is worse than most of us can imagine.

THE FUTURE OF AUTHORITARIANISM

Between 1974 and 1990, more than thirty countries in Latin America, Asia, and Eastern Europe shifted from a nondemocratic to a democratic form of government.[22] During the 1980s, Ecuador, Bolivia, Peru, Brazil, Uruguay, Argentina, Chile, and Paraguay replaced military rulers, opting for more democratic alternatives. Central American nations followed suit. In 1989, a wave of revolutions swept communist regimes from power across Eastern Europe.

Democracy also made inroads in parts of sub-Saharan Africa. In the early 1990s, many African countries held multiparty elections or adopted reforms designed to lead to such elections.[23] At the same time, South Africa's repressive **apartheid system**, based on a racist ideology of white supremacy, was abolished and replaced by majority rule.

How deep and enduring the trend away from authoritarian governments will be is still an open question. Can we look forward to a future when, for the first time in human history, democracy will be the global norm? Or will the inherit difficulties and defects of democratic rule give rise to growing disappointment until people become so disillusioned that they turn away?

Certainly, the contemporary world features many examples of successful democracies and failed dictatorships, and the prosperity common to many democratic states encourages imitators. But the reverse is also true: successful dictatorships and failed democracies. The People's Republic of China, for example, combines a rigidly authoritarian political system with a dynamic economy, whereas the government of Greece, a democratic country, faced bankruptcy in 2010.

The rise of Islamism, a fanatical, violent, anti-Western form of Islam, is a reminder that Western-style democracy continues to face major challenges in many parts of the world. Another is the return of the centralized authoritarian state in Russia, which is "run largely in the interests of a ruling clique."[24] Democracy has often suffered reversals even in the West, where popular rule has the deepest roots.[25]

In Latin America, democracy is widespread yet in places remains fragile and unstable. Several countries, including Colombia, Peru, and Mexico, face internal threats from guerrilla and terrorist groups. Back in 2004, a *New York Times* reporter painted this bleak picture:

> In the last few years, six elected heads of state have been ousted in the face of violent unrest, something nearly unheard of in the previous decade. A widely noted United Nations survey of 19,000 Latin Americans in 18 countries in April produced a startling result: a majority would choose a dictator over an elected leader if that provided economic benefits.[26]

He added, "Analysts say that the main source of the discontent is corruption and the widespread feeling that elected governments have done little or nothing to help the 220 million people in the region who still live in poverty, about 43 percent of the population."

Great disparities in wealth and living standards in today's world help explain popular discontent with democracy. There are many countries in Eastern Europe, Asia, Latin America, and sub-Saharan Africa where modern economies have yet to be created. Gross economic and educational inequalities

apartheid system The South African system designed to perpetuate racial domination by whites prior to the advent of black majority rule there in the early 1990s.

persist and worsen with the passage of time. Stagnant economies and tribal or ethnic divisions destabilize many developing societies.

Even in countries where the military has relinquished power, generals often continue to exert a behind-the-scenes influence over civilian governments. Where the principle of civilian rule is open to question, the government is fragile and the fear of anarchy is real, the abrupt return of military dictatorship remains an ever-present possibility. Dictators come and go, but it is too soon to write the obituary for authoritarian rule.

AUTHORITARIANISM AND U.S. FOREIGN POLICY

Soon after the end of World War II, the United States found itself engaged in a cold war with the Soviet Union. The Cold War was not a natural rivalry between two great powers but rather a struggle to the death between two rival systems of morality, economics, and government. The ideologies of these two rivals were absolutely incompatible. The United States pursued a policy of "containment" based on the theory that communism would eventually collapse of its own dead weight, while the Soviet Union drew upon Marx's prediction that capitalism was headed for the "dustbin of history."

The two principals in this contest divided the world in half—East and West, communist and capitalist, good and evil. One thing the implacable foes agreed on, however, was that neutrality was not an option: with few exceptions, the nations of the earth would have to choose between them.

In reality, the world was never so neatly divisible. Many developing countries preferred to remain nonaligned. Egypt, India, and Indonesia attempted to launch a nonaligned movement in the 1950s that, for a time, appeared to be getting off the ground. But the Cold War protagonists cajoled, pressured, and enticed the leaders of these fledgling states with foreign aid, weapons transfers, and cash. By the mid-1960s, most governments in Africa, Asia, and Latin America had chosen sides.

In the rush to recruit Third World leaders who would jump on the anti-communist bandwagon for a price, the United States frequently found itself using "dollar diplomacy" and other inducements to prop up right-wing dictatorships—and looking the other way when friendly regimes committed gross violations of human rights.[27]

Unfortunately, as events in the Balkans, West Africa, and elsewhere in the 1990s showed, when an autocrat dies or is ousted, the result is not always democracy, peace, and prosperity—that is one of the most important lessons of the post–Cold War era. Closer to home, as Robert Kaplan noted, "Look at Haiti, a small country only 90 minutes by air from Miami, where 22,000 American soldiers were dispatched in 1994 to restore 'democracy.' Five percent of eligible Haitian voters participated in [the last] election, chronic instability continues, and famine threatens."[28] Kaplan continued,

Those who think that America can establish democracy the world over should heed the words of the late American theologian and philosopher Reinhold

Niebuhr: "The same strength which has extended our power beyond a continent has also...brought us into a vast web of history in which other wills, running in oblique or contrasting directions to our own, inevitably hinder or contradict what we most fervently desire. We cannot simply have our way, not even when we believe our way is to have the 'happiness of mankind' as its promise."[29]

These words proved prophetic. In early 2004, exactly a decade after Kaplan's warning about the dangers of anarchy in impoverished, out-of-the-way countries like Haiti was first published in *The Atlantic Monthly*, Haiti's elected president, Jean-Bertrand Aristide, was forced to flee as mob violence threatened to plunge the country into chaos. The crisis ended only after a U.S. Marine Corps contingent was deployed to restore calm. (See Landmarks in History: The Demise of Saddam Hussein.)

Autocrats are often brutal and even sadistic. But where the fear and awe they inspire, and the ruthless methods they employ, prevent a descent into anarchy, it is quite possibly the lesser of two great evils. In Kaplan's words:

THE DEMISE OF SADDAM HUSSEIN

In many respects the iron-fisted Saddam Hussein who ruled Iraq for twenty-four years was the "perfect" tyrant. Saddam's heroes were modern history's most ruthless dictators.

Saddam, called the Butcher of Baghdad, has been aptly compared with Joseph Stalin, the brutal Soviet dictator who summarily executed countless "enemies" and sent millions more to work and die in slave labor camps. Like Stalin, Saddam ruled through a tightly controlled monolithic political organization, the Ba'ath Party, which was virtually indistinguishable from the state. Like Stalin, he turned the country into a vast prison. And like Stalin, he perpetuated his rule through paralyzing fear, induced by highly publicized mock trials and police-state terror.

No one knows for certain how many Iraqis became victims of the Ba'athist regime during Saddam's rule. That he routinely imprisoned all whom he suspected of disloyalty, that he used poison gas against whole villages to punish rebellious Kurds in the north, and that he tortured many of his victims without mercy are facts well known to Iraqis. Iraqi "traitors" and "enemies of the state" were not safe even abroad. At Saddam's behest, secret agents murdered scores of dissidents in exile in the 1980s and 1990s. As Saddam put it, "The

hand of the revolution can reach out to its enemies wherever they are found."*

Saddam emulated Stalin's use of ideology and propaganda to justify or legitimize his crimes against humanity by extolling the "historical mission" of the Ba'ath Party. If the regime brutalized and dehumanized anyone who got in its way, it was always for a "higher purpose."

In fact, Saddam's purposes were purely self-serving: to stay in power and live like a king while his people sank ever deeper into poverty. Between 1991 and 1995, he reportedly built fifty new palaces at a cost of $1.5 billion; the largest was bigger than Versailles. Saddam displayed no conscience and no remorse in doing whatever he deemed necessary to control Iraqi society while he plundered the economy.

In the wake of the U.S.-led invasion of Iraq in the spring of 2003, Saddam was captured, put on trial, and convicted of mass murder. He was hanged in Baghdad on December 30, 2006, defiant and unrepentant to the end.

---

*Quoted in Elaine Sciolino, *The Outlaw State: Saddam Hussein's Quest for Power and the Gulf Crisis* (New York: Wiley, 1991), p. 91.

The lesson to draw is not that dictatorship is good and democracy bad but that democracy emerges successfully only as a capstone to other social and economic achievements....Tocqueville showed how democracy evolved in the West not through the kind of moral fiat we are trying to impose throughout the world but as an organic outgrowth of development.[30]

In recent times, the United States has invaded and occupied two countries, Iraq and Afghanistan, vowing to bring freedom and democracy to both despite the fact that the peoples of neither of these fractious societies had ever experience anything of the sort. More than a decade later, it is clear that Iraq will not become a stable democracy, and quite possible it will not survive as a single state. Ditto for Afghanistan. In Iraq, as in Afghanistan and other troubled parts of the world, the choice is between the risk of anarchy and the reality of authoritarianism. It's a stark choice, but if history is any guide, it is one they and they alone can make.

SUMMARY

When one or more self-appointed rulers exercise unchecked political power, the result is a dictatorship. Benevolent autocrats (who are somewhat concerned with advancing the public good), ordinary dictators (who are concerned solely with advancing their own interests), and tyrants (who exhibit great enthusiasm for violence and bloodletting) all qualify as dictators, but even slight differences can make a significant alteration in the lives of the people who, by definition, have no voice in how they are governed.

Historically, authoritarian rulers have provided the most common form of government. Yet despite their prevalence, authoritarian regimes have been regarded as perversions of good government because they almost always place the ruler's interests ahead of the public good. Nigeria provides a good example of a contemporary authoritarian state.

Misconceptions about authoritarian regimes abound. It is not true that dictatorial rule is a modern phenomenon or that all authoritarian states are identical, illegitimate, or unpopular with their citizens. Further, we can differentiate such governments on moral grounds: Some seek to promote the public interest; others do not. Moreover, authoritarian regimes do not represent the worst possible form of government in all cases.

Finally, despite some evidence that authoritarian government is giving way to democracy, it is too early to draw any definitive conclusions. The record of U.S. relations with authoritarian states is replete with inconsistencies and contradictions. The latter have weakened the U.S. moral position in international politics, complicated its diplomatic efforts, and led to charges of hypocrisy.

KEY TERMS

authoritarian states 90	junta 92	Democracy Wall 105
theocracy 90	coup d'état 96	Tiananmen Square massacre 106
autocracy 92	Politburo 100	charismatic leader 111
oligarchy 92	sovereign wealth funds 103	apartheid system 114

REVIEW QUESTIONS

1. What are the two basic types of nondemocratic government? What are the chief characteristics of authoritarian governments?
2. Are authoritarian governments becoming less prevalent? Where are such governments found today?
3. Are all autocrats tyrannical? Explain.
4. What kind of "advice" did Machiavelli give to rulers bent on maintaining their power?
5. Summarize the six myths that surround authoritarian governments. What fallacies underlie these myths?

The Totalitarian Model

A False Utopia

THINK ABOUT IT

What is totalitarianism?

What is the role of ideology in totalitarian states?

Who are the three most infamous totalitarian rulers, and what did they do to earn that reputation?

What are the three developmental stages in the life of a totalitarian state?

Why continue to study totalitarianism now that the world's worst examples of totalitarian rule have passed into the pages of history?

totalitarianism
A political system in which every facet of the society, the economy, and the government is tightly controlled by the ruling elite. Secret police terrorism and a radical ideology implemented through mass mobilization and propaganda are hallmarks of the totalitarian state's methods and goals.

A new and more malignant form of tyranny called **totalitarianism** reared its ugly head in the twentieth century. The term itself denotes complete domination of a society and its members by tyrannical rulers and imposed beliefs. The totalitarian obsession with control extends beyond the public realm into the private lives of citizens.

Imagine living in a world in which politics is forbidden and *everything* is political—including work, education, religion, sports, social organizations, and even the family. Neighbors spy on neighbors and children are encouraged to report "disloyal" parents. "Enemies of the people" are exterminated.

Who are these "enemies"? Defined in terms of whole *categories* or groups within society, they typically encompass hundreds of thousands and even millions of people who are "objectively" counterrevolutionary—for example, Jews and Gypsies (Romany) in Nazi Germany, the bourgeoisie (middle class) and kulaks (rich farmers) in Soviet Russia, and so on. By contrast, authoritarian governments typically seek to maintain political power (rather than to transform society) and more narrowly define political enemies as individuals (not groups) actively engaged in opposing the existing state.

Why study totalitarianism now that the Soviet Union no longer exists? First, communism is not the only possible form of totalitarian state. The examples of Nazi Germany and Fascist Italy are reminders that totalitarianism is not a product of one ideology, regime, or ruler. Second, totalitarianism is an integral part of contemporary history. Many who suffered directly at the hands of totalitarian dictators or lost loved ones in Hitler's Holocaust, Stalin's Reign of Terror, Mao's horrific purges, or other, more recent instances of totalitarian brutality are still living. The physical and emotional scars of the victims remain even after the tyrants are long gone. Third, totalitarian states demonstrate the risks of idealism gone awry. Based on a millenarian vision of social progress and perfection that cannot be pursued without resort to barbaric measures (and cannot be achieved even then), they all have failed miserably as experiments in utopian nation-building. Finally, as we will see, totalitarianism remains a possibility wherever there is great poverty, injustice, and therefore the potential for violence and turmoil—recent examples include Iran, North Korea, and Burma.

One of the lessons of 9/11 is that extremism remains a fact of political life in the contemporary world. It can take many malignant forms. Terrorism is one; totalitarianism is another. This chapter demonstrates clearly that totalitarianism and terror go hand in hand.

THE ESSENCE OF TOTALITARIANISM

Violence is at the core of every totalitarian state—at its worst, it assumes the form of indiscriminate mass terror and genocide aimed at whole groups, categories, or classes of people who are labeled enemies, counterrevolutionaries, spies, or saboteurs. Mass mobilization is carried out through a highly regimented and centralized one-party system in the name of an official ideology that functions as a kind of state religion. The state employs a propaganda and censorship apparatus far more sophisticated and effective than that typically found in authoritarian states. As the late William Kornhauser, a sociologist, wrote in a highly acclaimed study, "Totalitarianism is limited only by the need to keep large numbers of people in a state of constant activity controlled by the elite."[1]

Totalitarian ideologies promise the advent of a new social order—whether a racially pure "Aryan" society envisioned by Adolf Hitler, or the classless society promised by Lenin and Josef Stalin, or the peasant society in a permanent state of revolution Mao Zedong imagined. All such totalitarian prophets "have exhibited a basic likeness...[in seeking] a higher and unprecedented kind of human existence."[2] We can trace the totalitarian leader's claim of political legitimacy directly to this self-proclaimed aim of creating a new utopian society.[3]

Totalitarian societies are "thoroughly egalitarian: no social differences will remain; even authority and expertise, from the scientific to the artistic, cannot be tolerated."[4] Thus, individualism is rejected and even criminalized. The rights of society are paramount, leaving no room at all for the rights of the individual.

At the heart of this harmonious community lies the concept of a reformulated human nature. The impulse to human perfection was reflected in Lenin's repeated references to the creation of a "new Soviet man" and in the Nazi assertion that party workers and leaders represented a new type of human being or a new breed of "racially pure" rulers. Mao Zedong displayed a near obsession with something he called **rectification**—the radical purging of all capitalist tendencies, such as materialism and individualism, at all levels of Chinese society.

The clearest examples of such utopian political orders have been Nazi Germany, the Soviet Union (especially during Stalin's Reign of Terror), and Maoist China. Other examples in recent history include Pol Pot's Cambodia (1976–1979) and Mengistu's Ethiopia (1977–1991), and North Korea is a contemporary case. In the following section we examine the stages in the evolution of totalitarian regimes.

rectification
In Maoist China, the elimination of all purported capitalist traits, such as materialism and individualism.

THE REVOLUTIONARY STAGE OF TOTALITARIANISM

How do totalitarian movements start? Typically, they emerge from the wreckage of a collapsed or collapsing state. In such turbulent times, a charismatic leader sometimes steps onto the scene. Leadership is crucial to the success of any revolution. In the case of *total* revolution, leadership is one of five key elements. Ideology, organization, propaganda, and violence are the other four.

Leadership

Perhaps the most conspicuous trait of total revolution has been reliance on what we may term the *cult of leadership*. Virtually every such revolution has been identified with—indeed, personified in—the image of a larger-than-life figure. The Russian Revolution had its Lenin, the Third Reich its Hitler, the Chinese Revolution its Mao, Cuba its Castro, and so forth. Each of these leaders became the object of hero worship. "An outstanding leader is indispensible" observed

Eric Hoffer in a brilliant little book entitled, *The True Believer*. Without such a leader "there will be no [mass] movement." Hoffer continues:

> It was Lenin who forced the flow of events into the channels of the Bolshevik revolution. Had he died in Switzerland or on his way to Russia in 1917, it is almost certain that the other prominent Bolsheviks would have joined a coalition government. The result might have been a more or less liberal republic run chiefly by the bourgeoisie. In the case of Mussolini or Hitler the evidence is even more decisive: without them there would have been neither a Fascist nor a Nazi movement.[5]

Revolutionary leaders instinctively understand that the masses possess the raw power to change the world but lack the will and direction. Without a charismatic leader—one who can read their minds, capture their imagination, and win their hearts—there is nothing to act as a catalyst. A leader such as Lenin or Mao, then, is to a mass movement what a detonator is to a bomb.

Ideology

Whatever the quality of leadership, total revolutions depend in the final analysis on the willingness of converts to engage in extraordinary acts of self-sacrifice in the name of the cause. Such reckless devotion cannot be inspired by rational appeals. It must arise, rather, from the true believer's blind faith in the absolute truth provided by a comprehensive political doctrine.

Consider what an ideology must do for its followers if it is to be successful:

> It must claim scientific authority which gives the believer a conviction of having the exclusive key to all knowledge; it must promise a millennium to be brought about for the chosen race or class by the elect who holds this key; it must identify a host of ogres and demons to be overcome before this happy state is brought about; it must enlist the dynamic of hatred, envy, and fear (whether of class or race) and justify these low passions by the loftiness of its aims.[6]

The Need for a Scapegoat: Reinterpreting the Past As a critique of the past, ideology generally focuses on some form of absolute evil to which it can attribute all national (or worldwide) wrongs and social injustices. To the revolutionary ideologue, the true causes of economic recession, inflation, military defeat, official corruption, national humiliation, moral decadence, and other perceived problems are rooted in the mysteries and plots of a rejected past.

If an enemy does not exist, it is necessary to invent one. Usually it is an individual or a group that was already widely feared, hated, or envied. Lenin blamed the plight of workers on money-grubbing capitalists. Hitler blamed Jews and communists for the German loss in World War I and the economic crises that preceded his assumption of power. Mao found his enemy first in wealthy landlords and later in "capitalist roaders." Clearly, the purpose of these ploys was to focus mass attention on a readily identifiable scapegoat on whose shoulders all the nation's ills could be placed.

According to Hoffer, "Mass movements can rise and spread without a belief in God, but never without a belief in a devil."[7] Hate and prejudice, rather than love and high principle, seem the most effective forces in bringing people together in a common cause.

Revolutionary Struggle: Explaining the Present As a guide to the present, ideology provides the true believer with keys to a "correct" analysis of the underlying forces at work in contemporary society. Concepts such as class struggle for Marxist-Leninists, *Herrenvolk* (master race) for the Nazis, and "contradictions" for Mao's followers were used to explain and predict social reality. Yesterday the enemy was preeminent; today the enemy will be defeated.

Advocates of total revolution believe struggle is the very essence of politics. For Marxist-Leninists, class struggle was the engine of progress in history. For Maoists, struggle was a desirable end in itself; only through the direct experience of revolutionary struggle, they believed, could the masses (and especially the young) learn the true meaning of self-sacrifice. Hitler glorified the struggle for power by proclaiming war to be the supreme test of national greatness. (Revealingly, Hitler outlined his own path to political power in a book titled *Mein Kampf*, "my struggle.") Whether the aim is to overthrow monopoly capitalists or to purify a race, revolutionary struggle is always described in terms of good versus evil. It was common for leading Nazis to depict Jews not simply as enemies of the state but as *Untermenschen* ("subhumans") and, frequently, as insects or lice.[8] The repeated use of such degrading characterizations dehumanizes the victims; it is a lot easier to justify the extermination of insects than human beings.

Utopia: Foretelling the Future As a promise of the future, ideology tends to paint a radiant picture of perfect justice and perpetual peace. Marxist-Leninists envisioned this utopia as a classless society, one from which all social and economic inequality would be abolished. Similarly, the Nazi utopia was a society from which all racial "impurities" would be removed through the extermination or enslavement of racial "inferiors."

Whatever its precise character, the vision of the future always included a radical redistribution of wealth and property. Marxism-Leninism promised to take from the rich (the bourgeoisie) and give to the poor (the proletariat). Hitler made a similar promise when he proclaimed his intention to provide *Lebensraum* ("living space") in the east; he would take land from the land-rich but slothful Slavs and give it to the land-poor but industrious Germans.

Marxism is based on a deterministic worldview in which the success of the proletarian revolution is dictated by inflexible "laws" of history. Hitler, too, was an unabashed determinist. In *Mein Kampf*, he wrote, "Man must realize that a fundamental law of necessity reigns throughout the whole realm of Nature."[9] Hitler also frequently ranted about "the iron law of our historical development," the "march of history," and the "inner logic of events." No less than Lenin, Stalin, or Mao, he claimed that he (and the German people or *Volk*) had a world-shattering mission to accomplish, and that success was inevitable. He expressed this notion in what is perhaps his most famous (or infamous) pronouncement: "I go the way that Providence dictates with the assurance of a sleepwalker."[10]

Ideology and Truth The past, present, and future as described by a given revolutionary ideology may seem far-fetched or even ludicrous to a disinterested observer. The racial theory put forth by the Nazis utterly lacked historical,

Image of Vladimir Ilyich Lenin, leader of the October Revolution, on a Soviet postage stamp. The letters "CCCP" stand for Union of the Soviet Socialist Republics (USSR) in the Russian-language Cyrillic alphabet.

sociological, genetic, and moral foundations. By the same token, the economic facet of Hitler's ideology—the "socialism" in National Socialism—lacked any meaningful content. So watered down was Hitler's conception of socialism that in the words of one authority, "Anyone genuinely concerned about the people was in Hitler's eyes a socialist."[11]

Why would any sane person embrace such an ideology? First, it appealed to popular prejudices and made them respectable. Second, it was not the message that counted so much as the messenger—the leader's personal magnetism attracted a following, whether the words made sense or not. Third, certitude was far more important than rectitude. Fourth, ideologues can often get away with absurd allegations and gross falsehoods if they also address real problems faced by ordinary people.

Many Germans recognized the extremist nature of the Nazis' racial theories but probably believed Hitler would discard such absurdities once the work of unifying the country, reviving the economy, and restoring the nation's lost honor had been accomplished. By the same token, even if many of Lenin's followers did not truly believe the workers' paradise was just around the corner, the Russian peasants did believe in land reform, an end to Russia's disastrous involvement in World War I, and improvements in nutrition, medical care, and education as promised by Lenin.

Organization

Cohesive structure was one of the missing ingredients in pre-twentieth-century rebellions. Most such outbreaks were spontaneous affairs—they burst into flame, occasionally spread, but almost always burned themselves out. The October Revolution, however, was a different story.

Lenin founded the Bolshevik Party more than fourteen years before seizing power in 1917. Admitting only hard-core adherents into the party, Lenin reasoned the czar could be defeated through a long, clandestine struggle led by a small group of disciplined revolutionaries (a "vanguard") rather than by a large, amorphous mass of unruly malcontents.

cells
Small, tightly knit organizational units at the grassroots level of V. I. Lenin's Bolshevik Party.

To ensure secrecy, discipline, and centralized control, Lenin organized the Bolshevik Party into tiny **cells**. As the Bolsheviks grew in number and established cells in cities outside Saint Petersburg, intermediate layers of authority became necessary, although the principles of strict party discipline and total subordination of lower levels to higher ones were not relaxed (see "Landmarks in History"). Factionalism was not tolerated; party members were still expected to place party interests above personal interests at all times. This spirit of self-sacrifice and total commitment to the party was called **partiinost**.

partiinost
The spirit of sacrifice, enthusiasm, and unquestioning devotion required of Communist Party members.

Unlike its Russian counterpart, the Chinese Revolution was primarily a rural uprising by a mass of discontented peasants. Mao's most pressing organizational problem was to mold the amorphous peasant mass into an effective military force capable of carrying out a protracted guerrilla war. His success won over many leftists (especially in developing nations), who admired and

THE OCTOBER REVOLUTION

In October 1917, the Russian capital of Saint Petersburg (also called Petrograd) was in turmoil, due to hardships and popular anger caused by the long years of World War I and bitter capitulation to Germany. The October Revolution was led by Nikolai Lenin and the Bolsheviks, with the backing of the Mensheviks, the Left Socialist revolutionaries, and an assortment of anarchists.

There were actually two revolutions in Russia in 1917. The first, the so-called February Revolution, brought about three dramatic results: the ouster of Czar Nicholas II, the end of the Russian monarchy, and the creation of a power vacuum. Following a failed attempt by Aleksandr Kerensky to form a Western-style parliamentary democracy, Lenin and Trotsky masterminded a power seizure in the capital in October. This move had a dual character—half popular uprising and half *coup d'état*.

In fact, the revolution *did* spread, and it *was* fomented by Lenin's Bolsheviks. However, it was not entirely, or even mainly, a proletarian revolution of the kind Marx had imagined. Instead, it included disaffected soldiers and sailors, as well as land-hungry peasants. Russia did not have an extensive industrial labor force in 1917. It was still primarily a peasant society with an agrarian economy. Moreover, the "revolution" in Saint Petersburg was actually led by Leon Trotsky, not Lenin.

Nonetheless, Lenin was the prime mover. His role in creating a conspiratorial organization, orchestrating events between February and October 1917, and inspiring the masses made him the undisputed leader of the revolutionary Soviet state—so much so that Saint Petersburg was renamed Leningrad three days after Lenin's death in 1924. The name was changed back to Saint Petersburg in September 1991, shortly before the Soviet Union was formally dissolved.

FIGURE 6.1   Map of Russia.

even imitated Mao's theory and practice of peasant-based revolution in a poor and benighted rural society.

Mao's long march to power contrasts with Hitler's quixotic rise in Germany, which started with a violent, abortive coup in the early 1920s and culminated in a kind of constitutional *coup d'état* in the 1930s. A compliant organization in the form of the Nazi Party was crucial to Hitler's ultimate success. Hitler made extensive use of brute force to intimidate his opposition, but he also created numerous party-controlled clubs and associations. The Hitler Youth, a Nazi women's league, a Nazi workers' organization, a Nazi student league, and various other academic and social organizations gave the Nazis considerable political power even before Hitler took over the reins of government. Later, under an innocuous-sounding policy called **Gleichschaltung** ("coordination"), he destroyed virtually all preexisting social organizations and substituted Nazi associations in their place. Partly for this reason, Hitler's promises and threats carried great weight throughout German society. Like all modern revolutionaries, Hitler understood the value of a carefully constructed revolutionary organization.

Gleichschaltung
Hitler's technique of using Nazi-controlled associations, clubs, and organizations to coordinate his revolutionary activities.

propaganda
The use of mass media to create whatever impression is desired among the general population and to influence thoughts and activities toward desired ends.

Propaganda

As more people have become engaged in modern political life, **propaganda**—the dissemination of information based on falsehoods and half-truths designed to advance an ideological cause—has become a potent political weapon. To be successful, as Hitler noted, propaganda must address the masses exclusively; hence, "its effect for the most part must be aimed at the emotions and only to a very limited degree at the so-called intellect."[12]

An avid student of the science of propaganda, Hitler proposed that "all propaganda must be popular and its intellectual level must be adjusted to the most limited intelligence among those to whom it is addressed." Hence, "the greater the mass it is intended to reach, the lower its purely intellectual level will have to be.…Effective propaganda must be limited to a very few points and must harp on these in slogans until the last member of the public understands what you want him to understand." Given these premises, it follows that the "very first axiom of all propagandist activity [is] the basically subjective and one-sided attitude it must take toward every question it deals with."[13] And the bigger the lie, the better.

Hitler theorized that the success of any propaganda campaign depends on the propagandist's understanding of the "primitive sentiments" of the popular masses. Propaganda cannot have multiple shadings: Concepts and "facts" must

AP PHOTO

Through the implementation of an immense propaganda campaign in combination with the inculcation of the Nazi ideology, Adolf Hitler (1889–1945) was able to persuade the German people of the need to persecute Jews, the necessity of an eventual war, and the radical transformation of German society.

be presented to the public as true or false, right or wrong, black or white. In *Mein Kampf*, Hitler heaped high praise on British propaganda efforts in World War I and expressed contempt for German propaganda, which he faulted for not painting the world in stark black-and-white terms.

Unlike Hitler, who was a highly effective orator, Lenin was a master pamphleteer and polemicist who relied most heavily on the written word. In the infancy of his movement, Lenin's chief weapon was the underground newspaper. Endowed with such names as "The Spark" and "Forward," these propaganda tabloids were printed clandestinely or smuggled into the capital, Saint Petersburg, in false-bottom briefcases.

Violence

The fifth and final characteristic of totalitarian revolution is the use of violence and terror as accepted instruments of political policy. According to the Nazi theorist Eugene Hadamovsky, "Propaganda and violence are never contradictions. Use of violence can be part of the propaganda."[14] Assassinations and kidnappings, indiscriminate bombings, and sabotage are all part of the totalitarian tool box. Sabotage is designed to disrupt production, transportation, and communications systems; terror is aimed at a greater, pervasive sense of insecurity (see Chapter 15).

State terror—violence perpetrated by the government—has played a prominent role in mass movements of both the Right and the Left. The notorious "combat groups" (*fasci di combattimento*) Italian Fascist Party leader Benito Mussolini formed shortly after World War I provide a striking example. After attempts to woo the working class away from the Socialist Party failed, Mussolini began to cultivate the middle classes and seek financing from wealthy industrialists and big landowners. One of the more novel forms of terror the fascists devised was the *punitive expedition*, in which armed bands conducted raids against defenseless communities. The local police would often cooperate by looking the other way.

Mussolini's aim was threefold: (1) to create an artificial atmosphere of crisis; (2) to demonstrate that the state was no longer capable of providing law-abiding, taxpaying citizens with protection from unprovoked attacks on their persons and property; and (3) to prod an increasingly fearful, desperate, and fragmented citizenry to turn for refuge and order to the very same political movement that was deliberately exacerbating the problem.

The Nazis in Germany used the same sort of tactics. The similarities between this kind of organized violence and plain gangsterism are obvious—the crucial difference has to do with ends rather than means: Gangsters seek to gain control over lucrative (and often illegal) businesses, not to overthrow the government.

THE CONSOLIDATION OF POWER

Once the old order has been overthrown or fatally discredited, the totalitarian leadership can operate from a solid power base within the government. The next task it faces is to eliminate any competing political parties and factions. The final step in the consolidation process is the elimination of all those within the party who pose a real or potential danger to the totalitarian leader. At this stage, Machiavelli's advice is especially valuable: "One ought not to say to someone whom one wants to kill, 'Give me your gun, I want to kill you with it,' but merely, 'Give me your gun,' for once you have the gun in your hand, you can satisfy your desire."[15]

Eliminating Opposition Parties

Any opposition group, no matter how small or ineffectual, poses a potential danger to the ruler. By the same token, the mere existence of political opponents inhibits the kind of radical change mandated by the movement's ideology.

In dealing with rival political parties, Lenin famously employed **salami tactics**[16]—the practice of marginalizing or eliminating opposition by slicing it into pieces and playing one group off against the other. Thus, after the new Constituent Assembly (legislature) was elected, Lenin exploited an already existing division in the dominant Socialist Revolutionary Party by forming an alliance with its left wing. This alliance enabled Lenin to move against the party's more moderate wing, as well as against other rightist parties.

Lenin also repressed Russia's huge peasant population. The lack of peasant support for the Bolshevik regime became a particularly acute problem during the civil war (1918–1920), when foodstuffs and other basic necessities were extremely scarce. In response, Lenin "instituted in the villages a 'civil war within a civil war' by setting poor peasants against those who were less poor,"[17] thereby helping to undermine the political opposition.

Hitler employed a different strategy. Bolstered by his Nazi Party's steadily growing popularity in the polls (thanks to a formidable following of true believers), his superb oratorical skills, and a special group of shock troops known as storm troopers, he played a waiting game. Once in office, he gradually expanded his authority, first by gaining passage of new emergency powers and suspending civil liberties. Only then did he move to shut down all opposition parties. Hitler thus used the charade of legality to destroy his opponents politically before using the power of the state to destroy them physically.

Purging Real or Imagined Rivals within the Party

Political **purges** involve removing opponents from the party leadership or from positions of power, or rounding up whole (often fictitious) categories of people ("bourgeois capitalists" or "enemies of the people") but not necessarily killing them. Arresting people you don't trust and either imprisoning or exiling them can be just as effective as killing them—and ostensibly more civilized. In carrying out purges, totalitarian governments almost invariably accuse their victims of subversive activity or treason—a convenient rationale for eliminating individuals who are perceived as threats or political liabilities.[18] Thus, Hitler turned on Ernst Röhm and other party members who had been instrumental in the Nazis' rise to power; on the Führer's orders, the Röhm faction was murdered in June 1934. Blaming the whole incident on his political enemies, Hitler used the Röhm purge to solidify his popular support and give credence to his fear-mongering propaganda.

Purges played an even bigger role in the consolidation of power in the Soviet Union. In 1921, thousands of trade unionists and sailors, formerly the

salami tactics
The methods used by Vladimir Lenin to divide his opponents into small groups that could be turned against one another and easily overwhelmed.

purges
The elimination of all rivals to power through mass arrests, imprisonment, exile, and murder, often directed at former associates and their followers who have (or are imagined to have) enough influence to be a threat to the ruling elite.

backbone of the Bolsheviks' popular support, were murdered by the secret police when they demanded free trade unions and elections. Next, Lenin purged the so-called Workers' Opposition faction of his own Bolshevik Party, which demanded worker self-management of industry. Lenin pronounced the group guilty of "factionalism" and accused it of endangering both the party and the revolution. The members of the Workers' Opposition group were expelled from the party but not murdered.

Such relatively mild actions were not characteristic of Lenin's successor, Joseph Stalin, who, as the head of the Soviet Communist Party (1924–1953), did not hesitate to murder those whom he perceived to be his political enemies. How Stalin gathered total power in his hands is a textbook example of cutthroat power politics. He shrewdly adapted Lenin's salami tactics. However, whereas Lenin set rival parties against one another, Stalin set rivals within his own party—virtually all the great Bolshevik heroes of the October Revolution—against one another. Stalin purged and eventually murdered virtually the entire top party leadership after Lenin's death in 1924.

Creating a Monolithic Society

The totalitarian state stops at nothing short of total control over the economy, the arts, the military, the schools, the government—every aspect of society. As Nazi propaganda chief Joseph Goebbels (1897–1945) remarked, "The revolution we have made is a total revolution.... It is completely irrelevant what means it uses."[19] Ironically, the golden society at the end of the utopian rainbow is incompatible with intellectual freedom. Thus, one Nazi official asked this rhetorical question: "If the brains of all university professors were put at one end of the scale and the brains of the Führer at the other, which end, do you think, would tip?"[20]

Total control requires total loyalty. During the Nazi era, even in small towns, any magistrates and petty officials who had not publicly supported the Nazis were removed from power. Simultaneously, numerous "enemies of the people" were identified and punished by the brutal **Gestapo** or secret police.[21] The effectiveness of these terror tactics helps explain why there was so little overt resistance to the Nazi takeover, but it does not tell the whole story. Cowardice, apathy, and self-interest played important roles as well. A true story told by a German refugee who had been on the faculty of the prestigious University of Frankfurt speaks directly to this point. Following the appointment of a Nazi commissar at the university, every professor and graduate assistant was summoned for an important faculty meeting:

> The new Nazi commissar...immediately announced that Jews would be forbidden to enter university premises and would be dismissed without salary on March 15....Then he launched into a tirade of abuse, fifth, and four-letter words such as had been heard rarely even in the barracks and never before in academia. He pointed his finger at one department chairman after another and said, "You either do what I tell you or we'll put you into a concentration camp." There was silence when he finished; everybody waited for the distinguished biochemist-physiologist.
>
> The great liberal got up, cleared his throat, and said, "Very interesting, Mr. Commissar, and in some respects very illuminating; but one point I didn't

Gestapo
In Nazi Germany, the secret state police, Hitler's instrument for spreading mass terror among Jews and political opponents.

get too clearly. Will there be more money for research in Physiology?" The meeting broke up shortly thereafter with the commissar assuring the scholars that indeed there would be plenty of money for "racially pure science."[22]

The English philosopher Edmund Burke is reported to have said, "All that is necessary for evil to succeed is for good men to do nothing." Indeed.

THE TRANSFORMATION OF SOCIETY

The transformation stage generally coincides with the regime's assumption of control over the economy and requires active government planning and intervention.[23] In justifying the drive for a new social order, totalitarian regimes typically blame everything that is wrong with the country on counterrevolutionaries, spies, and saboteurs.

Carl Friedrich and Zbigniew Brzezinski, two respected students of this subject, have identified six characteristics shared by all totalitarian governments—an official ideology; a single, hierarchical party; a secret police; a tightly controlled armed forces; a media monopoly; and central control over the economy.[24] These characteristics derive from the main features and functions of the revolutionary movement we have discussed (leadership, ideology, organization, propaganda, and violence), now redirected to the state's day-to-day administration and transformation.

The attempted transformation of the state follows a predetermined ideological path, with some concessions to pragmatism where necessary. But practicality is rarely of prime importance for the total tyrant bent on transformation. Examples from the political careers of Stalin, Hitler, and Mao illustrate this point.

The Soviet Union under Stalin

In 1928, having defeated his political rivals, Stalin stood poised to launch his drive to collectivize and industrialize the Soviet economy. His first Five-Year Plan for the Soviet economy (1928–1932) marked the beginning of a cataclysm. Over the next ten years, millions of innocent people were killed or sent to labor camps, and a whole class of relatively well-to-do landholders, the **kulaks**, ceased to exist. In addition, the whole pattern of Soviet agricultural production was radically reshaped.

To understand why Stalin would inflict so much suffering on the Soviet farm population, we must first understand the role of ideology in totalitarian systems. Stalin's first Five-Year Plan, which instituted a highly centralized economic system designed to foster rapid development of the Soviet economy, was motivated by a lust for power. However, Stalin was also committed to creating an advanced industrial society based on collective, rather than capitalist, principles. The way to accomplish this remarkable feat in the shortest possible time, Stalin reasoned, was to invest massively in heavy industry while squeezing every last drop of profit from agriculture, the traditional foundation of the Russian economy.

Private ownership of farmland, animals, and implements would have to be eliminated and farming "collectivized." Under Stalin's **collectivization** plan, most agricultural production took place in large cooperative units known as

kulaks
A class of well-to-do landowners in Russian society that was purged by Joseph Stalin because it resisted his drive to establish huge collective farms under state control.

collectivization
The belief that the public good is best served by common (as opposed to individual) ownership of a political community's means of production and distribution; derived from "collective," denoting a form of community or commune in Marxist ideology.

kolkhozy (collective farms), whose members shared whatever income was left after making compulsory deliveries to the state, or in *sovkhozy* (state farms), whose laborers received wages.

Soviet agriculture was collectivized to underwrite Soviet industrialization. Through a massive transfer of resources from farms to cities, Stalin believed industrial production could double or even triple during the period of the first Five-Year Plan. But doing so would necessitate crushing all pockets of rural resistance, herding the peasants into collective farms, and imposing a draconian system of "tax" collections or compulsory deliveries of scarce food supplies to the state in order to feed the growing army of industrial workers and to pay for imported capital goods.

One reason the plan failed was the excessive and indiscriminate brutality Stalin employed. Stories spread through the countryside of how Stalin's agents had machine-gunned whole villages. Many Russian peasants deliberately burned their crops and killed their cattle rather than cooperate with Stalin's requisition squads. Despite an all-out national effort, industrial production grew only slightly, if at all. In the meantime, famine depopulated the countryside.

Stalin made no apologies and no policy adjustments. Instead, he fabricated statistics, which no one dared question, to "prove" that real progress was being made. In the words of one expert, "The Stalin regime was ruthlessly consistent: All facts that did not agree, or were likely to disagree, with the official fiction—data on crop yields, criminality, true incidences of 'counterrevolutionary' activities…were treated as nonfacts."[25]

In 1934, as the death toll mounted and the first Five-Year Plan came to an unspectacular end, the Soviet dictator declared he had uncovered a far-reaching conspiracy, orchestrated by foreign agents and counter-revolutionaries, to resurrect capitalism in Soviet Russia. This conspiracy theory gained credibility when Sergei Kirov, the dynamic young leader of the Leningrad party organization, was assassinated in December 1934. Harsh reprisals, numerous arrests, phony trials, summary executions, and large-scale deportations followed. Many of the victims were loosely identified as members of a fabricated conspiracy called the Leningrad Center. The alleged plot furnished Stalin with the pretext for a purge of Lenin's original circle of revolutionary leaders, the so-called Old Bolsheviks.

During the first phase of the Great Terror (January 1934 to April 1936)—also known as the Great Purge—Communist Party membership fell by nearly 800,000, or approximately 25%. The Soviet press denounced these excommunicants as "wreckers, spies, diversionists, and murderers sheltering behind the party card and disguised as Bolsheviks."[26]

The second phase of the Stalin purges (1936–1938) was highlighted by the infamous *show trials*, in which the Old Bolsheviks, along with many other top-ranking party leaders, were placed on public trial and forced to make outrageous "confessions." The trials represented only the tip of the iceberg (see "Landmarks in History").

One of the most ruthless dictators of the twentieth century, Joseph Stalin (1879–1954) moved away from the Soviet model of an international communist revolution proposed by Marx and Lenin to focus on "socialism in one country." In pursuit of his aims, Stalin committed mass murders on a grand scale and enslaved millions in a vast system of gulags (forced-labor camps). It's amazing, even shocking, given what we now know about Stalin that he was named *Time* magazine's "Man of the Year" in 1942.

THE GREAT PURGE

Between 1934 and 1938, Stalin ordered most of the Soviet political and military elite executed as enemies of the state, including:

- 1,100 delegates to the 17th Party Congress (more than half)
- 70% of the 139-member Party Central Committee

- 3 of 5 Soviet marshals (the highest-ranking generals)
- 14 of 26 army commanders
- All 8 admirals
- 60 of 67 corps commanders
- Half the 397 brigade commanders
- All but 5 of the 81 top-ranking political commissars

gulag archipelago
Metaphorical name for the network of slave labor camps established in the former Soviet Union by Joseph Stalin and maintained by his secret police to which nonconformists and politically undesirable persons were sent.

Nor were the rank-and-file workers spared. Throughout the mid- to late 1930s, Stalin collectivized the Soviet labor force by means of forced-draft or conscript labor. Work units were structured and regimented along military lines. This policy gave birth to the so-called **gulag archipelago**, a network of draconian slave-labor camps maintained and operated by the Soviet secret police where social and political undesirables were forced to live. Through the gulag system, railroads, canals, and dams were constructed in remote and inaccessible areas where workers would not voluntarily go. Aleksandr Solzhenitsyn, the celebrated dissident writer who chronicled life in the labor camps, estimated that they held as many as 12 million prisoners at any given time, perhaps half of them political prisoners. "As some departed beneath the sod," he noted, "the Machine kept bringing in replacements."[27]

At the close of 1938, Stalin stood alone at the top. Industrial development had been spurred, but the Soviet Union was anything but a worker's paradise. Terror had brought about great political changes, with many luminaries from the pages of Soviet Communist Party history uncovered as traitors and placed on public trial. The list of the accused read like an honor roll of the October Revolution. The military high command had been sacked, the party rank and file cleansed of all political impurities, and the "toiling masses" reduced to a new level of industrial serfdom. Although he ruled until his death in 1953, Stalin (and the legacy of Stalinism) would be identified, above all, with the bloody purges of the 1930s.

Germany under Hitler

The overriding theme of National Socialist (Nazi) Party ideology during the Third Reich (1933–1945) was the elimination of the Jews and other "social undesirables" and the ascendency of the "Aryan" race—a fiction that nonetheless obsessed Hitler and his followers. Through Nazi ideology and propaganda, the German people came to accept the persecution of the Jews, the necessity of eventual war, and the radical transformation of society. Every aspect of German life became politicized. Dissident artists, journalists, and academicians were silenced. New state organs, including the Reich chambers for literature, press, broadcasting, theater, music, and fine arts, were created for the primary purpose of censoring or quelling potentially "dangerous" forms of written or artistic expression.

In the realm of music, German folk tunes were exalted over "decadent" modern music and classical music written by composers of Jewish lineage, such as Felix Mendelssohn and Gustav Mahler. Modern art was likewise condemned, and the works of virtually every well-known contemporary artist were banned. Literature under the Nazi regime fared no better. According to one chronicler of the Third Reich, "Blacklists were compiled ceaselessly and literary histories were revised....The 'cleansing' of libraries and bookstores presented some problems, but the destruction and self-destruction of German literature was achieved within a matter of months through the substitution of second- and third-rate scribblers for first-rate writers and by inhibiting contacts with the outside."[28]

The Nazi attack on the arts was indicative of the lengths to which Hitler would go to ensure that Nazi values were propagated. But perhaps no part of German life more vividly demonstrated Hitler's commitment to a new future than the Nazi school system. As Bracher pointed out, "While National Socialism could substitute little more than ideology and second-rate imitators for the literature and art it expelled or destroyed, its main efforts from the very outset were directed toward the most important instruments of totalitarian policy: propaganda and education."[29]

Nazi educational policy was implemented in three principal ways. To begin with, educators and school administrators who were suspected of opposing Hitler, Nazism, or Nazi educational "reform" were promptly removed from their positions. Then all academic subjects were infused with ideological content reflecting Hitler's anti-Semitic racial theories. History became "racial history," biology was transformed into "racial biology," and so on. Finally, the Nazis established special schools to train a future party elite, including military leaders, party officials, and government administrators. Students were assigned to these schools according to age group and career orientation. The Adolf Hitler Schools, to cite one example, taught twelve- to eighteen-year-old students who wished to become high party functionaries. In general, all special schools taught certain basic core courses (such as racial history and biology) and emphasized military drill (for example, the training of the infamous Hitler Youth).

The Nazi educational program turned out to be all too successful. In the judgment of one authority, "Just as teachers and parents capitulated to the pressures of the regime, so on the whole did the indoctrination of the young succeed. The young, who were receptive to heroic legends and black-and-white oversimplifications, were handed over to the stupendous shows of the regime."[30] Education of the young was reinforced by carefully planned pomp and ceremony: "From earliest childhood, they were exposed to flag raisings, parades, nationwide broadcasts in the schools, hikes, and camps."[31] Indoctrination and propaganda, not terror, became the instruments by which the children of the Third Reich were initiated into the new order.

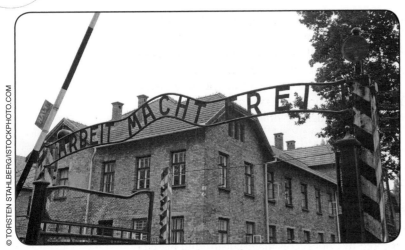

The overriding theme of Nazi Party ideology was the elimination of the Jews and other "social undesirables" and the subsequent creation of a "racially pure" Aryan nation. Between 1933 and 1945, at least 6 million European Jews plus countless others perished in Nazi death camps. The entrance to the infamous Auschwitz death camp is pictured here. The sign above the gate reads "Work makes you free."

Mass indoctrination combined with a preexisting anti-Semitism made it possible for Hitler to carry out the murderous racial policies that culminated in the Holocaust. After seizing power, Hitler implemented his anti-Jewish policy in stages, each more radical than the one before.[32] First came the attempt to define who precisely was and was not a Jew. Then the regime launched a systematic campaign to isolate Jews from the mainstream of German life and to expropriate their property. Next all Jews who had not fled the country between 1933 and 1938 were forcibly removed from German society and sent to the infamous concentration camps. This mass deportation presaged the fourth and final step—genocide.

Hitler's maniacal obsession was ultimately his undoing. Even on the brink of defeat, Hitler continued to divert resources needed to prosecute the war to the Final Solution (the liquidation of the Jews). In the end, some 6 million European Jews plus countless others, including the mentally ill, physically disabled, Soviet prisoners of war, gay men, Gypsies, Jehovah's Witness members, Polish intellectuals, and many Polish Roman Catholics, were annihilated.

China under Mao

Mao Zedong's rise to power in China is an epic example of revolutionary struggle—a true mass movement in a poor, peasant-dominated society. For more than twenty years (1927–1949), Mao waged a bitter "war of national liberation" against the **Kuomintang**, headed by Chiang Kai-shek, as well as against the Japanese during World War II. In the mid-1930s, Mao was one of the leaders of the legendary Long March, a 6,000-mile trek, during which his ragtag band of guerrillas repeatedly evaded capture or annihilation by the numerically superior and better-equipped forces of Chiang's Nationalist army. By 1949, when Mao finally won the last decisive battle and assumed command of the Chinese nation, Mao had been waging class war in the name of the Chinese masses for more than two decades.

Kuomintang
The Chinese Nationalist Party, led by Chiang Kai-shek, defeated by Mao Zedong in 1949.

Mao prided himself not only on his revolutionary exploits but also on his political thought. In time, the "thoughts of Chairman Mao," compiled in his pocket-sized little Red Book, of which millions of copies were printed and mass distributed, attained the status of holy scripture in Chinese society. His vision of a new, classless state and of the exemplary communist cadres and comrades who would typify this morally reeducated society inspired the radical policies that have become known collectively as Maoism.

Although Mao's worldview was undoubtedly shaped by the basic tenets of Marxism, 1920s China was a preindustrial society without a true proletarian (industrial-worker) class or a "monopoly capitalist" class of the kind Marx had described in *Das Kapital*. The bane of China's peasant masses was not factory bosses but greedy landlords and bureaucratic officials preoccupied with the preservation of the status quo and of their own power and privilege. If the oppressed majority were to be liberated, those in power would have to be overthrown. To accomplish such a historic mission, Mao believed, violent revolution "from below" was an unavoidable necessity. "Political power," he wrote, "grows out of the barrel of a gun."[33]

As part of his adaptation of Marxism, Mao glorified the Chinese peasants— whom he described as "poor and blank"—as models of communist virtue because they had never been corrupted by "bourgeois materialism" and big-city decadence. Mao thus made the peasantry (not the proletariat) the cornerstone of his visionary utopian society.

Once in power, Mao turned China into a kind of social laboratory. The first step included campaigns to eradicate specific evils such as individualism and bourgeois materialism by "reeducating" the masses or exterminating undesirable social elements (landlords, counterrevolutionaries, and "bandits"). Accompanying mass reeducation was a sweeping land reform program culminating in the wholesale collectivization of Chinese agriculture. This bitter pill was administered with massive doses of propaganda, as well as brute force. In the early 1950s, a major push to industrialize China along Stalinist lines was also launched.

Alternating periods of freedom and repression marked Mao's rule. In 1956, for example, he announced the beginning of the **Hundred Flowers campaign**, which promised a relaxation of strict social discipline. As a high-ranking party official put it at the time,

> The Chinese Communist party advocates [that] one hundred flowers bloom for literary works and one hundred schools contend in the scientific field … to promote the freedom of independent thinking, freedom of debate, freedom of creation and criticism, freedom of expressing one's own opinions.[34]

What followed probably caught Mao by surprise. Public protests and antiparty demonstrations occurred at Beijing University and other campuses. Strikes and scattered riots, even isolated physical attacks on party officials, occurred in various parts of the country. Instead of a hundred flowers, thousands of "poisonous weeds" had grown in the Chinese garden. The incipient rebellion was rapidly suppressed in a brutal "anti-rightist" crackdown. The official party newspaper, *People's Daily,* announced the whole Hundred Flowers campaign had been a ploy to lure the enemies of the state into the open.

In retrospect, the Hundred Flowers episode was a mere warm-up for Mao's **Great Leap Forward** (1957–1960)—a spectacular but ill-conceived attempt to catapult China onto the stage of "full communism" by means of mass mobilization. Mao set out to prove that anything is possible, and that subjective factors

Hundred Flowers campaign
A brief period in China (1956) when Mao Zedong directed that freedom of expression and individualism be allowed; it was quashed when violent criticism of the regime erupted.

Great Leap Forward
Mao Zedong's attempt, in the late 1950s and early 1960s, to transform and modernize China's economic structure through mass mobilization of the entire population into self-sufficient communes in which everything was done in groups.

Following his successful war of national liberation against Chiang Kai-shek's Kuomintang, Mao's rule between 1949 and 1976 was characterized by periods of vast social experimentation, as well as by violent periods of political repression. Here a youthful looking Mao is depicted on Chinese currency officially known as the Renminbi (more commonly called the yuan).

like human will can triumph over objective conditions such as poverty, illiteracy, and external dependency. According to China scholar John King Fairbank (1907-1991), the idea "was to take advantage of China's rural backwardness and manpower surplus by realizing the Maoist faith that ideological incentives could get economic results, that a new spirit could unlock hitherto untapped sources of human energy without the use of material incentives."[35] Thus did Mao's brand of "Marxism" stand Marx on his head.

The most visible and dramatic symbol of the Great Leap was the establishment of communes—relatively large and self-sufficient residential, social, economic, and political-administrative units. Private plots were absorbed into the communal lands, and private belongings, including pots and pans and other domestic items, were pooled. In addition, as Fairbank noted,

> Many peasants for a time ate in large mess halls. All labor was to be controlled. Everyone was to work twenty-eight days of the month, while children went into day nurseries. This would bring large-scale efficiency to the village and get all its labor, including its womanpower, into full employment.[36]

Why were the unprecedented measures associated with Mao's grandiose concept instituted? "The result, it was hoped, would be agricultural cities with the peasants proletarianized and uprooted from their own land"—with an overall view toward giving the state increased control over labor resources and changing the peasants' attitudes.[37]

The Great Leap Forward was a colossal failure with disastrous consequences for the Chinese people, including severe crop failures and food shortages. But Mao was undeterred. After a brief period of retrenchment, he launched a second "revolution from above." From 1966 to 1969, the **Great Proletarian Cultural Revolution** shook Chinese society to its very foundations. In the first stage, designed to wash away all that was "decadent" in Chinese life, Mao closed all schools and urged his youthful followers, called the Red Guards, to storm the bastions of entrenched privilege and bureaucratic authority. Millions of Maoist youths obligingly went on a rampage throughout the country for many weeks. This phase of the revolution accomplished its intended purpose, as the Red Guards "smashed most of the Republic's bureaucratic institutions"

Great Proletarian Cultural Revolution
A chaotic period beginning in 1966, when the youth of China (the Red Guards), at Mao Zedong's direction, attacked all bureaucratic and military officials on the pretext that a reemergence of capitalist and materialist tendencies was taking place. The offending officials were sent to forced-labor camps to be "reeducated."

and "invalidated [the government's] authority and expertise."[38] Officials were dragged out and put on public display to be ridiculed and humiliated, accompanied by purges and summary executions; temples and historical treasures lay in ruins, as did the party, government, and armed forces.

The second stage of the Cultural Revolution called for positive action to replace the previous order with a new and better one. Unfortunately, the economy and society, especially in urban areas, had been severely disrupted. Factories and schools, shut down by marauding Red Guards, did not reopen for months or even years.

The ultimate cost of the Cultural Revolution is incalculable. One fact, however, is clear: Mao's unrelenting efforts to prove that human nature is infinitely malleable—and society, therefore, infinitely perfectible—foundered on the rocky shores of political reality, not to mention the folly of eliminating a whole generation of educated citizens. His death in 1976 closed a unique chapter in the political history of the modern world.

THE HUMAN COST OF TOTALITARIANISM

Totalitarian regimes present a stark contrast between ends and means—diabolical deeds in pursuit of utopian dreams. The death camps of Nazi Germany and the labor camps of Stalinist Russia stand as the essence of twentieth-century totalitarianism.

By one estimate, about 110 million people have died in the name of the three revolutions—in Nazi Germany, Stalinist Russia, and Maoist China—featured in this chapter.[39] The number defies imagination; but these estimates, which include World War II casualties, are quite plausible and may actually be low.[40] War-related deaths in the European theater during World War II numbered "about six million for Germany and Austria, 20 million for the Soviet Union, and about 10 million for all other European countries, for a total of about 36 million."[41] Hitler's Final Solution was estimated to have resulted in the deaths of an estimated 5 to 6 million European Jews, not to mention an indeterminate number of non-Jews whom Hitler considered "social undesirables." All in all, perhaps 42 million people died directly or indirectly as a result of Hitler's policies.

The Russian Revolution of 1917 and its aftermath were hardly less costly in terms of human life. Between 1918 and 1923, approximately 3 million Soviet citizens died of typhus, typhoid, dysentery, and cholera, and about 9 million more disappeared, probably victims of the terrible famine that scourged the country in the early 1920s. Many perished in a severe drought in 1920–1921, but others died of direct or indirect political causes.

In the late 1920s, during Stalin's titanic industrialization drive, the kulaks were annihilated as a class. In addition, another killer famine—at least partially self-inflicted—occurred in the early 1930s. When deaths associated with the early stages of collectivization are combined with deaths brought on by famine, the mortality figures range in the millions for the period from 1929 to 1934.

But the worst was yet to come. After 1934, Stalin's purges directly claimed hundreds of thousands of lives and led to the premature deaths of some 2 million "class enemies" in Siberian forced-labor camps. Nor did the end of the great purges in 1938 stop the political hemorrhaging that, together with World War II, drained Soviet society of so much of its vitality. Millions of labor camp inmates died between 1938 and 1950 due to the inhumane treatment and harsh conditions they had to endure on a daily basis.

The human cost of the revolution in Maoist China exceeds that of Stalinist Russia. Between the time of the communist takeover in 1949 and the Great Leap Forward in 1957, several mass campaigns were launched to combat allegedly counterrevolutionary forces. After the Chinese Communist takeover, the land reform program cost the lives of several million "landlords" and rich peasants between 1949 and 1952. Other campaigns against counterrevolutionaries in the early 1950s cost another million and a half lives. Periodic anti-rightist campaigns and collectivization of agriculture after 1953 also took a toll. According to scholar C. W. Cassinelli,

> Accurate information is not available—and often even informed guesses are lacking—on the cost of the *first decade* [emphasis supplied] of the People's Republic. An estimate of twelve million lives is modest but reasonable.[42]

These figures do not include deaths caused by hardship and privation, most notably those traceable to the dislocations that accompanied the Great Leap Forward in the late 1950s.

The Cultural Revolution (1966–1969) was another bloody episode in Chinese history, although firm estimates of the number of casualties are impossible to make. A much heavier toll was probably taken by the Chinese gulag system. As many as 15 million may have perished as a direct result of inhumanly harsh labor-camp conditions. When Cassinelli tallied the total number of politically related deaths, including "another million from miscellaneous causes," he arrived at the astonishing figure of "about 33.5 million."[43] Though unverifiable, this number is consistent with the available evidence. The mere fact that it is not implausible speaks volumes.

Totalitarian regimes typically refuse to concede that any goal, no matter how visionary or perverse, is beyond political reach. The compulsion to validate this gross misconception may help explain the pathological violence that marks totalitarian rule.

THE SANGUINARY IMITATORS

Stalin's Russia, Hitler's Germany, and Mao's China are the best-known examples of totalitarianism, but not the only ones. A surprising number of dictatorships have tried to copy or imitate totalitarianism's Big Three. Incredibly, one went to even greater extremes to purge society than either Stalin or Mao did, and in this case, to which we now turn, the tyrant committed genocide against his own nation.

Pol Pot governed Cambodia (renamed Kampuchea) from 1975 to 1979. He and his followers sought to create a radically new society, based on the rustic and Spartan life of peasant cadres. All vestiges of the old order—everything from the calendar to the family—were eradicated. Pol Pot proclaimed 1978 "Year Zero," which turned out to be grotesquely appropriate, for at the end of his brief rule, some 2 million Cambodians (of a population of 7.5 million) would be dead—the victims of purges, starvation, or persecution.[44]

Another example of totalitarian rulers is Ethiopia's Colonel Mengistu, who ruled from the mid-1970s until 1991. Mengistu attempted to reorganize the nation by physically relocating its people into regimented population and refugee centers for the purposes of permitting intensive governmental surveillance as well as encouraging systematic propaganda and indoctrination. His efforts destroyed the nation's agriculture, and a killer famine resulted. Although the West made efforts to feed the starving children of Ethiopia, the Mengistu regime appeared curiously detached and indifferent. While his people went hungry, Mengistu staged lavish military parades, sold wheat to neighboring nations, and used the money he received to buy weapons.[45] In May 1991, with his regime under siege by a coalition of rebel forces, Mengistu fled the country.

North Korea is the last Soviet-style totalitarian state still in existence. Kim Il Sung ruled over the Hermit Kingdom (so named for the nation's self-imposed isolation from the outside world) until his death in July 1994. He was succeeded by his son, Kim Jong Il, who ruled from 1994 to 2011 as a brutal and lunatic tyrant bent on building nuclear weapons and indifferent to the suffering and starvation of his own people. The second Kim's claim to rule was hereditary— his father not only founded North Korea's totalitarian dictatorship after World War II but also established a ruling dynasty.

Kim Jong Il ruled North Korea the same way his father did—by perpetuating a personality cult similar to those once perpetrated in Russia by Joseph Stalin or in China by Mao Zedong. In a bizarre twist, when his father died, Kim Jong Il made him (the father) president for eternity. North Korean propagandists ascribe to Kim (the son) the authorship of 1,000 books while he was a college student. When Kim Jong-Il died in 2011 he was succeeded by (guess who) his son, Kim Jong-un.

North Korea maintains a huge army, entrenched along the 38th parallel that divides Korea, and poses a standing threat to South Korea, a close ally of the United States since the Korean War (1950–1953). That major war was started when northern Korea invaded the south, a fact that continues to shape Western perceptions of North Korea today. The war ended in a draw and without a peace treaty.

In stark contrast to the prosperous south, North Korea remains one of the poorest countries on earth. Malnutrition and even starvation threaten the population—children in North Korea are, on average, considerably shorter and weigh less than children of the same age in South Korea. North Koreans are not allowed to have contact with South Koreans, including family members.

After 9/11, President Bush declared North Korea to be part of an "axis of evil" along with Iraq and Iran. North Korea again found itself in the international spotlight when the late Kim Jong Il defied the Bush administration's demand for a "complete, verifiable, and irreversible" halt to its nuclear weapons program. U.S. relations with North Korea did not greatly improve in the ensuing years. A preoccupation with the wars in Iraq and Afghanistan, as well as a deepening recession in the wake of the U.S. financial crisis in 2008–2009, led President Obama, like his predecessor, to seek an accommodation with Pyongyang (the capital).

North Korea conducted a nuclear test in 2006 and in April 2009 attempted to launch a long-range missile, but the test failed. North Korea is also thought to have stockpiles of chemical and biological weapons. North Korea's extreme self-isolation and secrecy make it impossible to know for certain how the power transition is playing out in Pyongyang since the death of Kim Jung-Il in December 2011. So if the Hermit Kingdom does have a nuclear "six-shooter." nobody knows for sure *whose* finger is on the trigger.

Khomeini's Iran displayed most of the elements normally associated with totalitarian rule: an attempt to transform society; a dictatorship that demanded abject loyalty, obedience, and self-sacrifice; an all-encompassing creed that rationalized, explained, and justified arbitrary rule; press censorship; and secret police, show trials, summary executions, and holy wars.

Eventually, no aspect of life in Iran lay outside governmental control. Teachers, textbooks, education, entertainment, the legal system, even courtship and sexual mores were made to conform to fundamental Islamic beliefs. The regime declared war on civil servants, intellectuals, professional and entrepreneurial elements of the middle class, and all others who had endorsed modern Western ways and culture.

After Khomeini's death, his successors relaxed some of the strict moral and social controls but maintained a rigidly theocratic police state fiercely opposed to the West and, in particular, to the U.S. presence in neighboring Iraq and the Persian Gulf. In addition, Tehran launched a major nuclear research and development program, raising a general alarm in the international community and causing the United States to orchestrate a global campaign to stop Iran from building nuclear weapons.

When President Obama assumed office, he lost little time in attempting to break the diplomatic impasse with Iran. During the 2008 presidential campaign, Obama had roundly criticized President Bush for refusing to engage in direct talks with Tehran. In early 2009, the new administration expressed a willingness to meet with Iran "without preconditions," and on April 16, 2009, Iran's hard-line President Mahmoud Ahmadinejad declared in a televised speech, "We have prepared a package that can be the basis to resolve Iran's nuclear problem. It will be offered to the West soon."[46]

The Iranian case demonstrates three important points. First, totalitarian regimes, like democracies and traditional dictatorships, can share a single essence and assume many different guises. Second, although totalitarian regimes appear to be rigid and unchanging on the outside, they are, in fact, not impervious to change on the inside. Third, in the modern world of the twenty-first century, totalitarian regimes cannot succeed *economically* in isolation—that is, without access to global markets, the latest technological advances, and sources of investment capital.

Ironically, as totalitarianism disappeared in Russia and Eastern Europe, it sprang up in Afghanistan—a country the Soviet Union had invaded in 1979. It is generally accepted that the protracted and costly conflict in Afghanistan hastened the demise of the totalitarian Soviet state. It turned out to be Moscow's Vietnam, but with more dire consequences.

In the 1990s, totalitarianism in a different guise arose from the ashes of the war that had ravaged Afghanistan during the previous decade. That regime—the Taliban—captured the world's attention after September 2001 because the mastermind behind the 9/11 operation, the actual perpetrators, and the organization that carried it out were all based in Afghanistan. The Taliban was providing sanctuary for Osama bin Laden, who had set up training camps for his stateless "army."

But the Taliban was not only *harboring* a terrorist organization; it was itself a terrorist organization—a full-blown totalitarian regime complete with a single all-powerful ruling clique, harsh and arbitrary laws, kangaroo courts, predictable (guilty) verdicts, summary executions turned into public spectacles, severely restricted personal freedoms, closed borders, and a captive population. Afghans were not allowed to emigrate or travel abroad. Girls were not allowed to go to school. Boys were not allowed to fly kites. Women had no rights, had to be completely covered in public, and could not work outside the home. Wife beating, no matter how severe, was not a crime—not even when the victim died.

THE TWILIGHT OF TOTALITARIANISM?

Hitler boasted that his would be a thousand-year empire, but it lasted less than a decade. In fact, in stark contrast to the great autocratic empires of ancient history, totalitarian regimes are short-lived. They tend to burst on the scene like a meteor and burn out. Why?

Fatal wars with other nations, such as Hitler's defeat by the Allies in World War II, can bring a sudden end to totalitarian states. The death of a particularly charismatic or successful ruler—Mao or Stalin, for instance—can precipitate an extended downward spiral. Drab, indistinguishable successors who rule by coercion and terror rather than by consent may undermine the economic efficiency, moral vitality, and political idealism on which legitimate political power ultimately rests. Thus, the collapse of the Soviet Union was preceded by both a prolonged period of economic disintegration and a widespread loss of faith in the regime and its political ideals; a period of "totalitarianism in decline."[47]

The Peoples' Republic of China, to cite a key example, has morphed into a one-party authoritarian system with a transitional economy falling somewhere between a Soviet-style command economy and a Western-style market economy—a hybrid form sometimes called **state capitalism**. Iran after Khomeini remains a **theocracy** with limited personal freedoms but it cannot in fairness be called totalitarian. North Korea alone still qualifies as unambiguously totalitarian. The totalitarian regimes in Kampuchea and Ethiopia are long gone—only the scars and bitter legacies remain.

state capitalism
An economy falling somewhere between a Soviet-style command economy and a Western-style market economy. The economy in Communist China after Mao is one contemporary example.

theocracy
A state like present-day Iran in which religious leaders monopolize political power, legitimate authority derives from a common belief in one god, and there is no separation of church and state.

BRYANT ARNOLD

Comic fans know all about Captain America. Here cartoonist Bryant Arnold depicts him as an old man. In real life he'd have to be in his 90s. (According to the legend he enlisted in the U.S. Army in 1940 to fight the Nazis.) The 2011 movie *Captain America: The First Avenger* involves a Super-Soldier serum, a top secret research project, and a Nazi plot to take over the world. The Nazi era is over but it's not forgotten.

In sum, the best thing about the worst regimes in today's world is that they tend to be short-lived. Unfortunately, totalitarian tyrants need only a little time to do a lot of damage.

SUMMARY

Totalitarian states attempt to realize a utopian vision and create a new political order. Like authoritarian states, totalitarian states are nondemocratic. Yet these two regime types differ in several important respects. In particular, totalitarian regimes seek total control over all aspects of their citizens' lives and demand active participation, rather than passive acquiescence, on the part of the citizenry.

The three major totalitarian states of the past century—Soviet Russia, Nazi Germany, and Maoist China—appear to have gone through several distinct stages of development. The first stage coincides with a period of violent revolution. The five major elements necessary for a successful revolution are charismatic leadership, ideology, organization, propaganda, and violence. During the second stage, power in the hands of the totalitarian ruler is consolidated, opposition parties are eliminated, the party faithful are put in charge, and real or imagined rivals within the party are killed.

The third stage attempts to bring about the total transformation of society. In the Soviet Union, Stalin launched this effort in 1928 with the first Five-Year Plan. In Nazi Germany, Hitler's goal of "racial purification" provided the rationale for a totalitarian drive that culminated in World War II and the Holocaust. In Maoist China, the first attempt to transform Chinese society, the Great Leap Forward, failed miserably in the late 1950s and was followed by the Cultural Revolution of the 1960s.

The human costs of totalitarianism have been staggering. Actual numbers cannot be verified, but even the roughest estimates suggest the totalitarian experiments of the twentieth century brought death or appalling hardship to many millions of people.

Totalitarian states appear in many guises, and there is no guarantee new ones will not emerge in the future. Indeed, the ousted Taliban regime in Afghanistan qualified as a new form of totalitarianism that used a perverted form of Islam as a political ideology.

KEY TERMS

totalitarianism   120
rectification   121
cells   124
partiinost   124
Gleichschaltung   126
propaganda   126
salami tactics   128
purges   128

Gestapo   129
kulaks   130
collectivization   130
gulag archipelago   132
Kuomintang   134
Hundred Flowers
   campaign   135

Great Leap
   Forward   135
Great Proletarian
   Cultural
   Revolution   136
state capitalism   141
theocracy   141

REVIEW QUESTIONS

1. What sets totalitarianism apart from other nondemocratic forms of rule?
2. What is required for a successful total revolution to take place?
3. How do totalitarian states consolidate power?
4. What are the basic characteristics of the totalitarian system of rule?
5. What were the primary aims of Stalin's drive to transform Soviet society in the 1930s? What methods did he use?
6. How and why did Hitler try to reshape German society?
7. What was the impetus behind the Great Leap Forward and the Cultural Revolution? What methods did the Maoists employ? What kind of a society did they envisage?
8. What have been the costs of totalitarianism, as measured in human terms?
9. "Totalitarianism passed away with the deaths of Hitler, Stalin, and Mao." Comment.
10. Name two or three recent examples of totalitarianism. Which one(s) are still in existence? Write a short essay on an existing totalitarian state, answering the following three questions: Who rules? How? To what ends?
11. Hitler's totalitarian state ceased to exist after a crushing military defeat. Does the evidence suggest that totalitarian regimes can ever change from within—that is, without being defeated in war?
12. "As the world's oldest democracy, the United States government should never engage in direct talks with totalitarian states." Do you agree or disagree? Explain your position.

Established and Emerging Democracies

Parliamentary Democracy

THINK ABOUT IT

What is Aristotle's concept of a mixed regime, and which modern political system best embodies the Aristotelian model?

Why is Britain often called the "mother of all parliaments"? Compare the British and U.S. systems of government. What are the advantages of the British system?

Which legislative body functions best, the British parliament or the U.S. Congress, and why? Which country has the strongest executive, the UK, Germany, France, or Japan?

It has been said that Japan is a Western-style democracy in form but Japanese in substance. What does that mean?

India and Israel are both democracies—what's the big deal? Is democracy a bigger challenge in India or in Israel? Be sure to explain the difficulties both face.

We have not only to study the ideally best constitution. We have also to study the type of constitution which is practicable [that is, the best for a state under actual conditions].... The sort of constitutional system which ought to be proposed is one which men can be easily induced, and will be readily able, to graft onto the system they already have.

—Aristotle, *The Politics*[1]

Long ago, the great Greek philosopher Aristotle made a compelling case for the systematic comparison of political systems. Today, the value of comparative political analysis is widely recognized in the discipline. We have seen that strikingly different forms of government are possible—democratic, authoritarian, and totalitarian—and that there are many permutations of each form. Authoritarian regimes, for example, can be monarchies, military juntas, theocracies, and so on. Democracies also vary widely, as we noted in Chapter 4. The form of democracy found in the United States is the one Americans know best, of course, but most Europeans are far more familiar with a very different model of democracy, one that originated in England—a country that is separated from the Continent by a narrow expanse of water and a wide expanse of history and culture.

In this chapter, we compare parliamentary democracies with a view to identifying how they differ between and among each other. We also ask what variations appear to result in dysfunctional systems and whether or not remedies are available. Finally, we ask how parliamentary systems compare to our own and revisit the question asked in Chapter 4: Which model of democracy works better?

GREAT BRITAIN: MOTHER OF ALL PARLIAMENTS

The British system has its origins in horticulture, not architecture. Unlike the U.S. Constitution, it is not based on a blueprint devised by rational minds. Instead, it grew out of England's unique history and geography and its evolving political culture. The organic nature of the British parliamentary system raises an obvious question about whether it can be transplanted, but first we take a closer look at this unique representative democracy.

The political system that formed after the American Revolution represented a sharp break with the European autocratic tradition, and it required a fresh political theory. Although there is no British counterpart to the Federalist Papers, we find a sort of homegrown theory of British-style democracy in the writings and speeches of Edmund Burke. Burke detailed Britain's long unbroken chain of political development, during which, significantly, economic equality and political liberty expanded together. As the monarchy declined in power, British government became increasingly democratic, evolving into a **parliamentary system**. It was gradually established that the British monarch would automatically accept Parliament's choice of prime minister (PM). In time, the PM

parliamentary system
In contrast to the U.S. presidential model based on the separation of powers, parliamentary systems feature a fusion of powers in which Parliament chooses the prime minister who then forms a government; Parliament can in turn force the government to resign at any time by a simple majority no-confidence vote.

The United Kingdom's Queen Elizabeth II is a beloved monarch who reigns but does not rule. As the ceremonial chief of state, she has served a nation proud of its traditions with dignity and grace since 1952.

mixed regime
A nation in which the various branches of government represent social classes.

eclipsed the monarch as the head of government. Today, the monarch Queen Elizabeth II is the head of state with no executive power—a beloved figurehead.

A Mixed Regime

From the seventeenth century on, the British parliamentary system became a prime example of what Aristotle called a **mixed regime**, in which different institutions represent different classes. The House of Lords represented the interests of the traditional governing classes, whereas the House of Commons gradually came to represent the interests of the general electorate, expressed through free elections and increasing suffrage.

Great Britain's mixed regime historically promoted stability by providing representation for classes that otherwise might have become openly hostile toward one another. The famed British welfare state of today is designed to perpetuate a large middle class through an elaborate system of income redistribution. Although the traditional representation of separate social classes has become largely irrelevant, the two major parties—the Conservatives and Labour—continue to retain the distinctions, attitudes, and values of a class-conscious society.

The supreme legislative body is the popularly elected House of Commons, while the aristocratic House of Lords has been reduced to little more than a debating society. The Parliament Acts of 1911 and 1949 made it impossible for the House of Lords to block legislation passed by the Commons. Today the Lords can do no more than propose amendments or delay a bill from taking effect for one year.

About 800 individuals (including appointed life peers and hereditary peers, plus twenty-five Anglican bishops and archbishops) claim formal membership in the House of Lords, but only about 300 play an active role.[2] The British upper house can easily be seen as an anachronism in the modern age, perhaps even a little ridiculous—and not only to outsiders. Indeed, in 2012 a major reform bill pushed by the Liberal Democrats (junior partners in a Conservative Government headed by David Cameron) and designed to democratize the Lords (four-fifths of the members would be elected for nonrenewable fifteen-year terms) was under serious consideration in the House of Commons. Tory backbenchers (junior MPs relegated to the back benches) and Labour demanded a popular referendum to decide the matter. One editorial in a prominent British news weekly jumped into the controversy without equivocation: "Reform will profoundly change Britain's political system.... Let the people break the deadlock."[3] The Cameron Government abandoned this bill in August–September 2012 in response to strong opposition from within the Conservative Party.

Fusion of Powers

Under the British parliamentary system, the executive branch—the prime minister and the cabinet—is formed after each election and consists of the leaders of the victorious party within the House of Commons, endorsed by the Parliament and appointed by the queen. Although all members of Parliament, including those in the opposition party, are free to question and criticize, the victors control the government.

When a victorious party leader takes over in the United Kingdom, it is understood the new government will serve for no more than five years before seeking a new mandate from the voters. A British prime minister's job security entirely depends on his or her ability to maintain "confidence"—an elusive but vital intangible in British politics. Think about what the ever-present possibility of falling from power means in practice.

In the United States, elections are held at regular intervals that never change; voters always know exactly when the next election will be held. Not so in the British system. Parliament is required to stand for election every five years, but the prime minister (PM) can call for elections earlier if it looks as though the mood of the electorate momentarily favors the ruling party. By the same token, Parliament can force the government to resign by a vote of "no confidence." In this event, either a new government is formed under new leadership or the queen dissolves Parliament and calls new elections.

The authority to decide when to call new elections can be a big advantage for the party in power. Prime Minister Margaret Thatcher made particularly shrewd use of this authority in 1983, for example. After serving only four years, the "Iron Lady" (as she was often called) capitalized on a surge of British patriotism, spurred by a war with Argentina over the Falkland Islands, to renew the Conservative Party's mandate to rule for another five years.

In 1987, she again called for an election four years into her term and won. Three years later, Thatcher's popularity fell as a result of her support for a poll tax that many Britons considered regressive and unfair. Under attack within her own Conservative Party, she resigned, turning over the reins of government to her successor, John Major. But by then she had already held the United Kingdom's highest office for more than a decade—a twentieth-century record.

More recently, Prime Minister Tony Blair was forced to resign due to his unstinting support for the U.S.-led war in Iraq—a war strongly opposed by the vast majority of British voters. In the summer of 2007, Blair gave way to his chief rival in the Labour Party, Gordon Brown. In 2010, Gordon Brown was ousted when the British voters deserted Labour in large numbers, giving the Conservatives and a third party, the Liberal Democrats, a sweeping victory in national elections (Figure 7.1). The upshot was a coalition government under Conservative Party leader David Cameron in partnership with "Lib Dem" party leader Nick Clegg.

In the United Kingdom, the resignation of a chief executive who has lost public confidence is expected. Prime Minister Neville Chamberlain (1869–1940) resigned in 1940, despite the fact that his party still commanded a majority in the House of Commons. So widespread was his unpopularity after his "appeasement" of Adolf Hitler at Munich that he stepped aside and let another Tory leader take charge—a chap named Winston Churchill. The redoubtable, gravel-voiced, cigar-smoking Churchill, of course, proved to be one of history's great wartime leaders.

FIGURE 7.1   Map of United Kingdom. Although the UK, like the United States, has two major parties, several other parties can and do win seats in Parliament. The Liberal Democrats are the major spoiler in British elections and became partners with the Conservatives in a coalition government after the 2010 elections.

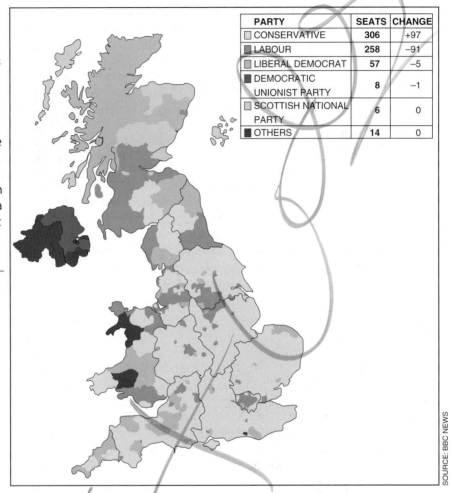

PARTY	SEATS	CHANGE
CONSERVATIVE	306	+97
LABOUR	258	−91
LIBERAL DEMOCRAT	57	−5
DEMOCRATIC UNIONIST PARTY	8	−1
SCOTTISH NATIONAL PARTY	6	0
OTHERS	14	0

SOURCE: BBC NEWS

no-confidence vote
In parliamentary governments, a legislative vote that the sitting government must win to remain in power.

party discipline
In a parliamentary system, the tendency of legislators to vote consistently as a bloc with fellow party members in support of the party's platform.

Other circumstances may cause a government to fall before its five-year term has expired. If the majority party's policy is unpopular or if the government becomes embroiled in a scandal, a motion of no confidence can be introduced. If the motion passes in a **no-confidence vote**, the government resigns. The prime minister then asks the monarch to dissolve Parliament and call for new elections. In countries with multiparty parliamentary systems, governments come and go frequently in this manner, but it is rare in the United Kingdom, where it has not happened since Prime Minister James Callaghan lost a no-confidence motion in 1979.

Disciplined Parties

Party discipline in the United Kingdom manifests itself in a ritual show of public unity, coherent party platforms, and bloc voting. British parties differ sharply in this respect from U.S. parties, which are more loosely organized and often less important to voters than are the personal traits of the candidates.

In Parliament, the government demands unwavering support from its majority-party members. Strong party discipline does not mean that MPs never cross the aisle to vote with the opposition, however. They can also abstain on an important vote or even engineer a party realignment. In the early 1900s, for example, when the trade union movement transformed the British working class into a powerful political force, the Labour Party eclipsed the old Liberal (or Whig) Party as the Conservative (or Tory) Party's chief rival.

The party-out-of-power—formally called Her Majesty's **Loyal Opposition**—criticizes the majority's policy initiatives and holds the government accountable for its actions. Criticism is usually tempered by civility, because the Opposition "thinks of itself as the next government, and a wise Opposition operates within those limits which it hopes its own opponents will respect when the tables are turned."[4] In fact, the Leader of the Opposition is considered an essential role player in the British system and since 1937 has been given a special salary paid out of public funds.

Prime Minister David Cameron led the Conservative Party to victory in the May 2010 national elections, but they failed to win a clear majority of seats in Parliament and had to form a coalition government with the Liberal Democrats as the junior partner.

Are Two Heads Better Than One?

Unlike the United States, where one chief executive (the president) serves as both the head of state and the head of government, Great Britain separates these functions. The British head of state is the reigning monarch. Queen Elizabeth II, "arguably the most famous person in the world," has occupied the British throne for over half a century. The monarch is a national symbol and a source of unity, personifying the state but not wielding its powers.

The actual head of the government is the prime minister, who, in close consultation with key cabinet members (often called the *inner cabinet*), sets domestic and foreign policy. National policy emerges from this leadership core, which then presents it to the cabinet as a whole. Cabinet members who are out of step with the government on an important policy matter are expected to resign quietly.

Loyal Opposition
The belief, which originated in England, that the out-of-power party has a responsibility to formulate alternative policies and programs; such a party is sometimes called the Loyal Opposition.

A Model with Legs

Most European democracies are patterned after the British system, although with mixed results. France under the Third and Fourth Republics (1876–1958) and Italy since World War II came to be dominated by political parties and a parliament. The political party system became fragmented, internal party discipline broke down, and the government fell victim to never-ending legislative skirmishes. Strong executive leadership was often missing in France before 1958 and remains a chronic problem in Italy to this day.

Such conditions have led to political stalemate in both countries at different times. In France, during the entire life span of the Third and Fourth Republics, no single party ever won a majority of seats in the National Assembly, and no fewer than 119 governments ruled the country, each with an average life of less than a year. A similar malaise has plagued Italy, which had more than forty prime ministers between 1945 and 1986 (one per year on average).

THE BRITISH AGENDA: A SAMPLER

The Economy

Under Labour leadership, Britain developed a model welfare state in the 1950s and 1960s but was stricken by stagflation, or simultaneous recession and inflation, in the 1970s. In 1979, Margaret Thatcher led the Conservative Party to victory and set about reprivatizing state-run industries and systematically deregulating the British economy.

Voters turned the Conservatives out of office in 1997 for the first time in nearly two decades. Under Labour Prime Minister Tony Blair's market-friendly policies, the British economy managed to outperform Europe's other major economies (Germany, France, and Italy) for a time.

Gordon Brown moved into 10 Downing Street when Blair moved out in 2007. As Chancellor of the Exchequer (or Finance Minister) in the Blair Government, Brown was in charge of economic policy. Although few disputed his qualifications for the job, Prime Minister Brown's personal popularity hit a low ebb even before the 2008 global financial crisis took its toll. Public confidence in Brown's economic crisis-management skills briefly boosted his standing in opinion polls, but his lackluster personality and a sluggish economy set the stage for the Conservatives to make a comeback in the May 2010 elections.

The Voting System

In a referendum held in May 2011, British voters roundly defeated a proposal championed by the Nick Clegg, leader of the Liberal Democratic Party (aka "Lib Dems"), to change the UK's tradition-bound first-past-the-post electoral system (see Chapter 11, "Landmarks in History: The 2011 UK Referendum on Electoral Reform," for more details).

Paying for the Welfare State

In the spring of 2010, Conservative leader David Cameron campaigned on the vague promise of "hope and change." The following fall, he unveiled a plan calling for deep cuts in public spending as a cure for Britain's chronic budget deficits. This austerity plan, however, came at a

time when sluggish growth and rising unemployment prompted many economists to call for stimulus rather than austerity. But Cameron stuck to his position even as the British economy continued to lag, unemployment remained high, and his government's deficit reduction target for 2012 was missed. News of a sharp drop in the quarterly jobless rate at the end of 2012 occasioned no celebrations as Finance Minister George Osborne let it be known that austerity budgets would continue in effect until 2018—three years more than originally planned.

Northern Ireland

The four options for settling the decades-old civil war in Northern Ireland (Ulster) are (1) reunification of Ulster with Ireland, (2) independence from Britain, (3) devolution (home rule), or (4) integration with Britain. Before a 1994 ceasefire, the provisional Irish Republican Army (IRA) repeatedly carried out terrorist attacks in an effort to force the British from Northern Ireland and made bold attempts to assassinate both Thatcher and Major. By the time of the ceasefire, some 3,000 people had been killed on both sides—Catholic and Protestant.

In January 2013, news of loyalist youths "fighting street battles with police on an almost nightly basis over the last six weeks" shattered any illusions about an end to sectarian violence in Northern Ireland. There was a dismaying sense of déjà vu in the reportage: "some of the most sustained violence in the British-controlled province since a 1998 peace deal ended 30 years of conflict." Despite relative calm in recent years, any lasting solution must balance the interests and claims of British-backed Protestants ("loyalists" and/or "unionists"), who slightly outnumber Catholics in Northern Ireland, against those of Irish Catholics ("nationalists"), who constitute an overwhelming majority in the Irish Republic.

The European Union

The United Kingdom joined the European Union in 1973. However, its policy toward the EU has been

(Continued)

characterized by continuing ambivalence. In the 1990s, when the adoption of the euro went into effect, British popular opinion was strongly against a common currency, and London opted out. In the minds of most British voters, the euro crisis has vindicated the UK's decision not to join the euro zone.

Prime Minister Cameron is an outspoken Eurosceptic, saying there is "a lack of democratic accountability and consent that is....felt particularly acutely in Britain." In early 2013, he pledged to hold a national referendum— an in-or-out vote—on British EU membership after the next UK general election.

Yet today parliamentary governments are found all over Europe, with rare exceptions—a major triumph in a region divided by war, revolution, and totalitarian rule until recently. Parliamentary rule is Britain's gift to Europe and the world—a model with "legs."

Are All Parliamentary Systems Alike?

No. Most parliamentary systems function in ways similar to the British system, but in countries with multiple parties and proportional representation (see Chapter 11), the government often cannot count on a clear parliamentary majority. Where there are five or six parties in parliament—and none with a popular base to match either of Britain's two major parties—it often happens that no single party has enough seats to form a government. In this event, coalitions, or two or more parties joining forces, are necessary. Sometimes coalition governments work fairly well; in the worst cases such as Italy, however, parliamentary rule can be unstable and even chaotic.

FRANCE: PRESIDENT VERSUS PARLIAMENT

The U.S. presidential and British parliamentary systems represent two different approaches to democratic government. Under the Fifth Republic founded in 1958 and forged in the crucible of a constitutional crisis, France fashioned a unique form of representative democracy that combines elements of both models. Today France is the world's fifth-ranked economy, sixth-ranked exporter; in the first half of 2012, it was the fourth-largest recipient of foreign direct investment and has more multinational corporations in the global *Fortune* 500 than the United Kingdom.

In June 2012 French voters brought François Hollande's Socialists to power, replacing Nicolas Sarkozy's center-right government. It was a stunning victory for a party that in the United States is wrongly perceived as incompatible with a stable democratic order. Wrongly, because it's not the first time it's happened in France and, despite all sorts of dire Chicken Little predictions emanating from the land of the Anglo-Saxons, the sky over ancient Gaul has not fallen.

FIGURE 7.2   Map of France. Divided into 22 regions, 95 departments, and 36,851 communes, France is a political-administrative jigsaw puzzle. Mayors of major cities often become prominent national politicians and are often also members of the National Assembly (the French parliament) at the same time.

© CENGAGE LEARNING

The Fifth Republic: A Hybrid System

The Fifth Republic was meant to overcome what its founder, Charles de Gaulle, understood to be the great nemesis of French politics: impotent executives dominated by fractious legislatures (Figure 7.2). As de Gaulle was fond of pointing out, France's first three experiments in republican government all ended in dictatorship.

Under the Fourth Republic (1946–1958), governments had lasted an average of six months. A profusion of political parties, some of fleeting duration, turned France's parliamentary system into a travesty. Worse, parties at opposite ends of the political spectrum—Gaullists on the right and Communists on the left—both sought to undermine the Fourth Republic's constitution and force the resignation of weak coalition governments.

The Fifth Republic's constitution was short and simple. Its provisions were guided by de Gaulle, who, in a famous address twelve years earlier, declared:

> The unity, cohesion, and internal discipline of the Government of France must be sacred objects or else the country's leadership will rapidly become impotent and invalid.... The executive power should, therefore, be embodied in a Chief of State, placed above the parties....to serve as an arbiter, placed above the political circumstances of the day, and to carry out this function ordinarily in the Cabinet, or, in moments of great confusion, by asking the

nation to deliver its sovereign decision through elections. It is his role, should the nation ever be in danger, to assume the duty of guaranteeing national independence and the treaties agreed to by France.[5]

In sum, the centerpiece of the constitutional system, de Gaulle insisted, would be a strong executive branch to counterbalance the perennially divided parliament. The centerpiece of the executive, however, would be the chief of state (president) rather than the prime minister.

France's Dual Executive

The basic elements of de Gaulle's diagnosis are etched into nearly every provision of the 1958 constitution that pertain to the organization of public powers. In accordance with the parliamentary model, the French executive is divided (a **dual executive**). On paper, the prime minister (or *premier*) is the head of government; the president is head of state. Unlike the British monarch, however, the French president is democratically elected and wields executive powers similar, though not identical, to those of the U.S. president. As France's leading political figure, the president is independent of the legislative branch, possesses a wide array of powers, and serves a fixed term in office (seven years from 1962 to 2000, but now five years).

France's constitution positioned the president as the arbitrator of conflicting interests and competing political parties. As the nation's chief diplomat and foreign policy decision maker, the president appoints and dismisses the prime minister, dissolves the legislature, calls for new elections, declares a state of emergency, issues decrees having the force of law, and presides over cabinet meetings. In addition, the president can call for a national referendum, a device used a number of times since the 1960s. For example, in 1962, de Gaulle's popular referendum to replace the electoral college with direct election of the president passed by an overwhelming majority. In a democratic age, nothing gives a political leader more legitimacy or moral authority than a mandate from the voters.

Compared with the president, France's prime minister generally exercises less power and influence, although there is now a greater balance between these two offices than there was in de Gaulle's time. As head of the government, the prime minister presides over the cabinet and is responsible to the legislature. Together, the prime minister and the cabinet oversee the running of government and the bureaucracy.

In general, however, the constitution of the Fifth Republic does not clearly delineate which powers or functions belong to the president and which belong to the prime minister. Due to his unrivalled stature in French politics, de Gaulle enjoyed considerable latitude in interpreting the constitution. Thus, during his tenure, the presidential powers were elastic—de Gaulle could, and did, stretch them to fit the needs of the moment.

No president after de Gaulle, however, has so dominated French politics. François Mitterrand, a Socialist, served as France's president for fourteen years (1981–1995), but he was no de Gaulle. Neither was his center-right successor, Jacques Chirac. Not until the election of Nicolas Sarkozy (2007–2012)—a one-term wonder—did France have a charismatic center-right president with a Napoleon-sized ego to match de Gaulle's (and a diminutive stature to match

dual executive
In a parliamentary system, the division of the functions of head of state and chief executive officer between two persons; the prime minister serves as chief executive, and some other elected (or royal) figure serves as ceremonial head of state.

Napoleon's). By that time, France had endured (and the Fifth Republic had survived) three periods of cohabitation in which the president and prime minister were from opposing political parties.

Reduced Role of the National Assembly

If the presidency was clearly the big political winner under the Fifth Republic, the legislature was the loser. France's parliament is divided into two houses, the Senate and the National Assembly. The French Senate, which has only limited powers, is indirectly elected. The **National Assembly**, its parliament, is popularly elected from multimember districts in a double ballot (two-stage) election process. As the focal point of legislative power, the National Assembly must approve all proposed laws. However, the word *law* is rather narrowly defined by the 1958 constitution; in fact, many matters are left to the executive branch, which has the power to issue "decree laws."

The National Assembly is more interesting for the powers it does *not* have. For example, the French parliament has no power to introduce financial bills. If it fails to approve the government's budget by a certain deadline, the executive can enact the budget by fiat (presidential decree).

Rival Parties and Seesaw Elections

Unlike the United States, France has a wide spectrum of political parties. Rival parties exist on both the left and the right, as well as in the center, and both the Far Right and the Far Left often play a significant role in elections.

The two most important parties of the Left are the Communist Party and the Socialist Party. When left-leaning voters began turning away from the Communists in the late 1970s, the Socialist Party was the primary beneficiary on the left. In 1981, the Socialists won a resounding victory at the polls, and Socialist leader Mitterrand was elected president (a post he held for fourteen years after winning reelection in 1988).

In 1993, however, the center-right won a landslide victory, retaking control of the National Assembly; two years later, the neo-Gaullist candidate Jacques Chirac was elected president. Combined with the decisive center-right triumph in Senate elections that same year, Chirac's election put the conservatives back in the driver's seat—but not for long.

In the June 1997 elections, parties of the Left, again led by the Socialists, won overwhelmingly. Chirac bowed to the will of the electorate and named Socialist Party leader Lionel Jospin the new prime minister. Jean-Marie Le Pen's far-right National Party received more votes than the Gaullist UDF (Union for French Democracy)—14.9% to 14.2%—and nearly as many as Chirac's RPR, which had 15.7%. Yet the two center-right parties garnered 242 seats in the National Assembly, while the National Party won but a single seat. Why?

France's electoral system stacks the deck against fringe parties by requiring a second round of balloting when no candidate receives an absolute majority of votes in the first round. In practice, this means parties with similar (and less uncompromising) ideological stances can form temporary alliances between the two balloting rounds. As a result, the influence of fringe or extremist parties is greatly diminished.

National Assembly
Focal point of France's bicameral legislative branch that must approve all laws.

In 2002, Chirac's new center-right umbrella party called Union for a Popular Movement (UMP) won a clear majority in the National Assembly (357 seats, or 62% of the total) in the second round of balloting, but the result was misleading. The UMP, despite the preelection realignment that merged three center-right parties into one, received only 33% of the votes in the first round (just 7% more than the Socialists). The election outcome once again underscored the way France's two-step electoral process produces a parliamentary majority out of a fragmented party system.

When center-right candidate Nicolas Sarkozy was elected president in May 2007, French voters gave the center-right a solid majority in the National Assembly, but the Socialists were not shut out: in fact, they made a net gain of forty-six seats while the UMP actually lost forty-four seats. In the 2008 local and regional elections, the UMP lost numerous city mayoral races and eight departmental presidencies.

In the 2012 national elections, Sarkozy and the center-right parties suffered a stinging defeat. Not only did François Hollande trounce Sarkozy in the presidential election, but the new French president's Socialist Party also won 314 parliamentary seats, 25 seats more than the 289 needed to command an absolute majority. Exactly what it meant for Hollande to have "a free hand to govern as he sees fit," as *The Economist* wrote in June 2012, was anybody's guess. One result of the 2012 elections was not in doubt: "The new parliament will be younger, more feminine, and more ethnically diverse than the old one, which was dominated by grey hair and suits."[6] Many were first-timers too—about 40%.

Constitution under Pressure: Testing the Balance

The Fifth Republic has brought stable democracy to France for more than six decades now. De Gaulle's influence has extended well beyond his presidency, and his broad interpretation of presidential powers prevails to this day. De Gaulle's preference for a strong national economy that mixes a large role for the state (a French tradition) with a healthy respect for free-market principles remains firmly fixed as a part of his legacy. Nonetheless, without de Gaulle's firm hand on the tiller, "long-range programs gave place to expediency, and party alignments obeyed the logic of electoral tactics rather than policy making."[7]

From the start of the Fifth Republic, France faced the danger of a **divided executive:** when the president and prime minister represented two different parties, embraced different ideologies, and advanced different policies. Although a deadlocked government remains a hazard in France's dual executive system, France has survived three periods of cohabitation, most recently from 1997 to 2002.

Justice à la Française

The French judicial system is divided into two basic types of courts—ordinary courts and administrative courts—with different jurisdictions. Despite this rather routine distinction, France's legal system has some interesting twists. For example, the High Council of the Judiciary, chaired by the president, decides on judicial promotions and discipline, whereas the High Court of Justice has the power to try the president for treason and members of the government for crimes related to abuses in office.

divided executive
Situation in French government in which the president and the prime minister differ in political party or outlook.

THE FRENCH AGENDA: A SAMPLER

The Economy

High taxes, mounting public debt, double-digit unemployment, an inflexible labor market, and a generally sluggish economy plagued France even before the global Great Recession brought a sharp downturn in the European Union's single-market economy. The 2008 Wall Street banking crisis exposed the dire financial straits of Greece and several other EU countries, which in turn put Europe's common currency—the euro—in jeopardy.

The euro crisis destabilized France not least because French banks held more than 90 billion euros of Greek sovereign debt (government bonds) and Greece was teetering close to default (bankruptcy). If France's banks were crippled, the lumbering French economy would also be crippled.

Sarkozy faced a dilemma: adopt unpopular austerity measures or continue to pile bigger and bigger budget deficits on a rapidly rising national debt. With public spending approaching three-fifths of national output (57%) and chronic budget deficits rising above 90% of GDP, France was losing its competitive edge within the EU, making it too difficult for companies to lay off workers, running a risk that businesses would relocate to more business-friendly countries.

Of course, France's economic woes did not disappear when Sarkozy was turned out of office in 2012. It then fell to Hollande to pick up the pieces, including an unemployment rate hitting 10% in the first quarter of 2012; the youth unemployment rate (workers under age twenty-five) was more than twice as high (22.7% in May 2012).

Hollande swept into office promising to stimulate the economy and reduce France's chronic budget deficit, and to do so without major cuts in social spending or middle-class tax increases. Instead he proposed to raise taxes on the rich, on large companies, and on financial transactions, among other things. But many analysts believed stark realities would force Hollande to cut spending and pressure labor unions into making concessions: in other words, to adopt policies not so different from those of his predecessor.

The Welfare State

France's cradle-to-the-grave social-spending model is facing huge challenges in the new era, which some are calling the decline of the West. France's much-remarked thirty-five-hour workweek is immensely popular, but critics say it places France at a competitive disadvantage. France, they say, is paying the price for profligate spending and pandering to labor unions, farmers, pensioners, and other special interests. Without a major overhaul of pensions—a highly charged political issue—the French treasury faces a rising tide of red ink. Wealth, corporate profits, and high incomes are heavily taxed, a fact dramatized in early 2013 when famed French film star Gerard Depardieu, protesting a new tax hike on the rich, left his native France for Russia where he will pay a flat 13% income tax rate rather than the 75% on income over 1 million euros ($1.3 million) in France.

Immigration and National Identity

There are an estimated 14 million French citizens of foreign ancestry (about 23% of the total population) and more than 3 million Arabs, mostly from Algeria, Morocco, and Tunisia. High unemployment and urban decay have eroded traditional French hospitality toward political exiles, refugees, and asylum seekers, as well as immigrants in general. Immigrants often willing to work for low wages crowd into cities and compete for scarce jobs.

The election of Nicolas Sarkozy, a hard-liner on immigration, put the issue of "national identity" high on the French government's policy agenda. In 2009, France's Minister for Immigration and National Identity, Eric Besson, kicked off a three-month national debate on "what it means to be French." Muslim headscarves, citizenship classes, and a proposal to make schoolchildren sing France's national anthem ("La Marseillaise") were among the issues raised—symptoms of a deeper vein of race-tinged social tension in France not likely to disappear any time soon.

(Continued)

(CONTINUED)

In 2010, 120,000 people became naturalized French citizens, but this number fell by more than 30% in 2011-2012. With an eye to the 2012 elections, the Sarkozy government deported 33,000 illegal immigrants in 2011 and moved to introduce a multiple-choice history and culture test for would-be citizens. But the new Socialist government scrapped this plan, easing the path to citizenship. A good proficiency in the French language is still required.

No one knows how many illegal immigrants reside in France at present. But with the Socialists back in power more will likely seek legal status.

Foreign Policy

De Gaulle's disdain for the "special relationship" between the United States and the UK, and the mutual mistrust it fostered, played a key role in shaping France's postwar foreign policy. France participated in the U.S.-led campaign against the Taliban regime in Afghanistan after the 9/11 attacks, but President Chirac opposed the invasion of Iraq in 2003, defiantly blocking U.S. efforts in the UN Security Council to get the United Nations to endorse the action.

A virtual partnership between France and Germany has been an essential pillar of the European Union from its origins. Differences over how to deal with the euro crisis has led to severe strains in Franco-Germany relations in recent years. How this bilateral relationship at the core of the European Project is managed in a time of crisis will go a long way toward deciding the fate of France and Europe in the coming years.

President Sarkozy sought to repair France's strained relations with Washington and London. France rejoined NATO's integrated military structure in 2009 after a forty-year absence. In November 2010 Britain and France signed a landmark fifty-year treaty on defense and security, envisaging the joint use of aircraft carriers, a 10,000-strong joint expeditionary force, and unprecedented levels of collaboration on nuclear missiles. Whether this new look in French foreign policy will survive now that Sarkozy has left the scene only time will tell.

The Constitutional Council is composed of nine justices—three nominated by the president of the republic, three by the president of the National Assembly, and three by the president of the Senate—plus all the past presidents of the republic. This judicial watchdog plays several vital roles in the French system. It supervises presidential elections and can investigate and resolve contested legislative races. Under certain conditions, it can also render opinions on laws and the constitution. The cases that come before the Council deal with political issues brought by either the president of the republic, the prime minister, the two presidents of the legislature, or at least sixty members of the National Assembly or the Senate.

The Balance Sheet

From the social and political upheavals of the late eighteenth century to the launching of the Fifth Republic in 1958, France's quest for national unity and constitutional democracy was troubled and turbulent, but in the past half-century it has enjoyed the most stable government

Socialist Party leader François Hollande was elected president of France in May 2012; he succeeded center-right President Nicolas Sarkozy.

for the longest period since the French Revolution. This political system has proven to be more durable and adaptable than its predecessors, but the nation now faces big problems and avoiding unpopular solutions is not an option for Hollande's Socialist government.

Of course, France is not alone in facing many daunting challenges that call for creative policy responses. Europe is struggling, which only complicates matters for any country on the Continent trying dig out of a deep hole. The big question now is whether the *dirigiste* (state-directed) French economic model is sustainable without dismantling the entrenched welfare state—a move almost certain to have profoundly destabilizing effects on a society accustomed to benefits its government can no longer afford.

GERMANY: FEDERALISM AGAINST MILITARISM

Modern Germany burst onto the scene in the second half of the nineteenth century with sweeping military victories over Austria in 1866 and France in 1871. Those two wars were a prelude to two world-shattering wars in the first half of the twentieth century.

The two world wars changed Europe in fundamental ways. Germany started both of these calamitous conflagrations—a fact Europeans will never forget and never let Germany forget. After World War II, Germany and its former capital were partitioned and divided between East and West for fifty years. In 1989 the infamous Berlin Wall was dismantled and the country reunited following the collapse of the communist regime in East Germany.

Germany's postwar responsibility for Europe's condition is still costing Germans in all sorts of ways—in 2011–2012, for example, with the "euro crisis" threatening to spread like a contagion, Europe expected Germany to bear the burden of bailing out Greece and saving Europe's common currency. Meanwhile, in Greece and elsewhere Germany was despised—and Angela Merkel, the chancellor, demonized—for demanding tough austerity measures as the price of bolstering the embattled euro. To understand Germany's turbulent history, it is necessary to go back to the bitter (for Germans) legacy of World War I.

The Weimar Republic

Weimar Republic
The constitutional democracy founded in Germany at the end of World War I by a constitutional convention convened in 1919 at the city of Weimar; associated with a period of political and economic turmoil, it ended when Hitler came to power in 1933.

Hitler's Third Reich sprang from the ashes of the **Weimar Republic**, Germany's first experiment with constitutional democracy. The Weimar Republic was ill fated from the moment of its inception because it was associated with Germany's humiliating defeat and the harsh peace terms imposed by the Allied powers after World War I. Burdened by punitive reparations, Germany fell victim to high unemployment, widespread business failures, and rampant inflation.

In the face of such turbulence, German society became polarized between the extreme Right and the extreme Left. In the words of one authority, "Stable democratic government was in jeopardy throughout the life of the Weimar Republic. The country was governed....by unpopular minority cabinets, by internally weak Grand Coalitions, or finally, by extra-parliamentary authoritarian

Presidential Cabinets."[8] Between the two world wars (1919–1939) the country's fragile political institutions were put to a test that proved fatal.

Given this background, the founding of the Federal Republic of Germany in 1949 was risky. Whether democracy could ever be made to work in a country that had only recently bowed to a deranged dictator, served a totalitarian state, and looked the other way while millions of innocent people were systematically murdered was an open question.

Divided Germany: The Cold War in Microcosm

World War II destroyed Germany. The nation and its capital, Berlin, were subsequently bifurcated into the German Democratic Republic (GDR), or East Germany, and the Federal Republic of Germany (FRG), or West Germany. From 1949 to 1990, Germany and Berlin, the historical capital, became powerful symbols of the Cold War—the ideological rivalry between the United States and the Soviet Union—and the unbridgeable East–West divide.

The West German "economic miracle" in the 1950s was unmatched. In the 1960s it was the main engine driving the newly established Common Market, a six-nation trading bloc that in time evolved into the world's largest single economy—the European Union. West Germany's success stood in stark contrast to the dismal Stalinist state of East Germany. The building of the Berlin Wall in 1961 aimed at keeping East Germans from escaping to the West highlighted the dramatic difference between the two Germanys. Berlin and "the Wall" became a metaphor for the Iron Curtain, proof that the peoples of the East living under communism were "captive nations" in the most literal sense, and a reminder to all in the West of the need for vigilance and unity in the ongoing struggle between freedom and tyranny.

The Great Merger: Democracy Triumphant

For three decades, East Germans, whose living standards were far below West Germans', had not been allowed to emigrate or even to visit relatives across the border.[9] It was the reform-minded Soviet leader Mikhail Gorbachev who opened the floodgates.

East Germany's end came at a time when rebellion was rife in central and Eastern Europe: Poland and Hungary had already taken giant steps toward dismantling communist rule, and Czechoslovakia, Romania, and Bulgaria were not far behind. For East German communism, the unraveling started with a mass exodus and ended with the bulldozing of the Berlin Wall following the collapse of the East German regime in late 1989.

Following free elections in the former GDR in the spring of 1990, the two Germanys entered into a formal union, with Berlin restored as the capital. Together, the nearly simultaneous collapse of Soviet power and German reunification set the stage for the eastward expansion of the European Union.

The remaking of Germany carried a big price tag. West Germans paid for the economic rehabilitation of East Germany with a 7.5% income tax surcharge and a higher sales tax. Nonetheless, unemployment in eastern Germany remained high in the 1990s, hovering around 18%, nearly twice the rate in western Germany.

German Federalism

Prior to 1989, the Federal Republic of Germany consisted of ten states, or *Länder* (singular, *Land*), plus West Berlin. It was about equal in size to the state of Oregon. The merger of the two German states in 1989 added six new *Länder* to the federal structure (see Figure 7.3). Even so, no fewer than

FIGURE 7.3   Map of Germany. Note that Berlin, once again the capital, is located in the state of Brandenburg. During the Cold War and before Germany's reunification in 1990, it was deep inside East Germany. The provinces (now federal states) that comprised the former East Germany were Brandenburg, Mecklenburg-Vorpommern, Saxony-Anhalt, Saxony, and Thuringia.

twenty-five countries the size of the united Germany would fit comfortably into the territory of the United States.

The main reason for German federalism is political rather than geographic—namely, to act as a barrier to overcentralization of power. The primary responsibility of the *Länder* or state governments is to enact legislation in specific areas, such as education and cultural affairs. They alone have the resources to implement laws enacted by the federal government, exercise police powers, administer the educational system, and place (limited) restrictions on the press. The federal government in Berlin has the exclusive right to legislate in foreign affairs, citizenship matters, currency and coinage, railways, postal service and telecommunications, and copyrights. In other areas, notably civil and criminal law, as well as laws regulating the economy, the central government and the *Länder* have shared powers, although the European Union plays a large and ever-greater role in regulating the economies of its twenty-seven member-states.

The *Länder* are more powerful and receive a larger proportion of tax revenues than U.S. states do. For example, individual and corporate income taxes are split between Berlin and the *Länder* in equal 40% shares; the remaining 20% goes to the cities. The *Länder* also receive one-third of the value-added tax, the large but hidden sales (or turnover) tax used throughout Europe.

The Executive

Germany has a parliamentary form of government with a divided executive. The most important government official is the chancellor, akin to a prime minister. The head of the majority party in the lower house of parliament becomes the chancellor; if no one party enjoys an absolute majority, as has often been the case, a coalition government chooses the chancellor. The chancellor, with parliamentary approval, appoints and dismisses cabinet members. In case of a national emergency, the chancellor becomes commander in chief of the armed forces (which are integrated into the NATO alliance structure) and is responsible for the formulation and implementation of public policy. In 2005, Angela Merkel became the first woman chancellor in German history.

The president, as the titular head of state, serves a largely symbolic function, except in the event of a political stalemate in parliament. Chosen indirectly for a seven-year term, the president, like the king or queen of Great Britain, is above party politics.

The Legislature

The legislative branch of the German government is divided into a lower house, known as the **Bundestag**, and an upper house, called the **Bundesrat**. In this bicameral setup, as in France and Britain, the lower house is the more important of the two. In Germany, however, the upper house is a far bigger player than in France and Britain.

Bundestag
The lower house in the German federal system; most legislative activity occurs in this house (see also *Bundesrat*).

Bundesrat
The upper house in the German federal system; its members, who are appointed directly by the *Länder* (states), exercise mostly informal influence in the legislative process (see also *Bundestag*).

The Bundestag The presiding officer of the Bundestag is always chosen from the leadership of the majority party. Procedural matters are based on rules inherited from the Reichstag, the prewar legislature. Elections to the Bundestag are normally held every four years.

In Germany, the Basic Law (the constitution) requires a "constructive vote of no confidence," meaning a chancellor cannot be ousted by a no-confidence vote unless the Bundestag simultaneously chooses a successor. This provision was intended as insurance against a recurrence of the governmental instability associated with Hitler's rise to power.

Because the most important work is done in legislative committees, it is especially vital that political parties gain enough seats for a *Fraktion*, a block of at least fifteen legislative seats. It is only through this unit that deputies can be assigned to committees and political parties can receive formal recognition.

The Bundesrat The upper house must pass to the lower house any measure that would alter the balance of powers between the national government and the *Länder*. Members of the Bundesrat are not directly elected; the *Länder* governments appoint them, and they must vote as a bloc. This arrangement gives the German states a powerful weapon to protect themselves against federal encroachment and makes the Bundesrat one of the most important upper houses anywhere in the world. Germany's state governments play a primary role in implementing federal policy as well as in helping to shape that policy in the concurrent areas designated under the Basic Law.

Political Parties

Germany's political party system was consciously designed to keep the number of parties from getting out of hand and to prevent tiny extremist groups from playing a significant role in the country's political life. To gain Bundestag representation, parties must receive a minimum of 5% of the national vote and must win seats in a minimum of three electoral districts.

Another factor strengthening the major parties is the mode of elections to the Bundestag. Each voter casts two votes, one for the individual and another for a *list* of names determined by the party. This method of election gives the major parties a significant role in determining the future of those who aspire to careers in politics and public service, because fully half the members of the Bundestag are elected from party lists in multimember districts by proportional representation.

Since 1949, the German Federal Republic has had two major parties—the center-left Social Democratic Party (SPD) and the conservative Christian Democratic Union/Christian Socialist Union (CDU/CSU). Because the two major parties have frequently evenly divided the popular vote (and the seats in the Bundestag), the small Free Democratic Party (FDP) has often held the key to forming a government. Both the SPD and the CDU/CSU have courted the FDP at different times but for the same reason. As a result, the FDP has had power disproportionate to its popularity at the polls and has been a junior partner in several coalition governments.

In recent years, the Green Party, which started as a social protest movement emphasizing environmental issues, has gained in popularity. In 1998, when the SPD defeated the CDU/CSU but failed to win a majority of the seats in the Bundestag, the Social Democrats, then led by Gerhard Schröder, entered into a coalition with the Green Party to form a center-left government. Schröder, who succeeded Christian Democrat Helmut Kohl (and preceded Angela Merkel) as chancellor, named Green Party leader Joschka Fisher as his foreign minister.

In 2005, Angela Merkel, leader of the Christian Democratic Union, became the first female chancellor in German history. Chancellor Merkel's party won a major victory in national elections in the fall of 2009. Her handling of the euro crisis—in particular Germany's role in bailing out Greece and Ireland, and support for a plan to create a euro zone rescue fund to recapitalize banks in Spain and Italy directly—dealt a serious blow to her prestige and popularity at home.

The Judiciary

Besides its ordinary judicial functions, the German court system is designed to act as a barrier against abuses of executive or legislative power and as a guardian of civil liberties. The regular judiciary, headed by the Supreme Court, operates alongside a set of four specialized federal tribunals, Labor Court, Social Court, Finance Court, and Administrative Court. From a political standpoint, the most important judicial structure is the Constitutional Court, which deals exclusively with constitutional questions and has the express power to declare the acts of both federal and *Land* legislatures unconstitutional.

The Bundestag elects half the judges for the Constitutional Court, and the Bundesrat elects the other half. Most judges, however, are chosen on the basis of competitive civil service–type examinations and are appointed for life by the minister of justice, with the assistance of nominating committees selected by the federal and *Land* legislatures. Indefinite terms help ensure judicial independence.

In some eyes, the Constitutional Court is Germany's most powerful institution. It is certainly the most popular: almost 80% of Germans trust it, whereas fewer than half express confidence in the federal government and the Bundestag. One big reason: The court is widely seen as being above politics. Any German citizen can bring a case before the Constitutional Court, and over the years many have done so.

THE GERMAN AGENDA: A SAMPLER

Reunification and Its Aftermath

Merging the two German states in the 1990s was costly, and West Germans had to pay the price. East Germany's infrastructure was inadequate, factories were obsolete, and unemployment was high due to numerous plant closings. More than two decades after the Berlin Wall came down, per capita GDP in eastern Germany pales in comparison with the western part; although GDP has more than doubled in eastern Germany, the economic behemoth in western Germany still dwarfs the east.

Welfare State versus Competitive Economy

The German economy stalled in the mid-1990s and unemployment hit a postwar high of 12.8% in 1998, helping the Social Democrats win control of the government. By 2005, some 5.2 million Germans were jobless—a post–World War II record. German voters brought the center-right Christian Democrats, led by Angela Merkel, the first woman Chancellor in Germany's history, back to power.

As Chancellor, Merkel engineered major labor market and pension reforms. The Germany economy bounced back strongly in 2010 despite the lingering effects of the 2008–2009 global recession. But chronic budget deficits and crushing public debt in Greece, Portugal, Ireland, and Spain sent the euro area into the doldrums and put the brakes on the German recovery in 2011–2012. Although the resilient German economy has weathered the storm better than most, the euro crisis has nonetheless roiled German politics.

In May 2012, the center-left (Social Democrats and Greens) combined to win 50.4% of the votes in a bellwether election in North Rhine-Westphalia. Merkel's CDU/CSU garnered only 26.3% (down from 34.6% in 2010), its worst showing there since World War II. That result gave the two main opposition parties a majority in the state legislature, and set the stage for a test of Merkel's leadership in the 2013 national elections. Despite it all, polls show German voters still trust her to lead the country in difficult times.

The Euro Crisis and the EU

Germany has been the bulwark for European unity and integration since the early 1950s, but bailing out EU governments teetering on the verge of bankruptcy was never part of the plan. Germany under Merkel and the Christian Democrats reluctantly agreed to go along with big (critics say not big enough) rescue plans for Greece and Ireland in the face of considerable domestic opposition. But Merkel, a fiscal conservative, has demanded painful and unpopular austerity (spending cuts and tax increases) in return. (Keynesian economists favor strong state action and deficit spending to create jobs and boost consumer demand.)

It fell to Germany, the "locomotive" of Europe's Single Market economy, to decide what to do to save the euro and how to do it. A fiscal conservative in a country where inflation and deficits are anathema for reasons deeply embedded in the nation's history and culture, Merkel was loathe to act in haste. Critics from afar accused her of fiddling while Europe burned, while the German public and her own party urged her not to bail out prodigal governments (above all, Greece) that caused the problem.

Merkel reluctantly backed two key confidence-building measures to save the euro—a euro zone fiscal compact to impose a set of standard rules on member-state budgets and a permanent European Stability Mechanism (ESM) to provide emergency rescue funds. Few thought these measures would suffice without a third, namely, creation of euro bonds and mutualization of euro debt (a transfer of debt obligations from debtor to creditor nations within the EU).

Germany is one of the world's largest exporters (behind only China and the United States in 2011) and benefits more than any other country from having free access to a single market of 500 million consumers. Even in the 2012 slowdown, German exports were "buoyant" according to The Economist: "The German trade surplus is so huge—nearly €100 billion ($123 billion) in the first half of the year—that it has drawn flak from the OECD club of rich countries, and from the European Commission."*

(Continued)

(CONTINUED)

Climate Change and Energy Policy

Germany has been actively pursuing an ambitious policy of energy transformation (*Energiewende*) since the year 2000. This policy was accelerated after the Fukushima disaster in March 2011 when Merkel ordered an immediate shutdown of seven reactors and reaffirmed Germany's clean-energy goals—to cut greenhouse gas emissions from 1990 levels by 40% by 2020 and by 80% by 2050 and to do so without nuclear power. That means Germany will have to make a major push to develop wind energy and solar power. Will it succeed? Nobody knows, but with German engineering prowess it would not be surprising if Germany emerges as a leading exporter of alternative energy technologies and systems one day soon.

Foreign Workers, Illegal Immigrants, and Skinheads

Germany has been a magnet for temporary workers and illegal immigrants from Eastern Europe and elsewhere. Ten of the twelve countries that have recently joined the EU are in Eastern Europe, where with few exceptions per capita income and living standards remain relatively low. Xenophobic extremists, including neo-Nazis and "skinheads," have tried to capitalize on popular fears over immigration—so far with little success. In October 2010, Chancellor Angela Merkel declared that Germany's attempt to create a multicultural society had "utterly failed"; and Horst Seehofer, the leader of the CSU, the CDU's sister party, said there was no room in Germany for more people from "alien cultures."

Germany's Changing Role in Europe and the World

When Germany participated in the UN peacekeeping mission in Bosnia in the mid-1990s, it was the first time German soldiers had been sent abroad since World War II. In 1999, Germany contributed 8,500 combat troops to the NATO operation in Kosovo (Serbia), and after 9/11 it sent 2,000 troops to Afghanistan. Germany's opposition to the U.S.-British invasion of Iraq in 2003 was the first time Germany openly opposed the United States on a major foreign policy issue since World War II. Most Germans alive today were born after 1945. Any knowledge they have of World War II, Hitler, and the Holocaust is second hand or from history books.

---

*See "Europe's Tired Engine, *The Economist*, August 18, 2012 (online edition).

The Basic Law and Civil Liberties

In the realm of civil liberties, as one student of German politics declared, "The relevant historical experience was that of the Third Reich, with its oppressive flouting of all human liberties."[10] The first 19 articles of the Basic Law—Germany's constitution—are devoted to a careful elaboration of the unalienable rights of every German citizen.

All forms of discrimination, including religious and racial discrimination, are expressly prohibited. Freedom of speech, movement, assembly, and association are guaranteed, except when used "to attack the free democratic order." This last proviso was clearly aimed at the two extremes: Communism on the left, Nazism on the right. Fear of a right-wing resurgence has never been far beneath the surface. Indeed, in postwar Germany, neo-Nazi activity has generally been interpreted as constituting an "attack on the free democratic order."

Does Democracy Work in Germany?

One of the principal purposes behind the Basic Law was to arrange the institutional furniture in the "new Germany" to preclude a repeat performance of the "old Germany." By any standard, Germany's performance since World War II has been impressive.

JAPAN: BETWEEN EAST AND WEST

When a powerful earthquake in the Western Pacific in 2011 caused one of the world's worst nuclear accidents and displaced more than 150,000 people living in the vicinity of the Fukushima nuclear power plant, it put Japan in the global spotlight—and not in a good way. Massive internal dislocations during the Fukushima reactor meltdown and questions surrounding the way high-level government officials handled the crisis focused international attention on Japan's hidebound political culture, its inaccessible power elite, and the opaque inner workings of its powerful and insulated bureaucracy.

Like other Asian societies, Japan had no democratic traditions prior to 1947. In fact, its history, geography, and culture often worked against Western democratic ideas (see Figure 7.4). Yet today, Japan is one of Asia's oldest parliamentary democracies (the other, India, came into being at the same time but under very different circumstances). To see how this remarkable transformation came about, we start by sketching Japan's path from its feudal and imperial past to the present.[11]

Historical Background

Japan's feudal era lasted until the **Meiji Restoration** in 1868. At that time, under the guise of recapturing ancient glories, Japan crowned a new emperor, of the Meiji dynasty, and embarked on the path to modernization. Meiji Japan remained oligarchic, paying lip service to democracy. A group of elder statesmen, or *genro*, dominated the government, and the emperor, worshiped as a flesh-and-blood deity, personified national unity. He probably also played an important role in decision making on crucial issues.[12]

Domestically, Japan made great progress during the latter part of the nineteenth century. A modernizing elite promoted, protected, and subsidized a Western-style economic development program. Despite periodic opposition from rural landowners, the government force-fed the economy with infusions of capital designed to promote heavy industry. Only basic or strategic industries were state owned. Within a few decades, the leaders of the Meiji Restoration, according to one authority, "abolished feudal institutions, legalized private property in land, started a Western-style legal system, established compulsory education, organized modern departments of central and local government, and removed the legal barriers between social classes."[13]

After World War I, Japan entered a new phase of political development. Nationalism, taught in the schools, became a kind of religion. Governments blossomed and withered in a rapid and bewildering succession. All attempts at instituting democratic reforms were submerged in the tidal wave of militarism that swept over Japan in the 1930s. Charging that effete politicians infatuated with democracy had kept Japan down, ultranationalists looked to a strong military for

Meiji Restoration
The end of Japan's feudal era, in 1868, when a small group of powerful individuals crowned a new, symbolic emperor, embarked on an economic modernization program, and established a modern governmental bureaucracy.

FIGURE 7.4   Japan. Note Japan's proximity to the Korean peninsula and, in the north, to Russia.

CHINA

RUSSIA

Hokkaido

●Sapporo

NORTH
KOREA

☆Pyongyang

*East Sea
(Sea of Japan)*

Japan

Aomori●

Morioka
●

Akita●

●Seoul

SOUTH
KOREA

Yamagata● Sendai●

0   50   100 Miles
0   50   100 Kilometers

Niigata● Fukushima●

Toyama● Nagano Utsunomiya
Kanazawa● ●   ●   ●Mito
●Fukai *Honshu* Maebashi●
        Kofu● Urawa●
Matsue● Tottori●   Gifu● ●Tokyo
●Pusan   Kyoto● Otsu● Nagoya● Yokohama● ●Chiba
Hiroshima● Okayama● Kobe●●● Tsu● Shizuoka●
Yamaguchi● Takamatsu● Nara
Fukuoka● Matsuyama● Tokushima● Osaka
    ●Saga   ●Kochi Wakayama
●Oita

*East China
Sea*

RYUKYU ISLANDS

Naha●

Nagasaki● Kumamoto●
Kyushu
Kagoshima● ●Miyazaki

*East China
Sea*

PACIFIC OCEAN

PACIFIC OCEAN

Shikoku

© CENGAGE LEARNING

leadership. Japan had never truly embraced Western concepts of constitutionalism and liberal democracy. Sovereignty, according to popular belief, issued from the emperor-deity, not from the people. Thus, prior to 1945, Japan had dallied with democracy in form but not in substance.

The 1947 Constitution

The 1947 Japanese constitution, imposed by the victors after World War II, sought to remake Japan's political system. Henceforth, sovereignty would reside in the Japanese people, not in the emperor. U.S. influence on the new Japanese constitution is readily apparent in its preamble:

> We, the Japanese people, acting through our duly elected representatives in the National Diet, determined that we shall secure for ourselves and our posterity

the fruits of peaceful cooperation with all nations and the blessings of liberty throughout this land, and resolved that never again shall we be visited with the horrors of war through the action of government, do proclaim that sovereign power resides with the people and do firmly establish this Constitution.... Government is a sacred trust of the people, the authority for which is derived from the people, the powers of which are exercised by representatives of the people, and the benefits of which are enjoyed by the people.

Like weavers of a fine tapestry, the framers of the 1947 constitution sought to construct an elaborate system of representative democracy. Among the fundamental rights guaranteed by the constitution were the rights to receive an equal education and to organize and bargain collectively. In another extraordinary feature, the Japanese constitution explicitly renounced war and pledged, "land, sea, and air forces, as well as other war potential, will never be maintained." (This provision has not, however, prevented the government from building limited "self-defense forces.")

Parliament above Emperor

The constitution establishes a parliamentary form of government. The emperor remains the head of state, although as a merely ceremonial figure. The prime minister is the real head of government. The authors of the constitution, however, placed a preponderance of *formal* power in the new bicameral legislature. That body, called the Diet, is divided into a 480-member House of Representatives elected at least every four years (elections can be more frequent when the House is dissolved) and a relatively less powerful House of Councilors, whose 250 members serve six-year terms (half being elected every other three years).

Originally, members of each house were elected by universal suffrage from multimember districts (each having three to five seats, depending on population) in which voters made only one selection. This system endured until 1994, when calls for election reforms led to the redrawing of district boundaries and a major change in the electoral process for the lower house: there are now 300 single-seat constituencies, while the remaining 180 seats are decided by proportional representation.

The constitution explicitly states that popular sovereignty is to be expressed through the Diet, the only institution of the government empowered to make laws. Whereas in the past the prime minister and cabinet were responsible to the emperor, they are now responsible to the Diet, the "highest organ of state power." Japan's Supreme Court is empowered to declare laws unconstitutional (which it rarely does), and justices are to be approved by the voters every ten years after their appointment, a process that has become virtually automatic.

As we will see, however, the Japanese have adapted Western institutions to fit Japan's own rich and resilient cultural traditions. The result is a unique system that combines democratic politics and market economics—the new—with political hierarchy, economic centralization, and social discipline—the old.

The Party System

With one brief exception in 1993–1994, the Liberal Democratic Party (LDP) dominated Japanese politics from 1955 to 2009. Among the smaller parties, the

Socialists and Communists occasionally garnered significant numbers of votes, but their legislative role was to provide parliamentary opposition. For four decades, the actual governing of the country fell almost exclusively to the LDP.

When a single party retains a majority of seats in a freely elected legislative assembly over an extended time, it usually means the party has satisfied a broad range of social interests. In Japan, the LDP succeeded because it embraced pragmatism over ideological purity, enjoyed the backing of powerful special interests, and benefited from the sheer force of political inertia. According to two authorities,

> The changes they [the LDP] made toward a more strongly centralized system of government corrected some of the most obvious mistakes of the Occupation. The Liberal Democratic Party, being in power, also controlled a considerable amount of patronage and had the advantage when seeking the support of economic and professional interest groups. With the support of the majority of the rural vote and access to the resources of the business community, the party was in a strong position. It was on intimate terms with the bureaucracy,....[but these efforts] were not sufficient.... Beginning in 1955, the Liberal Democratic Party attempted to build up a national organization with mass membership.[14]

The LDP's consensus-building role became a defining feature of Japanese politics. Delegates to the LDP conference choose the party leader—called the president—before a national election. Until the 1990s, the LDP leader was assured of being elected prime minister. Getting elected president of the party, however, is not easy: A victor emerges only after intense bargaining by party factions, each of which has its own leader, its own constituencies to protect, and its own interests to promote.

The LDP nearly self-destructed in the early 1990s when a series of political scandals severely tarnished the party's image. A rising tide of social discontent over the rigors of daily life, high prices, long workdays, and a sluggish economy also contributed to the party's unprecedented defeat in the historical national elections, shattering the one-party-dominant system. What followed was a chaotic period during which Japan would see five different governments come and go. The LDP was the clear loser, but there were no clear winners.

In the fall of 1996, disgruntled voters handed the LDP a slim victory at the polls, but control of the party remained in the hands of a change-resistant old guard, and the LDP again fell out of favor with the public as the economy continued a downslide throughout the 1990s. The promise of change came in 2001, when Junichiro Koizumi, an LDP maverick, won a hard-fought battle to become the LDP's new president. He was reelected with a large popular vote majority in September 2003. Reform-minded and opposed to cronyism, Koizumi did not enjoy the support of his own parliamentary party, but the party rank and file (and the public in general) responded enthusiastically to his personal charm, fresh ideas, and candor.

Promising reform "without any sacred cows," Koizumi was rewarded for his efforts as the country's economy revived. However, many members of his own party in the Diet opposed his prize proposal—privatization of Japan's massive postal savings system. When the bill was defeated in the upper house in

2005, Koizumi dissolved the Diet and called new elections. The vote, which the LDP won by the largest majority since 1986, was a referendum on Koizumi's leadership *and* the postal privatization issue. The bill passed in 2005.

After serving five years as LDP party leader and prime minister, Koizumi stepped down in 2006, having won his biggest political battle: Japan's postal system was privatized in 2007. Although Japan has never fully recovered from the stock market crash in 1990–1991 (see "Ideas and Politics: The Japanese Agenda") and the subsequent implosion of its "bubble economy," it still boasts one the world's five largest national economies (the other four are the United States, China, Germany, and India).

Patron–Client Politics

Japanese democracy is a unique blend of imported democratic ideals and native culture—in particular, Japan's traditional *patron–client system,* which has long characterized Japanese politics. Factional leaders called patrons attract loyal followers or clients. The leader is expected to "feed" his faction, mainly by doling out campaign funds; in turn, faction members are obliged to vote as a solid bloc in the party conference and Diet.

Personal loyalty is the basis of financial support, intraparty power, and the prestige of individual leaders within the LDP. The vaunted political reform of 1994 that changed the electoral system temporarily disrupted the traditional behind-the-scenes collusion among government, bureaucracy, and the business elite, but it did not fundamentally change the patron–client system or practices. Nor is it likely to change the nation's preference for consensus seeking:

> This method rests on the premise that members of a group—say, a village council—should continue to talk, bargain, make concessions, and so on until finally a consensus emerges....Despite the spread of democratic norms, this tradition of rule by consensus still has its appeal and sometimes leads to cries against the "tyranny of the majority"—for example, when the ruling party with its majority pushes through legislation over the strong protests of the opposition.[15]

When Japan's economic miracle gave way to a severe and prolonged slump in the 1990s, the LDP's popularity faded with it. After an eleven-month hiatus in 1993–1994, however, the LDP regained control of the government. But then a new rival party emerged—the Democratic Party of Japan (DPJ). In the 2007 upper-house elections, the DPJ outpolled the LDP 39% to 21%, but the LDP still had a large majority in the Diet (300 seats to the DPJ's 113).

The LDP's long run as Japan's ruling party appeared at an end in August 2009 when Japanese voters handed the DPJ a stunning victory, giving the DPJ 308 seats and leaving the LDP with a mere 119 seats. Japanese voters rejected rule by Tokyo's "iron triangle" of party bosses, bureaucrats, and business elites—a closed and corrupt system that was tolerated so long as Japan's economy was robust. (In a practice known as *amakudari* [literally, "descent from heaven"], retiring Japanese high-level bureaucrats often take lucrative jobs at firms they previously regulated.)

After the earthquake-induced nuclear power accident at Fukushima, public confidence in the government of Naoto Kan plummeted. When Prime Minister

Kan and his cabinet resigned in the fall of 2011, the DPJ tapped Yoshihiko Noda to step in as Japan's sixth head of government in five years. Among the policy dilemmas Noda faced was whether to raise the consumption tax to deal with Japan's mounting public debt (see "Ideas and Politics: The Japanese Agenda").

In December 2012 voters made yet another U-turn, handing former prime minister Shinzo Abe and his Liberal Democratic Party (LDP) a landslide victory in national parliamentary elections (294 seats in the 480-seat lower house). (Naoto Kan lost his Diet seat to a relatively unknown LDP challenger.)

The Judiciary and Japanese Culture

The Japanese judicial system displays a curious combination of U.S. and European influences. The U.S. influence is evident in the name of Japan's highest judicial body, the Supreme Court. The Chief Justice is appointed by the Emperor but is nominated by the government; the cabinet appoints all other justices. The Supreme Court, like its U.S. counterpart, enjoys the power of judicial review, meaning it can declare acts of the legislature unconstitutional. Few other constitutional democracies permit judges to second-guess legislators.

Japan's legal system as a whole is modeled after the European civil law system, but again with some U.S. influences. Culturally, the Japanese are far less prone to sue each other than are U.S. citizens. They are also less likely to resort to the courts as a means of settling civil disputes or to seek redress for alleged injuries and injustices. In Japan, social, rather than judicial, remedies are still the norm. Often, successful intervention by a respected member of the community, the head of a family, or a supervisor at work makes legal action unnecessary.

Does Democracy Work in Japan?

Despite the turbulence of the 1990s, Japan has successfully blended Western political forms and Japanese political culture. As in Germany, economics played a key role in the success of the nation's shotgun democracy. ("Shotgun" because it was the result of defeat in war and military occupation.)

Japan's economic revival after World War II was hardly less miraculous than Germany's, as bombed-out cities, symbolized by Hiroshima and Nagasaki, were turned into models of efficient and innovative industrial production. Deliberate planning by a modernizing entrepreneurial elite was important to Japan's resurgence; a rising volume of world trade and massive U.S. purchases during the Korean War (1950–1953) were also crucial. Within two decades, Japan's export-oriented mercantilist economic strategy produced huge advances in heavy industry—notably, automobile manufacturing, robotics, and consumer electronics. Despite "the loss of 52 percent of Japan's prewar territories, the return of five million persons to a country about the size of California, the loss of 80 percent of Japan's shipping, and the destruction of one-fifth of [its] industrial plants and many of [its] great cities,"[16] Japan is now a major global economic power. China, with a population more than ten times larger, is only now beginning to catch up with Japan in GDP; India, despite its impressive strides in recent times, remains far behind.

After the 1980s bubble burst, Japan's economic growth rate slowed dramatically under the impact of four recessions in a dozen years. When the 1997 "Asian flu" financial crisis hit, Japanese banks were trapped in circumstances they themselves had done much to create by lending vast sums for speculative investments in construction, real estate, and retail trade with little security or scrutiny—like a dress rehearsal for the global financial meltdown that started on Wall Street in September 2008.

Japan is and will remain a major economic power, but its technological prowess no longer sets it clearly apart from its Asian competitors. The worldwide recession derailed reforms aimed at lifting the economy out of its malaise after 2008.

THE JAPANESE AGENDA: A SAMPLER

Nuclear Power, Energy Security, and Public Safety

The earthquake and tsunami in March 2011 that caused three of the six nuclear reactors at the Daiichi Fukushima nuclear power plant to melt down claimed some 15,700 lives and left thousands more unaccounted for, and forced 80,000 people to evacuate to temporary living quarters (where many remained six months later). The twin natural disasters compounded by a manmade disaster raised questions about the wisdom of Japan's heavy reliance on nuclear reactors for electric power

© FRANK RAMSPOTT/ISTOCKPHOTO.COM

The map marks the spot where the tsunami that caused the Fukushima meltdown slammed into northeastern Japan and inundated the coastal city of Sendai in Kagoshima Prefecture.

generation. What followed was intense public scrutiny and severe criticism of the government's mismanagement of Japan's nuclear power industry—in particular, its alleged failure to properly monitor and enforce safety standards.

A blue ribbon panel of experts set up by the Japanese Diet issued a scathing report in July 2012, concluding, "The Fukushima nuclear power plant accident was the result of collusion between the government, the regulators and Tepco [Tokyo Electric Power Company, the owner of the six Fukushima plants] and the lack of governance...." Further, the culpable parties, "effectively betrayed the nation's right to be safe from nuclear accident." And, finally, "the accident was clearly 'man-made.'"

The policy dilemma, however, is not easily solved. Japan's energy security is extremely tenuous: it has an export-oriented manufacturing economy, a modern, highly urbanized population, and at best modest indigenous fossil-fuel resources. Japan thus has to import almost all its coal, oil, and natural gas.

A Culture of "Reflexive Obedience"

The chairman of the above-mentioned expert panel, Kiyoshi Kurokawa, a medical doctor, declared Fukushima "a profoundly man-made disaster—that could and should have been foreseen and prevented." But he also placed blame on Japanese culture: "What must be admitted—very painfully," wrote Dr. Kurokawa, "is that this was a disaster 'Made in Japan.' Its fundamental causes are to be found in the ingrained conventions of Japanese culture; our reflexive obedience; our reluctance to question authority; our devotion to 'sticking with the program'; our groupism; and our insularity."

In this view, Japan's current problems are self-inflicted and not likely to be addressed until or unless something is done to change the socialization process. That implies major changes in education from teacher training, to pedagogy, to the basic curriculum. The paradox of an open society with a closed culture

impenetrable to outsiders is one key to understanding the challenges Japan faces in the new global economy of the twenty-first century.

Sustaining a High Standard of Living

Despite its prolonged economic downturn, Japan remains an affluent society. Even so, it is a relatively small, mountainous country with a large urban-dwelling population and relatively little land suitable for agriculture or settlement. The problems of overdevelopment—stress-related health problems, rush-hour crowds, and traffic congestion—are readily apparent in present-day Japan. Japan's demographic crisis—steeply declining birthrates and high life expectancy—means that the ratio of workers to pensioners is getting steadily worse. Is Japan's ultramodern mass-consumption economy sustainable under these circumstances?

Asian Challengers

Japan has largely lost its position as the preeminent economic power in Asia. In the 1980s, its main challengers were the so-called newly industrialized countries (NICs)—South Korea, Taiwan, Singapore, and Hong Kong. More recently, the surging economy of the People's Republic of China has registered double-digit annual growth rates and will soon overtake Japan in absolute GDP size; India's economy is also growing rapidly; with a population of more than 1 billion, and therefore an abundant supply of comparatively cheap labor, India is also a potential economic superpower. Indonesia, Malaysia, and Vietnam are three other countries in the region capable of competing with Japan in major export markets.

Foreign Policy: Japan's China Problem

The United States is Japan's most important ally and trading partner. Until recently the reverse was also true: Japan was America's most key trading partner in Asia. But the meteoric rise of China signifies a major strategic shift in the balance of power in Asia and the Western

(Continued)

(CONTINUED)

Pacific. Today, China rivals Japan as a partner in U.S. foreign policy calculations, not only because of trade but also as America's largest creditor—in October 2012 China's official holdings of U.S. bonds rose to $1.1535 trillion. Japan was second at $1.1215 trillion. As Japan's largest export market, the United States is vital to Japan's economic health (and vice versa). The United States is also China's largest export market.

The U.S. air and naval bases in the western Pacific, as well as the massive U.S. Pacific Fleet, have enabled Japan to concentrate on development of high-technology consumer industries and overseas markets while spending less than 1% of its GDP on defense, but for how long? In recent years, an escalating dispute with China over uninhabited islands in the East China Sea threatened to erupt into a shooting war. The feud reached a dangerous new level in January 2013 when both sides scrambled jet fighters over the area in dispute. Under the terms of the U.S.–Japan security treaty, Washington is obligated to defend the islands, which it handed back to Japan in 1972 along with the return of Okinawa.

After the Tsunami: Recovery and Reconstruction

The massive earthquake and tsunami in the spring of 2011 devastated the city of Sendai, not only killing thousands of people but also causing monumental damage to property and infrastructure. The World Bank estimated rebuilding costs at some $235 billion, and Japan's government put the total cost much higher—up to $309 billion.

INDIA AND ISRAEL: CHALLENGED DEMOCRACIES

Even if parliamentary rule works in Europe, where it started, and in Japan, where it was imposed by an occupying military power, can it work in other nations and regions where representative government has no roots in native traditions, or even in a country that finds itself in a perpetual state of war with its neighbors? The experiences of India and Israel suggest that it can.

Amazing India: A Parliamentary Miracle?

India is home to an ancient Hindu civilization and great empires, including that of the **Moghuls** or Muslim conquerors. Colonized by Great Britain in the nineteenth century, India regained its independence after World War II. The questions then were: Would the former colony become one country or two? Or would it fragment into a dozen or more ethnolinguistic states?

India is a paradox—an immense and extremely diverse established democracy in which poverty and illiteracy remain widespread despite great progress in recent times. With a population of 1.1 billion, it is the world's second most populous country. Some 70% of India's people still live in villages, making India a rural society in a postindustrial world.

Many children in rural India lack basic skills (reading, writing, and arithmetic) necessary to find productive work in a modern, urban economy. About two in five will be physically stunted by malnutrition. Roughly half of all Indian women are illiterate, compared with a ratio of about one in seven in China. Although

Moghuls
Muslim invaders who created a dynastic empire on the Asian subcontinent; the greatest Moghul rulers were Babur (1526–1530), Akbar (1556–1605), Shah Jahan (1628–1658), and Aurangzeb (1658–1707); Shah Jahan was the architect of the Taj Mahal.

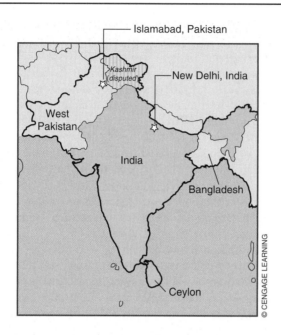

FIGURE 7.5 Pakistan at Independence in 1947. Note that West and East Pakistan (present-day Bangladesh) were on opposite sides of India. In 2012, the population of India was 1.2 billion and Pakistan had 180 million people.

a recent five-year growth spurt saw India's economy grow by nearly 9% a year, China's GDP was still three and a half times larger than India's in 2008–2009, and in the first three months of 2012 India's GDP growth fell to 5.3%.

Two large and distinct populations—the larger one Hindu and the other Muslim—inhabited the subcontinent of India. The heaviest concentration of Muslims is in the northwestern and eastern areas; the vast lands in between, constituting the bulk of the territory under the **British Raj** (the colonial ruler), were dominated by Hindus. To avoid conflict between these two religiously distinct communities, the retreating British created two states: India and Pakistan. The western part of Pakistan was separated from the eastern part with India in the middle (Figure 7.5).

This geographic anomaly was only one of the problems the British left unresolved. Another was the Hindu-Muslim split within India. Although most Muslims inhabited the territory of Pakistan, a large Muslim minority remained within the territory of the newly independent state of India. Even more problematic was the fact that India is a mosaic of diverse ethnic and cultural minorities, each speaking a different language. There are also several religions, including Sikhism, Jainism, and Christianity, as well as Hinduism and Islam.

Finally, no account of contemporary India is complete without mentioning poverty and population. Next to China, India is the most populous country in the world, with more than 1 billion souls. To this day, tens of millions are illiterate, and hundreds of millions are desperately poor, living in rural areas with little or no access to basic services, schools, health clinics, jobs, and the like.

Indeed, millions of India's poor have no identity—literally—because they lack birth certificates and school records. Imagine if you had no way to prove

British Raj
British colonial rule on the Asian subcontinent from the eighteenth century to 1947, when India and Pakistan became independent.

who you are. You could not open a bank account, get a job, enroll in college, get a post office box, travel abroad (sorry, no passport), or get a driver's license, to cite but a few examples. In 2010, India launched the Unique Identity (UID) project aimed at providing an exclusive number, based on biometrics (photo, all ten fingerprints and iris scans) to every resident in the country—more than a billion people. At the end of 2011, some 30 million had enrolled, setting the stage for a large-scale enrollment in 2012 projected at some 200 million, and 600 million (!) by the end of 2014.

Lok Sabha
The lower house of India's Federal Parliament; the directly elected House of the People. In India, as in the United Kingdom and other parliamentary systems, governments are formed by the majority party (or a coalition of parties) in the lower house following national elections (see also *Rajya Sabha*).

Rajya Sabha
The upper house of India's Federal Parliament; the indirectly elected Council of States (see also *Lok Sabha*).

India *is* changing. After decades of sluggish growth barely keeping pace with the "exploding" population, economic reforms put in place by Prime Minister Manmohan Singh in the 1990s galvanized the Indian economy. "The Indian tiger is on the prowl," wrote *The Economist* in 2007, and "at some point, India's growth rate could even outpace China's; and if you measure things by purchasing power parity, India should soon overtake Japan and become the third-biggest economy, behind only America and China."[17] In fact, India's economy is growing almost as fast as China's.

Despite all its recent achievements, however, India still faces huge challenges. Ethnic clashes and communal conflict among Hindus, Muslims, and Sikhs have plagued the country since independence. Nor has trouble been strictly internal; India has fought wars with both China and Pakistan. The bitter dispute between India and Pakistan over the territory of Kashmir (see Figure 7.5) has never been resolved, turning the two countries into perennial foes. One of the most dangerous moments came in the early 1970s, when East Pakistan broke away and became the present state of Bangladesh. India and Pakistan both possess nuclear weapons. India's border dispute with China has included military confrontation and conflict in the past but is now on the back burner, if not entirely forgotten.

As for India's economic prospects, the picture is brighter but far from rosy. India's sustainable rate of growth is lower than its historically high rates in recent years. Despite clear signs that the country is on the move, modernization and the rise of a prosperous middle class have done little, so far, to pull hundreds of millions at the bottom out of poverty. People in rural India still "waste hours queuing for drinking water," children still have no chance to go to school, and "around half of all Indian women are still illiterate."[18]

IDEAS AND POLITICS

INDIA'S FEDERAL GOVERNMENT

On the face of it, the idea of India as an independent republic is absurd. And yet there it is: India is a federal system comprising twenty-eight states and seven union territories. Power resides in a freely elected parliament and a prime minister who is the leader of the majority party (as in other parliamentary systems). The prime minister chooses a cabinet that is presented for approval to the **Lok Sabha**, the lower house. The **Rajya Sabha** or upper house is indirectly elected; it plays second fiddle to the lower house, but it debates and can delay passage of legislation, thus giving its members a real voice in the policy-making and law-making processes.

India is a parliamentary democracy (see "Ideas and Politics") that has functioned for more than half a century in a society faced with staggering challenges and presented with such extremes of size and diversity that its very existence for five decades as a single state under a single form of government—*any* form of government—is nothing short of miraculous. Except for one brief interlude in the late 1970s, when Prime Minister Indira Gandhi declared a state of national emergency and assumed dictatorial powers, India's leaders, starting with the great Jawaharlal Nehru, have operated within the framework of a British-style parliamentary democracy.

In the May 2009 national elections, with some 300 parties and independent candidates vying for votes, over 417 million ballots were cast across India during a period of several weeks. The turnout rate was an impressive 58% (in contrast to the 2009 European Union elections in which the turnout rate was a mere 43%). Prime Minister Manmohan Singh's Congress Party won a large plurality of the votes, by far the biggest bloc of seats in parliament, and thus retained control of the government. But Singh turned eighty in 2012 and many other top Congress leaders who run the country are getting old, so much so that critics are dusting off an old pejorative to describe this government: gerontocracy.

Israel: A War Republic

Like India, Israel came into being after World War II. Unlike Indians, most Israelis are relatively recent immigrants to the territory once known as Palestine. Also in stark contrast to India, Israel's population and territory are tiny—thus, the problem Israel faced was being too small, not too large. From its inception as a state, Israel was awash in controversy and surrounded by hostile Arab neighbors. In fact, Israel's very birth was violent, resulting from a bitter and prolonged struggle with the indigenous population of Palestinian Arabs.

Zionism
The movement whose genesis was in the reestablishment, and now the support, of the Jewish national state of Israel.

Balfour Declaration
Named for the British foreign secretary who, in 1917, declared that the United Kingdom favored "the establishment in Palestine of a national home for the Jewish people" and pledged to "facilitate the achievement of this object, it being clearly understood that nothing shall be done which may prejudice the civil and religious rights of the existing non-Jewish communities in Palestine or the rights and political status enjoyed by Jews in any other country."

The Western Wall ("Wailing Wall"—a sacred relic of the ancient Jewish temple and courtyard in Jerusalem destroyed by the Romans in the first century (CE). Ultra-orthodox Hasidic Jews are recognizable by their long beards and braids and traditional black attire.

Israel is a secular state but a Jewish society. A great influx of Jews into Palestine followed on the heels of Hitler's rise to power in Germany in the 1930s; however, the movement for a Jewish state in the modern era dates back to the 1890s. **Zionism,** as this movement was called, gathered momentum in 1917 with the famous **Balfour Declaration,** named for the then British foreign minister who authored the first official endorsement of the idea of a Jewish state. (At the time, Palestine was a virtual colony of Great Britain.)

MAPS THAT MATTER

THE LAND(S?) OF ISRAEL

FIGURE 7.6   Israeli Jews and Palestinian Arabs claim the same historic land of Palestine, which has been at the epicenter of the Middle East conflict since the state of Israel was founded in 1947. President Obama gave a major speech on the Middle East in May 2011, calling on Israel to return the lands it seized in the 1967 Six-Day War to the Palestinians. But Israeli Prime Minister Benyamin Netanyahu vowed that Israel would never give up control of a "united Jerusalem" and blamed Hamas and Palestinian extremists for the long-standing stalemate in peace negotiations. In 2012, the bloody protracted civil war in Syria threatened to spill over into neighboring states, including Israel, Lebanon, Jordan, and Turkey (not shown on the map but on Syria's northern border).

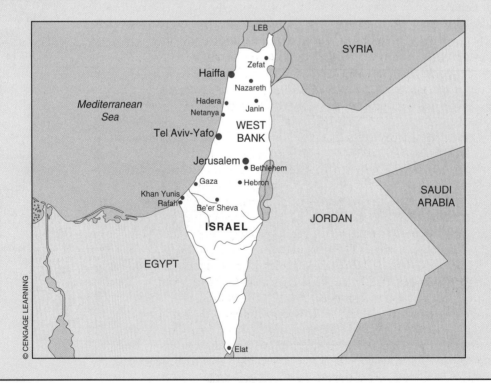

Israel and the Holocaust are inextricably intertwined. The original idea backed by the United States, the United Kingdom, and the United Nations after World War II was to carve two states out of the historic territory of Palestine—one for Jews and the other for Palestinian Arabs—and to make Jerusalem, sacred to three religions (Judaism, Christianity, and Islam), an international city under the auspices of the United Nations. That idea died when the Palestinian Arabs rejected the deal they were offered in 1947—though the Jewish side accepted it. As a result of the ensuing war, most Palestinian Arabs were displaced by Jewish settlers and became refugees living in squalid camps in the Gaza Strip, the West Bank of Jordan, and Lebanon (see Figure 7.6).

This situation left a legacy of bitterness and despair that has inscribed itself indelibly in modern Middle Eastern history, pitting the Arab-Islamic world against a diminutive but invincible Jewish state. Facing hostile Arab neighbors on all sides, Israel fought and won three wars of self-defense with Egypt, Syria, Jordan, and Lebanon: the Suez Crisis in 1956, the Six-Day War in 1967, and the Yom Kippur War in 1973. In the 1967 war, Israel seized and kept control of the Gaza Strip and the Sinai Desert (Egypt), the West Bank (Jordan), and the Golan Heights (Syria). In the 1973 war, Israel was in a position to conquer all of Egypt but—under heavy diplomatic pressure from the United States—decided against doing so. In 1978, President Jimmy Carter brokered the **Camp David Accords**—a peace treaty between Egypt and Israel. This historic deal included large U.S. subsidies to both parties, but it worked: Egypt and Israel have not exchanged blows since 1973.

Sadly, the Middle East in general and Palestine in particular continue to be turbulent and violent. In the 1980s and 1990s, a protracted Palestinian uprising called the **intifada** in the occupied territories (disputed Arab lands Israel seized in the 1967 Six-Day War) caused deaths and suffering on both sides. Although it is common to speak of two such uprisings, it was really only one that was interrupted during part of the 1990s when the hope of a peace settlement hung in the balance.

Relations between Israel and the Palestinians went from bad to worse in 2006 after voters in the West Bank and Gaza gave the militant group Hamas a big majority in the new Palestinian parliament. The sweeping victory set the stage for a struggle within the Palestinian territories between the militant Hamas and the more moderate Fatah. The struggle split the territories politically, with Fatah controlling the West Bank (under the leadership of Palestinian President Mahmoud Abbas) and Hamas controlling Gaza. Thereafter, Israel was hit by rocket attacks from Gaza; at the end of 2008, after stern warnings to Hamas, Israel invaded Gaza, killing many militants and some civilians; destroying buildings, including residences, thought to be harboring Hamas fighters; and leaving an otherwise poor and isolated Gaza in ruins.

In 2009, parliamentary elections in Israel resulted in a virtual tie between Tzipi Livni, the centrist leader of the Kadimi party, and Benyamin Netanyahu, the right-wing leader of Likud. The hawkish Netanyahu, who as prime minister in the 1990s had turned his back on a possible peace settlement with the Palestinians, was once again in the political cockpit.

Camp David Accords

A 1979 agreement by which Israel gave the Sinai back to Egypt in return for Egypt's recognition of Israel's right to exist; the two former enemies established full diplomatic relations and pledged to remain at peace with one another.

intifada

An Arabic word meaning "uprising"; the name given to the prolonged Palestinian uprising against Israeli occupation in the West Bank and Gaza in 1987–1993 and again in 2001–2002.

The dramatic events in the Arab World—including the Arab Spring and Egyptian Revolution, the overthrow of Muammar Qaddafi in Libya, Iran's nuclear ambitions, and the civil war in Syria—again brought that troubled region to the brink of war in 2011 and 2012. In the Middle East, the more things change, the more they stay the same.

Despite all, Israel is a functioning parliamentary democracy. Like the United Kingdom, it does not have a written constitution. But that's where the similarity ends. In Israel, security takes precedence over all other values, including the rule of law: Thus, to protect the 5.7 million Jews who comprise the 75% majority, there are severe restrictions on the civil liberties of the roughly 1.14 million Arabs who are also citizens of Israel but now constitute only 20% of the population. Nonetheless, all Israeli citizens enjoy the right to vote in free elections, criticize the government, engage in peaceful protests, and emigrate.

Knesset
The unicameral Israeli parliament.

In one sense, Israel is too democratic. Elections based on a wide-open system of proportional representation, in which even small upstart parties can often win a few seats, mean Israel's **Knesset** or parliament is a free-for-all that is often confusing and chaotic. Governments are forged from coalitions ranging from the center-left to the far right, depending on the mood of the country, the state of relations with Arab neighbors, and the outcome of the most recent election. The elections in January 2013, for example, kept the right-wing Likud coalition and incumbent Prime Minister Netanyahu in office, but this surprised even close observers and gave hawkish politicians pause. Why? The simple answer is contained in a *New York Times* headline: "Tepid Vote for Netanyahu in Israel Is Seen as a Rebuke." The article noted: "Over all, his conservative team came in first, but it was the center, led by the political novice Yair Lapid, 49, that emerged newly invigorated, suggesting that at the very least Israel's rightward tilt may be stalled."[19]

The occurrence of one crisis after another has probably saved Israel from the consequences of a contentious political culture and a chaotic party system—among them a great deal of governmental instability. Nonetheless, Israel remains a marvel of economic and political survival in a hostile environment. The examples of India and Israel as parliamentary democracies functioning under extremely adverse circumstances do not prove that popular self-government can work everywhere, but they demonstrate that it can work in some very unlikely places.

THE ADAPTABILITY OF DEMOCRACY

The examples of France, Germany, Japan, India, and Israel suggest that democracy is surprisingly adaptable. There are always idealists and dreamers who choose to believe it can be made to work everywhere, but that is probably not the case. One of the lessons of Vietnam, Iraq, and Afghanistan is that democracy can seldom be imposed on a society against its will. The imposition of democratic rule in Germany and Japan after World War II occurred under extraordinary circumstances—these two defeated powers were at the mercy of the victors and, as such, were only too grateful to have a second chance at self-governance. At the same time, the fact that democracy has now taken root in these two countries points to its adaptability.

Virtually every government in the world today, no matter how tyrannical, tries to give the *appearance* of constitutionalism and claims to be democratic. Indeed, democracy is, by definition, popular. It is no surprise that the idea of government "of the people, by the people, and for the people" has broad appeal—broad, but by no means universal.

The Islamic societies of North Africa, the Middle East, and South Asia, for example, have religion-based cultures and legal systems incompatible with the individualism, secularism, religious tolerance, and permissiveness inherent in the idea of liberal democracy. If it's true that people cannot be forced to be free, it's equally true that starving people cannot eat freedom. For people who are starving, democracy is a vague and meaningless abstraction. Any government that can alleviate the misery of daily existence is a good government.

But it would also be a mistake to sell democracy short. Many commentators attributed the failure of Germany's Weimar Republic to an allegedly ingrained antidemocratic passion for order and authority among the Germans. By the same token, Japan had virtually no experience with democracy before World War II, and its consensus-based patron–client culture appeared to be at odds with the basic principles of democracy. And who would have thought democracy had any chance of succeeding in India?

Are these nations exceptions that prove the rule? The experiences of such diverse countries as France, Germany, Japan, India, and Israel suggest that constitutional democracy is a surprisingly adaptable form of government that can work in a variety of social, cultural, and economic contexts. But the fact that it has yet to take root in the Islamic world or Africa is a cautionary note—one we ignore at our own peril.

PARLIAMENT OR PRESIDENT? A BRIEF COMPARISON

The purpose of legislatures in both systems is to enact laws, levy taxes, control expenditures, and oversee the executive. But, despite these similarities, the British parliament is surprisingly different from the U.S. Congress.

In the British tradition, Parliament is sovereign. According to Sir William Blackstone (1723–1780), the famed British jurist, Parliament can do "everything that is not naturally impossible." In the words of another authoritative writer, "This concept of **parliamentary sovereignty** is of great importance and distinguishes Britain from most other democratic countries. Parliament may enact any law it likes, and no other body can set the law aside on the grounds that it is unconstitutional or undesirable."[20] In contrast, the U.S. system places the Constitution above even Congress. Ever since the 1803 case of *Marbury v. Madison*, in which Chief Justice John Marshall used an obscure provision in the Judiciary Act of 1789 to establish the principle of **judicial review**, the U.S. Supreme Court has successfully asserted its right and duty to overturn any law passed by Congress it deems unconstitutional.[21]

In both systems, of course, legislatures can pass or defeat proposed new laws, both confirm new cabinet ministers, and both have oversight powers. But there

parliamentary sovereignty
In the United Kingdom, the unwritten constitutional principle that makes the British Parliament the supreme law-making body; laws passed by Parliament are not subject to judicial review and cannot be rejected by the Crown.

judicial review
The power of a court to declare acts by the government unconstitutional and hence void.

Question Time
In the United Kingdom, the times set aside Monday through Thursday every week for Her Majesty's Loyal Opposition (the party out of power) to criticize and scrutinize the actions and decisions of the government (the party in power); each week, the prime minister must answer hostile questions fired at him or her by the opposition or backbenchers.

is nothing in the U.S. Congress to compare with the **Question Time** in the British Parliament, when the various government ministers are required to answer questions submitted by MPs. Question Time occurs Mondays through Thursdays. On Wednesdays, the prime minister answers questions from 12:00 to 12:30 P.M. The questions, which run the gamut from the trenchant to the trivial, are aimed at clarifying issues, focusing public attention, eliciting information, and holding the government accountable for its actions (or its failure to act). Question Time is when the Opposition can and does go on the attack. It is representative democracy at its best.

A key difference between the two political systems lies in the extent to which the legislature determines the makeup of the executive branch. As we noted earlier, the prime minister is the leader of the majority party in Parliament. Government ministers (the cabinet) are prominent members of the majority party. Because the parliamentary system blurs distinctions between legislative and executive powers, it is often difficult to determine where the authority of one branch begins and that of the other leaves off.

No such fusion of powers exists under the presidential system of government. Unlike senators and representatives, presidents enjoy a *national* popular mandate, and the presidency derives its powers from a separate section of the Constitution. But Congress can refuse to confirm cabinet appointments, hold public hearings, subpoena government officials, censure those who violate the law or the public trust, and, in extreme cases, impeach presidents for abuse of power (the Constitution cites "treason, high crimes, and misdemeanors").

Unlike Parliament, however, Congress does not have the power to bring down the executive by a vote of no confidence. Even if Congress votes down a key program proposed by the White House, the president will normally remain in office for a full four-year term. Unless a president dies in office or resigns, he or she can be removed only by impeachment, and no U.S. president has ever been impeached *and* convicted.

The executive branch of government comprises the head of government and the head of state, the cabinet, and the bureaucracy. In the U.S. system, the president is the head of government *and* the chief of state; in the British system, the executive is divided between the prime minister (head of government) and the monarch (head of state).

Presidents in the United States also enjoy the security of a fixed term. By contrast, the British prime minister's position depends on his or her ability to retain the confidence of a majority in the House of Commons. Prime ministers frequently are forced to step down either because public opinion turns against them or because they lose on a key vote in Parliament.

Common law
In Great Britain, laws derived from consistent precedents found in judges' rulings and decisions, as opposed to those enacted by Parliament. In the United States, the part of the common law that was in force at the time of the Revolution and not nullified by the Constitution or any subsequent statute.

Despite significant differences in the structures of their court systems, both the United States and Great Britain share what is generally known as the common law tradition. **Common law** is based on decisions made by judges rather than laws promulgated by legislatures. The idea dates back at least as far as the twelfth century, when Henry II sought to implement a system by which judges were charged with enforcing the king's law while taking into account local customs. In the process of resolving disputes, each judge made, and sent to London, a record of the legal proceedings. Over the years, certain common themes and legal principles emerged from these records, and magistrates turned to certain celebrated judicial decisions for guidance. In time, these precedents and decisions were codi-fied by judicial commentators—the most famous being William Blackstone—and were carried to all corners of the globe, including the American colonies.

Notwithstanding this shared common law background, the legal systems of the United States and Great Britain differ with respect to selection of judges, organiza-tion of the judiciary, powers of judicial review, and other key structural matters.

Perhaps the most important *political* difference between the two judicial systems has to do with the power of judges to uphold or strike down legislative or executive actions. In the United States, both state and federal courts review the acts of the other branches of government—state courts on the basis of state constitutions and federal courts on the basis of the U.S. Constitution.

In contrast, British judges play only a limited role in governing. Whereas the question of constitutionality hovers over every legislative and executive act in the United States, in Great Britain the judiciary does not possess the power to overturn an act of Parliament. Nor do British judges act as constitutional guardians of civil liberties, as U.S. judges do whenever they assert the primacy of individual rights over legislative acts. Only rarely do British judges rule that the executive branch has overstepped its legal bounds.

In the view of one scholar, "The parliamentary system is a Cadillac among governments" and the presidential system is a "Model T."[22] Parliamentary sys-tems are often highly sensitive to public opinion. Political parties campaign on distinct, well-defined platforms. If the election outcome results in a strong mandate for one party, the resulting government is likely to succeed in pushing its program through Parliament. If government policies prove unpopular or impracticable or if the government falls into disrepute for any reason whatso-ever, the prime minister or the ruling party can be replaced with no major shock to the political system as a whole. Party discipline in the British parliamentary system makes it more efficient than the often deadlocked U.S. Congress.

The U.S. presidential system, critics have asserted, is too often marked by deadlocks stemming from the checks and balances built into its tripartite struc-ture. Too often, one party controls the presidency and another controls the Congress. Moreover, it is very difficult to remove an incompetent or unpopular president from office. In addition, an ossified two-party system leaves many groups and interests underrepresented in the Congress.

Finally, many critics contend that the Electoral College is a dinosaur that makes the popular election of the president a farce. In this view, the practice of choosing electors on a winner-takes-all basis puts the will of the people in jeopardy—witness the 2000 election in which Al Gore won the popular vote but George W. Bush won the White House.

SUMMARY

The British parliamentary model features a fusion of powers, indefinite terms of office, disciplined parties, and a dual executive. This model of constitutional democracy has been imitated more widely (except in Latin America) than the U.S. model. It is especially influential in Europe, where it has inspired most of the constitutional democracies in existence.

France is a hybrid form of constitutional democracy, combining features of both the U.S. and the British systems. Germany features a parliamentary system but differs from both France and Great Britain in that it is federal (comprising states called *Länder*), rather than unitary. Japan is also a parliamentary democracy. Politically, it differs from Europe in its political culture rather than its political structure. Japan has incorporated a consensus-based society with informal, highly personal networks of political power based on patron–client relations into a set of political institutions that, on the surface, appear to be made in Europe. (Actually, they were made in America during the U.S. occupation after World War II.)

India and Israel are two unlikely candidates for republican rule, yet they have both survived as parliamentary democracies for more than half a century. Their examples suggest the parliamentary model is highly adaptable and has wide application, even in places that appear too troubled or turbulent for elections to occur or stable governments to endure.

The U.S. and British systems invite comparisons and offer provocative contrasts in the legislative, executive, and judicial areas. It is difficult to say which system is better in the abstract; the answer exists only within the specific context and circumstances of each nation.

KEY TERMS

parliamentary
  system   147
mixed regime   148
no-confidence vote   150
party discipline   150
Loyal Opposition   151
dual executive   155
National Assembly   156
divided executive   157
Weimar Republic   160

Bundestag   163
Bundesrat   163
Meiji Restoration   168
Moghuls   176
British Raj   177
Lok Sabha   178
Rajya Sabha   178
Zionism   179
Balfour
  Declaration   179

Camp David
  Accords   181
intifada   181
Knesset   182
parliamentary
  sovereignty   183
judicial review   183
Question Time   184
common law   184

REVIEW QUESTIONS

1. Why is the British political system often considered a model of parliamentary democracy?
2. What are the basic operating principles of the parliamentary system?
3. How can the British manage without a written constitution?
4. When did the current French republic come into being and under what circumstances?
5. Compare and contrast democracy in France with democracy in the United States and the United Kingdom. (Trick question: Which country did France model its own political system after?)
6. When did Japan adopt the parliamentary system and under what circumstances?
7. Compare and contrast democracy in Japan with democracy in France and Great Britain.
8. Comment on the significance of parliamentary democracy in India and Israel.
9. Compare the strengths and weaknesses of parliamentary versus presidential rule.

States and Economies in Transition

Between Democracy and Yesterday

The Collapse of Communism
Russia: Old Habits Die Hard
Eastern Europe: Two-Track
    Transition

Two Asian Tigers: Still Role Models?
Latin America: A New Day
    Dawning?

THINK ABOUT IT

What is a transitional state?

Is Russia a constitutional democracy or an authoritarian state disguised as a democracy?

How close are the former Soviet "satellite states" to completing the transition process?

What Asian states have made significant progress toward liberal democracy in recent times?

What are four major transitional states in Latin America, and why is liberalization in these countries a big deal?

On December 31, 1991, the Union of Soviet Socialist Republics (USSR), one of two superpowers that had dominated world politics for nearly half a century, ceased to exist. The demise of the Soviet Union (as it was commonly called) stands as one of the most momentous political events of the twentieth century. Although the end came as a surprise, it was not without warning signs. The Soviet Union had been going through a fascinating but turbulent period of change since 1985, when Mikhail Gorbachev, the country's charismatic leader, launched a series of bold reforms.

The disintegration of the Soviet order ushered in a new era in world politics. It also drew attention to fatal flaws in the nature and structure of centrally planned economies lacking the flexibility, efficiencies, and incentives built into competitive markets. In Russia, the tradition of autocratic rule continues to cast a long shadow over a society that has never known the constitutional guarantees and civil liberties taken for granted in the West. In most of the other former communist states, the transition has gone farther, faster.

The concept of "states in transition" applies to many countries in the so-called developing regions of the world as well: Asia, Africa, and Latin America. Following a look at the problems facing Russia and Eastern Europe, we take a brief look at several Asian and Latin American countries in various stages of transition toward a market-based representative democracy.

THE COLLAPSE OF COMMUNISM

For all practical purposes, the Communist World ceased to exist in 1989. In 1988, before the end of the Cold War, fifteen states could be classified as Communist. A decade later, the number had shrunk to only five or six states—China, Cuba, Laos, North Korea, Vietnam, and perhaps Cambodia—each pursuing independent policies. Only North Korea remains an unreconstructed Stalinist state. It no longer makes any sense to talk about a "Communist threat." What happened?

Eastern Europe abruptly abandoned Communist rule in 1989, ahead of the collapse of the Soviet Union in 1991. Thereafter, democracy and privatization (the process of turning formerly state-run enterprises over to the private sector) advanced rapidly in Poland, Hungary, the Czech Republic, and Slovakia, as well as in the Baltic States (Latvia, Lithuania, and Estonia). Romania and Bulgaria have followed suit, but at a slower pace. The former East Germany is a special case, having merged with West Germany in 1990.

RUSSIA: OLD HABITS DIE HARD

As the 1990s began, the Soviet Union—or "Russia" prior to the end of World War I in 1918—stood as one of the last of the world's great empires (the United States and Communist China were two others) (see Figure 8.1). The Stalinist state that remained in place until 1991 displayed all the classic features of totalitarian rule, including centralized control over the armed forces, the media, and the economy; a dominant monopoly party; an official ideology; and

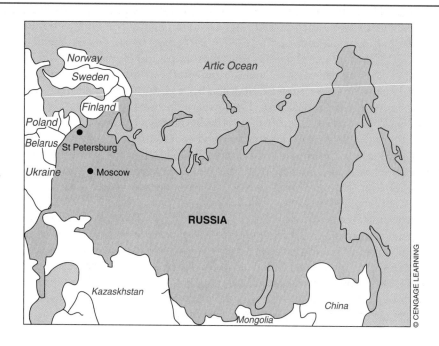

FIGURE 8.1 Sixty percent of Russia (including Siberia) is located east of the Urals, in Asia. Russia is so vast that if you board a train in St. Petersburg and go all the way to Vladivostok you pass through no fewer than eleven time zones.

a systematic program of terror against suspected political opponents and the mass murder of innocents deemed unworthy (or dangerous) by the regime. The story of how the former Soviet Union emerged from the long dark winter of totalitarianism provides the essential background for understanding the nature of Russian politics today.

The Decline and Fall of a Superpower

When Mikhail Gorbachev became General Secretary of the Communist Party in 1985, the Soviet Union faced daunting political and economic problems. The USSR was falling behind the West and, looking east, the People's Republic of China was stirring. Gorbachev recognized the need for radical reforms; and because the Communist Party monopolized power, he made a risky decision—a kind of wager with the devil—to transfigure the Soviet political system in order to save it.

From the time Lenin assumed power in 1917, the Soviet Union had featured a *command economy* in which all important economic decisions (such as what and how much was to be produced and so on) were made at the uppermost level of the Communist Party. Competition, the pursuit of profits, and most forms of private ownership were forbidden as inconsistent with the tenets of Communism.

This system of central planning succeeded in making the Soviet Union a first-rate military power, but at a crushing cost to the consumer economy, which was all but nonexistent. Grossly distorted budget priorities and mounting debt were disguised by artificial prices, press censorship, and secrecy. By the mid-1980s, the Soviet Union was at a huge competitive disadvantage with industrialized democratic nations such as the United States, Japan, and the members of the European Union, and it was falling further behind all the time.[1]

Most Soviet citizens led relatively austere lives with few of the conveniences Westerners took for granted. Soviet economists estimated about one-fourth of all grain harvested each year was lost before it got to the market. As a result, meat and dairy consumption for the average Soviet citizen declined nearly 30%.[2] Store shelves were often empty and spare parts unavailable. According to one estimate, women spent an average of two hours a day, seven days a week, waiting in line to purchase the few basic goods available.[3] In the twilight of the Soviet era, an estimated 28% of the Soviet population lived below the official Soviet poverty line.[4]

While the Soviet economy decayed and the quality of life for the general populace deteriorated, growing social problems threatened the very fabric of Soviet society. Among the worst were alcoholism and corruption. Another major problem was a widening technology gap. Soviet managers had little encouragement to invest in new technologies (computers, cell phones, robotics), and the party feared (rightly, it turned out) that the coming Digital Age and the Internet (already on the horizon in the 1980s) would jeopardize its information monopoly.

At the root of these problems was central planning, which discouraged initiative. Plant managers and directors of government-run farms remained tied to a central plan that imposed rigid quotas on factory and farm production. Plan fulfillment was the highest priority for all Soviet economic administrators. The Stalinist system sacrificed quality for quantity. Because of relentless pressures to meet overly ambitious production quotas, managers often took shortcuts and cooked the books to conceal failures or paper over problems.

The cynicism of the managers was matched by the low morale of the Soviet workers, who were underemployed, unhappily employed, or simply not motivated to work. "The party pretends to pay us, and we pretend to work." This cynicism was fed by the hypocrisy of high party officials, who espoused egalitarian ideals but lived in secluded luxury while the proletariat they glorified had to stand in long lines to buy bread and other staples.[5] The result was appallingly low productivity, shoddy work, and poor quality.

An entrenched elite known as the **nomenklatura** occupied all the top positions in the Soviet system.[6] Included in this system of power and privilege were key members of the party and state bureaucracy. The hidden world of luxury apartments, specialty shops, vacation resorts, hospitals, health spas, and schools was an open secret—one that stood in sharp contrast to the bleak existence of ordinary Soviet citizens and made a mockery of the "classless society" Marx had envisioned.

In short, Gorbachev faced a stark choice: push reforms or preside over the death of the Soviet state. In the end, he did both.

nomenklatura
The former Soviet Communist Party's system of controlling all important administrative appointments, thereby ensuring the support and loyalty of those who managed day-to-day affairs.

perestroika
Term given to Mikhail Gorbachev's various attempts to restructure the Soviet economy while not completely sacrificing its socialist character.

The Politics of Reform

Gorbachev's reforms became known to the world as **perestroika** (restructuring) and **glasnost** (transparency), plus a promise of **democratization**. Clearly, what Gorbachev had in mind was nothing less than a state-controlled revolution from above. Unfortunately, the revolution spun out of control.

The goal of perestroika was to revitalize the ossified system of central planning. Gorbachev endeavored to reduce the power of the entrenched party and state bureaucracy; improve worker productivity; change the culture of cheating, stealing, and cynicism; and so on. But serious market reforms—breaking up the woefully inefficient state enterprises, introducing real competition, or privatization—were not in the picture. Hence, perestroika became a catchy political slogan rather than a coherent economic policy. By 1989, the Soviet economy was rapidly disintegrating, and within two years it had plunged into a depression.

Glasnost brought a major relaxation of media censorship, and for a time won popular sympathy for Gorbachev, while distracting public attention from the disastrous war in Afghanistan, the poor economy, and the disarray in the party and state bureaucracies. Glasnost also had wide appeal beyond Soviet borders, making Gorbachev the darling of the world press and a popular figure in many Western countries.

The real purpose behind glasnost was to expose the official corruption and incompetence Gorbachev blamed for the country's economic malaise. He wanted to shake the change-resistant Soviet bureaucracy out of its lethargy and change the public attitude toward work and the workplace.

But glasnost quickly became a force unto itself. Previously censored books and movies flourished; the state-controlled mass media dared to criticize the government; newspapers and magazines published scorching articles challenging the official version of history and current events. By allowing public dissent, glasnost severely undermined the legitimacy of the ruling Communist Party and dispelled the fears that kept the Soviet system afloat.

Finally, Gorbachev also called for democratization of the political system, including elections that allowed voters a limited choice at the polls. Taken together these reforms, in effect, let the genie out of the bottle.

glasnost
Literally "openness"; this term refers to Mikhail Gorbachev's curtailment of censorship and encouragement of political discussion and dissent within the former Soviet Union.

democratization
Mikhail Gorbachev's policy of encouraging democratic reforms within the former Soviet Union, including increased electoral competition within the Communist Party.

Mikhail Gorbachev instituted bold political and economic policies to reform communism and the Communist Party during his leadership from March 1985 until August 1991. Ultimately, these initiatives exacerbated the crisis of the Stalinist state and helped precipitate the downfall of communism throughout Eastern Europe. Ironically, Gorbachev was far more liberal and reform-minded than Russia's longest ruling, popularly elected, post-Communist leader, President Vladimir Putin.

© ITAR-TASS PHOTO AGENCY / ALAMY

The Collapse of the Soviet Empire

Gorbachev's reforms failed miserably. Popular expectations rose while living standards fell dramatically, creating a politically volatile situation. Galloping inflation and labor strikes, both previously unheard of, dangerously destabilized the Soviet state.

As the end of the Soviet empire drew near, the so-called Nationality Question loomed ever larger. In 1991, the seventeen largest nationalities accounted for more than 90% of the Soviet population (about 294 million people). The majority Russians accounted for only slightly more than half the total. Some twenty ethnic groups numbered more than 1 million. Among the largest were the fifteen nationalities for whom the union republics are named plus the Tatars, Poles, Germans, Jews, and others less familiar to the outside world (Table 8.1). In total, the Soviet Union encompassed more than one hundred different nationalities, speaking some 130 languages.

Historically, the Kremlin was not averse to the use of brute force to assimilate non-Russian groups. Another primary instrument of state policy was the education system. All schoolchildren throughout the Soviet Union were required to learn Russian.

Gorbachev's reforms emboldened non-Russian nationalities to demand self-determination. Glasnost, in particular, encouraged criticism of local officials. The independence movement broke out in the Baltic States first. The spirit of rebellion swept across the Soviet empire, as republic after republic declared its independence.

TABLE 8.1   Major Nationalities in the Soviet Union at the Time of Its Demise (1989).

Nationality	Percent of Total Population[a]	Nationality	Percent of Total Population[a]
1. Russian	50.78	11. Moldovan	1.17
2. Ukrainian	15.47	12. Lithuanian	1.07
3. Uzbek	5.84	13. Turkish	0.95
4. Belarusian	3.50	14. Kirgiz	0.85
5. Kazakh	2.84	15. German	0.71
6. Azerbaijani	2.38	16. Chuvash	0.64
7. Tatar	2.32	17. Latvian	0.51
8. Armenian	1.62	18. Jewish[b]	0.50
9. Tajik	1.48	19. Bashkir	0.50
10. Georgian	1.39	20. Polish	0.39

[a]These figures are adapted from the last official census of the Soviet Union.
[b]The former Soviet Union classified Jews as a nationality.

SOURCE: *Population Today*, November 1991, Population Reference Bureau. Reprinted by permission.

In August 1991, a group of eight hard-line Communist Party traditional-ists with ties to the army and the KGB (the Soviet secret police) staged a coup, which ultimately failed. Boris Yeltsin, the president of the Russian republic, saved the day, rallying demonstrators who had taken to the streets to fight for democracy. The Soviet Union ceased to exist on the last day of 1991.

Contemporary Challenges

A downsized Russian state and a loose, face-saving confederation consisting of all former Soviet republics except the Baltic States emerged from the ashes of the extinct Soviet Union. Boris Yeltsin turned out to be a colorful but quixotic character, ill suited to the big tasks he faced as the new Russia's first elected president. By contrast, his successor is the exact opposite: a no-nonsense politi-cal boss with little imagination and a notable lack of charisma, but an iron will (see "Ideas and Politics").

Russia has roughly three-fourths the landmass, about half the population, and approximately three-fifths the GNP of the Soviet Union. Even so, it is still by far the world's largest country, encompassing an area roughly twice the size of Canada, the United States, or China, and possesses the massive nuclear arsenal it inherited from its superpower predecessor. Ukraine, Kazakhstan, and Belarus fell heir to the nuclear weapons deployed outside Russia proper. Ukraine and Kazakhstan promised to relinquish control of these weapons to Moscow, but they demanded economic and financial concessions in return. Belarus demurred. All three eventually came around to the view that possessing nuclear weapons was a liability. The 9/11 terrorist attacks on the United States raised new fears that weapons of mass destruction might fall into the hands of international terrorists. Fortunately, by that time all ABC weapons (atomic, biological, and chemical) stamped "Made in the USSR" had reportedly been removed to Russia.

Economic Dislocations In the 1990s, the Russian economy went from bad to worse. By the middle of the decade, output dropped by one-third and hyperin-flation stalked Russian consumers like a great plague.[8] Year after year, the vital statistics—GDP growth, productivity, prices, wages—told a grim story.[9] Failure to crack down on organized crime was partially to blame for the deep malaise, as was official corruption that, among other things, turned the privatization program into a bonanza for crooks.

A grossly mismanaged privatization program allowed crooks—operating behind the scenes, greasing palms, and using Kremlin connections—to gain control of huge chunks of the Russian economy. In this way, the sell-off of state assets at fire sale prices created multimillionaires ("oligarchs") while most Rus-sians sank deeper into poverty. Meanwhile, Russia lacked the legal and financial structures necessary for the development of a diversified economy capable of competing in a global marketplace.

Under Yeltsin most Russians perceived they were worse off than under Com-munism. A decade later with Putin at the helm the picture was much brighter.[10] The reason: a sudden steep rise in oil and natural gas prices on the world market

PUTIN: The "Black Belt" Tsar

Russians often express nostalgia for a strong leader ("boss") like Stalin, Nicolas II, or Ivan the Terrible. Vladimir Putin is the latest incarnation of a strong Kremlin boss. A former KGB agent with a black belt in karate, Putin is ruthless and rock-ribbed in his determination to stay in power.

Several examples illustrate his no-nonsense style of leadership: Putin withdrew from the START II treaty in June 2002, one day after the United States withdrew from the antiballistic missile (ABM) treaty.[7] (SALT II was the successor to the original Strategic Arms Limitation Treaty, or SALT I, between the United States and the Soviet Union in 1972, cutting the number and type of nuclear weapons each side could deploy.) In October 2002, when fifty Chechen rebels seized 800 hostages inside a Moscow theater, Putin ordered Russian commandos to move in, using poison gas to incapacitate the guerrillas. Nearly all the guerillas died, as well as 129 hostages.

In October 2003, Putin ordered Mikhail Khodorkovsky, the richest man in Russia at the time, arrested and jailed on charges of tax evasion. Khodorkovsky was sentenced to nine years in prison in 2005. In December 2010, after serving seven years of his original nine-year prison term, Khodorkovsky was once again placed on trial—this time on new charges of embezzlement. To no one's surprise, he was again found guilty and sentenced to an additional fourteen years in prison. Critics of both trials suggested the motive was political; in 2003, Khodorkovsky had been a potential candidate for president. In 2010, Putin wanted to make certain that Khodorkovsky would still be in prison in 2012, when he (Putin) would again be eligible to run for president.

Putin won reelection in 2004 by a landslide. Under the Russian constitution, a sitting president can serve no more than two consecutive terms. In 2008, Putin's protégé, Dimitry Medvedev, was elected to succeed his boss, winning about 70% of the popular vote with Putin's endorsement. Medvedev then named Putin prime minister—a convenient arrangement that honored the letter of the law but left Putin in charge.

As planned, in 2012 Medvedev and Putin again traded places with what critics viewed as only a

Vladimir Putin is Russia's second president since the fall of Soviet communism. When Yeltsin named him premier in 1999, Putin was an obscure figure who had served for many years as a KGB recruiter. In 2001, this former Soviet spy became an important U.S. ally in President George W. Bush's war on terror. However, relations soured after the U.S. invasion of Iraq; and at the Munich Security Conference in February 2007, Putin bitterly denounced the United States for allegedly provoking a new global arms race.

paper-thin veneer of constitutional legitimacy. Putin tightly controlled the state-run television. Meanwhile, reports of widespread vote rigging led Putin's detractors and much of the world press to dismiss the election as a sham.

Ironically, Putin is now a very divisive force in a country with a history of mass action that produced one of the most consequential revolutions of the last century. The biggest demonstrations in Moscow since the collapse of the Soviet state more than two decades ago were provoked by Putin's decision to grab another term as Russia's president. To that end, Putin applied the full power of the state apparatus—including state-controlled media—to ensure the "election" would have the outcome he desired.

in the post-9/11 period. A major producer and exporter of fossil fuels (oil and natural gas), Russia reaped windfall profits before the global recession drove world oil prices down in 2008.[11]

In short order, Russia paid off its external debt and amassed one of the world's largest foreign-currency surpluses during this period of irrational exuberance, but ultimately failed to capitalize. By failing to diversify the Russian economy or to create a business environment attractive to foreign investors, Putin squandered Russia's energy-export windfall. The downside of Russia's extreme dependence on energy exports became evident when world oil and gas prices collapsed and export revenues plummeted in 2008 and 2009.

Ethnic Conflict Civil war, religious persecution, and ethnic strife followed in the wake of the Soviet breakup in 1991. Centrifugal forces—antagonistic ethnic groups, demands for independence, and terrorist acts—have taxed the Kremlin's patience and resources, and marred its image in the eyes of the world.

Under the 1993 constitution, ethnic groups form the basis for the twenty-one republics in the new Russian Federation (successor to the USSR). These federal units, similar to state governments in the United States, are represented as *republics* in the upper house of the Russian legislature.

Unfortunately, enmities rooted in history, culture, and prejudice born of rivalry, injury, and envy are not easily erased. Russia's nationality problem was put on display in December 1994, when Russia attacked Chechnya, a Muslim republic the size of Connecticut. When Chechnya declared independence and talks failed to produce a settlement, Yeltsin sent Soviet troops to put down the revolt. In the ensuing war, Russian warplanes bombed the Chechen capital of Grozny. Russian troops—reflecting widespread public skepticism (and mindful of Russia's disastrous war against Afghanistan in the 1980s)—lacked the same high level of

The wars in Bosnia and Chechnya are often called "dirty wars" because uniformed soldiers (not insurgents or "terrorists") as a matter of strategy and policy deliberately attacked and targeted civilians. Such acts are outlawed under the rules and conventions of warfare going at least as far back as the Geneva Convention of 1864. No wars are civilized; the wars in Bosnia and Chechnya were particularly barbaric (hence the term "dirty").

OLEG NIKISHIN/AFP/GETTY IMAGES

commitment as the Chechens. Not surprisingly, the invaders suffered heavy casualties.

Faced with a formidable enemy, a failing economy, a demoralized public, and a rising tide of negative world opinion, Yeltsin moved to end the dirty war in Chechnya. A truce signed in late 1996 put the question of Chechnya's independence on the back burner; in other words, it settled nothing. In 1999, it was Yeltsin's deputy, Vladimir Putin, who directed the brutal crackdown that subdued the Chechen rebels. Putin's success made him a hero to nationalists still fighting mad over Russia's lost empire.

Family Matters: Ukraine For Russian nationalists, losing Ukraine was the biggest blow, akin to losing a family member. Russians and Ukrainians come from the same ethnic stock and (to a larger extent than Ukrainian nationalists care to admit) share a common history, religion, and culture.

Family feuds can become very nasty, very fast. Nations are no different. In 2005–2006 in the middle of a cold hard winter, when Moscow announced a fourfold increase in the price of natural gas, Kiev balked. Putin cut off natural gas supplies to Ukraine, but eventually agreed to a compromise somewhat more acceptable to Kiev.

Russia again cut off natural gas supplies to Ukraine in the winter of 2008–2009. Why? Putin used an economic tool (natural gas) as political leverage. Specifically, Ukraine's dependence on Russia for its energy supplies meant (means) the Kremlin could (and still can) punish Kiev for being too pro-EU, pro-NATO, and pro-Western at will—a classic example of one state using economic means to coerce or blackmail another state.*

Tensions between Russia and Ukraine are based on history as well as economics and international politics. Ukraine, and specifically the city of Kiev, is the ancient birthplace of Russia. It is one of the largest countries in Eastern Europe, with a population of approximately 40 million, roughly the size of neighboring Poland's population. Within Ukraine, situated on a strategic peninsula, is the Crimea, an important piece of real estate on the banks of the Black Sea.

Crimea's current inhabitants are Great Russians, who replaced the indigenous population after Stalin sent the Crimean Tatars (famous as formidable warriors) into internal exile to Siberia in the 1930s. A dispute in the mid-1990s over control of former Soviet naval facilities and forces at Sevastopol, a historic Crimean port city, arose from ambiguities and conflicting interests. Although it was resolved peacefully in 1997 (Russia got 80% of the fleet but conceded the port to Ukraine), it resurfaced again in 2008 during Russia's war with Georgia (see "Maps That Matter").

Relations between Russia and other former republics, for example, Kazakhstan and Moldova, are often strained as well. Troubled ethnic relations on Russia's borders continue to be mirrored by tensions inside the Russian Republic. Chechnya is by no means the only potential internal trouble spot: In fifteen of

---

*It's not nice, but in politics nothing succeeds like success. Economic coercion often works better than military coercion (think USSR in Afghanistan in the 1980s, the United States in Iraq from 2003 to 2011, or the United States in Afghanistan today).

GEORGIA: Between Russia and the West

FIGURE 8.2 Map of Caucus Region.

SOURCE: University of Texas Perry-Castañeda Library Map Collection.

No Trespassing: Georgia*

Russia's military invasion of Georgia, a small country of less than 5 million on its southern flank, rekindled memories of the Cold War when the United States and the Soviet Union were bitter rivals. In happier times, the United States made a show of promising Georgia it would not stand alone as it embarked on the path of democracy.

But when Russia attacked in August 2008, the United States was embroiled in two dirty wars (Iraq and Afghanistan) of its own. George W. Bush—a lame duck president already badly overextended in the Middle East and Central Asia—was in no position to do anything but join the chorus of feckless diplomatic protests. On its own, tiny Georgia was no match for the Russian Goliath.

Georgia's desire to join NATO gave Moscow a motive to match its means, a powerful mixture of geopolitics and national pride. From the Kremlin's vantage, the West had profited at Russia's expense, using NATO and the EU to fill the vacuum created by the Soviet collapse. Any further encroachment on Russia's periphery was a provocation to be met with deadly force. Seen in this light, the attack on Georgia put the West on notice: No (more) trespassing!

Nor was the war just about politics. It was also about control of vital oil and natural gas pipelines to the West, about Russia's debut as a post-Soviet global power (which it clearly is by any geopolitical reckoning), and about drawing a line in the sand on Russia's western and southern frontiers. Georgia always has been important to Russia because of its strategic position on the Black Sea, the gateway to the Mediterranean, and its proximity to Iran, Turkey, and the Middle East.

Russia's use of force against a sovereign state friendly to the West was reminiscent of the Cold War. Some things never change.

---

*Adapted from the author's op-ed article in the *Kansas City Star*, August 18, 2008, p. B6.

the twenty-one ethnic republics in Russia today, the titular nationality is in the minority (see Figure 8.2).[12]

State Building Putin recentralized state power at great cost to Russia's fragile democratic institutions. We can summarize the effect of his reverse reforms as follows:

- *A Tattered Constitution.* Putin has greatly enhanced the powers of the executive at the expense of the legislative branch and used the judicial system to intimidate and punish his opponents.

- *Feeble Parties and Fewer Elections.* The Russian party system is weak and badly fragmented. Putin places formidable obstacles in the path of political parties and party leaders who dare to oppose his policies; he abolished elections for regional governors altogether (he handpicks them now).

- *Organized Crime.* According to one estimate, organized crime employed some 3 million people in the mid-1990s; it infiltrated the police and bureaucracy; it also clouded Russia's relations with the West on many levels.[13] Organized crime remains a major blight on civil society in Russia to this day.

- *Disrespect for the Law and the Police.* Crime, corruption, and collusion have contributed to a culture of illegality that's been called "Russia's biggest blight."[14]

Putin: President or Czar?

In August 1999, Yeltsin named Putin, a political unknown, to be his new prime minister; eight months later Putin was the newly elected president of the Russian Federation. As the new boss in the Kremlin, Putin quickly moved to put his personal stamp on Russia's domestic and foreign policies. At home, he moved against Russia's notorious "oligarchs" (wealthy tycoons who gained control over gigantic pieces of the old Soviet economy in the botched privatization program carried out during the Yeltsin era). Abroad, he gave Russia's foreign policy a new look, strongly backing the U.S. campaign against terrorism in the fall of 2001.

Putin also paid tribute to economic reforms, including changes in the tax laws and creation of a financial intelligence service to fight money laundering. Buoyed by high oil prices, the Russian economy revived (Table 8.2). But the basic structures of Russia's protectionist, cartel-dominated, red tape–ridden

TABLE 8.2   Russian Economic Performance, 1992–2010 (% annual change).

	1992	1994	1996	1998	2000	2002	2004	2006	2008	2010	2012
GDP	−14.5	12.6	−6.0	−5.0	9.0	4.0	6.4	7.5	6.0	3.5	3.7
Inflation	2323	202	21.8	82.0	20.2	14.0	12.7	9.2	14.1	7.0	5.1

SOURCE: World Bank and *The Economist* ("Emerging Market Indicators"), July 1, 2000; December 7, 2002; March 27, 2004; February 19, 2005; and December 2, 2006. Data for 2008 and 2010 from Economist Intelligence Unit estimates, *The Economist*, January 31, 2009, p. 101, and December 11, 2010, p. 117.

economy, including such key sectors as utilities, banks, and state-owned enterprises, remain largely unchanged.

Putin's instincts are authoritarian; his methods are Machiavellian. He has eviscerated the independent news media. He relies heavily on the so-called *siloviki* (antidemocratic hard-liners from the old KGB, police, and the army) to run the country and maintain his grip on power.

The fatal poisoning of Alexander Litvinenko in a London restaurant in November 2006 was a chilling reminder that the ghost of Stalin lives on. Litvinenko, who had defected to the United Kingdom six years earlier, was a former colonel in the Russian secret service (the FSB, successor to the KGB) and a vitriolic critic of Putin.

The independent press in Putin's Russia gets little or no protection from the state. Quite the opposite: Journalists and writers who criticize Putin often have a difficult time getting published. Putin's critics are threatened, assaulted, arrested on false charges, and in a few instances, murdered. Politically motivated trials typically result in convictions and imprisonments. A month before the Litvinenko incident, Anna Politkovskaya, a popular and courageous journalist who dared to criticize Putin despite repeated threats and intimidation, was shot dead in Moscow in what many believed to be a contract killing.

Strong-arm methods to intimidate Russia's independent press continue to be reported. To cite one recent example, the head of Russia's Investigative Committee, Alexander Bastrykin, did not like something Sergei Sokolov, the deputy editor of *Novaya Gazeta* (a popular opposition newspaper), wrote about him so Bastrykin arranged a meeting in a forest and threatened to kill him! (Bastrykin first disputed the story, but later made a public apology.) In August 2012, Bastrykin charged Alexander Navalny, a harsh critic of Putin and a leader in the anticorruption movement, with embezzlement (stealing 16 million rubles worth of lumber!)—a crime that carries a maximum prison sentence of ten years. On the same day, the feminist punk rock band Pussy Riot went on trial for blasphemy against the Russian Orthodox faith. Specifically, the three female band members were arrested and jailed in February 2012 after they performed an anti-Putin song in a Moscow cathedral.

Such incidents illustrate the severe limits to press freedom in Putin's Russia. As we are about to see, the same can be said of political opposition.

The Two Faces of Post-Communist Russia

Clearly, Russia has emerged from the dark days of its totalitarian past. Stalin is dead but the legacy of Stalinism is still present in the political culture, and courts of law are tools of state power. The fate of investigative journalists such as Anna Politkovskaya and Putin opponents such as Alexander Litvinenko and Mikhail Khodorkovsky attests to the continuing use of police-state tactics and a corrupt judicial system reminiscent of the Stalinist show trials to suppress dissent.

Legislation in the summer of 2012 was Putin's iron-fisted response to Russia's rising middle class—a phenomenon he helped to create but which has spawned a highly vocal liberal opposition to his rule. One measure imposes heavy fines on protestors who attend unsanctioned street demonstrations. Another forces NGOs receiving funding from abroad to declare themselves "foreign agents" and submit to extraordinary financial audits. A third recriminalizes libel, with fines as high as 5 million rubles (over $150,000). A fourth creates a "blacklist" of websites to be blocked—a thinly disguised form of state censorship.

Even so, Putin is not Stalin and today's Russia is not the Soviet Union. Queuing up for a loaf of bread or a kilo of meat in the freezing cold is no longer part of daily life. The dreaded knock on the door in the middle of the night is a thing of the past, as is the infamous Soviet gulag archipelago—the vast chain of forced labor camps in the Siberian wilderness. Gone too is the Soviet ban on foreign travel.

The horrors of Soviet history are no longer locked away: "*Gulag Archipelago* and other literature, fiction and nonfiction, about Stalin's terror are easily available in bookstores and libraries; academic research is unconstrained."[15] In 2007, Putin visited Butovo, one of the sites where mass executions occurred under the Stalin terror in 1937 and 1938, calling it "insanity"; and in November 2010 the Kremlin admitted that the Soviet Union—*not* Nazi Germany—carried out the atrocity known as the Katyn Forest massacre near the Russian city of Smolensk in 1943.[16]

But Putin continues to rely heavily on Russia's law enforcement agencies—specifically the Federal Security Service (the FSB) and the new Investigative Committee under a Putin crony—to maintain his grip on power. FSB officers and veterans still proudly call themselves *chekisty*—heirs of the Cheka (Lenin's secret police). (Putin himself got his start as a KGB officer under the old Soviet system.)

Putin's relations with the West have been less than cordial and cooperative. From Iran's advancing nuclear ambitions to the civil war in Syria, Russia (along with China) has backed the "wrong" side and blocked attempts to use the UN Security Council to rebuke or punish "bad" actors.

Will Russia Ever Change?

Does Russia represent the remains of a great empire in decay or will it reemerge as a major world power? Is it unalterably authoritarian? The answer to the first question is probably "neither"—Russia will neither self-destruct as the Soviet Union did nor will it recapture the status of world-class superpower the Soviet Union achieved. The answer to the second question is probably "yes"—there is little reason to believe Russia's governmental institutions, power structure, or political culture will change any time soon.

Though the era of totalitarian rule has ended, Russia remains a riddle to the West and the world. The show trial of the rock band in 2012 for blasphemy (since when is that a *crime* rather than a "sin"?) underscored the tenuous and tentative status of democracy in Putin's Russia, as well as the collusive ties, reminiscent of pre-Soviet Russia, between church and the state, patriarch and potentate. Given centuries of despotism and centralized rule, the political culture necessary for liberal democracy to take root and flourish is too weak and the inertia of the past too strong.

Still, in the early 1990s, many dared to hope that Russia was finally shedding its authoritarian habits. But that hope soon faded. With Putin at the helm, it all but vanished—a victim of an autocratic Kremlin boss who recentralized the political system and restored order, but failed to take advantage of windfall profits from Russia's oil and gas exports to modernize and diversify the Russian economy. Failed also to prevent corrupt insiders from secretly diverting billions of rubles into private bank accounts abroad.

Russia's new beginning at the end of the last century contemplated a federation with a parliament and a president whose powers were defined in and limited by a written constitution. Today, Russia is neither federal nor democratic in character. In September 2010, then-President Dmitry Medvedev, Putin's puppet, sacked the powerful mayor of Moscow, Yuri Luzhkov, one of the last of the post-Soviet regional bosses capable of challenging Putin's authority from within.

Still, Putin is not as powerful as his autocratic predecessors, as the mass protests in 2012 against his grab for a third presidential term show. The rise of a predominantly liberal Russian middle class wishing for a government modeled on the parliamentary democracies of Western Europe is now a major impediment to Putin's autocratic ruling style and heavy-handed methods—what one Western journalist has called Russia's "mafia state."[17]

Putin and the old-style Russian politics are now badly out of step with changes in Russian society. At first, high oil prices allowed Putin to restore a measure of popular trust in the paternalistic state, which had fallen into disrepute in the decay, despair, and turbulence of the 1990s. By the late 2000s, however, Russia's newly emerging middle class constituted 25% of the population and nearly 40% of the workforce. In Russia's major cities, notably Moscow and St. Petersburg, these numbers were even higher.

Considering that until now Russia has never had a middle class, this socioeconomic transformation promises to create ever-greater pressure on Russia's political rulers and institutions. As more and more Russians are advancing economically, they are finding it less and less tolerable to be shut out politically. This fact is reflected in polls showing that many Russians have lost trust in Putin and believe the country is stagnating.

Russians are realists: The perception of stagnation is firmly rooted in facts. Revitalizing the Russian economy is one of the big challenges facing Putin in the coming years. Corruption—fraud, bribery, blackmail—are pervasive problems. Bureaucratic red tape is yet another. Foreign investors are understandably reluctant to take the risks associated with doing business in Russia.

But Russia is a big country with vast human and natural resources. In 2012, Russia finally joined the World Trade Organization (WTO), a major step toward opening the Russian economy to global competition and establishing normal trade relations for the first time in Russian history. Russia has considerable potential for creating export markets beyond oil and natural gas, including passenger cars, vans, commercial vehicles (ambulances, fire engines, trucks, and buses), as well as helicopters, electronics, optical instruments, and metallurgy. Perhaps Russia's biggest gamble in its bid for an industrial revival is on the MC-21, a commercial airliner designed to challenge Boeing and Airbus.

Starting in 2009, Russia kicked off the new campaign to reindustrialize with the creation of a restructuring agency called Russian Technologies (RT).[18] Since that time, some 600 industrial firms and an estimated 900,000 employees have been transferred to RT's control. The strategic plan calls for RT to float high-quality companies on the stock market eventually. Interestingly, RT is required to find new jobs for any workers laid off (a rather different approach to "creative destruction" than the one venture capitalist and 2012 presidential candidate Mitt Romney put into practice at Bain Capital).

Finally, Moscow is making a bid to create a Russian "Silicon Valley" at a place called Skolkovo outside Moscow. This ambitious project is a special economic zone (SEZ), modeled after China's SEZs (see Chapter 5), credited with catapulting the PRC to the front ranks of the world's major economies in the short span of three decades. Whether Skolkovo will materialize into something more than a pipedream remains an open question. Nonetheless, it is a sign of the times—and Putin's sense of urgency—in the face of new forces and rising powers in the global economy that are rapidly leaving Russia in the dust.

We turn next to a brief look at Eastern Europe, a region of nations in transition. No two countries have approached the problems of political and economic reform in exactly the same way; there is a widening gap between the most and least successful countries; and the process of integration into Europe's single economy is going forward at different speeds from country to country.

EASTERN EUROPE: TWO-TRACK TRANSITION

The newly independent states of Eastern Europe were Communist-ruled during the Cold War era, which lasted for more than four decades. All were saddled with centrally planned economies patterned after that of the Soviet "Big Brother." Just as central planning did not work in the long run in the Soviet Union, neither did it work anywhere else. But it is easier to demolish than to construct; for rebuilding, Eastern Europe had to look to the West. The West stood ready to help, but first the former Communist states would have to create democratic institutions and market-based economies.

Poland

The boldest reforms were adopted in Poland, the Czech Republic, and Hungary. (The Baltic states of Estonia, Latvia, and Lithuania also moved quickly to jettison all vestiges of the Stalinist police state and central planning following the breakup of the Soviet Union.) Poland showed the way, launching "shock therapy" policies designed to create a functioning market and to privatize the notoriously inefficient state enterprises that were a legacy of Communist rule. Unlike the Soviet Union, Poland had never banned small-scale private enterprise, and a decade after its democratic revolution private enterprise was flourishing as never before (with some 2 million registered businesses).

Poland's tough approach to reform yielded impressive results in the 1990s, when its economy grew faster than that of its ex-Communist neighbors, averaging over 5% a year between 1995 and 2000. Poland also managed to tame inflation, a major threat to social and economic stability throughout the region. As a direct result of these market-friendly reforms, Poland attracted infusions of foreign investment that were, in turn, a tonic to its reviving economy.

But relatively high unemployment (hovering above 12% in 2012) remains a nettlesome issue, especially in a country where jobs had been guaranteed to all adults during two generations of Communist rule. A growing wealth gap is also a problem, as the relatively poor rural populations continue to lag behind the urban middle class. Because Polish agriculture was never collectivized (as in the Soviet Union), many of Poland's impoverished villagers still live and work on its 2 million family farms.[19]

Although polls show crime and official corruption have undermined public confidence in government, the Polish economy continued to improve year after year, turning in steady growth rates (5 to 7%) with modest inflation (2 to 4%) prior to the global recession in 2008. Poland's economy was projected to grow at a modest 2.6% in 2012. Poland joined NATO in 1999 and the European Union in 2004—before the euro crisis cast a pall over Europe's single market.

Poland is a parliamentary democracy with a popularly elected president. Prime Minister Donald Tusk's center-right Civic Platform won the 2011 elections with nearly 40% of the popular vote and a gain of 63 seats in the Sejm (parliament). Civic Platform (PO) and the agrarian Polish People's Party (PSL) formed a coalition government, with the PSL as a very junior partner. President Lech Kaczynski, leader of the main opposition party called Law and Justice, was killed in a plane crash in April 2010. Bronislaw Komorowski (a Civic Platform leader from 2001 to 2010) was elected president in August 2010.

The Czech Republic

Unlike Poland, caught between two totalitarian states (Nazi Germany and Soviet Russia) in World War II, Czechoslovakia was betrayed at the Munich meeting between British Prime Minister Neville Chamberlain and German Reich Chancellor Adolf Hitler. (It's fair to call the Munich Pact a betrayal because Britain and France chose not to honor a preexisting military alliance with Czechoslovakia.) Hitler's Wehrmacht invaded and occupied Czechoslovakia in 1939. In 1945, as the war was drawing to a close, it was the Red Army, ironically—not the U.S. Army—that "liberated" most of Czechoslovakia, thus helping to boost the image of the Czech Communist Party. In the 1947 elections, Czech Communists won a majority of seats in the national parliament, formed a government, and quickly moved to establish a Stalinist dictatorship.

This bit of history is especially important both because the Communists came to power in a free election rather than a revolution (the only such instance in European history) and because Czechoslovakia was the *last* country where anyone who knew anything about Eastern (or Slavic) Europe would have expected that to happen.

Czechoslovakia came into being after World War I as a full-fledged parliamentary democracy—the only instance of popular self-government in Eastern Europe prior to 1989. In the Czech Republic, Prime Minister (now President) Václav Klaus extolled the virtues of the marketplace and implemented an ambitious coupon-redemption scheme that theoretically gave all Czech citizens shares of newly privatized (formerly state) enterprises. But the distribution was done without adequate safeguards and thus failed to accomplish one of its primary aims—to give Czechs a stake in the new market economy. In fact, crooks and insiders (a distinction without a difference) grabbed up the high-quality stocks, most of which never became available to the public, and used connections to get operational control of the "hottest" properties.

Unsurprisingly, this bungled attempt at reform soured many ordinary Czechs toward democracy and capitalism rather than solidifying popular support as it was intended to do. Inflation, fear of job losses, corruption in high places, a growing gap between the *nouveaux riche* and the majority, and a heightened awareness of how far behind the West Eastern Europeans in general—and Czechs in particular—had fallen all contributed to a deepening disillusionment. In the eyes of the people, the shady entrepreneurs and self-aggrandizing politicians became synonymous with "the system."

Despite popular dissatisfaction with politics, the Czech Republic is a free country with a popularly elected president and parliament and an independent judiciary. The Czech economy, having stumbled along for most of the 1990s, made a good recovery following the recession of 1997–1999. Structural reforms (for example, in the banking sector) helped achieve this result. Voters strongly endorsed the Czech Republic's entry into the EU in 2004, a move that opened Europe's huge Single Market to Czech-built automobiles, armaments, machinery, and other exports and could well make the Czech Republic a magnet for foreign investment.

In the five-year period 2003–2008, the Czech economy grew at an annual rate of 5.2%, while inflation averaged just below 3.0%. The manufacturing-based economy was especially hard-hit by the global recession in 2008–2009—industrial output fell by more than 17.4% in November 2008, the highest of any EU country. (Spain was close, but the overall drop in industrial activity for the EU as a whole was a less dramatic 7.7%.) Due to budget constraints at home and Europe's painfully slow recovery from the global recession—exacerbated by the euro crisis after 2010—Czech GDP was set to shrink in 2012, while inflation was rising by 3.5% and unemployment remained above 8%.

After more than two decades of freedom and independence, Czechs embrace constitutional democracy as an ideal but remain cynical about the existing political system and the politicians who run it. And for good reason: The Czech party system is fragmented (no fewer than nine political parties contested the 2010 elections), the Czech parliament is fractious (five parties claimed seats in the new parliament), and coalition governments are often unstable.

In March 2009, Czech Prime Minister Mirek Topolanek was forced to resign following a vote of no confidence—at a time when the Czech Republic held the six-month presidency in the European Council (the supreme decision-making body of the EU). It was an embarrassment that was finally erased when for the first time in more than a decade elections held in 2010 resulted in a center-right coalition government with a solid majority and common policy goals.

Hungary

In 1968, the same year as the ill-fated Prague Spring ("socialism with a human face") in Czechoslovakia, the Budapest government launched the New Economic

Mechanism (NEM). The NEM, aimed at limited decentralization of the economy and other market-oriented reforms, was a promising experiment in the early going. Production of consumer goods (always a low priority in Soviet-type economies) rose, and the quality of life for Hungarians generally improved. But hard-line Communists at home and abroad (particularly in the Soviet Union) opposed these reforms, and in the 1980s, the NEM was abandoned.

Even so, as the economy steadily declined, Hungary turned to the West for trade, aid, and investment. The liberalization that accompanied this policy included a new tolerance of private businesses and partnerships with foreign multinational companies. Thus, Hungary's reform efforts—though limited in scope and scale by a combination of politics, ideology, and Soviet interference—gave it a head start when Communism self-destructed at the end of the 1980s.

After 1989, Hungary's popularly elected government accelerated the pace of free-market reforms. In particular, as the leading emerging market in the region, Hungary attracted more than half of all direct foreign investment in Eastern Europe, even though its population (about 10 million) was a mere 25% of Poland's and a tiny fraction of Russia's.

Post-Communist Hungary moved swiftly to break up and privatize its huge state-owned enterprises; by 1993, the private sector's share of the GDP was about 50%. The pace of privatization slowed temporarily when the Socialists gained a majority in the parliament in 1994, but the following year, the same parliament passed legislation to speed the sale of state-owned enterprises and prepare to sell off public utilities and strategic industries such as steel and electricity.

Despite these bold restructuring efforts, Hungary has suffered high levels of inflation and unemployment. In the five years preceding the 2008 global recession, Hungary's economy grew at an annual rate of only 2.8%, while inflation averaged more than 5%. In 2009, the economy was in dire straits as demand for the country's manufactured goods crumbled—exports account for about 80% of Hungary's GDP and industrial output fell by almost 30% in February.

To make matters worse, Hungary's currency (the forint) dropped sharply. Because it depends so heavily on exports to the EU (and especially Germany), Hungary was especially vulnerable as Europe and the world sank into recession in 2009. Hungary's economy, flat in 2010, was expected to grow by a mere 0.8% in 2012. The slow economy has not slowed inflation, which remains at 5 to 6%. Meanwhile, double-digit unemployment continues to cast a shadow over the country's recovery.

Like Poland and the Czech Republic, Hungary is a multiparty parliamentary democracy. In the first three free elections after 1989, a different party won control of the government each time—a sign of party competition and political pluralism at work. Currently, both president and prime minister are leaders of the right-wing Fidesz Party, which won a two-thirds majority in Hungary's unicameral legislature in the 2010 national elections—the biggest electoral margin since the end of Communist rule.

Like Poland and the Czech Republic, Hungary joined the EU in 2004. By a twist of fate, it was Hungary's turn to take the six-month rotating EU presidency in 2011. But the first acts of Hungary's new government—including a tough new law aimed at restricting the independent media—left many observers questioning its commitment to liberal democracy. Luxembourg's foreign minister even asked whether Hungary should be allowed to hold the seat at all.

In sum, Hungary's political future is under a cloud while its economic problems are raising tensions within Hungarian society. Will these tensions undermine Hungary's fledgling democratic institutions? Will the government start a fight with Slovakia to whip up nationalism and distract the public from Hungary's domestic ills? If so, Hungary's standing in Europe will be placed in grave jeopardy at a time when the EU can ill afford another crisis emanating from within.

Many other former Communist states in Eastern Europe have also joined both NATO and the European Union, including Slovakia, Slovenia, the Baltic States (Estonia, Latvia, and Lithuania), Bulgaria, and Romania. Tiny Slovenia (population 2 million) has outshined all the others, achieving a per capita GDP that puts it well ahead of the Czech Republic, Poland, and Hungary—and even one Western European country, Portugal. All have made—or are in the process of making—the transition from authoritarian one-party rule and Soviet-style command economies to pluralistic representative democracy and market economies. Failure to make this transition means the door to the European Union remains shut.

Among the countries standing in line to join the West are Albania, Croatia, Montenegro, and Serbia. Ukraine and Georgia have also expressed a desire to join both NATO and the EU. But the euro crisis that started with a small country (Greece) and now threatens to spread and possibly call into question the survival of a common currency has created new burdens for EU members (especially Germany) and a collective sense of self-doubt in Brussels. Whether the new realities translate into a greater reluctance to admit new members only time will tell.

Amid all of Europe's "negatives" in these difficult times, it's easy to lose sight of the positives. For all practical purposes, totalitarianism (Communism, Nazism, Fascism) has disappeared from the map of Europe. There are still countries in which elections are a farce and freedom of the press is a fairytale (Russia and Belarus, for example), but they are now few and far between.*

TWO ASIAN TIGERS: STILL ROLE MODELS?

Like Eastern Europe, much of Asia is also in transition. South Korea, Taiwan, Singapore, Thailand, Malaysia, and Indonesia all compete with Japan—and now China—for export markets. Unlike China, however, these countries have also taken steps toward political liberalization.

---

*Belarus is a perennial Putin nemesis. Historically part of the Kremlin's "inner empire" from the time of Catherine the Great (1762–1796) to the breakup of the Soviet Union in 1991, Belarus has blocked Putin's efforts to resurrect the Old Russian Empire, resisted Putin's move to create a customs union (with Kazakhstan), and refused to recognize the independence of South Ossetia and Abkhazia (two provinces of Georgia that seceded with Russia's military backing).

South Korea: Crisis-Prone but Resilient

The economic transformation of South Korea, from a poor country dependent on agriculture to a modern industrial state powered by a technologically advanced manufacturing sector, was complete by the turn of the twenty-first century (see Figure 8.3).

Although China now has the world's second largest national economy, South Korea's per capita national wealth (GDP) was roughly six times mainland China's and twenty times that of Pakistan in 2010. To put South Korea's achievement in even better perspective, South Korea's GDP per capita is nearly double that of Chile, currently the richest country in Latin America, and more than double that of Brazil, the region's largest country.

Still, South Korea lags well behind the two poorest countries in Western Europe, Greece and Portugal. It has come far in the half-century since World War II and the Korean War left its economy in a shambles and its people traumatized and destitute. But it has a long way to go to catch up with Japan. Indeed, Japan's GDP per capita (roughly $39,500 in 2011) is twice that of South Korea, putting Japan's economy in the same league as those of Germany, France, and the United Kingdom.

In the 1990s, huge industrial conglomerates and largely unregulated big banks dominated South Korea's economy. These special interests had become so powerful and entrenched as to stifle competition. Although Asia's financial crisis of 1997–1998, known as the **Asian flu**, did not start in South Korea, it had a devastating impact there. Big banks had been lending money to big business without regard to the underlying financial condition of the borrowers. This situation, as well as the general need to revitalize the country's economy, compelled South Korea's popularly elected president to undertake aggressive state intervention—not to put the government in control of the economy but to give greater play to free-market forces. Seoul launched a program of bold reforms in the late 1990s designed to resuscitate the economy after it contracted by more than 6% in 1998.

The reforms proved to be a tonic: Although the country experienced a recession in 2003, South Korea's economy grew at an average annual rate of more than 4.0% between 1995 and 2008, when the global recession deepened. The country's resilient export-driven, trillion-dollar economy was slowed but bounced back quickly, growing at a rate of 6.3% in 2010 (8.7% in the second quarter of that year). Much of the credit was given to a bold $38 billion economic stimulus program aimed at creating new jobs in green industries and technologies, but any self-congratulations in Seoul (the capital) would have been premature: In 2011, South Korea's economy slowed to 3.6% and continued to fall in 2012.

Korea's political traditions are authoritarian. North Korea has been Communist-ruled since World War II, while South Korea, a close ally of the United States, is anti-Communist. Even so, South Korean "democracy" was little more than a façade for a pro-Western police state until 1997, when Kim Dae Jung became the first opposition candidate ever elected in South Korea. Kim won the Nobel Peace Prize in 2000 for his valiant efforts to improve relations between the two Koreas.

Asian flu
A term used to describe the widespread financial turmoil in Asian stock markets, financial institutions, and economies in 1997.

FIGURE 8.3   Map of South Korea. Note the vulnerable geostrategic location of the capital, Seoul, perilously close to the Demarcation Line (border zone) with South Korea's archenemy, North Korea.

But South Korea's democracy is still relatively fragile. Kim Dae Jung's successor, Roh Moo Hyun, won the 2002 presidential election but immediately faced a recalcitrant legislature controlled by opposition parties. Dissension within the ruling party led to a split, weakening it badly in the run-up to parliamentary elections in April 2004. In these tumultuous circumstances, Roh Moo Hyun called for a referendum on his presidency, giving rise to speculation that without a strong popular mandate he might resign. In March 2004, the National Assembly, in a recriminatory and unprecedented move, impeached him. After a sixty-three-day hiatus, the Korean Constitutional Court overturned the impeachment action and reinstated Roh, thus ending a perilous political crisis in one of East Asia's pivotal states.

The year 2012 was a year of elections in the Republic of South Korea (ROK). Voters cast ballots both in parliamentary and presidential elections—a rare occurrence in the ROK because national assembly elections are held every four years in contrast to presidential elections held every five years. Only once in every twenty years are both held in the same year but not at the same time.

Despite the initial predictions of a landslide victory for the main opposition Democratic United Party (DUP), the ruling conservative Saenuri Party staged an upset, winning 152 seats, enough for a clear majority in the 300-member national assembly (the DUP won 127 seats). The stage was set for the presidential election later in the year.

There was one new twist to add even greater drama to this election: Park Geun-hye, the daughter of General Park Chung-hee (South Korea's ruler from 1961 to 1979) was credited with engineering a major makeover of the conservative party in the run-up to the 2012 parliamentary elections. As such, she was well positioned to make a run for the presidency, which is precisely what happened. Park Geun-hye won, thus becoming her country's first woman president. In her new role, she faced daunting challenges. South Korea's export-led economy, stunted by the lingering effects of the global recession, has been slow to recover and forced to compete with China, Japan, and Taiwan. Sluggish growth has been accompanied by rising poverty. One sign of the times: In October 2012 the Bank of Korea lowered its growth forecast for 2013 from 3.0% to 2.4%. Another sign: The number of South Koreans living in relative poverty jumped 10% between 2006 and 2012. Meanwhile, roughly one-fifth of the population earned less than half the national average income.

Business executive and former mayor Lee Myung-bak won the December 2007 presidential election, but five years later his approval rating had plummeted to an abysmal 30%. Rising food and gas prices, high education and housing costs, inadequate job opportunities for university graduates, and a weak social safety net were among the primary sources of public disenchantment with the government.

Although Korea remains a divided country, South Korea has made the transition from an authoritarian state with a democratic veneer to a political system based on regular elections, civilian authority, and the rule of law.

Taiwan: Asia's Orphan State

Taiwan is another of Asia's success stories, but it exists in a kind of diplomatic twilight zone. For more than three decades, despite determined efforts by the People's Republic of China to isolate it on the global stage, Taiwan has managed to prosper.

Taiwan became an independent state after World War II when the Chinese Communists, led by Mao Zedong, defeated Chiang Kai-shek's Kuomintang. Until 1972, the United States recognized Taiwan as the legitimate government of China, although it was clear the Communist regime in Peking was in control of the mainland. In 1972, the People's Republic of China replaced Taiwan at the United Nations, and the United States decided to "derecognize" Taiwan in order to restore full diplomatic ties with Beijing for the first time since 1949.

The decision was a devastating blow to Taiwan. Although it has remained independent, it no longer enjoys diplomatic recognition by other sovereign states and is no longer a member of the United Nations. The reason for this unique state of affairs is that the People's Republic of China has successfully pressed its claim that Taiwan is part of China, there is only one China, and Beijing is its capital.

Nonetheless, Taiwan—officially the Republic of China—continues to enjoy the military protection and diplomatic goodwill of the United States, as well as close economic ties. Taiwan's economy is one of the most dynamic in Asia, outpacing even South Korea's. If Taiwan were in Europe, it would rival Portugal and Greece and would outrank nearly all the EU's new members, including the

Czech Republic, Hungary, and Poland. Its economic success is nothing new, but its movement toward liberal democracy is.

In 1988, Lee Teng-hui became the first native Taiwanese leader to assume the office of the presidency, and in the 1996 election he became the first popularly elected president in Taiwanese history. Lee instituted sweeping political reforms during his twelve-year tenure, continuing a process initiated in the mid-1980s by his predecessor, Chiang Ching-kuo (Chiang Kai-shek's son). In 2000, Taiwan's voters elected Chen Shui-bian president—the first time ever that the Taiwanese government was not headed by the leader of the Kuomintang.

With the formation of the Kuomintang-led Pan-Blue Coalition of parties and a Pan-Green Coalition led by the ruling Democratic Progressive Party, politics in Taiwan has become polarized. The Pan-Blue Coalition favors eventual Chinese reunification, whereas the Pan-Green Coalition favors an official declaration of Taiwan independence. In September 2007, the Democratic Progressive Party approved a resolution asserting Taiwan's separate identity from China, expressing a desire to become a "normal country" under a new constitution, and calling for general use of "Taiwan" as the island's name.

Chen assumed office pledging to clean up government. But his tenure was marred by allegations of corruption that came against a background of public discontent over a slowing economy and legislative gridlock. Chen and several family members allegedly embezzled millions of dollars while he was in office, charges that led to a high-profile trial in March 2009. If convicted, Chen faces life in prison.

The Kuomintang increased its majority in Taiwan's parliament in January 2008, and its nominee Ma Ying-jeou won the presidency in March of that year, taking office in May. Ma's campaign platform promised more robust economic growth and better ties with the People's Republic of China.

Taiwan is a geographic pygmy compared to the PRC, but its per capita GDP, only slightly lower than South Korea's, dwarfs that of its giant rival on the mainland. Exports—especially electronics, machinery, and petrochemicals—are the main drivers of Taiwan's economic growth. A heavy dependence on exports exposes Taiwan's economy, like South Korea's, to fluctuations in global demand. Little surprise, then, that in 2009, Taiwan's GDP contracted 1.9%. In 2010 exports bounced back and the economy raced ahead by 10.9%. It grew 5.2% in 2011 and slowed to little more than 1.0% in 2012.

Taiwan's economy grew at an average annual rate of 4.6% from 2003 to 2008—before the financial meltdown that plunged the world into the Great Recession. That's the kind of "normal" to which most countries, Taiwan included, would no doubt be only too happy to return.

LATIN AMERICA: A NEW DAY DAWNING

Whereas Asia's transitional states started with economic reforms, Latin America's led with political change. Democracy has finally taken root, but most countries in Latin America still have not found a recipe for economic revitalization.

The modern states of Latin America (formerly colonies of Spain or Portugal) gained independence in the 1820s—long before Europe's colonial empires were dismantled elsewhere. With few exceptions, military-bureaucratic rule was the norm in Latin America until quite recently. Only in a few countries, such as Colombia, Venezuela, and Costa Rica, had popularly elected civilian governments ever succeeded. The wave of liberalizing reforms that swept across Latin America in the 1980s ushered in a whole new age in the region's history and opened a fresh page in its politics.

The ABCs of Reform: Argentina, Brazil, and Chile

In the 1980s, one Latin American military dictatorship after another stepped aside in favor of a democratically elected civilian government. Today, virtually every government in the region qualifies as a liberal democracy.

What drove these regime changes was the need for economic reforms, evidenced, above all, in the huge foreign debts many Latin American countries had amassed. The burden of these debts, combined with outmoded economic structures and uncompetitive (protected) industries, high inflation, mass unemployment, widespread poverty, and gross inequality between the rich and poor, plunged the region into a crisis of self-confidence and underconsumption. Millions of people, especially *campesinos* (peasants) in rural areas, continue to struggle to survive at a bare subsistence level.

Chile Although in most of Latin America political change preceded economic reforms, Chile instituted market reforms *before* it democratized its political system. General Augusto Pinochet, who seized power in a bloody coup in 1973 by overthrowing the elected Marxist government of Salvador Allende, led one of the harshest military dictatorships in the region. During Pinochet's long rule, more than 3,200 people were executed or disappeared. Yet despite this reign of terror, the Chilean economy—spurred by market forces and a cozy relationship with the United States—performed remarkably well.

Chile is now the most prosperous country in South America, and despite a corrupt civil service and deep social divisions, its economy continues to grow. Exports, a major factor in this success story, rose sharply in subsequent years. In addition, Chile signed free trade agreements with the EU in 2003, and similar agreements with the United States and South Korea went into effect in 2004.

Pinochet gradually eased his iron grip on the Chilean political system in the 1990s. Today, Chile holds free elections and civilians run the government.

In 2005, Michelle Bachelet, running as the candidate of the Socialist Party of Chile, won in a run-off to become Chile's fourth elected president since the end of the Pinochet era. The election of a Socialist and a woman (the first ever in Chile) to lead the country reflected a deep vein of social discontent over the issue of equality—or rather the lack of it.

Bachelet's popularity fell sharply in the first year when massive demonstrations involving high school students broke out all over the country. The students were difficult to dismiss as immature or irresponsible: They were demanding a better education. There was also a fiasco over a major change in Santiago's transportation system that damaged the new president's popularity.

But she won most Chileans back in the second half of her four-year term. When Bachelet left office in March 2010 she had a record 84% approval

She is called the "angel of liberty" by her admirers. Camila Villejo led mass university student protests against social injustice and inequality in Chile. There are many YouTube videos of Ms. Villejo on the Internet (http://www.youtube .com/watch?v=se1cwgnMk9g).

rating according to one opinion poll. Presidents under Chile's constitution cannot succeed themselves. Bachelet has not ruled out running for a second term in 2013, however.

Billionaire businessman Sebastián Peñera, leader of the opposition center-right Alliance Party and the man Bachelet narrowly defeated in the 2005 election, was elected president in 2009. Peñera faced his first major test as president in the aftermath of the devastating 2010 earthquake. Peñera directed the dramatic rescue of thirty-three trapped miners—a story that was closely followed by the media around the world for many months. His approval rating soared to 63% in late 2010; over the next two years it plunged to a paltry 29%.

What happened? In 2011, a Chilean winter of discontent followed—and was perhaps inspired by—the tumultuous Arab Spring. Why? Often the causes of social unrest are rooted in a failed or failing economy. Not so in Chile, where the economy has been growing at a brisk annual rate of 6%, unemployment is low, and wages are steadily rising.

So what *is* the problem? In a word: fairness. In 2010 Chile joined the Organization of Economic Cooperation and Development (OECD), an international organization consisting of thirty-one of the world's most advanced economies. Chile is at the very top of this group in one key but unenviable category: income inequality. The problem is not that most Chileans are so poor; the problem is that a few Chileans are super rich and getting richer all the time. The upshot is a pervasive sense of unfairness expressed in a class-conscious confrontational stance toward Chile's elites and strident demands for major changes in education, transportation, and energy policy. In Chile, it's the students who have taken the lead in demanding a more just society. Camila Villejo, a twenty-three-year-old university student, is a prominent figure in the protest movement; she is also one of many young, university-educated Chileans who openly embrace Communism two decades after its widely (but perhaps prematurely) celebrated death. According to opinion polls, 70 % of Chileans supported the students' demands, even though some respondents had reservations about the students' methods (for example, violent clashes with police).

Brazil In Brazil the generals finally relinquished control of the government in 1985. Three years later, the country adopted a new constitution that provides for a direct election of the president. Fernando Henrique Cardoso, an economist, was elected in 1995 promising to reform and restructure Brazil's economy. Despite his best efforts, Brazil continued to be plagued by heavy external debts, chronic budget shortfalls, extensive rural poverty, and glaring inequalities when Cardoso left office in 2002.

Cardoso's successor, Luis Inácio Lula da Silva, presented a stark contrast in both political philosophy and leadership style. A charismatic union leader and reformer, the new president was affectionately known as "Lula" to millions of Brazilians. Under Lula's direction the state ratcheted up pensions and the minimum wage by 50%. In 2006, the voters rewarded Lula's efforts by reelecting him to a second term. Four years later, Worker's Party candidate Dilma Rousseff, Brazil's first woman president, rode to office on Lula's coattails.

Lula was a tough act to follow. As president from 2003 to 2010, he managed to balance economic reforms and social justice. With Lula at the helm, the richest Brazilians (top tenth) got 11% richer, while the poorest (bottom tenth) gained 72%, thanks largely to a plan called the *Bolsa Familia* (Family Allowance). The program uses tax revenues to give cash subsidies to the poorest Brazilians provided they send their kids to school and get regular checkups at free public health clinics.

Despite a sluggish economy slowing to a nearly zero growth rate, Rousseff's personal approval rating hit record highs in the summer of 2012. "We are living in a period of crisis for the advanced economies," Rousseff wrote in an article on the Brazilian model. "Debt accumulation is no substitute for rising wages, and market self-regulation is no substitute for government regulation. The rich world is now searching for a more balanced economic model and there are some common policies we should all pursue in 2012...." According to Rousseff, in the short span of eight years more than 40 million Brazilians have been lifted "out of poverty and into the middle classes, with access to health, education, credit and formal employment."[20]

Notwithstanding, bureaucratic obstruction, corruption, poverty, illiteracy, and inequality remain major obstacles to a Brazilian economic miracle. Brazil *does* have a lot going for it. Measured by both population and landmass, it is the fifth largest country in the world. Measured by GDP at purchasing-power parity, it ranked as the eighth largest economy in the world in 2013.

In the summer of 2013, mass protests erupted in Brazil's cities triggered by a 20 percent rise in the cost of public transportation but more generally attributable to growing discontent over government policies and a pervasive sense of social injustice rooted in a history of extreme wealth for a few amidst extreme poverty for the many. Hundreds of thousands of Brazilians, perhaps as many as a million on a single day in June, streamed into the streets. Publicly President Rousseff expressed tolerance, declaring that "Peaceful demonstrations only strengthen our democracy." But for her government the demonstrations could hardly have come at a worse time. A popular football event (The Confederations Cup) was currently underway and Pope Francis was scheduled to arrive for a weeklong stay in July. Brazil hosts the World Cup in 2014 and the Olympic Games in 2016. The world will be watching.

Thanks to Lula's popularity and political skills, Rousseff inherited a strong and stable government, a fiscally sound state, and a large, diversified service sector and modern industries including automotive, aeronautical, and electronics. That's the good news. The bad news: mother nature is paying a heavy price.

In 2009, Brazil made a commitment to reduce deforestation of its Amazon rainforest by 80% by 2020. The Amazon rainforest is one of the natural wonders of the world and a major mechanism for the exchange of carbon dioxide and oxygen in the earth's atmosphere. But clear-cutting for roads and agriculture is massively reducing the area it covers. In 2013, the government ordered an inventory of the trees in the Amazon—perhaps a step in the right direction.

FIGURE 8.4 Map of Brazil. With the exception of Ecuador and Chile, every country in South America borders on Brazil, the fifth-largest country in the world by total landmass.

Along with China and India, Brazil is one of three major economic powers to rise to prominence on the world stage in recent times (see Figure 8.4). But it is increasingly clear that economic success is not a cure-all. Rising expectations, demographic realities, and energy demands all contribute to an ecological conundrum now often oversimplified in terms such as "climate change" and "global warming." These are problems not only for ecologically challenged BRICs (Brazil, Russia, India, and China), but also for the richest countries. The BRICs have the most to gain; the West has the most to lose.

Argentina Argentina's military rulers bowed out in 1982 after the country's humiliating defeat by the British in the Falklands War. Argentina was then the richest country in South America in per capita GDP, but in the years that followed, corrupt politicians and economic mismanagement reduced its economy to ruins.

To hold down inflation and budget deficits, the government had little choice but to adopt unpopular policies, including high taxes and spending restraints. This policy of fiscal austerity, in turn, led to rising unemployment and social unrest. But the government feared that if it relaxed fiscal discipline, foreign investors would turn away. This dilemma led to a political crisis in 2001 as the slumping economy went from bad to worse. With the country on the verge of economic collapse, popular anger boiled over. Argentina became the scene of widespread riots and looting. Then it defaulted on its $155 billion foreign debt payments—the largest default of its kind in history. One president resigned,

LANDMARKS IN HISTORY

THE ARREST OF LEOPOLDO GALTIERI

Following a military coup in 1976, Argentina's junta (ruling clique) declared martial law and began the "dirty war" to restore order and eradicate opponents. No one will ever know how many people perished in this brutal campaign of repression, but the Argentine Commission for Human Rights charged the junta with 2,300 political murders, more than 10,000 political arrests, and the disappearance of 30,000 people.

Blanket amnesty laws protected the perpetrators of Argentina's dirty war for many years. In July 2002, former junta leader Leopoldo Galtieri and forty-two other military officers were arrested and charged with the torture and execution of twenty-two leftist guerrillas during the country's seven-year military dictatorship (1976–1983). In June 2005, the Supreme Court ruled the amnesty laws unconstitutional. The following year, numerous military and police officials went on trial. But it was too late to save the victims or to find any trace of the "disappeared."

another could not calm the storm; finally, in 2003, Néstor Kirchner, the governor of Santa Cruz, was elected president.

Kirchner vowed to reform the courts, police, and armed services and to prosecute perpetrators of the dirty war (see "Landmarks in History"). Argentina's economy rebounded after 2001, growing at an impressive rate of 8% a year under Kirchner's guidance. In March 2005, Kirchner announced the successful restructuring of the country's debt. In January 2006, Argentina paid off its remaining multimillion dollar IMF debt ahead of schedule.

Kirchner was not eligible to run again in 2007, but his wife, Cristina Fernández de Kirchner, ran instead—and won (like Isabella Perón, who famously succeeded her husband, Juan Perón, in 1974). Néstor Kirchner died of heart disease in 2010 amid calls for his wife's impeachment.

Cristina Kirchner's presidency has been marked by controversy over both policy and persistent questions about the couple's personal finances, which reportedly have increased exponentially since they acceded to the presidency. Her attempt to dismiss the Central Bank President Martin Redrado by presidential decree for refusing to carry out an order to transfer $6.7 billion into an escrow account to retire high-interest bonds failed when Redrado refused to step down and a judge annulled the decree. Kirchner used a 1983 truth-in-advertising law adopted during the rule of a brutal military dictatorship to levy stiff fines on ten maverick economists for allegedly misleading consumers; she has also deployed the national tax agency against some of her critics. (Tax evasion is rampant in Argentina, so the potential for highly selective prosecution is enormous.)

The problems facing Brazil and Argentina are fairly typical for the region as a whole. In Latin America, political reforms have often proven easier to implement than economic reforms. The reasons are many and varied, but the most intractable problems are rooted in a history of injustice and extreme inequality. The potential for social and political instability inherent in such conditions goes far toward explaining the appeal of radical populist and socialist ideas, as was evidenced in the rise to power of Hugo Chávez in Venezuela and Evo

Morales in Bolivia, as well as the persistence of violent Marxist and Maoist insurgent groups, most notably in Colombia and Peru.

Mexico

Last, we turn to Mexico, the United States' "distant neighbor" to the south.[21] Mexico is a good example of the historical contradiction found in so many Latin American countries—a romantic attachment to democratic ideals coexisting with an authoritarian regime disguised as a republic.

On paper, Mexico has been a liberal democracy since World War I. In reality, however, there has rarely been anything resembling genuinely competitive elections in Mexico—until 2000. Finally, after decades of one-party rule under the **Institutional Revolutionary Party (PRI)**, Mexican voters were given a real choice. The result was a bombshell: Opposition candidate Vicente Fox, representing the **National Action Party (PAN)**, won in a run-off election.

The **North American Free Trade Agreement (NAFTA)** boosted Mexico's economic prospects in the 1990s, but internal market reforms had been half-hearted, at best, due to Mexico's inefficient state-owned companies (for example, PEMEX, the oil monopoly), entrenched interests, and a corrupt bureaucracy fearful of losing its privileges. Membership in NAFTA gave Mexico easy access to U.S. markets, but it also gave the United States leverage to pressure the Mexican government into accelerating economic reforms.

President Fox came into office vowing to do just that. It would not be any easier in Mexico than elsewhere in Latin America, but Mexico had to agree if it wanted to compete as an equal NAFTA partner with the United States and Canada. The 2003 national elections produced no clear majority in Mexico's federal legislature—for the third time in a row.[22] President Fox's efforts to reform the Mexican government and economy were effectively blocked. In 2006, the PAN candidate, Felipe Calderón, was elected president in the closest Mexican election ever, with a 0.58% lead over a center-left opponent. His opponent, Andrés Manuel López Obrador, claimed fraud and called for "pacific civil resistance" but an electoral tribunal upheld the outcome.

Calderón pledged to fight crime and corruption. His campaign slogan, "Clean hands, firm hands," struck the right chords, but changing a political culture is easier said than done. In office, Calderón has placed a high priority on illegal immigration and security policy—especially the drug war and narco-terrorism (drug-related murders and kidnappings). His answer to rising world corn prices, the main food staple of Mexico's poor, was the Tortilla Price Stabilization Act. Unfortunately, it did not work—at least not well enough to counteract the lingering popular distaste left over from the ugly 2006 election. Similarly, Calderón's well-intended First Employment Program, aimed at creating new jobs for first-time new entrants into the labor force, has been criticized for not going far enough.

Enrique Peña Nieto, leader of the Institutional Revolutionary Party that had ruled the country for seventy years until 2000, was elected president in July 2012. The PRI also won the most seats in Congress in Mexico's parallel election cycle, but fell short of a clear majority in the legislature. Peña pledged transparency in government; action to curb organized crime (especially violence against citizens at the hands of the vicious Mexican drug cartel); economic revitalization; and improved relations with the United States.

Institutional Revolutionary Party (PRI)
The dominant political party in Mexico from 1929 to the present. The PRI had never lost an election until 2000, when Vicente Fox of the National Action Party won the presidency.

National Action Party (PAN)
The main opposition party in Mexico; the PAN's candidate, Vicente Fox, was elected president in 2000.

North American Free Trade Agreement (NAFTA)
An agreement signed in 1994 by the United States, Mexico, and Canada that established a compact to allow free trade or trade with reduced tariffs among the three nations.

Too good to be true? If the past is any guide, Peña will be the latest in a long line of leaders who overpromised and underperformed.

Official corruption, fiscal mismanagement, gross social inequality, and endemic poverty are problems by no means unique to Mexico. They are all too common in Latin America—and not just "Latin" America. (Corruption, fiscal mismanagement, and gross inequality are familiar problems in the United States too.) When people do not have good jobs or benefits or steady income, they lack the kind of security we tend to take for granted. Without a circulation of wealth throughout the whole society, it is difficult, if not impossible, to complete the transition from a rural-based, slow-growth, inward-looking protectionist economy to a modern, urban, market-based, mass-consumption, export-oriented economy. The latter is where Latin America is headed, but for the region's poor it is taking too long to get there.

In sum, Latin America has made a turn toward political pluralism, but the social and economic transition is incomplete. In the year 2000, around 225 million people were considered poor (43.9% of the total population), according to the Economic Commission for Latin American and the Caribbean (ECLAC); by 2012 that number had fallen to 167 million (28.9%)—the lowest in three decades. For millions of Latin Americans, the promise of a better life is no longer an empty one.

SUMMARY

With the demise of the Soviet Union in 1991, Communist rule ended nearly everywhere in the world. Nonetheless, a few exceptions remain, including China, Cuba, and North Korea. The collapse of Communism brought the problems of transition in the former Soviet-bloc states to the fore. Other countries launched major political and economic reforms in the 1990s, including South Korea and Taiwan in Asia and Argentina, Brazil, and Chile in Latin America.

The Soviet political system was an outgrowth of the Stalinist totalitarian model. In trying to reform and restructure this system, Mikhail Gorbachev followed in the footsteps of an earlier Soviet leader, Nikita Khrushchev. In the Soviet system, the Communist Party ruled, and a person's ranking in the party was the best indication of that individual's political power. When Gorbachev rose to the top post in the Communist Party in 1985, he faced both acute economic problems and associated social problems, each related to the failure of central planning.

Gorbachev's reforms proved inadequate to save the former Soviet Union. His successor, Boris Yeltsin, failed to guide Russia through a smooth transition. His successor, Vladimir Putin, inherited a mess—economic dislocations, ethnic fragmentation, and poorly established state institutions. Putin turned out to be a decisive leader who was twice elected by large majorities but has ruled as a traditional strong Russian boss.

China instituted major free-market reforms and downplayed much of its Communist ideology after Mao's death, but remains a country headed by a single party that brooks no political or religious dissent. As China modernizes its armed forces and attempts to become a world power, it faces increasing social problems as well as economic and border tensions among its provinces.

India, South Korea, and Taiwan are three other examples of Asian societies in transition. All three countries made the transition to market-based (though semiprotectionist) economies first, but have more recently instituted meaningful political reforms.

The transition process in Latin America is the reverse of the pattern found in Asia. Argentina, Brazil, Chile, and Mexico are four key countries in the region. In three of the four, political reforms came before economic reforms (Chile is the exception). In Venezuela and Bolivia, market reforms have taken a back seat to social reforms—a reversal of what has happened elsewhere in the region and the world. The extremely unequal distribution of wealth and official corruption remain obstacles to progress.

KEY TERMS

nomenklatura   190
perestroika   190
glasnost   190
democratization   190
Asian flu   207

Institutional
   Revolutionary Party
   (PRI)   216
National Action Party
   (PAN)   216

North American Free
   Trade Agreement
   (NAFTA)   216

REVIEW QUESTIONS

1. What problems did the Soviet Union face in 1985 when Mikhail Gorbachev came to power, and how did Gorbachev respond? With what consequences?
2. "One of the most important questions facing Russia today is whether it can become a stable democracy." What do you think? Explain.
3. What countries in Eastern Europe, Asia, and Latin America have made the most successful transitions so far? Explain your choices.
4. Comment on the economic transition in China since Mao's death. What reforms did Mao's successors institute and with what results?
5. Compare and contrast the transitions in Eastern Europe on one hand and Latin America on the other relative to (a) economic reforms, (b) political stability, (c) the rule of law, and (d) human rights.
6. Compare and contrast the transitions in Asia on one hand and Latin America on the other relative to (a) economic reforms, (b) political stability, (c) the rule of law, and (d) human rights.
7. What region of the world has experienced the most success in making the transition from dictatorship to democracy in the past two decades? Justify your view.
8. Has Russia or China been more successful in making the transition from a centrally planned economy to a market-oriented economy? Compare and contrast the way the two countries have approached problems and assess the economic reform strategies of each. Which country has had a better outcome so far? What is the evidence?

CHAPTER 9

Development
Myths and Realities

THINK ABOUT IT

What is development in the study of politics?

What are four challenges in building a new nation-state?

From a developmental perspective, how do India and Nigeria compare?

What are four obstacles to development?

What are five examples of failed states?

least developed
countries (LDCs)
Countries where the
ratio of population
to land and jobs is
unfavorable to growth,
where the economy
is not diversified, and
where literacy rates are
low; three criteria used
to classify LDCs also
indicate the challenges
they face: (1) low
income; (2) human
resource weakness
(nutrition, health,
education, adult literacy);
and (3) economic
vulnerability.

This chapter focuses on the problems arising in the context of too little development too late, rather than too much too soon. We use the term **least developed countries (LDCs)**, a term adopted by the United Nations, instead of "developing countries" (Table 9.1) because LDCs encompass the poorest of the poor.

During the second half of the last century, the West lumped Africa, Asia, and Latin America together into what was commonly called the Third World. In this narrative, the First World was epitomized by the United States, Western Europe, and Japan, plus Canada, Australia, and New Zealand—rich countries with stable societies and well-established democratic political institutions. The citizens of these fortunate states were free to criticize the government. The Communist states—Soviet Russia and Eastern Europe—comprised the Second World. All the rest—formerly known as the Third World—were categorized as "underdeveloped" or "less developed" countries. The term "Third World" is seldom used now that the Cold War is a distant memory, but the problems remain.

Today, it is considered politically incorrect to use such pejorative terms. Indeed, the term "developing countries" is rarely used to describe the former colonies. Many of these countries now have diversified economies, meaning they are no longer simply agrarian or nomadic but have industries and service sectors as well. Indeed, major companies in the United States and Europe outsource manufacturing and services to China, India, Malaysia, and Indonesia where labor costs (wages) are low.

In fact, *all* countries are developing, no matter how rich or how poor. Indeed, if some countries are not developed enough to sustain themselves, other countries are, arguably, not sustainable for the *opposite* reason: development driven by the latest advances in science and technology has given rise to major new problems and huge challenges (carbon pollution, climate change, pandemics, water wars, nuclear accidents, etc.).

By definition, LDCs display all or most of the following features: endemic poverty; ethnic, religious, or tribal conflict; widespread illiteracy; political turmoil; and glaring inequalities. Although the picture is changing in much of Asia and, to a lesser extent, in Latin America, many sub-Saharan African nations continue to face great obstacles on the path to full political, economic, and social development.

In the worst cases, the economy goes into a tailspin, the government collapses, societies erupt, and entire populations are plunged into anarchy. In the 1990s, this chilling possibility became a reality in places like the former Yugoslavia, Rwanda, Sierra Leone, and the Côte d'Ivoire (Ivory Coast); more recently, forces of anarchy have ravaged societies in the Middle East, Central Asia, and West Africa.

In 2011–2012 the so-called Arab Spring was accompanied by social and political upheavals in Egypt and Tunisia, and rulers were overthrown following violent clashes between demonstrators and security forces. In Libya a civil war broke out, and a dictator on the run was captured and killed by rebels in Sirte. In Syria, a full-scale civil war dragged on through 2012 and into 2103 with no end in sight.

West Africa has been in crisis for more than two decades. Insurgencies, atrocities, kidnappings, "child soldiers"—these horrors were the stuff of daily

TABLE 9.1 The World's Least Developed Countries*

Africa (33)

1	Angola	18	Madagascar
2	Benin	19	Malawi
3	Burkina Faso	20	Mali
4	Burundi	21	Mauritania
5	Central African Republic	22	Mozambique
6	Chad	23	Niger
7	Comoros	24	Rwanda
8	Democratic Republic of the Congo	25	São Tomé and Príncipe
9	Djibouti	26	Senegal
10	Equatorial Guinea	27	Sierra Leone
11	Eritrea	28	Somalia
12	Ethiopia	29	Sudan
13	Gambia	30	Togo
14	Guinea	31	Uganda
15	Guinea-Bissau	32	United Republic of Tanzania
16	Lesotho	33	Zambia
17	Liberia		

Asia and Pacific (15)

1	Afghanistan	9	Samoa
2	Bangladesh	10	Solomon Islands
3	Bhutan	11	Timor-Leste
4	Cambodia	12	Tuvalu
5	Kiribati	13	Vanuatu
6	Lao People's Democratic Republic	14	Yemen
7	Myanmar	15	Maldives
8	Nepal		

Latin America and the Caribbean (1)

1	Haiti

*This is the list drawn up by the United Nations' Office of the High Representative for the Least Developed Countries. It can be accessed on the Internet at http://www.unohrlls.org/en/home/. Click on "least developed countries" and "country profiles" on the drop-down menu.

SOURCE: United Nations Office of the High Representative for the Least Developed Countries. http://www.unohrlls.org/en/home/.

life in this all but forgotten corner of sub-Saharan Africa during the 1990s. Although troubles persisted into the 2000s, a modicum of stability and peace was restored. But in 2012 a new crisis boiled over when jihadist insurgent groups in northern Mali seized the country's largest city, Gao, and the fabled town of Timbuktu. France sent troops to help Mali's army put down the Islamist rebellion in 2013.

The background to the crisis in Mali involved a military coup détat in 2012 that overthrew an elected president and scrapped the country's constitution. Given the endemic political instability of both West and North Africa, and Mali's geographic proximity to both regions, there was (is) a danger of spillover to neighboring states. Across the border in Algeria, jihadists attacked a BP gas facility and seized hostages. A shootout with Algerian security forces left some sixty-nine people dead, including thirty-nine foreigners and an Algerian, presumed to be hostages. It is unknown whether this incident was linked to events in Mali.

A bloody civil war consumed Sri Lanka for twenty-five years until the Tamil Tiger rebels were finally crushed in 2009. In Haiti, a near total collapse of the state was triggered by a natural disaster (a devastating hurricane) in January 2010. Pakistan, a big country (population 170 million) of major strategic importance located in one of the most volatile regions of the world, teeters on the edge of open rebellion. Pakistan's per capita GDP is lower than India's and roughly one-tenth that of New Zealand or South Korea.

With few exceptions, endemic poverty is the root cause of the worst problems facing most of the least developed countries—some 3 billion people, almost half the world's population, live on less than $2.50 a day (Figure 9.1). According

FIGURE 9.1   Percent of People in the World at Different Poverty Levels, 2005. How many people in this world are poor? The answer depends on who is counting and how national governments and international organizations define poverty. At $1.00 a day "only" about 880 million people were poor in 2005; but if we draw the poverty line at $2.00, that number climbs to 2.6 billion. In 2010 the World Bank estimated the number of hungry people in the world at 925 million.

SOURCE: World Bank Development Indicators, 2008.

Poverty Line (USD Dollars a Day at 2005 Purchasing Power Parity)
Numbers inside bars are world population at that indicator, in billions

■ Below the poverty line   ▨ Above the poverty line

to the World Bank, the poorest 40% of the world population accounts for 5% of global income; the richest 5% accounts for three-quarters of global income. Some 25,000 children die *every day* due to poverty. More than one-fourth of the children in LDCs are stunted or underweight due to chronic malnutrition, and about two-thirds live in South Asia or sub-Saharan Africa—two of the most conflict-ridden regions on the planet.

Nearly 1 billion people entered the twenty-first century unable to read or write, but the correlation between poverty and illiteracy is just part of the story. In the least developed countries, unemployment is the norm and only the most fortunate few have access to a health clinic or doctor. Preventive health care is also beyond reach. The lack of mosquito nets is a major reason for half a billion new cases of malaria and as many as 2 million deaths, mostly children, in the LDCs each year. Add an estimated 50–100 million cases of dengue fever and approximately 25,000 deaths annually, and the magnitude of the problem of poverty becomes all too apparent.[1]

Poverty, malnutrition, illiteracy, tribal and ethnic rivalries, official corruption, and violence against women are among the many problems we often associate with the regions formerly known as the Third World. What we often forget is that these problems are not unrelated to the bitter legacy of colonialism, and they continue to be exacerbated by the fact that many of the world's poor countries are not bereft of resources the world's rich countries desire—a mixed blessing, to be sure, as the turm*oil* (emphasis on oil) in the conflict-ridden Middle East attests.

World poverty, of course, raises profound moral issues. In this chapter we focus on two basic questions. First, what are the causes of poverty and instability in least developed countries? Second, is a world divided into rich ("us") and poor ("them") sustainable—otherwise put, can the problems of poverty be contained, or will they inevitably spill over? A look at the context of politics in what used to be called the Third World will shed light on the extreme challenges these countries face.

DEVELOPMENT AS IDEOLOGY

During the Cold War, the Third World was also called the South, which highlighted the great disparities between the industrially developed states in temperate climates above the equator (North), and the former colonies in the tropical and semitropical zones below it (South). According to a view known as **neocolonialism**, the rich nations of the North continued to exploit the poor nations of the South even after the latter gained independence in the post–World War II period. This view both reflected and fed into notions about the existence of an ill-defined **North-South conflict**.

Several prominent Third World figures promulgated the idea of a Manichean struggle between the rich (north) and the poor (south) in the 1950s and 1960s. Ghana's Kwame Nkrumah published a book in 1956 titled *Neo-Colonialism, The Last Stage of Imperialism*. "Faced with the militant peoples of the ex-colonial territories in Asia, Africa, the Caribbean and Latin America," Nkrumah wrote, "imperialism simply switches tactics." Nkrumah called for solidarity

neocolonialism
A theory holding that unequal and exploitative economic arrangements created by former colonial powers continued to be used to maintain control of former colonies and dependencies long after they gained formal independence in the 1950s and 1960s.

North-South conflict
A shorthand term for the tensions and disputes that arose between the rich industrialized countries and the former colonies during the Cold War era.

among the former colonial peoples, railing against the "extended tentacles of Wall Street" and Washington (in particular, the Pentagon and the CIA) as the "very citadel of neo-colonialism."

All such attempts to bring about solidarity among the LDCs were doomed to fail, however. As memories of colonial rule fade, the anti-imperialist rhetoric that resonated throughout much of Africa, Asia, and Latin America has lost its relevance. More than half a century after independence, blaming the old over-lords for new problems no longer rings true. Official corruption and misman-agement is a widespread and well-known fact. Even more telling is the fact that some former colonies are racing ahead as others slide into the abyss.

The West countered neocolonialist ideology with its own capitalist ideol-ogy, extolling the virtues of freedom, democracy, and commerce. The fact that capitalism grew out of the Western experience and was tainted by its close asso-ciation with colonialism made it a hard sell. But strategic grants of foreign aid and trade concessions, and the implicit or explicit threat to intervene militarily, provided the West with a good deal of leverage nonetheless.

THE IDEA OF DEVELOPMENT

What exactly does development mean in a global economy undergoing such rapid change? For better or worse, the definition is based on the Western experience and the yardstick in common use is a Western measure of eco-nomic and political success. That doesn't make it good or bad, right or wrong, but it does raise questions about its applicability and acceptability outside the West.

In the least developed countries the vast majority still do not enjoy access to education, jobs, health care, or the other good things in life that are the hall-marks of modernity in the West. Moreover, few LDCs have governments that are accountable, stable, and clean (as opposed to corrupt). When we in the West say a country is "developing," we are usually thinking of an LDC, and what we mean is that it is not *yet* truly modern—that is, resembling the Western-ized world. Westerners tend to assume that as, or if, these countries develop, they will look increasingly like us—urbanized, secularized, materialistic, and technology-dependent—and will want what we want.

The LDC countries come in all shapes and sizes. Some are huge—Brazil has a territory of 3 million square miles (larger than the continental United States) and a population of 160 million; India's territory of 1 million square miles supports a population of more than 1 billion. Others are tiny—for example, Barbados in the Caribbean (territory, 166 square miles; population, 252,000) and Kiribati in the Pacific (territory, 266 square miles; population, 61,000). The Pacific island of Nauru wins the prize: it has 8,000 people living on 8 square miles of land.

Nauru is small but not poor, thanks to a brisk trade in phosphate exports. Most of the poorest countries depend primarily on agriculture. LDCs are often dependent on a single commodity or raw material for export, but a few, such as the oil-rich states of the Persian Gulf—Bahrain, Kuwait, Oman, Qatar, Saudi Arabia, and the United Arab Emirates—rely largely on a single natural resource,

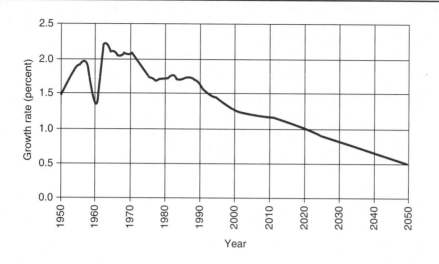

FIGURE 9.2   World Population Growth Rates, 1950–2050.

SOURCE: U.S. Census Bureau, International Data Base, December 2008 Update.

as does Russia, a country much poorer than Saudi Arabia and the others, which are anything but poor.

The world's poorest countries generally have the highest population growth rates; the richest often have the lowest. The world's population, surpassing the 7 billion mark in 2012, has more than doubled since 1969. As Figure 9.2 and Figure 9.3 show, population growth rates have been steadily declining since the 1960s, but the world's total population continues to climb and is projected to reach 9 billion by 2050.

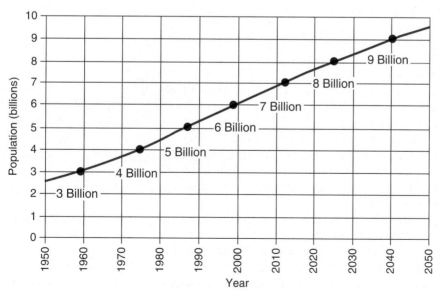

FIGURE 9.3   World Population, 1950–2050.

SOURCE: U.S. Census Bureau, International Data Base, December 2008 Update.

Population pressure places onerous burdens on economic, social, and political structures in many poor countries, but comparisons can be misleading and often yield surprises. The Gaza Strip, one of the most wretched places on earth, has one of the fastest growing populations in the world. Arab and sub-Saharan countries generally have higher birthrates than Asian or Latin American nations. Although much higher than in Europe or North America, India's birthrate is low compared with most countries in the Arab World and sub-Saharan Africa, while China's is about the same as France's (and lower than the United States').

Asia, the most densely populated region of the world, has about 57% of the world's population but only about 18% of its landmass, much of which is arid or mountainous. Apart from Asia (and with a few exceptions, such as Egypt, whose population is clustered around the Nile River), population density in least developed countries is relatively low. Africa's average population density is only 24 per square kilometer, as opposed to India's 296, the United Kingdom's 646, Japan's 880, and Singapore's 5,571. Africa has more arable land per capita than any other so-called developing region.

Why are so many of the least developed countries in the world located in sub-Saharan Africa? We turn next to a consideration of this question.

THE LEGACY OF COLONIALISM

Only twenty-three countries among the current United Nations membership were independent in 1800. More than half of these states were in Europe, with Afghanistan, China, Ethiopia, Japan, Iran, Nepal, Oman, Russia, Thailand, Turkey, and the United States rounding out the list.[2] Since then, the number

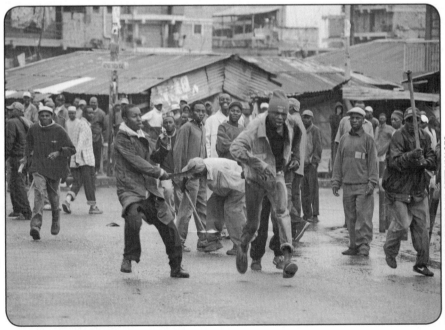

Ethnic strife is an all too common legacy of colonialism and remains a problem for many developing nations. Here a member of the Luo tribe is attacked by a Kikuyu gang in January 2008 in the northeast Nairobi slum of Huruma.

BONIFACE MWANGI/BLOOMBERG VIA GETTY IMAGES

THE AGE OF IMPERIALISM

FIGURE 9.4   The World in 1914. Note how many European countries, including small countries such as Belgium, Denmark, and Holland (the Netherlands), had far-flung colonial empires at the beginning of the twentieth century. Note also that these empires encompassed nearly all of Africa and much of Asia but had all but disappeared from Central and South America.

Belgium		Spain
Denmark		United States
France		Independent States
Germany		Bodies of Water
Great Britain		American sphere of influence
Holland		British sphere of influence
Italy		French sphere of influence
Japan		German sphere of influence
Portugal		Japanese sphere of influence
Russia		Russian sphere of influence

© CENGAGE LEARNING

(Continued)

(CONTINUED)

A new wave of European colonial expansion occurred in the second half of the nineteenth century, sometimes called the Age of Imperialism. Earlier in that century, popular revolutions in the Americas against England, Spain, and Portugal had led to disillusionment with empires and colonies. Industrialization diverted attention from external expansion in favor of internal development, and the new emphasis on free trade removed much of the rationale for global empire building. British Prime Minister Benjamin Disraeli expressed the tenor of the times in 1852. "These wretched colonies," he said, "will all be independent too in a few years and are a millstone around our necks."

But as industry grew, Europe's economic and political leaders began to seek new sources of raw materials and new markets for their products. After 1870, free trade gave way to protectionist policies, and soon a race for new colonies began (Figure 9.4). Various theories defending colonial expansion were expounded.

Alfred T. Mahan's geopolitical concepts were used to "prove" great powers could not survive without overseas possessions. Charles Darwin's concept of the survival of the fittest was used to "prove" colonialism was in accordance with the inexorable laws of nature. Rudyard Kipling wrote about the "white man's burden" of spreading civilization to a benighted world. Even U.S. President McKinley claimed God had spoken to him on the eve of the Spanish-American War (1898), commissioning the United States to take the Philippines and Christianize "our brown brothers."

By the end of the nineteenth century, all Asia and Africa had been colonized. Even China had lost its sovereign status: It was subjugated through a series of treaties that gave various European powers special rights and prerogatives. Africa in 1914 was under the colonial sway of no fewer than seven European nations—Belgium, France, Germany, Great Britain, Italy, Portugal, and Spain. In fact, only two independent nations remained—Ethiopia and Liberia.

of independent states has risen to more than 190. World War II (1939–1945) was a watershed because it led to the rapid deconstruction of the European colonial empires (see "Landmarks in History"). Most of the countries existing today came into being during this recent period, and all but a few were least developed countries. Also, the breakup of the Soviet Union led to the creation of some twenty-five new independent states in Eastern Europe, Transcaucasia, and Central Asia by 1994.[3]

colonialism
The policy of seeking to dominate the economic or political affairs of underdeveloped areas or weaker countries (see also *imperialism*).

imperialism
A policy of territorial expansion (empire building), often by means of military conquest; derived from the word *empire*.

For centuries, the great powers of Europe competed for colonial holdings, ruling and administering over weaker and technologically less-advanced peoples and territories located in faraway places around the globe. These colonial empires were a source of great prestige and wealth. In the nineteenth century, European powers scrambled to colonize Africa. At the beginning of the twentieth century, Britain, France, Belgium, Germany, Portugal, Holland, Italy, Spain, and Turkey all possessed overseas colonial empires. This European intrusion—which came to be known as **colonialism** or **imperialism**—became synonymous with subjugation and exploitation in the minds of the indigenous peoples.

Colonialism *did* include Europeans dominating native peoples, and it *was* based on implicit or explicit notions of racial superiority or religious zeal (or both). However, there were great differences in the methods and means employed by the colonial powers. For instance, the British approach was far milder than Spanish colonial rule, which was notorious for its rapacity and cruelty. The Portuguese and French tried to assimilate colonized peoples. France even granted Algerians seats in the national legislature and positions in the national cabinets. The Dutch in Indonesia allowed native rulers to remain in power. Great Britain pursued both strategies, relying on local authorities to maintain law and order and allowing natives to pursue careers in public administration, attend British schools and universities, and enter the professions.[4]

Nonetheless, the idea of being governed by a distant country was repugnant to most colonial peoples. In many cases, independence and violence went hand in hand. In India, however, Mahatma Gandhi led a nationwide mass campaign of **nonviolent resistance** (*satyagraha*), a strategy later adopted by Martin Luther King Jr. in the United States. (Ironically, both Gandhi and King were assassinated.)

Colonialism's legacy remains controversial. Any advances in health (hospitals), education (schools), and transportation (roads) generally came at a high price for the native peoples—including disruption of traditional ways of life and epidemics caused by the introduction of European germs into populations with no resistance.[5]

The extent to which Western countries continued to exploit former colonies *after* independence is debatable. Today, trade issues top the political agenda in relations between the rich and poor countries. Although agriculture constitutes only 8% of the world's total merchandise trade, exports of food and fiber so vital to the LDCs are among the hardest hit by protectionist policies of rich countries (see "Ideas and Politics").

nonviolent resistance
A passive form of confrontation and protest; also called civil disobedience at times.

FREE TRADE

In 2001, the 150-member World Trade Organization (WTO) focused on agricultural protectionism in the Doha Round of trade negotiations. The least developed countries (the G33 nations), many heavily dependent on agricultural exports, feared rising protectionist sentiment in the West would cut off vital markets. Therefore, the G33 nations urged the United States and Europe to eliminate or greatly reduce tariffs and farm subsidies. But for political reasons—mainly the influence of powerful farm lobbies—the talks stalled. In July 2008, it appeared a compromise agreement was finally in the works. But the talks broke down, and protectionism was once again on the rise following the near-collapse of the global banking system in the fall of 2008.

In early 2010, Brazil and the WTO's Director-general Pascal Lamy focused on the role of the United States in breaking the deadlock. Brazil's President Lula de Silva urged Barack Obama to end the trade dispute between Brazil and the United States over cotton subsidies following Lula's decision to ratchet up tariffs on more than 100 U.S. goods. One consequence of the 2008–2009 global recession is the desire of political leaders to protect domestic markets from foreign competition, especially in tough times. A 12% drop in trade in 2009, reportedly the largest annual drop since World War II, pointed to the urgency of new trade talks. In early 2011, there was still no sign of movement in that direction.

Despite globalization, trade is still far from free. The rich debate; the poor wait. Some things never change.

The consequences of colonialism are still with us. Colonial empires were created without regard to preexisting ethnic identities, territorial boundaries, and the like. When the European powers withdrew, they typically created artificial new states by stitched together a crazy quilt of incompatible peoples and cultures. (Iraq, Sudan, and Nigeria are three prime examples.) Chronic political instability, coups, revolutions, civil wars, and even genocide—these are bitter fruits of colonialism. Simply listing *some* of the least developed countries that have been wracked by conflict in recent years proves the point: Afghanistan, Angola, Burma, Burundi, Cambodia, Chad, the Democratic Republic of the Congo (formerly Zaire), Côte d'Ivoire, Ethiopia, Iraq, Liberia, Nigeria, Pakistan, Rwanda, Sierra Leone, Somalia, Sudan, and Sri Lanka.

The fragility of these societies has led to dire warnings about the "coming anarchy" in Africa and elsewhere.[6] Raising the specter of anarchy is perhaps overly pessimistic, but Somalia has experienced a calamitous breakdown in civil order in recent times, as have Sudan, the Congo (DRC), and, in 2012, Syria.

BUILDING A NEW NATION-STATE: FOUR CHALLENGES

political development
A government's ability to exert power effectively, to provide for public order and services, and to withstand eventual changes in leadership.

Building a new nation-state is an exercise in **political development**. Rich countries often display certain common traits: a stable government, a merit-based civil service system, basic public services (police and fire protection, education, health, and sanitation), and legal structures (law codes and courts). All these traits are typically lacking in poor countries. Imagine growing up in a society where not only schools but also drinking water and basic sanitation do not exist. How can people who have no money, no police protection, and who cannot read or write lift themselves out of poverty or demand decent government?

The development process can be, and often is, destabilizing. It is therefore no great surprise that governments in least developed countries are often authoritarian, prone to coups, and beset by crises. Poor countries typically face four fundamental developmental challenges: nation-building, state-building, participation, and distribution.[7]

The first and most basic challenge is *nation-building*—the process of forming a common identity based on the notion of belonging to a political community separate and distinct from all others. Often the concept of "nation" is based on common ethnolinguistic roots. The countless conflicts in Africa and Asia in the post–World War II era testify to the extreme difficulty (if not impossibility) of artificially building something as natural as a nation within a territory containing multiple ethnic and religious communities. The lessons of recent U.S. attempts at nation-building in Iraq and Afghanistan also point to the conclusion that it cannot be done from the outside by outsiders.

Having a *charismatic* leader present at the creation is a key variable in the initial nation-building stage (try to imagine the founding of the United States without George Washington). Notable Third World examples include Egypt's Gamal Abdel Nasser (who ruled from 1954 to 1970), Kenya's Jomo Kenyatta

(1964–1978), India's Jawaharlal Nehru (1947–1964), Indonesia's Sukarno (1945–1967), and Libya's Muammar el-Qaddafi (1969–2011). Flags and celebrations also help instill a sense of national identity, and threats from a neighboring state—real, imagined, or manufactured—can galvanize unity, at least until the perceived danger subsides.

The second challenge, **state-building**, is the creation of political institutions—in particular, a central government—capable of exercising authority and providing services throughout the length and breadth of society. A functioning state bureaucracy promotes economic development and social unity by such mundane means as creating the infrastructure (roads, bridges, telephone lines) necessary for an integrated national economy. To achieve this essential result, the government must be capable of levying and collecting taxes. But in countries with traditional economies based on subsistence agriculture, there is often little or nothing to tax, which leads to a vicious cycle that can only be broken with infusions of foreign capital (trade, aid, and investment). But foreign investment (an external variable) depends on political stability (an internal variable).

A third challenge facing the LDCs is *participation*. For new societies to prosper and grow economically, the people must be actively engaged in the development process. This kind of mobilization gives rise to a political dilemma: As people become more actively involved and feel the effects of government (good and bad), they begin to demand a greater voice in determining who governs and how. But what if rising expectations strain the capacity of the state to respond? Hence, the challenge of participation is how to harness popular energies without setting in motion the forces of political disintegration or revolution.

The fourth and final challenge is *distribution* to reduce the extreme inequality that often characterizes **traditional societies**. Extremes of wealth and poverty can easily lead to a pervasive sense of injustice and, in turn, to mass revolt (see Chapter 14), as Marxism's popular appeal in the Third World during the Cold War demonstrated. In some cases, attempts have been made to address the challenge of distribution through land reform, but often only half-heartedly. Readjusting tax burdens and instituting income redistribution are two other obvious approaches to this problem, but the cost of Western-style social welfare programs is prohibitive for least developed countries.

Problems arising from the unequal distribution of wealth are now also arising in some of the world's most advanced economies. The United States, where the extreme concentration of wealth now resembles Argentina and other Latin American countries, is a prime example.

THE STRATEGY OF DEVELOPMENT

As we have seen, political development and popular participation often go hand in hand. But not all forms of popular participation are bottom-up (democratic); some are top-down (coercive). The latter are associated with authoritarian or totalitarian regimes. Democratic states are, by definition, limited in what they

state-building
The creation of political institutions capable of exercising authority and allocating resources effectively within a nation.

traditional societies
A common term for often resource-poor societies that continue to observe pre-modern ways of life, work, and worship; often associated with high infant mortality rates, low life expectancy, poverty, illiteracy, hunger, and lack of the most basic medical services.

can do by constitutions, laws, and public opinion. For this reason, democracy and development often do not easily coexist, and dictatorships have been (and still are) all too common in the LDCs.

To say that democracy is a sign of development is true, but it begs the question: What explains development? In fact, democracy is a sign of wealth. Not all democracies are rich (although most are), nor are all rich nations democratic (although, again, most are). But there are precious few examples of democracy and poverty coexisting for very long.

Democracy and Development

democratic correlates
A condition or correlate thought to relate positively to the creation and maintenance of democracy within a nation.

Why does democracy work in many rich countries but not in most poor countries? One way to approach this question is to look for factors most democracies have in common—in other words **democratic correlates**. In theory, where these correlates exist in the greatest number and measure, the probability of democracy is greatest; conversely, where they are largely absent, democracy has the smallest chance of succeeding.[8] But in the real world, theory and practice often diverge.

Economic correlates include:

- *National Wealth.* Prosperity and democracy are often found in the same place, as are poverty and autocracy, but not always. India, for example, has been democratic since independence, despite being poor and extremely diverse, and oil-rich Saudi Arabia is autocratic.

- *A Market Economy.* Market economies generally favor private enterprise over state ownership of the means of production. Competition rewards efficiency and innovation. Supply and demand drive decisions about what to produce and how. Self-interest and the need for self-reliance encourage savings and investment.

- *A Middle Class.* A sharp class division with no buffer between rich and poor is not conducive to a sustainable democracy. Sooner or later, the many will strike back against the few—either rising up in open rebellion or simply slacking off on the job, placing either the state or the economy, or both, in grave jeopardy.

- *The Internet.* Access to the latest knowledge and information is vital to economic success; in the age of globalization, access to the Internet is essential.

There are also certain political, cultural, historical, and geographic correlates of democracy. Political correlates include civilian control over the military, a strong independent judiciary, and the existence of a differentiated civil society (civic clubs, trade unions, business organizations, and the like).[9] *Cultural* correlates such as tolerance of diversity, respect for the rule of law, and belief in democracy are also important. Obviously, the greater the distribution of wealth and education in a given society, the more likely the spread of the seeds of democracy.[10] But that doesn't solve the problem for the LDCs that, by definition, lack the resources to build schools or the wealth to spread around.

Development and Democracy

What comes first, democracy or development? The stunning success of China in reducing poverty provides dramatic proof that development without democracy is possible. Indeed, civil rights are hardly a top priority for people who are starving, sick, or homeless.[11] A vibrant economy is more likely to have an immediate impact on the quality of life, social services, infrastructure, and educational opportunities than, say, free elections.

The reforms necessary to spur economic development inevitably have spillover effects on society and the political system. For example, privatization and foreign investment give rise to a nascent middle class. To be competitive, it is necessary to cultivate a professional class with the same type of educational opportunities and financial rewards. To gain access to foreign markets, least developed countries face pressures to open up their own markets. Western products and services—from music to fashion—give rise to individualism, materialism, and a desire for freedom of expression, especially among youth. In these and countless other ways, market-oriented economic reforms impart a bias toward democratization. Where such reforms bring new hope and prosperity, they help ensure that if and when democracy finally arrives, it does so without plunging society into a state of anarchy.[12]

Africa: Neither Democracy nor Development

Between 1974 and 1990, more than thirty countries in southern Europe, Latin America, East Asia, and Eastern Europe replaced authoritarian with democratic governments. One noted observer wrote that it was "probably the most important political trend in the late twentieth century."[13] Everywhere, that is, except Africa.

Then in the early 1990s a democracy wave rolled across sub-Saharan Africa, where at least nine countries—including Benin, Cape Verde, and Gabon in West Africa—held free elections, in most cases for the first time ever.[14] It was South Africa that witnessed the most stunning changes, however, as black majority rule supplanted apartheid (white-supremacist rule). Democratic reforms were changing the face of politics in Benin, Botswana, Guinea-Bissau, Madagascar, Mali, Namibia, and São Tomé as well during this time.[15]

Elsewhere in Africa, however, things fell apart. In 1993, Nigeria's military rulers rescinded election results that displeased them. Côte d'Ivoire's government did the same. Elections in Kenya, Cameroon, and Gabon were marred by irregularities and corruption. Rwanda was the scene of genocidal violence in 1994. In 1996, military governments in Chad, Gambia, and Niger rigged national elections to achieve the outcomes they desired. During the 1990s, Somalia sank deeper into chaos and anarchy. Bloody civil wars wrought havoc in Liberia and Sierra Leone, and conflict in the Democratic Republic of the Congo (formerly Zaire) was accompanied by unspeakable atrocities. More than a decade later, the Congo is still a war zone. Thus, despite democratic gains, clan or tribal tensions destabilized much of sub-Saharan Africa in the 1990s.[16]

NIGERIA VERSUS INDIA: TWO CASE STUDIES, ONE RIDDLE

Nigeria is a giant with few equals on the African continent. India dwarfs Nigeria in nearly every category. The world's tenth largest oil exporter, Nigeria is resource rich; India, the world's seventh largest oil importer, is not. Nigeria's natural wealth to population ratio is favorable to successful nation-state building; India, with well over a billion people is not so fortunate.

And yet India has had a long run as a parliamentary democracy, interrupted only once (in 1975) by then Prime Minister Indira Gandhi who declared a state of emergency amid escalating riots. She allowed free elections in 1977 and was voted out of office. Nigeria, on the other hand, was under military rule during most of its post-independence history. When the military finally relaxed its chokehold on the government in 1999, it ushered in a decade of turmoil and misery.

Today, not only is India more democratic than Nigeria, but it is also achieving more rapid and diversified development. Why? Let's take a closer look at these two countries in search of clues to solve this riddle.

Nigeria: World's Poorest Oil-Rich Country

A large country in West Africa, Nigeria includes several distinct ethnic groups that predominate in different parts of the country, many smaller tribes, and several hundred distinct languages spoken.[17] Potentially one of sub-Saharan Africa's great powers, Nigeria endured inept military rule for much of its brief history as an independent state. Although the country accounts for only 3% of Africa's landmass, its population (estimated at 170 million in 2012) makes up some 20% of sub-Saharan Africa's total.

Nigeria is not a natural nation-state. Originally a British colony, it was drawn up for the administrative convenience of its colonial rulers who were only dimly aware of the ethnographic map of Africa at the time. Within its borders are peoples divided by region, religion, ethnicity, language, and culture. Nigeria's astonishing diversity also makes it a breeding ground for social conflict. The country is also divided along religious lines: Muslims dominate in the north, and Christians in the south.

Tensions simmer between Christians and Muslims. Regional animosities, exacerbated by religious, ethnic, and linguistic differences, erupted in a bloody civil war in 1967, when eastern Nigeria seceded as the independent state of Biafra. The war, which lasted about three years and ended in defeat for the rebels, claimed at least 600,000 lives.

After 1967, corrupt and incompetent military regimes ruled Nigeria. Despite huge state-owned oil reserves that produced a steady flow of export revenues, the nation's economy sank into a deepening morass with the vast majority of the population living in abject poverty.

In the 1990s, Nigeria's economy stagnated, growing by less than a half percent per year while corruption reached new heights. A 1996 UN fact-finding mission did not mince words: Nigeria's "problems of human rights are terrible and the political problems are terrifying." A succession of military dictators and ruling cliques enriched themselves shamelessly while neglecting the country's economic and social needs. According to *Transparency International*, a research institute based in Berlin, Germany, Nigeria had the most corrupt government in the world in the mid-1990s.[18]

By this time, bribery and extortion had become a way of life in Nigeria, where the system of "patronage" (with the military rulers bestowing government jobs and other favors on supporters of the regime) produced a bloated, inefficient, irresponsible, and unresponsive bureaucracy that absorbed more than 80% of the annual budget. Even today, it is not unusual to find petty civil servants sleeping at their desks or asking visitors for cash. Higher-level officials routinely inflate the contracts for everything the state procures and embezzle untold sums of money.

The average per capita income in oil-rich Nigeria (about $2,600 at purchasing power parity in 2011) is substantially lower than that of India, which has a population more than six times larger. High world oil prices have boosted Nigeria's oil-dependent economy in recent years, but most Nigerians have experienced few benefits. (Ninety-five percent of Nigeria's foreign exchange earnings derive from oil exports and 80% of budgetary revenues.)

There is no good reason for Nigeria or Nigerians to be poor. With a gross national product second only to South Africa's, Nigeria is a major oil producer, but its petrodollar bounty has not been invested in infrastructure, public works projects, or job-creating private business enterprise. In addition to suffering atrocious macroeconomic mismanagement, the country has been plagued by tribal and ethnic rivalries.

The complexity and diversity of Nigerian society partially explains the failure of two previous experiments with democracy and elected civilian government (in 1960–1966 and 1979–1983). Nigeria's military rulers repeatedly promised free elections, but these promises were not kept. When elections were held in 1993, the results displeased the generals, who nullified the election, imprisoned the winner, and charged him with treason. Thereafter, many other critics of the military regime were also imprisoned and persecuted; some were even executed.

In 1999, a former military leader, Olusegun Obasanjo, became Nigeria's first democratically elected president since 1983. Obasanjo was a rarity in Nigeria— a public figure with a military background and a reputation, justified or not, for personal integrity.

President Obasanjo promised to root out corruption but, despite some eventual arrests and convictions, he had limited success. Here is how one *New York Times* reporter described the situation at the end of 2005:

> Corruption touches virtually every aspect of Nigerian life, from the millions of sham e-mail messages sent each year by people claiming to be Nigerian officials seeking help with transferring large sums of money out of the country, to the police officers who routinely set up roadblocks, sometimes every few hundred yards, to extract bribes of 20 naira, about 15 cents, from drivers.[19]

Corrupt military regimes ran the country almost continuously from 1967 to 1999. The generals would promise—and occasionally stage—a national election, but it would turn out to be a sham (as in 1993). Mounting international pressure no doubt played a large role in compelling Nigeria's military rulers to allow free elections in 1999 and to permit the results—the election of the first popular presidential candidate in nearly twenty years—to stand.

But corruption did not end with the return of civilian government, and a decade later the morally debasing effects of easy money from a grossly mismanaged oil industry with few links to the national economy were still everywhere apparent. Indeed, for a time Nigeria—the richest poor country in Africa—was actually *importing* gasoline. Although Nigeria has extensive fossil fuel resources, crooked officials who control the state-monopoly oil company have used it as a cash cow for personal enrichment rather than as a resource for national economic development.

Hopes for a new beginning in Nigeria were dashed in 2007 by widespread reports of fraud in local and parliamentary elections and a sham election for president. What some were calling "gangster politics" eclipsed outgoing President Obasanjo's failed reforms.[20] When Umaru Yar'Adua succeeded Obasanjo as president in 2007, he inherited an improved economy but not a particularly healthy one. Nearly halfway through his first term, nothing was yet being done about the country's inadequate infrastructure, nationwide electricity cuts were still a common occurrence, and continuing attacks by militants in the oil-rich Delta region were severely disrupting oil production, which provides 95% of Nigeria's export revenues. All but a few Nigerians continued to languish in poverty—and frequently darkness as well. Meanwhile, the Economic and Financial Crimes Commission (EFCC), set up to enforce the new anticorruption laws, was spinning its wheels.[21]

Yar'Adua died in office after an extended illness that left him incapacitated and the government in limbo. Vice-president Goodluck Jonathan (yes, that's his real name) formally succeeded Yar'Adua as president in May 2010 pledging to fight endemic corruption, clean up the electoral process, and fix the electricity grid. As a member of the Ijaw, an ethnic group native to the Niger delta where rebels have engaged in a prolonged and bloody battle for a bigger share of the oil income that makes up 80% of the central government's revenues, Jonathan is perhaps Nigeria's best hope of ending this bitter dispute.

Jonathan won the presidential election in 2011, a mixed blessing for any Nigerian civilian leader intent on improving the life of the long-suffering Nigerian people. It goes without saying that Nigeria continues to be plagued by a dysfunctional economy and a corrupt state bureaucracy.

Nigeria's oil-wealth has not led to diversification of its economy or any significant redistribution of income. The annual per capita gross national product was about $2,600 (PPP) in 2011, compared to $6,200 in Egypt, $8,400 in China, $8,600 in Algeria, $13,400 in Turkey, and $14,940 in Latvia (one of Europe's poorest countries). The unemployment rate was 21% (!) and most Nigerians— as much as 70% of the population—live below the poverty line.

In sum, Jonathan has his work cut out for him. If he can make a good start on the work of bringing peace and stability to Nigeria, ending rampant corruption, promoting greater social justice, improving the country's infrastructure, and moving the economy away from a dangerous overdependence on oil, he will secure for himself an exalted place in the history of Nigeria—and the whole of sub-Saharan Africa. Meanwhile, millions of Nigerians are still waiting for the curtain to go up.

India: Elephant or Cheetah?

With its 1.2 billion people—17% of the world's population—India accounts for only about 2% of global GDP and about 1% of trade.[22] India is the second-largest country in the world and one of the most diverse. The Indian constitution recognizes 16 languages, though census data indicate more than 1,500 languages are spoken, including dialects. The "big three" official languages are English, Hindi, and Urdu. Hindi is spoken by about one-third of all Indians. English is the elite language, spoken by all university-educated Indians. Urdu is the language of Indian Muslims, the nation's largest minority group.

India is also home to various religions. Hinduism predominates, but there is also a large Muslim population (about 12% of the total), as well as Sikh, Jain, Parsi, Buddhist, and Christian minorities. Since Indian independence in 1947, communal violence—between Hindus and Muslims or Hindus and Sikhs—has erupted periodically. In some instances, members of one religious group have massacred members of another. In 1984, Prime Minister Indira Gandhi was assassinated by her Sikh bodyguards. In 1991, her son, former Prime Minister Rajiv Gandhi, was assassinated while campaigning to regain office.

The traditional caste system in India also created a barrier to development—everyone was born into a particular caste and remained there for life. Professions, occupations, and social status were all governed by the rules of the caste system. Members of a lower caste could not aspire to a profession or occupation reserved for a higher caste, nor could anyone marry outside his or her caste. Obviously, this rigid framework greatly impeded social mobility—the very mobility needed to transform a traditional society into a modern one. A vast underclass, called the untouchables, had no rights or opportunities in traditional India. The Indian government has since outlawed untouchability, but old attitudes die slowly, especially in tradition-bound rural societies. (Seven in ten Indians still live in small villages.)

Societal divisions tend to be reinforcing rather than crosscutting. Thus, Indian Muslims practice their own distinct religion and live in their own insular areas, have a distinct ethnic heritage, and speak their own language. Much the same can be said of Sikhs, Jains, and other groups. In extreme cases, these divisions can lead to calls for separatism or communal violence. Militant Sikhs have called for an independent state in northwestern India (where they are concentrated).

Hindu-Muslim hatred has led to periodic massacres. In the state of Gujarat in March 2002, Hindus slaughtered as many as 2,000 Muslims. In August 2003, two bombs blamed on Muslim militants killed 52 people in Mumbai (formerly Bombay). On November 26–29, 2008, ten coordinated shooting and bombing attacks occurred in Mumbai, killing at least 173 people and injuring more than 300. The split between Hindus and Muslims continues to destabilize India—and therefore South Asia as a region—more than six decades after independence.

India was long the indigent giant of Asia (see Figure 9.5) , a society with a rich history and a civilization symbolized by the splendor of the Taj Mahal but unable to cope with the challenges of the modern world. Just as Hong Kong,

FIGURE 9.5 Map of India. Note India's lengthy border with Pakistan; note also the geographical triangle formed by New Delhi (north central) and Mumbai (formerly Bombay) on the Arabian Sea and Calcutta on the extreme eastern edge by the Bay of Bengal.

Taiwan, South Korea, and Singapore were often called "dragons" or "tigers" not long ago, India was likened to an elephant—huge and magnificent, but encumbered by the weight of its massive body. Anyone familiar with the contemporary Asian scene, however, is more likely to think of India as a cheetah than an elephant. Neither image quite fits; paradoxically, each is half true.

Despite gains and an impressive growth spurt in recent years (see "Landmarks in History"), India remains a poor country even by comparison with China (the only country with more people). One reason: India's population is growing much faster than China's. Until recently, demography has overwhelmed development in India.

Although a recent five-year growth spurt saw India's economy grow by nearly 9% a year, China's GDP was still 3.5 times larger than India's in 2008–2009. China needs 8% annual growth to provide jobs for the roughly 7 million new members of its workforce each year; India's workforce is growing by about 14 million a year—that is, it is producing about 25% of the world's new workers. Like China, India is vulnerable to a drop in global demand for its exports. And when the Indian economy retreated in 2008–2009, Delhi's ability to provide the needed stimulus was hampered by a budget deficit approaching 8% of GDP.[23]

Today's India is a study in contrasts. In the 1990s, Manmohan Singh, now the prime minister, opened up India's economy by privatizing publicly owned enterprises, easing protectionist trade practices, cutting red tape, and making it possible for foreign firms in certain sectors to set up operations in India for the first time since independence.

LANDMARKS IN HISTORY

INDIA: Miracle of Democracy

India gained its independence in 1947, thus becoming one of the very first former colonies to break away. Mahatma Gandhi's leadership, exemplified by the strategy of nonviolent resistance, was a major factor in India's successful campaign against the British *raj*. India's extreme poverty and diversity at the time of independence made any attempt to create a democracy in the power vacuum that resulted from the British departure precarious. Even so, India's early leaders, including Gandhi (who was assassinated in 1948) and Jawaharlal Nehru, India's first elected president, resolved to bring India into the world as a democracy. And so they did.

India's achievements since independence:

- Maintaining parliamentary democracy
- Reducing absolute poverty by more than half
- Dramatically improving literacy and health care delivery
- Becoming one of the world's fastest-growing economies, with an average growth rate of 9% over the past four years
- Emerging as a global player in information technology, business process outsourcing, telecommunications, and pharmaceuticals

SOURCE: The World Bank, "India Country Overview 2009."

India's five-year plan set in 2007 called for a sustained growth rate of 9%. The downturn in 2008–2009 put a dent in the plan (the projected growth rate in 2012 was 6 to 7%, well below both inflation and unemployment rates). India's road to prosperity is strewn with potholes, including woefully underdeveloped infrastructure (roads, bridges, airports, electricity, and clean water), runaway inflation, overextended commercial bank credit, and a chronic double (trade and budget) deficit.

India's economy is growing but its population is growing even faster, threatening to overwhelm all efforts to provide a better life for millions of Indians with little or no education and mired in poverty. The young woman pictured here ekes out a living selling brooms on the street.

OBSTACLES TO DEVELOPMENT

The steeplechase is a challenging track-and-field event— a race over fences and ditches and hurdles—in a word, an obstacle course. As such, it's an apt metaphor for the problems facing developing nations. They, too, are in a race— against the clock and the competition. And they, too, face all sorts of obstacles.

Self-Identity: Who Am I? Where Do I Belong?

When modernization occurs, traditional ties are undermined, people are uprooted, and beliefs are challenged. Villagers tend not to trust strangers; social interaction is generally confined to family, clan, or village members. Fear of the unfamiliar, fatalism in the face of nature's accidents, and a low sense of individual efficacy combine to make traditional peasants and villagers averse to risk-taking. Modernization often forces villagers to move to cities in search of work; to interact with strangers; and to redefine themselves. Traditional people are less time-conscious than modern urbanites. Punching a clock is alien. Personal success and the spirit of free enterprise associated with entrepreneurship and competition are also alien to people accustomed to thinking in group terms (family, clan, or tribe).

Status in traditional societies is **ascriptive**; that is, it is *ascribed* by society on the basis of religion, age, and the like. In contrast, modern societies are (or claim to be) merit based. The Indian caste system is an extreme example of ascriptive status.

Gender is another key status factor. Male dominance is prevalent in most traditional societies, where a low level of technology, ranging from the lack of modern machines to absence of birth control, combines with high infant mortality rates to reinforce traditional gender roles and attitudes. Thus, in developing nations, the communal nature of traditional life precedes, and often precludes, individualism, entrepreneurship, and self-expression.

ascriptive status
An individual's status and position in society are ascribed on the basis of religion, gender, age, or some other attribute.

Greed: West Africa's Deadly Diamonds

Wars interfere with a nation's development efforts by diverting the government's attention and sapping its limited resources. Nearly all the wars since World War II have been fought in the Middle East, Africa, and Asia. Rivalries in the Middle East and Asia have also culminated in wars at various times, including those between Iran and Iraq, Pakistan and India, Vietnam and China, and China and India. Many Latin American countries also have long-standing disputes and rivalries with neighbors. Chile, for example, has engaged in military clashes with all three adjacent states: Argentina, Bolivia, and Peru.

In the 1980s, a conflict between Ethiopia and Somalia over the Ogaden region, worsened by a famine that spread across the Horn of Africa, led to a humanitarian crisis for some 1.5 million Somali refugees. This conflict was the background for the ill-fated 1992–1994 intervention by U.S. military forces, which was ostensibly to safeguard food deliveries to the starving (see discussion later in this chapter). Anarchy stalked West Africa during these years. In Sierra Leone, the diamond trade drove the violence. For years, so-called "conflict diamonds" from rebel-held mines allowed the brutal Revolutionary United Front (RUF) to arm and equip armies.

Between 1994 and 2007, sub-Saharan Africa was the scene of four major wars (conflicts causing at least 800,000 deaths each) in Rwanda, Sudan, Congo,

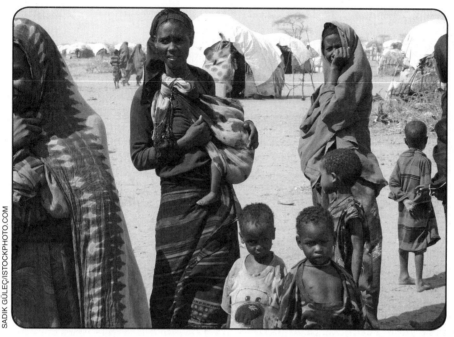

War, revolution, ethnic rivalry, famine, drought, and epidemics cause widespread human misery and destabilize governments on the African continent every year. These Somali women and children are living in the Dadaab refugee camp in Kenya; thousands of Somalis fled from hunger and starvation in 2011.

and Angola, and eighteen smaller wars. Armed conflicts in sub-Saharan Africa have not only taken a terrible toll in human life; they have also destroyed and disrupted fragile economies.

Ethnic Hatred: Taming the Tigers

Many least developed countries were carved out of former colonial holdings with little concern for the geography or history of the area or indigenous ethnic, religious, tribal, or linguistic patterns. Too often the result has been interethnic strife and even civil war.

Modernization (another name for development) poses daunting problems for indigenous peoples. Western concepts of "nation" and "nationalism" have little relevance, and yet success in forging a single national identity is crucial. Often, militant groups or movements hostile to social integration and modernization (Westernization) obstruct efforts at nation-building. For example, Islam's emphasis on piety, devotion to Allah, prayer five times each day, and strict rules of moral conduct are at odds with secularization, the sexual revolution, materialism, and self-gratification—in other words, the kinds of social change associated with modernization in the West.

Specific examples best illustrate the practical problems associated with diverse populations. Nigeria and India are both least developed countries with very diverse populations. Although we have focused on India and Nigeria, many other least developed countries face similar problems. Sri Lanka is one example.

Sri Lanka is split between the majority Sinhalese (74%), who are mostly Buddhist, and the Tamils (18%), who are mostly Hindu and predominate in the northern and eastern parts of the country. Militant Tamil groups seeking to secede—notably the Tamil Tigers—have carried out terrorist acts and conducted guerrilla warfare against the central government since 1983, when an outbreak of communal riots left at least 2,000 Tamils dead.[24] After a quarter-century of civil war, Sri Lanka has still not defeated this insurrection, but in February 2009, the United States, the European Union, Japan, and Norway issued a joint statement saying it was "just a short time before the Tigers lost all the territory still under their control." Like India, Sri Lanka displays a pattern of cultural diversity that impedes the search for a national consensus.

Rwanda and Burundi became genocidal killing fields in 1993–1994 as a result of hatred and mistrust between Hutu and Tutsi tribes. A decade later, a tragedy of similar proportions unfolded in eastern Sudan, where a government-sponsored campaign to crush rebels turned into a policy of **ethnic cleansing**, the unconscionable practice of rape, pillage, and mass murder in the remote Darfur region. Some 2 million refugees—mostly women and children who managed to escape—were displaced during the genocidal civil war.

Peace talks finally produced an accord in 2005 calling for a six-year period of autonomy for South Sudan followed by a referendum on independence. The outcome was no surprise: the people of South Sudan voted overwhelmingly to divorce Sudan. South Sudan became independent in July 2011.

Development is necessary, but it is no guarantee of peace or prosperity. But as the case of South Sudan demonstrates, the reverse is also true: Peace does not necessarily bring development and prosperity.

In sum, ethnically diverse societies are the rule in the LDCs. More than half of the nations created by decolonization in the postwar period are home to more than five major ethnic groups.[25] Ethnic diversity has made the problems of nation-building in these countries complex and conflict an all too common occurrence.

Poverty: First Things First

Despite significant differences in economic development and national wealth, many former colonies are still poor more than half a century after independence. Why?

Premodern economies are based on agriculture and mining. Excessive dependence on agricultural commodities and raw materials makes these societies vulnerable to the ups and downs of global markets. Some poor countries raise only one major export crop. Bangladesh, for example, produces nothing but jute for export. When the price of jute declines, Bangladesh—one of the poorest developing nations—has nothing to fall back on. Ethiopia's monoculture economy is based on coffee exports; Cuba mainly produces sugar for export; Honduras exports bananas, and so on. Some LDCs are economically addicted to illegal cash crops: Peasants in Colombia, Ecuador, and Peru, for example, produce coca (cocaine) for export; Afghanistan is the world's primary source of heroin (made from poppy seeds). Though many LDCs have more than one crop or mineral resource, few are highly diversified in both agriculture and industry. And even some oil-rich countries are poor despite having an abundance of "black gold." As a result, great economic disparities still exist, not only from one country to another but also from region to region (Table 9.2).

To modernize, poor countries need to import industrial goods. To pay for manufactured goods, LDCs need to export food, fiber, and minerals. But the **terms of trade** tend to work against them—the price of industrial goods is high,

ethnic cleansing
The practice of clearing all Muslims out of towns and villages in Bosnia by violent means; the term has also been used to characterize genocidal assaults on minority populations in other parts of the world, including the Darfur region of Sudan.

terms of trade
In international economics, the valuation (or price) of the products (commodities, manufactures, services) that countries buy on the world market relative to the valuation of the products they sell; the structure of prices for different kinds of goods and services in international trade—for example, if manufactured goods are generally priced high relative to minerals and agricultural products, then the terms of trade are unfavorable for countries that produce only farm commodities or raw materials.

TABLE 9.2   Per Capita Gross National Income (purchasing power parity) by Region.

Region	Per Capita GNI (in U.S. dollars)
Arab World	9,577
Sub-Saharan Africa	2,240
North America*	47,912
Latin America and the Caribbean	11,950
South Asia	3,315
East Asia and Pacific	10,313
EURO area	35,250

*This number is for the United States; Canada's per capita GNI was just under $42,000, but Canada, with a population of just 34.5 million represents less than 7% of the population of North America (California alone, for example, is over 38 million).

SOURCE: The World Bank 2011. http://databank.worldbank.org/data/views/reports/tableview.aspx.

while the price of agricultural products and raw materials is often low. Commodity prices on the world market fluctuate wildly at times, creating uncertainties and mounting foreign debt.

Some LDCs also face a serious population problem. The industrial democracies have population growth of less than 1%, and several western European countries reached zero or negative population growth by 1990. By contrast, many of the poorest countries still have birthrates in the range of 2 to 3% annually (compare Figure 9.6 and Figure 9.7). In some African countries (Niger and the Democratic Republic of the Congo), as well as in parts of the Middle East (notably the Palestinian territories and Yemen), annual birthrates are greater than 3%.

Rapid urbanization poses acute problems because LDCs do not have the resources to support public services, build roads and bridges, or create new schools, hospitals, housing complexes, and, most important, jobs. Clean water is basic to good health and a decent living standard, yet countless millions of men and women do not have easy access to a water pump,

This young man in Angola is pushing a cart by hand. Angola is poor despite being one of sub-Saharan Africa's largest oil-producing countries.

JOSE MANUEL LIMA DE SILVA

FIGURE 9.6   World Population, 1995: 5,692,210,000.

SOURCE: Boyce Ransberger, "Damping the World's Population: Birthrates Are Falling Now but More Needs to Be Done in the Long Term," Washington Post National Weekly Edition. September 12–18, 1994, 10–40. ©1994 The Washington Post. Reprinted with permission.

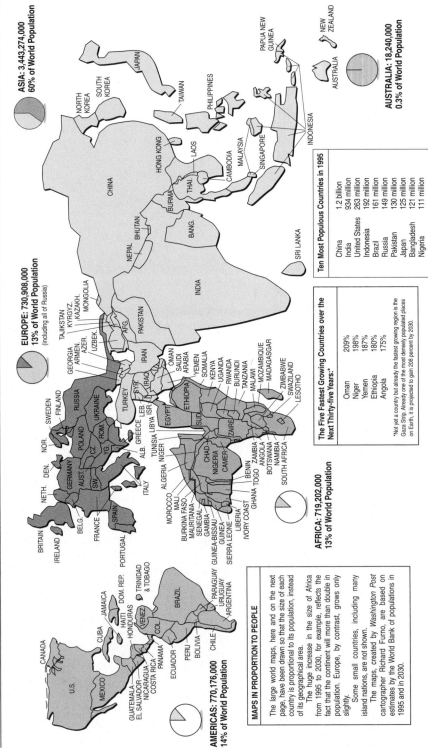

ASIA: 3,443,274,000
60% of World Population

EUROPE: 730,908,000
13% of World Population
(including all of Russia)

AFRICA: 719,202,000
13% of World Population

AMERICAS: 770,176,000
14% of World Population

AUSTRALIA: 18,240,000
0.3% of World Population

Ten Most Populous Countries in 1995

China	1.2 billion
India	934 million
United States	263 million
Indonesia	192 million
Brazil	161 million
Russia	149 million
Pakistan	130 million
Japan	125 million
Bangladesh	121 million
Nigeria	111 million

The Five Fastest Growing Countries over the Next Thirty-five Years:*

Oman	209%
Niger	198%
Yemen	187%
Ethiopia	180%
Angola	175%

*Not yet a country but already the fastest growing region is the Gaza Strip. Already one of the most densely populated places on Earth, it is projected to gain 208 percent by 2030.

MAPS IN PROPORTION TO PEOPLE

The large world maps, here and on the next page, have been drawn so that the size of each country is proportional to its population, instead of its geographical area.

The huge increase in the size of Africa from 1995 to 2030, for example, reflects the fact that the continent will more than double in population. Europe, by contrast, grows only slightly.

Some small countries, including many island nations, are not shown.

The maps, created by *Washington Post* cartographer Richard Furno, are based on estimates by the World Bank of populations in 1995 and in 2030.

© CENGAGE LEARNING

FIGURE 9.7 World Population, 2030: 8,474,017,000 (a 49% increase from 1995 world population). These two maps show the projected change in population growth between 1995 and 2030. The maps have been drawn so that each country's size is proportional to its population. As these maps dramatically illustrate, much of the projected population increases will occur in developing nations.

SOURCE: Boyce Ransberger, "Damping the World's Population: Birthrates Are Falling Now but More Needs to Be Done in the Long Term," Washington Post National Weekly Edition. September 12–18, 1994, 10–40. ©1994 The Washington Post. Reprinted with permission.

ASIA: 5,053,974,000
60% of World Population
+47%

EUROPE: 741,707,000
9% of World Population
+1.5%
(includes all of Russia)

AUSTRALIA: 22,824,000
0.3% of World Population
+25%

AFRICA: 1,556,723,000
18% of World Population
+116%

AMERICAS: 1,082,702,000
13% of World Population
+41%

Ten Most Populous Countries in 2030		
China	1.5 billion	+25%
India	1.4 billion	+53%
United States	328 million	+25%
Indonesia	275 million	+43%
Pakistan	259 million	+100%
Nigeria	233 million	+110%
Brazil	231 million	+43%
Bangladesh	191 million	+58%
Ethiopia	158 million	+180%
Russia	153 million	+3%

© CENGAGE LEARNING

much less indoor plumbing. In LDCs open sewage systems are common and toilets rare.

Those of us fortunate enough to live in rich countries take the basic human needs—food and shelter, as well as clean water—for granted. Not so for people, especially women and children, in the world's poorest countries. The **Green Revolution**, the application of agricultural technology and modern irrigation and synthetic fertilizers to produce high-yield strains of wheat, rice, and corn, has helped ease the food-population crisis in India, Mexico, the Philippines and elsewhere, but as we now know, at a high cost to the environment.[26] Unfortunately, the promise of ending world hunger through modern technology has yet to be fulfilled (see "Ideas and Politics").

People who subsist on severely limited diets do not have the energy to be productive, leaving many developing nations caught in a vicious cycle: they are poor because they are not productive enough, and they are not productive enough because they are poor.

Land tenure also poses a significant problem in many least developed countries. In some areas, land ownership—and local power—is highly concentrated; in others, land is fragmented into parcels too small to be profitable. In Africa, communal ownership of rural land is (or was) common. But as commercial plantations encroach on village land, cash crops such as maize, rice, and coffee replace traditional food crops. Young men and women are forced leave in search of work. Many become migrant farm workers, earning paltry wages during the crop-growing season.

Green Revolution
A dramatic rise in agricultural output, resulting from modern irrigation systems and synthetic fertilizers, characteristic of modern India, Mexico, Taiwan, and the Philippines.

A WORLD WITHOUT HUNGER

Some facts about world hunger:

- Across the world, 63 million people are hungry.
- Every day, almost 16,000 children die from hunger-related causes—one every five seconds.
- Poor nutrition and calorie deficiencies cause nearly one in three people to die prematurely or develop disabilities.
- Hunger manifests itself in many ways other than starvation and famine. Most poor people who battle hunger also face chronic undernourishment and vitamin or mineral deficiencies, which result in stunted growth, weakness, and heightened susceptibility to illness.
- Countries in which a large portion of the population goes hungry are usually poor and lack social safety nets; when a family cannot grow enough food or earn enough money to buy food, there is nowhere to turn for help.

- In 2006, about 9.7 million children died before they reached their fifth birthday. Almost all these deaths occurred in least developed countries, four-fifths of them in sub-Saharan Africa and South Asia, the two regions that suffer the highest rates of hunger and malnutrition.
- In the developing world, 26% of children under age five are moderately to severely underweight, and an overwhelming 32% are moderately to severely stunted.

A world without hunger is a wonderful idea. Unfortunately, it does not exist, never has, and, unless lots of things change, it never will.

SOURCE: Adapted from Bread for the World website at http://www.bread.org/learn/hunger-basics/hunger-facts-international.html.

Finally, damage to the environment is an ever-growing problem in the least developed countries. Native plants and animals are disappearing in many places, water and air pollution are rising, soil degradation and deforestation are occurring at an alarming rate from Indonesia to Brazil and in many parts of sub-Saharan Africa, causing floods, soil erosion, and loss of wildlife habitat.

The idea of progress and the closely related concept of development are both outgrowths of the Western experience. But we now know that societies in the throes of modernization are also, paradoxically, among the most vulnerable to disintegration and decay—from better to worse. As the famed political scientist, Samuel Huntington, wisely observed: "Modernization in practice always involves change in and usually the disintegration of a traditional political system, but it does not necessarily involve significant movement toward a modern political system.... Yet the tendency is to think that because social modernization is taking place, political modernization must also be taking place."[27]

FAILED STATES

The promise of development all too often collides with the realities of poverty, corruption, and ethnic hatred in the former colonial areas. In recent decades, the world has witnessed a grim spectacle of states and societies self-destructing and in the process destabilizing neighboring states. Clearly, development has its discontents and comes with no guarantees, no owner's manual. In many parts of the world, it has not come at all.

The most dysfunctional ("failed") states are wretched places where extremes are the norm, where government is either repressive or too weak to maintain a modicum of law and order. Under such circumstances, the most violent elements in society take over. Both criminal and political violence stalk the city streets and threaten villages unprotected by police or a vigilant free press.

When the world is not watching, atrocities can go unnoticed for days, weeks, even months. This image may be disturbing, but it is all too real. Among the world's most dysfunctional states, Haiti is the one geographically closest to the United States. In this section, we look at Haiti and four other failed states: Somalia, Sierra Leone, Afghanistan, and Zimbabwe. These examples by no means exhaust the list of candidates. Before the collapse of Communism (1989–1991), Soviet Russia and the Central and Eastern European countries probably belonged on that list as well. After the collapse, the former Soviet Union, Czechoslovakia, and Yugoslavia broke apart—in other words, failed.

Haiti

Haiti banished French colonial control and slavery in a series of wars in the early nineteenth century. In so doing, it became the first republic ruled by people of African descent in world history, as well as the first independent Caribbean state. But after decades of poverty, environmental degradation, and political instability—as well as a series of brutal dictatorships and natural disasters—Haiti is the poorest country in the Western Hemisphere and was one of the poorest in the world even before the devastating 2010 earthquake.

An estimated 300,000 people were killed in the January 2010 earthquake, which left the capital of Port-au-Prince in ruins and prompted a major international aid effort. Near the end of 2010 (October–December), Haiti's population of 10.2 million was hit by a major cholera outbreak. Meanwhile, despite massive outside aid, the rubble had not been cleared away, reconstruction had barely begun, and hundreds of thousands of people were still living in tents (the number was reported to have declined to 810,00 in January 2011, down from a peak of 1.5 million in July 2010).

Somalia

The Horn of Africa is home to several of the poorest countries on earth, including Sudan, Somalia, Eritrea, and Ethiopia. In the 1980s and 1990s, this region was afflicted by drought, famine, international conflict, civil wars, and all manner of violence. In the early 1990s, the most critical food shortages occurred in Somalia, where civil war and drought conspired to cause terrible human suffering. In August 1992, the United Nations Children's Fund (UNICEF) triggered a massive international relief effort when it warned that 2 million Somalis, of a total population of slightly more than 8 million, faced starvation within six months.

Against this backdrop of violence and misery, rebels ousted Somalia's long-time dictator, Siad Barré, in January 1991. Fighting and famine followed, leaving 300,000 people dead and millions at risk of starvation. A near-total breakdown of law and order plunged the country into anarchy and placed women and children at the mercy of armed bandits, who disrupted relief efforts by international agencies, stole food intended for starving children, and murdered relief workers. At the end of 1992, outgoing U.S. President George H. W. Bush ordered a military intervention to safeguard relief supplies and workers. The scene was so chaotic that restoring law and order proved impossible. Long after the U.S.-led UN forces departed in March 1995 (following the brutal killing of several U.S.

Following the 7.0 magnitude earthquake that hit Haiti's capital city of Port-au-Prince in January 2010, some 1.5 million people were housed in temporary shelters. Many families were still living in tents one year later.

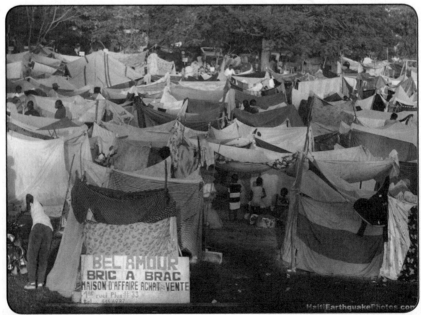

soldiers), Somalia remained a country without a national government. Maps showing which areas were controlled by which factions looked more like a jigsaw puzzle than a political configuration.

Somalia was one of the poorest countries in Africa in the 1990s, with a per capita GNP of less than $500 and an illiteracy rate of more than 75%. Moreover, it is underdeveloped both politically and economically. The structure of Somali society is based on kinship ties, or clans—in fact, the civil war was a clan war. If Somalia cannot find a formula for political stability, it cannot rebuild its economy. The reverse is also true: Stability depends on economic and social progress.

Somalia today remains a failed state. Anarchy is a boon to thieves, and Somalia is the world's number-one haven for pirates. In 2009 it once again became the focus of world attention when Somali pirates seized a merchant ship flying the U.S. flag and held the captain hostage, provoking President Obama to authorize the use of force if it appeared the captain's life was in imminent danger. Three of the hostage takers were killed by sharpshooters and a fourth was captured and brought back to the United States to face trial on criminal charges. The rescue operation succeeded: The captain's life was saved. But who will rescue Somalia?

Sierra Leone

We've seen that functioning democracy is rare in sub-Saharan Africa. Even where it once appeared to be working, it has failed—in some cases miserably, and nowhere more so than in Sierra Leone.

When legislative elections were held in Sierra Leone in 1986, the aptly named All People's Party approved 335 candidates to contest 105 elective seats. The party typically offered at least three contestants for each seat, a common practice among one-party states in sub-Saharan Africa. Voters in Sierra Leone actually had more choices—relative to personalities, at least—than voters in most U.S. legislative races.

Nonetheless, in the 1990s, Sierra Leone began a steady descent into anarchy. Between 1996 and 1998, the government changed hands four times. Then all hell broke loose, and rebel members of the so-called Revolutionary United Front (RUF) began chopping off hands right and left. They chopped off heads too. They kidnapped small boys and girls and abused them in unspeakable ways. The RUF was notorious for turning boys into drug-addicted killers and sex slaves—so-called child soldiers. Kidnapped girls became sex slaves and sometimes fighters as well.[28]

The conflict officially ended in January 2002. It is estimated that 50,000 people were killed in the decade-long civil war, but there is no way of knowing for sure and no way of measuring the cost in shattered lives. The United Nations installed a peacekeeping force of 17,000 troops—the largest ever. The incumbent president, Ahmad Tejan Kabbah, was reelected with 70% of the vote in May 2002. The disarmament of 70,000 soldiers was completed in 2004, and a UN-sponsored war crimes tribunal opened.

In June 2007, three former rebel leaders were found guilty of rape and enlisting child soldiers—the first time an international tribunal ruled on the recruitment of child soldiers under age fifteen. In September 2007, in the first elections since the departure of the UN peacekeeping force in 2004, voters in Sierra Leone chose a new president. War crimes trials in The Hague continued for the next five years, including the highly publicized trial of Charles Taylor, the former Liberian president, for "crimes against humanity"—specifically, aiding and abetting the violent rebel group (RUF) mainly responsible for the atrocities committed in the civil war. (A gruesome practice of the RUF was to terrorize the population by hacking off victims' hands or feet.) The last case ended in The Hague in April 2012, with judges finding Taylor guilty as charged.

Sierra Leone is an object lesson in what can happen when a failed state sinks into anarchy. Neither the civil institutions nor the political culture necessary to support and sustain democracy were present. For a time, the appearance of democracy masked the reality of a society capable of erupting into volcanic civil violence at any moment. Today, the UN classifies Sierra Leone as one of the world's "least livable" countries.

Zimbabwe

Robert Mugabe has been the face of Zimbabwe since its inception in 1980. Mugabe was born in 1924 in what was then the British colony of Southern Rhodesia. He rose to prominence in the 1960s as the leader of the Zimbabwe African National Union during a long and bitter guerrilla war against white minority rule. In 1980, he became the prime minister of the new Black African government of Zimbabwe and gradually gathered dictatorial powers in his own hands, assuming the presidency in 1987. As president, Mugabe has enriched himself and his cronies while plunging his country into a degrading and desperate state of poverty. Today Zimbabwe is a failed state.

At first hailed as a symbol of the new Africa, Mugabe, a lifelong Roman Catholic, has presided over one of the worst and most corrupt governments in the world, while utterly mismanaging Zimbabwe's postcolonial economy. Under his despotic rule, the health and well-being of the people has dropped dramatically, in a natural result of widespread poverty, unemployment, malnutrition, and the absence of medical care—as well as a costly war with the Democratic Republic of the Congo (1998–2002).

The government's chaotic land reform program, which seized white-owned farms with the avowed aim of redistributing the land, effectively destroyed the only functioning sector of the economy and turned Zimbabwe into a net importer of food. Mugabe's response to the economic crisis he created was to print money to cover soaring government deficits while stubbornly refusing to institute economic reforms. The IMF eventually stopped lending to Zimbabwe because of arrears on past loans.

Despite humanitarian food aid from the United States and the EU, according to the World Health Organization, Zimbabwe has the world's shortest life expectancy (thirty-seven years for men and thirty-four years for women), the most orphans (about 25% of the country's children, according to UNICEF), and the highest inflation rate (skyrocketing from more than 1,000% in 2006 to 11.2 million percent in 2008). An estimated 3,800 Zimbabweans died of cholera in the last half of 2008. In January 2009, a newly released $50 billion note was just enough to buy two loaves of bread. Zimbabwe's annual GDP per capita in 2010 was estimated at a paltry $169 (PPP).

Mugabe "won" reelection in 2002 only after having his leading opponent arrested for treason. In March 2007, a popular opposition leader named Morgan Tsvangirai was beaten and hospitalized in Zimbabwe after the country's eighty-three-year-old virtual dictator, Robert Mugabe, ordered police to break up a protest rally in the capital of Harare. Despite all, Tsvangirai defeated Mugabe in the 2008 presidential elections, but Mugabe refused to relinquish power, unleashing a spasm of violence that saw 163 people killed and some 5,000 tortured or brutally beaten.

Under enormous international pressure and facing a reenergized domestic opposition, Mugabe finally agreed to a power-sharing deal in September 2008, allowing Tsvangirai to become prime minister in a new dual-executive government. But, true to form, Mugabe broke the agreement, installing his own loyal lieutenants in every ministry. Mugabe, at age eighty-five, remains Zimbabwe's president. In 2009, *Parade* magazine named Mugabe the world's worst living dictator.

During his twenty-seven years in power, Mugabe has plunged Zimbabwe into utter ruin. When he finally goes, he will leave a bitter legacy of chronic unemployment, hyperinflation (the highest in the world), and an impoverished society where the oft-repeated promise of democracy was repeatedly broken.

Mugabe is an example of the kind of corrupt and incompetent leadership that has plagued sub-Saharan Africa since the end of the colonial era. Sadly, at the end of the first decade of the twenty-first century, what distinguishes Zimbabwe's government from that of most other countries in the region is a difference in degree, not in kind.

Afghanistan

The United States invaded Afghanistan when it became known that the 9/11 attacks were carried out by a militant Islamic group called al-Qaeda and that the Taliban, Afghanistan's fundamentalist political regime, was allowing al-Qaeda's leader, Osama bin Laden, to use Afghanistan territory as a base of operations. What was less well known at the time (and what decision makers in Washington appear to have forgotten or overlooked) is the historical background. For nearly three decades prior to the landing of U.S. Special Forces on Afghan soil, Afghanistan had been one of the world's most dysfunctional states. Even prior to the overthrow of the monarchy in the 1970s, the country was poor and backward, but thereafter it spiraled into two decades of bloody turmoil. By 2001, the entire country was a shambles, and millions of people—especially women and children—were living on the very edge of a precipice.

Home to many ethnic groups, Afghanistan reflects the disparate populations around its periphery—Pakistan, Iran, Turkmenistan, Tajikistan, Uzbekistan, and China. The largest group, the Pashtuns, constitute about 40% of the total population (about 26 million people). Thus, there is no majority group, only minorities of different sizes. Roughly 99% of all Afghans are Muslims; about 15% are Shi'ite Muslims (as are most Iranians).

Afghanistan was a monarchy from 1747 to 1973, when the country came apart at the seams. Various factions fought for supremacy after 1973, until the Soviet Union made the fateful decision to intervene on behalf of its favorite thug (a Communist) in 1979. A brutal and protracted war ensued; the Soviet Union finally withdrew in defeat in 1989 after a decade of debilitating (and humiliating) warfare. The United States had secretly backed the Islamic resistance, called the mujahedeen, by supplying weapons and other aid to the rebel forces. Amazingly, the United States and Osama bin Laden were fighting side by side at this time.

Opponents overthrew the Communist regime and seized power in 1992. The new strongman refused to relinquish power when his term officially expired, but Taliban forces assaulted the capital and ousted him in 1996. The Taliban regime instituted a totalitarian system of rule couched in the language and concepts of Islam but based on a perversion of the Qur'an (holy scripture) and Sharia law (based on the teachings of Muslim clerics or mullahs). Women and girls were forced to wear the burka (a one-piece, head-to-toe garment) in public and were forbidden to work outside the home, to go to school, or to express opinions at variance with the government. The government banned television, movies, music, dancing, and most other forms of "decadent" entertainment.

The Taliban was a brutal and repressive regime that clearly did not enjoy the support of the people. It seized control of a fragile and dysfunctional state and turned it into a tool of domestic and international terrorism. Instability in Afghanistan poses a grave danger to neighboring Pakistan as well. As a failed state, Afghanistan illustrates a stark and sobering lesson: dysfunctional states can become a threat to regional stability and world order. The solution—economic growth and development—is obvious but elusive.

In June 2011, President Obama unveiled his plan for the withdrawal of U.S. troops from Afghanistan to be completed by the end of 2014. Despite a sizeable drawdown in 2011–2012 some 68,00 US troops remained in Afghanistan at the beginning of 2013. After more than a decade of war, the prospects for peace in Afghanistan are bleak—with or without a U.S. military presence.

DEVELOPMENT: TONIC OR ELIXIR?

In the West, we think of development as a good thing. But we are seeing lots of signs that point to a different and disturbing conclusion: that it's possible to get too much of a good thing; that *overdevelopment* can be as detrimental to the health and sustainability of a state and society as underdevelopment. Signs and symptoms of overdevelopment are all around us but are often too easily ignored unless we happen to be visiting Beijing during an "orange smog" alert; or living on the Jersey Shore when a super storm like Hurricane Sandy makes landfall; or caught in an afternoon rush-hour traffic jam on a Los Angeles freeway in mid-July. (You can probably think of examples close to home. Go ahead. Try. Start with what you know from first-hand experience. One example: massive multiacre high school parking lots filled with cars. You won't see anything like it anywhere else on the planet. By the way there were about 20 million students in grades 9 through 12 in the United States in 2012—if, say, one-third of these students drive to school....)

All societies are in a constant state of flux, rising or falling. They develop in different ways, at different rates, and at different times. In the modern era, Western societies have led the way, developing economically and technologically along lines congruent with the political institutions that evolved at the same time. In this sense, development was a natural process originating *within* these societies.

For least developed countries, development is often just the opposite: an alien process that originates from the outside. Development is always disruptive, but even more so when it is forced on societies, whether by foreign powers or by external circumstances.

The story of development does not end with the arrival of the postindustrial state. Most rich states boast high-tech economies offering a vast array of commercial and financial services. They still engage in agriculture, mining, and industry, but these sectors of the economy are eclipsed in importance by high-tech goods that drive the global economy—computer software, pharmaceuticals, and financial services.

The new global economy brings a higher quality of life to consumers but comes with a price—outsourcing of jobs and chronic unemployment, urban congestion and crowding, air and water pollution, epidemics and stress-related illnesses, illegal drug use, overconsumption, energy shortages, waste disposal problems, global warming, extinction of countless plant and animal species, and others.

Thus late-stage development is no more free of challenges than early-stage development. The challenges are different, but no less daunting. Overdeveloped countries—where development has outrun society's capacity to deal with undesirable side effects of rapidly accelerating technological and social change—might do well to focus more attention on solving the problems they face and less on telling so-called underdeveloped countries what to do and how to do it.

In the West, politicians and scholars alike often uncritically accept the proposition that development is the answer to all the world's problems. Sometimes, in an effort to be politically correct, political scientists use the term *premodern* to describe societies in an early stage of development. Development theory often *assumes* development is good—always and everywhere—and that tradition and superstition, the "dead hand of the past," are impediments to progress. Critics argue that musings on development often amount to little more than praise for all things Western, and that Western experts on the subject are guilty of ethnocentrism.

In 1750, the French philosopher Jean-Jacques Rousseau observed, "Our souls have been corrupted in proportion to the movement of our sciences and arts towards perfection."[29] Rousseau's political philosophy sprang from the notion that science and technology were eroding, rather than enhancing, our humanity. Overstated? Perhaps, but there's no denying that development—what we often equate with the greatest advances in modern civilization—can be a double-edged sword.

SUMMARY

The least developed countries (LDCs) are so named because they are poor and lack basic features of modern postindustrial states. Although generalizations and clichés are common (for example, rural poverty and urban crowding), these nations are highly diverse. The enduring legacy of European colonialism is a political map that makes little sense: borders that do not reflect indigenous ethnic, religious, and tribal patterns. The upshot in many cases is chronic instability: social unrest, rebellions, civil wars, and even genocide.

State-building requires leaders that can effectively unify the population (nation-building), political institutions that respond to people's needs and encourage citizen participation, and an honest government that can transfer power smoothly.

Democracy correlates with the existence of certain identifiable economic, political, social, and attitudinal variables. In most LDCs, the failure of democracy and development have gone hand in hand.

Development is an arduous task and often fails. Socially, populations are often fragmented. Psychologically, individuals are heavily dependent on tradition and frequently oppose change. Economically, problems range from unfavorable terms of trade and high foreign debt to rapid population growth, a low level of technology, entrenched land tenure problems, and environmental difficulties.

States and societies frequently disintegrate rather than develop. The Soviet Union provides the most stunning example in recent decades. Other examples include Iraq, Congo, Ethiopia, Haiti, Lebanon, Liberia, Sudan, Somalia, Sierra Leone, Yugoslavia, and Afghanistan.

Overdevelopment (the opposite of "underdevelopment") is a problem afflicting many Western societies today. Contemporary ideas about development tend to assume its desirability despite such postindustrial problems as pollution, congestion, and drug addiction, as well as overpopulation, climate change, and pandemic diseases.

KEY TERMS

least developed countries (LDCs)   220
neocolonialism   223
North-South conflict   223
colonialism   228
imperialism   228
nonviolent resistance   229
political development   230
state-building   231
traditional societies   231
democratic correlates   232
ascriptive status   240
ethnic cleansing   242
terms of trade   242
Green Revolution   246

REVIEW QUESTIONS

1. What are the salient characteristics of the Third World of yesterday and the Least Developed Countries of today? How do these relate to the development process?
2. Are most WTO members rich or poor? Do the majority of the world's nations and peoples have fair access to global markets?
3. Elucidate the correlates of democracy. How compelling is this line of analysis? Comment.
4. What are the incentives for modernization? What sources of resistance can you identify?
5. Does development always lead to democracy? Is the reverse true? List some examples.
6. All things considered—India's political system, the current state of the Indian economy, and the broader question of social justice—would you say India's successes outweigh its failures or vice versa? Explain.
7. Nigeria is most likely to become sub-Saharan Africa's first major global power. Do you agree or disagree with this statement? Explain.
8. What are the barriers to development? If development is so difficult, why do nations undertake it?
9. How are development and decay related? Are states and societies ever static? Comment.
10. Name three dysfunctional states and use one as an example to illustrate the nature of this type of state.

PART 3

Politics by Civil Means

Citizens, Leaders, and Policies

CHAPTER 10

Political Socialization

The Making of a Citizen

THINK ABOUT IT

What is the good citizen, and how do we know?

What is socialization, and why is it important?

By what means and mechanisms does a disparate population of individuals and groups (families, clans, and tribes) become forged into a cohesive society?

How does socialization affect political behavior, and what happens when socialization fails?

The year is 1932. The Soviet Union is suffering a severe shortage of food, and millions go hungry. Joseph Stalin, leader of the Communist Party and head of the Soviet government, has undertaken a vast reordering of Soviet agriculture that eliminates a whole class of landholders (the *kulaks*) and collectivizes all farmland. Henceforth, every farm and all farm products belong to the state. To deter theft of what is now considered state property, the Soviet government enacts a law prohibiting individual farmers from appropriating any grain for their own private use. Acting under this law, a young boy reports his father to the authorities for concealing grain. The father is shot for stealing state property. Soon after, the boy is killed by a group of peasants, led by his uncle, who are outraged that he would betray his own father. The government, taking a radically different view of the affair, extols the boy as a patriotic martyr.

Stalin considered the little boy in this story a model citizen, a hero. How citizenship is defined says a lot about a government and the philosophy or ideology that underpins it.

THE GOOD CITIZEN

Stalin's celebration of a child's act of betrayal as heroic points to a distinction Aristotle originally made: The *good citizen* is defined by laws, regimes, and rulers, but the moral fiber (and universal characteristics) of a *good person* is fixed, and it transcends the expectations of any particular political regime.[1]

Good **citizenship** includes behaving in accordance with the rules, norms, and expectations of our own state and society. Thus the actual requirements vary widely. A good citizen in Soviet Russia of the 1930s was a person whose first loyalty was to the Communist Party. The test of good citizenship in a totalitarian state is this: Are you willing to subordinate all personal convictions and even family loyalties to the dictates of political authority, and to follow the dictator's whims no matter where they may lead? In marked contrast are the standards of citizenship in constitutional democracies, which prize and protect freedom of conscience and speech.

When the requirements of the abstract good citizen—always defined by the state—come into conflict with the moral compass of actual citizens, and when the state seeks to obscure or obliterate the difference between the two, a serious problem arises in both theory and practice. At what point do people cease to be real citizens and become mere cogs in a machine—unthinking and unfeeling subjects or even slaves? Do we obey the state, or the dictates of our own conscience?

This question gained renewed relevance in the United States when captured "illegal combatants" were subjected to "enhanced interrogation techniques"—an Orwellian euphemism for torture—during the Bush administration's war on terror following the 9/11 attacks. One prisoner was waterboarded 183 times (strapped to a board with towels wrapped around his head while water was poured slowly onto the towels until he smothered).[2] Other harsh interrogation methods were also used.

The Third Geneva Convention (1949), to which the United States is a party, outlaws torture, as does the U.S. Code (Title 18, Chapter 113C). In addition, torture is a gross violation of the *moral* code we are taught to observe in our everyday lives

citizenship
The right and the obligation to participate constructively in the ongoing enterprise of self-government.

In January 2010, members of a group called Witness Against Torture, wearing orange jumpsuits and black hoods, staged a protest in Washington, D.C., and called on the Obama administration to close down the Guantanamo detention camp.

ALEX WONG/GYI NSEA/ISTOCKPHOTO.COM

from earliest childhood. As a presidential candidate, Barack Obama denounced torture and the use of "extraordinary" methods and procedures in the war on terror. As president, he ordered an end to waterboarding but, to the dismay of his critics on the left, failed to close the Guantanamo Bay ("Gitmo") detention camp.

President Obama's decision to sign the 2012 National Defense Authorization Act (NDAA) disappointed and angered many of his erstwhile supporters, not least because he had threatened to veto it. "The fact that I support this bill as a whole does not mean I agree with everything in it," he said. "In particular, I have . . . serious reservations with certain provisions that regulate the detention, interrogation, and prosecution of suspected terrorists." Few friends of the U.S. Constitution and Bill of Rights—in particular the Fourth, Fifth, and Sixth Amendments—were placated.

> Question 1: Can anyone in any position of authority who orders the use of torture be justified in so doing?
>
> Question 2: Can anyone who carries out such an order be a good citizen?
>
> Question 3: Is it ever right to obey orders that are wrong—that is, illegal and (or) immoral?

Keep these questions in mind as you read.

Defining Citizenship

Throughout history, people of diverse moral character have claimed to be models of good citizenship. The relationship between the moral character of citizens and different forms of government underscores Aristotle's observation that the true measure of a political system is the kind of citizen it produces.

According to this view, a good state is one whose model citizen is also a good person; a bad state is one whose model citizen obeys orders without regard for questions of good or evil. Simple though this formulation may sound, it offers striking insights into the relationship between governments and citizens, including, for example, the fact that we cannot divorce civic virtue or public morality from our personal integrity or private morality.

It is little wonder that different political systems embrace different definitions of citizenship. In many authoritarian states, people can be classified as citizens only in the narrowest sense of the word—that is, they reside within the territory of a certain state and are subject to its laws. The relationship between state and citizen is a one-way street. Ordinary citizens have no voice in deciding who rules or how, or even whether they have a vote. In general, the government leaves them alone as long as they acquiesce in the system.

By contrast, in totalitarian states, where the government seeks to transform society and create a new kind of citizen, people are compelled to participate in the political system, but popular participation is meaningless because it is not voluntary and stresses duties without corresponding rights. Loyalty and zealotry form the core of good citizenship in such states, and citizens may be forced to carry out orders they find morally repugnant.

In democratic societies, people define citizenship very differently. In elementary school, the good citizenship award typically goes to a pupil who sets a good example, respects others, plays by the rules, and hands in assignments on time. Adults practice good citizenship by taking civic obligations seriously, obeying the laws, paying taxes, and voting regularly, among other things. In a democracy, the definition of good citizenship is found in the laws, but the legislators who write the laws are freely elected by the people—in other words, a true republic at its best erases (or at the very least eases) the tension between citizenship and moral conscience.

Many individuals, including civil libertarians, emphasize that the essence of citizenship lies in individual rights or personal liberties. The formal requirements of citizenship in the United States are minimal (see "Ideas and Politics: Military Conscription"), even though people the world over envy its rewards (hence the steady flow of immigrants into the United States, compared with the trickle of U.S. citizens emigrating to other countries). According to the Fourteenth Amendment, "All persons born or naturalized in the United States, and subject to the jurisdiction thereof, are citizens of the United States and of the State wherein they reside." Note that citizens of the United States are distinguished from aliens not on the basis of how they act or what they have done but simply on the basis of birthplace—to be born in the United States is to be a U.S. citizen. Moreover, the presumption is once a citizen, always a citizen, barring some extraordinary misdeed (such as treason) or a voluntary renunciation of citizenship.

A Classical View

The minimalist view of citizenship described in the "Ideas and Politics" feature may provide a convenient way of distinguishing citizens from aliens (foreigners), but it does not do justice to a time-honored concept in Western civilization.

Fringe right-wing opponents of Barack Obama have claimed that he was not born in the United States and therefore is not eligible under the Constitution to serve as president. The so-called Birthers refused to drop this spurious objection to his presidency even after Obama published this official long-form birth certificate proving that he was, in fact, born in the state of Hawaii.

MILITARY CONSCRIPTION: Democracy, Duty, and the Draft

In the United States, apart from paying taxes and obeying laws, the demands of citizenship are quite limited. One major obligation for males of a certain age—namely, military service—ended after the Vietnam War as a result of the backlash against the **Selective Service System** (often called "the draft"), which many considered unfair. Although males over the age of 18 are still required to register for the draft, the practice of military conscription in the United States ended in 1973 with the establishment of an all-volunteer military.

Defenders of an all-volunteer military argue that it is more professional and proficient, that willing recruits are likely to make better soldiers than are conscripts, and that the military provides excellent opportunities for young men and women from minority and low-income groups to acquire the self-confidence, discipline, and technical skills that can lead to high-paying jobs in the civilian economy.

Many veterans of past U.S. wars, among others, decry the ending of the draft. Others advocate making at least one year of national service mandatory for young adults who do not enlist in the armed forces. Supporters of the draft stress that military service builds character, teaches teamwork, and inculcates important moral values such as honor, duty, self-discipline, respect for authority, and courage.

Some who argue for bringing back the draft do so on the surprising grounds that it would make war less likely. Why? Because voters are often apathetic when an issue does not affect them directly and are too easily swayed when patriotism is invoked—as it always is in war. This issue resurfaced in 2003 when President George W. Bush, in effect, declared a "presidential war"—defined as the use of force outside the United States without a formal declaration of war by Congress as required under the Constitution—on Iraq.

Was President Bush justified in ordering U.S. troops to invade a country that did not (and could not) attack the United States? Is it fair to ask the sons and daughters of minorities and the poor to fight our wars, while the rich are called upon to make no sacrifices? Why not reinstitute the draft, or at least a universal national service of some sort? What do you think?

I WANT YOU
FOR U.S. ARMY
NEAREST RECRUITING STATION

LIBRARY OF CONGRESS PRINTS AND PHOTOGRAPHS DIVISION [LC-USZC4-595]

After the unpopular Vietnam War, the United States abolished the draft in favor of an all-volunteer armed forces.

Selective Service System
The means by which the United States keeps a list of all individuals eligible for the draft; upon turning 18, male citizens between the ages of 18 and 25 are required by law to register within thirty days.

To the ancient Greeks, the concept of citizenship was only partly related to accidents of birth and political geography; rather, responsible and selfless participation in the public affairs of the community formed the vital core of citizenship. Aristotle held that a citizen "shares in the administration of justice and in the holding of office."[3] The Athens of Aristotle's time was a small political society, or city-state, that at any given time accorded a proportionately large number of citizens significant decision-making power (women and slaves were excluded). Citizenship was the exalted vehicle through which public-spirited and properly educated free men could rule over, and in turn be ruled by, other free men and thereby advance civic virtue, public order, and the common good.

In eighteenth-century Europe, the Greek ideal reemerged in a modified form. *Citizen* became a term applicable to those who claimed the right to petition or sue the government. Citizens were distinguished from slaves, who had no claims or rights and were regarded as chattel (property). Citizens also differed from subjects, whose first and foremost legal obligation was to show loyalty to and obey the sovereign. According to the German philosopher Immanuel Kant (1724–1804), citizens, as opposed to slaves or subjects, possessed constitutional freedom; that is, the right to obey only laws to which they consented. Kant also contended that citizens possessed a civil equality, which relieved them of being bound by law or custom to recognize any superior among themselves, and political independence, meaning a person's political status stemmed from fundamental rights rather than from the will of another.[4] No longer were citizens to be ruled arbitrarily by the state.

Republican government came the closest to this ideal of citizenship. In the final analysis, as Kant and other eighteenth-century thinkers recognized, the freedom and dignity of the individual inherent in the concept of citizenship could flourish only under a republican government, and such a government could function only if its rank-and-file members understood and discharged the responsibilities of citizenship.

One distinguishing feature of the modern era is the extension of citizenship. In the United States, for instance, it took many years for racial minorities, women, and individuals without property to gain the right to vote and the right to protection under the law in the exercise of their civil rights. Yet, as the number of citizens (and of people in general) has risen, effective political participation for individuals has often become more difficult. It is one thing for society to embrace ideas such as citizenship for all and equal rights in theory; it is quite another to provide the civic education and social development necessary to make the ideal of a society of political equals a practical reality.

POLITICAL CULTURE: DEFINING THE GOOD

The Greek view of what constituted the good citizen was a reflection of the way the Greeks defined the word *good*. Every language in the world has a word meaning "good," and it is arguably the most important word in any language. But every language is embedded in a culture, and no two cultures are identical. We are all products of the culture into which we are born. From our earliest infancy, and long before we know how to read or write, we learn to talk.

Along with language, we also learn about our environment, which includes both tangible and intangible things. Among the most important intangibles are values—that is, what our parents or other guardians say is "good" or "bad." In the process of learning the difference between good and bad (picking up our toys is "good" and not eating our vegetables is "bad"), we also learn about right and wrong. Crossing the line from "good" and "bad" in word and deed to "right" and "wrong" in thought and sentiment is a giant step across a great chasm—it is the difference between outward behavior and inner motives, beliefs, and desires. Culture, in the sense that anthropology and political science use the word, is all about established norms, customs, and traditions—in other words, how *society* defines right and wrong and about what "the good life," or the word *good* itself, means in a given place and time. There is no universally accepted definition of "the good life" in this world for the simple reason that there is no universal culture.

Culture has many meanings. Here we are interested primarily in the aspects of culture that are related to politics—what scholars often call **political culture**. Political culture encompasses the prevailing moral values, beliefs, and myths people live by and are willing to die for. It also includes the **collective memory** of a society—the history we learn about in grade school; what we come to know about our leaders, about crises we have survived as a nation, and about wars we have fought. Virtually anything and everything that shapes our shared perceptions of reality is part of our political culture. This collective memory and these shared perceptions differ depending on the specifics of geography, climate, terrain, and other physical circumstances, as well as certain accidental factors—for example, the presence or absence of hostile and aggressive neighbors.

Small nations often have a history of being subjugated by powerful neighbors. Island peoples, such as the British and the Japanese, have a history that differs in fundamental ways from landlocked nations, owing to the absence of shared borders. The success of the thirteen American colonies in breaking away from the British Empire, as well as the United States' historic isolationism, would not have been possible without the benevolent presence of two great oceans. Clearly geography matters.

Religion plays a major role in shaping political cultures. We cannot understand Western civilization without reference to Roman Catholicism, the Reformation, and Christianity. By the same token, Islam forms the moral core of life in the Arab Middle East, as well as in much of South, Central, and Southeast Asia (Figure 10.1). The same is true of Hinduism in India; Buddhism in Cambodia, Tibet, and Thailand; Taoism and Confucianism in China and other Asian countries; and Shinto, as well as Buddhism, in Japan. Even where secularization has eroded religious beliefs (as in the West), the stamp of religion on political culture is both undeniable and indelible (see "Ideas and Politics").

We are often bemused, perplexed, or outraged by the reactions and perceptions of others. We wonder what they must be thinking. How could anyone, for example, condone the actions of terrorists whose victims are often innocent bystanders? We tend to judge anyone with extreme views as ignorant, misguided, or even depraved. In fact, however, profound differences in perception,

political culture
The moral values, beliefs, and myths by which people live and for which they are willing to die.

collective memory
The history we learn about in grade school; what we come to know about our leaders, about crises we have survived as a nation, and about wars we have fought.

FIGURE 10.1   Map of Islamic Faith. Religion exerts a powerful influence on the political ideas, values, and aspirations of people all over the world. With an estimated 1.5 billion adherents, Islam is the second-largest body of believers in the world. (Christianity is the first, with roughly 2.1 billion.)

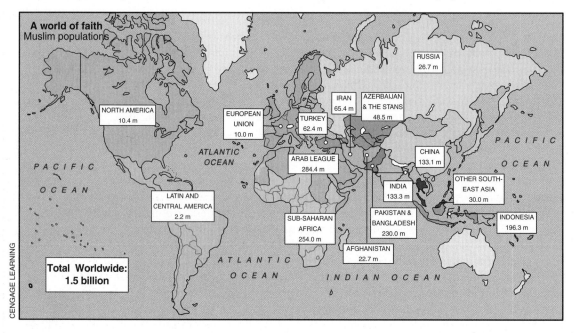

outlook, and behavior can often be traced to differences in national history, personal experience, and political culture.

A political culture is like a filter for our personal experiences, without it we lack any common interpretation of reality. Without a shared reality, we lack the basis for a community or society.

We can study political culture in several different ways. We can look at its sources in society (geography, climate, history, religion, and the like); at its manifestations (attitudes, perceptions, beliefs, and prejudices); or at its effects (actions and public policies). As is often the case, however, the closer we look, the more complicated the picture becomes.[5]

Another way to think about political culture is in terms of one national political culture and many regional and local political *subcultures*. College students have an opportunity to research this question themselves by simply engaging classmates from different states or regions of the country—and from different countries—in conversations about growing up. Comparing your own upbringing with those of others from different backgrounds can be both fun and enlightening.

In the next section, we look at the ingenious ways societies sow the seeds of political culture. Consider this: Are our ideas about "first things" (good and bad, right and wrong) really *our* ideas at all—or were they implanted at a young age, long before we had any idea of them?

THE TAO AND THE CLASH OF CIVILIZATIONS

In his provocative little book *The Abolition of Man* (New York: Macmillan, 1947), C. S. Lewis argued that "the Tao" could be found in civilizations, cultures, and religions the world over. Taoism originated in China in ancient times. The Tao is "the way"—the source of all knowledge about nature and truth, the key to inner peace and social harmony. Lewis noted that this type of metaphysical reasoning and the moral values it fostered are found in religions and ethical systems all over the world. He cites many "Illustrations of the Tao" drawn "from such sources as come readily to the hand of one who is not a professional historian."

Lewis makes a powerful case for humanistic education—that is, for teaching people to love truth and justice. Learning to love truth and justice, Lewis suggested, is the key to civil society, because people are not simply rational beings and do not naturally behave according to reason. It is necessary, therefore, that society finds ways to link human emotions with positive attitudes and good acts, which brings us back

to the Tao. What Lewis called the Tao teaches respect for authority, humility, honesty, charity, generosity, and so forth—in short, the way to live in harmony with oneself, others, and nature.

Political culture cannot be distilled from moral and religious teachings alone; indeed, politics is not what Lewis's book is about. But his views on the role of public education in developing a sense of right and wrong—a civic culture that supports democratic processes and institutions—have significant implications for students of politics.

The late Harvard scholar Samuel Huntington wrote a best-selling book in the mid-1990s titled *The Clash of Civilizations and the Remaking of the World Order*. The book's thesis highlights the prevalence and intensity of faith-based politics in today's world. Indeed, the nexus between education and values, the province of religion and morality, remains an important question—one involving a global battle for the hearts and minds of people with little understanding of international politics.

POLITICAL SOCIALIZATION: FORMING CITIZENS

Though we can dispute the proper definition of citizenship, most people agree that good citizens are made, not born. Children grow up to be responsible citizens through the interplay of various influences and institutions—including family, religion, school, peer groups, the mass media, and the law. The process of being conditioned to think and behave in a socially acceptable manner is called *socialization*.

Every self-sustaining society inculcates in its citizens certain basic values necessary to establish and perpetuate a political order. Even as staunch an individualist as the British philosopher John Stuart Mill (1806–1873) acknowledged that the sense of citizen loyalty or allegiance "may vary in its objects and is not confined to any particular form of government; but whether in a democracy or in a monarchy its essence is always . . . that there be in the constitution of the state something which is settled, something permanent, and not to be called into question; something which, by general agreement, has a right to be where it is, and to be secure against disturbance, whatever else may change."[6]

U.S. NAVY PHOTO BY PHOTOGRAPHER'S MATE 1ST CLASS ARLO K. ABRAHAMSON

Political socialization The process by which members of a community are taught the basic values of their society and are thus prepared for the duties of citizenship.

Political socialization is the process whereby citizens develop the values, attitudes, beliefs, and opinions that enable them to support the political system.[7] This process begins with the family.

The Family

The family exerts the first and most important influence on the formation of individual values. Different political regimes view the family in different ways. Some governments support and nurture the family; others choose to remain indifferent toward it; a few seek to undermine it and regard the love and loyalty that flow from family ties as subversive to the state. Despite these varying reactions, all governments recognize the importance of the family in the socialization process.

Even nations that publicly proclaim the value of the traditional family may not be able to ensure its success in society. The number of children living in single-parent households in the United States, for example, has risen dramatically since the 1960s, due to rising divorce rates, changes in sexual mores, teenage pregnancies, and other social changes. In 1980 single-parent households constituted 19.5% of the total, but that figure had risen to 29.5% in 2008. Another sign of the times: in 2009, 7.8 million children lived with at least one grandparent, a 64% increase since 1991, according to a U.S. Census Bureau report released in mid-2011.

Poverty and lack of education are major causes of divorce. Moreover, the problem is self-perpetuating. Studies confirm that children raised in single-parent families are at greater risk than those in two-parent families to drop out of school, to become involved with crime and illegal drugs, to be unemployed (or underemployed) and poor, and to have failed marriages and personal relationships as adults—a vicious cycle.[8] Of course, single-parent families are often successful, and many children raised by single parents become well-adjusted adults. Indeed, if one parent is physically or emotionally abusive, it is often better for a child to be nurtured (and protected) only by the parent who is not.

Children are first socialized at home, within the family structure, learning what is and what is not permissible, with rewards and punishment to reinforce daily behavior. In this manner, parents make the obligations of children to the family and to others clear. Slowly, children become citizens of the family, often with clearly defined responsibilities and occasionally with rights or privileges. Parents emphasize moral ground rules, even if they don't always specify the reasons for them ("Do it because I said so"). Trust, cooperation, self-esteem, respect for others, and empathy, each rooted in family relations, bear on the behavioral and moral development of individuals.[9]

When discipline is lacking and parents are overly permissive, children are given rights and privileges with few

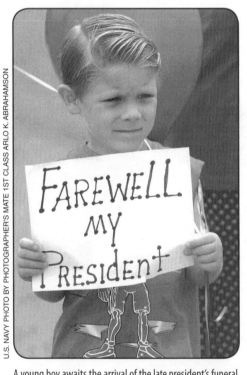

A young boy awaits the arrival of the late president's funeral motorcade at the gate of the Ronald Reagan Presidential Library in Sim Valley, California, on June 7, 2004. Children begin learning to be good citizens and to show respect for legitimate authority—important lessons in political socialization—at an early age.

if any responsibilities. In such cases, socialization is impeded to the extent it fails to produce behaviors conducive to social harmony, civility and civic duty, or leads to narcissism, self-promotion, and a tendency to exploit others.

The family also helps determine the direction the ultimate political socialization of children takes and how successful it will be. Party orientation and even affiliation often derive from the family, especially when both parents belong to the same party. In the United States, about 70% of children whose parents both have the same party affiliation favor that party too.[10] In addition, the family exerts a powerful influence on religious persuasion, which tends to correlate highly with party affiliation, as well as with certain political opinions (fundamentalist Protestants tend to oppose abortion; Jews tend to support Israel; and so on).[11] However, studies indicate that when it comes to opinions about more abstract political issues, parental influence is quite limited.[12] As adults, we may find ourselves at odds with our parents' ideas about politics (among other things), a fact often attributed to "generational" differences.

Social Class and Minority Status Family interest in politics tends to increase with social standing. Middle- and upper-class children are most likely to become actively engaged in politics; children from lower-class families are typically uninformed about politics and participate less often.[13] There are many exceptions, however, including Abraham Lincoln, Harry S. Truman, Richard M. Nixon, William Jefferson Clinton, and Barack Obama, all rising from humble origins to become president of the United States.

Former Secretary of State Madeleine Albright, current president of Liberia Ellen Johnson Sirleaf, and Josephine Baker, the first African American female to star in a major motion picture, are examples of women not born to privilege who rose to great heights. Josephine Baker was born in St. Louis in 1902 and dropped out of school at the age of 12. She is best known as a recording artist and stage performer, but she was decorated for her undercover work in the French Resistance during World War II. When she died in Paris in 1975, she became the first American woman to receive French military honors at her funeral. Condoleezza Rice, born in Birmingham, Alabama, in 1954 at a time when blacks were not allowed to have a hamburger at Woolworth's, became the first black woman (and only the second woman) ever to serve as U.S. Secretary of State (2005–2009).

Minority status can play a significant role in political socialization. Some researchers have found that in the United States, African American children tend to place less trust in government, and to feel less confident of influencing it, than do white children.[14]

Not surprisingly, such attitudes correlate with political opinions; thus, holding social-class differences constant, black adults in the United States tend to be less conservative than whites on most economic and foreign policy issues, although not on the issue of crime. Politically, though not necessarily socially and culturally, Asian Americans tend to resemble white ethnic groups more closely than black groups, particularly on domestic social issues. Hispanic Americans tend to fall between blacks and whites. However, family socialization and the transmission of political beliefs have exerted an influence on Cuban Americans, who, as a group, tend to be more hard-line conservative, especially on foreign policy

In the race to succeed in business, politics, and most professions, women in economically advanced societies have made substantial gains in recent decades, but men still enjoy a big advantage at the highest levels of government and the corporate world.

PETER GRIFFIN/PUBLICDOMAINPICTURES.NET

questions, than are other Hispanic American groups, including Mexicans and Puerto Ricans. One reason for this is that when Cubans fled to the United States at the time of the Cuban Revolution, Cuban leader Fidel Castro confiscated their property and persecuted family members they had left behind.

Gender and Politics Like class and race, gender differences can be important independent correlates of political behavior and opinions. In the United States, the so-called **gender gap**—differences in the ways men and women think and vote in the aggregate—has gotten a lot of attention in recent decades. For instance, in the 1992 general elections, Bill Clinton won the women's vote by 8 points, but won the men's vote by only 3 points. Women thus helped a challenger defeat a sitting president. In 1996, the gender gap was even bigger. In 2008, women favored Barack Obama over John McCain by a wide margin, despite the fact that McCain's running mate was a woman, Sarah Palin. But that number does not tell the whole story: In all, 8 million more women voted for Obama than for McCain, and women voters accounted for 53% of all the votes cast. Obama thus received a double boost from women voters—a larger percentage of a bigger vote. In 2012, Obama again won the female vote by a solid margin (55% to 45%), but his Republican opponent, Mitt Romney, won the male vote (52% to 44%). The pattern is different in congressional races, however, where the gender gap is generally less apparent.

Some researchers tie gender differences to early family experiences and expectations; others contend there are innate differences in the way men and women develop moral and political awareness. One theory postulates that due to some combination of socialization and biology, women—as mothers and primary caregivers for children—tend to develop a moral and political perspective

gender gap
Differences in voting between men and women in the United States; this disparity is most obvious in political issues and elections that raise the issue of appropriateness of governmental force.

that emphasizes compassion and the protection of human life.[15] An alternate theory holds that gender-based political differences are rooted in *some* women's later life experiences.[16] For example, working women who have been paid less than men doing the same job are likely to vote for a party or candidate that stresses fairness and equal rights.

One important political difference between the sexes revolves around the government's use of force. Women tend to be more reluctant to support war, more opposed to capital punishment, and more inclined to support gun control. Women also tend to give more support to social welfare programs intended to help families, the working poor, and the economically disadvantaged. These differences help explain why the gender gap has aided Democrats in recent years. We turn now to a factor that has greatly aided Republicans in recent times.

Religion

Either the church or the state may present itself as the true source of moral authority, which makes religion particularly important in the socialization process. And just as religion can influence a young person's developing political opinions, so can politics decisively shape the role of religion within the family and the place it ultimately occupies within the larger political order.

Sometimes religion can legitimize existing practices and lend stability to a society in transition. Hinduism in India, for instance, has proved compatible with changing political institutions. Described by one expert as having "a multilayered complexity allowing for the existence of many gods, many incarnations, many layers of truth,"[17] Hinduism has tended, historically, to support the status quo. Even when the status quo allowed systematic discrimination against a lower, "untouchable" class, Hinduism counseled patience and perseverance in anticipation of future lives to come. In other parts of the world, however, religious doctrine has ignited aggressive policies. In Libya and Iran, for instance, Islamic fundamentalism has helped fuel belligerent foreign policies and contributed to a periodic fervor for war.

Religion and politics sometimes conflict. In Nazi Germany, the government steamrolled the Lutheran and Catholic churches. In the former Soviet Union, the regime allowed the historically entrenched Russian Orthodox Church to continue functioning but restricted and monitored its activities, frequently persecuting believers.[18]

In the United States, religion and politics reinforce one another at a number of levels. Although the Supreme Court has interpreted the Constitution to prohibit government from directly supporting religion, the First Amendment also clearly prohibits government from denying an individual's free exercise of religion. Religion continues to flourish in the United States. In the mid-1980s, "More than 90 percent of all Americans identify with some religious faith, and on any given Sunday morning more than 40 percent are to be found in church"; furthermore, by "most measurable indices the United States is a more religious country than any European nation except Ireland and Poland."[19] But this picture appears to be changing—about 15% of survey respondents in the United States say they have "no religion."[20]

THOMAS M. MAGSTADT

The separation of church and state is a principle enshrined in the Bill of Rights. Thomas Jefferson famously described it as a "wall of separation." Nonetheless, religion has always played a big role in U.S. politics and still does. Indeed, some critics, alarmed at what they see as an improper and increasingly aggressive use of the pulpit to influence voters, argue that overtly political religious institutions deserve to lose their tax exempt status. The sign in this picture was planted amidst rows of crosses symbolizing the graves of aborted fetuses on the grounds of a Roman Catholic Church in a Midwestern city only days before the 2012 election. What do you think?

The Judeo-Christian tradition continues to be dominant in the United States, yet there is significant diversity within that tradition. Census data show numerous Protestant denominations constitute about 51% of the population (with Baptists constituting the largest groups at about 16%); Roman Catholics, 24%; and Jews, 1.7%. After the terrorist attacks of September 11, 2001, both the public reaction and the mass media focused attention on the fact that there is also a Muslim minority in the United States, although it is relatively small (0.6%). There are more Buddhists in the United States than Muslims.

Important political differences correlate with these differences in religious orientation, some even arising from the religious doctrines themselves. Quakers and Mennonites tend to be pacifists, fundamentalist Protestants tend to oppose abortion, and Jews generally favor Israel. By the same token, members of black Protestant churches tend to be more politically liberal than are Protestants affiliated with mainstream churches, and members of mainstream churches tend to be more politically liberal than their evangelical Protestant counterparts.

More generally, on a scale measuring political conservatism and liberalism, Protestants tend to be somewhat more conservative than Catholics and much more conservative than Jews. Jews, Catholics, and religiously unaffiliated voters have historically identified more with the Democratic Party, and Protestants have leaned toward the Republican Party, though the correlation between religion and party affiliation appeared to be weakening until George W. Bush received 56% of the Protestant vote and Al Gore (the Democratic candidate) only 42% in the 2000 presidential election. (Gore won among Roman Catholic voters, however, with 50% to Bush's 47%.) In 2010 Roman Catholics joined Protestants in voting Republican in the midterm elections, a shift reflecting the Vatican's staunch "pro-life" (anti-abortion) position. But in 2012 a majority of Roman Catholics voted for Obama despite a strong pro-life stance on the part of the church hierarchy. (The literal meaning of the word "hierarchy" is "holy government").

Religion can be used to edify and elevate as well as divide. Sometimes political leaders draw on religious imagery to unite citizens in a common understanding of the present or to point them toward a more noble vision of the future.[21] For example, the famous U.S. clergyman and civil rights leader Martin Luther King Jr. inspired the nation with his dream of a day "when all of God's children— black men and white men, Jews and Gentiles, Protestants and Catholics—will be able to join hands and sing in the words of the old Negro spiritual 'Free at last! Free at last! Thank God Almighty, we are free at last.'" The tragic assassination of King, like the assassination of Abraham Lincoln a century earlier, helped rally the U.S. people to the cause of racial equality.

The role of religion in U.S. national politics has risen sharply in recent years. As part of his "faith-based initiative," George W. Bush asked Congress to allow religious organizations to compete for government contracts and grants without a strict separation of religious activities and social service programs.

But it was the shock of September 11, 2001, that changed everything. Suddenly, religion was at the heart of a great menace, namely, international terrorism. The late Osama bin Laden and his al Qaeda terrorist network gave the world a horrifying glimpse of religion's dark side when they attempted to unite the world's 1.5 billion Muslims against the "Crusaders" (Christians and Jews) in a jihad, or holy war. Al Qaeda obliterated the distinction between religion and ideology and used Islam as an instrument of war against the West.

Schools

Schools play a vital role in **civic education**. In effect, the state uses schools as instruments of political socialization. Some governments merely prescribe one or two courses in civics or history, require students to salute the flag, and hang a few pictures of national heroes on school walls. Other governments dictate the entire school curriculum, indoctrinate the children with slogans and catch phrases, heavily censor textbooks and library acquisitions, and subject teachers to loyalty tests.

civic education
The process of inculcating in potential citizens the fundamental values and beliefs of the established order.

Different regimes inculcate different values. Under some regimes (for example, the Soviet Union in the 1930s), blind obedience to authority is the norm. In others, patriotism is encouraged, but so is the habit of critical and independent thinking. One other key variable is the *priority* given to education (see "Ideas and Politics").

Socialization studies tell us a lot about how children learn civic values in school.[22] During the elementary school years children develop positive *emotional* attachments to key political concepts such as liberty and democracy and respect for others. Young children also learn to think of the government in terms of an authority figure—a police officer, the president, and so on.

As we mature, *cognition* comes into play; we begin to grasp abstract concepts such as democracy. During adolescence and early adulthood, our attitudes toward authority often change radically. We cease to obey authority without question. Increasingly, we want to decide things for ourselves—a sentiment readily transferable to the political realm.

High school civics classes are probably less important than the total educational experience.[23] Lessons and stories on the nation's history, formal rituals such as reciting the Pledge of Allegiance, patriotic music, and extracurricular activities such as sports, band, debate, and writing for the school newspaper all can convey the importance of responsible participation and working toward a common goal. Electing class officers and participating in student government is typically our first exercise in democracy.

CONFUCIAN VS. CONFUSION: A Reverence for Education

An international study published in December 2010, compared students in 65 countries representing all different faiths in math, science, and reading. The winner? Confucianism!

China's Shanghai was at the top of all three lists by a wide margin. *New York Times* columnist Nicolas Kristof observed, "Three of the next top four performers were also societies with a Confucian legacy of reverence for education: Hong Kong, Singapore and South Korea."*

Finland was the only non-Confucian country in the mix. The United States came in fifteenth in reading, twenty-third in science, and thirty-first in math.

No less worrying is a study published a month later, in January 2011, reporting that 45% of undergraduates in the United States show almost no gains in learning in the first two years.† The research

indicated that colleges don't make academics a priority, that professors are primarily interested in research, and that students spend 50% less time studying compared with students several decades ago.

Other details in the research: more than a third of U.S. students surveyed reported spending no more than five hours per week studying alone (research shows that students who study in groups learn less); half reported never taking a course in which they wrote more than twenty pages; nearly one-third said they never took a course in which they read more than forty pages per week.

---

* Nicolas Kristof, "China's Education System," *New York Times*, January 15, 2011.Online at http://kristof.blogs.nytimes.com/2011/01/15/ chinas-education-system/.

† Richard Arum et al., *Academically Adrift: Limited Learning on College Campuses* (Chicago, IL: University of Chicago Press, 2011).

In general, higher education and political participation go hand in hand. Higher education also correlates positively with personal self-confidence and trust in others—personality traits that democratic political systems, based on citizen participation, require.[24]

In the United States, the college curriculum often represents a blend of vocational training and liberal arts—with the latter, which includes literature, philosophy, science, history, and linguistics, placing great emphasis on the development of critical thinking.[25] Advocates of the liberal arts stress the importance of education not only for citizenship but also for leadership. What such an education does, at its best, is produce *politically literate* adults. Evidence suggests it tends to produce more liberal adults as well.[26]

liberal education
A type of education often associated with private colleges in the United States; stresses the development of critical thinking skills through the study of literature, philosophy, history, and science.

The ideal of **liberal education** fits easily with constitutional guarantees that protect the right to question authority. It also prepares citizens to do so.[27] With rare exceptions, democracies alone tolerate independent thinking and dissent. Recall that the Greek philosopher Socrates was considered subversive and sentenced to death not for teaching his students *what* to think but for teaching them *how* to think.

peer group
A group of people similar in age and characteristics—for example, college students.

Peer Groups

A **peer group** can refer either to a group of people who are friends, or to people of similar age and characteristics. The concept of peers itself arises from "the tendency for individuals to identify with groups of people like themselves."[28] Peer groups exert considerable influence over our political activities and beliefs, but there has been little research on the influence of peer groups in politics.[29]

The relationship between gang membership and the development of antisocial attitudes by adolescent male lawbreakers, for example, is a matter of more than academic interest. Studies indicate that gang membership and teenage crime are linked. According to one study, peers and gangs "can affect the value a person assigns to the rewards of crime (by adding the approval of colleagues to the perceived value of the loot or the direct gratification of the act)."[30] But it's still not clear whether gangs *cause* teenagers to commit crimes or attract teenagers predisposed to criminal behavior in the first place. In all probability, the answer is both.

Psychologically, peer groups satisfy our need for approval. Peer groups are often formed voluntarily and informally, but organizations such as the Girl Scouts, the Young Democrats, or a high school journalism club are also peer groups. As such, they satisfy the same need for approval and a sense of belonging that totalitarian tyrants like Hitler, Stalin, and Mao deftly exploited (see Chapter 6).

The state can create peer-group structures for youth, as well as adults. These involuntary associations are typically designed to infuse ideological fervor and abject loyalty into young hearts and minds. Under the Nazi Party, for example, German life was organized through an elaborate network of state-controlled associations of peers to ensure that every German would, in time, adopt correct political attitudes and be properly socialized into the new Nazi order. Similarly, the Communist Party of the Soviet Union created an all-encompassing set of centrally controlled peer organizations in the guise of clubs and civic associations.

In liberal democracies, the state plays a role in the socialization process but does not control it. Peer groups form naturally, and civic associations are independent of the state.

The Mass Media and Internet

The media and the Internet also play a significant role in political socialization. In nondemocratic states, **mass media**—that is, television, radio, newspapers, and large-circulation magazines—are almost always owned or controlled by the state, and the Internet is monitored and websites the government finds objectionable are blocked (as in China, North Korea, and Iran). Even some democratic governments monopolize radio and television broadcasting (as in Denmark) or own and operate television networks (as in Great Britain) but strive to ensure fairness and objectivity.

mass media
The vehicles of mass communication, such as television, radio, the Internet, film, books, magazines, and newspapers.

The Internet is especially crucial in shaping attitudes now because young people generally have a high level of computer skills and spend more hours each day on the Internet than watching TV. For American youth between the ages of 12 and 24, one recent study found that in "daily time spent" the Internet soared from 10% in 2000 to 30% in 2010. The same respondents reported watching TV almost as much, but spending almost no time reading newspapers and magazines.[31]

Television is still popular most everywhere in the world, of course, even in some strict Islamic societies, where the state now uses this otherwise "decadent" source of Western pop culture to inculcate Islamic moral values. Thus, in Saudi Arabia, a traditional monarchy, state-owned television holds an annual "Miss Beautiful Morals" pageant that is the exact opposite of our beauty pageants— the physical appearance of the contestants is irrelevant (in fact, they are covered from head to foot). Rather, the winner is the contestant who is judged to have the most devotion and respect for her parents.[32]

FREE SPEECH: The FCC vs. Fox Television

The late comedian George Carlin created a sensation when he did a stand-up routine about the "seven dirty words" you cannot say on television. That routine secured Carlin's place as one of the most famous nightclub and television comedians in recent U.S. history. But it was more than a knee-slapping shtick; it was also political satire at its most biting, for Carlin was raising a serious question: Does the state's action in restricting indecent speech on television violate the citizen's right to free speech?

For several decades, the FCC's restrictions on indecent speech allowed a fleeting swear word or curse word—that is, so long as it was not repeated. In 2003, the FCC changed the rule to make even a fleeting indecent word impermissible, and to impose severe penalties in the form of steep fines for violations. Fox TV then sued the FCC and in November 2008 the case came before the U.S. Supreme Court.

The issue: Whether the FCC provided an adequate explanation, or instead acted arbitrarily and capriciously, in changing its policy to permit isolated uses of expletives on broadcast television to be considered "indecent" under federal law. The Court narrowly backed the FCC in a 2009 ruling, but sent it back to the court of appeals for further consideration of the First Amendment question. It remains unclear whether and under what conditions the state can censor speech on radio and television, much less the Internet.

In the United States, where mass media are privately owned, the Federal Communications Commission (FCC) regulates radio and television. FCC rules are designed to discourage ideas, attitudes, or behavior the agency considers undesirable or unhealthy. For example, certain words cannot be uttered on television in the United States (see "Ideas and Politics"), full nudity is banned from 6:00 a.m. to 10 p.m. daily, and broadcasters are not permitted to air commercials for cigarettes.

The FCC is also charged with promoting and preserving media competition, but in December 2007 it lifted the so-called cross-ownership ban in the twenty largest U.S. markets. Radio and television broadcasters are now allowed to own newspapers as well. Critics contend that consolidation of the media has greatly harmed competition and undermined the quality of news and diversity of views available to the public.

The Internet and television have become critical sources of information as U.S. adults read fewer newspapers and attend fewer political party functions.[33] The high cost of television advertising—and, therefore, of running for office—adversely affects the quality of campaigns and candidates (see Table 10.1). The same is true of the content. Attack ads are often intentionally unfair, misleading, and manipulative. They typically impugn the character and motives of the other candidate and deliberately misrepresent his or her voting record.

How news is presented, particularly on television, is important. Fairness and objectivity are vital. Some conservative critics contend that television news shows a liberal bias. The media's emphasis on rumor and innuendo—as well

TABLE 10.1   The Best Government Money Can Buy.

Campaign Spending in the 2008 Elections			
	House	Senate	President
Democratic Party	$489.7 million	$217.1 million	$1.12 billion
Republican Party	$442.5 million	$200.6 million	$630.3 million
Total	$936.8 million	$418.4 million	$1.75 billion

Total campaign spending in 2008 hit a record high of $5.4 billion. The cost of the 2012 elections was a soaring 7% higher; estimates placed the final figure at a record $5.8 to $6.0 billion.

SOURCE: Open Secrets.Org at http://www.opensecrets.org/overview/index.php.

as the ranting of popular media personalities on both the right and left—has blurred the line between sensationalism and straight news.

One view holds that media consolidation (especially for radio and newspapers) is leading to homogenized news, keyed to conservative audiences and corporate agendas. Critics fear the daily news will reflect right-wing biases while also becoming more and more like tabloid journalism or mind-numbing entertainment.

There is no denying the radio and television media are often superficial and sensationalistic. Television coverage of election campaigns, for example, stresses candidates' attempts to gain strategic advantage, instead of focusing on issues and policy differences. One mainstream political scientist argues, "the United States cannot have a sensible campaign as long as it is built around the news media."[34]

Television executives know that conflict and confrontation are entertaining and that, as a rule, bad news makes good ratings. For this reason also, television almost always emphasizes the "horse race" aspect of presidential elections, dwelling on who is ahead, who gained, and who lost because of this gaffe or that revelation. The networks all want to be the first to call every contest. The race becomes an end in itself, and the "product" (where the candidates stand on the issues) takes a back seat to the process.

In one study of network news coverage between 1968 and 1988, the average length of presidential quotations shrank from 45 seconds to 9 seconds— truncated sound bites.[35] The old form of coverage—a short setup and a relatively long presidential comment—was reversed. By the late 1980s, reporters were regularly upstaging the president, commenting on his comments rather than letting him speak for himself. The ratio of paid political ads to political news has also shifted dramatically. In 2006, a study at the University of Wisconsin–Madison found that "local newscasts in seven Midwest markets aired 4 minutes, 24 seconds of paid political ads during the typical 30-minute broadcast while dedicating an average of 1 minute,

IDEAS AND POLITICS

OPPOSITION RESEARCH

Increasingly, the mass media broadcast negative political advertisements. These ads may or may not be entirely truthful, but they are often very effective. Sometimes viewed as a kind of political ambush, they are the product of extensive research into the background of political opponents and are aired at strategic times during the campaign. The Internet has made this kind of dirty work much easier for those who do it. Dirt diggers can request (and often obtain) telephone records, credit checks, and court records. Opposition research—or "oppo"—is a multimillion-dollar business employing investigators, consultants, lawyers, pollsters, and media experts.

Go to a website operated by Investigative Research Specialists, LLC touting "The Opposition Research Handbook" to get a better idea of what these for-profit dirt-dealing firms actually do. The URL is http://researchops.com/ or simply Google "research ops".

SOURCE: Michele Norris, "Opposition Research: Know Thine Enemies," National Public Radio (NPR), *All Things Considered*, February 6, 2007.

43 seconds to election news coverage."[36] In-depth analysis, critics say, has become a casualty of Madison Avenue marketing techniques, the Nielsen ratings, and outright manipulation by highly paid professionals (see "Ideas and Politics")—political gurus, media consultants, and spin doctors (public relations specialists).

In short, a drift toward tabloid journalism and the use of the airways as a vehicle for propaganda have severely compromised the integrity of television news reporting and talk radio. This type of coverage, pandering to prurience and prejudice, increasingly crowds out honest attempts to fulfill the vital "news and information" function of the mass media.[37] To make matters worse, newspapers—long the main source of information on current events for most citizens—are rapidly losing readership (see "Ideas and Politics").

Consumers are also to blame for the state of the news. The news is "dumbed down" and entertaining because that is what attracts the largest number of viewers. Knowing the average viewer has a short attention span, television news directors spotlight the razzle-dazzle of video technology, flashy computer graphics, fast-paced interviews, and rapidly changing stories, locations, and camera angles. After a hard day's work, most viewers are not in the mood for an in-depth story or analysis that confuses, upsets, or makes them think too much. The problem is that the most important political issues tend to do all three.

The media's tendency to focus on negative news serves as a reminder that freedom of speech and criticism of the government are protected rights in liberal democracies. Indeed, the content and quality of the daily news in any given country is one indicator of how much freedom exists there. Where criticism of the government is allowed, freedom is usually the norm. In the final analysis,

MEDIA CONSOLIDATION

Who needs newspapers or media competition? Either Congress or the FCC is asleep at the switch—or they are looking the other way. The facts speak for themselves:

- In early 2009, the *Seattle-Post Intelligencer* shut its printing presses after 146 years in business; two weeks later, the *Rocky Mountain News* folded. The *Tucson Citizen* suffered the same fate.
- Daily print circulation dropped from a peak of 62 million circa 1990 to around 49 million two decades later. Online readership has risen faster, to almost 75 million people and 3.7 billion page views in January 2009, according to Nielsen Online.
- In 1950, the total daily paid circulation relative to the number of U.S. households was 120%; by 2010, this figure had dropped to under 40%; similarly, total daily circulation of U.S. *national* dailies fell from just under 60% in 1995 to well below 40% in 2010.
- In the middle of the twentieth century, 80% of all newspapers were independently owned. By 2004, more than 7,000 cities and towns had no locally owned newspaper.
- There are 2,500 book publishers in the United States, but five giant companies produce most of the revenue; two retail chains (Barnes & Noble and Amazon.com) accounted for well over half of all retail book sales in the United States in 2008.
- Four major companies account for half of the movie business.
- Six companies account for at least 90% of all domestic music sales, and Apple (iTunes) became the biggest single U.S. music retailer in 2008 (19%), beating out Wal-Mart (15%) for the first time.
- The 1996 Telecommunications Act doubled the number of local radio stations a single company can operate and removed all limits on how many one company can own nationwide; a single company—Clear Channel Communications—owns more than 1,200 radio stations.
- By one count, the forty-five top-rated talk radio shows ran 310 hours of conservative talk to a mere 5 hours that were not patently right-wing.

SOURCES: *NOW with Bill Moyers* on PBS, February 13, 2004, http:// www.pbs.org, and author's updates from various Internet databases.

mass media in democratic states are both gauge and guarantor of individual freedom.

The Law

The law plays an important role in socialization. Some laws are designed to promote public order (by having cars drive on the right side of the street, for example). Other laws prohibit violent or antisocial behavior in society, such as murder, false advertising, theft, and racial discrimination. Equally important, the very idea of "law and order" is ingrained in us at an early age and the "rule of law" is an essential feature of liberal democracy. Thus, the law conditions our behavior in all sorts of subtle and not-so-subtle ways.

SOCIALIZATION AND POLITICAL BEHAVIOR

Fortunately, most citizens who participate in the political process choose, most of the time, to do so legally.

Political Behavior

Most of us participate in politics in largely symbolic, passive, or ritualistic ways—for example, by attending a political rally, responding to a political poll, watching a candidate on television, or putting a bumper sticker on our cars. Some volunteer on political campaigns (witness the huge volunteer "army" that helped Barack Obama get elected in 2008) or join liberal public interest groups such as the Sierra Club, the American Civil Liberties Union, or MoveOn.Org, or conservative ones such as the National Right to Life Committee, the National Taxpayers Union, or the Christian Coalition. Others participate in political protests of one kind of another.

Even during the turbulent Vietnam War era, however, only 2% of U.S. citizens surveyed believed violence was justified to achieve political aims.[38] Support for milder forms of protest is much higher, but this support falls off sharply as the action in question approaches the line between legal and illegal behavior. In general, protests, mass marches, and street demonstrations are far less common in the United States today than they are in Europe and elsewhere in the world.

Illegal Political Behavior

Some illegal acts—in particular, those classified as civil disobedience—are intended to stir a nation's conscience. Taking his cue from Mahatma Gandhi, Martin Luther King Jr. advocated civil disobedience in the struggle for racial equality in the 1960s. Civil disobedience stresses nonviolence and encourages demonstrators to accept the consequences of breaking the law, including arrest and detention.

Students marching for freedom of speech in Caracas, Venezuela, after President Hugo Chávez closed down a popular television channel. Note that many of the student demonstrators' hands are painted white as a sign of peaceful intentions, but the government nonetheless accused them of being violent.

AP PHOTO/HOWARD YANES

Whether a particular form of illegal political behavior is morally wrong depends on the context—and the beholder. When people are victimized by government or by a dominant class or ethnic group, the moral basis for law and authority often erodes. Even in the United States, illegal forms of political behavior have not always been considered "un-American." Agitating for independence from Great Britain in colonial times, for example, was treasonous. Had the American Revolution failed, Benjamin Franklin, Thomas Jefferson, and George Washington, among other leaders of the revolt, would probably have gone to the gallows.

Before the Civil War, the "underground railroad" that helped fugitive slaves escape bondage was a clear violation of federal law by many otherwise law-abiding citizens, especially in the northern states of Massachusetts and New York. The underground railroad could not have existed without a network of activists who considered slavery a desecration of a "higher law," nor could these activists have themselves escaped prosecution without the cooperation of family, friends, and neighbors.

That the legal system does not always serve the cause of justice is, in fact, a kind of cliché even in the United States where most people express a strong belief in the rule of law. It's the theme of popular books, movies, and television shows. Thus, for example, in the popular TV series *Person of Interest* a billionaire computer genius and a former Green Beret and CIA field officer who have lost faith in the system go outside the law to protect intended victims from violent crimes that fall outside the government's narrow definition of a terrorist threat.

But, of course, illegal political behavior—sabotage, assassinations, and terrorist acts—aimed at elected officials and legitimate governments cannot be tolerated. Examples of such acts are all too common even in stable democracies. The attack on Arizona Congresswoman Gabrielle Giffords at a shopping mall in Tucson, Arizona, in early 2011, resulting in the death of six people, including a 9-year-old girl, is a recent case in point.

WHEN POLITICAL SOCIALIZATION FAILS

A nation's political culture reflects the fundamental values its people hold dear. These values need not be entirely consistent and may even conflict at times. Nor will day-to-day political beliefs and actions of individual citizens always conform to the ideals people hold dear in the abstract.[39] But a steady state requires an established political culture consisting of shared values. In democracies, these values set a very high standard—too high, in fact, to be fully attainable. Yet the standard is kept at the forefront, and it is the striving for a perfection never achieved that, in many ways, defines democracy and distinguishes it from its alternatives.

In the United States, private values correlate highly with key public (or civic) values.[40] Accordingly, U.S. adults generally profess a strong belief in basic liberal values: personal freedom, political equality, private ownership of property, and religious tolerance. Not only are these values expressed in the nation's fundamental documents and writings, including the Declaration of Independence, the Constitution, and *the Federalist Papers*, but they are also instilled in U.S. youth by a variety of socialization strategies.

In other democratic societies, the process of socialization works the same way and serves the same purposes. But the *expression* of such core values as liberty, equality, security, prosperity, and justice (see Chapter 13), as well as the precise content and balance among them, vary significantly from one country to another. In Europe, "equality" is more often about class-consciousness than civil rights. As a result, the state provides a much wider range of social services (including guaranteed universal health care) than in the United States. By the same token, love of liberty in Europe does not impede the police in criminal investigations the way it often does in the United States, nor does it entail the right of private citizens to own deadly weapons.

When a multiethnic nation fails to politically socialize large numbers of citizens as members of a single community—in effect, a new nation—the consequences are far-reaching. If there are multiple communities, there will be multiple processes going on and multiple political cultures being perpetuated. Members of the various subnational communities will not be successfully integrated into the political system, and they will not share the norms, rules, and laws of the society.

Some citizens may never become fully socialized politically. A state's failure to socialize its citizens may result from its unequal or unfair treatment of them. Citizens may then become angry, cynical, or embittered, and they may turn to crime or even revolution. In extreme cases of unjust, tyrannical government, citizens' "crimes" may be viewed as actions taken justifiably. Although the failure of political socialization is always detrimental to the government in power, the moral and political implications of that failure are not as easy to evaluate.

SUMMARY

Different governments treat the concept of citizenship in different ways. All states demand adherence to the rules (laws), of course, and most treat birth in, or naturalization into, the political order as a requirement of citizenship. In democratic states, the concept of citizenship is also tied to the ideas of equality and liberty, as well as to meaningful participation in politics, such as voting in periodic elections. This ideal of democratic citizenship dates back to the ancient Greek city-states, which were small enough to permit direct democracy (self-representation of enfranchised adults through public assemblies and plebiscites).

Political socialization is the process whereby citizens develop the values, attitudes, beliefs, and opinions that enable them to relate to and function within the political system. Specific influences on the developing citizen include the family, religion, public education, mass media, the law, peer groups, and key political values. Political socialization is of paramount importance; if a nation fails to socialize its citizenry on a large-scale basis, its political stability can be endangered.

KEY TERMS

citizenship 257
Selective Service
  System 262
political culture 263

collective memory 263
political socialization
  266
gender gap 268

civic education 271
liberal education 272
peer group 272
mass media 273

We begin with a checklist of sorts. Many of us hold certain basic beliefs about participation and the political process:

- Participation is a right.
- Voting matters.
- Every vote is equal in value.
- A large voter turnout is good.
- Elections are fair.
- Majority rule determines outcomes.

These assumptions are worth examining, but first let's look at the various ways ordinary citizens can participate in the political process.

DEFINING PARTICIPATION

Citizens in democracies participate in politics by expressing opinions and casting votes. Polls focus attention on public opinion and give it clear definition (see "Ideas and Politics: Public Opinion").

Public Opinion

In theory, citizens in a democracy have a powerful voice in shaping government policies. In practice, it's not so simple. The public is often divided; attitudes

IDEAS AND POLITICS

PUBLIC OPINION: Just How Stupid Are We?

In his book titled *Just How Stupid Are We?* (New York: Basic Books, 2008), historian Rick Shenkman asks, Why do we value polls when most citizens do not know enough to make a reasoned judgment? He is not alone in wondering.

"Americans are too ignorant to vote." That was the conclusion of a report from the Intercollegiate Studies Institute on the state of civic literacy in the United States, published in late 2008.* Nearly half the 2,500 voting-age adults in the study (including college students, elected officials, and other citizens) flunked a thirty-three-question test on basic civics. Consider these results:

- Only 17% of college graduates knew the difference between free markets and central planning.

- Only 27% of elected officials could name a right or freedom guaranteed by the First Amendment.

- Asked what the Electoral College does, 43% of elected officials were stumped.

- Almost half the elected officials (46%) did not know that the Constitution gives Congress the power to declare war.

The authors of this study recommended reforms in the higher-education curriculum to correct the problem. Shenkman, founder of George Mason University's History News Network, suggests requiring students to read newspapers and giving college freshmen weekly quizzes on current events. He would subsidize newspaper subscriptions and college tuition for students who perform well on civics tests.*

In the meantime, don't expect government to do anything about the problem. After all, most elected officials can't pass a basic civic literacy test themselves.

*Kathleen Parker, "Disheartening Finds about Civic Literacy," *Washington Post*, November 26, 2008, online at http://www.washingtonpost.com.

STRATEGIC POLLING

Traditionally, polls measured public opinion *after* political leaders took positions or enacted legislation. Increasingly in election campaigns, however, polling has become future oriented, to determine what positions candidates *ought* to take or how positions are to be advanced or what advertisements will project positive candidate images. This use of public opinion is *strategic polling*.

To gauge whether a political advertisement or position will be popular, *focus groups*, small numbers of people led by a professional communications expert, are asked to react to and discuss particular agenda items. Electronic polling has made possible the *dial group*, in which individuals use a dial to register instant approval or disapproval.

Strategic polling, even among incumbents, has become a fact of political life. In the 2008 presidential election, the Obama campaign was particularly adept in using polls to determine how to frame not only the issues but also the message, including slogans like "Yes, we can" and "Change you can believe in."

---

change over time, vary from place to place, and are difficult to measure accurately. Different polls on the same issue or candidate often produce conflicting results.

Politicians do pay attention to opinion polls, but is public opinion a reliable guide? (See "Ideas and Politics: Strategic Polling.") Should elected officials follow or lead? As we will see in Chapter 12, this fundamental question is at the root of two opposing theories of representation.

What is **public opinion**? Is it a fine blend of collective wisdom and rational thought or a witch's brew of gut feelings, prejudices, and preconceptions based on scanty information? The short answer: both. Let's look a little deeper.

Polls

The first attempts to measure public opinion were **straw polls**—unscientific opinion samples nineteenth-century newspapers used to predict a winner in the run-up to elections. Local news sources still sometimes use straw polls today.

But there is never any guarantee that the sample in such a poll is representative of the population as a whole. The *Literary Digest* poll that predicted Alf Landon would defeat Franklin D. Roosevelt in 1936 is a famous case in point. Although the *Literary Digest* had correctly predicted the outcome of the three previous presidential elections, in 1936 its poll missed by a mile: Roosevelt won big. Where did this particular poll go wrong? The names in the sample were taken from the telephone directory and automobile registration lists—two very unrepresentative rosters at the time, because only rich people could afford telephones and cars during the Great Depression. Incidentally, that was the end of the *Literary Digest*'s polling and, for all practical purposes, of the *Literary Digest* itself. In 1938, it went out of business.

Over the past few decades, opinion polling has improved. To obtain the most objective results, a **random sampling** of citizens is drawn from the entire population, or universe, being polled. (Statisticians have deemed a sample of

public opinion
In general, the ideas and views expressed by taxpayers and voters. When a majority of the people hold strong opinions one way or the other on a given issue or policy question, it tends to sway legislators and decision makers who know they will be held accountable at the next election.

straw poll
Unscientific survey; simple, inexpensive poll open to all sorts of manipulation and misuse.

random sampling
A polling method that involves canvassing people at random from the population; the opposite of stratified sampling.

JON SCHEIBER

Polls predict who will win an election before voters cast ballots. But they are not infallible. The same can be said of voters who often pay little attention or spend little time studying the issues and vote mindlessly. Only fourteen of the fifty states allow straight-ticket voting—for example, selecting all the Democrats or Republicans on the ballot by checking a single box.

1,500 respondents ideal for polls of large numbers of people.) In a cross-section of this kind, differences in age, race, religion, political orientation, education, and other factors approximate those within the larger population.

Because it is not always possible to conduct hundreds of separate interviews, pollsters sometimes use a method called **stratified sampling** in which they select small population sets with certain key characteristics (age, religion, income, party affiliation, and so on) in common. **Exit polling**, which permits television networks to predict political winners as the polls close by surveying departing voters, illustrates two levels of stratified polling. Pollsters first identify precincts that statistically approximate the larger political entity (a congressional district, a state, or the nation) and then try to select a sample that reflects the overall characteristics of the precinct.

Tracking polls repeatedly sample the same voters during the course of a campaign to identify shifts in voter sentiment and correlate them with media strategy, voter issues, candidates' gaffes, and so forth. To discover which campaign strategies are working and which are not, candidates often use tracking polls in conjunction with focus groups and other campaign instruments.

Polls are useful predictive instruments, but they are not infallible. The exact wording of a given instrument is important for issues about which most people do not have well-formed opinions. Given a choice between two policy alternatives (for example, "Should the federal government see to it that all people have housing, or should individuals provide for their own housing?"), some respondents can be so influenced by the order in which the policies appear that a 30% variance between them may result, depending solely on which policy option is stated first in the question.[1] The *way* a question is phrased can also make a big difference. For example, "Do you support the right to life?" is likely to produce very different results from, "Do you support the right to terminate a pregnancy in the first trimester?"

stratified sampling
A manner of polling in which participants are chosen on the basis of age, income, socioeconomic background, and the like, so that the sample mirrors the larger population; the opposite of random sampling.

exit polling
Voters leaving the polling place are asked how they voted; designed to provide a snapshot of the likely outcome of an election before the actual votes can be tallied.

tracking poll
Repeated sampling of voters to assess shifts in attitudes or behavior over time.

Polls not only *measure* public opinion but also *influence* it. A question that frames smoking in terms of freedom to exercise a personal choice will yield a higher rate of approval for smoking than a question that mentions the health risks of secondhand smoke. Candidates, corporations, and organized interest groups of all kinds can often obtain the results they want by carefully phrasing their questions. Unfortunately, stacking the deck this way is a common practice in both the public and the private sectors.

Today, literally hundreds of polls are taken in a presidential election year. More polls do not necessarily mean better results,[2] though in the last three presidential elections they have been quite accurate. Indeed, the "poll of polls" (the average of all the major surveys) in the 2008 presidential election was right on the money. Polls taken on the eve of the election projected an Obama advantage of 7.52 percentage points on average; Obama's actual margin of victory was 7.2%.[3]

Political polling presents certain hazards. First, polls are only snapshots of public opinion, and public opinion is subject to rapid change. Second, as polling has become more widespread and intrusive, citizens are becoming less cooperative (despite pollsters' assurances of anonymity) and probably less truthful as well. Third, there are important methodological differences among the various polls. The biggest is the way polling organizations count the "undecided" voter and how they predict who the "likely" voter will be. Even the most scientific polls typically have a margin of error of 3% at the .05 level of confidence, which means 95 in 100 times the error is no more than 3% in either direction.

Elections

Polls and elections are closely related. In fact, elections *are* polls—the most accurate ones of all because the "sample" includes everybody who actually votes. Free elections are tied to the concept of representation—indeed, *representative democracy* and *republic* are synonymous.

Limitations of Elections Ideally, elections should enable a democratic society to translate the preferences of its citizens into laws and policies. In reality, elections often produce disappointing or indecisive results for a long list of reasons, including the following:

- If public opinion is ill defined or badly divided, elected officials get mixed signals.
- The great expenditure of time and money required to run for public office gives a huge advantage to incumbents and discourages many potential challengers.
- To attract as many voters or interest groups as possible, candidates often waffle on issues, giving voters a choice between Tweedledee and Tweedledum.
- Powerful lobbies and a convoluted budget process preoccupy, and occasionally paralyze, Congress.
- Politicians frequently say one thing and do another.

Despite these limitations, elections are indispensable to democracy. Contrary to popular opinion, campaign promises are often kept.[4] Elected officials sometimes turn out to be duds or disappointments, but seldom are they total surprises. In this sense, voters often get what they deserve.

Electoral Systems

Electoral systems vary greatly. We begin with the familiar and then look at some of the alternatives.

Winner-Takes-All Systems Most voters in the United States would have difficulty explaining how the U.S. electoral system works. Members of Congress are elected by plurality vote in single-member districts—that is, in the **winner-takes-all system**, which means that only one representative is elected from each electoral district, and the candidate who gets the most votes in the general election wins the seat. Because a state's two senators are elected in different years, entire states function as single-member districts. The fifty states are each single-member districts in presidential races as well, because *all* the electoral votes in any state are awarded to the electors of the presidential candidate who receives the most popular votes in that particular state.

The practical implications of such a system are wide-ranging. In any election within a single-member district, if only two candidates are seeking office, one of them necessarily will receive a **plurality**, defined as the largest bloc of votes. If three or more candidates are vying for a seat, however, the one who receives the greatest number of votes is elected. In a five-way race, for example, a candidate could win with 25% (or less) of the votes. As we shall see, this method of election strongly favors the emergence of a two-party system.

The effects of winner-takes-all electoral systems, also known as **first past the post**, are graphically illustrated by the hypothetical U.S. congressional race depicted in Table 11.1. This system has at least one important advantage: it produces clear winners. A plurality—as opposed to a majority (over half the total votes cast)—decides who will represent the district. In the table, John Liberal is the clear winner. But there is a price to be paid for this convenient result—a majority (57% of the electorate) did not vote for him. For all it mattered, they might as well have stayed home. Neither the policies advocated by candidates Jane Conservative and Ima Nothing nor the preferences of the majority in this congressional district will be represented.

Under this system, one of the two major parties in every election invariably gains seats disproportionate to the actual percentage of the total votes it receives—a built-in bonus that comes at the expense of the other major party and any minor parties in the race. Hence, a party receiving, say, 42% of the popular vote may win a clear majority of legislative seats, as normally happens in British elections. In the United Kingdom a major party receiving fewer than half the votes can sometimes win in a landslide (an election resulting in a huge

winner-takes-all system
Electoral system in which the candidate receiving the most votes wins.

plurality
Something less than an absolute majority. Where the plurality vote principle applies, the candidate or party receiving the largest number of votes wins; where there are multiple parties or candidates, winners typically receive fewer than half the total votes cast.

first past the post
An electoral method used in the United States and the United Kingdom whereby candidates run in single-member districts and the winner is decided by plurality vote; favors broad-based, entrenched political parties and tends toward a two-party configuration.

TABLE 11.1   Hypothetical Political Race.

Party	Candidate	Votes Received	Percent of Vote
Democratic	John Liberal	25,800	43
Republican	Jane Conservative	24,600	41
Independent	Ima Nothing	9,600	16

© CENGAGE LEARNING

LANDMARKS IN HISTORY

UNITED KINGDOM: 2011 Referendum on Electoral Reform

In May 2011 British voters were given an opportunity to change the existing first past the post electoral system to a new Alternative Vote (AV) system. Voters under an AV system rank candidates in order of preference, and anyone getting more than 50% in the first round is elected. If that does not happen, the candidate with the fewest votes is eliminated, and voters' second choices are allocated to the remaining candidates. This process continues until a winner emerges.

The Conservative-Lib Dem coalition was pushing for the change. Labour opposed it, fearing a new way of

electing MPs was a part of a larger Tory strategy aimed at changing constituency boundaries (redistricting).

Electoral systems affect different political parties differently, so any change in the electoral system was bound to be controversial; that's true in spades in a country like the UK where tradition is treasured. In the UK, even resort to a referendum is rare (indeed, the 2011 referendum was only the second in British history; the first gave the voters the final decision on whether or not to enter the European Union). Given this context, no one was surprised at the outcome: Fully two-thirds (68%) voted against the change (only 10 of 440 districts voted "Yes").

parliamentary majority). A referendum on electoral reform in Britain was overwhelmingly rejected in May 2011 (see "Landmarks in History").

The winner-takes-all electoral system encourages the emergence of two major political parties and hampers the growth of smaller political parties and splinter groups. The advantage is greater political stability compared with many multiparty systems. But critics argue that stability in this case is achieved at too high a price. Because the winner-takes-all system does not represent the total spectrum of voter opinions and interests, they point out, it severely limits voter choice and stifles attempts of minor parties to compete in elections.

proportional representation (PR)
Any political structure under which seats in the legislature are allocated to each party based on the percentage of the popular vote each receives.

PR Systems   The main alternative to a winner-takes-all system is **proportional representation** (PR). PR systems typically divide the electorate into *multimember* districts, with a formula awarding each district's seats in proportion to the fractions of the vote the various parties receive in that district. The result is that representation in the legislature accurately mirrors the outcome of the election. Hence, if a party wins 42% of the vote, it will get 42% of the seats—in other words, not enough to form a government without the support of at least one other party.

Among the many countries using this system are Israel, Italy, Belgium, Norway, and Ireland. Germany also uses proportional representation to elect half the members of the Bundestag (the lower house of parliament). Candidates in a district win office if they receive at least a specified number of votes, determined by dividing the number of votes cast by the number of seats allocated. For example, assume in Table 11.1 that a proportional representation system is in place, the district has been allocated three seats, and 60,000 votes have been cast. A representative will thus be elected for every 20,000 votes a party receives. According to this formula, John Liberal and Jane Conservative would both be elected because each received more than 20,000 votes.

But no votes are wasted. The district's third representative would be determined by a regional distribution, which works like this: 5,800 Democratic votes, 4,600 Republican votes, and 9,600 Independent votes are forwarded to the region, to be combined with other districts' votes and reallocated. Where regional distributions fail to seat a candidate, a final *national* distribution may be necessary. In this manner, proportional representation guarantees that everyone's vote will count.

Some countries have modified this system to prevent the proliferation of small fringe parties, requiring that minor parties receive a certain minimum of the national vote to qualify for district representation. In Germany and Russia, this figure is 5%; in other countries, it can be 15% or even higher.

The **list system** is by far the most common. Parties choose the candidates and rank them on the ballot in each electoral district. If a party receives enough votes to win one seat, the candidate ranked first on the list gets that seat; if it garners enough votes to elect two, the candidate ranked second also gets a seat; and so on. The list system strengthens political parties significantly because citizens vote primarily for the party (as opposed to the candidate), and the party controls the ordering of the candidates on the ballot.

The **Hare plan** is based on a single transferable vote and emphasizes individual candidates or personalities rather than parties. Voters indicate a first and second preference. A quota—the number of votes required to win a seat—is set, and when a candidate has met the quota, the remainder of votes cast for that candidate are transferred to the second preference on those ballots, and so on until all available seats have been awarded.

Electoral Systems Compared Proportional representation systems have certain advantages over the winner-takes-all method. Few votes are "wasted," more parties can gain seats in the legislature, and fairness—to voters, candidates, and parties—is emphasized because seats are apportioned according to the vote totals that each party actually receives.

The winner-takes-all system has the advantage of stability. It effectively bars the door to upstart and single-issue splinter parties. By frequently magnifying a plurality of votes into a majority of seats, it often obviates the need for **coalition governments**. Finally, it boils down choices for the voters, typically between two or three middle-of-the-road parties.

Direct Democracy

Voters can also be legislators. Perhaps the most easily recognized model of direct democracy is the New England town hall meeting. By providing for elected representatives, however, the U.S. Constitution rejects the idea of a direct democracy in favor of a representative one.

Today, direct democracy coexists with representational democracy in many places. In some democracies, such as Switzerland and Australia, as well as a number of U.S. states, citizens can bypass or supersede the legislature by voting directly on specific questions of public policy in a **plebiscite**. In the United States, a plebiscite can take three forms.

A **legislative referendum** occurs when the state legislature puts a proposal to repeal an existing law or policy on the ballot; in states that allow for a

list system
Method of proportional representation by which candidates are ranked on the ballot by their party and are chosen according to rank.

Hare plan
In parliamentary democracies, an electoral procedure whereby candidates compete for a set number of seats, and those who receive a certain quota of votes are elected. Voters vote only once and indicate both a first and a second choice.

coalition government
In a multiparty parliamentary system, the political situation in which no single party has a majority and the largest party allies itself loosely with other, smaller parties to control a majority of the legislative seats.

plebiscite
A vote by an entire community on some specific issue of public policy.

legislative referendum
A measure placed on the ballot by a legislature through which citizens vote directly to adopt or repeal a law.

IDEAS AND POLITICS

INITIATIVE AND REFERENDUM

There are two types of initiative—direct and indirect—and two types of referendum—popular and legislative. Legislative referendum is divided into two categories: amendments and statutes. Twenty-three states give their legislatures *discretionary power* to place statutes on the ballot. Delaware is the only state that does not *require* placement of *constitutional amendments* on the ballot.

- Twenty-seven states have some form of initiative or popular referendum.
- Twenty-four states have a form of initiative.
- Twenty-four states have popular referendum.
- Eighteen states allow citizens to fire state officials by means of a recall.
- All fifty states have some form of legislative referendum.
- The first state to hold a legislative referendum to adopt its constitution was Massachusetts, in 1778.

- The first state to adopt the initiative and popular referendum was South Dakota, in 1898.
- The first state to place an initiative on the ballot was Oregon, in 1904.
- The first state to allow cities to use initiative and popular referendum was Nebraska, in 1897.
- The first state to provide for initiative and popular referendum in its original constitution was Oklahoma, in 1907.
- Four states have adopted initiative or popular referendum since 1958.

SOURCE: Adapted from Initiative and Referendum Institute, "Quickfacts," http://www.iandrinstitute.org/factsheets/quickfacts.htm.

---

popular referendum
A device that allows citizens to approve or repeal a legislative act; the measure is placed on the ballot via a petition signed by voters.

initiative
A mechanism by which voters act as legislators, placing a measure on the ballot by petition and directly deciding whether or not to make it a law on election day.

recall
Direct voting to remove an elected official from office.

popular referendum, citizens can petition to repeal a law by a direct vote. Sometimes the vote is merely advisory, indicating the electorate's preferences; in other cases, voter approval is required before a ballot item can be enacted into law. In an **initiative,** the voters themselves put a measure on the ballot by filing petitions containing a stipulated number of valid signatures (see "Ideas and Politics: Initiative and Referendum").

The **recall** is a political device intended to remove an elected official from office. It works much like an initiative and is also placed on the ballot by the signatures of a predetermined number of citizens. One famous example in recent history was the recall of California Governor Gray Davis in 2003 and his replacement by the movie star, Arnold Schwartzenegger (aka "The Terminator").

Some major issues decided by direct vote in Europe include the following:
- French President Charles de Gaulle used a referendum to amend the French constitution to provide for the direct election of the president (de Gaulle himself) in 1962.
- The United Kingdom held its first referendum in 1973 to decide whether the nation should join the Common Market (a narrow majority voted in favor); in its second ever referendum in 2011, voters rejected a proposal to change the way MPs are elected.

- Denmark, Ireland, and Sweden, among others, have put issues such as whether to join the **euro area**—the EU countries that have adopted the euro—on the ballot. (Danish voters rejected it, but Denmark plans to hold another referendum on it; Irish voters said yes, and Swedish voters said no.)
- Direct popular vote in several Central and East European countries determined whether they would join the European Union. (All countries invited said yes.)

We can trace the modern era of direct democracy in the United States to 1978 and California's passage of the famous Proposition 13, which not only halved property taxes there but also spurred many initiatives and referendums throughout the nation.

Many direct democracy measures are divisive and "too hot to handle" for elected representatives seeking to avoid alienating voters on either side of the issue. In 1996, for example, voters approved Proposition 209 (aka, the California Civil Rights Initiative) limiting affirmative action programs by amending the state's constitution to prohibit discrimination against, or preferential treatment of, "any individual or group on the basis of race, sex, color, ethnicity, or national origin in the operation of public employment, public education, or public contracting."

Opponents of the initiative challenged the new law in federal court on grounds it was unconstitutional, but lost. In 2006, voters passed an amendment banning affirmative action in university admissions in Michigan, but in 2011 a three-judge panel of the 6th Circuit Court of Appeals voted to overturn the new law. In March of 2013, the U.S. Supreme Court announced it would consider the Michigan case. A ruling was expected sometime between the fall of 2013 and 2014. Depending on the high court's ruling, California's Proposition 209 will also stand or fall.

Even more controversial is Proposition 8, another California ballot initiative, passed in 2008. Prop 8 amended the state constitution to restrict the definition of marriage to opposite-sex couples and eliminate same-sex couples' right to marry. The "yes" vote overrode portions of a California Supreme Court decision affirming marriage as a fundamental right earlier in 2008. In December 2012, the U.S. Supreme Court agreed to consider a constitutional challenge to Proposition 8.

Direct democracy is often championed as a means of revitalizing public faith in government, improving voter participation, and circumventing corrupt, cowardly, or incompetent officeholders.[5] Opponents argue that money and special interests can too easily engineer the outcome of an initiative or referendum. They also say ballot measures are often so complex and technical the average voter cannot understand the issues. At least one student of plebiscites disagrees: "On most issues, especially well-publicized ones, voters do grasp the meaning…and…they act competently."[6]

But opponents of direct democracy argue that too much democracy can perhaps be as bad as too little. When measures are too numerous and issues are complex, the opportunity for demagoguery grows, and the possibility of rational voter choice diminishes. For these reasons, direct democracy is, at best, a supplement to, rather than a substitute for, representative democracy—one that should be used sparingly and with caution.

euro area
In the European Union, the euro zone refers to the twelve member states that have adopted the euro, including Germany, France, and Italy, but not the United Kingdom.

Opponents of direct democracy argue too much democracy can be as bad as too little. The anger displayed in this photo is inimical to reason or calm deliberation.

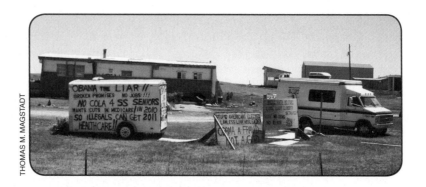

THOMAS M. MAGSTADT

WHO VOTES FOR WHAT, WHEN, AND WHY?

The right to vote is not a foolproof defense against tyranny and oppression, but it is the best one available. Yet later generations often take for granted rights earlier generations won at a very dear price. The United States offers no exception.

Voting in the United States

Voter turnout in the United States is often low by comparison with many other democracies.[7] In Europe voter participation in national elections typically averages more than 80%. Imagine a U.S. presidential election with an 85% voter turnout (that was the actual turnout in France in April 2007).

In 1996, a presidential election year, fewer than half of voting-age adults in the United States voted (Figure 11.1); by contrast in the 1960 Kennedy–Nixon election, nearly 63% of eligible adults voted. In recent elections, however, turnout has climbed back up but still remains well below 60%.

In 2000, a slightly larger turnout in Florida (where less than half the voting-age population cast a ballot) might have changed the outcome—and the course of U.S. history (see "Maps that Matter"). In the hotly contested 2004 presidential

FIGURE 11.1   Voter Turnout in U.S. National Elections 1996–2012. Color indicates presidential election years.
SOURCE: Federal Election Commission. Data drawn from Congressional Research Service reports, Election Data Services Inc., and state election offices.

Year	Voting age	Voter registration	Voter turnout	Voting-age turnout
2012	240,926,957	180,345,625	NA	NA
2010	235,940,406	NA	90,732,693	37.8%
2008	231,229,580	150,000,000	132,618,580	56.8%
2006	220,600,000	135,889,600	80,588,000	37.1%
2004	221,256,931	174,800,000	122,294,978	55.3%
2002	215,473,000	150,990,598	79,830,119	37.0%
2000	205,815,000	156,421,311	105,586,274	51.3%
1998	200,929,000	141,850,558	73,117,022	36.4%
1996	196,511,000	146,211,960	96,456,345	49.1%

THE ELECTORAL COLLEGE IN 2000

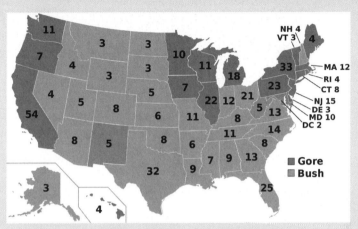

SOURCE: 2000 Electoral College Map, public data. © Cengage Learning.

The 2000 presidential election came down to 537 votes separating the "winner" (Bush) from the "loser" (Al Gore) in one state, Florida, where the chief election official, Katherine Harris, was also co-chair of the Florida Bush campaign. In that race, thousands of Florida voters were "wrongly purged" according to the *New York Times*.*

Florida was the most notorious case of voting list irregularities in the 2000 election, but it was not the only one, nor was it the most egregious. The *New York Times* cited another example:

> In Missouri, St. Louis election officials kept an "inactive voters list" of people they had been unable to contact by mail. Voters on the list, which ballooned to more than 54,000 names in a city where only 125,230 voted, had a legal right to cast their ballots, but election officials put up enormous barriers. When inactive voters showed up to vote, poll workers had to confirm their registration with the board of elections downtown. Phone lines there were busy all day, and hundreds of voters travelled downtown in person, spending hours trying to vindicate their right to vote. The board admitted later that "a significant number" were not processed before the polls closed.

What happened in Florida and Missouri in 2000 could happen elsewhere. According to the *New York Times*, "Voters would have no way of knowing [if there was a problem] because of the stunning lack of transparency in election operations." Election board officials often make decisions about removing voters from the rolls without any written rules or procedures.

The power to decide who gets to vote has both social and political implications. In both Florida and St. Louis, disenfranchised voters were disproportionately black. In Florida, African Americans are one of the strongest Democratic voting groups.

In the 2012 election, liberals accused Republican strategists of attempting to prevent high voter turnout especially in key "swing states" (Ohio, Virginia, North Carolina, Wisconsin, Colorado, and Florida, among others). How? By putting strict photo ID laws in place (thus, critics claim, targeting minorities, the poor, and elderly citizens) and restricting early voting, for example.

What is to be done? The *New York Times* recommends a three-step remedy: (1) clear standards—the policy for purging voting lists ought to be based on clear, written guidelines; (2) transparency—the public has a right to know when voting list purges are under way; and (3) nonpartisanship—election board officials should not be connected to candidates or parties.

---

*Editorial, "How America Doesn't Vote," *New York Times*, February 15, 2004, <http://www.nytimes.com/2004/02/15/opinion/how-america-doesn-t-vote.html?

FIGURE 11.2   Midterm Election Turnout, 1962–2010, based on House Votes Cast (percentage of voting-age population).

SOURCE: Adapted from Congressional Quarterly Weekly Report, February 23, 1991, p. 484; and the United States Elections Project, Department of Public and International Affairs, George Mason University, http://elections.gmu.edu/Voter_Turnout_2006.htm.

The voter turnout rate in midterm elections remains low. It fell abruptly after the voting age was lowered to 18 in 1971 and has trended downward, with a mild reversal in the recession year of 1982 and a significant upturn in 1994. In Tennessee, Mississippi, and Louisiana (where only one district was decided in November), the turnout rate did not reach 20 percent. In only four states did a majority of the voting-age population participate in voting for the House: Maine (55.6 percent), Minnesota (54.8 percent), Montana (54.6 percent), and Alaska (52.5 percent).

motor voter law
A statute that allows residents of a given locality to register to vote at convenient places, such as welfare offices and driver's license bureaus; the idea behind laws of this kind is to remove technical obstacles to voting and thus promote better turnouts in elections.

election (George W. Bush vs. John Kerry), as the electorate became polarized over the war in Iraq, voter turnout climbed to 55% and in 2008 reached nearly 57%, the highest since 1968.

Midterm elections (when there is no presidential race) provide another measure of voting behavior in the United States. In general, turnout is low in these years (Figure 11.2). Even in the highly charged 2006 midterm elections, only 37% of the eligible population turned out to vote; in 2010 the figure was a bit higher—about 41%.

As noted earlier, low voter turnout remains the pattern in the United States despite changes that ought to have brought more voters to the polls. Laws and rules designed to block or burden access to the ballot, such as poll taxes, literacy tests, and lengthy residence requirements, are gone. The voting age has dropped to 18. The potential for virtually all U.S. adults to vote now exists.[8] Moreover, since passage of the **motor voter law** in 1993, new voters can register while obtaining or renewing their driver's licenses. In sum, low voter participation flies in the face of "broad changes in the population [that] have boosted levels of education, income, and occupation, all associated with enhanced rates of turnout."[9]

Who votes is a key question in any democracy. Perhaps even more important, however, is the question many nonvoters ask: Why bother? Unless the defenders of democracy can continue to give them a meaningful answer, there is always a danger that liberty itself will lose its hold on the popular imagination.

People who believe it is possible to make a difference, who are self-confident and assertive, are more likely to become engaged in public affairs, including political activity, than people who lack these attributes. Why then do some people lack a sense of **political efficacy** and why do so many U.S. adults not even vote?

Patterns of Participation

Most people in the United States value private property over public goods—from national parks and vital water resources to the air we breathe. Oddly, citizens who belong to service clubs and donate to charities are often reluctant to get involved in "politics" or community action or to run for local office. A pioneering 1950 study by Julian L. Woodward and Elmo Roper revealed that about 70% of U.S. adults were politically inactive.[10] A later study found approximately 26% of the U.S. population could be classified as activists; the rest either limited participation to voting or avoided politics altogether.[11]

The rate of political literacy—people with the knowledge, skills, and values essential to make informed decisions and participate effectively in the democratic process—is low in the United States and falling. According to one study by the UCLA Higher Education Research Institute, a mere 29.4% of college freshmen considered political awareness a "very important" or "essential" life goal in 1996, down from 38.8% in 1992 and 57.8% in 1966. (Say you were to take an informal poll in your dorm or dining hall. Do you expect today's college students to be as apathetic as they were in 1996? Less? More?)

Who votes in the United States? According to U.S. census data, women are more likely to vote than men, and whites are more likely to vote than blacks or Hispanics. People over age 65 are much more likely to vote than young adults 18–24. Midwesterners are more likely to vote than people in the South or West. People with a college education vote more than people who never finished high school, and white-collar workers vote more often than blue-collar workers. Clearly, socioeconomic factors affect participation rates.

The 2008 general election, however, "the most diverse in U.S. history," saw a marked difference in certain voting patterns. Minorities and youth voted in record numbers. African Americans cast nearly 3 million more ballots in 2008 than in 2004 (up 21%); 1.5 million more Latinos voted in 2008 than in 2004 (up 16%); and the youth vote (aged 18–29) climbed by 1.8 million votes (a 9% rise). Black women had the highest voter turnout rate (68.8%)—a first.[12]

Whether 2008 was indicative of a trend toward greater diversity in elections is unclear. Voter turnout in 2012 was indeed higher than in 2010, but lower than in the two preceding presidential elections—57.5% compared to 62.3% in 2008 and 60.4% in 2004. (It was only 54.2% in 2000, however.) There were some 219 million eligible voters in the United States in 2012. Postelection estimates put the number of votes cast at 126 million, meaning 93 million "eligibles" failed to vote.

Generational factors are increasingly important in U.S. elections. In three recent general elections—2004, 2006, and 2008—voters 18–29 were "the Democratic party's most supportive age group. In 2008, 66% of those under age 30 voted for Barack Obama, making the disparity between young voters and other age groups larger than in any presidential election since exit polling began in 1972."[13] In 2012, exit polls had Obama carrying 60% of the youth vote, less lopsided than in 2008, but still far above Mitt Romney's 36%. Voters 18–29 represented 19% of the total turnout in 2012.

Until recently observers tended to blamed low voter turnout rates on the lowering of the voting age to 18. But this explanation is too simplistic. Other relevant factors include a declining sense of civic duty, lengthy campaigns that dull the senses, voter cynicism over the rising role of Super PACs and stories in the press about billionaires who pour millions into candidates and causes they favor,[14] and negative television ads that turn people off.

Private Pursuits and the Public Good

In the 1830s, French writer Alexis de Tocqueville observed that wherever a widespread belief in equality exists, and established sources of moral instruction like religion, family, monarchy, and tradition fail to carry the weight they once did, individuals tend to be morally self-reliant.

For Tocqueville the resulting **individualism** is detrimental to a sense of social and civic duty and thus diminishes the life of the community. "Individualism," he wrote, "is a mature and calm feeling, which disposes each member of the community to sever himself from the mass of his fellow creatures; and to draw apart with his family and friends; so that, after he has thus formed a little circle of his own, he willingly leaves the society at large to itself."[15] People live in a state of constant agitation arising from personal ambitions, he noted. "In America the passion for physical well-being...is felt by all" and "the desire of acquiring the good things of this world is the prevailing passion of the American people."[16]

Tocqueville thought that individualism in the United States was counteracted, to some extent, by the fact that people belonged to an enormous number and variety of civic associations. But participation in groups and group activities of all kinds has declined in the United States. Observing that the number of bowlers had increased 10% whereas league bowling decreased 40% between 1980 and 1993, Robert Putnam concluded in the mid-1990s that bowling symbolized life as we know it in the United States.[17] Putnam also pointed out that participation in organized religion, labor unions, the PTA, traditional women's groups such as the League of Women Voters, and service clubs such as the Shriners and Masons had declined during the past thirty years, as had volunteering.

In April 2009, President Obama signed the Edward M. Kennedy Serve America Act committing $5.7 billion over five years to promoting volunteerism. It is doubtful whether this program will make much of a difference, but in an age when a "wireless culture" is transforming the character of postmodern societies, there can be no denying the importance of civic-minded citizens in the life of a community—or a nation.

Affluence and Apathy

Political apathy and indifference, expressed as a lack of curiosity about what is going on in Washington or the world, persisted in the United States even after 9/11 and the invasion of Afghanistan and Iraq. The apathy turned to alarm, if only momentarily, in 2008 when the financial crisis suddenly jeopardized the

individualism
According to Alexis de Tocqueville, the direction of one's feelings toward oneself and one's immediate situation; a self-centered detachment from the broader concerns of society as a whole. According to John Stuart Mill, the qualities of human character that separate humans from animals and give them uniqueness and dignity.

political apathy
Lack of interest in politics resulting from complacency, ignorance, or the conviction that "my vote doesn't really count" or "nobody cares what I think anyway."

fortunes and future of millions of U.S. workers with investments in mutual funds and retirement plans. The conclusion that wallets are more important than wars in the public mind is difficult to escape (see "Ideas and Politics: Australia's Mandatory Voting Law").

AUSTRALIA'S MANDATORY VOTING LAW

Noted scholar and political observer Norm Ornstein wants to make voting mandatory in the United States. He believes lower turnout is the cause of "ever-greater polarization in the country and in Washington, which in turn has led to ever-more rancor and ever-less legislative progress." He makes a persuasive case:

> With participation rates of about 10 percent or less of the eligible electorate in many primaries, to 35 percent or so in midterm general elections, to 50 or 60 percent in presidential contests, the name of the game for parties is turnout—the key to success is turning out one's ideological base. Whichever party does a better job getting its base to the polls reaps the rewards of majority status. And what's the best way to get your base to show up at the polls? Focus on divisive issues that underscore the differences between the parties.

Ornstein points out that several countries, including Austria, Belgium, and Cyprus, as well as Australia and Singapore, have adopted mandatory voting. In Australia (Figure 11.3), "no-shows" at the polls pay a modest fine of about $15 the first time and more with each subsequent offense. The result: a turnout rate greater than 95%. "The fine, of course, is an incentive to vote. But the system has also instilled the idea that voting is a societal obligation." No less important, "It has elevated the political dialogue," and it places a premium on "persuading the persuadables."

Ornstein surmises, "If there were mandatory voting in America, there's a good chance that the ensuing reduction in extremist discourse would lead to genuine legislative progress." But, he argues, political reform is urgent: "These days, valuable congressional time is spent on frivolous or narrow issues (flag burning, same-sex marriage) that are intended only to spur on the party bases and ideological extremes. Consequently, important, complicated issues (pension and health-care reform) get short shrift."

Note: Norm Ornstein is a scholar in residence at the American Enterprise Institute and coauthor (with Thomas Mann) of *The Broken Branch: How Congress Is Failing America and How to Get It Back on Track* (New York: Oxford University Press, 2006).

SOURCE: Norm Ornstein, "Vote—Or Else," *New York Times,* August 10, 2006 (online edition).

FIGURE 11.3   Map of Australia. Australia is a continent, as well as a country, that is roughly the size of the "lower 48" (the continental United States minus Alaska). It is a parliamentary democracy with a mandatory voting requirement.

Perhaps thinking we can afford to be nonchalant about politics so long as we ourselves are not insecure or oppressed is just human nature. Or maybe Tocqueville was right: People in the United States are too predisposed to individualism to care if somebody they don't know is fighting a war in a place they can barely find on a map.

Political apathy is the luxury of an affluent society where the majority does not feel threatened and people's basic needs are met. Under such circumstances, apathy is understandable, predictable, and perhaps even rational. When people who are normally indifferent or inattentive to politics grow restive, it's a sure sign that all is not well. In the 1850s, for example, apathy gave way to antipathy between North and South over slavery and states' rights, leading to secession and the Civil War. In the 1930s, the Great Depression galvanized the nation.

In 2008–2009, the deepest recession since the 1930s briefly banished voter apathy in the United States. But voters quickly shrugged off the Great Recession: As noted previously, voter turnout in 2012 was well below 2008 and even 2004 despite a bitterly contested cliffhanger presidential race, an estimated $6 billion spent in campaigns, and 8 million more eligible voters.

In sum, participation is not always a good thing. But neither is apathy. If the only time we take a keen interest in politics is when we are personally affected, if our *only* motive is self-interest as opposed to the public interest or the common good, that points to a serious defect in our national character—one that, over time, will manifest itself in undesirable ways. Try explaining what went wrong on Wall Street in August 2008, for example, without mentioning the role of greed. A steady and sober interest in public affairs stemming from a well-ingrained sense of civic duty is a healthy antidote to excessive individualism—and a far better solution to the problem of apathy than an aroused but ignorant majority (see "Ideas and Politics: Australia's Mandatory Voting Law").

PARTICIPATING AS A SPECTATOR: OUTSIDERS

In the competitive "game" of politics, most people are outsiders. As outsiders, we are at a disadvantage because (a) we don't understand the game very well; (b) we don't get to make the rules; and (c) unlike the insiders, we can't break the rule and get away with it.

One study in the 1990s found nearly half of respondents did not know the Supreme Court has final authority to determine whether a law is constitutional, and three of four were unaware senators serve six-year terms.[18] Can government by majority rule work if the majority—the outsiders—do not know *how* it works (or why it doesn't work the way we want it to or think it should)?

Many believe politicians rarely if ever say what they mean or mean what they say. Studies of voter awareness paint a portrait with few distinct lines. First, whereas only a minority of the voting-age population votes, those who do vote generally are better informed than are those who do not. Second, U.S. adults as a whole probably know as much about politics today as they did in the 1940s.[19] Third, many find it more worthwhile to engage in private pursuits and leave politics to others.[20] Fourth, candidates often take no clear political stance, so many citizens may wonder, What's the point? Finally, many voters make reasonable judgments about issues and candidates despite being poorly informed.[21]

According to a theory called **low-information rationality**, ill-informed voters use shortcuts (for example, does a candidate look the part?) and simplifying assumptions (such as party identification) to make political judgments.[22] This theory assumes picking a candidate for office is like buying a car. But when voters go to the polls, they have a far narrower range of choices than car buyers and far less information about the "product"—problems that can be fixed only by elected representatives, who unfortunately often have a vested interest in *not* fixing them.

Why do supposedly rational voters almost always reelect incumbents while mistrusting Congress as an institution? According to rational actor theory (which holds that human behavior is a product of logical reasoning rather than emotion or habit), they are "voting for the devil they know rather than the devil they don't" and for representatives with seniority who have proven they can produce "pork" (federal funding) for local projects.

Enlightened or not, this type of voting behavior is rational in the short term and on the local level. The dilemma for democracy arises from the fact that "comfort zone" voting is not necessarily rational in the aggregate or in the long run—that is, on the national level, where the big-picture decisions, laws, and policies are made.

PARTICIPATING AS A PLAYER: INSIDERS

Some say a power elite controls the political process from top to bottom. The most popular version of this theory holds that ordinary citizens never exercise much influence, elections and public opinion polls notwithstanding, and the political system is manipulated from above rather than below. The manipulators are the power elite, a small group of plutocrats who go back and forth through a "revolving door" between the commanding heights of the economy (megabanks and multinational corporations) and the rarefied echelons of government, exercising enormous power over the nation's destiny. The status, wealth, and power of this self-perpetuating political class ensure that access to the levers of government is monopolized by the few to pursue private interests, not the public interest.

The close links between personal business interests of the Bush family and the oil industry gave new credence to this theory (especially after the ill-fated invasion of Iraq), as did the fact that Halliburton, the huge multinational corporation formerly headed by Vice President Cheney, was awarded billions of dollars in no-bid contracts to operate in Iraq. The nomination of venture capitalist and multimillionaire Mitt Romney as the Republican candidate for the presidency in 2012 gave rise to numerous books and articles about the rise of a Super-Rich, plutocratic, and self-perpetuating "meritocracy" in American politics.

Elitist Theories: Iron Laws and Ironies

Elitist theories of democracy hold that neither the voters nor public opinion nor a variety of competing interests but rather a small number of wealthy individuals governs democracy. This theory was propounded most influentially in the 1950s by sociologist C. Wright Mills and has recently been expanded

low-information rationality
The idea that voters can make sensible choices in elections even though they lack knowledge and sophistication about public policy, candidates, and current events.

elitist theories of democracy
In political thought, the theory that a small clique of individuals (a "power elite") at the highest levels of government, industry, and other institutions exercise political power for their own interests; according to elitist theories, ordinary citizens have almost no real influence on governmental policy.

and updated by a growing number of distinguished journalists, economists, and policy analysts—Robert Reich, Christopher Hayes, Joseph Stiglitz, Paul Krugman, and Matt Taiibi, to name a few.[23] By putting the power elite in the spotlight, Mills challenged the idea of "government by the people" and called into serious question whether it exists (or ever existed) in the United States. Contemporary critics focus on the erosion of the middle class and the great divide between the "plutocracy" (the so-called super-rich) and the rest of us.

Robert Michels, a German sociologist, also advanced a theory of elitism, but his study applied to all modern bureaucratic organizations. His findings were distilled from an analysis of the German Social Democratic Party, which before the outbreak of World War I had been the largest socialist party in the world. Michels reasoned that because the party favored equality in wealth and status, it should be sufficiently committed to democratic principles to put them into practice. He found instead that elite groups that derived their power and authority from well-honed organizational skills ran the party.

iron law of oligarchy
According to this theory, the administrative necessities involved in managing any large organization, access to and control of information and communication, inevitably become concentrated in the hands of a few bureaucrats, who then wield true power in the organization.

This discovery led Michels to postulate his famous **iron law of oligarchy**, which holds that all large organizations, including governments, are run in the same fashion. He believed organizations naturally become increasingly oligarchic, bureaucratized, and centralized over time, as those at the top gain more information and knowledge, greater control of communications, and sharper organizational skills, while the great mass of members (or citizens) remain politically unsophisticated, preoccupied with private affairs, and bewildered by the complexity of larger issues. According to this view, the people, for whose benefit democratic institutions were originally conceived, are inevitably shut out of the political or organizational process as corporate officers or bureaucratic officials govern in the name of the rank-and-file shareholder or citizen.

In elitist theories, democracy is seen as a sham or a myth: It does not matter what the people think, say, or do, because they have no real influence over public policy. If most people believe public opinion matters, it is only because they are naive and do not really understand how "the system" works.

Logically, "democracy for the few" is a contradiction in terms incompatible with the core principle of government by consent. But some close observers argue that the many are unfit to govern themselves. The "masses are authoritarian, intolerant, anti-intellectual, atavistic, alienated, hateful, and violent."[24] The irony of democracy is then clear: Allowing the people real power to rule will only result in the expression of antidemocratic preferences and policies.

Pluralists versus Elitists

Pluralists and elitists agree that in any society there are gradations of power and certain groups or individuals exercise disproportionate influence. They disagree, however, about the basic nature of the political system itself.

According to pluralists, the U.S. political system is decentralized. They concede that organized interest groups with lots of money to dole out, by concentrating on a single issue, can exert disproportionate influence in that specific policy area. They also admit that from time to time certain disadvantaged or unpopular groups may not be adequately represented. Nonetheless, no single individual or group can exercise total power over the whole gamut of public policy. The political system is too wide open, freewheeling, and institutionally fragmented to allow for any such accumulation of power. In the opinion of one prominent pluralist,

> The most important obstacle to social change in the United States, then, is not the concentration of power but its diffusion.... If power was concentrated sufficiently, those of us who wish for change would merely have to negotiate with those who hold the power and, if necessary, put pressure on them. But power is so widely diffused that, in many instances, there is no one to negotiate with and no one on whom to put pressure.[25]

Pluralists don't deny that those who hold the highest positions in government and business tend to have similar backgrounds and characteristics: Admittedly, many are males from well-to-do WASP (white Anglo-Saxon Protestant) families who have had Ivy League educations. However, that wealth, status, and education correlate closely with political influence does not prove the system is closed, they argue, nor does it mean participatory democracy is a sham. In fact, there are opportunities for most everyone to exert political pressure at the local, state, and national levels. The public interest—defined as the aggregation of private interests—is generally better served under constitutional democracy than under any other system. So say the pluralists.

So who's right? There is more than a grain of truth in elitist theory, as the concentration of wealth in the United States, with its market economy and business-friendly tax system, attests. But politicians and public policy *are* affected by public opinion. There's no denying that widespread and steadily growing popular sentiment against the Vietnam War was instrumental in pressuring the government to withdraw from that conflict. In 2006, growing opposition to the war in Iraq cost the Republicans control of the Congress. Similarly, in 2010 voters turned against the convoluted "ObamaCare" plan in large numbers, helping Republicans win a solid majority in the House of Representatives. Republican presidential candidate Mitt Romney tried to capitalize on this divisive issue in 2012 but the effort was awkward because as governor he had signed a similar plan into law in Massachusetts—one that served as a model for the Affordable Care Act of 2010 (aka, ObamaCare).

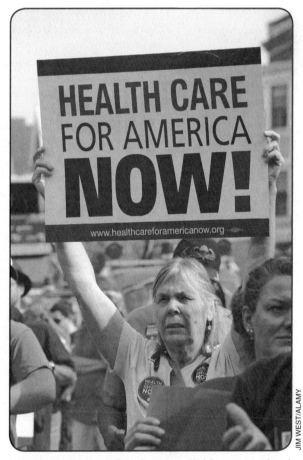

Interest groups take many different forms. Some, like labor unions, are formal and highly structured with dues-paying members and professional staffs; others, like these demonstrators on behalf of health care reform, are informal, spontaneous, narrowly focused, and often short-lived. Public opinion has the potential to influence elected officials and force action on pressing issues, but it plays little or no role when the citizenry is deeply divided.

Public opinion in the United States is often fragmented, but that does not render it nonexistent or irrelevant. Whether elections are meaningful or the outcomes rational, however, are very different questions (ones we take up later in this chapter).

PARTICIPATION AND POLITICAL PARTIES

One major purpose of a **political party** is to select, nominate, and support candidates for elective office. Another is to bring various interests under one tent—a process called **interest aggregation**. Political parties have become permanent fixtures in all liberal democracies, including the United States.

American Democracy: No Place for a Party?

The Constitution makes no mention of political parties; some Founders abhorred them. George Washington sought to avoid partisanship by forming a cabinet composed of the best available talent, including Thomas Jefferson as secretary of state and Alexander Hamilton as secretary of the treasury.

Washington's noble attempt to avoid partisan politics ultimately failed. Personal animosities developed between Jefferson and Hamilton, in large part due to conflicting understandings of government and public policy, and the two became fierce rivals. In the late 1790s, Jefferson and his followers founded a loosely organized Republican Party to oppose the strong anti-French policies of Federalists such as Hamilton and John Adams. Yet in 1789, Jefferson himself had written, "If I could not go to heaven but with a party, I would not go there at all."[26]

Why did so many statesmen of Jefferson's generation distrust political parties? In Jefferson's case, dislike stemmed from a peculiarly American brand of individualism that has survived to this day. "I never submitted the whole system of my opinions to the creed of any party of men whatever, in religion, in philosophy, in politics, or in anything else, where I was capable of thinking for myself," he observed, concluding that "such an addiction is the last degradation of a free and moral agent."[27] Other thinkers of Jefferson's generation believed political parties fostered narrow self-interest at the expense of the general or public interest. They saw parties as the public extension of private selfishness.

Fast forward to the present. Partisanship in U.S. politics still has a bad name. Witness the calls for a "bipartisan" approach to legislation in Congress, often by the very politicians who are the least willing to compromise or work with a president of the opposing party.

Many commentators see Republican leaders such as Speaker of the House John Boehner, House Majority Leader Eric Cantor, 2012 vice-presidential candidate Paul Ryan, and several state governors, including Scott Walker of Wisconsin and Bobby Jindal of Louisiana, in this light. For example, Andrew Sullivan, a conservative *Daily Beast* political columnist, appeared on Comedy Central's *Colbert Report* (August 26, 2012) and denounced Republicans in Congress because, in his words, he expected them "to have the good grace and patriotism to cooperate with an incoming president" but instead "they set out to destroy this guy from the get-go."

---

political party
An organization whose adherents share a political philosophy and common interests and whose primary reason for existing is to win control of government.

interest aggregation
How the interests, concerns, and demands of various individuals and groups in society are translated into policies and programs; in constitutional democracies, a major function of political parties.

Sullivan's criticism was remarkable mainly because his is the voice of a popular conservative with a big amplifier. But polls consistently show that the spectacle of a mudslinging Congress and a dysfunctional government is repulsive to citizens on both sides of the partisan divide.

General Aims

Political parties strive to gain or retain political power; in practical terms, this means capturing control of the government. Because voters decide who rules, political parties concentrate on winning elections, but they also engage citizens as volunteers, recruit candidates, raise money, and launch media campaigns. In the party platform, proposals and policies are formulated to appease key interest groups, which, in turn, support the party's candidates with money and votes.

In the United States, candidates frequently appeal for votes by promising to deliver on bread-and-butter issues rather than taking strong stands on ideological issues or advancing bold domestic and foreign policy proposals. The idea is to build a consensus around a vague set of principles rather than detailed policies. The presidential candidate perceived to be closest to the political center is usually elected. An opposing strategy is to offer voters clear alternatives, which is how elections are structured in most democratic countries—and, arguably, how the Obama campaign won in 2008 and how the Romney campaign lost in 2012.

In Europe's parliamentary systems, multiple parties vie for votes and each formulates more or less distinctive policy alternatives. Parties are generally more important than personalities, because winning a majority of seats in parliament is the key to controlling the government. Where the stakes are so high, party discipline is at a premium and mavericks rarely prosper.

Political Party Systems

By definition, liberal democracies have competitive party systems. In theory, more competitive party systems are better than less competitive ones—democracy, after all, implies meaningful choices. Thus, multiparty systems have this advantage over two-party systems: they offer voters real choices. Two-party systems sometimes do offer "a choice, not an echo," but often the choice is between Tweedledee and Tweedledum (two middle-of-the-road parties). On the other hand, two-party systems often result in more stable governments than multiparty systems.

At one time or another **one-party dominant** systems existed in Mexico (the Institutional Revolutionary Party), Japan (the Liberal Democratic Party), India (the Congress), Taiwan (the Nationalist Party), and the U.S. Deep South (the Democratic Party). One-party dominant systems resemble the one-party systems found in authoritarian states, but they hold regular elections, allow open criticism of the government, and do not outlaw other parties.

However, the line between authoritarian and democratic rule is not always clear. In Mexico, for example, the Institutional Revolutionary Party (PRI) long maintained its dominant position through corruption, intimidation, and voting fraud. One-party dominant systems invite official interference in elections—including ballot box stuffing and other blatantly unfair practices.

one-party dominant
One-party dominant systems are different from authoritarian one-party systems in that they hold regular elections, allow open criticism of the government, and do not outlaw other parties. Until recently, Japan operated as a one-party dominant system, as did Mexico; South Africa is one current example.

The nearly century-long dominance of the PRI in Mexico is a notorious example of the correlation between concentration and corruption, and the corrosive effects of this nexus on a society (see Chapter 8). But Americans north of the border too often failed to recognize that official corruption is not confined to Latin America or the Southern Hemisphere.

Excessive concentrations of wealth are closely linked to a narrow distribution of political power manifested in cozy arrangements among business leaders, bankers, entrenched bureaucrats, and top government officials. This is the message of the Occupy Wall Street (liberal) and Tea Party (conservative) movements in the United States, where the copious mixing of money and power is perfectly legal under the U.S. Supreme Court's interpretation of the First Amendment right of free speech (the "corporations are people" argument).[28] To understand how and why things happen the way they do in Washington, the best advice is "follow the money." When and where the exchange of votes for money (say, in Congress) follows the exchange of money for votes (say, in campaigns) how is that different from bribery? How can the conflation of private motives and public service fail to foster corruption?

Designing Democracy: Electoral Systems

Political parties allow citizen participation; they are thus an important part of the architecture of democracy. But this architecture is not entirely accidental—in fact, party systems are not an accident of nature. Rather, they are the result of human engineering.

The design element is found in the *rules* governing elections, sometimes spelled out in a constitution, which limit the number of political parties that can exist and thus shape the choices available to voters. The success of minor parties is discouraged in systems based on single-member districts, where any candidate with a one-vote advantage (a plurality) wins the only available seat. Smaller parties find it difficult to attract voters simply because their candidates have such a small chance of winning. By contrast, in proportional representation systems, where several candidates are elected from each district, minor parties enjoy a far greater chance of being elected. Thus, to repeat a key point, proportional representation is far more likely than the first past the post system to produce a multiparty political system.

Another structural consideration is whether the political system is centralized or decentralized. Parties in federal systems organize themselves along the federal structure of the government. In the United States vote totals in presidential elections are determined nationally but counted (and weighted) state by state in winner-take-all contests. Thus George W. Bush won the 2000 election despite the fact that Al Gore received more total votes nationwide.

U.S. presidential candidates and the political parties they lead face the challenge of winning not one election, but fifty. And though the United States has only two major parties, fifty state parties exist alongside each *national* party. Thus, for example, the Democratic Party in Massachusetts has borne little resemblance to the Democratic Party in Mississippi, historically. Strong state-level party organizations help elect senators, representatives, and state and local officials. In 2012, the Republicans won thirty-three more seats in the U.S. House of Representatives than Democrats despite the fact that Democratic candidates received over a million more votes.

The U.S. federal structure also strongly favors small states over large and gives small-state voters far greater weight in Congress. In the Senate Rhode Island and Texas have the same weight. The twenty-six smallest states have a mere 18% of the population but a majority of the votes; conversely the nine states with a majority of the population have only 18% of the votes. States reshape congressional districts every ten years (called reapportionment) so the party that controls the legislature can stack the deck by a method called "gerrymandering" (drawing up voting districts most likely to produce the desired outcome). And the Electoral College can hand the White House over to a candidate who loses the popular vote (as happened in 2000).[29]

Structural factors are thus clearly important, but culture also influences a nation's form of government and the party system it designs by the electoral rules it prescribes. Multiparty systems are most likely to thrive in countries that value ideology and group solidarity over compromise and stability.

Is the Party Over?

Some now say neither major party reflects U.S. society's values or diversity.[30] Others see the rancor between the two parties as evidence of a dysfunctional political system.

Ironically, opportunities to participate are at an all-time high. State presidential primary elections, once the exception, have become the rule. States now compete to hold the earliest primaries. (The elections themselves have become a bonanza for some states, attracting revenue and wide media attention.) Other states hold party caucuses, where rank-and-file party members choose delegates who later attend state conventions that, in turn, select delegates pledged to support particular candidates at the party's national convention.

On the other hand, presidential campaigns are costly and prolonged in the United States; the nomination and election process can last well over a year. (By contrast, British parliamentary elections often last less than a month and cost a tiny fraction of what U.S. elections cost.) Fundraising is a full-time endeavor, not only for presidential hopefuls but also for serious candidates in Senate and House races, prompting cynics to remark that U.S. elections have become nonstop events.

The 2012 campaigns saw record spending (both presidential candidates spent more than $1 billion, for example: Obama: $1.123 billion; Romney: $1.019 billion). No other liberal democracy in the world spends so much time and treasure choosing its chief executive. Parties play a role in elections, but money plays a far bigger role. Where do candidates turn for financial backing? Next we look at the role of interest groups in contemporary U.S. politics.

PARTICIPATION AND INTEREST GROUPS

Interest groups—also known as special interest groups, pressure groups, and advocacy groups—try to influence legislation, policy, and programs. Interest groups that operate in Washington, D.C. or state capitals are known as **lobbies**. They often concentrate on specific areas or issues, including corporate taxes and subsidies for big business, banking regulations, farm subsidies, federal aid to education, or wildlife conservation, to name a few.

interest group
An association of individuals that attempts to influence policy and legislation in a confined area of special interest, often through lobbying, campaign contributions, and bloc voting.

lobby
An interest group that operates in Washington, D.C., or in a state capital, and attempts to influence legislators, decision makers, and regulators to bend laws, policies, and rules in ways that benefit its membership or constituency.

special interests
An organization or association that exists to further private interests in the political arena; examples in the United States are the U.S. Chamber of Commerce or the National Association of Manufacturers (business), the AFL-CIO (labor), and the National Farmers Organization (NFO).

public interest
The pursuit of policies aimed at the general good or the betterment of society as a whole; in contrast to special interests that pursue laws or policies more narrowly favoring individuals or groups.

One way to categorize interest groups is to distinguish between those that represent **special interests** and those that represent the **public interest**. The Audubon Society, the Aspen Institute, Greenpeace, Friends of the Earth, the Sierra Club, The Fund for Peace, Worldwatch Institute, and the Earth Policy Institute are examples of familiar public interest advocacy groups in the United States. The Royal Society for the Protection of Birds, with more than a million members, is the largest advocacy group in Europe. Public interest groups promote causes they believe will benefit society as a whole. The Sierra Club, for example, backs environmental causes and sound conservation policies.

Special interest groups differ not only in the issues they emphasize, but also in scope. Most ethnic groups (the National Italian American Foundation, for example), religious groups (the American Jewish Congress), occupational groups (the American Association of University Professors), age-defined groups (AARP), and a variety of groups that cannot be easily categorized (such as the Disabled American Veterans) are narrowly focused. Each fights for laws and policies that benefit the exclusive group it represents—for private rather than the public interest.

One common classification scheme distinguishes four basic types of interest groups.

- Associational interest groups have a distinctive name, national headquarters, professional staff, and political agenda tied to specific group characteristics, goals, beliefs, or values. Examples include the National Association of Manufacturers (NAM), the National Rifle Association (NRA), the National Association for the Advancement of Colored People (NAACP), the United Auto Workers (UAW), the Christian Coalition of America (CCA), the Sierra Club, and AARP (formerly the American Association of Retired Persons).

- Nonassociational interest groups lack formal structures but reflect largely unvoiced social, ethnic, cultural, or religious interests capable of coalescing into potent political forces under the right circumstances. Informal groups are most common in the developing countries of Asia, the Arab world, Latin America, and sub-Saharan Africa.

- Institutional interest groups exist mainly within the government, although some outside groups—major defense contractors, for example—are so intertwined in the operations of government that we can include them in this category. In the United States at the federal level, departments and agencies have vested interests in policies and programs for which they lobby from the inside, often out of public view. The Pentagon lobbies for new weapons systems, airplanes, warships, and the like, and Labor, Agriculture, and Education become captives of the special interests most directly affected by the programs they administer.

- Anomic interest groups sometimes develop spontaneously when many individuals strongly oppose specific policies. The nationwide student demonstrations against the Vietnam War in the late 1960s and early 1970s are one example. Political scientist Gabriel Almond suggested that street riots and even some assassinations also fit this category.[31]

Sources and Methods of Influence

Interest groups attempt to sway public policy by influencing elected officials and public opinion at the national or state level in three primary ways: (1) by seeking the election of representatives they trust, (2) by seeking access to elected officials, and (3) by mounting mass media campaigns.

Interest groups prize access to decision makers, especially on a one-on-one basis. Many employ **lobbyists,** who cultivate credibility and influence with legislators in various ways. They testify before legislative committees on the basis of their expert knowledge and arrange for intermediaries—close personal friends or constituents—to advance their viewpoints. Lobbyists also mount public relations, fax, telephone, telegraph, or Internet campaigns; cooperate with other like-minded lobbyists for common legislative objectives; and increase communication opportunities between themselves and legislators (for example, by throwing a party or sponsoring a charitable event).[32]

lobbyist
A person who attempts to influence governmental policy in favor of some special interest.

Money and membership are vital to the success of interest groups. Organizations representing a large and distinct group of citizens with identical interests have a clear advantage. AARP is a prime example, with tens of millions of like-minded members (some 36 million) and clear aims (for example, protecting senior-citizen entitlement programs such as Social Security and Medicare).[33] Roughly half of all U.S. adults over the age of 50 (some 20% of all voters) belong to AARP, making it the second-largest nonprofit organization in the country, trailing only the Roman Catholic Church. Employing eighteen registered lobbyists and a staff of 1,800 people, maintaining a budget of nearly $600 million, and portraying itself as the guardian angel of the U.S. elderly, AARP is a key player on legislation affecting pensions, health care, and the rights of the elderly.

The American-Israel Political Action Committee (AIPAC), the National Right to Life Committee (NLRC), and the National Rifle Association (NRA) are three powerful single-issue interest groups. Each focuses on a single objective: support for Israel (AIPAC), opposition to abortion (NLRC), and the right to bear arms (NRA).

A highly motivated mass membership is important, but money is crucial. Major corporations, interest groups, and wealthy private citizens can exert

THOMAS M. MAGSTADT

In September 2012, the City Council of Overland Park, Kansas, passed a law permitting residents who are at least 18 years old to openly carry a gun without completing any gun safety or weapons training classes. Such laws are applauded by the National Rifle Association (NRA), but the Overland Park City Council had second thoughts when the new law created a public outcry. Only two months earlier in neighboring Colorado a gunman entered a movie theater and opened fire, killing twelve people and injuring fifty-eight others. Three months later another gunman killed twenty children and six adults at an elementary school in Newtown, Connecticut. Meanwhile, the NRA, which claims to have nearly 4 million members, calls itself "the most powerful lobbying organization in the country."

great influence on the political process by launching expensive media campaigns or contributing large amounts to political campaigns. In addition, the personal networks and political contacts of the super-rich are often advantageous in influencing elected officials.

Interest groups are sometimes closely tied to political parties. In Western Europe, the giant trade unions maintain close ties with working-class political parties. (The British Labour Party and Trades Union Congress have the support of some 85% of organized labor in Great Britain.) In the United States, by contrast, interest groups increasingly bypass political parties entirely, providing direct financial support to candidates they favor. Indeed, in a recent landmark decision the U.S. Supreme Court ruled that under the First Amendment the funding of independent political broadcasts in elections cannot be limited.

Soliciting funds through computerized direct-mail appeals and the Internet is one key to interest group success, but personal connections are also important. In Washington, it's often said, "It isn't *what* you know, but *whom* you know that counts." For this reason, interest groups often compete to hire former presidential advisors, ranking civilian and military Pentagon officials, and members of Congress as "consultants." A rose by any other name is still a rose, and lobbyists by any other name are still lobbyists, paid handsomely by defense contractors, arms manufacturers, oil companies, and the like to open doors on Capitol Hill, at the Pentagon, wherever power resides, policies are shaped, and decisions are made (see "Ideas and Politics: Clean Government vs. the Best Congress Money Can Buy").

Upon taking office, President Obama laid down a marker for members of his administration: "If you are a lobbyist entering my administration, you will not be able to work on matters you lobbied on, or in the agencies you lobbied during the previous two years." Ironically, it was soon disclosed that Obama's choice for Secretary of Health and Human Services, former Senator Tom Daschle, a liberal and longtime advocate of universal health care, not only had not paid all the federal income tax he owed and but also after leaving the Senate had lobbied for clients in the health care industry, among others—using his personal contacts and political ties in Congress to line his own pockets.

The Great Race: Getting Ahead of the PAC

Although estimates differ significantly, experts agree the number of interest groups in the United States, and the lobbyists they employ, has increased by at least 50% over the past three decades. Today lobbying is the third-largest industry in Washington, D.C., behind only government and tourism. There were about 5,000 registered lobbyists in the nation's Capital in 1956. One source estimated that in 1991 there were still fewer than 6,000.[34] That number jumped to 20,000 by 1994 and kept rising; in 2005, there were 34,750, whereas the fees lobbyists charged clients rose by as much as 100%.[35]

Why this population explosion? It results from the dramatic increase in government benefits, the declining influence of political parties, the increasing diversity of U.S. society, and the rise of single-issue movements.[36] At the

IDEAS AND POLITICS

CLEAN GOVERNMENT VS. THE BEST CONGRESS MONEY CAN BUY*

In January 2007, shortly after midterm elections, the new U.S. Congress, now controlled by the Democrats, launched a major drive to curb unethical ties between Washington lobbyists and legislators. House Democrats pledged to crack down on the use of corporate jets by members of Congress and to adopt stricter rules on gifts and travel

Not to be outdone, President George W. Bush, taking aim at the widespread use of "earmarks" by Congress, denounced "the secretive process by which Washington insiders are able to get billions of dollars directed to projects, many of them pork barrel projects that have never been reviewed or voted on by the Congress." This issue became a major bone of contention at the end of 2010 when the senators on both sides of the aisle stuffed 6,000 earmarks totaling $8 billion into the proposed budget bill, while blaming each other and vowing to cut the deficit. (Budget stalemates threatened to shut down the federal government in the spring of 2011 and drive the economy over a "fiscal cliff" in 2012.)

Who's to blame? Both Republicans and Democrats in Congress use lobbyists and earmarks to get what they want—votes in the next election. The real problem: all too often when a lawmaker finds out how much his or her vote is worth, he or she sells it to the highest bidder.

*Based on Carl Hulse and David D. Kirkpatrick, "Ethics Overhaul Tops the Agenda in New Congress," *New York Times*, January 4, 2007 (electronic edition).

same time, mass mailings and computer technology make new start-ups relatively easy. Higher levels of education have increased individuals' interest in such associations, and relative prosperity has made them better able to pay dues.

In the early 1970s, a new kind of interest group, known as **political action committees** (PACs), became prominent in the United States. In 1971, Congress attempted to curb election abuses by prohibiting corporations and labor unions from contributing directly to political campaigns. However, the law did not prohibit special interests from spending money *indirectly* through specially created committees, and the number of PACs rose dramatically until the mid-1980s. Interest groups with large and influential PACs include the American Medical Association; the National Association of Realtors; the National Automobile Dealers Association; the National Association of Letter Carriers; the American Institute of Certified Public Accountants; the American Dental Association; and the American Federation of State, County, and Municipal Employees.

PACs have played a key role in financing candidates and causes at both the national and state level as the cost of elections, increasingly dependent on television advertising, has escalated. Dianne Feinstein, a Democratic senator from California, raised $22,000 a day during the seven months before the 1994 election; if "Feinstein Inc. were a business, its projected revenue would place it among the top 5 percent of U.S. corporations."[37] Incredibly, Feinstein's wealthy Republican opponent, Michael Huffington, actually outspent her in that campaign, squandering $29 million of his own money only to lose the election!

political action committees (PAC) Group organized to raise campaign funds in support of or in opposition to specific candidates.

SPECIAL INTEREST MONEY: The Record Breaking 2010 and 2012 Elections

The 2010 midterm election—the most expensive ever—cost more than $4 billion, compared to $2.6 billion in 2006.

- According to the nonpartisan Center for Responsive Politics, $293 million came from groups operating independently of the candidates or political parties. Under the Supreme Court's controversial *Citizens United* ruling, these groups, including Super PACs, 527 organizations, and 501(c) organizations, are free to spend without limits and accept unlimited donations from corporations, trade associations and unions.
- Slightly less than half of the independent money—$138 million—came from 501(c) and 527 organizations that are not required by law to disclose donor names when they file spending reports with the Federal Election Commission (FEC).
- Independent money, including donations made in secret, was instrumental in election outcomes. Figures compiled by Public Citizen show independent groups spent an average of $764,000 on behalf of the winners and just $273,000 on behalf of the losers.
- Republicans were the major beneficiaries of secret 501(c) money; these groups spent some $183 million on behalf of GOP candidates.
- Democrats were the biggest beneficiaries of donations by 527 organizations to political party committees; these groups can accept unlimited corporate and union funds; they spent $102.7 million on behalf of Democratic candidates. Most 527 contributions focused on a single issue or a particular ideology. Money spent by union-aligned 527s—over $42 million in 2010—is subject to FEC disclosure requirements.

- Independent money, including some $252 million from 527 groups, also figured prominently in campaigns for governor and other state and local races.

The 2012 general election set an all-time spending record, estimated at $7 billion, compared to $5.4 billion in 2008.

- The $7 billion total breaks down as follows: $3.2 billion in spending by candidate committees, $2 billion from party committees, and at least $2 billion from outside groups (the major source of "dark money"—i.e., from undisclosed sources).
- Obama for America reported receipts of $746.9 million in the 2012 presidential campaign; Romney for President, Inc. reported receipts of $485.8 million.
- Political Action Committees (PACs) reported giving $48.9 million to House and Senate candidates in 2012—including $29.9 million (61% to Republicans) and $18.8 million to Democrats (39%).
- Democrats spent $919.3 million on advertising in 2012, including payroll, TV and Radio ads ($420 million), online ads ($118 million), telemarketing ($35.2 million), fundraising, and polling.
- Republicans spent $885.6 million on ads, including $270 million for TV and radio ads, $100.6 million for online ads, and $74.5 million for telemarketing.

SOURCE: Common Cause, Public Citizen, the Center for Responsive Politics, Political MoneyLine, and the Sunlight Foundation, plus various major news outlets. http://www.commoncause.org/ See "Money in the 2010 Election."

Given the high cost of campaigns, it is hardly surprising to find more, not less, PAC involvement in elections. In the 2005–2006 election cycle, industry group PACs alone gave $311 million to federal candidates, an increase of $45 million since the 2003–2004 election cycle.[38]

Many observers decry the growing influence of money in U.S. politics. Although money has always been a factor in politics, in recent decades it has become *the* factor without which winning is virtually impossible. The average cost of winning a House seat jumped from $73,000 in 1976 to $680,000 in 1996 and to roughly $1.1 million in 2008; for a Senate seat, it rose from $595,000 to $8.5 million during the same period.[39] In 2012, the cost of winning a seat in the Senate rose to $10.5 million; for the House it was a bargain—"only" $1.7 million. According to the Pew Charitable Trusts, "Money is the fuel that powers the current campaign system. In a circular fashion, interest groups, candidates, and parties raise money to pay consultants to launch expensive television ad campaigns."[40]

As a rule, Republicans raise more money than Democrats, and incumbents have a huge financial advantage over challengers. In 2004, 98% of House incumbents and 96% of incumbent senators won reelection. In 2008, five U.S. senators lost their seats to challengers, but only 23 incumbents in the House of Representatives were defeated (6 Democrats and 17 Republicans), for a total of 435. In 2012, 90% of House members and 91% of senators seeking re-election won, a higher rate than in 2010. Senators' 2012 re-election percentage was the highest since 2004.

Interest groups are essential, but in the absence of any effective curbs on **soft money**—money given to political parties ostensibly for purposes other than campaigning and money spent independently *on behalf* of candidates or parties—they are increasingly drawn into a kind of systemic corruption for which there currently are no adequate legal or political remedies. To expect the very politicians who benefit most from the existing system to change it is unrealistic. So long as voters continue to elect incumbents who don't want to fix the system, the system will not get fixed.

Citizens United v. Federal Election Commission

The Bipartisan Campaign Reform Act of 2002 (BCRA)—commonly known as the McCain-Feingold Act—prohibited corporations and unions from making campaign contributions out of their general treasury fund, to include "any broadcast, cable, or satellite communication" that "refers to a clearly identified candidate for Federal office" and "is made within 30 days of a primary election." McCain-Feingold allowed corporations and unions to establish a political action committee (PAC) to express advocacy or media ads.

In January 2008, Citizens United, a nonprofit corporation, released a documentary critical of then-Senator Hillary Clinton, a candidate for her party's presidential nomination. Anticipating that it would make the *Hillary* documentary available on cable television through video-on-demand within thirty days of primary elections, Citizens United produced television ads to run on broadcast and cable television. To head off civil and criminal penalties for violating federal law, it sought injunctive relief, arguing that the McCain-Feingold Act is unconstitutional.

soft money
Campaign contributions to U.S. national party committees that do not have to be reported to the Federal Election Commission as long as the funds are not used to benefit a particular candidate; the national committees funnel the funds to state parties, which generally operate under less stringent reporting requirements. Critics argue that soft money is a massive loophole in the existing system of campaign finance regulation and that it amounts to a form of legalized corruption.

The District Court denied Citizens United a preliminary injunction and ruled in favor of the Federal Election Commission (FEC) summary judgment.

In a landmark decision in 2010, the nine-member U.S. Supreme Court overturned the lower court ruling by a vote of 5 to 4, holding corporate campaign spending cannot be limited under the First Amendment. Critics argued that this ruling places elective office on the auction block and a "for sale" sign on Capitol Hill.

The upshot of the controversial *Citizens United* ruling is to reaffirm the status of corporations as "citizens" under the U.S. Constitution, declaring that money donated to political campaigns is a form of speech and giving businesses with billions of dollars in assets such as Wal-Mart, Exxon Mobil, and General Electric the same First Amendment rights as an individual. Given the huge sums

IDEAS AND POLITICS

OPEN SECRETS: How Open?

The Center for Responsive Politics publishes extensive campaign finance data at its OpenSecrets.org website. Google "open secrets" or go to http://www.opensecrets.org and explore. You can point and click and find out how much Super PACs spent on both candidates in the presidential election, compare candidate spending, find out who gives what, who funds your representatives, what lobbies spend the most on behalf of candidates and causes, learn all about outside spending, and so on.

According to OpenSecrets.org:

A January 2010 Supreme Court decision (*Citizens United v. Federal Election Commission*) permits corporations

and unions to make political expenditures from their treasuries directly and through other organizations, as long as the spending—often in the form of TV ads—is done independently of any candidate. In many cases, the activity takes place without complete or immediate disclosure about who is funding it, preventing voters from understanding who is truly behind many political messages. The spending figures cited are what the groups reported to the FEC; it does not account for all the money the groups spent, since certain kinds of ads are not required to be reported.

Here's a glance at "outside spending," much of which can be done anonymously. In other words, not all the open secrets of campaign finance are open any more.

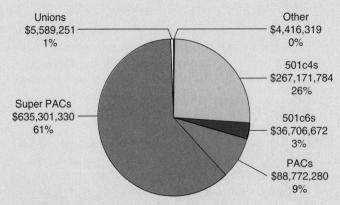

Reported outside Spending by Source, 2012 Cycle

SOURCE: Dēmos and U.S. PIRG Education Fund analysis of FEC and Sunlight Foundation data.

corporations can and do spend electing candidates, influencing Congress, and swaying public opinion (think TV ads), critics argue that it's impossible for ordinary citizens, individually or collectively, to compete with corporations in today's political arena. Indeed, record spending in the 2010 midterm elections approached $4 billion—a figure that exceeds the gross national product of Georgia and Armenia, as well as more than sixty other small countries.

Rise of the Super PAC: Death of the Republic?

In the aftermath of the *Citizens United* ruling and following the outcome of a federal court case known as *SpeechNow.org v. Federal Election Commission* in July 2010, a new kind of political action committee known as the Super PAC came into being. Super PACs are free to raise unlimited sums of money from corporations, unions, associations, and individuals. There are no limits to the sums Super PACs spend electing or defeating targeted candidates. But they must report the names of donors to the Federal Election Commission on either a monthly or quarterly basis and they cannot donate money directly to—or coordinate with the campaigns of—candidates.

By contrast, 501(c)(4) organizations do not have to disclose the names of donors. In theory, they operate exclusively to promote "social welfare"—that is, to further, in some way, the common good and general welfare of the people of the community. But here theory and practice part company—a major loophole in the law allows these organizations to engage in lobbying and to promote political causes and candidates without jeopardizing their tax-exempt status. The only "catch": The donations they receive are not tax-deductible donations.

The impact of Super Pacs and 501(c)(4)s was tested for the first time in the 2012 elections. Big contributions from a small number of individuals loomed larger than ever but in the end it failed to achieve what for a few ultra-conservative billionaires like Charles and David Koch and Sheldon Adelson was the desired outcome: namely, defeating Obama's bid for a second term and electing a slate of Tea Party Republicans who campaigned against abortion, gay marriage, ObamaCare, state regulation, and higher taxes for the super rich. To learn about the role of money in the 2012 election, check out an e-book called "Billion Dollar Democracy" at www.demos.org.[41]

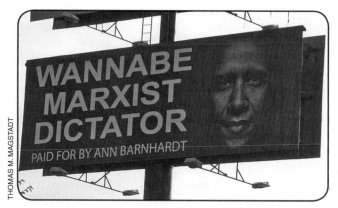

Many wealthy individuals who back political candidates prefer not to disclose to whom or how much they shell out. Here's one example of the exact opposite. The person who paid for this billboard located on I-70 near Fort Riley, Kansas, is obviously proud of it and wants the world to know what she thinks of President Barack Obama (aka, the Commander in Chief).

THE INTERNET REVOLUTION: POWER TO THE PEOPLE?

Until the advent of the Computer Age, few advances in technology have had a more profound or sudden impact on politics than television. In the United States, television became available in most homes in the 1950s, computers only in the 1980s. When the first desktop computers started showing up in people's homes, however, they were usually not connected to the outside world, which meant that TV and telephones were still essential to remain "connected." How the world has changed!

Imagine living without your "tablet" and "handheld device" today. Staying connected without email, Facebook, and Twitter would be like going back to the horse and buggy days. Getting the information you want and need is so easy now compared to the "good old days" when college students had to trudge to the library and go to the card catalog, search through stacks for books that may or may not contain the information you need, go through reels of microfiche to find archived newspaper stories, and the like.

Just as the Internet has transformed the way we study, play, and learn about the wider world, it has also transformed politics. In theory, this transformation is a great victory for democracy, transparency, and participation.

Information is power—a cliché to be sure, but one worth pondering. By placing massive amounts of information at the fingertips of anybody with a computer and a "wifi" hookup, the Internet gives potential power to the previously powerless. The Internet also makes it much harder for governments to hide inconvenient truths or to censor the news. It also greatly facilitates bottom-up, grassroots political action: It is now possible to spark a mass movement with little or no money using existing social networks. The Tea Party movement that played a crucial role in the 2010 midterm elections is one example. Another example: the huge demonstrations in Cairo, Egypt, in January 2011 aimed at overthrowing the autocratic rule of President Hosni Mubarak, which began on a popular Facebook page with some 90,000 pledges to participate. Fearing a spillover effect, China blocked "Egypt" from Internet searches, as a growing number of Chinese rely on microblogging sites for news and information.

But it works both ways: governments can use the Internet to monitor the activities of ordinary citizens. Or they can block certain Internet sites—witness Google's recent troubles operating in the China. Then, too, international terrorists can use the Internet it to plan and coordinate attacks, and hackers use it to steal your credit card information.

Finally, the Internet is changing the way political campaigns are conducted. In 2008, Barack Obama's campaign demonstrated the power of the Internet to reach masses of people and coordinate grassroots political action across the length and breadth of the fifty states. Few observers dispute that the Obama campaign changed politics, that presidential campaigns in America will never be the same. Thus, "by using interactive Web 2.0 tools, Mr. Obama's campaign changed the way politicians organize supporters, advertise to voters, defend against attacks and communicate with constituents."[42] Obama's campaign videos were watched on YouTube for 145 million hours. To buy the same amount of exposure on broadcast TV would cost $47 million.[43]

The Internet has changed the way we live and learn. Will the tenor and tone of politics change for better or worse? So far, at least, the vulgar partisanship that has characterized the political scene in recent years does not bode well.

THE ECLIPSE OF THE PUBLIC INTEREST

Often, when citizens complain about influential "special interests," they mean lobbyists or pressure groups that advocate *other people's* interests. Farmers back the farm lobby in Washington, millions of senior citizens (defined as anybody over 50 years of age) join the AARP every year, and so on.

What problems do interest groups *objectively* pose to the public interest? Some critics argue that the power of interest groups imposes a particular hardship on the most disadvantaged segments of society. The poor have too little influence and the rich have too much, in this view.

Critics also express alarm at the number of government officials who leave high positions to lobby on behalf of major corporations and defense contractors. In 1978, Congress banned high-ranking, ex-government officials from any contact with the agencies for which they previously worked for a year and prohibited them from attempting to influence the government on policies for which they had "official responsibilities" for two years. But the rules did not prevent government officials from going back and forth between the public and private sectors in a kind of revolving door. Thus, Dick Cheney, a former secretary of defense under George H. W. Bush, left his job as CEO of Halliburton, a major defense contractor, to become George W. Bush's running mate in 2000. This practice raises serious ethical issues involving conflicts of interest and the public trust. President Obama issued an executive order aimed at stopping this practice, but whether anything will change is open to question.

When a single-issue interest group champions an obscure regulation or law, there is little incentive for lawmakers or bureaucrats to resist pressures from special interests. In a large country with numerous levels of government, important matters, especially tax laws in the United States, are decided with little debate or media attention.[44] When well-financed lobbies operating under the radar or behind the scenes push for laws and regulations that bear little, if any, relationship to the public interest, the policy process is likely to be corrupted.

In politics, money talks. To the extent that participation and democracy go hand in hand, it follows that the super rich can participate to a far greater degree than the rest of us. If so, and if the trend is toward an ever-greater concentration of wealth (as it has been at least since the early 1980s), then democracy becomes less and less meaningful for the vast majority of Americans—the middle class long recognized as the backbone of democracy. Can anything reverse the trend toward an ever-greater concentration of wealth and power? Or is the coin of democracy in the United States destined to be permanently debased?

The same technology that has revolutionized political campaigns is also revolutionizing the way government works. At this point, it's anybody's guess what that means for the future of democracy.

SUMMARY

Citizens can participate in politics in a variety of legal ways: conventionally, by voting and taking part in public opinion polls; organizationally, by joining political parties or interest groups; or professionally, by working full time for such organizations. Street demonstrations and economic boycotts are unconventional forms of participation. Illegal participation runs the gamut from nonviolent actions (civil disobedience) to extremely violent acts (terrorism).

Public opinion polls can influence the political process in various ways. Elections, despite inherent limitations, are the democratic way to translate mass preferences into public policy. The two major types of electoral systems are first past the post (found in the United States and Great Britain) and proportional representation (used in most representative democracies). In democratic republics, voters elect legislators, chief executives, and sometimes judges. Forms of direct democracy include referendums, initiatives, and recalls.

Voting rates in the United States are low, especially in midterm elections. Voters are generally ill informed. According to elitist theories, political power is always concentrated in the hands of the few. Madisonian pluralists, who argue that power in democratic societies is diffused, dispute this elitist theory.

Political parties perform several key functions in republics. They facilitate participation, aggregate interests, recruit qualified candidates for office, raise money for political campaigns, and help organize governments by building a national consensus and offering alternatives, especially during the election process. One-party systems are generally associated with authoritarianism. Multiparty systems typically offer voters clearer alternatives than do two-party systems. The type of party system found in a given country is determined by its traditions, constitution, and culture.

In modern democracies, interest groups and lobbies play an important role in influencing public policy. Some say they distort the democratic process and serve special interests rather than the public interest. Defenders say they offset one another and ensure a competitive political system.

The Internet has transformed politics. It both facilitates popular participation and places a new control tool in the hands of governments.

KEY TERMS

public opinion   284
straw poll   284
random sampling   284
stratified sampling   285
exit polling   285
tracking poll   285
winner-takes-all
   system   287
plurality   287

first past the post   287
proportional
  representation
  (PR)   288
list system   289
Hare plan   289
coalition
  government   289
plebiscite   289

legislative
  referendum   289
popular
  referendum   290
initiative   290
recall   290
euro area   291
motor voter law   294
political efficacy   295

REVIEW QUESTIONS

1. How do citizens participate in politics?
2. What are the different forms of electoral systems? What are the advantages and disadvantages of each?
3. Some say apathy is a problem in democratic societies. Do you agree or disagree? Explain.
4. How do the elitist theories of democracy differ from the pluralist model? What political implications follow from the elitist theories?
5. What assumptions do we generally make about political participation in democracies? Are they correct? Explain.
6. What kinds of party systems are found in democracies? How do they differ? Why do the differences matter? Finally, in your opinion, which one is best?
7. To what extent does the functioning of interest groups depend on the political system in which they operate?
8. Why has the power of interest groups increased as the power of political parties has decreased? To what extent are these two phenomena related?
9. What does this statement mean: "Not all interest groups are created equal"?

CHAPTER (12)

Political Leadership
The Many Faces of Power

THINK ABOUT IT

What is statesmanship, and why do some leaders aspire to it?

What do Rómulo Betancourt and Anwar al-Sadat have in common with Abraham Lincoln and Winston Churchill?

Why is leadership important?

Who is Tom Delay, and how was his leadership style in Congress reminiscent of Aaron Burr, Theodore Bilbo, Huey Long, and Joseph McCarthy?

What are two opposing theories of representation, how do they differ, and why does it matter?

The implied meaning of words we use in everyday language and life is often more important than the dictionary definitions. Contrast the implied meanings of the word "physician" and the word "politician." Both denote a practitioner of a profession, but that is where the similarity ends. One is accorded automatic respect; the other is often a term of derision and disdain.

Perhaps more than any other group, politicians are lumped together and stereotyped. We rarely see politicians in a positive light—as leaders with the knowledge, experience, and strength of character to guide the nation in times of crisis; find solutions to big problems; and act in the public interest even when it means taking political risks. Imagine parents saying, "Our daughter is in college now and wants to become a cardiologist, but we're hoping she goes into politics."

For a long time politics was off-limits to women, but not anymore. Women now occupy key positions of leadership in many countries. Nancy Pelosi was the first woman in U.S. history to become the Speaker of the House (2007–2011); Madeleine Albright became the first woman to serve as U.S. Secretary of State (1997–2001), and two others—Condoleezza Rice (2005–2009) and Hillary Clinton (2009–2013)—have followed in her footsteps.

In President Barack Obama's first term (2009–2013), women held four cabinet posts and several other key positions, including EPA administrator and White House Senior Advisor. Elizabeth Warren, a Harvard Law School professor, led the effort to establish a U.S. Consumer Financial Protection Bureau in the wake of the tumultuous 2008 financial crisis (and ran successfully for the U.S. Senate in 2012). Gender roles and attitudes are changing in the United States and around the world (including the Middle East and North Africa) with profound implications for politics and society.

Whether we know it or not, politics plays a huge role in our lives, and what politicians do with the power we give them matters a great deal. When we make a campaign contribution or cast a ballot in an election, we are not only choosing one politician over another but also one political path over another. Few things are more important than the wisdom, knowledge, character, and judgment of the people we elect to high office.

The news headlines constantly remind us that the fate of the nation and the world depends on the capacity of leaders to choose wisely and to act prudently. History offers many examples of misguided policies leading to tragic consequences. President Lyndon Johnson's decision to escalate the Vietnam War in the mid-1960s—eventually committing more than 500,000 U.S. troops, alienating friends and allies abroad, and damaging the nation's prestige in the eyes of the world—cost him his job, but it also cost the lives of 58,193 U.S. military personnel. And it was all for naught: the United States lost the war and a whole lot more.

The Vietnam War proved the undoing of Johnson's successor, Richard Nixon, as well. The Watergate affair involving dirty tricks in the 1972 presidential campaign led directly to impeachment proceedings—and Nixon's resignation. Now let's look at a very different set of foreign policy decisions with very different consequences.

After World War II, President Truman made a series of historic decisions— to rebuild Europe by means of the Marshall Plan, to create new military alliances such as the North Atlantic Treaty Organization (NATO), and to confront

Sir Winston Churchill (1874–1965) was an indomitable wartime leader who opposed the policy of appeasement toward Hitler and, when his dire warnings turned out to be true, led his country through its darkest days to its finest hour. As bombs fell on London and other British cities, Churchill declared, "We shall not flag or fail. We shall go on to the end.... We shall never surrender."

the Soviet Union's perceived expansionism with a strong policy of containment. Few historians doubt that firm and decisive leadership was a crucial factor in shaping the postwar world and in creating the structures at home and abroad whereby the West eventually prevailed in the Cold War.

The late political scientist and historian Robert C. Tucker's dictum that "politics in essence is leadership"[1] continues to ring true. Political leaders have the potential for doing good or evil on a vast scale. Whether we like it or not, they are role models for civil society; they set a moral tone that affects the behavior of the citizens they purport to serve. A chronic and conspicuous absence of civility in public life (such as mudslinging and smear tactics in political campaigns) inevitably infects the way people treat one another. Most people are naturally good and decent; but because power corrupts, leaders often are not worthy of the people they lead.

In this chapter, we examine four types of leader—the **statesman, demagogue, politician,** and **citizen-leader.** These leadership types are different in many ways, including methods used and purposes pursued. A few are notable for the good they accomplish. Some are placeholders who do no harm. Still others are remembered for audacious abuses of power. You will encounter some household names; others will be new to you. All are chosen because they illustrate certain problems, pathologies, and patterns of leadership behavior—and how power corrupts many who exercise it, but raises a few to sublime heights and even a kind of immortality.

Often these distinctions are easier to make in theory than to apply in practice. Nonetheless, there are enormous differences between the best and the worst of leaders. For example, most observers would agree that Adolf Hitler, a mass-murdering madman who led Germany to disaster in World War II, exemplifies the worst. At the same time, few would dispute that Winston Churchill—who recognized the dangers of totalitarianism in Nazi Germany earlier than most, led his nation's heroic defense in the darkest days of the war, and played a major role in shaping the postwar world—exemplifies the best.

statesman
A political architect who creates new states, a peacemaker who resolves conflicts, or an orator who inspire the popular masses in times of national crisis. He or she is yesterday's founder, today's pathfinder, and tomorrow's legend.

demagogue
Someone who uses his or her leadership skills to gain public office through appeals to popular fears and prejudices and then abuses that power for personal gain.

politician
A public officeholder who is prepared to sacrifice previously held principles or shelve unpopular policies to get reelected.

citizen-leader
An individual who influences government decisively even though he or she holds no official government position.

THE IDEAL LEADER

The concept of the ideal leader has been around for a long time. Plato and Aristotle both examined it. Indeed, Plato depicted Socrates engaging in a dialogue about *statesmanship*, the term often used to refer to the role of a gifted leader or national hero. Typically, it is only after a leader has departed the scene that he or she comes to be regarded as a statesman in the popular mind.

Until quite recently, politics and government were almost exclusively male bastions, but times are changing. Golda Meir (Israel), Indira Gandhi (India), Margaret Thatcher (United Kingdom), Benazir Bhutto (Pakistan), and Dilma

Rousseff (Brazil) are five examples of women among a growing number of others whose personal charisma, political skills, and leadership qualities propelled them to international preeminence in the post–World War II era.

Great men and women in history are often exemplars of **statecraft**—the art of leading in difficult times. Founders of new nations are often revered and remembered as heroes. George Washington is such a larger-than-life figure, but many nations have iconic leaders steeped in legend and lore. Examples include Simón Bolívar (1783–1830), a Venezuelan statesman who led the revolt against Spanish rule in Latin America; Kwame Nkruma (1909–1972), who led Ghana to independence from the United Kingdom in 1957; Nelson Mandela (b. 1918), who led the struggle to end *apartheid* (white minority rule and strict racial segregation) in South Africa; and Ho Chi Minh (1890–1969), Vietnam's "George Washington," who masterminded a protracted guerrilla war for national independence from France and subsequently led the war against the United States to unite North and South Vietnam. Think of other examples and ask yourself what special qualities these heroic figures have in common.

Even most revered and admired leaders are not above reproach, however. Washington and the founders did not abolish slavery (or free their own slaves), nor did they see fit to give women the right to vote. Nearly a century later, Abraham Lincoln was instrumental in freeing the slaves, but the Civil War did not advance the cause of women's suffrage (voting rights) in America. Between the Civil War and World War I, women's rights activists arose to fight for the franchise. The names of these courageous leaders—Isabella Baumfree (aka, Sojourner Truth), Susan B. Anthony, Louisa May Alcott, Mary Baker Eddy, and Jeannette Rankin, to name a few—until recently were often absent in standard American history textbooks. The rise of the Suffragettes in England paralleled this historic women's rights movement in the United States.

Statesmanship

Defining the ideal leader is not easy. Most of us would agree that we want our leaders to possess certain qualities or virtues we look for in our friends, qualities others look for in us. We want our friends to be fair-minded and faithful, generous and compassionate. Intelligence is important, but common sense is essential. Some of the most gifted and famous people—geniuses and virtuosos of all kinds—are deeply flawed. The bravado of a Donald Trump may be useful in high-stakes business dealings, but it does not translate into political appeal or leadership potential. The brilliance of Albert Einstein did not overbalance the eccentricities that made him unfit for high office (to which, fortunately, he never aspired).

In *A Preface to Morals*, the late Walter Lippmann, a famed American philosopher and columnist, attempted to isolate the key factors and character traits that distinguish leaders from run-of-the-mill politicians. Lippmann suggested that most politicians work only "for a partial interest." Examples include politicians who feather their own nests or slavishly follow the party line. The word *statesmanship*, in contrast, "connotes a [person] whose mind is elevated sufficiently above the conflict of contending parties to enable him to adopt a course of action which takes into account a great number of interests in the perspective of a longer period of time."[2]

statecraft
The art of leading in difficult times, promoting the common good, and protecting vital national interests while avoiding unnecessary conflict.

AP PHOTOS

The late Golda Meir (1898–1978), who served as Israel's prime minister from 1969 to 1974, is remembered today as an exceptional leader; in her public life, she exemplified the traits of personal charisma, practical wisdom, political skills, and moral integrity often associated with statesmanship.

Lippmann recognized that the line between an ordinary politician and a real leader is often blurred. In a democracy, even the most high-minded leaders have to be politicians to gain and hold office. A trenchant observation attributed to H. L. Mencken (1880–1956) speaks directly to this point: "The men the American people admire most extravagantly are the most daring liars; the men they detest most violently are those who try to tell them the truth." Nonetheless, a true leader is not content merely to satisfy the momentary wishes of his or her constituents. The wiser course is to persuade voters that the pursuit of the public interest is in everyone's interest and that private interests are not (and ought not to be) the primary concern of public policy.

Pursuit of the Public Good The best leaders are motivated not by crass self-interest but by the public good. By choosing what "the people will in the end find to be good against what the people happen ardently to desire," Lippmann contended, true leaders resist opinion polls and popular impulses. In refusing to promise the impossible, they choose honesty and moderation over self-flattery. Such a decision, he continues, requires the "courage which is possible only in a mind that is detached from the agitations of the moment," as well as the "insight which comes from an objective and discerning knowledge of the facts, and a high and imperturbable disinterestedness."

Virtue in public life is not identical to virtue in private life. Honesty is a virtue, but in political life it is not always possible. When the stakes are high, when complete honesty is an impediment to success, and when the best interests of the nation are served by stealth or dissimulation, a true leader will sometimes resort to deception. For example, both before and during the Civil War, President Lincoln consistently downplayed the slavery issue, preferring to keep the political spotlight on the overriding importance of preserving the Union. Lincoln understood that a call for immediate abolition risked alienating many moderates in both the North and South, ultimately harming the cause of both black emancipation and the Union.[3]

Practical Wisdom Belief in the public good is useless without a way of achieving it. Effective leaders display common sense—a quality not always present among wielders of much power. They understand the relationship between ideals and implementation, between actions and consequences. Statecraft—the art of diplomacy—distinguishes between the possible and the unattainable. In this sense, political leaders are a lot like physicians, whose success is ultimately measured not in dollars and cents they earn, but in the health of the community they serve.

Political Skills Law and policies (and in the case of elections, the leaders themselves) require the consent of the governed. Reconciling wisdom and consent in the often-turbulent public arena is one of the primary tasks of leadership in a democracy.

Successful leaders are also good judges of talent and know how to delegate. Managing a vast bureaucracy, directing a large personal staff, working with the legislature to ensure a majority for the passage of the administration's programs, and rallying public opinion behind the administration's policies—these complex and demanding tasks are too much for any one individual to handle.

Of course, political skills are not always put at the service of the public good. Demagogues often seek to remove obstacles to needed social reforms by ruining, jailing, or killing opponents; even when they bring about progress and a measure of prosperity, the ends do not justify the means.

Perilous Times Historians have frequently observed that great times make great leaders. To become an iconic figure like Washington or Lincoln, it is necessary to guide the nation in a time of war or revolution. At such times, moral inspiration and political expertise are essential if the nation is to endure; such a situation is tailor-made for the exercise of statecraft. During times of "politics as usual," even the most capable leader will lack the opportunity to become a hero in history.

Good Fortune The final prerequisite of exceptional leadership is good luck. No political leader can be successful without a certain amount of good fortune. A turn in the tide of a single battle, a message thought about but not sent (or sent too late), or any number of other seemingly unimportant incidents or actions may prove decisive. Great leadership can never be attributed entirely to good luck, but considering the complex environment in which such leaders operate, good luck often makes the difference between success and failure.

The Lure of Fame Office holders often get into politics at significant cost to themselves, relinquishing more lucrative careers and facing constant public scrutiny. The question inevitably arises: Why would men and women of outstanding ability devote the best years of their productive lives to the pursuit of political excellence? What would inspire such individuals to work for the public good, often at the expense of more obvious and immediate self-interests?

According to historian Douglass Adair (1912–1968), the Founders were motivated primarily by the idea of fame. For George Washington, James Madison, Alexander Hamilton, and Benjamin Franklin, narrow self-interest, defined in terms of personal power or wealth, was not an overriding concern. Nor was individual honor, which Adair defined as a "pattern of behavior calculated to win praises from [one's] contemporaries who are [one's] social equals or superiors."[4] Rather, the Founders' great motivating force was a desire for fame—a concept that, according to Adair, has been deeply embedded in the Western philosophical and literary tradition since the classical era. Applying this interpretation to the U.S. Founders, Adair wrote:

> Of course they were patriots, of course they were proud to serve their country in her need, but Washington, Adams, Jefferson, and Madison were not entirely disinterested. The pursuit of fame, they had been taught, was a way of transforming egotism and self-aggrandizing impulses into public service; they had been taught that public service nobly (and selflessly) performed was the surest way to build "lasting monuments" and earn the perpetual remembrance of posterity.[5]

Alexander Hamilton observed that a love of fame is "the ruling passion of the noblest minds."[6] The desire for immortality was a powerful elixir in Hamilton's time, when only wealthy, property-owning white men dared aspire to high office.

But times have changed. Today, you don't have to be rich to get into politics in the United States, but it helps (witness Wilbur Mitt Romney). On the other hand, an African American named Barack Hussein Obama, whose father was born in Kenya and who was raised in a small Kansas town (by his grandparents), can become president. But he couldn't have done it without raising millions and millions of dollars. As noted in Chapter 11, Obama raised a lot of money in small donations using the Internet; but he also had the backing of billionaires George Soros in 2008, and Jon Stryker, David Shaw, Anne Cox Chambers, Irwin Jacobs, Haim Saban, and Stephen Spielberg in 2012.

National politics is now a very lucrative profession. Former Senator Tom Daschle is one example among many. When Daschle went to Washington as a freshman congressman in 1979, he had no money. An unknown even in his home state of South Dakota, he had campaigned by going house to house, knocking on doors, and introducing himself to the voter: "door-to-door Daschle," people called him. But in Congress, he prospered. In 1987, he was elected to the Senate, where he rose to become Senate Majority Leader. Having lost his bid for reelection in 2005, he left the Senate but did not leave Washington. He became a "consultant" (a euphemism for lobbyist) like his second wife, Linda, a former deputy Federal Aviation Agency (FAA) administrator. Known as "one of Washington's most prominent aviation lobbyists" whose clients notably include American Airlines, Linda Daschle (a former Miss Kansas) was so successful that she started her own lobbying firm, LHD and Associates, in January 2009. It goes almost without saying that today the Daschles are multimillionaires.

GREAT LEADERS IN HISTORY

We all know something about great rulers in history. In some cases, it's ridiculously easy to identify them: Alexander the Great (356–323 BCE), Asoka the Great (c. 304–232 BC), Darius the Great (550–486 BC), Peter the Great (1672–1725), Frederick the Great (1712–1786), Catherine the Great (1729–1796), and the list goes on. Such heroic figures in history are often called "great" because they fought and won military battles and conquered new lands. But that's not how we use the term in this book.

At least since the dawn of the Nuclear Age at the end of World War II, militarism and expansionism have not been associated with virtuous leadership. As we saw in Chapter 6, the most militaristic leaders of the twentieth century were totalitarian dictators bent on conquest—greatly cruel, greatly destructive, and greatly evil, but not great. The adverb works, but not the adjective.

If not conquest, what is it that distinguishes great leaders from all the others in today's world? Obviously, leaders are not all cut from the same cloth. Some are courageous and incorruptible. Others are cowardly and crooked. Most of them fall somewhere in the middle. Here, we reserve the term "great" for the best ones.

It is easy to become cynical about the possibility of good government or honest leaders (two sides of the same coin). If we believe politicians are *all* alike or power *always* corrupts, we run the risk of creating a self-fulfilling prophecy. If we have low expectations and reward elected officials by reelecting them *automatically*, we devalue the very idea of leadership.

Good leaders do not come along every day; great ones are rare. Throughout history, exemplary leaders—the best of the best—have appeared at various times and places. As the following political biographies of six world-famous leaders demonstrate, the backgrounds, qualities, and motives of those who have risen to the first rank of leadership display both remarkable similarities and wide disparities. Setting a good example is the mark of a good leader—hence the term *exemplary* to characterize the best of them.

Rómulo Betancourt (1908–1981)

Venezuela's President Hugo Chávez was a left-leaning populist and strident critic of U.S. foreign policy. As such, he is reminiscent of a certain type of leader in Latin American history, namely, the *caudillo* (in Spanish, a strong leader, especially a military dictator). Thus, despite his image as part demagogue and part Robin Hood, Chávez was not really so different from other leaders in Venezuelan history. Indeed, the famous "liberator" of Latin America, as noted earlier, was a charismatic, populist Venezuelan military leader named Simón Bolívar.

Against this backdrop of populist dictators, the story of Rómulo Betancourt, a towering figure in the checkered history of Latin American democracy who remains little known in the United States, appears all the more remarkable.

Venezuela became a nation in 1830. From then until 1959, when Betancourt assumed the elected presidency, no democratic ruler had survived in office for even two years. Yet not only did Betancourt survive, battling seemingly insurmountable obstacles, but his public career prospered, giving life to his country's fledgling democracy.

JOHN DOMINIS/TIME LIFE PICTURES/GETTY IMAGES

Romulo Betancourt (1908–1981), president of Venezuela, 1945–1948 and 1959–1964. Betancourt first became president of Venezuela in the old-fashioned Latin American way: by a military coup. Today he is most often remembered as "The Father of Venezuelan Democracy," one of Latin America's great post–World War II statesmen and a vigorous defender of constitutional government. Among his most notable achievements in office were the declaration of universal suffrage, many progressive social reforms, restructuring of Venezuela's oil contracts to keep over half the profits in the country and for the public benefit, and, finally, the famous "Betancourt Doctrine," which denied diplomatic recognition to any government that came to power by military force. Betancourt's last major contribution as president was to direct what is generally believed to have been the most honest election in Venezuela's history; and in March 1964 he handed over the reins of government to the winner, Raul Leoni. Betancourt thus became the first elected Venezuelan president ever to serve a full term in office and the first to transfer power constitutionally from one elected chief executive to another.

Betancourt's political career began when he was still a university student. At that time, a military dictator named Juan Vicente Gómez ruled Venezuela. In 1928, at the age of 20, Betancourt became a student leader in a failed revolution, eventually ending up in jail. After his release, he went into exile in Costa Rica for eight years, returning to Venezuela shortly after the death of the dictator in 1935. Afterward, Betancourt became a prominent political figure, though from the mid-1930s until 1959, he was a political maverick—often on the run, active in the underground, and sometimes living in exile as he continued his opposition to the dictator of the day. During his early years in opposition, he sympathized with the communists, but he moderated in time, favoring democratic socialism instead. Betancourt's most notable achievement during this time was laying the groundwork for what would become Venezuela's leading party—Acción Democratica.

Throughout most of his years in opposition, both Betancourt and his party consistently championed broad democratic participation for all citizens, agrarian reform, guaranteed universal education, national health care, and economic diversification (Venezuela was heavily dependent on oil exports). Betancourt joined and, according to some versions, headed a group of military reformers in a coup d'état (power seizure) against Venezuela's military government in October 1945. He ended up as president.

In office Betancourt championed a foreign policy in which Venezuela refused to extend diplomatic recognition to dictatorships and urged other governments in the region to follow suit. Domestically, he decreed that the large oil companies in Venezuela turn over half their income, enabling the government to undertake a far-reaching program to establish schools, hospitals, public water and sanitation facilities, and low-cost housing developments. He sponsored a new constitution in 1947, promoted elections, and declared he would not be a candidate for office. The candidate who succeeded Betancourt lasted only nine months before being ousted by another military coup. It was not until Betancourt was elected president in 1959 that democracy returned to Venezuela.

During his five-year term, Betancourt pursued the progressive policies he had always advocated. Particularly notable were his efforts to encourage foreign investment and improve urban housing. Betancourt also initiated a program of land reform. His economic and political achievements were all the more remarkable because when he took office, his nation was facing an economic crisis, the military did not support his rule, and coup attempts from both the Left and the Right punctuated his term. (Betancourt survived more than one assassination attempt.)

Although he was decisive and governed with a firm hand, Betancourt exemplified the differences between democratic leadership and dictatorial abuse of power. He encouraged the politics of moderation, compromise, and toleration. He heeded the powers and prerogatives of the other two branches of government, followed the constitution, respected the rights of citizens, and did not use his high office for material advantage (or permit anyone under him to do so).[7]

Betancourt prevailed in the end and was beloved by his people. What accounted for his success as a democratic leader in a country with an autocratic tradition? Betancourt appears to have possessed an uncanny ability to judge the motives and character of others; almost unerring judgment about when to stand firm and when to compromise; a capacity to listen to advice but to keep his own counsel; an ability to make difficult decisions; self-control; and great personal valor, both moral and physical. He combined all these qualities with a high degree of practical idealism—a clear vision of what he wanted to accomplish for his country and a commitment to values that, together with ambition, had motivated him in national politics for decades.[8]

Betancourt can justly be considered the founder of Venezuelan democracy. As one of his foremost biographers, Robert J. Alexander, observed, "No other Venezuelan political leader of his time could have succeeded under all these circumstances."[9] A historian who specialized in Latin America wrote, "If moral authority and high principles counted, Rómulo Betancourt loomed as a titan in the history of Venezuela."[10] In the end, he did what no Venezuelan had ever done before, something demagogues never do: he bowed out gracefully, handing power over to a democratically elected successor.[11]

Winston Churchill (1874–1965)

Winston Churchill became Britain's prime minister in May 1940, at a time of great peril to his country. A colorful personality, Churchill was brilliant, charming, and witty; he was also courageous, controversial, and cantankerous. In the 1930s, he recognized and warned Britain of the menace posed by the rise of Nazi Germany in the heart of Europe. When war broke out, Churchill had already had his share of ups and downs in government, but his career reflected a steadfast devotion to the cause of freedom.

Churchill was born into a prominent English family that traced its lineage directly back to John Churchill, the first duke of Marlborough. Winston's father had been a distinguished member of Parliament and cabinet minister; his mother was American. He himself was elected to Parliament at the tender age of 25 and almost immediately acquired a reputation as an eloquent and outspoken maverick. In 1911, he was appointed First Lord of the Admiralty, a high office he held through the first year of World War I. He was forced to resign in 1915, after the dismal failure of an amphibious attack on Turkey, by way of the Dardanelles, that he had sponsored. Churchill's political prestige then fell to an all-time low, although he managed to recoup sufficiently to be appointed minister of munitions in 1917.

Churchill remained a Conservative Member of Parliament (MP) throughout most of the 1920s and even held the prestigious position of chancellor of the exchequer (comparable to the U.S. secretary of the treasury) for an extended period. Despite a solid record of public service, he entered the 1930s as something of a political outcast, having alienated the leadership of his party. Even though the Conservatives held power, he was excluded from the government, and he found himself increasingly isolated in Parliament. At the age of 56, he was facing a premature end to his political career.

But Churchill had a kind of clairvoyance rare in politics. From the time of Hitler's ascent to power, he tried to alert Britain, Europe, and the United States, warning of the danger posed by Nazi Germany's rapid rearmament and the comparative weakness of Britain's armed forces—especially its air power. Many mainstream politicians and commentators ridiculed him as an alarmist. In the words of his foremost biographer, Churchill was a voice in the wilderness.[12]

As the 1930s progressed and Churchill's alarms began to arouse the nation, there still was no place for him in his party's cabinet. Only after Britain entered World War II was he asked to return to the government, initially in his former post as First Lord of the Admiralty, and then as prime minister.

After France had fallen and before the United States relaxed its policy of strict neutrality, Britain was the only power standing between Hitler and his goal—the total conquest of Europe. Churchill's inspiring words and example proved decisive. As Churchill later wrote, "Alone, but up-borne by every generous heartbeat of mankind, we had defied the tyrant in his hour of triumph."[13]

Churchill had rare leadership qualities. He understood the darker side of human nature and thus grasped the danger Hitler posed to civilization. Churchill had the courage of his convictions, never yielding to the voices of appeasement in his own party or the pressures of public opinion. His rhetoric inspired the nation in the face of a mortal threat and relentless bombardment. Above all, events proved him tragically right—right about the imminent threat, right about the malignant evil Hitler represented, and right about the urgent need for military preparedness. His message—that another terrible war was coming—was one his compatriots did not want to hear, but he never confused what the nation wanted to hear with what it *needed* to hear. And so he became the savior of his country.

Abraham Lincoln (1809–1865)

Churchill saved Britain from Hitler's Germany; Abraham Lincoln saved the United States of America from itself. The pivotal political issue in Lincoln's time was slavery. The South's economic dependence on it, along with the persistence of racial prejudice in the North, meant that advocating the immediate abolition of slavery was incompatible with winning the presidency. But preventing the "westward" spread of slavery, as it turned out, was incompatible with maintaining the peace.

This was the context in which Lincoln decided to run for president, a decision that culminated in his election to the nation's highest office in 1860. Lincoln's politics were guided by a basic moral precept and a profoundly practical judgment. The moral precept, which he repeatedly voiced in his debates with Stephen Douglas during his 1858 campaign for the Senate, held that slavery was wrong in principle, everywhere and without exception. In declaring slavery unjust and immoral, Lincoln did not resort to abstract philosophy; rather, he based his judgment squarely on the Declaration of Independence, which states, ". . . all men are created equal." Thus, for Lincoln, slavery violated the most basic principle of the U.S. political order.

Lincoln exercised uncommon practical judgment in evaluating the conditions under which slavery might be eradicated in the United States. He believed above all that it was necessary to maintain the Union as a geographic entity, as well as to preserve its integrity as a constitutional democracy. Only through a single central government for North and South alike could slavery be ended, although this was by no means inevitable. Conversely, any breakup of the Union would mean the indefinite extension of slavery, at least in the South.

Lincoln's belief in political equality and his conviction that such equality could be achieved only by preserving the Union help explain the pre–Civil War stands he avoided taking, as well as the ones he adopted. Although he believed slavery was morally wrong, he did not propose its immediate abolition; he knew such a proposal would prompt the South to secede and ensure the survival of slavery in that region. Nor did he support northern abolitionists who sought to disassociate themselves from the Union so long as it continued to countenance slavery. Here again, Lincoln recognized that such a policy would only entrench the very institution it was designed to eliminate. Finally, he opposed Stephen Douglas's formula of popular sovereignty, under which each new state would be allowed to declare itself for or against slavery. The question of slavery, Lincoln believed, was too fundamental to be submitted to the vagaries of the political marketplace.

Rather than pursue any of these policies, Lincoln favored an end to the extension of slavery into the territories, so that from then on, only free states would be admitted to the Union. In Lincoln's mind, this was the only antislavery policy that had any chance of gaining popular acceptance. The keys to his strategy were patience and perseverance. Adoption of his plan would ultimately bring about an end to slavery in the whole United States, as the relative weight and legislative strength of the slaveholding states diminished with the passage of time and the admission of new non-slaveholding states.

When it became evident that Lincoln's policy would not win the day, he accepted the Civil War as inevitable. Yet during the course of this conflict, his approach to the slavery question varied according to the circumstances of the war. As noted earlier, when the tide of battle ran against the Union and victory seemed to depend on not alienating several of the slaveholding Border States, Lincoln went out of his way to soft-pedal the slavery issue. The North needed military victories, not pious pronouncements, if the Union were to endure. It could not endure, he believed, if it remained "half slave and half free." In the final analysis, the reason Lincoln was willing to countenance civil war was, paradoxically, to preserve the kind of Union the Founders had intended.

Both before and during the Civil War, Lincoln's policies were aimed at achieving the maximum amount of good possible within the confines of popular consent. As commander in chief, he pushed his constitutional authority up to, and arguably beyond, its legal limits. But just as his ultimate political purposes were not undermined by the compromises he accepted to save the Union in time of peace, so too his moral integrity was not corrupted by the dictatorial powers he wielded in time of war. For all these reasons, Lincoln stands out as an exemplary political leader whose resolute actions and decisions under fire were instrumental in saving the Union.

Anwar al-Sadat (1918–1981)

The Middle East is one of the world's most unstable and violent regions. Miraculously, in late 1993, Israeli Prime Minister Yitzhak Rabin and Palestine Liberation Organization leader Yasir Arafat, bitter enemies, agreed to a deal that gave limited autonomy to the Palestinians in the Israeli-occupied West Bank and Gaza Strip. The agreement was a big step toward a possible peace, but it was not the *first* step. In fact, there was a precedent in the Middle East, one that suggested even the deadliest of enemies can live together in peace. Anwar al-Sadat was the political architect of that peacemaking precedent.

Sadat was president of Egypt from 1970 until his assassination in 1981. He succeeded Gamal Abdel Nasser, the acknowledged leader of the Arab world and a prime mover in the post–World War II anti-colonialist movement. Nasser was an autocratic ruler who governed Egypt with an iron fist and staunchly opposed the existence of the state of Israel. When Nasser died in 1970, Sadat succeeded him. (As vice president, Sadat was Nasser's handpicked successor.)

Like Nasser, Sadat was a fighter for Egyptian independence from Great Britain. His anti-British activities during World War II included contacts with Germans aimed at collaboration against the British imperialists. For these efforts, Sadat spent two years in a detention camp. Later, he would spend three more years (1946–1949) in prison, charged with attempting to assassinate a British official. In pursuit of a nationalistic strategy that sought to capitalize on anti-British sentiment in Egypt, Sadat and Nasser cooperated closely. It was Sadat who publicly announced the overthrow of the Egyptian monarchy and the establishment of the new, independent republic of Egypt under Nasser's leadership in July 1952.

Given this history, it seemed inevitable that as president Sadat would continue Nasser's policies. Events seemed to bear out this expectation. In 1971, he was instrumental in forging the Federation of Arab Republics, an alliance of Egypt, Libya, and Syria motivated by Nasser's policy of uniting the Arab world. The federation ultimately failed, but not for want of trying on Sadat's part.

In 1973, Sadat led Egypt in a war against Israel. Although Egypt was defeated, Sadat stressed that the Egyptian army had won a major battle at the outset of the war; this victory, he maintained, restored Egypt's national honor. In the aftermath of the war, Sadat switched from belligerent Arab nationalist to committed advocate of peaceful coexistence. This transformation was capped by a precedent-shattering state visit to Israel, where Sadat delivered a memorable speech before the Israeli Knesset (parliament) on November 20, 1977. More important than the speech was the symbolic significance of his official presence in the Israeli seat of government: Egypt had become the first Arab country to recognize Israel as a sovereign state.

This dramatic act of conciliation by Sadat paved the way for the Camp David Accords between Egypt and Israel the following year. The Egyptian-Israeli agreement at Camp David, Maryland, which set the stage for Israel's withdrawal from the Sinai peninsula, caught foreign observers by surprise and stunned the Arab world. Sadat was bitterly attacked by many of his fellow Arab rulers as a traitor to the Palestinian cause. To the Arabs, and to many of the most astute observers, Sadat's bold step toward a lasting Arab-Israeli peace was as unexpected as it was unprecedented.

Why did Sadat take this extraordinary step? Given the serious economic and social problems (poverty, overpopulation, urban crowding, and a growing generation gap) facing Egypt, Sadat, some argue, had little choice but to seek peace with Israel. Others emphasize Israel's value as a source of intelligence about Libya, Egypt's neighbor and rival in North Africa. A more plausible explanation is that Sadat the pragmatist concluded the only way Egypt was ever going to regain the Sinai (which Israel had occupied since 1967) was by signing a peace treaty.

Pragmatism explains Sadat's political-strategic calculations, but not the intensity of his peace efforts or the magnitude of the personal and political risks he was willing to take. He knew his actions would alienate most of the Arab world, including many of his fellow citizens. It seems likely that just as the young Sadat was moved by the ideal of a free and independent Egypt, which he helped to bring about, so too an older Sadat was inspired by an even more noble vision. As he expressed it on the occasion of the signing of the Camp David Accords:

> Let there be no more wars or bloodshed between Arabs and Israelis. Let there be no more suffering or denial of rights. Let there be no more despair or loss of faith. Let no mother lament the loss of her child. Let no young man waste his life on a conflict from which no one benefits. Let us work together until the day comes when they beat their swords into plowshares and their spears into pruning hooks.[14]

The eradication of hatred, religious bigotry, and incessant warfare from a region where they had been a way of life for as long as anyone could remember would indeed be a great act of statecraft. The attempt to bring peace to the Middle East may well have been Sadat's own personal bid for immortality. He may or may not have been aware of Alexander Hamilton's views on the subject of leadership, but through his actions, Sadat bore out the truth of Hamilton's observation that love of fame is the "ruling passion" of history's most exceptional leaders.

Like Lincoln, Sadat was assassinated by one of his own countrymen. Oddly, such is often the fate of history's peacemakers. Thus, Mahatma Gandhi, the charismatic leader of India's independence movement and a champion of non-violent resistance, was himself assassinated.

Paradoxically, making peace often entails greater political and personal risks than making war. The tragic fate that befell Sadat also befell Israeli Prime Minister Rabin who was gunned down in Tel Aviv in 1995. The assassin was Yigal Amir, 25 years of age, a fanatical Zionist opposed to the Oslo Peace Accords (for which Rabin, along with Shimon Peres and Arafat, won the Nobel Peace Prize). A lasting peace in the Middle East has been elusive, but Egypt and Israel have been at peace for more than two decades thanks to the treaty that stands as a fitting memorial to the wisdom and courage of Anwar al-Sadat.

Benazir Bhutto (1953–2007)

In December 1988, Benazir Bhutto of Pakistan became the first female prime minister in a Muslim country in history. She was born into politics in a country where politics was off limits to women, but broke through the plate glass ceiling that still reserves most professions and most well paying jobs for men. Her father, Zulfikar Ali Bhutto, founded Pakistan People's Party, the largest political party in Pakistan, and served as Pakistan's president (1971–1973) and prime minister (1973–1977).

The Army deposed Zulfikar Ali Bhutto in a coup in 1977 and effected his judicial execution (by hanging) two years later (allegedly for ordering the assassination of a political opponent). Educated in the United States (Berkeley) and in the United Kingdom (Oxford), Bhutto favored Western-style progressive economic policies. Such policies are often controversial in tradition-bound Islamic societies. In addition, the generals did not like playing second fiddle to a modernizing civilian leader.

Benazir Bhutto returned to Pakistan when her father was arrested and jailed. She moved to England in 1984, but became the joint PPP leader in exile. In 1986, she returned to Pakistan and led a successful nationwide campaign for open elections. In 1988, Benazir Bhutto, at the ripe young age of 35, led the PPP to victory. Like her father, Bhutto was educated in the United States (Radcliffe and Harvard) and in the United Kingdom (Oxford). And like him, she embraced modernity, democracy, and liberalism.

As prime minister, one of her first acts on taking the oath of office was to lift the ban on student unions and labor unions. She also directed negotiations leading to three peace agreements with India, Pakistan's archenemy since independence in 1947. But in 1990, her government was accused of corruption and dismissed under a controversial provision of the Constitution (Amendment Eight) that allows the president (usually a military figure or a civilian under the Army's boot heel) to take such action at virtually any time he chooses.

Bhutto's PPP won the elections in 1993 and she again served as prime minister until 1996 when her government, in the face of fierce opposition from conservative politicians and the army, was again dismissed. Threatened, she again went into self-imposed exile only to be accused in absentia of corruption and sentenced to three years in prison. Unable to return to Pakistan, she continued to work for liberal reforms and social justice from abroad.

Bhutto returned to Pakistan in October 2007 after President Musharraf (a former Army General) granted her amnesty on all corruption charges. A suicide attack at her homecoming rally killed 136 people, but she survived by ducking down behind her armored vehicle. When Musharraf imposed a state of emergency in early November, Bhutto pronounced it Pakistan's "blackest day" and threatened to call on her supporters to stage mass demonstrations. In the showdown that followed, Musharraf place Bhutto under house arrest; she, in turn, called for his resignation. Under heavy Western pressure, Musharraf lifted emergency rule in December.

Bhutto was assassinated and twenty-eight others died in a suicide attack after an election campaign rally in Rawalpindi on December 27, 2007. The attack left at least another hundred wounded. Some died in a hail of bullets; others were killed in the bomb blast.

The attack plunged Pakistan into turmoil. Bhutto's supporters went on a rampage in several cities. The fact that Pakistan and India both have nuclear weapons added drama and danger to the crisis.

The political murder of Benazir Bhutto was a tragedy on many levels—for her family, her country, the war-torn region of Central Asia (Afghanistan is Pakistan's next-door neighbor), and the turbulent Muslim world. But it was also a tragedy for the West and for women the world over. Because her life and work were cut short, we will never know what might have been. But it is clear that Benazir Bhutto was an uncommonly courageous woman who dedicated her life to making Pakistan a better place for her people and the world a better place for us all. To that end, she fought and died.

Aung San Suu Kyi (b. 1945)

"It is not power that corrupts, but fear. Fear of losing power corrupts those who wield it and fear of the scourge of power corrupts those who are subject to it."

Like Benazir Bhutto, Aung San Suu Kyi was born into politics. Her father, Aung San, a major military and political leader in Burma's struggle for independence after World War II, was assassinated by rivals for power in 1947. Suu Kyi earned degrees from Oxford (BA,1969) and the University of London (PhD, 1985).

From 1962 until 1988—that is, during Suu Kyi's entire adult life to that point—Burma (also known as Myanmar) was ruled as a military dictatorship under Genera Ne Win. During the Ne Win dictatorship, Suu Kyi lived abroad in the United Kingdom (London) and in the United States (New York City). In 1988, two events signaled a watershed in Burma's history: Ne Win stepped down, and Suu Kyi returned from her long self-imposed exile. In August, she addressed a huge throng (estimate at half a million people) in the capital, Rangoon, calling for democracy. In September, even as a military junta usurped power, Suu Kyi and others launched the National League for Democracy (NLD). Placed under house arrest, the junta invited her to leave the country in July 1989. She refused.

When the military called a general election in 1990, Aung San Suu Kye's NLD received 59% of the popular vote and, in theory, 80% of the assembly seats. The balloting turned out to be a feckless exercise because the military promptly nullified the elections and again placed Suu Kyi under house arrest, where she would remain for fifteen of the next twenty-one years. During these years, however, she continued a solitary fight for democracy in personal isolation, against all odds, in poor living conditions, and under constant threat from the military rulers.

Finally released from house arrest in November 2010, she plunged right back into the roiling waters of Burmese politics. In a 2012 by-election she ran for a seat in parliament and won.

During the two decades she was barred from politics and kept a prisoner in her own home, Aung San Suu Kyi became the stuff of legend. Many honors and awards were bestowed on her (in absentia, of course), including the Nobel Peace Prize and the Congressional Gold Medal. Today, she is the face of a newly emerging Burma (much as Nelson Mandela became the face of the new South Africa), a living symbol universally admired for her courage and resistance to tyranny.

WHERE HAVE ALL THE LEADERS GONE?

Living politicians have a lot in common with the late comedian Rodney Dangerfield: They get no respect. In politics, sometimes "losers" come to be admired as leaders, and winners suffer the opposite fate (see "Ideas and Politics —Winners and Losers" and Figure 12.1). When politicians are beholden to special interests and

WINNERS AND LOSERS

Two examples of "losers" in recent U.S. history are Jimmy Carter (who lost his bid for reelection to Ronald Reagan in 1980) and Al Gore (who lost to George W. Bush in the controversial 2000 election). After his defeat in 1980, President Carter came to be widely admired for his unstinting humanitarian efforts—notably, his Habitat for Humanity project—as well as for promoting peace and democracy in troubled parts of the world. As a presidential campaigner, Al Gore was often dismissed as boring and was even blamed for the "historical debacle" that many believe resulted from his failure to win the presidency in 2000. But Gore revealed a very different side of his personality in 2006 when he starred in *An Inconvenient Truth*, the Academy Award–winning documentary about global warming and the dangers it poses to the health and survival of the planet. In 2007, he was awarded the Nobel Peace Prize for his work on climate change.

Gore's passion for environmental causes goes back to his college days, long before he ran for public office. Similarly, Carter's humanitarianism is rooted in long-held religious beliefs. In 1992, a decade before global warming became a major issue in the United States, Gore wrote *Earth in the Balance*, which called for eliminating the internal combustion engine by 2017 and for making environmentalism "the central organizing principle for civilization."

Both Al Gore and Jimmy Carter have arguably had a greater impact on public policy as private citizens than they ever did as politicians—even as the vice president or president of the United States. Both Carter and Gore did not let a defeat define them.

The moral of the story: The true test of leadership is what we do, not what we say. And doing something is more important than being something.

FIGURE 12.1   Winner/Loser Map. Al Gore and other crusaders for a clean environment have gradually gained adherents among voters and state legislators, but the green movement still faces an uphill battle. In 2009, 10 northeastern and mid-Atlantic states joined the Regional Greenhouse Gas Initiative (RGGI), a voluntary cap-and-trade program aimed at reducing greenhouse gases. In the U.S., three such regional schemes currently cover about twenty-six states, but these programs remain under challenge. In New Jersey, for example, Governor Chris Christie wants to pull out of the program. There have also been repeal efforts in New York and New Hampshire. California's program has survived various lawsuits and a ballot initiative to have it repealed. Advocates hope that the nascent RGGIs and California will act as models for other U.S. regions and states. At the federal level, however, lobbyists and lawmakers have blocked action on greenhouse gases and the EPA has resisted a crackdown on polluting coal-fired power plants.

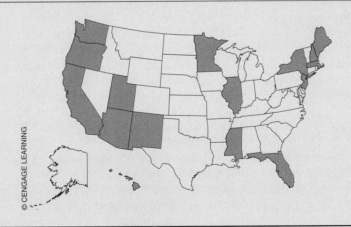

© CENGAGE LEARNING

use focus groups to formulate messages that will sell in a ten-second television sound bite, courageous political leadership often seems like a distant ideal.*

Leadership as a concept has virtually disappeared from the language and literature of U.S. politics. Significantly, the 1934 edition of the *Encyclopedia of the Social Sciences* included a brief but incisive essay on statesmanship by a celebrated British scholar, but a more recent edition omits all mention of statesmanship as a category of political thought.

In an age of equality, there is a danger that the idea of excellence will be debunked and dismissed as elitist.[15] To the debunkers, vague historical determinants or narrow self-interest, not free will, are the true motive forces in history, and it is naïve to believe some leaders really care about the public good. This cynical view leads to a drastically reduced opinion of outstanding leaders in world history. It is as if "the old histories full of kings and generals whom our ancestors foolishly mistook for heroes are, we suppose, to be replaced by a kind of hall of fame of clever operators."[16]

One consequence of this tendency is that it makes political life less attractive to capable and conscientious individuals. By denying public officials the respect they are due, a democratic society can do itself considerable harm. As noted earlier, a pervasive belief that corrupt and mediocre politicians are the norm can become a self-fulfilling prophecy, causing only the corrupt or mediocre to seek public office.

DEMAGOGUES IN AMERICAN HISTORY

Originally, in ancient Greece, a demagogue was a leader who championed the cause of the common people. Today, the term *demagogue* is applied to a leader who exploits popular prejudices, distorts the truth, and makes empty promises to gain political power. In general, demagogues combine unbridled personal ambition, unscrupulous methods, and great popular appeal.

If true leaders represent the ideal, demagogues represent the perversion of both truth and leadership. Statesmen genuinely care about justice and the public good; demagogues only pretend to care in order to gain high office whence they inevitably betray the public interest they previously championed.

Demagogues are rarely long remembered. Occasionally, they leave an indelible mark.

Aaron Burr (1756–1836)

His name is one of the most notorious in the annals of early U.S. history. Schoolchildren learn at an early age that Aaron Burr was a "bad guy," but very few, including adults, know much about him or why he was a danger to the young republic he claimed to serve.

Burr had a tragic childhood. Born into a wealthy and famous family, he lost both his parents at a very early age. He was beaten by his guardian and ran away from home more than once. At the age of 10, he tried to stow away on a ship. Desperate not to be taken back to live with his tormentor, he climbed the ship's mast and refused to come down. In the end, he was delivered once again into his guardian's "care."

---

*Historians sometimes seek to refute the conventional wisdom about history's most famous figures. In the United States, recent books have cast doubt on the character and motives of even our most revered national icons, including George Washington and Thomas Jefferson.

Burr was a precocious child and a brilliant student. In time, he became a lawyer and then went into politics. He had an uncanny ability to beguile, to pretend he was someone other than who he really was. He was also an eloquent speaker and an agile debater, skills that served him well in a court of law. A great admirer of Thomas Jefferson, he was a candidate for president in 1800, the year Jefferson was elected. Because of the peculiar workings of the Electoral College, however, no candidate received the absolute majority required by the Constitution to claim the presidency, so the decision was thrown into the House of Representatives, dominated by the lame-duck Federalists, where the delegations from the various states each cast one vote. The contest in the House of Representatives was between Jefferson and Burr. The Federalists were determined to "elect" Burr, who refused to withdraw even though Jefferson was clearly the popular choice. Finally, after five long days, on the thirty-sixth ballot, a delegate from Virginia changed his vote, giving Jefferson the one additional state vote he needed to put him over the top. Thus, Burr became the vice president, having nearly stolen the presidency.

In Jefferson's time, vice presidents had very little to do. Burr kept himself busy, however, by undermining the president and the republic. The story of his seditious activities is too long and convoluted to be told here, but they included trying to organize a secession movement in New England and the territory north of the Ohio River, later plotting to assassinate Jefferson, and trying to lead an insurrection in New Orleans and what was then the Mississippi Territory. (His plans included creation of a western empire, under his control, in the lands acquired through Jefferson's leadership in the famed Louisiana Purchase.)

Burr was eventually captured and arrested on charges of treason. Brought to trial in Richmond, Virginia, in 1807, he was acquitted by the Chief Justice of the Supreme Court, John Marshall, who was also acting as federal court judge. Marshall was a die-hard Federalist and a rival of Jefferson's. Seldom, if ever, has there been a more blatant case in U.S. jurisprudence of politicizing a trial and showing contempt from the bench for the integrity of the Constitution. The evidence against Burr was abundant and damning, but neither Jefferson nor the Republican-controlled Congress had the stomach to see Burr hang once Marshall had rendered his verdict.

In sum, Burr failed to achieve his seditious intents, but his demagoguery had come dangerously close to catapulting him into the presidency in 1800. The fact that he became a U.S. senator and vice president shows that demagogues have long played a role at the highest levels of government. Burr's personal charisma and political skills in the end also probably helped him escape the gallows.

Theodore Bilbo (1877–1947)

As governor and senator, Theodore Bilbo dominated Mississippi politics from the 1920s through the 1940s. He campaigned equally hard against blacks and his political opponents, linking them whenever possible. His campaign rhetoric was colorful and outrageous. In the heat of one political campaign, he denounced his opponent as a "cross between a hyena and a mongrel...begotten in a [racial slur deleted] graveyard at midnight, suckled by a sow, and educated by a fool."[17] Although Bilbo's white supremacist politics and down-home language endeared him to a great many Mississippians, not everyone was impressed. Even political allies viewed him as a self-serving political operator.

According to one writer, Bilbo was "pronounced by the state Senate in 1911 'as unfit to sit with honest upright men in a respectable legislative body,' and described more pungently by his admirers as 'a slick little bastard.'"[18] And in the eyes of the editor of the *Jackson Daily News*, Bilbo stood "for nothing that is high or constructive,…nothing save passion, prejudice and hatred,…nothing that is worthy."[19] Bilbo was reelected to a third Senate term in 1946, but this time the Senate refused to seat him because of his alleged incitement of violence against blacks who tried to vote. Bilbo died of cancer a few months later at the age of 69.

Huey Long (1893–1935)

Theodore Bilbo has mercifully escaped the attention of most U.S. historians; Huey Long, a politician from the neighboring state of Louisiana, has not. Known to his Cajun constituents as the Kingfish, Long was far more ambitious than Bilbo. Of humble origins, he completed the three-year law program at Tulane University, passed a special examination from the Louisiana Supreme Court, and became a licensed attorney at the age of 21. In his own words, he "came out of the courtroom running for office."[20] Three years later he was elected state railroad commissioner, and in 1928 he gained the Louisiana governorship.

Long governed Louisiana with an iron hand during his four-year reign (1928–1932) and during his subsequent term as U.S. senator, which was cut short by his assassination in 1935. As governor, Long controlled every aspect of the state's political life. Surrounded by bodyguards and aided by a formidable political

As Governor of Louisiana, Huey Long seized control and acted as a virtual dictator. Then as senator during the Great Depression, he cast himself as a radical populist social reformer and had great ambitions on the national scene. But an assassin's bullet abruptly ended his career and his life in 1935. It is said that his last words were, "God don't let me die. I have so much left to do."

AP PHOTO

machine, he used state police and militia to intimidate voters, handed out patronage and political favors, created a state printing board to put unfriendly newspapers out of business, ordered a kidnapping on the eve of a crucial election vote to avoid personal political embarrassment, and generally acted more like a despotic ruler than a democratically elected governor. Under his autocratic rule:

> Men could be—and were—arrested by unidentified men, the members of his secret police, held incommunicado, tried, and found guilty on trumped-up charges. A majority of the State Supreme Court became unabashedly his.... A thug, making a premeditated skull-crushing attack upon a Long opponent, could draw from his pocket in court a pre-signed pardon.[21]

Despite these excesses and a penchant for luxury, Long always took care to portray himself as "just plain folks." The true villains in U.S. society, he said, were rich corporations such as Standard Oil, which consigned ordinary people to lives of poverty while enriching a few corporate officers.

To counteract this alleged thievery by big business and to create a popular platform for the upcoming presidential race in 1936, Long developed an unworkable (but popular) "Share the Wealth" program, tailor-made to appeal to people suffering through the Great Depression. Long's proposal included restrictions on maximum wealth, mandated minimum and maximum incomes, so-called homestead grants for all families, free education through college, bonuses for veterans, and pensions for the aged—as well as the promise of radios, automobiles, and subsidized food through government purchases. However implausible and impractical this program seems, it's worth remembering that the people to whom Long was appealing were not inclined to quibble or question. They needed someone to believe in.

Like many other demagogues, Long gained power by promising hope to the hopeless. Demagogues generally vow to defeat the forces of evil that, according to them, are solely responsible for the people's plight. Of course, those forces—blacks in the case of Bilbo, corporations for Long—invariably do not exercise anything like the controlling influence attributed to them. Nonetheless, once accepted as the champion of the little people against enemies they themselves have conjured up, demagogues often have been able to manipulate the unsuspecting populace for their own illicit ends.

Joseph McCarthy (1906–1957)

During the 1950s, an obscure politician from Wisconsin named Joseph McCarthy identified a demon that greatly alarmed the U.S. people and then claimed to find evidence of this malignant force in all areas of public life.

While serving as a Republican senator from Wisconsin, McCarthy attracted national attention by making the shocking "revelation" that the U.S. Department of State was infiltrated by communists. For approximately four years, he leveled charges of treason against a wide array of public officials, college professors, and Hollywood stars. Using his position as chair of the Senate Committee on Investigations, McCarthy badgered, intimidated, and defamed countless people in and out of government. As his accusations helped create a national climate of fear, his power grew, and those who opposed him did so at their own risk.

In 1954, McCarthy accused the secretary of the army of concealing foreign espionage operations. That accusation, along with innuendos aimed at General George C. Marshall—next to President Dwight D. Eisenhower, perhaps the most respected public servant in the United States—marked a turning point. McCarthy had gone too far. Ironically, his unscrupulous methods were exposed in Senate investigations that resulted from his own irresponsible accusations. The hearings received national radio and television coverage and made front-page headlines in every major newspaper in the country. In the end, McCarthy was cast into obscurity as rapidly as he had been catapulted into national prominence.

Tom DeLay (b. 1947)

Texas Republican Tom DeLay (b. 1947) was first elected to the U.S. House of Representatives in 1984 and served as House majority leader from 2003 to 2006, having been the House majority whip in the 1990s and subsequently serving as deputy majority leader. DeLay became known as "The Hammer" for his ruthless methods and questionable ethics. As House majority whip, he demanded strict party discipline and made anyone who crossed him pay. When he became House majority leader after the 2002 midterm elections, he rallied—or bullied—House Republicans to close ranks behind President George W. Bush's neoconservative agenda.

In the early 2000s, DeLay played a key role in a plan to gerrymander state legislative districts and later to redraw Texas's congressional districts in favor of the Republican Party. However, in October 2004, the House Ethics Committee voted unanimously to admonish DeLay on two counts relating to ethics violations, though it deferred action on another count related to fundraising while that matter was under criminal investigation in Texas.

In 2005, a Texas grand jury indicted DeLay on criminal charges of conspiring to violate campaign finance laws by engaging in money laundering during that period. Although he denied the charges, claiming they were politically motivated, he had no choice under existing rules but to step down temporarily as majority leader. Under heavy pressure from within his own party, he later announced he would not seek to return to his leadership position in the House. About this same time, two of DeLay's former aides were convicted in the Jack Abramoff scandal.

DeLay ran for reelection in 2006 and won the Republican primary but subsequently resigned his seat in Congress. He tried to have his name removed from the ballot to avoid a humiliating defeat, but he lost a court battle and had to remain, even though he had withdrawn from the race. In the annals of U.S. politics, there are few more ignominious endings to a politician's career. (The demise of Richard Nixon is one.)

Abramoff served a prison sentence for defrauding American Indian tribes and for corruption of public officials. Tom DeLay was sentenced to three years in prison in January 2011. As the saying goes, the bigger they are, the harder they fall.

LEGISLATORS

Solon was the great lawgiver of ancient Athens, the wise legislator who framed the laws of the city-state that became the first democracy in the history of Western civilization. Words like *great* and *wise* are seldom used in the same sentence as *legislator* these days; sadly, many today delegate and consider the very idea of a "great legislator" to be an oxymoron.

Most politicians are fairly average. On a day-to-day basis, they do the best they can, given the pressures and constraints they face. Much of the time, they want to do the right thing, although they have difficulty keeping moral or ethical issues in clear focus and even more difficulty taking political risks. Generally they are not corrupt, but they often *are* corruptible. They are no better, and no worse, than most people, but they are in a position to do more harm (or good) than most ordinary citizens.

As citizens, we often scorn "politicians."[22] They, in turn, lament the fact that voters fail to understand how the system really works—that without logrolling (trading votes) the legislative process would grind to a halt. The would-be leader in a democratic society faces the choice of whether to act as a delegate, carrying out the voters' (presumed) wishes, or as a trustee, exercising independent judgment on behalf of his or her constituents. The political system itself requires elected representatives to be responsive if they wish to be reelected. But those to whom the people have entrusted power are duty-bound to lead—and therein lies the politician's dilemma.

Legislators as Delegates

delegate theory of representation
The theory that elected officials should reflect the views of the voters back home, rather than following their own conscience or substituting their own judgment for that of their constituents; in other words, elected representatives should be followers rather than leaders.

According to the **delegate theory of representation**, a legislature "is representative when it contains within itself the same elements, in the same proportion, as are found in the body politic at large. It is typical of us; we are all in it in microcosm."[23] In this model of representative democracy, elected representatives are obliged to act as instructed delegates.

The delegate theory tends to legitimize the use of focus groups and opinion polls to help legislators decide what stands to take on important issues. One notable advocate of this theory holds there is a "relative equality of capacity and wisdom between representatives and constituents," it would be "arbitrary and unjustifiable for representatives to ignore the opinions and wishes of the people," and that political issues often involve "irrational commitment or personal preference, choice rather than deliberation, [making it all] the more necessary...that the representative consult with the people's preferences."[24]

Legislators as Trustees

Detractors say the delegate theory of representation requires elected officials to be too passive—in effect, to act as followers rather than leaders. One famous critic of this theory was Edmund Burke (1729–1797), the famed eighteenth-century British writer and legislator.

Burke believed legislators ought to retain a certain independence of thought and action. Specifically, according to Burke, the elected representative needs to isolate specific complaints about real problems from the grumbling of an irascible (and possibly irrational) electorate. He contended that the politician as legislator must listen to the complaints of constituents but not give all complaints equal weight: competent legislators distinguish between legitimate grievances and those that arise from defects in human nature.[25] For Burke's ideal lawmaker, public opinion is a useful barometer, rather than a guidepost.

Burke believed a natural aristocracy made up of the best and the brightest should govern and that elected officials should act as trustees, not puppets. As he declared in a famous speech to his own constituents, "Your representative owes you not his industry only, but his judgment; and he betrays, instead of serving you, if he sacrifices it to your opinion."[26] Burke's views were elitist: he posited a wide gulf in knowledge, wisdom, and virtue between those fit to be legislators and ordinary constituents. Seen in this light, true legislators are leaders rather than followers.

Burke's so-called **trustee theory of representation** fits into his larger philosophy of government. Good government, he argued, must include not only goodwill, but also "virtue and wisdom." Burke's Parliament is a place of "*one* nation, with *one* interest, that of the whole—where not local purposes, not local prejudices, ought to guide, but the general good, resulting from the general reason of the whole" prevails.[27] Did it ever exist or did Burke fall victim to wishful thinking? Looking at the U.S. Congress today, what do *you* think?

> **trustee theory of representation**
> The theory that elected officials should be leaders, making informed choices in the interest of their constituencies.

CITIZEN-LEADERS

Occasionally, an individual can decisively influence the course of political events without holding an official position in the government. An individual's unique dedication to a cause, personal magnetism, or even outright courage can garner an impressive political following. Such a person is called a *citizen-leader*. In the following section, we look at five examples of such grassroots leadership.

Václav Havel (1936–2011)

In the mid-1960s, at the age of 29, Václav Havel (1936–2011) gained worldwide acclaim for his satirical absurdist plays, including *The Garden Party* (1964) and *The Memorandum* (1965). In the summer of 1968, Havel and thirty other Czech cultural figures signed a statement calling for the revival of the outlawed Social Democratic Party in communist-controlled Czechoslovakia. In August of that same summer, the increasing, but cautious, trend toward liberalization within Czechoslovakia that had begun in 1963 was swiftly and successfully thwarted when the Soviet Union invaded the country to reassert hard-line Soviet control.

During the conflict, Havel played a key role in putting the Czech Radio Free Europe on the airways and used this underground radio broadcast to direct daily commentary to Western intellectuals as a plea for assistance. Over the next two decades, he became Czechoslovakia's most famous playwright. His plays often contained biting satire aimed at the communists who ruled in Prague. But his writings were not the only reason for his increasing notoriety. He also became Czechoslovakia's foremost dissident and human rights champion. In 1977, Havel coauthored the Charter 77 Manifesto, which denounced Czechoslovakia's communist rulers for failing to abide by Basket Three of the 1975 Helsinki Accords, in which all signatories promised to respect civil and political rights. For such acts of political defiance, Havel was jailed repeatedly, serving sentences that often included hard labor. Despite these punishments, he was not silenced.

In December 1989, after Czechoslovakia's communist regime collapsed under the crushing weight of popular civilian discontent, Havel became president by popular consensus. His rise from prison to the presidency in 1989 was unprecedented.

DENNIS VAN TINE /LANDOV

Václav Havel at Columbia University in November 2006; President of Czechoslovakia (1989–1993) and the Czech Republic (1993–2003). Havel led the revolution against Czechoslovakia's communist regime in 1989 and was instantly elevated to the presidency by popular acclamation. A courageous playwright and lifelong human rights activist who had been persecuted and imprisoned for daring to dissent against tyranny, Havel in office was even more poplar abroad than at home. As president, he was content to exercise moral power through his words and ideas, and, to the chagrin of critics and admirers alike, readily conceded political power to others. Renowned for his credo of "living in truth," Havel was the conscience of his country and a highly respected world leader.

But then, no other public figure in Czechoslovakia could come close to matching the moral authority Havel had accumulated during three decades of courageous citizen-leadership.

Havel remained in office for more than three years. Then, on the verge of Czechoslovakia's disintegration into two ethnic nation-states (the Czech Republic and Slovakia), he resigned. But he did not long absent himself from public life. On January 26, 1993—little more than six months after his resignation—the Czech parliament elected Havel to a five-year term as president of the Czech Republic.

Despite his prominent position, Havel did not always take an active role in governing his nation, yet he remained an important national figure. Although most Czechs distrusted and disavowed politicians, many respected Havel as the only living Czech leader who not only talked and wrote about "living in truth," but also practiced what he preached.

Martin Luther King Jr. (1929–1968)

An outstanding citizen-leader was the renowned civil rights champion Martin Luther King Jr. (1929–1968). From the moment he became president of the newly formed Southern Christian Leadership Conference in 1957, King's national prominence grew. He led sit-ins, marches, demonstrations, and rallies throughout the South, all aimed at ending racial segregation and overcoming racial discrimination in jobs and housing. Practicing nonviolent civil disobedience, protesters under King's leadership openly broke the law, which sanctioned segregated lunch counters, required parade permits, forced African Americans to sit at the back of buses, and so on, and then accepted punishment for their actions. King intended to stir the conscience of the nation by reaching legislators and judges and, in the end, the U.S. people. As he stated in his famous 1963 "Letter from Birmingham Jail":*

> I submit that an individual who breaks a law that conscience tells him is unjust, and willingly accepts the penalty by staying in jail to arouse the conscience of the community over its injustice, is in reality expressing the very highest respect for law.[28]

---

*King had gone to Birmingham, Alabama, to lead an economic boycott aimed at desegregating public facilities and was jailed for organizing an unlicensed parade.

King's hope was clear:

> We must see the need of having nonviolent gadflies to create the kind of tension in society that will help men to rise from the dark depths of prejudice and racism to the majestic heights of understanding and brotherhood.[29]

The influence of King and other African American civil rights leaders has been decisive. Although extremely controversial at the time, their courageous efforts proved crucial to the passage of the landmark 1964 Civil Rights Act, which banned discrimination in public accommodations and employment. Later, other civil rights legislation was passed, further ensuring equal treatment under the law for all citizens. In 1964, King was awarded the Nobel Peace Prize for his efforts. Four years later, at the age of 39, he was assassinated.

Rosa Parks (1913–2005)

Rosa Parks (1913–2005) stirred the conscience of a nation with a single act of courage. On December 1, 1955, she left work after spending a long day as a tailor's assistant at a department store in Montgomery, Alabama. Boarding a bus to go home, she found a seat. Soon, however, a white man who was standing demanded her seat. (Montgomery's customary practice required that all four blacks sitting in the same row with Rosa Parks would have to stand in order to allow one white man to sit, since no black person was allowed to sit parallel with a white person.)[30] Parks stayed put:

> I was thinking that the only way to let them know I felt I was being mistreated was to do just what I did—resist the order....I had not thought about it and I had taken no previous resolution until it happened, and then I simply decided that I would not get up. I was tired, but I was usually tired at the end of the day, and I was not feeling well, but then there had been many days when I had not felt well. I had felt for a long time, that if I was ever told to get up so a white person could sit, that I would refuse to do so.[31]

AP PHOTOS

Rosa Parks in Montgomery, Alabama, in 1956, after the Supreme Court banned segregation in public transportation.

The bus driver had Parks arrested.

Many historians date the origin of the U.S. civil rights movement to the Montgomery Bus Boycott—a reaction to the arrest of Rosa Parks. Her simple but courageous act of defiance is remembered today as one of political valor that drew attention to racial injustice and led to a chain of events that eventually changed the nation forever.

Nelson Mandela (b. 1918)

Born in Transkei, South Africa, on July 18, 1918, Nelson Mandela was the son of a tribal chief. He joined the African National Congress in

1944 and was engaged in resistance against the ruling National Party's apartheid policies after 1948. He went on trial for high treason in 1956–1961 and was acquitted in 1961. Meanwhile, resistance to apartheid grew, mainly against the new Pass Laws, which dictated where black people were allowed to live and work.

When the government banned the ANC in 1960, Mandela went underground. As one of the top leaders of the ANC, Mandela launched a campaign of economic sabotage and even advocated creation of a military wing within the ANC. He was arrested in 1962 and sentenced to five years' imprisonment with hard labor. In 1963 Mandela and other ANC militants were brought to stand trial for plotting the violent overthrow of the government, and in June 1964 eight of the accused, including Mandela, were sentenced to life imprisonment. At his trial, he said: "I have cherished the ideal of a democratic and free society in which all persons live together in harmony and with equal opportunities. It is an ideal which I hope to live for and to achieve. But if needs be, it is an ideal for which I am prepared to die."

While in prison, Mandela became the symbol of the anti-apartheid movement. "In prison," he later confessed, "you come face to face with time. There is nothing more terrifying." And yet, for more than a quarter of a century, he refused to compromise with South Africa's white minority government. "Only free men can negotiate. Prisoners cannot enter into contracts."[32]

Mandela was finally released on February 11, 1990. In 1991, Mandela was elected president of the newly legalized ANC. He was awarded the Nobel Peace Prize in December 1993. Five months later, as a widely revered statesman who was jailed for twenty-seven years and yet managed to lead the anti-apartheid struggle, Mandela emerged to became the country's first black president when, for the first time in South Africa's history, all races voted in democratic elections. He retired from politics—and largely from public life—in 1999.

Every community and every country is profoundly affected by the quality of its political leadership. The 75-year-old Mandela, who was self-taught, widely trusted, and world renowned, led a peaceful political transition, ending the rule of the white supremacist government.

Wael Ghonim (b. 1980)

In the early days of the Egyptian uprising that ended the rule of dictator Hosni Mubarak at the beginning of 2011, Google executive and political activist Wael Ghonim was arrested and held in detention for eleven days. Ghonim quickly became a symbol of the anti-Mubarak movement and a national hero. Protest organizers gave speeches in Cairo's central Tahrir Square vowing they would not leave the square until Ghonim was freed, but the government-controlled media suggested that Ghonim's political activities made him a traitor to the nation.

Ghonim's role in organizing the January 25 protest movement is unclear, but there is no doubt that his use of an Internet-based social network—Facebook—to communicate with a vast social network of Egyptian activists in the months preceding the uprising played a key role. Part of a cadre of young activists in Egypt who set the stage for the massive demonstrations in Cairo, Ghonim wrote on his personal Facebook profile for friends, "I said one year ago that the Internet will change the political scene in Egypt and some Friends made fun of me :)."

He posted this comment two days into the crisis that brought the Egyptian dictator down. The next day, January 28, Ghonim disappeared.

> Ghonim was one of four administrators running the first of the major Facebook pages that became a virtual headquarters for the protest movement, according to a collaborator in the political opposition, and also according to an Internet activist familiar with the situation. Ghonim also set up the official campaign website for opposition leader Mohamed ElBaradei and volunteered as a tech consultant for other opposition groups, according to Ziad Al-Alimi, a senior aide to Mr. ElBaradei.

> Online activists including Ghonim have played a central role in electronically sowing the seeds of the current protests. Ghonim joined ElBaradei's political campaign as a volunteer about a month before Mr. ElBaradei, winner of the 2005 Nobel Peace Prize and former head of the International Atomic Energy Agency, made a dramatic return to Egypt last February amid speculation he was seeking a wider political role. Ghonim's Facebook profile, which he updated often, lists Mr. ElBaradei as someone he admires along with Microsoft founder Bill Gates, billionaire investor Warren Buffett and Apple founder Steve Jobs.[33]

On March 2, 2011, Ghonim gave a ten-minute "TED" talk that was beamed to seventy locations around the world on closed-circuit television. He said that one reason the protestors succeeded in ousting Mubarak was because "we didn't understand politics." Another: The Egyptian people were no longer paralyzed by fear. Why? Because, he said, they finally had a way to talk to one another (Google, Facebook, Twitter) and discovered that they were not alone, that they were part of a community of people who desired freedom, and that they had the power to act on that desire.

One of the virtues of modern democracies is that citizenship is universal and leadership arises from the rank and file. Leadership can take many different forms—from the highest office to working at the local level. Exemplary leadership at the national level always has local consequences, but, as we have seen, it is also true that exemplary leadership on the local level can have national consequences. The quality of a nation reflects the quality of its leaders; in a democracy, where voters make choices, the quality of the nation's leaders reflects on its citizens too.

SUMMARY

We can classify political leaders who occupy government positions as statesmen, demagogues, or ordinary politicians. Citizen-leaders hold no official office but can exert significant political influence.

Exceptional leaders who display an overriding concern for the public good, superior leadership skills, and keen practical wisdom in times of crisis were long called statesmen; today, this term is not considered politically correct in some quarters, so it has fallen into disuse. The lure of fame has been one of the motivating forces for many great leaders. Modern neglect of the concept of statecraft has led some observers to view it as a dying art.

Most prevalent in representative democracies are ordinary politicians. All elected officials must decide whether to exercise positive leadership or merely represent the views of their constituents. According to the delegate theory of democratic representation, politicians should act primarily as conduits for the expressed wishes of the electorate; the trustee theory, by contrast, stresses the importance of independent judgment in political office. The demagogue combines reckless personal ambition, unscrupulous methods, and charismatic appeal. Demagogues are most prevalent in democracies, and their fall is often as sudden and spectacular as their rise to power.

Citizen-leaders combine dedication to a cause, personal ability or magnetism, and opposition to governmental policy (or established practice). They inspire others and attract a sympathetic following, frequently on a worldwide scale. They exert a moral force generated by the power of the cause they personify.

KEY TERMS

statesman   320
demagogue   320
politician   320
citizen-leader   320

statecraft   321
delegate theory of
   representation   340

trustee theory of
   representation   341

REVIEW QUESTIONS

1. How do we classify political leaders? Explain the differences between the various categories.
2. Why is the study of political leadership an important aspect of the overall study of politics?
3. What accounts for the rarity of exemplary leadership?
4. Describe two competing theories of representation. Which one makes the most sense to you and why?
5. Is it fair to lump all politicians together? Do politicians generally have a good reputation? Can they be found all over the world or only in certain countries? Explain your answers.
6. What is a demagogue? Name some demagogues. What motivates them?
7. Does democracy have any natural defenses against demagoguery? If so, what are they?
8. What is the nature of exemplary leadership? Name four exemplary leaders and explain in detail what makes any one of them exemplary.

CHAPTER 13

Issues in Public Policy

Politics, Principles, Priorities, and Practices

The Pursuit of Security

The Pursuit of Prosperity

The Pursuit of Equality

The Pursuit of Liberty

The Pursuit of Justice

Goals in Conflict

THINK ABOUT IT

Cite five policy areas corresponding to the core values in Chapter 2.

What is the highest policy priority in the United States today? Explain.

What competing principles and policy issues are entailed in the First Amendment? Are gifts to political campaigns a form of free speech?

Why was the Fourteenth Amendment necessary? Explain "due process" and "equal protection" in legal and constitutional theory?

The law locks up the man or woman
Who steals the goose from off the common
But leaves the greater villain loose
Who steals the common from off the goose.

—Seventeenth-century poem (author unknown)

In Chapter 2 we identified five core values: security, prosperity, equality, liberty, and justice. Translating values into law and public policy is the essence of politics. In this chapter, four "P" words provide the analytical framework for evaluating just how well our own government processes collective values into corrective policies.

In democratic societies, dialogue and debates over public policy are an integral part of the process. The quality of the process is critical to the quality of product. When the tenor and tone of politics are debased by politicians and pundits with personal agendas, the public interest is undermined and democracy itself is placed in jeopardy. Indeed, some close observers argue that the U.S. Congress is dysfunctional. Norman Ornstein and Thomas Mann—widely respected scholars based at Washington think tanks philosophically opposed to each other on most issues—collaborated to write *The Broken Branch: How Congress Is Failing America and How to Get It Back on Track* (New York: Oxford University Press, 2006).

In 2011 and 2012, for example, the U.S. Senate had the votes to pass three jobs bills, the DREAM Act, campaign finance reform, and equal pay for equal work, but they all fell victim to the filibuster. The DREAM Act, aimed at legalizing the status of several million undocumented youth, received 52 Senate votes in 2007 and 55 votes in 2010 (when it also passed in the House). But it did not become law because under Senate rules it takes 60 votes (a three-fifths majority) to break a filibuster.

Although this chapter focuses on contemporary issues in the United States, many of the same problems arise in other democracies as well. Some are part of a pattern—a kind of postmodern syndrome—in high-consumption, affluent Western societies. Others are universal—climate change and pandemics, for example. A few, such as the majority-rule defying filibuster and the legacy of slavery, are uniquely American. Problems facing many non-Western countries (such as overpopulation, hunger, and illiteracy) are discussed elsewhere in this book (see Chapter 9).

THE PURSUIT OF SECURITY

Every independent state seeks to safeguard the security of its population and territory. The political philosopher Thomas Hobbes (1588–1679), for example, argued that safety from harm constituted the chief justification for a government's existence. For Aristotle, too, the first goal of political life was the protection of life itself.[1]

Security from Foreign Enemies

national security
Protection of a country from external and internal enemies.

In the aftermath of World War II, the high priority Washington gave to **national security** was (and still is) reflected in staggering levels of defense spending. Today, the United States accounts for roughly half of world arms expenditures; China, now America's chief rival for world leadership, follows at less than 10%

FIGURE 13.1 U.S. Military Spending vs. the World (in billions of U.S. dollars and % of world total). The United States alone accounts for nearly half the world's total military spending every year. By comparison, Europe, with a larger total GNP, spends only about 40% as much as the United States and a mere fifth of global military outlays. Russia, the world's other superpower only two decades ago, now spends one-tenth as much as the United States on defense and only one-fourth as much as the European Union.* Globally, military spending leveled off in 2011–2012 after thirteen years of continuous increases after 1998, including an annual average increase of 4.5% between 2001 and 2009. The United States, United Kingdom, France, Germany, India, and Brazil made military budget cuts in 2011, but arms expenditures rose markedly in China and Russia.

SOURCE: From "World Military Spending" by Anup Shah, Global Issues, March 1, 2009, available online at http://www.globalissues.org. Reprinted by permission of the author.

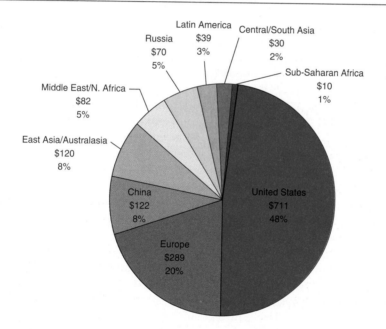

(Figure 13.1). Nearly two decades after the Cold War has ended, the United States still spends more on arms than the next fourteen countries combined.

From 1945 to 1991, foreign policy debate in the United States focused on the Soviet threat. Portraying the Soviet Union as an expansionist power bent on world domination, politicians of both major parties made support for ever-expanding arms expenditures into a virtual loyalty test. Today, the U.S. Department of Defense maintains hundreds of military bases overseas, plus thousands of military bases and facilities in the United States and its territories. In 2010, there were more than 1.4 million men and women in uniform. The Pentagon's natural

*For all practical purposes, Europe minus Russia.

constituents and biggest stakeholders are defense contractors who provide a vast array of arms and services to the military and profit from budget-busting military outlays.

In his 1961 farewell address to the nation, President Dwight D. Eisenhower, one of the most celebrated generals in U.S. history, warned of a growing "military-industrial complex":

> In the councils of government, we must guard against the acquisition of unwarranted influence, whether sought or unsought, by the military-industrial complex. The potential for the disastrous rise of misplaced power exists and will persist.
>
> We must never let the weight of this combination endanger our liberties or democratic processes. We should take nothing for granted. Only an alert and knowledgeable citizenry can compel the proper meshing of the huge industrial and military machinery of defense with our peaceful methods and goals, so that security and liberty may prosper together.[2]

President Eisenhower echoed James Madison who way back in 1795 observed:

> Of all the enemies to public liberty war is, perhaps, the most to be dreaded because it comprises and develops the germ of every other. War is the parent of armies; from these proceed debts and taxes…known instruments for bringing the many under the domination of the few.…No nation could preserve its freedom in the midst of continual warfare.[3]

With the collapse of the Soviet Union, the justification for Cold War levels of defense spending suddenly evaporated. President George H. W. Bush promised a "peace dividend" in the early 1990s.*

Defense budgets in the mid-1990s were a reflection of the "peace dividend" (scaled-down military commitments) when the Cold War ended in 1989–1991 (Figure 13.2). Thus, from the Cold War peak in 1986, Pentagon personnel—active, reserve, and civilian—declined by almost 20%. Active-duty military also underwent a 20% reduction, from 4.4 million to 3.5 million. But these figures are misleading. The Clinton administration contracted out to the private sector many services previously performed in-house (within the federal government); these outsourced services included military combat roles that in the past had been kept strictly under the executive branch's control.[4]

This practice was continued and extended under the Bush administration following the terrorist attacks of September 11, 2001. Congress and the country were back in the Cold War groove, ready to spend "whatever it takes" to make the world safe for democracy (see Figure 13.2). Gone was the euphoria of the 1990s. Gone, too, was the illusion of invulnerability. *They* (international terrorists) had attacked *us* in our own front yard.

Security from Enemies Within

This new climate of fear gave rise to a homeland security state similar to the national security state that came into being after World War II. Just as the National Security Act of 1947 had restructured the federal government to meet

---

*However, a behind-the-scenes group of conservative hard-liners, the so-called neocons, remained adamantly opposed to big defense cuts in the 1990s. When George W. Bush ran for president in 2000, members of this group, calling themselves the "Vulcans," served as Bush's team of foreign policy advisors.

FIGURE 13.2 Military Spending, 1981–2008. In 2004, total military spending in the United States was about $534 billion, including $87 billion for military operations in Iraq and Afghanistan passed by Congress and other arms-related expenditures. In that year "national security"—including the portion of the national debt attributable to past defense budgets—totaled more than $700 billion. In 2006, military spending rose to $626 billion; total spending for national security past, present, and future totaled about $800 billion. In 2008, defense spending alone climbed to $710 billion (an increase of 25% since 2004), and dropped to $612 billion in 2012. The United States still accounts for 41–42% of total world military expenditures; the second biggest military spender, the People's Republic of China, accounts for 8% of the total.

SOURCE: The author wishes to thank G. Ross Stephens, Professor emeritus at the University of Missouri–Kansas City, for supplying much of the information shown in this graph. Most of the data are based on official U.S. budget reports; some are taken from the *Stockholm International Peace Research (SIPRI) Yearbook 2012*.

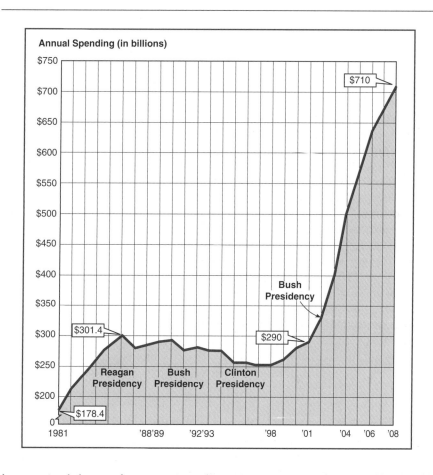

the perceived threat of communism, the USA Patriot Act of 2001 (officially the Uniting and Strengthening America by Providing Appropriate Tools Required to Intercept and Obstruct Terrorism Act) restructured the machinery of the state to fight international terrorism (see "Ideas and Politics").

WAR ON TERROR OR WAR ON THE CONSTITUTION?

The USA Patriot Act, passed by Congress in response to the September 11, 2001, attacks, was signed into law by President George W. Bush on October 26, 2001. In May 2011 and to the dismay of his liberal base, President Obama extended several key provisions of this act due to expire. Critics contend it severely erodes privacy rights long upheld by the U.S. Supreme Court, for the following reasons:

- **It expands the power of the federal government to conduct surveillance of U.S. citizens**. The government can monitor individual Web-surfing records, use wiretaps to monitor phone calls of persons "proximate" to the primary person being tapped, access Internet service provider records, and investigate anyone who participates in a political protest.

- **It is not limited to terrorism**. The government can add samples to DNA databases for anyone convicted of "any crime of violence." Wiretaps are now allowed for suspected violators of the Computer Fraud and Abuse Act, offering possibilities for government spying on any computer user.

- **Intelligence agencies can more easily spy on citizens**. Domestic eavesdropping powers under the existing Foreign Intelligence Surveillance Act (FISA) are broadened. The Patriot Act partially repeals legislation enacted in the 1970s that prohibited pervasive surveillance of citizens by U.S. agencies created to gather foreign intelligence.

- **It reduces government accountability**. Under the Patriot Act, the balance between the need for secrecy in government and the need for transparency (the public's right to know what the government is doing) is shifted sharply in favor of secrecy.

- **It authorizes the use of sneak-and-peek search warrants**. Such warrants authorize law-enforcement officers to enter private premises without the occupant's permission or knowledge and without informing the occupant that such a search was conducted. These warrants can be used against anyone suspected of a federal crime, including a misdemeanor.

The American Civil Liberties Union (ACLU) and other interest groups have pushed for a major overhaul of federal laws that allow the NSA and FBI to engage in warrantless domestic spying operations. The White House and Congress have turned a deaf ear.

In January 2012 journalist Chris Hedges and six other plaintiffs sued President Obama over Section 1021(b)(2) of the National Defense Authorization Act (NDAA), which authorizes the military to detain U.S. citizens indefinitely without due process. In September 2012, a federal district judge ruled for the plaintiffs and issued a permanent injunction—in effect, declaring the law unconstitutional, but an appeals court overturned the lower court ruling on October 3, 2012.

September 11 placed a premium on the role of government in protecting the lives and property of U.S. citizens from the enemies among us. But just how far does the Constitution allow the government to go?[5] Is terrorism a crime or an act of war?

Crime and Punishment   There is little agreement about what causes crime, what society ought to do about it, and whether some crimes ought to be decriminalized (the buying and selling or mere possession of marijuana, for example). What is not in dispute is that the long-term crime rate in the United States has risen steadily over the past fifty years (see "Ideas and Politics"). Why?

IDEAS AND POLITICS

DEFINING CRIME DOWN

Why has the United States accepted such a high level of crime? The late Daniel Patrick Moynihan (1927–2001), a U.S. senator and noted scholar, suggested one intriguing answer in a controversial article titled "Defining Deviancy Down: How We've Become Accustomed to Alarming Levels of Crime and Destructive Behavior."* Faced with a high crime rate, Moynihan contended, U.S. citizens have denied its importance by redefining (defining down) what they consider to be normal. Years ago, a high crime rate was understood to be a severe social pathology; now, it has become accepted as a normal condition of society about which little can be done.

Moynihan supplied a striking example. On February 14, 1929, four gangsters gunned down seven rivals in the infamous St. Valentine's Day Massacre. Moynihan observed that the nation was shocked, the event became a legend meriting two entries in the *World Book Encyclopedia*, and the "massacre" inspired an amendment to the Constitution that ended Prohibition (a policy thought to have caused much gang violence).

Moynihan noted that with illegal drug trafficking, this form of violence has returned, but, by contrast, "at a level that induces denial." Inured, U.S. adults now accept violence they once rejected as deviant and unacceptable. Sadly, concluded Moynihan, "Los Angeles has the equivalent of a St. Valentine's Day Massacre every weekend."

American Scholar, Winter 1993.

The End of Prohibition.

The late Daniel Patrick Moynihan (1927–2001), U.S. Senator and noted scholar.

According to some experts, crime is a social phenomenon, a reflection of personal frustration or alienation caused by poverty and neglect, racial discrimination, and unequal economic opportunity. Others stress the decline of the traditional family and community. Still others blame popular culture and the mass media.[6]

Some social critics would reduce crime by redefining it—for example, by decriminalizing prostitution. Advocates of this approach say it's illogical and unjust to punish "victimless" crimes. In this view, nobody is harmed when adults freely choose to engage in prostitution, for example. In 2003, the U.S. Supreme Court ruled state sodomy laws unconstitutional and unenforceable (*Lawrence v. Texas*)—a sign of the times and a deepening "values divide" along fault lines of religion, region, and sexual orientation.

Many violent crimes in the United States are drug related.[7] The problem may be clear but the solution is not. Drug addicts sometimes rob and steal to support a habit made artificially expensive by state action rather than market forces. Legalize drugs, some argue, and the price will drop dramatically, drug trafficking will become less profitable, and drug-related crime will decrease. That's what happened when the sale of alcohol was legalized. The Eighteenth Amendment and Volstead Act established nationwide Prohibition (making the manufacture, sale, transport, import, or export of alcoholic beverages a crime) that led to the rise of the mafia in the 1920s and 1930s. In December 1933, the Eighteenth Amendment was repealed, but by that time gangsters like Al "Scarface" Capone, Charles "Lucky" Luciano, and John Dillinger had written new pages in the history of organized crime in Chicago and other major cities.

Of course, times have change. Alcohol is legal everywhere now, but it is regulated in various ways in the fifty states. Marijuana, however, is a different story.

Why Not Pot?

Opponents of legalization fear that legalizing marijuana would increase the number of addicts and corrode the moral standards of the community. Perhaps, but historical evidence and recent experience demonstrate clearly that criminalizing a popular social activity such as drinking or smoking pot creates a highly lucrative, unregulated black market in which violence-prone thugs often thrive and places a heavy burden on law enforcement and the penal system without solving the problem.

Between 1980 and the mid-1990s, the U.S. prison population more than tripled, due in large part to a nationwide crackdown on illegal drugs, and rose from 1.1 million in 1990 to 1.6 million in 2010. (Counting the local jail population, the total number of inmates reached a record 2 million in 2002.) Meanwhile, the use of marijuana and other illegal substances has continued to trend upward, as has the burgeoning prison population.

The United States had the world's highest rate of imprisonment, with 743 persons per 100,000 incarcerated in 2011-2012. With only 4.5% of world population, the United States accounts for 23% of all prison inmates. California, Texas, and Florida lead the states in the rate of imprisonment, but the federal government is by far the nation's biggest jailer.

Drug laws and drug-related crimes account for a major share of all criminal trials and convictions in the United States. About half of all inmates in federal prisons are there for drug-related crimes. The social and economic costs of this zero-tolerance policy have been very high, by any measure, but have failed to produce the promised results.

Decriminalization of drugs and prostitution is extremely controversial in the United States, but the Netherlands has already done it. In the capital city of Amsterdam, "soft drugs" (including marijuana) and prostitution are allowed, but only in restricted areas under no-nonsense police supervision and control. Prostitutes are required to have frequent medical checkups, and social problems linked to illegal drug trafficking have been alleviated.

But the times are changing. Colorado began licensing medical marijuana dispensaries in 2010; a year later there were more than 400 marijuana businesses in Denver alone. In 2012, voters in Colorado, Washington, and Oregon were given the chance to legalize marijuana for recreational use by adults. Polls showed that Colorado's Amendment 64 legalizing recreational marijuana use for adults age 21 and older enjoyed the support of more than 60% of the voters. Why? A compelling argument for many voters is one most advocates overlook: tax revenue. If it's legal and transactions take place in the open, marijuana (like liquor and gasoline) can be taxed. Voters in Colorado and Washington approved the ballot initiative, but it failed by a large margin (went up in smoke?) in Oregon.

Guns "R" Us

In January 2011, a tragic shooting in a shopping mall in Tucson, Arizona, refocused national attention on the problem of gun control (Figure 13.3).

April 3, 2009	Immigration services center in Binghamton, New York: 13 dead plus gunman Jiverly Wong.
November 5, 2009	Soldier Readiness Processing Center at Fort Hood, Texas: 13 killed by Nidal Malik Hasan.
April 16, 2008	Virginia Tech campus, Blacksburg, Virginia: 32 dead plus gunman Seung Hui Cho.
April 20, 1999	Columbine High School in Littleton, Colorado: 13 dead plus gunmen, students Eric Harris and Dylan Klebold.
October 16, 1991	Luby's Cafeteria in Killeen, Texas: 23 dead plus gunman George Hennard.
August 20, 1986	Post office in Edmond, Oklahoma: 14 dead plus gunman Patrick Sherrill.
July 18, 1984	McDonald's restaurant in San Ysidro, California: 21 dead plus gunman James Oliver Huberty.
August 1, 1966	University of Texas at Austin: 16 dead plus gunman Charles Whitman.
September 6, 1946	Camden, New Jersey: 13 killed by Howard Unruh.

FIGURE 13.3   The Terrorists Within. Other worst mass shootings in the United States since World War II.

© CENGAGE LEARNING

The attack by a 22-year-old killer brandishing a 9mm Glock pistol with a 33-round magazine resulted in the death of six people, including a 9-year-old girl, and left Congresswoman Gabrielle Giffords in critical condition with a gunshot wound to the head at point blank range. In July 2012 at a midnight showing of *Batman 3* ("The Dark Knight Rises") in Aurora, Colorado, a lone gunman set off tear gas grenades and sprayed the theater with gunfire, killing twelve movie-goers and wounding fifty-eight, in the bloodiest mass shooting in U.S. history. Four months later in December 2012 another mass shooting occurred, this time at an elementary school in Newtown, Connecticut. The shooter killed twenty children and six adults and then committed suicide.

In the run-up to the November 2012 election, the presidential candidates of the two major parties, incumbent Obama and the challenger Romney, avoided the issue—one indication of the extent to which "gun control" has become a litmus test of freedom in the eyes of many Americans. After the election, however, President Obama came out strongly in favor of an assault weapons ban—in other words "gun control." Despite a rising call for action, and opinion polls showing the public solidly in favor of restricting the sale of assault weapons and high-capacity magazines, Congress dithered, holding hearings and making speeches, but putting off any definitive changes in the gun laws that would antagonize constituents or risk incurring the wrath of the NRA. Nonetheless, despite overwhelming public support for tightening gun control laws, the U.S. Senate voted down expanded background checks in April 2013.

The United States is the only postindustrial society in which private ownership of handguns is considered normal and private arsenals are not unusual. In the United States, the right to bear arms is guaranteed by the Second Amendment. Some 40% of households report having a gun (or guns), compared with only 4.7% in the United Kingdom and a mere 2% in the Netherlands. Other countries vary considerably. Among the countries that make these figures publicly available, not one comes close to U.S. levels (Table 13.1). Current estimates put the number of private firearms in the United States at 300,000,000 or close to 90 per 100 residents.

Changing gun laws to restrict access is controversial. Gun control activists argue that guns contribute to violent crime and point out that the murder rate in the United States is the highest in the Western world. Moreover, they argue, the Second Amendment says nothing about the right of individuals to own semi-automatic weapons with large-capacity magazines (such weapons did not exist when the Constitution and Bill of Rights were drafted). Nor does it say anything about the right of an individual to bear arms of any kind. Rather, it says "a well-regulated militia being necessary to the security of a free state, the right of the people to keep and bear arms shall not be infringed." Until the Reagan Revolution of 1980s, it was generally understood that the Second Amendment protected the right of state militias, not individuals, the right to bear arms. Then Chief Justice Warren Burger scoffed at this interpretation, calling it "a fraud."

Opponents of gun control, led by the National Rifle Association, began to push hard for the "individual-rights" doctrine in the late 1970s. The gun enthusiasts and the NRA point out that most gun owners have never committed a crime; that most private firearms are used for hunting, recreational shooting,

TABLE 13.1   **Armed Households 1992–1994** (% with guns in selected countries)*

Australia	19%
Belgium	16%
Canada	29%
France	22%
Italy	16%
Netherlands	1.9%
New Zealand	22%
Norway	32%
Spain	13%
Sweden	15%
Switzerland	27%
United States	40%

*Research note: Data of this kind is difficult to obtain and even more difficult to verify; data on gun ownership in most non-Western (and even some European countries) is simply not available.
SOURCE: United Nations Office on Drugs and Crime. From a 1992–1994 survey.

and home defense; and that the non-gun murder rate in the United States is higher than the total murder rate in many European countries.

But facts are stubborn, and United States, with the sole exception of Turkey, is by far the most violent major OECD* country, with a homicide rate much higher than most societies at a comparable stage of political and economic development. The gun culture in the United States not only correlates positively with a high homicide rate, it also correlates with an incarceration rate about seven times higher than the median rate for other OECD countries.

Social Security

When Americans think of social security, they think of the mandatory federal pension program established in 1935: the concept of social security is narrowly defined and limited. Contrastingly, Europeans take it for granted that the state has an obligation to provide a cradle-to-the-grave social safety net for all its citizens. Oddly enough, voters and taxpayers in the United States have long been staunchly opposed to a European-style "welfare state" or anything that smacks of "socialism."

What is the state's proper role in helping members of society in need? Food stamps, farm subsidies, pensions, health and unemployment benefits, and student aid are all forms of public assistance. In general, Americans disdain "welfare" (defined as any subsidies or benefits for which they themselves are not eligible) on the grounds that "giveaway" programs reward lazy people.

---

*OECD is the acronym for the Organization for Economic Cooperation and Development, which comprises thirty-four of the world's wealthiest countries.

Welfare reform was a big issue in the 1990s, when the federal government gave states more authority (and flexibility) to require welfare recipients to perform public service (called "workfare").

Social Security and Medicare are by far the biggest and most expensive public assistance programs in the United States. These are *compulsory* insurance programs, however, not "welfare." U.S. workers are required by law to pay into the Social Security pension fund until they retire (normally around age 65). Payouts from the fund are called **entitlements**, not to be confused with subsidies—government payments to a particular industry or sector (agriculture, for example) deemed vital to the economy. So-called entitlements are politically sensitive, not least because senior citizens typically turn out to vote in large numbers.

In the 2012 election, entitlements were at the center of a bitter political debate over how to cut deficit spending and balance the federal budget. Republicans insisted it be done by cutting social spending (Social Security, Medicare, and Medicaid); Democrats wanted to extend the Bush tax cuts for households making less than $250,000. So vitriolic was the fight that in the weeks after the election Republican leaders in Congress vowed to let the country go over a "fiscal cliff" (triggering automatic tax hikes and across-the-board spending cuts of 10%) if President Obama did not back down.

Social Security made monthly remittances to more than 35 million retirees in 2011, and Medicare provided health benefits to some 48 million people age 65 and above or disabled. Both programs have grown dramatically in recent decades and are projected to rise even faster in the future. In 2011, Social Security and Medicare distributions (payments to beneficiaries) totaled more than $1.2 trillion, accounting for 36% of the federal budget.[8] (Medicare costs rose sharply after Congress approved a prescription drug benefit in 2003.)

Social Security and Medicare expenditures are rising faster than projected revenues (Figure 13.4); at present depletion rates and without changes, the Social Security trust fund will be empty by 2037. One reason is that U.S. adults are living longer, making the programs more expensive. An even bigger reason is the large number of people born in the years immediately following World War II (the "baby boomers"), who have now reached retirement age and are eligible to draw monthly benefits.

Medicare has been hit hard by the demographic tidal wave, as well as escalating health care costs. When it was established in 1965, there were 5.5 people paying money into Medicare for each recipient drawing money out. Since then, the ratio has dropped to about 3 to 1 and is still falling. Since 1980, Medicare has been the fastest-growing federal program. At President George W. Bush's urging, Congress passed a controversial law in 2003 adding a prescription drug plan to Medicare at a projected long-term cost of as much as $8 trillion.[9] The federal government now calculates Medicare will run out of money by 2024.

What happened to the Social Security trust fund? When the federal government spends more than it raises in taxes and other revenues, it borrows money to cover the shortfall. Since the 1980s, the Treasury has quietly "borrowed" huge sums of money every year from Social Security. This transaction is conveniently left off the federal balance sheet—if the government tells taxpayers the federal budget deficit in any given year is, say, $1.3 trillion (the official figure for 2011),

entitlements
Federal- and state-provided benefits in the United States such as Social Security and Medicare funded by mandatory tax contributions; such benefits become a right, rather than a privilege, in the public mind because recipients typically pay into the system for many years before they are eligible to take anything out.

Social Security

	Number of years until depleted	Year depleted	Year change in projected depletion
	0 10 20 30		
1999		2034	
2000		2037	3
2001		2038	1
2002		2041	3
2003		2042	1
2004		2042	0
2005		2041	−1
2006		2040	−1
2007		2041	1
2008		2041	0
2009		2037	−4

Medicare

	Number of years until depleted	Year depleted	Year change in projected depletion
	0 10 20 30		
1999		2015	
2000		2025	10
2001		2029	4
2002		2030	1
2003		2026	−4
2004		2019	−7
2005		2020	1
2006		2018	−2
2007		2019	1
2008		2019	0
2009		2017	−2

FIGURE 13.4   Failing Health: Social Security and Medicare. At current rates, Social Security funds will run out in 2037, and the Medicare cash drawer will be empty in eight years.

SOURCE: Office of the Chief Actuary, Social Security Administration, 2009.

that figure—though an all-time record amount—*excludes* hundreds of billions borrowed from the Social Security cash drawer (these borrowings totaled $2.7 trillion in 2011). Thus, using standard accounting rules, the real deficit in 2005, for example, was $760 billion—more than double the official figure of $318 billion.[10]

The gross mismanagement of Social Security funds dates back to the start of the Reagan era in the early 1980s. In 1983, Congress "voted to raise Social Security taxes, changing it from a pay-as-you-go system to one in which people were required to pay 50 percent more than the retirement and disability program's immediate costs, to build a trust fund to pay benefits more than three decades into the future."[11]

Emissions Trading Scheme (ETS)
In the European Union, part of an antipollution drive aimed at significantly reducing Europe's carbon footprint by 2020 by assigning carbon-emission allowances to industries and factories and creating a carbon exchange, or a market where "clean" companies (ones that do not use their full allowances) can sell the credits they accumulate by not polluting to "dirty" companies (ones that exceed their allowances).

Kyoto Protocol
Countries that ratify this treaty, which went into effect in 2005, agree to cut emissions of carbon dioxide and five other greenhouse gases or to engage in emissions trading if they exceed a certain cap; the United States signed it under President Bill Clinton, but President George W. Bush renounced it shortly after taking office in 2001 and President Barack Obama, who was sympathetic to the Kyoto pact as a candidate, in office has shown little inclination to push for a new global climate-change treaty.

So far, partisan politics in the nation's Capitol has thwarted all efforts to place Medicare and Medicaid on solid, long-term financial footing. Doing so will necessitate unpopular changes: later retirement, less generous cost-of-living adjustments, payroll tax increases; not doing so will make it impossible to deal with the chronic federal deficit and risk a Greek-style debt crisis that would have disastrous consequences for the United States and for the global economy.

Security and the Environment

Hazards caused by humans can also endanger the health and safety of the public. Mandatory clean air standards, environmental impact statements, increasingly stringent waste disposal requirements, and vigorous recycling efforts all seek to protect the environment. Most scientists now agree global warming is a major threat to the security of the planet (and therefore to the life forms that inhabit it) in the coming century. Greenhouse gas (GHG) emissions, mainly from automobiles and coal-fired power plants, trap heat in the earth's atmosphere, causing climate change. The likely consequences, say the experts, are that glaciers will continue to melt at an accelerating rate, sea levels will rise, and ocean currents will be altered and degraded.

The European Union has adopted an **Emission Trading Scheme** (ETS) as part of a larger set of policy goals aimed at significantly reducing Europe's "carbon footprint" by 2020. In one of his first acts as president, George W. Bush announced that he was taking the United States out of the **Kyoto Protocol**

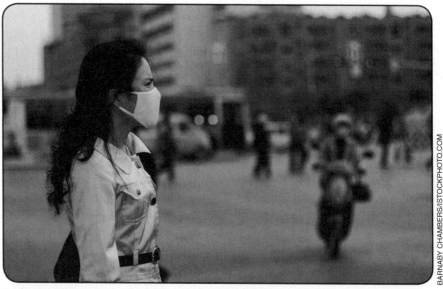

China and India are the two most populous countries and two of the fast-growing economies in the world. As such, they are the two leading examples of Asia's rapid rise in the global economy. But the price of progress in an overpopulated world comes very high. It creates massive problems of its own, which can easily overwhelm the resources and capabilities of governments. Here, pedestrians in one of China's many burgeoning cities with millions of migrants from poor rural areas are wearing masks in thick smog that makes breathing a health hazard.

THE KYOTO PROTOCOL AND CLIMATE CHANGE

The Kyoto Protocol is an addendum to the UN Framework Convention on Climate Change (UNFCCC). Countries that ratify this protocol agree to cut emissions of carbon dioxide and five other greenhouse gases or to engage in emissions trading if they exceed a certain cap. The protocol, which went into effect in 2005, now covers some 160 countries and more than 55% of greenhouse gas (GHG) emissions worldwide. The United States has signed, but not ratified, the agreement. After Australia embraced it toward the end of 2007, the United States was more isolated than ever. Upon taking office in 2009, President Obama pledged U.S. support for global efforts to curb climate change, but his critics say he has waffled on the issue and relegated it to the back burner.

Under Kyoto, developed countries are obligated to reduce GHG emissions to an average of 5% below 1990 levels by 2008–2012. For many countries, including EU member-states, meeting this goal means cutting to roughly 15% below 2008 GHG emissions levels. The Kyoto caps expire in 2013.

Parties to the UNFCCC agreed to a set of "common but differentiated responsibilities." The largest share of GHG emissions has originated in developed countries, and per capita emissions in developing countries were relatively low in the 1990s (and still are). China, India, and other developing countries were exempted from the Kyoto Protocol caps because, at least until recently, they have not been major contributors to GHG emissions nor, therefore, to past and present climate change. But critics of Kyoto argue that climate change is, above all, a future threat, and that developing countries—especially China and India—will be major contributors in the twenty-first century. In addition, unless developing countries are brought into the global warming tent, polluting industries in developed countries will simply move to the Third World, resulting in little or no net reduction in carbon pollution.

As a presidential candidate in 2008, Barack Obama pledged to renew U.S. leadership in the fight against global warming. But the issue of climate change was derailed by the global banking crisis after 2008. In the 2012 presidential debates, climate change did not get so much as a nod from either candidate.

Ironically, the devastating impact of Hurricane Sandy put climate change back on the national agenda just days before the election. But in his election-night victory speech, President Obama said his second-term goals were "reducing our deficit, reforming our tax code, fixing our immigration system, freeing ourselves from foreign oil." Climate change was mentioned only in a passing reference to "the destructive power of a warming planet." Having still not ratified the Kyoto treaty, the United States is the only holdout among the world's major countries.

(see "Landmarks in History"), which had been signed by his predecessor, Bill Clinton. The Bush White House favored corporate oil and energy interests over the environment and was generally at odds with the green movement, but the Obama administration has pledged cooperation with the global community to combat climate change.

Critics argue rightly that the United States alone cannot make a dent in the problem; unless China, India, and other Third World countries take action to cut GHG emissions, there is not much the United States can do to curb global

sustainable growth
A concept popular among environmentalists and liberal economists that emphasizes the need for economic strategies that take account of the high-cost and long-term impact on the environment (including global warming) of economic policies aimed at profit-maximization, current consumption, and the like.

warming. Advocates of **sustainable growth** point out that the United States ranks first in the world in total volume of GHG emissions. However, China and India both outrank the United States in emissions intensities (metric tons of carbon equivalent per million dollars of economic output), and energy-related carbon emissions increased not only in the United States, but also in six of the nine biggest polluting countries in recent decades.[12] One sign of the growing alarm over the dangers posed by global warming: in 2005, researchers at Yale and Columbia universities, in collaboration with the World Economic Forum and the European Union, published an Environmental Sustainability Index that ranked countries using a range of scientific indicators—the United States ranked forty-fifth, behind Japan, Botswana, Bhutan, and most of Western Europe.[13]

Environmentalists, naturalists, and conservationists around the world also seek to protect endangered species of wildlife, to prevent clear-cutting of tropical rain forests (sometimes called slash-and-burn agriculture), and to curb the use of deep-sea fishing nets, among other commercial fishing activities such as whaling. Although the 2008 presidential election pointed to growing public support for environmental action, the green movement in the United States still pales in comparison to Europe's. Meanwhile, the global recession that started with the meltdown on Wall Street in August 2008 is proving to be the biggest immediate threat to coordinated action on climate change, deflecting attention, derailing efforts, and dampening public enthusiasm for environmentalism on both sides of the Atlantic.

Security from One's Own Actions

Many states have adopted laws requiring motorists to wear seatbelts, motorcyclists to wear safety helmets, and small children to be strapped into special infant seats in cars. Examples of local, state, and federal attempts to legislate morality include Prohibition, pornography, and prostitution. Libertarians, among others, argue that the state has no right to interfere in citizens' private lives.

THE PURSUIT OF PROSPERITY

James Madison famously labeled the United States a commercial republic—salient characteristics include self-reliance, upward mobility, and the profit motive. There is a close link between the political philosophy of Madison, the nation's fourth president and a founding father, and Madison Avenue, a symbol of U.S. capitalism.[14]

The Founders launched a political experiment long championed by great thinkers like Locke and Montesquieu. The idea was compelling: A republic that encouraged entrepreneurship and innovation, protected private property, and rewarded hard work would generate great wealth, a burgeoning middle class, and a robust economy.

During the nineteenth century, the Industrial Revolution ushered in modern capitalism—the private ownership, manufacture, and distribution of goods and services free of heavy-handed state intervention or regulation. In the early twentieth century, the federal government enacted new laws to curb monopolies and encourage competition. The Great Depression of the 1930s witnessed a sudden expansion of the state's role in the economy. That legacy has coexisted with an aversion to state intervention and "welfare" ever since.

Beginning in the 1980s, a conservative backlash—often called the Reagan Revolution—swept the country. Reagan—and a decade later, Republican House Speaker Newt Gingrich—suggested government had gone too far down the road to becoming a "welfare state" (never mind that federal budget deficits soared to record heights during the Reagan presidency). In fact, however, the level of state intervention and social spending was still far below that found in most Western democracies.

The prosperity of the 1990s and early 2000s made many in the United States wealthy—at least on paper—as the stock market hit historic highs and the number of people investing in it through mutual and pension funds rose dramatically. Much of that paper wealth temporarily shrank in the bear market of 2001–2003 and then disappeared in the recession of 2008–2009, which saw the sharpest stock price declines since the 1930s.

Budget Deficits and the National Debt

Total federal spending as a share of gross domestic product (GDP) increased from about 17% in the mid-1960s to 24% in 1983, following the massive Reagan tax cut of 1981, dropped in the 1990s but returned to the Reagan-era levels under President George W. Bush (see "Ideas and Politics"). The **federal budget deficit** rose sharply in the 1980s and again after 9/11. In 2001, annual interest payments on the national debt amounted to $360 billion; in 2008, the last year of the Bush-Cheney administration, interest payments were more than $451 billion—a

federal budget deficit
In the United States, the difference between federal revenues and federal expenditures in a given year; the national debt is the cumulative sum of budget deficits over many years.

Balanced Budget Act of 1997
Passed by Congress in 1997, this historic measure mandated a balanced federal budget by 2001 but was ironically undone in that very year by the events of 9/11.

THE ILL-FATED BALANCED BUDGET ACT OF 1997

Between 1993 and 2000, President Bill Clinton, a Democrat, and the Republican-controlled Congress addressed the problems posed by the mushrooming national debt. As a consequence, budget deficits declined sharply in the 1990s. Later in the decade, amid a generally robust economy, Democrats and Republicans joined forces in the Congress to pass the historic **Balanced Budget Act of 1997**, which mandated a balanced federal budget by 2001. But tax revenues increased faster than expected due to the strong economy, resulting in budget surpluses—using official accounting rules—earlier than expected or required by law. (In fact, the only real surplus, when borrowing from the Social Security trust fund is factored in, was in 2001.)

All that changed suddenly after September 11, 2001, when Congress under President Bush voted huge sums for cleanup and reconstruction efforts in New York City, bailing out hard-hit airlines (among others), and prosecuting the "war" against international terrorism at home and abroad. The budget surplus quickly vanished, as did all talk of a balanced budget. At the same time, the Bush administration pushed hard for across-the-board tax cuts, which Congress approved.

Then came the financial crisis of 2008 followed by a deep recession, prompting President Obama to launch a massive **economic stimulus** program resulting in the nation's first trillion-dollar budget deficit. In 2009, the federal deficit hit $1.4 trillion and fell to $1.3 trillion a year during Obama's first term. Massive deficits and mounting debt, however, did not deter Congress and the White House from extending the Bush tax cuts for millionaires and billionaires.

economic stimulus
A fiscal tool of government designed to bolster a weak economy and create jobs via public works projects and deficit spending.

record that still stands. (Vice President Dick Cheney played a major role in shaping policy behind the scenes when George W. Bush was president.)

The U.S. federal budget for 2010—the first Obama budget—was about $3.4 trillion. In the fall of 2012 the national debt—the sum of accumulated annual federal deficits—had climbed to more than $16 trillion, rising at a rate of more than $4 billion a day. Each citizen's share came to around $51,000. The national debt—that is, the accumulated annual federal budget deficits—hit a record in 2008 and climbed above 100% of GDP in 2012—a benchmark to be sure but not one to celebrate (it stood at 31% in 1975).

In the United States *private* debt levels are also very high. One consequence of high debt levels combined with chronic balance of payments (current account) deficits is a steady decline in the value of the dollar vis-à-vis other convertible currencies, especially the euro. The euro–dollar exchange rate hit a peak ($1.58) in July 2008 before falling somewhat later in the year, but the dollar did not strengthen appreciably against the euro in 2010 despite the euro crisis triggered by fears that Greece's government was about to default on its sovereign debt.

Who's to blame for the federal government's chronic overspending depends on whom you ask. Democrats and Republicans blame each other, not surprisingly, but both major political parties are guilty. (If you want to know more about the national debt and Obama's efforts to revive the economy, use an Internet search engine and look up "Obama by the Numbers" an article by Mark Warren and Richard Dorment with lots of graphs and charts that appeared in *Esquire* magazine in October 2012.)

Losing Interest: The National Debt

The national debt has serious consequences that will likely have a greater impact on future generations than on the generations that have created it. By 2007, as we've seen, the federal government had "borrowed" more than $2 trillion from the Social Security trust fund. The government replaces the money by selling treasury bonds (that is, by borrowing more), but it conveniently omits these funds from the figure it calls Debt Held by the Public (DHP). That accounting sleight-of-hand makes the national debt look a lot smaller than it actually is, but of course the government is obligated to pay interest—a lot of interest—on the *entire* debt. Interest on the debt is now the third-largest line-item expenditure in the federal budget (Social Security/Medicare and defense are first and second).

The Tax Burden: Who Pays What, When, and How?

Until recently, most U.S. citizens shared three mutually reinforcing aversions: to socialism, to state ownership, and to high taxes. Of these, tax aversion is the oldest.

Taxes are a perennial issue. One easy way for a presidential candidate to win votes is to promise tax cuts, as did both Ronald Reagan and George W. Bush in making successful bids for the White House. In 1988, George H. W. Bush made a campaign promise not to raise taxes and was elected; four years later, he was turned out of office after going back on that promise. In the 2008 campaign, Barack Obama pledged to keep the Bush tax cuts except for those making more than $250,000 a year; as president, he succumbed to pressure by Republicans in Congress to accept an extension of the Bush cuts for all, including the richest of the rich.

Few political issues in the United States are inherently more complex—or surrounded by more deliberate obfuscation and statistical subterfuge—than taxes.

Revelations of corporate fraud, greed, and stock swindles following the 2008 Wall Street meltdown caused a furor and fueled a short-lived debate over tax fairness.

Tax loopholes allowing the super-rich to avoid paying millions of dollars in income tax every year have been shifting the overall tax burden downward since the early 1980s. A slogan commonly attributed to Benjamin Franklin says the two things nobody can avoid are death and taxes, but some of the richest people in the United States *do* manage to avoid taxes. What's more, it's perfectly legal in most cases.

Taxes for the vast majority of middle-class taxpayers rose during the 1990s, while the tax burden on the super-rich fell.[15] In the words of David Cay Johnston, a Pulitzer Prize-winning journalist who covers taxes for the *New York Times*:

> [In 1997] Congress passed what its sponsors promoted as a tax cut for the middle class and especially for families with children. Buried in that law were many tax breaks for the rich, some subtle and some huge, notably a sharp reduction in the tax rate on long-term capital gains, the source of two-thirds of the incomes of the top 400.[16]

Both major political parties are to blame. The trend toward downloading the tax burden began in the 1980s, when Ronald Reagan (a Republican) was president but the Democrats controlled the Congress, and accelerated in the 1990s, when Democrat Bill Clinton was president (but Republicans were in the majority). The result of this bipartisan failure at tax reform—which has made it steadily more unfair to the middle class—is that "wealth in America today is more highly concentrated than at any time since 1929." Astonishingly, "the richest 1 percent of Americans [own] almost half of the stocks, bonds, cash, and other financial assets in the country. The richest 15 percent control nearly *all* of the financial assets."[17]

According to a Federal Reserve survey in 2012, the net worth of a median American family fell almost 40% from 2007 to 2010 (from $126,400 to $77,300). Collapsing real estate values accounted for most of that loss. Median family income in 2010 was about the same as in the mid-1990s (but, of course, indebtedness and prices of everything from groceries to gasoline were much higher).

The beneficiaries of the tax bonanza for the rich include many members of Congress, a body that collectively posted a 16% gain on stocks alone during the steep market downturn in 2008–2009. Roughly half of all members of Congress are millionaires compared to 1.0% of the population at large—eight are multimillionaires with stock portfolios valued above 100 million dollars.[18]

That most voters don't understand tax issues is hardly surprising. President Franklin Roosevelt once said the federal tax code "might as well have been written in a foreign language." The federal income tax rules are a taxpayer's nightmare, but an accounting firm's dream come true.

Attempts at "tax simplification" have failed. In 1986, the U.S. Congress passed a law directing the IRS to fix the system. A few years later, a "hypothetical" tax return listing family income and expenses was sent to fifty tax experts. The result was fifty different "bottom lines" ranging from a tax bill of $12,500 to nearly $36,000.[19] Clearly, the Byzantine tax code is too complicated, but that's not the only—or worst—thing critics say is wrong with it (Figure 13.5).

FIGURE 13.5   Business Tax. The tax burden in the United States is lower than in most developed countries, but critics point out that U.S. taxpayers do not get key benefits, such as national health insurance, that taxpayers in most other developed countries receive. Critics also point out that corporations pay a relatively small portion of the total tax bill, smaller by far than they did in the first decade after World War II. Big business pays a lot less of the total tax bill than in 1950. Guess who pays a lot more? If you guessed the middle class and lower-income wage earners, you're right on the money.
SOURCE: OMB

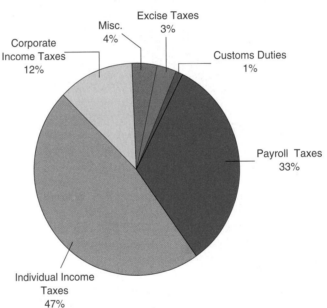

Projected Tax Revenues (FY 2013)

Misc. 4%
Excise Taxes 3%
Corporate Income Taxes 12%
Customs Duties 1%
Payroll Taxes 33%
Individual Income Taxes 47%

The U.S. tax system favors the rich over the middle class and poor. Due to various loopholes and tax shelters, the *actual* taxes its wealthiest citizens pay are low in comparison with other industrial democracies. Sales taxes hit the middle class much harder than the rich. If X and Y pay the exact same amount of sales tax in a year, but X earns 100 times more than Y, then X pays far less in sales tax than Y in proportion to income. For this basic reason, sales taxes are regressive.

Throughout the fifty states, sales taxes are common; in Europe, a *value added tax* (VAT) is the principal form of taxation. Unlike a sales tax, VAT is assessed at every stage in the manufacture and sale of a product—in this manner, the total tax "take" is built into the price of a finished product and passed along to

FIGURE 13.6   Federal Revenues by Source, Fiscal Year 2013. Individual income and payroll (Social Security) taxes together account for more than 80% of the U.S. government's annual revenues. Corporations pay only 13%. Today, corporations with powerful Washington lobbies get big tax breaks, and middle-class taxpayers foot the bill for both big business and big government.

SOURCE: The National Priorities Project. http://nationalpriorities.org/en/budget-basics/federal-budget-101/revenues/.

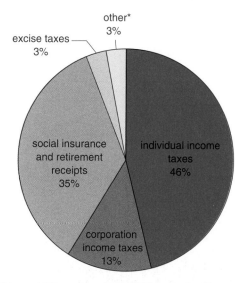

*Estate and gift taxes (1%), custom duties (1%), and miscellaneous receipts (1%).

the consumer. VAT rates among the twenty-seven countries of the EU range from 15 to 25%, but a high percentage of tax revenues are recycled into social welfare programs. By contrast, sales taxes in the United States are rarely more than 6%; in Minnesota, for example, groceries are exempt (eating in restaurants, however, is not), and in New Jersey, there is no sales tax on clothing.

Just under 60% of all federal revenue in the United States comes from personal and corporate income taxes, but the tax burden on individuals is far heavier than on corporations. In fact, corporate income tax amounts to only about 12% of federal revenues today, a dramatic decline from the 1950s and 1960s, when it stood at about 25% (Figure 13.6). (And don't be fooled by the *maximum* corporate tax rate of 39.2%—what pro-business interests like to trumpet as the "highest in the world"—corporations actually paid only about 12% in 2012, thanks to exemptions and a long litany of loopholes in the tax code; in fact, the ten richest U.S. corporations paid an average rate of only 9% in 2011.) Meanwhile, Social Security payroll taxes were the fastest-growing source of federal revenue (about one-third of the total).

TABLE 13.2   Tax Revenue as a Percentage of GDP by Country in 2013

Country	Tax Revenues (% of GDP)
India	07.4
Pakistan	10.1
United States	24.8
Australia	20.9
Japan	28.8
Switzerland	29.8
Canada	31.0
Spain	31.7
Poland	31.8
United Kingdom	35.0
Germany	36.3
EU27	40.0
Italy	43.0
France	42.9
Sweden	45.8
Denmark	48.2

SOURCE: "2013 Index of Economic Freedom" The Heritage Foundation at http://www.heritage.org/index/explore?view=by-variables and Eurostat at http://epp.eurostat.ec.europa.eu/statistics_explained/index.php/Tax_revenue_statistics.

U.S. taxpayers tend to think taxes are too high, yet the United States has low tax rates relative to other developed countries, especially the Scandinavian countries, but also France, the Netherlands, Germany, and the United Kingdom (Table 13.2). But, as noted earlier, in Europe income is widely redistributed through cradle-to-grave benefits to all citizens. In the United States, the federal income tax, instituted shortly before World War I, has become less and less progressive (or redistributive) since the early 1970s.

Comparisons between taxes and benefits in the United States and Europe raise two fundamental questions. First, is the tax system fair? Second, what do citizens actually get in return for the taxes they pay? Answering these questions necessitates a closer look at public policy in such areas as health and education.

Educational Malaise

We tend to measure the value of education primarily in monetary terms—how much more the average college graduate earns over a lifetime than someone with only a high school diploma. We want to know the practical value of a particular course, major, or degree, and implicitly we reject the inherent value of an education—knowledge for its own sake. "What can you do with a History major?" "There are no jobs for Philosophy majors." These are the kinds of questions and comments college students hear frequently if they are not pursuing a course of study that leads to a definite profession or occupation—prelaw, premed, nursing, accounting, and the like.

Critics frequently talk about the "crisis in education." In some schools, guns, drugs, and gangs endanger students and teachers alike. Declining college entrance examination scores, studies showing that our students score worse on mathematical tests than comparable European and Asian students, and high failure rates on elementary-level literacy tests administered to job applicants by many large corporations all testify to the seriousness of the problem. Studies have long shown that U.S. high school students consistently score lower than students in many other countries at a comparable level of development in English, mathematics, science, history, geography, or civics—even though the public schools are well funded.[20]

Grade inflation is widely recognized as a pervasive and corrosive force in education at all levels. Critics charge that teachers pamper students more and more and expect less and less. U.S. business spends billions of dollars every year training students in skills they should have learned in school. Who is to blame and what is to be done?

Until passage of the Elementary and Secondary Education Act of 1965 (ESEA), control of education had fallen primarily to the states. The 1965 law enhanced the role of the federal government. In 2001, Congress passed the No Child Left Behind Act (NCLB), which requires schools across the nation to administer standardized proficiency tests in reading and math and to improve on a yearly basis or face penalties. This law ties federal funding for public schools to compliance with federal educational policy, thus redefining—and greatly expanding—the federal role.

States and municipalities must now meet academic performance standards set by the federal government and measured by standardized tests administered yearly nationwide. Critics say NCLB was ill conceived from the start; that it forces teachers to change what and how they teach; that it is yet another example of the federal government burdening financially hard-pressed state governments and public schools with unfunded mandates; and that the requirements are unrealistic. They also point out that this movement toward frequent standardized testing (the magic word is "assessment"), which is now universally hated by teachers, was invented in Texas, where (they say) the educational system is an anomaly: highly state-controlled despite the fact that Texans are famously obsessed with private rights and fiercely opposed to big government.[21]

Although the Constitution prohibits Congress from making laws that would either establish religion or restrict its free exercise, many social conservatives favor a voucher system. Under such a system, parents with school-age children would first get money (vouchers) from the state, then freely choose a school—any accredited school (public, private, or parochial). Champions of free choice argue that competition would force all schools to excel or face extinction. Opponents argue that public support for private schools violates the First Amendment separation of church and state, discriminates against the poor and minorities, and perpetuates racial segregation.

In recent years, the idea of charter schools has gained ground in many states. As nonsectarian institutions independent of local school districts, charter schools are an attempt to revitalize public education while maintaining the "wall of separation" between church and state. Following Minnesota's lead, forty other states and the District of Columbia have passed laws allowing the creation of charter schools; Alabama, Kentucky, Maine, Montana, Nebraska, North Dakota, South Dakota, Vermont, Washington, and West Virginia are the only ten holdouts. In 2010, more than 1.7 million students were enrolled in thousands of charter schools across the country.

Are charter schools the answer? One study found that fourth-grade students in charter schools do no better than those in public schools on math and reading assessments. Good charter schools are often very good; bad ones are sometimes egregiously bad. Some simply fall by the wayside: between 1991 and 2004, more than 400 charter schools went out of business.

Public school administrators and teachers have generally opposed fundamental reforms. They contend that standardized tests are poor indicators of educational performance or potential. The whole idea of educational privatization, they argue, is politically motivated and pecuniary; the aims are to break teachers unions (notably, the National Education Association or NEA) and to shift billions of tax dollars from public schools to the private sector. Significantly, hundreds of charter schools are now run by for-profit education management organizations (EMOs).

Educators and researchers argue that problems in our public schools are reflections of the larger society—including crime, broken homes, bad role models, and drug use—and that public schools are powerless to solve these problems. They have a point.

Health Care: It Isn't for Everyone (Or Is It?)

A healthy society and a vibrant economy are two sides of the same coin. Individuals who suffer from malnutrition or are too ill to work are not productive. Societies ravaged by hunger and disease are not prosperous.

The moral/ethical/constitutional question can be simply put: is health care a business like, say, hair care or auto repair, or is it a fundamental right? If it is different, the implications are clear enough—the health care "industry" is inseparable from "life, liberty, and the pursuit of happiness" as enshrined in the Declaration of Independence. Without good health, there can be little happiness, and life itself is in jeopardy.

Modern postindustrial states, with one notable exception, guarantee basic health care to every citizen. The sole exception is the United States, where the bitterly partisan controversy over the Affordable Care Act (popular pejorative: "ObamaCare") demonstrates anew that health care is still widely viewed as a private good rather than a public right. In the field of health care, the United States is an "outlier" among rich countries. Health care facilities are among the very best in the world, the quality of medical care is generally high, the federal government spends far more money on biomedical research and development than any other country in the world, and, finally, its citizens spend more money on medical care than anybody else. And—outlays for Medicare and Medicaid are the largest single drain on the federal budget—larger than Social Security and larger than defense.

As noted, the United States is the only developed country in the world that does not treat basic health care as a fundamental human right. Everywhere in western Europe, for example, health care—like education—is something citizens of all ages can and do expect in return for paying taxes. (In fact, university education is also free or highly subsidized in Europe.)

Many countries with guaranteed universal coverage provide comparable medical services and at far lower overall cost than the United States. France's system, for example, is a mix of public and private provision that works well; it produces a healthy population at one-half the per capita cost in the United States with shorter waiting lists than in Britain, and the French live longer on average than both the British and the Americans.[22]

Most middle-class U.S. workers have some sort of private health insurance, but policies vary widely in cost and coverage. In 2009, 46.3 million Americans (15% of the population; 2 million in the middle class) had no health insurance at all. At least twenty countries have lower infant mortality rates than the United States; impoverished Cuba has a higher life expectancy. In the United States, health care costs have risen much faster than inflation rates or personal incomes, and patients often pay exorbitant prices for prescription drugs compared with the prices of the same drugs in other countries.

Who is to blame? The medical profession points to costly malpractice insurance, hospitals to costly new life-saving technologies, and pharmaceutical companies to R&D (research and development). Lost in the shuffle of self-absolution is the fact that consumers of medical care are *patients*, not customers shopping for a new pair of shoes. Compassion and common sense argue that sick people ought not to be denied medical care or driven into bankruptcy. After all, sick people do not choose to be sick.

Physicians point out that many people seek medical attention for trivial reasons, ask for prescription drugs they see advertised on TV, and are too ready to sue when something goes wrong. And as more people live to a ripe old age, hospitals and health care professionals are asked to devote more and more time and resources to geriatric care involving fragile patients facing end-of-life medical crises.

Campaigning for the presidency in 2008, Barack Obama promised to reform the system and once in office he tried to keep his promise. But a Republican majority in the House vehemently opposed what right-wing ideologues call "socialized medicine"—in particular, mandatory health insurance and cost controls. The result was a law that finally passed as the Affordable Care Act of 2010. It pleased few and did not fix the problem it purported to address, namely, "affordable care."

There is growing support for doing so among doctors and even within the traditionally conservative business community. In February 2007, the chief executives of retail giant Walmart and three other major U.S. companies joined hands with union leaders in calling for health care coverage for "every person in America and raising the value it [America] receives for every health care dollar." Walmart CEO Lee Scott declared, "We believe Americans can have high-quality, affordable, and accessible health care by 2012."[23] A 2007 *New York Times*/CBS News survey found that 90% of respondents believe the system needs either fundamental changes (54%) or a major overhaul (36%).[24]

Health care reform has become a major issue in U.S. politics. Critics denounce "ObamaCare" as a budget-busting step toward European-style socialism. Twenty-five challenges were filed in various states in 2010; in four separate cases, two federal judges found the law unobjectionable, two overturned all or part of it on constitutional grounds. A crucial test came in June 2012 when the U.S. Supreme Court upheld the constitutionality of the Affordable Care Act by a narrow 5–4 vote. The key question was over the law's controversial provision requiring everyone to buy health insurance and providers to insure individuals without regard to "preexisting conditions" (previous health problems).

When the new health care law was passed, an estimated 46–47 million Americans had no health insurance, roughly equal to the number who now live on incomes that fall below the official poverty line. That is scheduled to change by 2014, when all fifty states are required to have health insurance exchanges in place to broker mandated individual coverage for tens of millions previously having little or none. Advocates want more, namely, a nationwide single-payer system. Opponents want the new law struck down. The 2012 presidential contest was a referendum on health care reform. Tea Party Republicans in general and Mitt Romney in particular believed they could parlay opposition to "ObamaCare" into a winning strategy. It turned out to be a losing bet.

In Europe, health insurance is not an issue. France, for example, provides universal health care for its 62 million citizens, is healthier than the United States, and spends only about half as much per capita on health care—less than 11% of GDP, as against 16.5% in the United States. Indeed, no comparable society spends as much as the United States, and most provide universal coverage. Private spending for health care in the United States is astronomically higher than in Europe, and public spending under Medicaid and Medicare is also rising at what many (especially opponents of public health insurance) say is an unsustainable rate.

But many Americans are still ambivalent about health care reform. A Rasmussen Reports national telephone survey in January 2011 found that 55% of likely voters favored repeal of the new health care law. However, only 40% said they *strongly* favored repeal. Similarly, polls in 2012 depicted a society divided and ambivalent about the new law, but more against than for it. But, as noted above, the outcome of the 2012 presidential election suggests a growing public alarm at the high cost of health care and a willingness to accept an enlarged role for government in a realm once regarded as off-limits to state regulation or "interference."

Income Distribution: Who Gets What, When, and How?

Thomas Jefferson's declaration that "all men are created equal" was not a formula for the radical redistribution of property or wealth. It was an existential idea about how we start out, not how we end up. Far from it. But how much inequality is too much?

Prosperity depends not only on the amount of wealth in a society, but also on its distribution. Unless income is distributed widely in society, there will be too few consumers, or consumers with too little money to afford the goods and services the economy can produce, creating a vicious cycle in which everybody loses. Thus, recession (falling demand) causes unemployment, resulting in less demand (fewer consumers with money to spend), causing business profits to fall, and so on.

But the health of the economy is not simply an economic question. A faltering economy can also undermine political stability and governmental authority. Riots and revolts often have economic roots, as the American and French revolutions showed (see Chapter 14).

Glaring economic inequalities are difficult to justify from a moral standpoint as well. Indeed, in the United States, no politician seeking reelection would dare challenge the idea of "an honest day's work for an honest day's pay."

Yet, since 1980, the disparity between the incomes of the richest members of society and all the rest has grown. From 1949 to 1974, the share of family income of the poorest one-fifth of the labor force rose 26.7%, while that of the richest 5% of income earners fell 12.4%. Between 1980 and 2008, this trend was dramatically reversed, as the bottom one-fifth's share of family income fell 24.5%,

How wealth is distributed in a society says a lot about the character of its political institutions as well as the viability and sustainability of its economy.

while that of the top one-twentieth climbed 43.8%.[25] A Congressional Budget Office (CBO) study in 2011 found that the share of national income taken by the top 1% of earners has more than doubled since 1979 and noted, "The equalizing effect of federal taxes was smaller [because] the composition of federal revenues shifted away from progressive income taxes to less-progressive payroll taxes." And according to a Federal Reserve survey released in the summer of 2012, the median family's net worth fell nearly 40% between 2007 and 2010 (from $126,400 to $77,300) due in large part to collapsing real estate prices. Median family income also continued to decline, dropping from $49,600 in 2007 to $45,800 in 2010, a year in which 93% of the increase in total income went to the top 1%.[26]

Such numbers are startling, but they are not an accident of the so-called free market. On the contrary, government plays a major role through its power to tax—or not to tax. The taxes paid by the richest 400 taxpayers in the "roaring nineties" fell from 26.4 cents on every dollar of reported income to just 22.2 cents, while the overall federal income tax burden actually increased. This narrowing of the gap between what the super-rich pay and what everybody else pays equals a major upward redistribution of income.[27]

The phenomenon of top-loading wealth accelerated after 2000 as a result of the Bush administration's tax cuts. Studies show that middle-class workers have been running in place since the early 1970s. Between 1970 and 2000, average wages in the United States adjusted for inflation were flat. Meanwhile, the incomes of the elite top one-tenth of 1% climbed well over 300%.[28]

TALIA FELIX/PUBLICDOMAINPICTURES.NET

Using wealth as the yardstick, some analysts say that we are witnessing the disappearance of the American middle class. The top 20% of the populace holds 93% of the country's total financial assets, and the top 1% of the country holds approximately 43%. The middle 20% of the population—the official middle class—holds only 6% of the country's wealth. Even this shrinking share of the money pie dwarfs the bottom 40%, who get along on less than 1% of the country's wealth. One sign of the times: less than 10% of U.S. workers are employed in manufacturing now compared to just under 30% in 1960.[29]

Many conservatives take a different view of economic inequality. Rather than focusing on the extreme differences in income, they argue that the United States has always had a large middle class, still has, and it would be self-defeating to level society through legislative action aimed at redistributing incomes. Rather, policies that benefit those who work hard, take economic risks, invest wisely, and provide goods and services people want are proven to work best. Helping the poor is not the government's job, and "giveaway" programs only perpetuate poverty by rewarding laziness. In this view, charity belongs in the private sector—philanthropists, religious institutions, and charitable organizations.

Debates over income distribution in a given society are really about equality. Liberals and conservatives agree that equality is important in some sense, but they do not agree on what *kind* of equality is necessary or how much inequality is desirable—or tolerable.

THE PURSUIT OF EQUALITY

A century before the Declaration of Independence was written, the English political philosopher John Locke argued that "life, liberty, and property" are natural rights to which all human beings are entitled. The principle of *equal rights*—as distinct from equal results—has deep roots in the Anglo-American political tradition. Yet principle and practice often diverge, as the history of slavery in the United States attests.

Racial Discrimination

Until the 1860s, slavery made a mockery of the United States' commitment to liberty. On the eve of the Civil War, in the infamous *Dred Scott v. Sandford* (1856) case, the Supreme Court ruled that African Americans, whether slave or free, were not citizens. Chief Justice Roger Taney argued that "Negroes" were "so inferior" that they had "no rights which the white man was bound to respect."

The outcome of the Civil War meant an end to slavery, but it did not ensure equality under the law. Nor did enactment of the Fourteenth Amendment, which, among other things, guaranteed that no person shall be denied "the equal protection of the laws." Ironically, it was the Supreme Court, the supposed guardian of the Constitution, that largely nullified the intent of this amendment.

Two Landmark Cases   In the *Civil Rights Cases* (1883), the Court ruled that an act of Congress prohibiting racial discrimination in public accommodations (restaurants, amusement parks, and the like) was unconstitutional.[30] The Equal Protection Clause of the Fourteenth Amendment, the justices held, was intended to prohibit only *state* discrimination, not private discrimination. Discriminatory acts committed by individuals having no official connection with state government, in other words, were beyond the range of the federal government and, therefore, of the federal courts. If, for example, a restaurant owner turned away black citizens, the owner would merely be exercising the rights of a private individual, and no congressional remedy would be constitutional.

Thirteen years later, in *Plessy v. Ferguson* (1896), the Court went even further.[31] In upholding the constitutionality of a state law mandating racially segregated railway carriages, the Court in *Plessy* devised the notorious *separate-but-equal doctrine*.

Plessy (described by the Court as being of "seven-eighths Caucasian and one-eighth African blood") had taken a seat in the white section of a train, only to be told he was required to move to the "colored" section. A nearly unanimous Court rejected Plessy's claim that the segregation law violated his right to equal protection of the law, arguing that the law was neutral on its face; that is, it provided equal accommodations for persons of both races. The Court majority went so far as to suggest that if "the enforced separation of the two races stamps the colored race with a badge of inferiority," that "is not by reason of anything found in the act, but solely because the colored race chooses to put that construction upon it."

In two landmark Supreme Court decisions, *Civil Rights Cases* (1883) and *Plessy v. Ferguson* (1896), the strict racial segregation in the South was upheld by majority decision. Justice John M. Harlan's dissenting opinion in *Plessy*, that the Constitution is "color-blind," would not become law for almost fifty-eight years. Dr. Martin Luther King Jr., President of the Southern Christian Leadership Conference, at the Civil Rights March on Washington, D.C., August 28, 1963.

In both the *Civil Rights Cases* and *Plessy v. Ferguson*, only Justice John M. Harlan dissented. On each occasion, he argued the Court's decision had the effect of defeating the egalitarian purpose behind the Fourteenth Amendment, which, he declared, had "removed the race line from our government systems." Because he believed no government, at any level, possessed the constitutional power to pass laws based on racial distinctions, Harlan viewed the Constitution as "color-blind." His dissenting opinion in *Plessy* would not become law, however, for another fifty-eight years. Through the decisions handed down in the *Civil Rights Cases* and *Plessy v. Ferguson*, the Court not only sanctioned strict racial segregation in the South, but also helped legitimize a social system in which blacks were discriminated against, brutalized, and even murdered.

Racial Equality: Free at Last? Systematic racial segregation under law was the norm throughout the South well into the twentieth century; *de facto* segregation (neighborhoods and schools) was also widespread in the North, especially in urban areas. Beginning in the late 1940s, however, the Supreme Court began to reinterpret the old legal formulas with a view toward promoting racial equality. In *Shelley v. Kraemer* (1948), the Court held that judicial enforcement of discriminatory private contracts was unconstitutional.[32] The Court ruled that legal enforcement of such agreements amounted to "state action" for the purpose of discrimination, which was prohibited by the Fourteenth Amendment. In addition, though it declined to outlaw them outright, the Court began to insist that segregated state facilities be *truly* equal. Thus, in *Sweatt v. Painter* (1950), it held the University of Texas law school had to admit blacks because the state could not provide a black law school of equal quality and reputation.[33]

In the famous case *Brown v. Board of Education of Topeka* (1954), the Court finally overturned the separate-but-equal doctrine,[34] declaring segregated schools unconstitutional because "separate educational facilities are inherently unequal." The *Brown* decision sparked a heated political debate over the meaning of "equality" in the United States.

Congress eventually passed the Civil Rights Act of 1964, the first of a series of federal laws aimed at realizing racial equality. It was a sign of the changing times that the 1964 act contained an equal accommodations section very similar to the one ruled unconstitutional in the *Civil Rights Cases*.[35] By the late 1960s, after a decade of intense civil rights activities and the most serious civil disorders since the Civil War, the government was fully committed to ensuring equal rights under the law for all citizens. The public policy battle between advocates of racial equality and of white supremacy gave way to an increasingly complex and heated debate over the appropriate means to the goal of equality.

The Busing Controversy   The question of how far the government could and should go to promote equal rights was crystallized in the school busing controversy of the 1970s and 1980s, which grew out of an ambiguity in *Brown v. Board of Education*. Most blacks lived in the inner city and most whites in the suburbs—*de facto* segregation.

In 1971, the Supreme Court in *Swann v. Charlotte-Mecklenburg Board of Education* unanimously ruled in favor of a controversial remedy: to integrate school districts by transporting schoolchildren across district lines. Court-ordered school busing met with strong opposition from parents and school administrators on various grounds and coincided with a national "crisis of confidence" in the public schools.

Was busing a good idea? It *did* put pressure on local officials and school boards to improve facilities and conditions in inner-city schools. But busing often did nothing more than reshuffle minority schoolchildren from one part of the inner city to another. The Supreme Court invalidated most plans that involved reshuffling between black inner-city neighborhoods and white suburbs.[36]

Affirmative Action or Reverse Discrimination?

reverse discrimination In effect, going overboard in giving preferences to racial minorities and victims of gender discrimination in hiring, housing, and education; the U.S. Supreme Court has ruled that in some cases, affirmative action quotas are unconstitutional.

If the Constitution permits preferential treatment of minorities, does it also provide the majority with protection against **reverse discrimination**? The Supreme Court wrestled with this question in 1978 in a suit brought by a white student, Allan Bakke, who had unsuccessfully sought admission to the medical school of the University of California at Davis.[37]

Bakke contended that the medical school had unfairly undercut his chances of acceptance simply because of his race. In a close decision in *Regents of the*

University of California v. Bakke, the Court ruled rigid **affirmative action** quotas unconstitutional but said preference for minorities were allowable under certain circumstances.[38]

The Supreme Court has upheld broad-based preferential hiring programs, while drawing the line at preferential protection against layoffs.[39] It has upheld affirmative action for women in the workforce to improve gender balance in industry and many professions.[40] But the Court struck down governmental preferences for minority-owned businesses.[41]

In 2003, the Supreme Court in *Grutter v. Bollinger* ruled that race can be used in university admission decisions, voting 5–4 to uphold the University of Michigan Law School's affirmative action policy, which favors minorities—thus apparently reversing the decision in *Bakke*. But in a parallel case, *Gratz v. Bollinger*, the justices struck down the university's undergraduate affirmative action policy (which awarded twenty points to blacks, Hispanics, and Native Americans) on the grounds that the policy was not "narrowly tailored" to achieve the goal of diversity—thus apparently confirming the *Bakke* decision.

Exactly where affirmative action ends and reverse discrimination begins in the eyes of the Supreme Court is unclear. The Court adjudges the Constitution to give Congress more latitude than state and local governments to remedy discrimination past and present. Color-conscious affirmative action programs at the state and local levels are most likely to be upheld where there is clear evidence of specific (and not general social) discrimination against minorities.[42]

Who Deserves Preferential Treatment?

African Americans and Native Americans have historically been victims of injustice and discrimination. So, too, have Asian Americans.

During World War II, more than 120,000 Japanese Americans living on the West Coast were herded into concentration camps surrounded by barbed wire and armed guards until the end of the war. In the name of national security, whole families who had done nothing wrong were forced into internal exile, losing everything they had in the process. Not until 1988 did the U.S. Congress pass a law acknowledging "a grave injustice was done" and giving each victim $20,000 in compensation, along with an official letter of apology signed by the president.

Women, gays and lesbians, and Arab Americans are three other groups with a claim to preferential treatment based on past discrimination. After 9/11, Arab Americans were insulted, threatened, and in some cases physically attacked. The FBI placed many Arabs and Muslims under surveillance, questioned others, and arrested thousands, holding them without charges or access to an attorney for longer than the law allowed.[43]

Gender-based discrimination became a front-burner issue only in the 1970s. For a time, the debate centered on the ill-fated Equal Rights Amendment, which would have guaranteed that "equality of rights under the law should not be denied or abridged by the United States or by any State on account of sex." Do women need special protection as a historically disadvantaged "minority"? Are they entitled to preferential treatment to remedy the effects of past sex discrimination?

affirmative action
Giving preferential treatment to a socially or economically disadvantaged group in compensation for opportunities denied by past discrimination.

Gays and lesbians have long been the object of discrimination too. In 1992, Colorado voters passed a measure prohibiting the state from enforcing specific legal protections or extending preference to gay citizens who believed they were disadvantaged or discriminated against. The referendum was overturned in 1996, when the Supreme Court held the measure discriminatory and therefore unconstitutional.[44]

In 2008, California became the second state, after Massachusetts, to issue same-sex marriage licenses after the California Supreme Court ruled the state's ban on same-sex marriages unconstitutional. Later in 2008, however, California voters passed Proposition 8, a constitutional amendment intended to supersede the Court's ruling, but a federal judge in San Francisco negated this action. Next stop: the U.S. Supreme Court which began hearing arguments in the spring of 2013.

Same-sex marriages and civil unions are now legal in 15 U.S. States (and counting), as well as seven countries (Belgium, Canada, the Netherlands, Norway, South Africa, Spain, and Sweden). In December 2011, the lame duck Congress repealed the "don't ask don't tell" rule, the policy restricting the military from inquiring into sexual preferences of service members or applicants, while barring openly LGBT (gay, lesbian, bisexual, or transsexual) individuals from military service.

Today attitudes in the larger society are perhaps trending toward greater tolerance for diversity. Opinion polls in 2013 showed that more Americans favor same-sex marriage now than oppose it. Another sign "the times they are a-changin'": in his inaugural speech on January 21, 2013, President Obama dared to note the struggle for civil rights of "our gay brothers and sisters."

THE PURSUIT OF LIBERTY

What rights and legal protections are due all citizens? What does the U.S. Constitution have to say about liberty, and how can a government be designed to protect us (the citizens) from itself?

Liberty is often equated with freedom from governmental restraint. Free enterprise is necessary for a creative society and dynamic economy. Without freedom the spirit of invention and innovation is stifled. Freedom of expression keeps citizens informed and governments honest. When the state encroaches on anyone's liberty, it threatens everyone's liberty.

Liberty and the First Amendment

In the United States, legal questions about individual freedom often turn on the First Amendment, which provides that:

> Congress shall make no law respecting an establishment of religion, or prohibiting the free exercise thereof; or abridging the freedom of speech, or the press, or the right of the people peaceably to assemble, and to petition the Government for a redress of grievances.

The First Amendment protects four **civil liberties**: freedom of speech, freedom of the press, freedom of religion, and freedom of assembly. Because the language of the First Amendment is brief and intentionally vague, the first three rights in particular have required an unusual amount of judicial interpretation.

Freedom of Speech   Most constitutional experts agree the overriding purpose behind the First Amendment is the protection of *political* speech. In a republic, open debate between political opponents is vital to the effective functioning of the political system. Most of the time, the *exercise* of free speech is not controversial, even though the speech itself might be.

Freedom of speech can become a hotly contested issue even in the most open societies. Extremists often arouse strong passions, especially within minority groups they have victimized (Jews against Nazis, for example, or African Americans against the Ku Klux Klan).

In the United States, people often associate protesters and demonstrators with extremists and troublemakers. During the early days of the Vietnam War, youthful protesters were often depicted as unpatriotic and disloyal. Several years later, after the war had become unpopular, defenders of the U.S. role in Vietnam were booed and shouted down when they spoke on college campuses. But the First Amendment safeguards the right of *all* citizens to express political opinions, no matter how repugnant or unpopular. Freedom of speech is not absolute, however. For example, it does not entail the right to shout "Fire!" in a crowded theater, foment a riot, plot a terrorist act, or use "fighting words" in a dispute.

During the Vietnam War, the federal government engaged in domestic spying under the secret Counter Intelligence Program (COINTELPRO), aimed at monitoring the activities of antiwar activists. Subsequently, the FBI was banned from monitoring public events involving religious or political groups unless it had a specific reason for doing so. These post-Vietnam curbs on the FBI were effectively set aside after September 11, 2001. Thereafter, the FBI again set about collecting information on antiwar demonstrators, even if and when, in the words of its own internal memorandum, it "possessed no information that violent or terrorist activities are being planned."[45]

Antiwar protesters in masks demonstrate at the Colorado State Capitol during the 2008 Democratic National Convention in Denver, Colorado.

STUART SIPKIN/ISTOCKPHOTO.COM

> **civil liberties**
> Basic constitutional rights guaranteed to all citizens, including the right to life and freedom of speech, religion, and association, as well as freedom from arbitrary arrest and incarceration, torture, and slavery. But there is no universally accepted definition or list.

In early February 2004, a county deputy sheriff working closely with the FBI's Joint Terrorism Task Force served subpoenas on Drake University in Des Moines, Iowa, to turn over documents relating to an antiwar conference that had taken place there a few months earlier, "including any records relating to the people in charge, or to any attendees."[46] These subpoenas were withdrawn as a result of public outrage and criticism from members of Congress, most notably Senator Tom Harkin of Iowa, who likened it to "Vietnam when war protestors were rounded up [and] grand juries were convened to investigate people who were protesting the war."[47]

In office, President Obama faced a dilemma: whether to declare peace and return the nation to "normalcy" or appease the Republicans (and Democratic hawks) in Congress by continuing to wage a war on terror. The answer came in 2009 when Obama ordered a 30,000 troop surge in Afghanistan. In 2011 he signed a four-year extension of certain expiring provisions of the Patriot Act, including one that allows the government to engage in electronic surveillance (warrantless wiretaps) of private citizens.

The Supreme Court has placed a broad interpretation on the word "speech," defining it as synonymous with any form of *expression*. Flag burning, for example, has been upheld as a protected form of **symbolic speech**.[48] The context of symbolic free speech is almost always constitutionally more important than its content. The Ku Klux Klan's burning of a cross in an isolated field may be an objectionable act, but the Court has held that it is nonetheless a constitutionally protected form of symbolic expression.[49] Burning a cross on someone's lawn, however, is prohibited.[50]

symbolic speech
Forms of expression other than words: for example, flag-burning, provocative gestures, black armbands, and the like.

Freedom of the Press   The First Amendment protects publishers from almost all forms of official censorship. Newspapers and periodicals can publish what they wish, including criticisms and indictments of the government. The same holds true for the broadcast media. A free press is crucial to a democracy, because every citizen is a decision maker at election time and because the glare of publicity helps keep elected officials honest.

In the aftermath of 9/11, freedom of the press became a bone of contention as the Bush administration advocated greater governmental secrecy in order to prosecute the war on terror. But journalists and media executives expressed alarm at the way the Freedom of Information Act (FOIA) was being flouted. In May 2004, Tom Curley, CEO of the Associated Press, gave a chilling speech describing a culture of official secrecy and a growing hostility to the press at all levels of government and in the courts.[51]

The Supreme Court has consistently ruled in favor of a free press. Except in times of war or grave national emergency, the government does not have the power to engage in **prior restraint**—to prevent publication even of papers classified as secret or information a trial judge may later rule constitutes prejudicial pretrial publicity.[52] In the final analysis, however, only a free press and an alert public can prevent the abuse of power by a commander in chief.

prior restraint
The legal doctrine that the government does not have the power to censor the press, except in cases of dire national emergency.

Freedom of Religion   By prohibiting the establishment of a state-sponsored religion, the First Amendment requires the government to be neutral in religious matters—to neither help nor hinder any religion. This requirement comple-ments the guarantee of the free exercise of religion. Taken together, these two clauses ensure that citizens may practice any religion in any manner they like, within reasonable limits.

When religious practices pose a threat to society, however, government has the power to outlaw them. The free exercise of religion, for instance, does not include ritual murder or even certain religious practices that do not present any obvious danger to society, such as polygamy.[53] The Supreme Court has ruled the free exercise clause does include the right of conscientious objectors not to bear arms, Amish children not to attend public schools, and Jehovah's Witness schoolchildren not to salute the flag.

On the controversial issue of school prayer, the Supreme Court has held that prayer, even if nondenominational, and Bible-reading in public schools vio-late the Establishment Clause of the First Amendment.[54] Prayers at high school graduation exercises have also been ruled out.[55] Even a moment of silence in the public schools if a teacher suggests it be used for prayer.[56] Thus, the Court has consistently ruled school prayer unconstitutionally involves the state in the establishment of religion.

The Establishment Clause also plays a role in the debate over state aid to private schools. In 2002, the U.S. Supreme Court ruled in *Zelman v. Simmons-Harris* that a school voucher program in Cleveland, Ohio, did not violate the Constitution because the vouchers were intended for the secular purpose of helping children of low-income families attending failing schools. But in 2004, the Colorado Supreme Court ruled a school voucher program violated a pro-vision of the Colorado Constitution. Similarly, in January 2006, the Florida Supreme Court struck down a school voucher plan on grounds that it violated a section of the Florida Constitution providing "for a uniform, efficient, safe, secure and high-quality system of free public schools." In 2009, at the urging of the NEA, Democrats in Congress effectively killed the D.C. voucher pro-gram in a compromise plan one critic called "choosing attrition over summary execution."[57]

Although the National Education Association (NEA) is a staunch oppo-nent of voucher plans, the idea of an alternative to dysfunctional public schools is not likely to fade away. Even so, polls continue to show most voters still don't support school voucher programs that compete with public schools for tax dollars.

Privacy and the Right to Life

In 1973, the Supreme Court ruled in *Roe v. Wade* that most laws against abor-tion violated the right to privacy under the Due Process Clause of the Fifth Amendment. Since then, a more conservative Court has ruled that a woman's right to an abortion does not require the use of public funds to reimburse poorer women for the cost of abortions, nor is the state required to pay public employees for performing or assisting in abortions.[58]

Objections to *Roe v. Wade* have come largely from right-to-life groups, whose members believe human life begins at conception and abortion therefore amounts to legalized murder. Anti-abortion protesters have picketed and some-times blockaded abortion clinics, actions that are illegal under a federal law passed in 1994. The same year, the Supreme Court held that anti-abortion activists could be sued under the Racketeer Influenced and Corrupt Organization (RICO) law if blockading abortion clinics inflicted economic harm on those performing abortions.[59] But in 1997 the Court appeared to contradict itself when it ruled that anti-abortion demonstrators also enjoy constitutional protection under the First Amendment.[60]

Since the 1973 Supreme Court's ruling in *Roe v. Wade*, pro-choice and anti-abortion activists in the United States have demonstrated vocally and some-times violently. On a Sunday morning in late May 2009, a gunman entered the foyer of a church in Wichita, Kansas, then shot and killed Dr. George Tiller, a licensed physician who performed abortions at his local clinic. It was not the first instance of its kind and law-enforcement officials fear it will not be the last.

In 2004, the Bush administration served medical subpoenas on hospitals and clinics in California, Illinois, Kansas, Missouri, Michigan, New York, Pennsylvania, and Washington, demanding records of their patients who had undergone certain types of abortions over the previous three years. Under a 1996 federal law, critics noted, doctors, hospitals, and drugstores must give "notices of privacy practices" to patients and customers, assuring them personal information will be protected. [61] The federal government nonetheless sought the medical records of 2,700 patients from a public hospital and six Planned Parenthood clinics in San Francisco alone.[62]

The dispute involved legal challenges to the Partial Birth Abortion Ban Act (PBABA), which many legal experts argued was in conflict with a Supreme Court decision in a Nebraska case.[63] A federal judge in San Francisco denied the Justice Department access: "There is no question that the patient is entitled to privacy and protection." The information sought, the judge ruled, was potentially "of an extremely intimate and personal nature."[64]

Several Supreme Court justices have defended the pro-choice position by developing a new concept of privacy based on a right "to define one's own concept of existence, of meaning, of the universe, and of the mystery of human life."[65] On this basis, some also claim people under some circumstances choose death over life, as in a medically assisted suicide. In 1997, the Supreme Court unanimously refused to recognize a constitutional right to die.[66]

THE PURSUIT OF JUSTICE

In a just society laws are applied fairly and the punishment fits the crime. Viewed in this way, justice is not a pie-in-the-sky ideal, but a realistic political end achievable by means of proper courts and legal systems.

Crime and Punishment

No society can afford to let seriously antisocial or criminal behavior go unpunished. The four main most commonly cited reasons for punishment are pursuing security, government attempts to protect citizens from foreign enemies, from fellow citizens, from natural enemies, and, in some instances, from themselves.

In the United States, the goal of prosperity has historically been associated with a free-enterprise economy based on the idea of the commercial republic. In the twentieth century, however, the government has attempted to promote the economic well-being of individuals through social welfare and other programs. These programs have sparked heated debate over the proper role of government in economic matters, especially as the budget deficit has worsened. Problems in the educational system endangered U.S. competitiveness in the international economy. Income distribution also made for a lively topic of national debate in recent years and became a front-burner issue after the Wall Street meltdown in the fall of 2008. The election of Barack Obama and the economic recession have made extravagant executive bonuses and income disparities front-page news.

The goal of equality in the United States has been closely identified with the effort to end racial discrimination. Two landmark Supreme Court cases in the post–Civil War period helped perpetuate state laws and public attitudes upholding established patterns of racial inequality. Later, *Brown v. Board of Education* (1954) spearheaded the civil rights movement, which culminated in legislative, judicial, and administrative measures aimed at bringing about genuine racial equality. These civil rights gains were followed by new controversies over mandatory school busing to achieve racial integration and affirmative action guidelines designed to rectify past inequalities. Other major public policy issues related to equality have recognized the rights of various ethnic groups, women, and the poor and disadvantaged.

The pursuit of liberty is a core value of U.S. society. Among the personal liberties protected explicitly by the First Amendment are freedom of speech, freedom of the press, and freedom of religion. The right to privacy, or freedom of choice, is another significant aspect of personal liberty in the United States.

We can narrowly define the pursuit of justice as the government's attempt to ensure fair and impartial treatment under the law. In the United States, the criminal justice system strives to uphold a commitment to due process, or fair procedure. The controversial exclusionary rule attempts to balance the defendant's right to due process against society's right to be protected against criminals. Debates about judicial discretion and capital punishment also attempt to balance defendants' and society's rights.

Conflicts among these five goals prevent any one of them from being fully realized. A moderate, well-informed, and fair-minded citizenry is essential to sound public policy and a sustainable democratic order.

KEY TERMS

national security   348

entitlements   358

Emission Trading
  Scheme (ETS)   360

Kyoto Protocol   360

sustainable growth 362

federal budget
  deficit   363

Balanced Budget Act
  of 1997   363

economic stimulus   363

REVIEW QUESTIONS

1. What are some political issues that arise from security concerns?
2. What internal and external economic problems face the United States today? What triggered the current recession? What measures has the Obama administration taken to deal with it?
3. Contrast the ideal and the practice of equality in U.S. history.
4. Explain the idea of affirmative action. What groups, if any, deserve protection, and why?
5. What is reverse discrimination? How has the Supreme Court ruled in cases alleging discrimination of this kind? Do you agree or disagree with these rulings? Explain.
6. Why is liberty valuable? How is it protected in the United States?
7. What challenges currently plague the U.S. criminal justice system? Is the law color-blind? Comment.
8. Is mandatory sentencing a good idea in your opinion? Explain your point of view.
9. What is the relationship between the public good and moderation?

PART 4

Politics by Violent Means
Revolution, War, and Terrorism

CHAPTER (14)

Revolution
In the Name of Justice

The Frequency of Revolutions

Modern Revolutions: Two
   Traditions

Revolution—A Right or
   All Wrong?

The Causes of Revolution

THINK ABOUT IT

In what fundamental ways did the American and French Revolutions differ?

How did Edmund Burke's view of revolution differ from Thomas Paine's, and in what way(s) did John Locke's political theory both inspire and justify the American Revolution more than seventy years after his death?

What are the causes of revolution?

At the beginning of 2011, the eyes of the world were riveted on the turbulence in Egypt; then in 2012, all eyes were on Syria. Many in the mass media called the upheaval in Egypt a revolution and the one in Syria a civil war. What happened in Egypt was a mass uprising on a scale not witnessed in the Arab World at any time in recent memory. But was it a **revolution**? And what about Syria? When does a "civil war" morph into a "revolution"?

It's true that Egypt's dictator, Hosni Mubarak, was forced to flee the country, a victory for the antigovernment protesters in Tahrir Square. But the Egyptian military did not relinquish formal control of the government for a full year after the Arab Spring, and even then the generals kept a tight rein on the election process, media outlets, and state security organs. Given the long history of military rule in Egypt, the acid test comes down to whether or not real political power is transferred from military to civilian hands. By the same token, until Syria's ruthless ruler, Bashir Assad, abdicates or is forced out of power, there will be no regime change and therefore no revolution no matter how much blood is spilled.

What exactly is a revolution? Few words are used more loosely than "revolution" and "revolutionary." Television commercials abound with descriptions of "revolutionary" new anti-aging skin creams, Internet-enabled cell phones, or hybrid cars that represent a "revolution" in transportation. *Real* revolutions, however, are deadly serious business.

Revolutions are not to be confused with revolts. Any mass action that does not result in a fundamental change in the form of government is quite possibly a revolt, but it is not enough to qualify as a revolution. Revolts are often accompanied by violence and social upheaval, but they rarely result in a revolution. That's why it was premature to call the turbulence in Egypt a "revolution" before anyone knew the final outcome or *dénouement*. Nor is violence a sure sign of revolution. Some recent revolutions—in the former Soviet Union and Eastern Europe—have brought little or no bloodshed. In other cases, a great deal of social upheaval—and, yes, violence—has not resulted in a change of regime (such as Syria in 2012–2013).

The eighteenth century witnessed two great revolutions—one in the New World (the American Revolution) and one in the Old World (the French Revolution). But it was not until the twentieth century that revolutions swept across the globe—from Russia (1917) to China (1949) to the Third World (1960s and 1970s) to Eastern Europe (1989) and, coming full circle, back to (Soviet) Russia (1991). Great technological advances filled the years following World War II—space travel, organ transplants, computers, and the Internet. Those same years—coinciding with the Cold War—witnessed an eruption of revolutions in the Middle East, Africa, Asia, and Latin America.

The period after World War II saw the fastest and most far-reaching changes in world history so far. During this age of revolution, the dizzying pace of change was changing the nature of revolution itself. The Russian and Chinese revolutions occurred in agrarian societies. Although revolutions in the Third World were typically associated with Marxist ideologies and opposition to Western colonial rule, ethnic and religious conflicts often played a major role as well.[1] Unlike many anti-colonial independence struggles, the largely peaceful

revolution
A fundamental change in the rules and institutions that govern a society, often involving violent conflict in the form of mass action, insurrection, secession, or civil war.

revolutions in Eastern Europe following the collapse of communist rule led to democratization and liberal reforms (see Chapter 8).

Studying the contexts, causes, and consequences of revolution is essential to understanding the political forces that shape today's world. We begin with a look at the incidence of revolution in the modern world.

THE FREQUENCY OF REVOLUTIONS

Revolutions have occurred throughout human history, particularly during times of strong population expansion and rapid economic change.[2] Significant changes in governmental structure took place in many Greek city-states in the seventh and sixth centuries BCE, in Rome in the first century BCE, in the Islamic world in the eighth century CE, and in Europe, particularly from 1500 to 1650 and from 1750 to 1850.

In the twentieth century, revolutions occurred more frequently. In a sense, revolutions were part of a surge in national violence that marked most of the century. In the 1930s, the renowned Harvard sociologist Pitirim Sorokin studied "internal disturbances" in eleven political communities. In Western Europe alone, he was able to identify no fewer than 1,622 such disturbances in the post–World War I era, of which fully 70% "involved violence and bloodshed on a considerable scale."[3] Moreover, in each country studied, for every five years of relative peace Sorokin found one year of "significant social disturbance." He concluded that the twentieth century overall was the bloodiest and most turbulent period in history—and he made that judgment *before* World War II.

Subsequent events bore out his judgment. From 1945 to 1970, fully forty of the approximately one hundred developing countries witnessed at least one military takeover. Between 1943 and 1962, attempts to overthrow an existing government occurred in virtually every country in Latin America, in two-thirds of the countries of Asia, and in half the African countries that had gained independence.[4] Although the world has witnessed many revolutions, rebellions, and civil disturbances since the 1970s, the incidence of military coups has decreased in more recent decades. The *New York Times* reported that between 1946 and 1959, however, there were 1,200 separate instances of "internal war," including "civil wars, guerrilla wars, localized rioting, widely dispersed turmoil, organized and apparently unorganized terrorism, mutinies, and coups d'état."[5]

Not all revolutions are violent. In Eastern Europe, one country after another broke away from the Soviet Union in 1989, and most turned toward a market economy and parliamentary democracy. In all but a few instances—Romania, for example—these revolutions came about with a minimum of violence and bloodshed. In the former Czechoslovakia, it even came to be called the Velvet Revolution because the changeover from communist dictatorship to constitutional government was so smooth. The newly independent Baltic republics of Estonia, Latvia, and Lithuania are also notable examples of peaceful mass revolution. In each, a process of political transformation was initiated without great upheaval, destruction of property, or loss of life.

MODERN REVOLUTIONS: TWO TRADITIONS

Although revolutions date to the slave revolts of antiquity, we can trace to the late eighteenth century the idea of modern revolution—the belief "that a nation's people, by concerted political struggle, could fundamentally transform the political order that governed their lives and, with it, the social and economic structure of society."[6] Modern revolutions possess a distinctive attribute: the use of the anger of the lower classes not merely to destroy the prevailing social order but also "to create a new and different one in which the traditional forms of oppression did not exist."[7] For this reason, they are usually "characterized by a set of emotion-laden utopian ideas—an expectation that the society is marching toward a profound transformation of values and structures, as well as personal behavior."[8]

Modern revolution, and its desire to establish a new, just, social order, usually is traced to the **French Revolution** of 1789. But the **American Revolution**, begun in 1776, provides another model. Both revolutions, among the most important political events of the modern age, influenced the destiny of generations to come. Both championed profoundly important political changes animated by visions of a new kind of political order. Yet they differed dramatically in many other respects. As one astute observer contended:

> It is certainly indisputable that the world, when it contemplates the events of 1776 and after, is inclined to see the American Revolution as a French Revolution that never quite came off, whereas the Founding Fathers thought they had cause to regard the French Revolution as an American Revolution that had failed. Indeed, differing estimates of these two revolutions are definitive of one's political philosophy in the modern world: there are two conflicting conceptions of politics, in relation to the human condition, which are symbolized by these two revolutions. There is no question that the French Revolution is, in some crucial sense, the more "modern" of the two. There is a question, however, as to whether this is a good or bad thing.[9]

The American Revolution

There was no doubt in the minds of the Founders that the American War for Independence against the British Crown (King George III) was a revolution, or that signing the Declaration of Independence was an act of treason. Nor did they have any illusions about the grim fate that awaited them if the revolution failed. As Benjamin Franklin is reputed to have said, they needed to all hang together or they would hang separately.

In waging a war against England in the 1770s, the American colonists became the instigators of the modern world's first successful anti-colonial revolution. In time, the colonists' break with Great Britain became complete and irreparable. For that reason, it is tempting to say the American **Revolutionary War** created a model for later wars of national liberation. However, it differed decisively from subsequent revolutions prior to 1989.

Historical Significance To understand the historical significance of the American Revolution, we must first examine the political opinions of its leaders. They saw the Revolutionary War as a special and unique experience.

French Revolution
This 1789 war brought down the Bourbon monarchy in France in the name of *"liberté, egalité, et fraternité"* (liberty, equality, and fraternity); introduced the contagion of liberalism in a Europe still ruled by conservative, aristocratic, and royalist institutions; and ushered in the rule of Napoléon Bonaparte. Prelude to the First Republic in France and to the Napoleonic Wars.

American Revolution
Also called the War of Independence and the Revolutionary War (1775–1783), this epoch-making event led to the end of British rule over the thirteen American colonies and to the formation of the United States of America in 1787–1789; usually dated from the Declaration of Independence in 1776.

Revolutionary War
The American War of Independence (1775–1783).

The Battle of Lexington. The "first blow for liberty" in America's War for Independence was struck at the Battle of Lexington in April 1775; the American Revolution was the world's first successful anti-colonial uprising.

"From the very beginning," according to one authority, "it was believed by those who participated in it—on the western side of the Atlantic—to be quite a remarkable event, not merely because it was their revolution, but because it seemed to them to introduce a new phase in the political evolution of mankind, and therefore to be touched with universal significance."[10] The Founders were well acquainted with world history and with the writings of the great political philosophers, including Montesquieu, Locke, Rousseau, David Hume, and Voltaire.[11] Given this familiarity, they were not inclined to overestimate the value of new or experimental approaches to politics.

The revolutionaries of 1776 believed the divorce they demanded had universal meaning and that the Declaration of Independence was the timeless expression of it. In other words, they perceived an intimate relationship between the words (the "truths") they promulgated and the deeds they performed.[12] Thus, to discover what was truly revolutionary about the American Revolution, we first focus on what the revolutionaries wrote about government and then observe what they did about it.

Justification The clearest exposition of the American revolutionary credo can be found in the Declaration of Independence. In addition to proclaiming separation from Great Britain, the Declaration enunciated the reasons for it.

The British government, it asserted, had grievously violated the principles of good government. Following Locke's lead, Thomas Jefferson (the chief author) argued that those principles were twofold: (1) government must conform to the will of the majority (according to the Declaration's precise language, such a government must be based on "the consent of the governed"), and (2) it must protect the inalienable rights of all individuals to "Life, Liberty, and the pursuit of Happiness." These principles, in Jefferson's view, established the criteria by which to measure the legitimacy of all governments in all times and places. A good (or legitimate) government, in other words, draws its authority from the consent of the governed and acts to ensure the inalienable rights of all its citizens.

By making human rights the philosophical basis of good government, the Declaration departed significantly from past precedent and contemporary practice. Formerly, governments had come into existence to guarantee order, to build empires, to punish impiety, or to enforce obedience. Now, for the first time in history, a political regime dedicated itself unequivocally to the principle of securing popular rights and liberties.

It followed from the Declaration's principles that governments that repeatedly jeopardized, rather than protected, those rights forfeited their claim to rule. Having stated this conclusion in the Declaration, the colonists continued to wage their war for independence.

Although initially they desired only to be treated as equal British subjects, with the drafting of the Declaration they insisted on complete self-government. Nor would just any government do; they wished ultimately to create a government consistent with the self-evident truths they had pronounced in the Declaration. And these truths, they believed, were applicable far beyond the boundaries of the thirteen colonies. Jefferson found *universal* meaning in the enduring words of the document he had drafted:

> May it be to the world, what I believe it will be (to some parts sooner, to others later, but finally to all), the signal of arousing men to burst the chains under which monkish ignorance and superstition had persuaded them to bind themselves and to assume the blessings and security of self-government.[13]

Social and Political Changes Jefferson's sentiments were expressed in language that ranks with the best revolutionary rhetoric of his or any other time; certainly, it stirred citizens to fight and die for the cause. Even so, it would be a mistake to view the American Revolution solely in the context of the fighting that ensued. While the historic battles raged, great social, economic, and religious changes took place. Restrictive inheritance laws, such as primogeniture and entail, were abolished; large British estates were confiscated and redistributed in smaller holdings; royal restrictions on land settlements were repealed; important steps to secure religious equality and separation of church and state were taken; and old families lost power, their places "taken by new leaders drawn from younger men, from the common people, and from the middle classes."[14]

Political changes also occurred, as every colony wrote a new constitution. Drafted in the heat of war, these constitutions perpetuated existing systems of local self-government, especially the executive branch, while protecting individual liberties. The concepts and principles incorporated in these documents were then reflected in the Articles of Confederation and, eventually, in the U.S. Constitution. It is impossible to overemphasize the importance of this preoccupation with the rule of law, or legality, and procedural correctness.

The *constitution-writing process* culminated in the creation of a government by majority rule, at a time when Europe was still largely subject to the autocratic rule of monarchs. Moreover, the colonists' steadfast concern for constitutionality helped defuse or prevent conspiracies and cabals that could have divided the new nation into many feuding political subdivisions.

"A Revolution of Sober Expectations"   In retrospect, the American Revolution was marked by a "rare economy of violence when compared to other revolutions."[15] In comparison with later revolutionary conflicts (such as the French Revolution, the Russian Revolution, and the Spanish Civil War), civilian reprisals between insurrectionists and loyalists were mild. In addition, the leaders of the American Revolution were never purged or murdered, as so many instigators of later revolutions would be. To the contrary, the "military chief [Washington] became the first president of the Republic and retired at his own choice; the author of the Revolutionary Manifesto [Jefferson] was its first Secretary of State."[16]

What accounted for the unique orderliness of this revolution? Most important, the colonial leaders combined a Lockean attitude toward revolution with the pursuit of realistic, down-to-earth political goals. By "Lockean attitude," to which we will return later, we mean that, with few exceptions, the Founders regarded the revolution as a necessary evil. It was necessary because they knew of no other way of achieving independence from Great Britain, but it was evil insofar as it caused suffering, bloodshed, and devastation. The American Revolution remains unique precisely because it was not led by fanatics and zealots who embraced an inflexible ideology or who thought any means were appropriate to achieve their political ends. Rather, its leaders were contemplative individuals who continually questioned themselves (and one another) about the correctness of what they were doing.

Although there was no lack of enthusiasm on the part of the revolutionary leadership, "this enthusiasm was tempered by doubt, introspection, anxiety, and scepticism."[17] In short, the American Revolution never took its own goodness for granted. Its tempered revolutionary values were placed in the service of sober and clear-eyed goals. Essentially, what the colonial leaders wanted from the revolution was to separate from England and found a government on consent and respect for the rights and liberties of the people.

These objectives were ambitious but not unattainable, in contrast to the utopian aims of the French Revolution. The intertwined concepts of self-government and the protection of citizens' rights had been evolving in the colonies at both the state and township levels in advance of the revolutionary conflict. Unlike later revolutionaries, the colonial leaders did not attempt to immediately institute something radically new and different. Understanding the dangers inherent in quixotic or utopian idealism, they knew that "the political pursuit of impossible dreams leads to terror and tyranny in the vain effort to actualize what cannot be."[18]

Far from being an event marked by such terror and tyranny, the American Revolution was, in the words of one authority, "a revolution of sober expectations."[19] Sobriety, moderation, and prudence were the watchwords of this revolution and the chief characteristics of the "well-ordered union" the Constitution would later ordain.

The French Revolution

The French Revolution was quite a different affair. For years, France had experienced growing political instability and popular dissatisfaction. Seeking to preserve the sharp class distinctions that marked French society, the aristocracy had repeatedly frustrated attempts at economic and political reform. Furthermore, the government had demonstrated a clear inability to cope with changing circumstances.

Even a skilled and intelligent monarch, which Louis XVI (1754–1793) certainly was not, would have found it difficult to overcome the liability of governmental institutions that were decentralized and hard to coordinate. By the late 1780s, the government faced increasing difficulties in raising taxes to pay off massive debt from earlier wars. Then, just at the wrong time for those in power, economic reversals occurred.

Although the economy had been growing, the fruits of growth were terribly maldistributed. Many urban poor and peasants faced crushing material deprivation rather than the promise of economic development. By 1789, eddies of discontent had swelled into a sea of dissension. Middle- and upper-class reformers demanded both political and social changes, including restrictions on class privileges and reform of the tax system. Some leaders wanted more radical changes, including the creation of a political order governed by the principles of popular sovereignty.

The Storming of the Bastille. On July 14, 1789, in Paris, a mob attacked this prison, a hated symbol of state repression. It was a direct attack against the monarchy. Louis XVI conceded too little too late, and a revolutionary tidal wave in the name of "liberty, equality, and fraternity" swept France.

All these demands were put forward at the May 1789 meeting of the **Estates-General**, a giant parliament elected by broad male suffrage and divided into three estates, or houses, representing the clergy, nobility, and commoners. After considerable debate (and a good deal of turmoil), a majority of the delegates, led by the numerically preponderant Third (commoner) Estate, formed a popular National Assembly. In addition to asserting the right to approve or reject all taxation, the members of this body demanded an end to aristocratic privileges.

These actions constituted a direct attack on the monarchy. Louis XVI responded with predictable ineptitude, applying just enough force to incense his opponents. When he marshaled his troops in an effort to bar the National Assembly from meeting, the delegates promptly moved to a nearby indoor tennis court, where they resolved to draft a constitution. The king promised tax reforms later but refused to abolish the privileges of the aristocracy. At the same time, he deployed troops in strategic positions. Sporadic outbursts of violence, including the storming of the **Bastille**, followed swiftly, and Louis XVI, having lost control of the streets, was forced to accede to demands for a constitution.

Estates-General
Prior to the French Revolution, a quasi-legislative body in France in which each of the three estates (clergy, nobility, and commoners) was represented; it convened in 1789 for the first time since 1614.

An Ill-Fated Constitution Between 1789 and 1791, as the citizens of France awaited the unveiling of the new constitution, an egalitarian spirit swept the land. Aristocratic privileges were abolished, and church land was confiscated.

Bastille
At the time of the French Revolution (1789), the Bastille was the infamous royal prison in Paris; the mass storming of the Bastille on July 14, 1789, and the freeing of the prisoners constituted a direct attack against the monarchy and symbolized the end of an era in French history; the revolutionaries then used the guillotine against none other than the reigning Bourbon monarch, King Louis XVI, and his extravagant wife, Queen Marie Antoinette.

Declaration of the Rights of Man
Enacted by the French National Assembly in August 1789, this brief manifesto was intended as the preamble to a liberal-democratic constitution to be written later; it affirmed the sovereign authority of the nation but limited that authority by recognizing individual rights to life, property, and security.

A political document of fundamental importance, the **Declaration of the Rights of Man**, enshrined a slogan epitomizing the egalitarian spirit of the times: "liberty, equality, fraternity." The new constitution created a constitutional monarchy. No longer would Louis XVI rule autocratically according to divine right. Although the constitution placed the king at the head of the armed forces and charged him with responsibility for foreign affairs, it assigned most legislative powers to the National Constituent Assembly, which was given the power of the purse, as well as the power to declare war. A new elective administration was also created, and voting laws were liberalized. Thus, a stunning democratization of French political and social life was achieved in an amazingly brief period. The king's almost unlimited power had been undermined and radical social reforms implemented.

The constitutional monarchy set up by the 1791 constitution lasted less than one year, during which time the nation foundered without effective political leadership. Naturally, Louis XVI despised the new government imposed on him. (At one point, he even tried to flee the country to join opponents of the new government, but he was caught and returned to Paris.) The constitution barred former members of the National Constituent Assembly from serving in the new legislature, which meant inexperienced lawmakers held sway. Additional problems arose when the newly elected local administration failed to perform efficiently and interests that had lost power, especially the Catholic Church and the aristocracy, began to oppose the new regime. A war with Austria and Prussia exacerbated existing difficulties, and expected economic improvements were not forthcoming. Persistent rumors of the king's imminent return to absolute power swirled through Paris, inspiring a widespread fear of counterrevolution that undermined the political optimism brought on by the reforms.

Robespierre and the Reign of Terror   In the chaotic political and social environment of the early 1790s, events moved swiftly. Louis XVI was convicted of treason, deposed, and then beheaded in June 1793. A committee of political radicals intent on refashioning French society and unafraid to use violence took over the reins of government. The first priority of the new leader, Maximilien Robespierre (1758–1794), was to win the war against Austria and Prussia. In this atmosphere of external emergency, national unity at home was made paramount and all political opposition was considered treasonous. Then as now, political repression during times of war was common. But Robespierre was not satisfied simply to enforce national unity; he also wished to create a regime of virtue—to rebuild French society from the ground up, so to speak, by remaking the French citizenry in the image of moral perfection. According to one authority:

> Robespierre wanted a France where there should be neither rich nor poor, where men should not gamble, or get drunk, or commit adultery, cheat, or rob, or kill—where, in short, there would be neither petty nor grand vices—a France ruled by upright and intelligent men elected by the universal suffrage of the people, men wholly without greed or love of office, and delightedly stepping down at yearly intervals to give place to their successors, a France at peace with herself and the world.[20]

However grandiose, Robespierre's utopian idealism was not merely a statement of what *ought* to be; for him, it represented a call to action. Determined to create a "new citizen," Robespierre could not countenance the goal of individual freedom or the individual pursuit of happiness, as the American revolutionaries had. He was committed to a "despotism of liberty," rather than to a free society.

Institutionalizing virtue, however, was only one aspect of utopian idealism. Freedom from want, and even the promise of permanent abundance, became an important goal of Robespierre's revolution, waged in the name of the poor and oppressed against the greed and avarice of the oppressors.[21] Only through a policy motivated by compassion for the downtrodden, Robespierre believed, could a virtuous and contented citizenry emerge. Thus, the Biblical promise that "the meek shall inherit the earth" was an important part of his credo.

To advance virtue and end poverty in the shortest possible time, Robespierre proposed a sweeping reformulation of French life. Governmental institutions, legal arrangements, and social practices—everything was to be changed. Even a new calendar was proposed, as a symbol that a new era of history had dawned. The spirit of change was total, and heaven on earth was the ultimate goal. One observer has noted that the reigning spirit was that of "undiluted, enthusiastic, free floating messianism…satisfied with nothing less than a radical transformation of the human condition."[22]

But Robespierre and his compatriots soon discovered it was one thing to proclaim a new order and quite another to *keep* order. Policy disputes emerged as disillusionment reacted with unlimited expectations in a volatile mix. Active opposition to the new rulers began to spread.

Robespierre's response was to reinforce the regime of virtue with mass executions, which became known as the **Reign of Terror**. Executions by guillotine ordered by the Committee of Public Safety became commonplace, particularly in Paris. Originally aimed at active opponents, governmental violence soon gained a momentum of its own. It came to include people who shared Robespierre's vision but disagreed with his methods, and later, those merely suspected of dissenting became victims of the guillotine. Deep distrust enveloped those in power, as survivors feared for their safety. Eventually, collective fear led to the overthrow and execution of Robespierre himself. During his yearlong rule, some 40,000 people were summarily executed—an astonishing number in the eighteenth century.

Reign of Terror
During the French Revolution, Robespierre and his Committee of Public Safety arrested and mass executed thousands of French citizens for the "crime" of opposing the revolution or daring to dissent.

The King Is Dead, Long Live the Emperor The results of the French Revolution are not easy to evaluate. Clearly, it did not achieve its desired ends. After Robespierre's fall, a corrupt and incompetent government known as the Directory assumed power. In 1799, that regime gave way to the dictatorship of Napoléon Bonaparte, who managed to restore order and stability and crowned himself emperor in 1804. Under him, France tried to conquer all Europe in a series of ambitious wars that ultimately led to defeat and Napoléon's downfall.

No popular government followed on the heels of the French Revolution. In fact, after Napoléon's deposition, the monarchy was reinstituted. Many worthwhile and long-lasting changes did come about, however: The monarchy installed in 1815 was significantly limited in its powers, important social and political reforms stemming from the revolutionary era were retained, and the government was more centralized and more efficient. Despite these changes, the restored monarchy stood in sharp contrast to the egalitarian vision of a new society that had inspired Robespierre and his followers.

The Two Revolutions Compared

If the American Revolution was a revolution of sober goals, the French Revolution was one of infinite expectations. In the beginning, the French revolutionaries believed everything was possible for the pure of heart. The extremists' goals were utopian, and to realize them they were forced to use extreme means, including terror. Incredibly, America's best-known radical, Thomas Paine, found himself in a French prison during the revolution because his politics were not sufficiently extreme. In the thirteen colonies, most of the revolutionaries were political moderates. In France, moderates were executed or imprisoned.

The American Revolution, with its more modest aims, managed to produce the first great example of republican government in the modern age. France had no such luck. Yet the many revolutionary movements of the twentieth century were influenced far more by the French than by the American example.[23] It is understandable why the French Revolution—with its desire to eradicate poverty and its compassion for the oppressed—has fired the imagination of revolutionaries everywhere. But if concrete and lasting results are to be achieved, political ends must be realistic; otherwise, impossible dreams can turn into inescapable nightmares.

REVOLUTION—A RIGHT OR ALL WRONG?

"The tree of liberty must be refreshed from time to time with the blood of patriots and tyrants." These words were penned by Thomas Jefferson, who believed revolution was necessary to "refresh" democracy, as well as to establish it in the first place. But was he right? Is revolution more likely to improve the lot of the people or make things worse? British conservative Edmund Burke and American revolutionary Thomas Paine, Jefferson's contemporaries, engaged in a memorable debate over this very question during the early phase of the French Revolution. The pivotal issue was whether that revolution was really in the interest of the French people, in whose name it was waged, and, more generally, whether revolutions were beneficial or detrimental to society.

Burke's "Reflections"

The French Revolution inspired Edmund Burke (1729–1797) to write perhaps the most famous critique of revolution in the English language, *Reflections on the Revolution in France* (1790). Burke did not believe the French Revolution resulted from deep-seated economic and social forces. To his mind, the real revolutionaries were the philosophers who had expounded the subversive doctrine of rationalism and worshiped the god of science. By teaching that government existed to fulfill certain simple goals (for example, to secure individual rights), revolutionaries, Burke argued, created misleading impressions—most important among them that radical change almost always brought great improvements. This way of thinking undercut what Burke believed were the most important foundations of political society: religion and tradition.

Burke argued that dangerous political abstractions were at the heart of the French Revolution. By grossly oversimplifying politics and engendering unwarranted expectations at odds with French history and tradition, simplistic concepts such as "liberty, equality, fraternity" endangered the public order, on which all other political values and virtues ultimately rested. Good order, Burke noted, was the foundation of all good things.

The science of good government—how to run, maintain, or reform it—could not be mastered through philosophical speculations, Burke contended. He saw government as an "experimental science" whose practitioners needed the wisdom and insight born of experience. And experience, by its very nature, he argued, could not be acquired overnight; rather, it was accumulated, nurtured, cherished, and above all transmitted from generation to generation. Burke's view implied a veneration of the past, as well as a respect for age and achievement. Society, to his mind, was an intricate tapestry of laboriously handcrafted institutions possessing an inner logic and perpetuated by the force of habit, custom, and convention.

This sober view of government, and of human capacities and limitations, led Burke to stress the importance of pragmatism and prudence in politics. Prudence, he said, was the "first of all virtues." As for pragmatism, he maintained that given the complexity of humanity and society, no simple, all-embracing political formula could work the kind of profound changes promised by the French theorists.

Finally, Burke criticized the extreme impatience of those who glorified revolution. Arguing in favor of gradual and deliberate reform, he warned that unless political change occurred slowly and circumspectly, the main mass of the population would end up in worse straits than ever: "Time is required to produce that union of minds which alone can produce all the good we aim at. Our patience will achieve more than our force."[24]

Edmund Burke (1729–1797). Born in Dublin, Ireland, Burke is best known to the world as a British statesman and philosopher who abhorred revolution and advocated gradual change to conserve core values and institutions without which, he argued, societies risk descending into chaos and anarchy. "Our patience," Burke opined, "will achieve more than our force." Among his many quotable quotes, this one is perhaps the most famous: "All that is necessary for the triumph of evil is that good men do nothing."

By promising more than any political order can ever deliver and raising unrealistic expectations for some immediate utopian breakthrough, revolution may both dazzle the masses with visions of a bountiful (but unattainable) future and blind them to the wisdom of the past. In short, though politics can be understood as the "art of the possible," in the distorted mirror of revolution, it becomes the science of the impossible.

Paine's Rebuttal

Thomas Paine (1737–1809) attempted to refute Burke's view of revolution in his *Rights of Man*, written in two parts in February 1792 and addressed specifically to Burke. In defining the legitimacy of popular revolution, Paine stressed the many injustices perpetrated by the British monarchy on the American colonists. For him, tyranny and monarchy were as one. Monarchies, he declared, thrive on ignorance and are wrong in principle:[25]

> All hereditary government is in its nature tyranny. An heritable crown, or an heritable throne, or by what other fanciful name such things may be called, have no other significant explanation than that mankind are heritable property. To inherit a government, is to inherit the people, as if they were flocks and herds.[26]

In another passage, Paine wrote:

> When we survey the wretched condition of man under the monarchical and hereditary systems of government, dragged from his home by one power, or drived (sic) by another, and impoverished by taxes more than by enemies, it becomes evident that those systems are bad, and that a general revolution in the principle and construction of government is necessary.[27]

Thomas Paine (1737–1809) is best remembered for his ringing call to revolution in 1776 and his denunciation of monarchy in a pamphlet called *Common Sense*. Because this pamphlet inspired the American Revolution, Paine's place in history is secure, even though his role has often been overlooked in favor of iconic figures such as Thomas Jefferson, George Washington, John Adams, and Benjamin Franklin. This sign at a Tea Party rally features immortal words from another of Paine's revolutionary pamphlets called "The American Crisis."

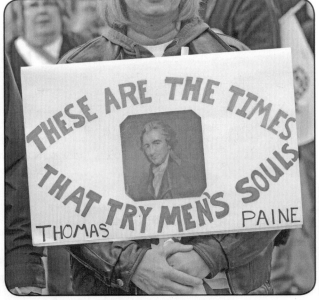

EDSTOCK/ISTOCKPHOTO.COM

Paine cited numerous examples of royal injustice and corruption. The greatest, he believed, was denial of the people's right to choose their own government. It seemed obvious to him that people should in no way be bound by their ancestors' decisions. "Every age and generation must be free to act for itself, in all cases, as the ages and generations which preceded it.... The vanity and presumption of governing beyond the grave is the most ridiculous and insolent of all tyrannies."[28]

Paine saw revolution in France as emphatically just. In seeking to overthrow the monarchy, he contended, the French were merely exercising a fundamental right, which grew out of their equal, natural right to liberty. Paine possessed an almost religious faith in the essential goodness and wisdom of the people. This pushed him to conclude that when the French Revolution is compared with that of other countries, it becomes apparent "that *principles* and not *persons* were the meditated objects of destruction."[29]

Locke's Right to Revolt

While Burke abhorred popular revolution, Paine glorified it.[30] Roughly a century earlier, John Locke had taken a middle ground between their two extremes in his *Second Treatise of Government*. Locke began with the premise that to escape the inconveniences of anarchy in the state of nature, human beings consent to be governed. Consent formed the basis for both civil society and formal government, with government existing chiefly to protect the rights deemed essential to human life. Locke then raised this question: What happens if the government endangers the life, liberty, and property of its citizens? In such a case, he concluded, the government has exercised "force without right," and the people have the right to resist and defend themselves. In Locke's words:

> The end of Government is the good of Mankind, and which is *best for Mankind*, that the People should be always expos'd to the boundless will of Tyranny, or that the Rulers should be sometimes liable to be oppos'd, when they grow exorbitant in the use of their power, and imploy (sic) it for the destruction, and not the preservation of the Properties of their People?[31]

Locke did not glorify revolution; he cautioned that popular rebellion should not be launched on a mere impulse. People will accept individual errors and instances of misrule, he asserted, but not "a long train of Abuses, Prevarications, and Artifices."[32] Locke even suggested his doctrine of rebellion could serve as a deterrent to revolution, by causing governments to respect the people's rights. Whether or not governments choose to recognize the *right* of the people to revolt, he pointed out, the people *will* revolt against a wicked government:

> If the majority of the people are persuaded in their Consciences, that the Laws, and with them their Estates, Liberties, and Lives are in danger, and perhaps their Religion, too, how they will be hindered from resisting illegal force used against them, I cannot tell. This is an Inconvenience, I confess that attends all Governments.[33]

In proclaiming the **right to revolution**, Locke may seem to have done little more than endorse what he saw as a fact of political life. But that does not diminish the importance of his doctrine of rebellion, which was itself

right to revolution
John Locke's theory that the end of government is the good of society and that when government deprives people of natural rights to life, liberty, and property, it is asking for trouble. If it fails to mend its ways, it deserves to be overthrown.

John Locke (1632–1704), English philosopher. Locke's magnum opus—*An Essay Concerning Human Understanding*—offers great insights into the limits of science and reason relative to what we can truly know about God, the natural order, and the self—and what we can never know. In Locke's view, the role of civil government is to preserve the life, health, liberty, and property of its subjects. When government fails, when it loses the consent of the majority, it naturally loses its legitimacy and risks overthrow. Locke's theory of revolution is not a prescription, but rather a description based on reasoned analysis of the conditions likely to give rise to rebellion.

JOHN LOCKE Efq.

revolutionary in the late seventeenth century. Even in England, where a few decades earlier King Charles I had been beheaded, the question whether dynastic rulers had a divine right to wield the scepter and command the sword was still being debated. In most other European nation-states, monarchs took the doctrine of divine right for granted. Not surprisingly, these kings did not trifle with anything so mundane as the will of the people, for they believed their authority stemmed from the will of God.

Locke's theory of revolution helped sound the death knell for the doctrine of divine right. Revolution, Locke claimed, becomes necessary when government acts contrary to its reason for being. Does revolution ensure good government? Of course not. It may lead to anarchy followed by a worse form of tyranny. But, Locke argues, popular revolution does create the *possibility* of government based on respect for life, liberty, and property.

Locke made no utopian claims about the relationship between revolution and political revitalization. As he saw it, revolutions may stem from the desire for better government, but they cannot guarantee that happy result. Like Aristotle before him, Locke assumed the existence of a finite number of governmental forms. New governments, he argued, are invariably new only in the sense that they supersede previous governments.[34]

Revolution, thus defined, hardly seemed a romantic endeavor. In Locke's view, it meant the exchange of one imperfect form of government for another, perhaps less imperfect form; it invariably encompassed great changes in the larger society; and it almost always implied the use of political force and violence. The tendency of revolutions toward upheaval meant the process was to be feared, even if the goal was desirable. Locke's sober view of rebellion has not been eclipsed; as one leading contemporary scholar pointed out, "A period of terror and the emergence of coercive and aggressive regimes are the outcomes of revolutions."[35]

THE CAUSES OF REVOLUTION

Locke held that revolutions are necessary and proper when citizens simply cannot endure any more. But what specifically is it they cannot endure? What causes citizens to discard ingrained political habits and support revolution?

The Classical View

To many observers, history and common sense suggest that injustices perpetrated by government over a prolonged period foster the conditions in which the seeds of revolution can germinate. This explanation of the cause of revolution originated with Aristotle, who observed in the fourth century BCE that although sedition may spring from small occasions, it ordinarily does not turn on small issues. The spark that ignites a revolution, in other words, should not be confused with the underlying causes of revolt.

Under every political order, competition for honors and wealth may give rise to the popular belief that one or both have not been fairly distributed. In most cases, Aristotle postulated, revolutions are caused by the administration of unequal justice.

Aristotle's concern with the perennial tension between rich and poor in political life established a theme in Western political thought that has gained importance over time. James Madison, for example, declared in *The Federalist* No. 10 that the "most common and durable source of faction is the various and unequal distribution of property" and then set out to develop a theory of government that might lessen this common source of political tension.

A half century later, Karl Marx declared inequality in wealth to be the ultimate cause of all revolutions. According to Marx, revolution is synonymous with class warfare and invariably stems from pervasive injustice. As the economic distance between wealthy capitalists and impoverished workers increases, so does the possibility of revolution.

What persuades the ordinary individual to disregard the strong social pressure for conformity and participate in a revolutionary movement? Marx held that desperation caused by poverty and social alienation is the chief psychological spur to revolutionary action, and his explanation has been widely accepted in modern times. A few years before Marx outlined this position in *The Communist Manifesto* (1848), however, Alexis de Tocqueville offered an alternative view. In studying the French Revolution, Tocqueville observed, "It was precisely in those parts of France where there had been the most improvement that popular discontent ran the highest. There, economic and social improvement had taken place, and political pressure had lessened, but still there existed the greatest amount of unrest."[36]

Tocqueville concluded that economic improvement leads to revolution because once the people see that some improvement is possible, they inevitably yearn for more. No longer are they willing to put up with inconveniences and annoyances—only *real* improvement, *immediate* improvement, will satisfy them. Thus is the incentive for revolution born, he argued.

Modern Theories

The positions of Marx and Tocqueville seem incompatible, but in 1962, James C. Davies wrote a celebrated article suggesting "both ideas have explanatory and possibly predictive value, if they are juxtaposed and put in the proper time sequence."[37] Davies came to this provocative conclusion after careful study of Dorr's Rebellion of 1842, the Russian Revolution of 1917, and the Egyptian Revolution of 1952. After seeing a remarkably similar pattern of revolutionary development, he concluded that revolutions are most likely to erupt when conditions have been getting better for a prolonged period of time and then suddenly take a sharp turn for the worse.

Elaborating on Davies's thesis, two authorities later argued that the rates of earlier economic growth (and the speed of any economic decline) are especially significant factors. The higher the growth rate in per capita GNP prior to a revolutionary upheaval and "the sharper the reversal immediately prior to the revolution," they declared, "the greater the duration and violence of the revolution."[38] In other words, revolutions stem not so much from terrible suffering as from crushing disappointment. Intense discontent, bred by the failure to acquire the goods and experience the conditions of life to which people believe they are rightfully entitled, induces them to revolt.[39]

A pervasive sense of injustice is typically at the core of revolutionary mass movements. But great social and economic injustice does not *always* lead to revolution. Modern theorists have tried to identify *specific* causes that can become the incubator of revolution. One way to go about this kind of academic detective work is through methodical case studies.[40]

According to political scientists Ted Gurr and Jack Gladstone, a revolution is best conceptualized as an interactive process that continues over time.[41] The machinery of government breaks down in stages as political crises ensue; both influential citizens and government leaders become alienated. Governmental leaders are increasingly perceived as inept: unable to exercise effective authority, incapable of stabilizing the economy, powerless to ensure domestic order, weak and irresolute in the face of external threats. Thus, nearly everyone (including the elites) comes to see the established government as illegitimate, and it loses its right to rule.[42] Precisely for these reasons, successful revolutionaries usually have the support of wealthy (possibly even aristocratic) patrons and are able to mobilize many discontented people as well.

Conceptualizing revolution as an interactive process is compatible with the traditional theory of revolution. It helps explain how injustice, or the perception of injustice, is at the root of revolution. Contemporary scholarship details how this process takes place. It examines the types of crises facing prerevolutionary states, the factors leading to a general loss of confidence in government, and the besieged governments' often hapless responses.

Invariably, societies on the verge of revolution face peril. Economic hardships can be particularly debilitating. Rapid population growth can slow or reverse economic growth and promote inequality. Ethnic, racial, or religious tensions may plunge a society into civil war, especially when one group grows or prospers at a faster rate than others. Rapid urbanization can create social problems, including inadequate housing, sanitation, and medical and educational services. Crime usually increases, particularly when there is a high percentage of alienated young males.[43]

Losing a war can be another prelude to revolution, because it is typically associated with severe economic hardships. In these circumstances, any government can lose its legitimacy in the eyes of the people.[44] Finally, upheavals in neighboring states can spill into and affect vulnerable governments in the vicinity.

Mounting economic, demographic, and political pressures in prerevolutionary nations can lead to criticism, lawlessness, riots, and acts of terrorism, forcing governments to act. If the bureaucracy includes officials from the landholding class, they may block or inhibit reforms designed to defuse a potentially revolutionary domestic crisis.[45] Or action may be inhibited by widespread internal corruption. But no government can tolerate long-term criticism, lawlessness, or acts of terrorism. If its response is unjust or inept, or if it fails to act at all, government risks losing the confidence of its supporters and becomes vulnerable to revolutionary demands.

Surprisingly, unpopular governments that equivocate or temporize in the face of a rebellion, rather than taking swift and decisive action to it in its infancy, are often at risk of being overthrown. In a study of the French Revolution, Tocqueville noted that French citizens took up arms against the government precisely when it began easing its crackdown. He concluded, "Generally speaking, the most perilous moment for a bad government is one when it seeks to mend its ways."[46]

Tocqueville believed that underlying this paradox (as well as his contention that reform, not repression, is the great accomplice of revolution) is a psychological truth:

> Patiently endured so long as it seemed beyond redress, a grievance comes to appear intolerable once the possibility of removing it crosses men's minds.... For the mere fact that certain abuses have been remedied draws attention to the others and now appears more galling; people may suffer less, but their sensibility is exacerbated.[47]

In sum, tyrants cannot afford to institute reforms because to do so would be to admit past injustices and activate "the rancor and cupidity of the populace."[48]

Modern studies provide some support for Tocqueville's observations. In a major analysis of the role of the armed forces in revolutionary episodes, one writer argued that revolution never succeeds when the armed forces remain loyal to the government in power and can be effectively employed.[49] When internal security measures are applied too late, too haphazardly, or as the last resort of a desperate government, there is a good chance that official acts of repression may only make matters worse. Apparently, governments that shrink from the systematic use of physical force in revolutionary situations run the greatest risk of being overthrown.

Some Tentative Conclusions

Theories of revolution abound, but despite many attempts, there is no definitive *general theory* of revolution. Nonetheless, we can draw some generalizations based on historical and sociological evidence.

For revolutions to occur, charismatic leaders must be willing to take the deadly risks associated with overthrowing an established (often repressive) regime.[50] They need the support of others in high positions and those with technical skills. The right moment to win over the elites is when the government offends, threatens, or undermines them in some way. Elite alienation poses the greatest danger to the prerevolutionary government when it occurs within the armed forces.[51] If the generals and other senior military officers withdraw support from or turn against the ruler(s), it is almost always fatal for the government in power.

Revolutionary change is frequently organized from above. However, all such change depends on the new government's success in gaining or holding a mass following, which, in turn, often depends on the degree of citizen discontent prior to the revolutionary events. The causes of popular discontent can include "widespread dissatisfaction over economic conditions, especially among urban peoples; frustration about the lack of opportunities for real political participation, especially among young students and the middle classes; widespread anger about foreign interventions and official corruption; and rural hostility toward the predatory and repressive policies of urban-based regimes."[52] In short, it is the popular perception of injustice, whether true or false, that fuels the fires of all-out revolution in the modern era.

Finally, revolutions are not likely unless most or all of the factors discussed earlier exist simultaneously. Thus, even a nation with economic and social problems would probably not be prone to revolution without the existence of other elements of prerevolution: revolutionary leaders, strong elite and citizen support for radical action, and a general loss of public confidence in the existing government's capacity to rule. It is the coincidence of these factors that makes revolutions happen.

The Spanish philosopher José Ortega y Gasset (1883–1955) published his famous book *The Revolt of the Masses* in 1930, after the fascists had taken over Italy, shortly before Hitler's accession to power in Germany, and just about the time Stalin was consolidating his power in Soviet Russia.[53] Ortega y Gasset wrote with horror about "the accession of the masses to complete social power" and argued that "the masses, by definition, neither should nor can direct their own personal existence, and still less rule society in general, [which means] that actually Europe is suffering from the greatest general crisis that can afflict peoples, nations, and civilizations."[54]

The twentieth century witnessed the bloodiest mass movements in history. All failed. The words of Ortega y Gasset are particularly poignant in the light of the calamitous results of modern revolutions:

> As they say in the United States: "to be different is to be indecent." The mass crushes beneath it everything that is different, everything that is excellent, individual, qualified, and select. Anybody who is not like everybody, who does not think like everybody, runs the risk of being eliminated.[55]

At the same time, the modern history of revolution provides significant counterexamples. Ironically, the United States would become the self-appointed global defender of the status quo after World War II, the archenemy of revolutionary movements in the Third World, where former colonies were fighting for independence as we ourselves had done nearly two centuries earlier. Those in the United States came to associate revolution with terror, totalitarianism, and tyrants. But when the Cold War finally drew to a close, the face of revolution suddenly changed, as dozens of dictatorships were swept away.

Today, democracies flourish where Communist police states ruled for nearly half a century, thanks to a series of stunning revolutions that occurred simultaneously with very little violence (with the exception of the Balkans). It was as if a massive earthquake shook Russia and Eastern Europe to their foundations but left nearly everything intact; instead of causing great death and destruction, it actually set the stage for a political and economic resurgence (see "Ideas and Politics: Nonviolent Revolutions").

NONVIOLENT REVOLUTION

History teaches that violent regimes are often the off-spring of violent revolutions. Between World War I (1914–1918) and the end of the Cold War (1989–1992), Russia (Lenin and Stalin), Germany (Hitler), Italy (Mussolini), Spain (Franco), China (Mao Zedong), Cuba (Castro), Cambodia (Pol Pot), Ethiopia (Mengistu), and Iran (Khomeini) endured bloody revolutions. Other notable revolutions after World War II occurred in Egypt (Nasser), Algeria (Ahmed Ben Bella), and Indonesia (Sukarno). All witnessed large-scale violence in varying degrees.

In sharp contrast, the overthrow of dictator Slobodan Milosevic (also known as the "Bulldozer Revolution") was the culmination of a long, sustained campaign of civil resistance —in other words, a nonviolent revolution. The overthrow was led by a largely student-based mass organization called *Otpor* (Resistance, in Serbian). Nine years later, Mohamed Abdel, a 20-year-old Egyptian blogger, frustrated at the failure of one previous attempt to launch a similar nationwide uprising against the autocratic rule of Hosni Mubarak, traveled to Belgrade, Serbia.* Abdel was on a mission:

> The Serbian capital is home to the Center for Applied Non Violent Action and Strategies, or CANVAS, an organization run by young Serbs who had cut their teeth in the late 1990s student uprising against Slobodan Milosevic. After ousting him, they embarked on the ambitious project of figuring out how to translate their success to other countries. To the world's autocrats, they are sworn enemies—both Venezuela's Hugo Chávez and Belarus's Aleksandr Lukashenko have condemned them by name.

Abdel went to Serbia to take "a week-long course in the strategies of nonviolent revolution." He did not need to learn how to communicate with others using Facebook or Twitter. He already knew that. In his own words, "I got trained in how to conduct peaceful demonstrations, how to avoid violence, and how to face violence from the security forces…and also how to organize to get people on the streets." Above all, he learned how to teach others.

Back in Egypt, Abdel began training young people. Out of these training sessions emerged two youth groups that "led the charge in actually getting organized and onto the streets," according to one report from Stratfor, a geopolitical analysis group.

Viewed in this light, the overthrow of Hosni Mubarak is one link in a lengthening chain of popular revolts using the strategy and tactics of civil resistance to bring about regime change. Before 1989, the Baltic states of Latvia, Lithuania, and Estonia were essentially Communist dictatorships ruled from Moscow. East Germany, Poland, Hungary, Czechoslovakia, Romania, and Bulgaria were also ruled by Soviet-style dictatorships. When Hungary revolted against Soviet rule in 1956, the Red Army quelled the uprising. In 1968, Moscow brutally suppressed a spontaneous mass revolt known as the Prague Spring in Czechoslovakia.

But two decades later, the Kremlin boss (Mikhail Gorbachev) looked the other way as Stalinist rulers in Eastern Europe tumbled like falling dominoes when the people streamed into the streets and refused to go home. Today the political map of Europe looks nothing like it did twenty years ago, thanks to a series of largely nonviolent revolutions that replaced one-party dictatorships with constitutional democracies. Hungary is an independent country with a parliamentary democracy, as are Poland and the Baltic states. East Germany has merged with the Federal Republic of Germany (West Germany). Czechoslovakia has split into two separate states, both democratically ruled. All are members of NATO and the EU. Romania and Bulgaria joined the EU in 2007 (Figure 14.1).

As products of the twentieth century, we naturally associate political revolutions with turmoil and tragedy, rather than peace and progress. In Serbia, an organized and energized mass of protesters succeeded

(Continued)

(CONTINUED)

FIGURE 14.1   Political Map of Europe. In 1989, the Communist regimes in Eastern Europe were overthrown in rapid succession and replaced by democratically elected governments. Except in Romania, this remarkable transformation was accomplished without bloodshed, and today, these emerging democracies belong to NATO and the European Union. EU members as of 2007 are highlighted in this figure.

(Continued)

(CONTINUED)

in overthrowing a brutal dictator and ushering in a parliamentary democracy. Remarkably, they did it by adapting the principles found in Lenin's revolutionary playbook (see Chapter 6). Unity, discipline, and planning—these are the three keys taught in the CANVAS seminars on nonviolent revolution. Unlike the Marxist-Leninist "dictatorship of the proletariat," in which violence plays a pivotal role, the emphasis on discipline in the Serbian and Egyptian uprisings was directed toward self-restraint in confrontations with security forces.

The triumph of democracy in Eastern Europe proves conclusively that under certain circumstances regime change can occur without violence. Only time will tell whether that good fortune will also fall to Egypt, Tunisia, Libya, and other Arab states beset by popular revolts in recent years.

---

*See Tina Rosenberg, "Revolution U," in *Foreign Policy*, February 16, 2011. Online at http://www.foreignpolicy.com/articles/2011/02/16/revolution_u.

Eastern Europe is not the only place where revolutions have occurred on the quiet. Several Asian states, including South Korea and Taiwan, have achieved major regime change with relatively little violence. Clearly, the notion that revolutions are *always* violent or that they are *always* inimical to peace and stability is false. Perhaps that is the most revolutionary change (and lesson) of all.

SUMMARY

Revolution brings significant changes in the form of a nation's government. There are two basic revolutionary traditions, the American and the French. The American Revolution was more limited and sought more moderate goals. The French revolutionary leaders, unlike their more pragmatic American counterparts, sought complete and radical change in the social, political, and moral fabric of their country.

Whether revolution is desirable has been fiercely debated since the late eighteenth century, when Edmund Burke stressed its many dangers and Thomas Paine its many benefits. Earlier, John Locke had taken a moderate position, calling revolution necessary and justified when directed against an oppressive government.

The precise causes of revolution are difficult to isolate. Aristotle argued that injustice is at the root of popular rebellion. But what convinces the ordinary citizen to participate in a revolution? Karl Marx contended that worsening economic and social conditions lead to participation in revolutions. Alexis de Tocqueville asserted that improving conditions are to blame, for they cause individual hopes to outrun social reality. A modern view put forth by James C. Davies combined Marx's and Tocqueville's positions in arguing that revolutions are most likely to erupt when sharp economic or social reversals follow a period of rising expectations and moderate improvements. More recent studies characterize revolution as an ongoing process, reflecting a crisis of government's legitimacy.

Facing difficult economic, political, or social problems, governments often act ineptly or unjustly. When they lose the confidence of elites in society, the masses are mobilized as revolutionary leaders plan the government's overthrow and the creation of a new political order. Mass-movement revolutions have ultimately all failed, and in the process they have ironically victimized many innocent people.

KEY TERMS

revolution   391
French Revolution   393
American
   Revolution   393

Revolutionary
  War   393
Estates-General   397
Bastille 397

Declaration of the
  Rights of Man   398
Reign of Terror   399
right to revolution   403

REVIEW QUESTIONS

1. In politics, what is the meaning of the word *revolution*? Have revolutions become more or less prevalent in the twentieth century in comparison with previous eras?
2. In what important respects were the American Revolution and the French Revolution similar? In what important respects did they differ?
3. In the debate over the desirability of revolution between Edmund Burke and Thomas Paine, what position did each take? What were Burke's chief arguments? How did Paine respond?
4. What was John Locke's view of revolution? Why did he assert the right of citizens to overthrow their government? In what sense does Locke occupy a middle ground between Paine and Burke?
5. According to Aristotle, what is the principal cause of revolution? How have modern social scientists sought to go beyond Aristotle's philosophical insights into revolution?
6. Has contemporary research shed any new light on the causes of revolution? If so, have any common elements arisen from recent theoretical research, or are the findings contradictory? What theories have been advanced to explain how and why individuals become sufficiently disenchanted to join a revolutionary movement?

CHAPTER 15

War

Politics by Other Means

THINK ABOUT IT

What are three theories on the causes of war (Hobbes, Rousseau, Locke), and who is right?

What is the difference between a total war and a nuclear war?

How does an accidental war differ from a proxy war?

Is there any such thing as a just war?

war
Organized violence, often on a large scale, involving sovereign states or geographic parts of the same state or distinct ethnic or social groups within a given state (civil war).

interstate wars
Armed conflict between sovereign states.

civil wars
A war between geographical sections or rival groups within a nation.

guerrilla warfare
The tactics used by loosely organized military forces grouped into small, mobile squads that carry out acts of terrorism and sabotage, then melt back into the civilian population.

low-intensity conflicts
Internal warfare that is sporadic and carried out on a small scale but often prolonged and debilitating to the state and society in which it occurs.

War is the central problem of world politics. In the famous words of Prussian military theorist Carl von Clausewitz (1780–1831), "war is a continuation of politics by other means." If anarchy is the absence of government and the rule of law, then world politics is an arena in which anarchy reigns. Small wonder that state actors are always conscious of war as an ever-present possibility and view peace as a precarious and perilous condition.

When people think of war, they usually have in mind **interstate wars**—that is, conflicts between two or more nation-states. **Civil wars** are conflicts within a single country; they have become more common than international wars today. **Guerrilla warfare** is a low-tech form of fighting usually waged in rural areas by small, lightly armed mobile squads (often fed and sheltered by sympathetic villagers). Guerrillas typically carry out selective acts of violence, primarily against the army, the police, and the government, in an attempt to weaken or topple the ruler(s). **Low-intensity conflicts**, a fourth category, occur when one state finances, sponsors, or promotes the sporadic or prolonged use of violence in a rival country (by hiring mercenaries or underwriting guerrillas, for example).

In terms of lives lost, property damaged or destroyed, and money drained away, war is undeniably the most destructive and wasteful of all human activities. Estimates of the war dead in the last century alone fall in the range of 35 million, including 25 million civilians.[1] General William Tecumseh Sherman knew firsthand the horror of war. As a military leader, he had, in fact, been a fearsome practitioner of it. In a speech delivered fifteen years after the American Civil War, Sherman declared, "There is many a boy who looks on war as all glory, but boys, it is hell."

Not everyone sees war the way an older and wiser General Sherman did. Some of history's most illustrious (or infamous) personalities have reveled in the "glory" of war or acknowledged its perverse attractions. In the eighth century BCE, the Greek poet Homer noted that men grow tired of sleep, love, singing, and dancing sooner than they do of war. In his poetry, he celebrated the self-sacrifice and courage war demanded. The Greek philosopher Aristotle, writing some 500 years later, listed courage as the first, though not the foremost, human virtue. To Aristotle, courage in battle ennobled human beings because it represented the morally correct response to fear in the face of mortal danger, danger that, in turn, imperiled the political community.

Perhaps no writer in modern times rationalized war better than the German philosopher G. W. F. Hegel, who argued, "If states disagree and their particular wills cannot be harmonized, the matter can only be settled by war." Hegel argued war is necessary because "corruption in nations would be the product of prolonged, let alone 'perpetual' peace." During times of peace, Hegel reasoned, society too easily grows soft and contentious: "As a result of war, nations are strengthened, but peoples involved in civil strife also acquire peace at home through making war abroad."[2]

Hegel contended that "world history is the world court." In other words, the ultimate test of validity or worth is not some abstract moral standard, but success. And because success in world politics is measured, above all, in terms of power and size, it follows that might and right are synonymous.

The German philosopher Friedrich Nietzsche (1844–1900) further radicalized this idea. Nietzsche disdained conventional morality in general and despised the Christian ethic of humility in particular (he regarded it as a weakness). What Nietzsche admired most, both in individuals and in nations, was the aggressive exercise of power. He celebrated the will to power and praised the curative effects of war on nations and civilizations.[3] This theme would be revived with a vengeance half a century later by Adolf Hitler and his ally, Benito Mussolini. Like Hegel and Nietzsche, Mussolini scoffed at pacifism. Said the father of Italian fascism, "War alone brings to their highest tension all human energies and puts the stamp of nobility upon the peoples who have the courage to meet it."[4]

Although war is a constant in human affairs, it has evolved over time. Technology has transformed its ways and means without mitigating its lethal effects or destructive consequences—indeed, quite the opposite. Today, old forms of guerrilla warfare coexist with ultra-high-tech robots, drones, and cyberwar.

This ever-present reality of war persists side by side with the dream of a world without war. Throughout the ages, philosophers and theologians have pondered the possibility of perpetual peace. But if war is ever to be eradicated, we must first isolate its causes.

THE CAUSES OF WAR

Why war? There is no simple answer. An observer living in Europe or the Middle East in the twelfth century would probably have attributed the frequency and ferocity of war at that time to religious zealotry. The Crusades, which began at the end of the eleventh century and continued for 200 years, were marked by the kind of unmerciful slaughter that, paradoxically, has often accompanied the conviction that "God is on our side."

Although religion did help fuel many regional and local wars, it played only a minor role in most of the major wars of the twentieth century. In no sense was religious fanaticism the cause of World War I, for instance. Many observers attribute the outbreak of that conflict to **nationalism** run amok, a phenomenon virtually unknown in the twelfth century. Others stress the **arms race** conducted by European nations, arguing that the momentum of military preparations carried Europe inexorably into war. Still others blame imperialism: The scramble for colonial territories in the latter half of the nineteenth century led to war, they contend, once there were no "unclaimed" lands left in Asia and Africa.

Nor did religion play a major role in World War II. Ideology was a factor (national socialism in Germany, fascism in Italy, and communism in the Soviet Union), but the main "ism" behind the aggressive policies of Germany, Italy, and Japan was **ultranationalism**, or what scholar Hans J. Morgenthau called **nationalistic universalism**. The Korean Conflict (1950–1953) and the Vietnam War (1963–1975) were fought for both geopolitical reasons, or **reasons of state**, and ideological reasons. Some historians have seen this mix of pragmatism and idealism as a factor in the unsatisfactory (for the United States) outcomes of both these wars, because military-strategic decisions were distorted by a crusading anticommunism that defined U.S. foreign policy during the Cold War.

nationalism Devotion to one's nation; closely akin to patriotism.

arms race Reciprocal military buildups between rival states; a process that tends to accelerate research, technology, and development in weapons systems and, according to some experts, is a potential cause of war.

ultranationalism Extreme nationalism often associated with fascism; a radical right-wing orientation typically characterized by militarism, racial bigotry, and xenophobia.

nationalistic universalism A messianic foreign policy that seeks to spread the ideas and institutions of one nation to other nations.

reasons of state The pragmatic basis for foreign policy that places the national interest above moral considerations or idealistic motives; also *raison d'état*.

On the surface, then, the causes of World War I and World War II differed radically from those of, say, the Crusades. But whatever their immediate causes, every war represents another outbreak of the same old disease, even if the symptoms and severity have changed.

Philosophers and theologians, hoping to find the keys to peace, have for 2,000 years attempted to discover war's root causes. After World War II, the most destructive war in history, political scientists tried using statistical and mathematical models to learn more. Quantitative research of this kind tries to match the methodological rigor and precision of the natural sciences. In the words of John Vasquez, one of the foremost advocates of this approach:

> Philosophical analyses of the physical world, for example,...even when conducted by such a brilliant thinker as Aristotle, did not produce a cumulative body of knowledge. A substantial advancement in our understanding came only with the development and application of the scientific method.[5]

What has the scientific approach to the study of war achieved thus far? According to Vasquez, it has "helped refine thinking about war and raised serious questions about existing explanations of war."[6]

Other political scientists are not so sure.[7] James Dougherty and Robert Pfaltzgraff concluded, "Despite the proliferation of statistical studies of war (both inductive and deductive),...[most] are more likely to be relegated to footnotes [in the long run] than regarded as classics."[8] Greg Cashman chose a middle-of-the-road position:

> Although no single theory seems to have anywhere near universal validity, social scientific research has not been completely fruitless....The investigations undertaken by social scientists during the last four decades have not culminated in the creation of a single, unified theory of war, [but] they have certainly added greatly to our understanding of the causes of war.[9]

What we know for certain is there is no simple explanation for war. To probe deeper, we turn to three broad theories of causation. One emphasizes flaws in human nature. A second stresses defects in society and its institutions. A third sees scarcity as the cause of conflict.[10] After examining each, we look at the findings of several quantitative studies to corroborate or refute them.

Christianity has had a profound influence on Western political thought in this regard. Drawing on the Old Testament, early Christian thinkers viewed the human race as irreparably flawed by original sin—that is, by Adam and Eve's violation of God's law in the Garden of Eden, as recorded in the book of Genesis. The story of the fall is, in a very real sense, a universal one with universal significance—world history in a nutshell.

According to Saint Augustine (354–430), an influential early Christian theologian, war is the price we pay for our corrupt nature. Many secular thinkers display a similar pessimism, without citing original sin as the cause. The Greek philosopher Plato attributed wars, at least in part, to the human passion for worldly possessions and creature comforts. The sixteenth-century

Italian thinker Niccoló Machiavelli painted an equally depressing picture of the interaction between human nature and politics. In *The Prince*, he asserted that political success and moral rectitude are often inversely related: Rulers tend to prosper in direct proportion to the dirty politics they practice for the sake of self-gratifying political ends.

The frequency of war shows the law of the jungle still governs human behavior much as it did before primates evolved beyond the state of nature. In the Nuclear Age, when all-out war is unthinkable, there is still no lasting peace on earth.

Whereas some have looked to religion and others to philosophy for an explanation of aggressive human tendencies, still others have turned to psychology. Sigmund Freud (1856–1939), the founder of psychoanalysis, believed human beings are born with a "death wish," or innate self-destructive tendencies, that they redirect into other activities most of the time. During times of conflict, Freud theorized, combatants direct these destructive tendencies against each other. Thus, wars serve a psychotherapeutic function: They offer an outlet for otherwise self-destructive impulses. Critics argue this theory is too clever by half—the soldiers who do the fighting and killing are not the ones who decide to go to war, and the decision makers, careful to stay out of harm's way, are not the ones who fight. Most soldiers kill because they have a job to do and because they do not want to be killed, not because they are violent or destructive by nature.

Other psychologists have called aggression an innate human drive constantly seeking an outlet, a normal human response to frustration, or the same "territorial imperative" that supposedly accounts for aggressive behavior in the animal kingdom. According to the territorial imperative theory, latent aggressions are lodged deep in human nature, and threats to an individual's or group's territory (property, loved ones, and so on) can trigger aggressive action.

Still other observers find the ultimate cause of war not in the human soul or psyche but rather in the brain. People are neither depraved nor disturbed but obtuse—too stupid to understand the futility of war. In the words of a prominent pacifist writing between World Wars I and II:

> The obstacle in our path…is not in the moral sphere, but in the intellectual.…It is not because men are ill-disposed that they cannot be educated into a world social consciousness. It is because they—let us be honest and say "we"—are beings of conservative temper and limited intelligence.[11]

Human Nature

Thomas Hobbes (1588–1679), living during the Puritan Revolution in England, had a different, but hardly more flattering, explanation for war. He was, above all, a realist who sought to understand human nature as it is, not as it ought to be. The only way to know what people are really like, Hobbes believed, is to look at how they would behave outside civil society as we know it—that is, as brutes of limited intelligence in a **state of nature**. The conclusions he drew from this exercise are fascinating and continue to influence how we think about politics, war, and the possibility of peace even today.

According to Hobbes, life in the state of nature would be "solitary, poor, nasty, brutish, and short." Human beings like other earth-bound creatures are governed by a keen instinct for self-preservation. They fear death above all and especially sudden, violent death. This fear does not, however, result in meekness or passivity; on the contrary, aggression and violent behavior are the norm. Hobbes identified "three principal causes" of war:

> First, Competition; Secondly, Diffidence; Thirdly, Glory. The first maketh man invade for Gain; the second, for Safety; and the third, for Reputation. The first cause [men to turn to] Violence to make themselves Masters of other men's persons, wives, children, and cattell; and the second, to defend them; the third, for trifles, at a word, a smile, a different opinion, and other signe of undervalue.[12]

The state of nature, for Hobbes, is a state of war—what he famously called a "war of every man, against every man."

Hobbes applied this same logic to international politics in his own time, which was a perpetual state of war. Just as individuals in the state of nature are governed by base motives and drives, he declared, leaders with similar motives and drives govern nations. And just as the state of nature lacks a government to protect people from one another, so the international system lacks a government to protect nations from one another.

Hobbes theorized that three kinds of disputes correspond to the three defects in human nature: aggressive wars, caused by competitive instincts; defensive wars, caused by fears; and agonistic wars, caused by pride and vanity. Through this compact theory, Hobbes sought to explain not only how human beings would act outside the civilizing influence of society and government (human beings constantly at each other's throats if not for government-imposed law and order), but also why nations sometimes go to war over issues that make no sense to outsiders.

The Hobbesian Legacy Hans Morgenthau, like Hobbes, argued forcefully that human beings are deeply flawed. According to Morgenthau, "Human nature, in which the laws of politics have their roots, has not changed since the classical philosophies of China, India, and Greece endeavored to discover these laws," and "politics, like society in general, is governed by objective laws that have their roots in human nature."[13] The key to understanding the operation of these laws is the "concept of interest defined as power." This means human beings are motivated by self-interest, which predisposes human behavior toward an eternal "struggle for power." Morgenthau made this point particularly clear when he stated, "International politics, like all politics, is a struggle for power.

---

state of nature
The human condition before the creation of a social code of behavior and collective techniques to control normal human impulses.

Whatever the ultimate aims of international politics, power is always the immediate aim." Like Hobbes before him, Morgenthau rejected the idealist view that "assumes the essential goodness and infinite malleability of human nature." Instead, he embraced the realist view "that the world, imperfect as it is from the rational point of view, is the result of forces inherent in human nature."[14]

According to Morgenthau and the realist school of political theory his writings inspired, human nature and the drive for self-aggrandizement are among the leading, if not the leading, causes of competition and conflict. Compelling, though not flattering, this view of humankind is not the only plausible explanation of why wars are fought.

Society

Not all political thinkers attribute war to the human psyche or human nature. Some blame modern society in general, organized into a state (an exclusive or "members only" political association), and others contend that particular kinds of political states pose disproportionate dangers to peace. In this section, we examine the different approaches of political theorists and leaders who blame society or the state (the political framework of society) for war's destructiveness.

Rousseau "Man is born free, and everywhere he is in chains." With this attack on the modern nation-state, the French philosopher Jean-Jacques Rousseau (1712–1778) began the first chapter of his classic *Social Contract* (1762), in which he directly challenged Hobbes's assertion that human beings are naturally cunning and violent. Rousseau started from the premise that human beings are naturally "stupid but peaceful" creatures, quite capable of feeling pity for those who are suffering. Hobbes simply erred, in this view, in attributing ambition, fear, and pride to human beings in the state of nature. Rousseau was convinced these are attributes of social man, not natural man (here the term *man* is used in the classic sense to mean all humans, irrespective of gender). Antisocial behaviors, paradoxically, have social causes; they are sure signs of human corruption. Society, not human nature, is to blame. Rousseau is quite explicit on this point: "It is clear that…to society, must be attributed the assassinations, poisonings, highway robberies, and even the punishments of these crimes."[15]

Indeed, Rousseau believed society is the cause of all kinds of problems, including war. Specifically, he blamed the institution of private property—a preoccupation of all eighteenth-century European societies—for the miseries that have beset the human race since it abandoned its natural innocence for the false pleasures of civilization. Property divides human beings, he argued, by creating unnecessary inequalities in wealth, status, and power among citizens within particular nations and, eventually, among nations:

> The first person who, having fenced off a plot of ground, took it into his head to say this is mine and found people simple enough to believe him, was the true founder of civil society. What crimes, wars, murders, what miseries and horrors would the human race have been spared by some-one who, uprooting the stakes or filling in the ditch, had shouted to his fellow-men: Beware of listening to this imposter, you are lost if you forget that the fruits belong to all and the earth to no one.[16]

Specifically, Rousseau postulated that just as the creation of private property led to the founding of the first political society, that founding mandated the creation of additional nation-states. And because each of these nations faced all the others in a state of nature, great tensions arose that eventually led to the "national wars, battles, murders, and reprisals, which make nature tremble and shock reason."[17] With the "division of the human race into different societies," Rousseau concluded:

> The most decent men learned to consider it one of their duties to murder their fellow men; at length men were seen to massacre each other by the thousands without knowing why; more murders were committed on a single day of fighting and more horrors in the capture of a single city than were committed in the state of nature during whole centuries over the entire race of the earth.[18]

Rousseau's view that private property is the root of all evil has exerted a profound influence on modern intellectual history. Even political thinkers who reject his specific diagnosis of the nation-state have widely accepted his general theory that "man is good but men are bad." Several twentieth-century variations on this theme have appeared. As we shall see, each differs in substantial ways from the others, but all assume the fatal flaw leading to war resides in society rather than in human nature.

Nationalism and War Many modern thinkers hold that war is inherent in the very existence of separate societies with sovereign governments. The manifestation of these potent separatist tendencies is nationalism, the patriotic sentiments citizens feel toward their homeland (sometimes referred to, in its most extreme forms, as *jingoism* or *chauvinism*). According to one authority:

> Each nation has its own rose-colored mirror. It is the particular quality of such mirrors to reflect images flatteringly: the harsh lines are removed but the character and beauty shine through! To each nation none is so fair as itself.... Each nation considers (to itself or proclaims aloud, depending upon its temperament and inclination) that it is "God's chosen people" and dwells in "God's country."[19]

Small wonder that nationalism has been called an idolatrous religion. Although it may foster unity and a spirit of self-sacrifice within a society, between societies it has led, directly or indirectly, to militarism, xenophobia, and mutual distrust.

Nationalism can be manipulated in support of a war policy, and warfare can be used to intensify nationalism. The chemistry between them is sufficiently volatile to have caused many **internationalists**, or theorists favoring peace and cooperation among nations through the active participation of all governments in some sort of world organization, to single out nationalism as the main obstacle to achieving peace and harmony in the world.

To the extent that nationalism is an artificial passion—one socially conditioned rather than inborn—political society is to blame for war. This type of reasoning has led some to suggest a radically simple formula for eliminating war: Do away with the nation-state and you do away with nationalism; do away with nationalism and you do away with war. Others have sought more practical remedies—fix the nation-state rather than abolish it.

internationalists
Theorists favoring peace and cooperation among nations through the active participation of all governments in some sort of world organization.

Tyranny and War: Wilson Many identify nationalism as the major cause of modern conflict, but others blame despotism for the two calamitous world wars of the last century. President Woodrow Wilson (1856–1924) championed this notion and actually tried to build a new world order on its conceptual foundations.

After World War I, Wilson sought to secure lasting peace through a treaty based on his Fourteen Points—principles he hoped would lead to a world without war. The cornerstone of this proposed new world order was the right of **national self-determination**, or the right of people everywhere to choose the government they wished to live under. Wilson expected self-determination to lead to the creation of democracies, which he viewed as being naturally more prone to peace than dictatorships.

But why should democracies be any more reluctant to go to war than dictatorships? The eighteenth-century German philosopher Immanuel Kant (1724–1804) first provided the explanation, one that appears to have deeply impressed Wilson. So germane are Kant's writings to Wilson's ideas that one authority suggested, "Woodrow Wilson's Fourteen Points were a faithful transcription of both the letter and spirit of Kant's Perpetual Peace."[20]

Kant postulated that to remain strong, nations must promote education, commerce, and civic freedom. Education, he theorized, would lead to popular enlightenment, and commerce would produce worldwide economic interdependence, all of which would advance the cause of peace. Most important, through expanded political freedom, individual citizens would become more competent in public affairs. And because liberty is most pronounced in republican regimes, such governments would be the most peace loving by nature. The reason is simple: in republics—unlike monarchies or aristocracies—the citizens who decide whether to support a war are the same citizens who must then do the fighting. In Kant's own words:

> A republican constitution does offer the prospect of [peace-loving behavior], and the reason is as follows: If…the consent of the citizens is required in order to decide whether there should be war or not, nothing is more natural than that those who would have to decide to undergo all the deprivations of war will very much hesitate to start such an evil game.…By contrast, under a constitution where the subject is not a citizen and which is therefore not republican, it is the easiest thing in the world to start a war…as a kind of amusement on very insignificant grounds.[21]

Kant envisioned an evolution, through steady if imperceptible progress, toward a peaceful world order as governments everywhere became increasingly responsive to popular majorities. Eventually, he felt, war would become little more than a historical curiosity.

Kant's linking of republicanism and peacefulness became Wilson's political credo. Both Kant and Wilson looked to the reconstruction of the nation-state as the key to a world without war. More specifically, both called for the global extension of

national self-determination
The right of a nation to choose its own government.

BETTMANN/CORBIS

Honored in Britain at the end of World War I, American president Woodrow Wilson hoped to make the world "safe for democracy" and end the scourge of war through a world organization—the League of Nations—based on the rule of law, collective security, and national self-determination.

democracy, education, and free trade to promote peace. Wilson, in particular, placed enormous faith in the morality and common sense of the ordinary person; he became convinced the ideal of national self-determination would be the key to humanity's political salvation. He also believed if the world's peoples were allowed to choose among alternative forms of government, they would universally choose liberal democracy and peace. Finally, Wilson felt, if democratic institutions existed in all nations, the moral force of both domestic and world public opinion would serve as a powerful deterrent to armed aggression.

Capitalism, Imperialism, and War: Lenin Among those who did not agree with Wilson was his contemporary, V. I. Lenin, leader of the Russian Revolution and the first ruler of the former Soviet Union. Lenin was as violently opposed to bourgeois democracy as Wilson was enthusiastic about it. Although both supported national self-determination, they held very different interpretations of it. Wilson assumed any nation would choose democracy over any other system. In contrast, Lenin assumed that given a choice between capitalism and communism, any nation should choose communism. For Wilson, the pursuit of power was an end in itself and both a necessary and sufficient cause of war; for Lenin, as a follower of Karl Marx, wars were waged solely in the interest of the monopoly capitalists.

In a famous tract titled *Imperialism: The Highest Stage of Capitalism*, Lenin advanced the Marxist thesis that Western imperialism—the late-nineteenth-century scramble for colonial territories—was an unmistakable sign that capitalism was teetering on the brink of extinction. Imperialism, according to Lenin, was a logical outgrowth of the cutthroat competition characteristic of monopoly capitalism. Lenin theorized (correctly) that capitalists would always seek foreign markets, where they can make profitable investments and sell (or dump) industrial surpluses. Thus, through their financial power and the political influence that accompanies it, monopoly capitalists push their societies into war for their own selfish purposes. In Lenin's words:

> When the colonies of the European powers in Africa, for instance, comprised only one-tenth of that territory (as was the case in 1876), colonial policy was able to develop by methods other than those of monopoly—by the "free grabbing" of territories, so to speak. But when nine-tenths of Africa had been seized (approximately by 1900), when the whole world had been divided up, there was inevitably ushered in a period of colonial monopoly and, consequently, a period of particularly intense struggle for the division and the re-division of the world.[22]

In sum, Lenin held that because war is good business for the capitalists of the world, capitalists make it their business to promote war.

Lenin's analysis of the causes of war seems far removed from the Wilsonian thesis that tyranny leads inevitably to international conflicts, and yet the two views coincide at one crucial point. Lenin and Wilson both believed a particular defect of a certain type of nation-state produces wars—the form of government for Wilson, the economy and resulting social structure (classes divisions) for Lenin. If it could be eradicated, lasting world peace would ensue. Change is the key.

The Environment

Other theorists argue that war is caused by scarcity and the insecurity brought by fear of cold, hunger, disease, snakes, storms, and the like. This view accords with the ideas of the philosopher John Locke.

Locke In his *Second Treatise on Civil Government* (1690), Locke argued forcefully that wars reflect conditions inherent in nature, rather than defects in human nature or society, that place human beings in do-or-die situations and make conflict inevitable. Like Hobbes before him, Locke saw the imperfections in human beings and believed self-preservation was the most basic human instinct. At this point, however, the two thinkers diverged. In the words of one authority:

> Locke's state of nature is not as violent as Hobbes's. If, as it seems, force will commonly be used without right in Locke's state of nature, it is not because most men are vicious or savage and bloodthirsty; Locke does not, as Hobbes does, speak of every man as the potential murderer of every other man. The main threat to the preservation of life in the state of nature lies not in the murderous tendencies of men but rather…in the poverty and hardship of their natural condition.[23]

Locke believed poverty and hardship are inevitable in the state of nature because great exertions are required to provide for our daily needs. Then we still have to protect our property, coveted by neighbors who have less and by others who are hungry and poor. Locke thus saw circumstances rooted in scarce resources as the principal cause of human conflict.

Locke's views on human beings, society, and nature have great bearing on the issues of war and peace. If the origins of war lie within human beings, as Hobbes believed, we can eradicate war only by changing the "inner self." If the problem lies in society, as Rousseau and Lenin contended, the solution is to reconstitute society (or the state) to remove the particular defects giving rise to aggressive behavior. If the problem lies neither in humans nor in society but in nature, the solution must be to transform nature.

The transformation of nature was precisely how Locke proposed to end human conflict in domestic society. Civil government, he asserted, must create the conditions to encourage economic development. Through economic development, a major cause of social tension—that is, the natural "penury" of the human condition—would be greatly eased. At the same time, if the formal rules of organized society replaced the uncertainties of nature, the need for every human being to constantly guard against the depredations of others would be lessened. Human beings would thus finally leave the state of nature, with all its anarchy and danger.

But in leaving one state of nature, humanity ironically found itself inhabiting another—the often-brutal world of international politics. Although Locke did not apply his theory of politics to the realm of international relations, his reasoning lends itself readily to such an application. Before the invention of government, human beings lived in domestic anarchy; likewise, in the absence of an effective world government, nations exist in international anarchy. In this sense, the relationships among nation-states differ little from relationships among individuals before the formation of civil society. The international state of nature, no less than the original, is a perpetual state of potential war.

Thus, each nation-state behaves according to the dictates of self-preservation in an environment of hostility and insecurity, just as each individual presumably did in the state of nature.

One of the most common spoils of war is territory. From all appearances, the desire for more land and resources—property, in the Lockean sense—is one of the most common objectives of war. Recall that Lenin attributed the European scramble for colonial territories toward the end of the nineteenth century to the search for new markets, cheap labor, and raw materials—that is, property. Significantly, Lenin held that the propensity to accumulate capital (money and property) that Locke described was directly responsible for imperialism, which Lenin predicted would lead inevitably to war. Even if Lenin overstated the case against capitalism, one thing is certain: Territoriality has always been associated with war, and it always will be.

When Locke wrote, plenty of land in the world remained unclaimed by Europeans and uncultivated. He noted that even in the state of nature, human relations were probably fairly harmonious, so long as no one crowded anyone else. It stands to reason, however, that as growing populations begin to place ever-greater pressures on easily available resources, the drawing of property lines becomes progressively more important. If, as Locke's analysis suggests, prehistoric people felt threatened by the pressures of finite resources, imagine how much greater those pressures have become in modern times.

Plagued by civil war and weakened by famine, an estimated 2 million people died in Somalia in the early 1990s. A similar tragedy occurred in the Darfur region of Sudan in 2004–2009, but much of the suffering there was due to atrocities and violence against unarmed civilians.

AP PHOTO/JEROME DELAY

Nature's Scarcity: Malthusian Nightmares Many contemporary writers have elaborated on the theme of resource scarcity propounded by Locke and, later, by Thomas Malthus (1766–1834) in his famous *Essay on the Principle of Population* (1798). Richard Falk, for example, identified "four dimensions of planetary danger," including the "war system, population pressures, resource scarcities, and environmental overload."[24] According to Falk, these are interrelated aspects of a single problem that must be treated as a group.

Falk's assumptions about the causes of international conflict are consistent with Locke's political understanding:

International society is, of course, an extreme example of a war system. Conflicts abound. Vital interests are constantly at stake. Inequalities of resources and power create incentives to acquire what a neighboring state possesses.[25]

Just as humans were constantly vulnerable to the depredations of others in the state of nature, so predatory neighbors continually threaten nation-states. Throughout history, then, violence has played a vital role in the conduct of foreign affairs because, Falk argued, conditions beyond the control of individual nation-states compel them to regard their own security as directly proportionate to their neighbors' distress.

Hence, even after the unprecedented destruction wrought by World Wars I and II, "many efforts were made, often with success, to moderate the scope and barbarism of war, but no serious assault was mounted to remove the conditions that cause war."[26] What exactly are these conditions? Professor Falk argued that access to food and water supplies had a great bearing on the earliest wars. These considerations remain relevant in the modern world:

> Given the present situation of mass undernourishment (more than two-thirds of the world population), it is worth taking account of the ancient link between war and control of food surplus, as well as the age-old human practice of protecting positions of political and economic privilege by military means.[27]

The population explosion exacerbates problems of food and water in the least developed countries (LDCs). Population pressures underlie the entire crisis of planetary organization, especially in light of what we now know about the linkages between economic development and urbanization, urbanization and pollution, and pollution and global warming. Nor are the LDCs the only (or primary) source of the problem.

Consider that developed countries, led by the United States, are by far the biggest global polluters at present; that China and India, both emerging economic giants, have a combined population of 2.4 billion, roughly three times that of the United States and the European Union put together; and that China and India are exempt from the carbon-emission limits established under the Kyoto Protocol (see Chapter 13). Under such conditions, no nation, no matter how powerful, feels terribly secure in our times. The 2008–2009 world financial crisis served as a dramatic reminder of the vulnerability of even the richest and most powerful countries. Not only oil, but also many other raw materials, such as bauxite, copper, and tin, are unequally distributed and in short supply. At the same time, the poorest countries continue to experience shortages in the most basic of all raw materials—food.

IN SEARCH OF A DEFINITIVE THEORY

The three alternative views on the ultimate causes of war identified in this chapter are based on one of the most fundamental concepts in Western political philosophy—the role of the individual in society, the role of society in shaping individual behavior, and role of nature in shaping the individual and society. All three theoretical approaches have some validity, and together they point to a multilevel theory on the origins of war. Individually or together, they help explain why war or the threat of war hangs over every nation like a dreaded sword of Damocles. And so long as war continues to plague humankind, the search for solutions and for a definitive theory will continue.

Beyond Politics

It seems reasonable to assume that, all else being equal, nations exhibiting intense nationalism are more warlike than are politically apathetic nations. But all else is seldom equal. Indeed, explanations that depend on nationalism "have done a relatively poor job in explaining the incidence of war."[28]

But what about the Wilsonian view that democracies are naturally peaceful, and tyranny is the primary cause of war in the modern world? Through the ages, political thinkers have stressed the relationship between dictatorial rule and belligerent or aggressive behavior. Aristotle called tyrants warmongers who plunge their nations into war "with the object of keeping their subjects constantly occupied and continually in need of a leader."[29] Some modern writers, such as Hannah Arendt, argue that totalitarian governments are inherently aggressive.[30] Two major modern conflicts—World War II and the Korean War—were initiated by totalitarian dictatorships. Stalin in the 1930s, Hitler in the 1940s, Mao in the early 1950s, and Pol Pot between 1975 and 1979 all waged war in the form of bloody purges and mass murder at home. These episodes of lethal state behavior strongly suggest totalitarian rulers are prone to coercive force.

Dictators also exercise absolute control over the armed forces, police, and instruments of propaganda. They have often been war heroes who rode to power on the wings of military victory—successful soldiers who take over governments are rarely squeamish about the use of force. For them, war can provide a popular diversion from the tedium and rigors of everyday life; it can act as an outlet for pent-up domestic hostilities that might otherwise be directed at the dictator; it can help unify society and justify a crackdown on dissidents; or finally it can rejuvenate a stagnant economy or an uninspired citizenry.

But these observations do not prove despotism often or always causes wars. The Kennedy, Johnson, and Nixon administrations blamed the Vietnam War on communist aggression. Critics of U.S. foreign policy, however, blamed it on misguided or provocative U.S. actions in Southeast Asia. Thus, depending on the evidence we accept, the Vietnam War can "prove" either that dictatorships are more prone to war than democracies or that democracies are no more immune to crusading militarism than are dictatorships.

Democracies have not been notably successful at avoiding war. In the second half of the twentieth century, for example, India, the world's largest democracy, waged several bloody wars against Pakistan, and the United States fought major wars in Korea, Vietnam, and Iraq. More recently, the United States spearheaded large-scale military actions against the Taliban regime in Afghanistan (2001) and against Saddam Hussein in Iraq (2003). Nor have democratic nations always been

"The Wall" containing 58,272 names of the deceased as of 2010 is part of the Vietnam War Memorial in Washington, D.C. That war dragged on for well over a decade. Many Americans said "never again." The U.S.-led military forces that invaded Afghanistan after 9/11 have been fighting a fierce Taliban insurgency in rugged mountainous terrain ever since—some claim it is the longest war in U.S. history (others say it isn't so). The conflict spilled over the border into northern Pakistan in recent years, and U.S. drone strikes against targets in Pakistani territory have cast a dark cloud over U.S.-Pakistani relations.

unwilling participants in war. The United States did not go out of its way to avoid fighting the Spanish-American War of 1898. And it is difficult to overlook U.S. intervention in the Mexican Revolution in 1914, when President Wilson ordered U.S. Marines to seize the Mexican port of Veracruz and later sent a punitive expedition into Mexico against the forces of Pancho Villa.

Research shows democratic nations are not less warlike than either authoritarian or totalitarian states.[31] In fact, they engage in military action about as often as other types of governments; some evidence suggests they may start wars less frequently but join them more often.[32] In one respect, however, the Kantian-Wilsonian pro-democracy, anti-dictatorship theory of war does hold true: In the so-called **paradox of democratic peace**, democratic states rarely, if ever, fight one another.[33] There has not been a real war between democracies in more than a century and a half.[34] One explanation for this paradox goes as follows:

> Expectations of war and threats of war between democracies are almost certainly reduced by the presence of a common political culture, by a mutual identity and sympathy, by stronger people-to-people and elite-to-elite bonds, by the ability of interest groups within these countries to form transnational coalitions, by more frequent communication, and by more positive mutual perceptions.[35]

Public opinion comes come into play because government is limited in constitutional democracies, political power is more or less widely distributed, popularly elected leaders are inclined to emphasize compromise over confrontation, and constitutional democracies generally respect the individual's rights. All these factors tend to promote the peaceful resolution of political disputes between democracies.

When democracies go to war, they fight nondemocratic states. This suggests that the degree of political difference (or distance) between governments, as well as economic and cultural differences, may be important.[36] Such findings support Wilson's conclusion that dictatorial regimes are the natural enemies of democracies, as well as Lenin's view that capitalist and communist nations are incompatible. As one study of Latin American politics notes, "The more similar two nations are in economic development, political orientation, Catholic culture, and density, the more aligned their voting in the UN" and the less conflict there will be between them. By the same token, "The more dissimilar two nations are in economic development and size and the greater their joint technological capability to span geographic distance is, the more overt conflict they have with each other."[37]

Beyond Economics

If politics provides only a partial and limited explanation for conflict, Lenin's theory that wars are caused by economic factors, particularly capitalism, explains even less. One problem with this proposition is that wars preceded both capitalism and imperialism, proving that capitalism is certainly not the only cause of war.[38] Furthermore, there is little in the historical evidence to support Lenin's economic theory that capitalist states (as opposed to socialist or communist states) are particularly warlike. Although some wars can be explained by national economic motives such as imperialism, most cannot.[39]

paradox of democratic peace Democratic states are often militarily powerful, fight other states, engage in armed intervention, and sometimes commit acts of aggression, but they rarely fight one another.

The relationship between capitalism and imperialism is not clear or consistent. Some capitalist states have practiced imperialism and waged war, whereas others, including Sweden and Switzerland, have avoided both. Lenin's economic theory has difficulty accounting for such differences or explaining why some socialist states have engaged in unprovoked armed aggression. Examples include the Soviet invasion of Estonia, Latvia, Lithuania, and Finland in 1939; North Korea's attack on South Korea in 1950; the Soviet invasion of Hungary (1956), Czechoslovakia (1968), and Afghanistan (1979); and China's attack on Tibet (1956), India (1962), and Vietnam (1979).[40]

There is little doubt that economics is a cause of specific wars, if not war in general. For instance, the U.S.-led coalition in the Iraq War was driven in part by economic motives: to protect the vast oil fields of Arabia and to keep the vital lifelines linking the Middle East with Europe, Asia, and North America from Saddam Hussein's control. But other motives are almost always present, as well. In the Iraq War these were the beliefs (false, as it turned out) that Saddam possessed weapons of mass destruction (WMD), that he was aiding and abetting international terrorists, that he represented a clear and present danger to Israel, and so on.

There is surprisingly little evidence to support the thesis that one kind of economic system or a country's particular stage of economic development or economics in general is decisive in motivating nations to fight wars. When academic studies point to economics as a contributing cause of war, they often rely solely on a statistical correlation between economics and war, which, as every scientist knows, does not prove causality.

Since World War II, wars have been fought within the territory of developing states. Does this mean countries with less-advanced economies are more warlike? Not necessarily, because it also appears these wars have often been instigated or even fought by industrialized nations. Post–World War II examples of such conflicts include those fought in Suez, Algeria, the Congo, Vietnam, Afghanistan, the Falkland Islands, and Iraq. Although we cannot make a strong correlation between economic development and the frequency of military conflicts, nations with more-developed economies may actually have greater warlike tendencies than the so-called lesser developed countries.[41]

The Danger of Oversimplification

Simplistic theories of war abound. Some quantitative theorists have described in fine detail recurring patterns that often lead to war-making military alliances, which are then followed by military buildups, the making of threats, a series of crises, and so on.[42] Such studies have also shown that certain actions political leaders take in an effort to reduce the possibility of war (for example, making alliances) may instead increase its likelihood.[43] However, none of these studies proves conclusively that creating military alliances or engaging in arms races, for example, are causes—rather than mere correlates—of war. Fear of war, for example, causes countries to join alliances, but joining alliances does not inevitably lead to war. Thus,

Western democracies with few exceptions joined the NATO alliance and all Communist states of Central and Eastern Europe joined the Warsaw Pact, but NATO and the Warsaw Pact never fought a war. Furthermore, the "typical" pattern is itself somewhat limited, as it represents only those conflicts fought between major states of approximately equal power.[44]

Most war theorists have long believed large states are more inclined to war than are small states,[45] and that powerful states are more inclined to fight than weak ones. That nations confident of winning are most inclined to fight wars makes intuitive sense.[46] However, defining a state's power is difficult; political leaders may overestimate their own strength and underestimate the adversary's (the Vietnam War is a sterling example).[47] Nations experiencing internal violence also are more likely to be war prone for several reasons. A war may help unify the nation, or internal conflict may make it an easy target.[48] Nations headed by risk-takers also are more likely to go to war.

Another relevant factor is common borders, particularly when there are many or when they are shared by long-standing rivals.[49] Nations with large and growing populations, limited access to necessary resources, and a high level of technology have an obvious environmental incentive to pursue expansionist foreign policy, whereas sparsely populated countries tend to fight fewer wars regardless of technology or access to natural resources. When these latter countries do fight, they tend to be victims rather than aggressors.[50] In sum, a large, powerful nation with a rapidly expanding population and advanced technology, that shares many borders with neighboring states or one border with a traditional enemy (or both), and is governed by a risk-oriented leader is a prime candidate for aggressive war, especially if it faces civil strife or armed rebellion.

Many factors we've discussed, from human nature to scarce resources, and many of the characteristics associated with war, including population size, economic development, and border problems, are difficult or impossible to change, especially in the short run. The humorist Will Rogers once suggested that world peace could be advanced if nations—like people—could move, but they can't (although populations can, and do, migrate).

In fact, the false belief that we can eradicate conflict or trace it to a single factor may increase the possibility of war. As European history from 1919 to 1939 illustrates, concentrating solely on rearranging the international system while ignoring the role of human nature can have the unintended effect of clearing obstacles from the path of megalomaniacs bent on aggression.[51] Had U.S., French, and British leaders in the 1930s heeded Churchill's warnings about the threat posed by Hitler and stood up to him earlier, they might have been able to defeat Nazi Germany quickly or prevent the war altogether. World War II had multiple causes, but that does not mean it was inevitable.

An understanding of the complex causes and factors of war can modestly improve the international system of conflict management by dispelling illusions about the prospects for peace. In such important matters, simple solutions can be worse than no solutions at all; some of history's foremost political simplifiers have also been among the foremost contributors to war.

TOTAL WAR: WARS EVERYBODY FIGHTS

Total war is a thoroughly modern phenomenon. It is different from the **limited wars** of the distant past in several crucial respects. First, it is unlimited in that one or more of the belligerents seek total victory and will stop at nothing short of **unconditional surrender**. Second, total war is unlimited as to means. States use advanced technology to enhance the range, accuracy, and killing power of modern weapons. Third, total war is unlimited as to participation: whole societies engage in the war effort.

The Napoleonic Wars are the prototype of total war and the first such war ever fought. Napoléon waged an all-out drive for hegemony that recognized no limits on ends or means. He sought total domination of Europe, and he possessed all the resources available to a modern, centralized state at that time. Of course, there were then no weapons of mass destruction, except conventional armies that could be used to this end once the enemy was defeated. Thus, Napoléon's forces burned much of Moscow, including the Kremlin, to the ground after Russia's defeat. Most important, Napoléon introduced the idea of mass conscription, drafting thousands of young men into the modern world's first people's army. (Prior armies had consisted of professional soldiers and paid mercenaries.) Napoléon also used nationalism, propaganda, and patriotic symbols to mobilize the entire society behind the war effort. These innovations were all harbingers of the future: We can consider the total wars fought in the first half of the twentieth century a single event with an interlude between two incredibly violent spasms—the horrific culmination of processes set in motion more than a century earlier.

After World War II, the concept of total war took on an even more ominous meaning due to major advances in the science and technology of war-fighting capabilities. The advent of the Nuclear Age utterly transformed both the strategy and tactics of war, the logic of military force and the battlefield. Like the new face of war itself, this transformation was total.

ACCIDENTAL WAR: WARS NOBODY WANTS

We like to think our leaders always know what they are doing, especially when it comes to matters of war and peace. But accidents do happen. What if a Pakistani arms smuggler were passing through India with a package containing weaponized anthrax? What if the spores were released in the center of New Delhi, the capital of India, when the Kashmiri taxi driver ran a red light and collided with a truck at a busy intersection? And what if that happened during a crisis with Pakistan? Might India think Pakistan was launching an all-out war? Pakistan had nothing to do with the incident, but India might decide to retaliate immediately and ask questions later (waiting would be extremely risky in such a situation). In this scenario, an all-out nuclear war could result from accident and misperception rather than from any rational choice on either side.

War by misperception, or war resulting from the misreading of a situation, is perhaps the most common kind of war nobody wants. **Accidental war** is another possibility. An incorrect translation, a message not delivered, a diplomatic signal missed or misinterpreted—accidents of this kind precipitated unintended wars well before the advent of space-age weapons systems. In a technological era dominated by nuclear weapons and ballistic missiles, the danger of war by accidental means has gone up dramatically, as have the stakes. Nuclear war by escalation could begin as a limited (and presumably localized) conflict between two nations in which neither side originally intended to use its most destructive weapons. But as casualties mount and battlefield reverses occur, one side (most likely the one losing) could be tempted to up the ante by introducing more powerful weapons, which the other side would have little choice but to match. If both sides possess nuclear weapons, the dynamics could move them toward nuclear war.

Catalytic war can also generate violence and destruction well beyond any nation's intention. Historically, such wars reflected alliance arrangements. If one member of the alliance was attacked, the other(s) sprang to its defense, enlarging the war. Nowadays, a catalytic war might originate as a localized conflict between, say, two developing countries that have powerful allies. Local wars have always had the potential to turn into regional or even global wars (as happened in both world wars). Or a saboteur or madman might somehow manage to "pull the nuclear trigger." All such scenarios—sabotage, misperception, accident, escalation, or a catalytic event—show how war can occur without any premeditation or intent.

catalytic war
A conflict that begins as a localized and limited encounter but grows into a general war after other parties are drawn into the conflict through the activation of military alliances.

NUCLEAR WAR: WARS NOBODY WINS

Weapons of mass destruction have been used only once. The United States dropped two atomic bombs on the Japanese cities of Hiroshima and Nagasaki to end World War II. President Truman waited for Japan's High Command to surrender after the first bomb leveled Hiroshima. When three days later they had not, he gave the order to drop the second bomb. This time Japan surrendered. But it would be a mistake to try to repeat that winning strategy. The reason is very simple. When the U.S. president decided to "go nuclear" in 1945, there were only two atomic bombs in the world, and they were both in the U.S. arsenal. Truman did not have to risk **massive retaliation** (a response in kind) from Japan or any other country. The United States had a (short-lived) **nuclear monopoly**.

The former Soviet Union quickly developed its nuclear weapons program. By the end of the 1950s, it had an arsenal of mass-destruction armaments and was even building long-range rockets called **intercontinental ballistic missiles** (ICBMs). Moscow beat the United States into outer space by launching *Sputnik,* the first earth-orbiting satellite, in 1957. During the 1960s, the United States lost not only its nuclear monopoly (if it had not already been lost a decade earlier) but also its aura of invulnerability. The era of massive retaliation and **brinkmanship**—reliance on nuclear weapons to intimidate adversaries—was superseded by the era of **mutual assured destruction** (MAD), or **mutual deterrence**, in which both superpowers had the ability to withstand a

Nuclear war survival skills.

nuclear first strike and still be capable of delivering a **second strike** that would result in unacceptable damage to the aggressor.

Neither superpower spared any effort to get (or stay) ahead in the nuclear arms race. By the early 1970s, both sides had a tremendous **overkill** capability; that is, each had enough weapons of mass destruction to destroy the other many times over. Even more alarming, both sides had built nuclear submarines to act as mobile platforms for launching ICBMs and were putting multiple warheads—called **multiple independently targeted reentry vehicles** (MIRVs)—on both land- and sea-based ICBMs, technically known as **submarine-launched ballistic missiles** (SLBMs). But whereas both sides wanted to win the arms race, neither wanted to lose a war with the other, and both knew there would be no winners if deterrence failed. This almost happened during the Cuban Missile Crisis (1963); it was a close call. As a result, the two sworn enemies quickly established the now-famous hotline—a direct communication link between the White House and the Kremlin—to avert a future calamity, one that might just happen by accident.

PROXY WAR: WARS OTHERS FIGHT

Civil wars and guerrilla wars typically pit established governments on one side against rebels or insurgents on the other. During the Cold War, the two superpowers frequently intervened directly or indirectly in civil wars or insurgencies in Third World countries. Vietnam in the 1960s and early 1970s and Afghanistan in the 1970s are two notable examples. In Vietnam, the United States intervened directly with military forces, and the Soviet Union intervened indirectly by sending massive amounts of military and economic aid. In Afghanistan, it was the other way around—the Soviet Union launched a military invasion, and the United States backed the freedom fighters (the mujahideen). Similarly, the Soviet Union intervened in Angola's civil war in the 1970s, and the United States intervened in Nicaragua and El Salvador in the 1980s. These conflicts were sometimes called **proxy wars** because the superpowers would back one side while relying on indigenous forces to do the fighting with the help of U.S. or Soviet "advisors."

With the collapse of the Soviet Union, only one superpower remained, and the ideological rivalry that fueled the Cold War became a thing of the past. Whether a proxy war will occur again is an open question; if so, it will be in a very different context and, in all likelihood, for different principles.

JUST WAR: WARS OTHERS START

So far, we have been looking at war primarily from the standpoint of the perpetrators of aggression. But what about the victims? Few observers would dispute that nations have the right to resist armed aggression. When national survival is at stake, self-defense is morally justified. So, despite Benjamin Franklin's assertion that "there was never a good war or a bad peace," some wars may be both necessary and proper, but which ones? Who is to say? And how can we know for sure?

The Just War Doctrine

The venerable doctrine of the **just war** holds that under certain circumstances, a war can be "good"—not pleasant or intrinsically desirable, but serving the welfare

---

massive retaliation
Strategic military doctrine based on a plausible standing threat of nuclear reprisal employed by the United States in the 1950s during the short-lived era of the U.S. nuclear monopoly. According to this doctrine, if the Soviet Union attacked U.S. allies with conventional military forces, the United States would retaliate with nuclear weapons.

nuclear monopoly
When only one side in an adversarial relationship possesses a credible nuclear capability; the United States enjoyed a nuclear monopoly for roughly a decade after World War II.

intercontinental ballistic missiles
A long-range missile armed with multiple nuclear warheads capable of striking targets anywhere in the world; both the United States and Russia possess large arsenals of these ultimate strategic weapons.

brinkmanship
In diplomacy, the deliberate use of military threats to create a crisis atmosphere; the calculated effort to take a tense bilateral relationship to the brink of war to achieve a political objective (for example, deterring a common enemy from carrying out an act of aggression against an ally).

WALTER E. THOMPSON

The U.S.-led military forces that invaded Iraq in the spring of 2003 quickly defeated Saddam Hussein's army, but the subsequent occupation gave rise to a protracted urban guerrilla war of attrition in which the enemy used terrorist tactics that turned key Iraqi cities, including the capital of Baghdad, into bloody battlegrounds. The United States withdrew the last combat troops from Iraq in December 2011, but the violence and fighting among factions competing for power continues. As part of a new war fighting doctrine, the U.S. Army endeavored to establish rapport with the civilian population in an effort to win hearts and minds. The soldier in this photo is deceased.

of a nation and the cause of justice. This concept was advanced by early Christian theologians such as Saint Augustine and refined by medieval philosophers. Hugo Grotius (1583–1645) and other natural law theorists later reformulated it.

Those who favor the concept of just war unanimously agree defensive wars are justified. A nation that suffers an unprovoked attack is justified in waging war against its assailant. Some theorists further give third-party nations the right to interfere on behalf of hapless victims of military aggression. The 1991 Persian Gulf War, preceded by Iraq's invasion and occupation of Kuwait, is a case in point.

Earlier writers did not limit the just war doctrine to defensive wars. Saint Augustine abhorred war in all its guises, but he justified even aggressive wars under some circumstances, as when a state "has failed either to make reparation for an injurious action committed by its citizens or to return what has been appropriated."[52] Another early Christian theologian, Saint Ambrose (339–397 CE), argued that nations have a moral obligation, not simply a right, to wage aggressive war for the sake of higher principle. "Man has a moral duty," he wrote, "to employ force to resist active wickedness, for to refrain from hindering evil when possible is tantamount to promoting it."[53] Ambrose was aware of the need for limitations on this kind of war. Aggressive wars, he declared, should be fought only for a clearly just cause.

The just war doctrine has five postulates. First, war must be the last resort of a legitimate government; there must be no other effective political alternatives available. Second, the conflict must be just, fought only for deterring or repelling aggression or righting a wrong. Third, the war cannot be futile; there must be some probability the nation undertaking it can succeed. Fourth, the war's purpose must justify the cost in money and lives; the means employed must be appropriate to the reason the war is fought. Finally, a just war must minimize injury and death to civilians.

In contrast to the simplistic nationalism represented by such slogans as "My country right or wrong," the just war concept suggests a standard of moral responsibility that transcends narrow national interest. Early Christian theologians based their notions of justice on theological doctrines and scriptural teachings.

mutual assured destruction (MAD) A nuclear stalemate in which both sides in an adversarial relationship know that if either one initiates a war, the other will retain enough retaliatory ("second strike") capability to administer unacceptable damage even after absorbing the full impact of a nuclear surprise attack; during the Cold War, a stable strategic relationship between the two superpowers.

mutual deterrence The theory that aggressive wars can be prevented if potential victims maintain a military force sufficient to inflict unacceptable damage on any possible aggressor.

Modern versions of the doctrine are grounded in a natural-law philosophy holding that there are self-evident truths about human welfare, and when taken together, they point toward the true meaning of the ideal of "justice for all."

Evaluating the Just War Doctrine

Of the criticisms leveled against the just war doctrine, we focus on three of the most substantial: that the doctrine represents moral relativism, that it embodies an ethnocentric bias, and that it is politically unrealistic.

Moral Relativism   Some critics contend the concept of the just war is based on highly subjective and, hence, unverifiable value judgments. Because governments rarely admit to starting wars and almost always blame the other side, any attempt to assign moral responsibility is bound to reflect the opinions of the observer more than the often uncertain facts of the situation. The only way to avoid this **moral relativism** is to confine ourselves to describing what happened before and during wars, sticking to accurate and verifiable facts.

Ethnocentric or Nationalistic Bias   Critics also say Western just war theorists reflect only their own culture, ignoring justifications for war advanced by other cultures or ideologies—an accusation of **ethnocentric bias**. For instance, the traditional Islamic concept of a jihad ("struggle" or "holy war") against temptation, evil, apostasy, or "infidels" offers a moral rationale for aggressive war rarely acknowledged by Western proponents of the just war doctrine. Just war theorists were similarly criticized for rejecting an interpretation advanced until recently by the former Soviet Union—that just wars are waged by the working class against their oppressors—for example, wars of "national liberation" fought by colonized peoples of the Third World against Western "imperialists," and wars waged to prevent the overthrow of socialist governments in Eastern Europe and elsewhere.

Political Naiveté   Several opponents of the just war doctrine raise the practical objection that even a universally accepted standard governing them would be extremely difficult to apply fairly. Just as individuals are not good judges in their own cases, it is argued, so nations are not competent to pass judgment on controversies involving their own interests and well-being. Without an impartial referee, critics contend, the just war doctrine remains a sham advanced by aggressor nations to justify self-serving policies and military interventionism.

Defenders of the just war doctrine point out that moral judgments concerning the conduct of wars have long been thought both natural and necessary: natural in the sense that "for as long as men and women have talked about war, they have talked about it in terms of right and wrong,"[54] and necessary because without them, all wars would have to be considered equally objectionable (or praiseworthy). Admittedly, we cannot prove scientifically that aggressive wars are any worse than preemptive or preventive wars, but nor do we need to prove cold-blooded murder is more reprehensible than killing in self-defense—a distinction both criminal law and common sense support.

In the real world, heads of state often engage in moral talk and immoral behavior. The idea of the just war is worth keeping, therefore, if not as a means of controlling that behavior, then as a method of evaluating it (see "Landmarks in History").

---

second strike
Retaliation in kind against a nuclear attack(er); this capability paradoxically minimizes the likelihood that a nuclear confrontation will lead to a nuclear exchange.

overkill
Amassing a much larger nuclear arsenal than is (or would be) needed to annihilate any adversary.

multiple independently targeted reentry vehicle (MIRV)
Intercontinental missiles containing many nuclear warheads that can be individually programmed to split off from the nose cone of the rocket upon reentry into the earth's atmosphere and hit different specific targets with a high degree of accuracy.

submarine-launched ballistic missile (SLBM)
Strategic missiles with multiple nuclear warheads launched from submarines that prowl the ocean depths and that cannot be easily detected or destroyed by a preemptive attack.

proxy wars
A war in which two adversaries back opposing parties to a conflict by supplying money, weapons, and military advisors, while avoiding direct combat operations against each other.

FIGURE 15.1 Nazi Death Camps. This map shows the location of the Nazi concentration and extermination camps. Notice that concentration camps existed in France, the Netherlands, Austria, Latvia, and Czechoslovakia, as well as in Germany. The infamous death camps were all located deep inside Poland. Strikingly, not one was located on or near German territory. Hitler obviously did not want the horrors of the Final Solution taking place in his own backyard.

SOURCE: From "Concentration and Death Camps" http://history1900s.about.com/library/holocaust/blmap.htm. Copyright © 2009 by Jennifer Rosenberg. Used with permission of About, Inc., online at www.about.com. All rights reserved.

(Continued)

(CONTINUED)

Following World War II, in history's most famous attempt to apply moral standards to wartime conduct, Nazi leaders were charged in Nuremberg, Germany, with several types of crimes. First, they were accused of **crimes against peace**, because they had waged aggressive war in violation of international treaties and obligations. Second, they were charged with war crimes, which encompassed violations of the accepted rules of war, such as brutality toward prisoners of war, wanton destruction of towns, and mistreatment of civilians in conquered lands. Third, they were accused of **crimes against humanity**, including the persecution and mass murder of huge numbers of noncombatants. Crimes against peace and war crimes were categories widely accepted under the just war doctrine; the category of crimes against humanity was designed to deal with a specific instance of genocide, the Holocaust.

The decision to punish Nazi leaders for genocide was prompted by an understandable desire for retribution. German actions could not be justified by the exigencies of war (which, of course, Hitler had started). The crimes against humanity concept provided firm support for the just war doctrine (and vice versa).

The Nuremberg trials were justifiable, but it is no simple task to apply the crimes against peace, war crimes, and crimes against humanity labels to concrete and often-unique situations. The death camps of the Holocaust violated all standards of law, justice, and decency (see Figure 15.1). But then what about the Allied firebombing of Dresden and many other German cities? Or the brutalities against German civilians tolerated (if not encouraged) by the Soviet army? Or the firebombing of Japanese cities and the dropping of the atomic bombs on Hiroshima and Nagasaki by the United States? These acts, which resulted in hundreds of thousands of civilian

UPI/USAF/HO/LANDOV

The United States uses drones like this one against the Taliban in Afghanistan and Pakistan. When civilians are killed, Washington calls it "collateral damage," but critics call it a war crime.

(Continued)

(CONTINUED)

deaths, were not covered under the war crimes labels. Critics argue this fact illustrates an important point: the victors write the history of a war. By the same token, the victors alone decide what is and what is not a war crime.

The United States is quick to label auto-genocide in Cambodia or "ethnic cleansing" (a euphemism for genocide) in Bosnia or genocide in Rwanda and Sudan as war crimes. On the other hand, when U.S. drone attacks targeting Taliban fighters in villages along the Afghan-Pakistan border kill civilians, it is labeled "collateral damage," which makes it legal. Critics of the Bush administration have argued that the methods used in the war on terror—"extraordinary rendition" (seizing

suspected terrorists on foreign soil), leaving detainees in legal limbo by creating a new classification of "illegal combatants," and "enhanced interrogation techniques" such as waterboarding—were war crimes.

As a candidate for the presidency, Barack Obama criticized the harsh methods President Bush approved in carrying out his war on terror. But as Bush's successor, President Obama disappointed many of his most ardent supporters by failing to close the infamous "Gitmo" detention center at Guantanamo Bay, Cuba. And in the spring of 2011, Obama backed off another key campaign pledge when he decided to resume military trials for terrorist detainees at Guantanamo Bay.

A WAR ON *WHAT*? THE POLITICS OF HYPERBOLE

The Bush administration's response to 9/11 was to declare a "war on terror" (see Chapter 16), but terror is not a state—not a place on the map. Waging "war" on terror is thus not like waging traditional war. In fact, calling it a war raises major conceptual and strategic problems. President Bush was not the first U.S. commander in chief to use the term *war* loosely. U.S. Attorney General Robert F. Kennedy declared a "war on organized crime" in 1961, and every president since John F. Kennedy (Robert's brother) has embraced the "war on crime" as his own. President Lyndon Baines Johnson waged a "war on poverty." LBJ's successor in the White House, Richard Nixon, declared a "war on drugs," calling drug abuse "public enemy number one in the United States." These and other domestic "wars" arguably made war appear a kind of permanent condition in a perilous world, rather than an extreme step taken only in the most extreme circumstances.

The war on terror identified a subversive organization—al Qaeda—as the source of all evil and a single individual, Osama bin Laden, as the mastermind behind it. Al Qaeda thus became the functional equivalent of world communism, and bin Laden was the new Stalin.

The Bush administration further linked several existing governments—Iraq, Iran, and North Korea—to this conspiratorial organization and branded these states the "axis of evil." (In the 1980s, President Reagan famously called the Soviet Union the "evil empire.") In addition, the war on terror, like the Cold War before it, would be open-ended. Unlike wars of the past, it would go on for generations, possibly forever. Finally, this new "war" was cast as a contest

just war
A war fought in self-defense or because it is the only way a nation can do what is right.

moral relativism
The idea that all moral judgments are conditional and only "true" in a certain religious, cultural, or social context; the belief that there is no such thing as universal truth in the realm of ethics or morality.

ethnocentric bias
The common tendency of human beings to see the world through a cultural lens that distorts reality and exaggerates the good in one's own society and the evil in others.

between good and evil, thus turning it into a religious-ideological crusade in much the same way as the Cold War was cast as a struggle between freedom and capitalism, and totalitarian tyranny and communism.

The means for fighting the war on terror are also reminiscent of the Cold War, including a major military buildup, a soaring defense budget, and a wholesale reorganization of the nation's intelligence, police, and defense establishment. The "national security state" was transformed by creating a new Department of Homeland Security. The central idea of this new department was to integrate the operational procedures of agencies, especially the FBI and CIA, which had operated independently or even competitively during the Cold War.

In the aftermath of the 9/11 attacks, what began as a surgical military operation to wipe out terrorist training camps in Afghanistan became a new global crusade pitting the United States and its allies against the so-called Axis of Evil—Iraq, Iran, and North Korea. Arguably, the prudent course of action was a limited response aimed at a finite evil and a specific target.

Not surprisingly, different observers interpreted the war on terror in very different ways. Conservatives were much more likely than liberals to accept the reasons given for launching an all-out "war" after 9/11, especially for the controversial decision to invade Iraq. But, in fairness, the war was not opposed by leading Democrats in Congress, and even liberal politicians, such as then-Senator Hillary Clinton, supported it. It was only after the occupation turned into a civil war that politicians of all stripes began to jump ship.

What are the lessons of this war? What does it tell us about war in general?

First, the Iraq War combined aspects of various war scenarios discussed earlier in this chapter—**inadvertent war** (war resulting from misperception, misinformation, or miscalculation), accidental war (war touched off unintentionally), catalytic war (war that starts small and gets bigger as other powers are drawn in), and **ABC war** (a war involving atomic, biological, or chemical weapons, otherwise known as weapons of mass destruction). The concept of a just war also came into play because the attack on Iraq was (wrongly) linked to 9/11. Thus the war was rationalized as a righteous way to punish an aggressor or to avenge a heinous act.

Second, the invasion of Iraq was conceived as part of a larger war; a war not against a specific enemy, but against a disembodied "ism." Terrorism, like poverty or crime, is a condition, a fact of life. It does not have a beginning or an end and therefore cannot be eradicated by military means. At best, it can be managed or brought under control. Whether the military as presently constituted is the best instrument for dealing with this type of threat is debatable. In Iraq, traditional military instruments—fighter-bombers, tanks, artillery, and the like—proved highly effective in defeating the Iraqi army but virtually useless in dealing with the guerrilla-style insurrection that followed.

Third, during the course of this war, the Bush administration switched enemies and changed the rationale for fighting. The real enemy was a secretive organization known as al Qaeda, rather than another state. To the extent that

---

crimes against peace
A Nuremberg war crimes trials category, covering the violation of international peace by waging an unjustified, aggressive war.

war crimes
Violation of generally accepted rules of war as established in the Geneva Conventions on the conduct of war. The Geneva Conventions call for the humanitarian treatment of civilians and prisoners of war, and respect for human life and dignity; crimes against humanity, such as genocide and ethnic cleansing, are also war crimes.

crimes against humanity
A category of war crimes, first introduced at the Nuremberg trials of Nazi war criminals, covering the wanton, brutal extermination of millions of innocent civilians.

inadvertent war
A war resulting from misperception, misinformation, or miscalculation; an unnecessary war.

ABC war
A general term for war involving weapons of mass destructions (WMD), especially atomic (nuclear), biological, and chemical weapons.

Soldiers in Afghanistan. In late 2009, President Obama ordered a "surge" in troop strength in Afghanistan. Washington pressured NATO allies to commit combat forces to an International Security Assistance Force (ISAF) under U.S. command. U.S. forces never serve under foreign command. PDD-25* decrees, "The chain of command from the President to the lowest U.S. commander in the field [is] inviolate." In this U.S. Army photo, a sniper team scans the area outside a leaders' shura from the rooftop in the village Baki Tana, January 30, 2013.

*PDD stands for Presidential Decision Directive.

this enemy had a face, it was the face of Osama bin Laden. For all its military might, the United States was unable to defeat al Qaeda by invading Afghanistan or even to bring the renegade bin Laden, who masterminded the 9/11 attacks, to justice for a decade until a U.S. Navy Seal team finally killed him in 2011. Instead, the Bush administration shifted the focus of attention from Afghanistan and bin Laden to Iraq and Saddam—in other words, from an elusive enemy who could not be defeated militarily to one who could, or so the architects of the Iraq War believed.

That belief proved to be false, as was the evidence that Saddam harbored WMD, which had been the reason given for launching the war in the first place. As the fighting dragged on and the death toll mounted, the Bush administration changed the rationale for the war once again. Clearly, the original objective—to locate and destroy Saddam's WMD labs and stockpiles—disappeared when no such weapons were discovered. The reason for ousting Saddam then became nation-building, to promote freedom and democracy in the world. Later, as the civil war raged, the reason was simply to stabilize the region because a hasty withdrawal would, it was argued, leave a dangerous power vacuum. What no one in Washington was saying, however, was what nearly everyone outside Washington was thinking all along: the real reason for invading and occupying Iraq was oil, still the world's most important strategic resource.

On the oil-rich Arabian peninsula, Iraq's petroleum reserves are second in size only to Saudi Arabia's. The possibility—indeed, the likelihood—that energy security (represented by Iraqi oil) played a major role in shaping the Bush administration's antiterrorism strategy points to one final "lesson learned." The pursuit of security in the modern world is too complex to be reduced to a simple formula or submitted to quick fixes. Any attempt to do so risks producing the opposite effect—that is, greater insecurity.

WEAPONS OF MASS DISRUPTION: CYBERWAR

In 2002, the U.S. Department of the Navy created the Naval Network Warfare Command, known as NETWARCOM. A key element of its mission is information operations (IO), "a warfare area that influences, disrupts, corrupts, or usurps an adversary's decision-making ability while protecting our own." NETWARCOM's "five core integrated abilities" include electronic warfare, computer network operations, psychological operations, military deception, and operational security.[55]

In November 2006, Chinese hackers attacked the U.S. Naval War College computer network, effectively forcing it to shut down for several weeks. Apparently, the attack was aimed at gleaning information about naval war games being developed at the Newport, Rhode Island, facility. The U.S. Navy estimates that hackers try to penetrate its computer systems, which are protected by the Navy Cyber Defense Operations Command, an average of 600,000 times per hour.

In May 2007, Estonia (Figure 15.2) was the target of an all-out cyberwar attack—the first ever against a sovereign state, but almost certainly not the last. The source of the attack was unknown, but Estonian authorities believed it was ordered by the Kremlin or launched by Russian nationalists in retaliation for Estonia's decision to move a World War II bronze statue of a Soviet soldier from a park in the Estonian capital of Tallinn, the previous month. Angry ethnic Russians living in Estonia staged street demonstrations that led to violent clashes with Estonian riot police. The Kremlin denied any involvement in the subsequent cyberattacks, directed against the executive and legislative branches of Estonia's government, as well as its mobile phone networks, banks, and news organizations.[56]

Although Estonia is a small country, electronic warfare is a big deal no matter what state happens to be the target. When the intended victim is a NATO member and the source of the hostile action implicates Russians (and perhaps Russia), the possibility of a good outcome is not high. Not surprisingly, the cyberwar against Estonia was a matter of intense interest to defense planning agencies, intelligence services, and computer security specialists the world over.

Finally, in the summer of 2009, the Obama administration unveiled a plan to create a new Pentagon "cyber command" as the centerpiece of its strategy for defending against a future attack on the nation's computer networks. The plan, still in its infancy, raised major privacy issues, as well as diplomatic questions. President Obama sought to allay fears of "Big Brother" watching what citizens were doing at home, saying the plan "will not—I repeat, will not—include monitoring private sector networks or Internet traffic." But a major architect of the new cyberstrategy was not so reassuring on this point: "How do you understand sovereignty in the cyber domain?" General James E. ("Hoss") Cartwright asked. "It doesn't tend to pay a lot of attention to geographic boundaries."[57]

Another complication raises a delicate diplomatic question: How does the U.S. military respond to a cyberattack initiated in another country without violating international law by invading that country's space? Otherwise put: Does the concept of sovereignty apply in cyberspace?

Clearly, the danger of cyberwar exists in today's world. But key questions have yet to be answered before adequate defenses can be designed and deployed.

FIGURE 15.2   Estonia is the smallest of the three Baltic states, which became independent when the USSR self-destructed in 1991. Ethnic Russians comprise more than one-fourth of Estonia's 1.3 million people. Tensions between native Estonians and Russians who settled in Estonia during the Soviet period have run high. As a member of both NATO and the EU, Estonia is now politically, economically, and militarily part of the West, but geographically it remains within easy striking distance of Russia's technologically sophisticated armed forces.

WAR AND DIPLOMACY

In a world of sovereign states, war is not only the absence of peace, but also the failure of diplomacy. Finding a way to keep the peace without compromising one's vital interests or basic principles is the acid test of diplomacy.

Conflict is endemic in international relations, as in everyday life. The mark of a great power is not how many wars it fights and wins, but how many conflicts it wins without a fight. Hence, the importance of an enlightened foreign policy is the focus of Chapter 17.

SUMMARY

Avoiding war is not always an objective of state policy. Some leaders—for example, Italy's fascist dictator Mussolini—have actually glorified it.

We can divide theories of the causes of war into three categories that blame human nature, society, and an unforgiving environment. Thomas Hobbes thought war was a product of human perversity; Jean-Jacques Rousseau maintained that human beings are basically good but society corrupts them; John Locke attributed human aggression to scarcities in nature, including hunger and famine, disease, storms, and droughts (that is, circumstances beyond human control).

All simplistic theories fall short of explaining the variety of factors that cause war—social, political, economic, and psychological. A large, powerful nation that shares boundaries with several neighboring states, is ruled by a risk-oriented leader, has access to modern technology, is experiencing (or expecting) internal conflict, and has a rapidly expanding population is likely to be predisposed toward war.

Under conditions of high tension, war may occur even if none of the principals want it. Such unintended wars may erupt because of misperception, misunderstanding, accident, escalation, or a catalytic reaction and make it difficult to assign moral responsibility. Often when war occurs, it is not clear who or what actually caused it.

Using war as an instrument of state policy violates international law and morality, but not all wars are equally objectionable. The just war doctrine holds that self-defense and the defense of universal principles are legitimate reasons for going to war. This doctrine is frequently criticized on the grounds of moral relativism, cultural ethnocentrism, and political realism.

International lawyers at Nuremberg developed a new category of war crimes—crimes against humanity. Although the trials were justified, such proceedings contain inherent pitfalls and must be approached with extreme caution.

KEY TERMS

war   414
interstate war   414
civil war   414
guerrilla warfare   414
low-intensity
   conflict   414
nationalism   415
arms race   415
ultranationalism   415
nationalistic
   universalism   415
reasons of state   415

state of nature   418
internationalist   420
national self-
   determination   421
paradox of democratic
   peace   427
limited war   430
unconditional
   surrender   430
war by
   misperception   430
accidental war   430

catalytic war   431
massive retaliation   432
nuclear monopoly   432
intercontinental ballistic
   missile (ICBM)   432
brinkmanship   432
mutual assured
   destruction
   (MAD)   433
mutual deterrence   433
second strike   434
overkill   434

multiple independently
   targeted reentry
   vehicle (MIRV)   434
submarine-launched
   ballistic missile
   (SLBM)   434

proxy war   434
just war   437
moral relativism   437
ethnocentric bias   437
crimes against
   peace   438

war crime   438
crimes against
   humanity   438
inadvertent war   438
ABC war   438

REVIEW QUESTIONS

1. Into what general categories do most explanations of the ultimate causes of war fall?

2. According to Thomas Hobbes, what is the root cause of all wars? What arguments did Hobbes offer in defense of his thesis?

3. What did Jean-Jacques Rousseau believe to be the root cause of war? How did his views differ from Hobbes's? What arguments did Rousseau advance to support his thesis?

4. Those who believe society is the ultimate cause of war differ about precisely what aspect of society is most responsible. What are the four alternative theories presented in the text?

5. How did John Locke explain the phenomenon of war? How did his view differ from those of Hobbes and Rousseau? What arguments did Locke offer in support of his thesis?

6. Which explanation of the causes of war seems most plausible? Explain your answer.

7. Why is it difficult simply to condemn the guilty party or parties whenever war breaks out?

8. With the technology of warfare advancing by leaps and bounds, it becomes increasingly probable that a war will start even though nobody intends it to. In what ways might this happen?

9. Are all wars equally objectionable from a moral standpoint? Why or why not?

10. Are the arguments, pro and con, concerning the validity of the just war doctrine equally balanced? Explain.

11. What prompted the Nuremberg War Crimes Trials? What are crimes against humanity? How does the just war doctrine fit into the picture? Should, or could, Nuremberg-type trials be conducted after every war?

12. Critique the concept of a "war on terror." Critique the strategy the Bush administration used in the conduct of that "war." Compare the Bush administration approach with that of the Obama administration. How do they differ? How are they the same?

CHAPTER 16

Terrorism
Weapon of the Weak

THINK ABOUT IT

What are the origins of terrorism?

Is terrorism heroic, an act of war, or a crime?

What is the best way to fight terrorism?

In February 1993, a yellow Ryder rental van containing a 1,200-pound bomb exploded in the parking garage of the World Trade Center in New York City, blasting a 200-foot crater in the basement. More than a thousand people were injured, and six died. Shocked citizens struggled to grasp the idea that a devastating terrorist attack had taken place against a symbol of U.S. economic might and one of the largest and most famous buildings in the world.

Eight and a half years later, on September 11, 2001, the United States watched in horror as the World Trade Center towers were hit again, this time by hijacked commercial airliners loaded with highly volatile jet fuel. The towers burned for a short time and then imploded with an incredible force that rocked downtown Manhattan, killing thousands of people still trapped inside the towers, creating a firestorm of debris, and sending a huge cloud of smoke, dust, and ash skyward that lingered over the city like an eerie, foul-smelling pall for many days.

No one knew in 1993 whether the first World Trade Center bombing was an isolated act or a sign of things to come. Now we know the answer: Terrorist attacks would become a grim reality of life nearly all across the globe in the coming decade (Table 16.1).

Between 2010 and 2013, terrorist attacks continued worldwide. Many of the worst ones resulted in multiple deaths and injuries occurred in Iraq, Afghanistan, and Pakistan. The last major terrorist attack of 2010 happened on

TABLE 16.1   Twenty-Five Year Terrorism Timeline—1983–2008.

April 18, 1983	Suicide bombing of U.S. embassy in Beirut kills 63.
October 23, 1983	Suicide truck bombing of Marine barracks in Beirut kills 241.
December 21, 1988	Pan Am flight 103 explodes over Lockerbie, Scotland, killing 270 people, including 11 on the ground.
February 26, 1993	Bomb in a van explodes beneath the World Trade Center in New York City, killing 6 and injuring more than 1,000.
March 12, 1993	13 coordinated bomb explosions in Mumbai (Bombay), India, kill 257 people and injure some 700.
June 23, 1993	Federal investigators break up a plot by Islamic radicals to bomb the United Nations and two Hudson River tunnels.
March 20, 1995	Members of Aum Shinrikyo release deadly sarin gas in the Tokyo subway in five coordinated attacks, killing 12, severely injuring 50, and causing temporary vision problems for many others.
April 19, 1995	A truck bomb destroys the federal building in Oklahoma City, Oklahoma, killing 168 and wounding more than 600. Two Americans are charged.
November 13, 1995	A car bomb explodes outside a U.S. Army training office in Riyadh, Saudi Arabia, killing 7, including 5 Americans, and wounding 60 others.

(continued)

TABLE 16.1   (continued)

April 3, 1996	The FBI arrests Theodore J. Kaczynski, a Montana hermit, and accuses him of an 18-year series of bomb attacks carried out by the "Unabomber."
June 25, 1996	A truck bomb explodes outside an apartment complex in Dhahran, Saudi Arabia, killing 19 Americans and wounding hundreds more.
July 1, 1996	Federal agents arrest 12 members of the Viper Militia, a Phoenix, Arizona, group accused of plotting to blow up government buildings.
July 17, 1996	A pipe bomb explodes at a concert during the Summer Olympics in Atlanta, Georgia, killing 1 and wounding more than 100.
August 7, 1998	The U.S. embassies in Kenya and Tanzania are bombed, killing 224 people, mostly Kenyan passers-by in the capital of Nairobi.
August 15, 1998	A large car bomb explodes in the central shopping district of Omagh, Northern Ireland, killing 29 people and injuring 330.
September 8, 1999	Bombs explode in an apartment block in Moscow, Russia, killing 94 and injuring 152, part of a series of bombings over a two-week period that altogether killed nearly 300 people.
October 12, 2000	A speedboat bomb attack on the USS *Cole* in Aden, Yemen, kills 17.
September 11, 2001	Four commercial jet airliners are hijacked from East Coast airports: two are crashed into the World Trade Center towers; one is crashed into the Pentagon; and the fourth one crashes into a field in Pennsylvania. Thousands are killed or injured.
October 12, 2002	Bomb blast in a Bali resort, blamed on militant Islamic group linked to Osama bin Laden and al Qaeda, kills an estimated 202 people.
August 8, 2003	Car bomb at Jordanian embassy in Baghdad kills at least 11 people.
August 19, 2003	Terrorist bomb attack destroys UN headquarters in Iraqi capital of Baghdad, killing 22, including Sergio Vieira de Mello, the top UN envoy in Iraq.
November 15 & 20, 2003	Suicide bombers in Istanbul attack two synagogues, a British-based bank, and the British consulate, killing as many as 50 people and injuring more than 600.
March 11, 2004	Ten bombs explode at train stations in and around Madrid during morning rush hour, killing 198 and wounding many more in Spain's worst-ever terrorist incident.
July 7, 2005	A series of bombs is detonated in three crowded subway trains and aboard a London bus during peak rush hour, killing at least 191 people and injuring some 1,755.
July 11, 2006	Seven bomb blasts kill 209 people on the Suburban Railway in Mumbai (Bombay), India; another 700 are injured.
September 17, 2008	Al Qaeda in Yemen carries out attack on U.S. embassy in Sanaa, killing 18 people.
November 26–29, 2008	A wave of 10 coordinated bombing attacks in Mumbai kills at least 173 and injures more than 300; allegedly carried out by Pakistani militants.

SOURCE: *Wall Street Journal*, July 29, 1996, p. A14; *The Economist*, September 15, 2001, p. 18; Country Reports on Terrorism, U.S. Department of State 2006, 2007, 2008; author's updates.

December 25 in Pakistan when a female suicide bomber blew herself up in the middle of a crowd at a United Nations food aid center, killing 46 people and injuring more than 100 others.[1]

In Iraq in 2011, Baghdad and other major cities (Fallujah, Karbala, Kut, Kirkuk, Najaf, and Tikrit, among others) suffered frequent car bombings, suicide bombings, and armed attacks; in Afghanistan, the cities of Kabul, Kandahar, and Lashkar Gah (the capital of Helmand province) were particularly hard hit; in Pakistan dozens of innocents were killed in attacks in the remote border regions of North Waziristan, Khyber Pakhtunkhwa, as well as in Islamabad, Bannu, Hangu, Karachi, Lahore, Peshawar, and other cities.

And in July 2011 one of the worst terrorist attacks of the year occurred in Norway when a lone gunman killed 77 people and injured 242. In a "manifesto" published electronically the day of the attacks, a right-wing blogger named Anders Behring Breivik expressed extreme antipathy toward Islam as a religion, immigrants in general, Muslims in particular, and "multiculturalism." In August 2012 a court in Oslo found Breivik sane and guilty of mass murder. What happened in Norway reminds us that Islam is by no means the only source of terrorism in today's world.

In 2013, terrorist attacks escalated in Iraq. In Pakistan, in the month before the General Elections held on May 11, at least 89 people, including candidates for office, were killed in terrorist attacks and another 418 were injured. Also in May, a British soldier was stabbed and hacked to death in broad daylight by two Islamic militants in the London suburb of Woolwich.

Terrorist attacks continue to plague many countries in Asia and Africa. Terrorism has become a harrowing fact of life not only in the Arab world and Pakistan, but also in Afghanistan, India, Indonesia, and the Philippines. Mexico and several Central and South American countries, including El Salvador, Guatemala, Honduras, Nicaragua, Peru and Colombia, have also suffered from widespread terrorism at various times in recent decades.

Nor is Europe immune. In the United Kingdom, Irish Republican Army (IRA) ultranationalists conducted a terrorist campaign against British control of Northern Ireland (also known as Ulster) that began in the late 1960s. In Spain, Basque separatists known as the ETA (Basque Homeland and Freedom) have conducted a long-running terrorist campaign against the Madrid government. In Russia, two female suicide bombers wearing explosive belts detonated the devices on the Moscow Metro system on May 29, 2010, at the peak of the morning rush hour, killing over 40 and injuring more than 100.

In May 2009, New York City police arrested four ex-convicts allegedly engaged in a plot to blow up two synagogues in the Bronx and shoot down a military aircraft. Among the weapons they had locked away in a storage container was a surface-to-air missile.

In 2013, more than a decade after 9/11, the United States remains officially at war against an elusive and amorphous enemy possessing no territory, no central authority, and no clear identity. In a major speech on terrorism at the National Defense University in late May 2013, President Obama appeared to signal a change in counter-terrorism policy, declaring that the United States cannot conduct a "boundless" war on terrorism. "Our systematic effort to dismantle terrorist organizations must continue," Obama said. "But this war, like all wars, must end. That's what history advises. It's what our democracy demands." Although these words clearly point to a shift in theory, words are not deeds. When and how the new theory will be applied in practice was an open question.

WHAT IS TERRORISM?

terrorism
Politically or ideologically motivated violence aimed at public officials, business elites, and civilian populations designed to sow fear and dissension, destabilize societies, undermine established authority, induce policy changes, or even overthrow the existing government.

Despite its prevalence, **terrorism** remains an elusive concept. Some definitions emphasize terrorism's use of violence in the service of politics. According to *Webster's New World Dictionary*, terrorism is "the use of force or threats to demoralize, intimidate, and subjugate, especially such use as the political weapon or policy." Another source defines terrorism as "the deliberate attack on innocent civilians for political purposes."[2] Terrorism has been defined in many ways, but most definitions take into account several factors, including violence, desire for publicity, political motive, and intimidation aimed at civilian populations.[3] As we see later in the chapter, our definition of terrorism implies both a strategy and tactics (see "Ideas and Politics").

Terrorism comes in many forms. Some experts attempt to designate terrorist activities according to whether they (1) are state controlled or directed or (2) involve nationals from more than one country (Figure 16.1).

IDEAS AND POLITICS

TERRORISM: Five Definitions

Terrorism, by nature, is difficult to define. Acts of terrorism conjure emotional responses in the victims (those hurt by the violence and those affected by the fear), as well as in the practitioners. Even the U.S. government cannot agree on one single definition. The adage "One man's terrorist is another man's freedom fighter" is still alive and well. Listed here are several definitions of terrorism.

- "Terrorism is the use or threatened use of force designed to bring about political change." —Brian Jenkins
- "Terrorism constitutes the illegitimate use of force to achieve a political objective when innocent people are targeted." —Walter Laqueur
- "Terrorism is the premeditated, deliberate, systematic murder, mayhem, and threatening of the innocent to create fear and intimidation in order

to gain a political or tactical advantage, usually to influence an audience." —James M. Poland

- "Terrorism is the unlawful use or threat of violence against persons or property to further political or social objectives. It is usually intended to intimidate or coerce a government, individuals, or groups, or to modify their behavior or politics." —Vice President's Task Force, 1986
- "Terrorism is the unlawful use of force or violence against persons or property to intimidate or coerce a government, the civilian population, or any segment thereof, in furtherance of political or social objectives." —FBI Definition

SOURCE: http://www.terror.com.

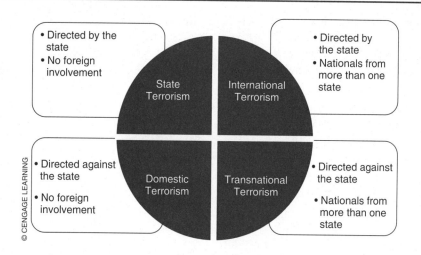

FIGURE 16.1
Classifying Terrorism.

State terrorism
Usually violent methods used by a government's security forces to intimidate and coerce its own people.

international terrorism
Terrorism that involves the governments, citizens, and interests of more than one country; terrorism that spills over into the international arena for whatever reason, whether state-sponsored or not.

state-sponsored terrorism
International terrorism that is aided and abetted by an established state; for example, Libya was linked to many terrorist acts against Western countries until Muammar el-Qaddafi made peace overtures in December 2003 and before he became an international pariah all over again in 2011 in the face of a popular rebellion.

State terrorism occurs when a government perpetrates terrorist tactics on its own citizens, such as occurred in Hitler's Germany. In contrast, **international terrorism**, sometimes called **state-sponsored terrorism**, happens when a government harbors international terrorists (as the Taliban government in Afghanistan did in the case of Osama bin Laden and the al Qaeda organization), finances international terrorist operations, or otherwise supports international terrorism *outside* its own borders.

During the Cold War, the United States frequently accused the Soviet Union of underwriting anti-U.S. terrorist groups around the world with money and arms. The Soviet Union responded that the U.S. government did the same when it was in U.S. interests to do so. Iran, Libya, Sudan, Syria, North Korea, and Cuba have all been on the United States' list of suspected state sponsors of terrorism for many years. Afghanistan and Iraq were also on this list prior to the fall of the Taliban regime in Afghanistan in late 2001 and the invasion of Iraq in 2003.

Libya was taken off the list when leader Muammar el-Qaddafi promised to scrap Libya's weapons research programs and open the country to international arms inspections in December 2003. In 2011 he again became a pariah in the eyes of the West when he turned his security forces against his own people in an attempt to resist the tide of democratizing reform—the so-called Arab Spring—sweeping across the region. With UN and NATO backing, President Obama ordered air strikes against the Qaddafi regime on humanitarian grounds (to protect the civilian population, especially in parts of the country, mainly in eastern Libya, known to be rebel strongholds). The rebels caught and killed the deposed tyrant in October 2011.

Domestic terrorism is practiced within a single country by terrorists with no ties to any government. The Tokyo subway sarin gas attacks in 1995, the Madrid commuter train bombings in 2004, and the Mumbai Suburban Railway

School shooting memorial following December 14, 2012, massacre at Sandy Hook Elementary School in Sandy Hook, Connecticut— 26 people died. The attack was carried out by a 20-year-old gunman brandishing three firearms including a Bushmaster semi-automatic AR-15 assault rifle. All 20 children killed were kindergarteners or in first grade. For the victims and families, the distinction between terrorism and what happened in Newtown that day is meaningless.

© GINA JACOBS/SHUTTERSTOCK.COM

domestic terrorism
A form of terrorism practiced within a country by people with no ties to any government.

transnational terrorism
Terrorist groups in different countries who cooperate with each other, or a group that crosses national boundaries to commit acts of terror.

bombings in 2006 (see Table 16.1) are examples of this type of terrorism. The aim of domestic terrorism is typically to strike fear and sow seeds of discord in society and to discredit or overthrow existing political institutions. Unlike the United Kingdom, Spain, and several other Western countries, the United States had been largely exempt from such acts until the Oklahoma City federal office building bombing in 1995, the summer 1996 bombing at the Olympics in Atlanta, and numerous bombings of abortion clinics.

Transnational terrorism arises when terrorists or terrorist groups not backed by any established state and operating in different countries cooperate with one another, or when a single terrorist operates in more than one country. Examples include the bombing of the U.S. embassies in Kenya and Tanzania in 1998, the World Trade Center attacks in 1993 and 2001, and the London subway bombings in 2005 (see Table 16.1). The global nature of terrorism today has blurred the distinction between domestic and international forms of terrorism.

Domestic terrorism is often directed against the state. Groups seeking to regain control over their homelands, such as Basques in Spain, Irish Catholics in Northern Ireland, Tamils in Sri Lanka, Sikhs in India, and Chechens in Russia, are motivated by *nationalist* or *separatist* aims. This type of terrorism is usually confined to a specific nation, although its practitioners may receive arms, money, and support from other radical groups, private donors abroad, or even foreign governments. But the distinction between domestic terrorism and violent crime is blurred when multiple killings of innocent civilians occurs, as it did in a movie theater in Aurora, Colorado, on July 20, 2012, and at Sandy Hook Elementary School in Newtown, Connecticut, on December 14, 2012.

Groups seeking to destabilize society in the name of some abstract belief are often inspired by *ideological* or *utopian* motives.[4] The specific ideology is less important than the fanatical behavior it encourages. Terrorism is a hallmark of fascism and anarchism, as well as distorted versions of Marxism and Islam.* Examples include the Red Army Faction in Germany, the Red Brigades in Italy, the Shining Path in Peru, the Islamic Jihad in Egypt, Osama bin Laden's al Qaeda (the Base), and certain far-right militia groups in the United States. Often such groups also have international links.

Some terrorist organizations defy simple description. Hamas (Islamic Resistance Movement), for example, which has violently opposed peace negotiations between Israel and the Palestine Liberation Organization (PLO) over the future of the Israeli-occupied West Bank and Gaza Strip, won a surprise victory in the Palestinian parliamentary elections of January 2006. Hamas is a nationalist-separatist movement that seeks the destruction of Israel and the establishment of a radical Islamic state. But it is also motivated by ideology, namely, a brand of Islamic fundamentalism that stresses militancy and jihad (holy war). Classifying terrorist groups is useful as a tool of analysis, but it is not always easy.

THE ORIGINS OF TERRORISM

There is clearly a link between terrorism and religious fundamentalism; Islamic extremism is an obvious case in point. However, many terrorists are not religious, and few religious fundamentalists engage in acts of terrorism. Still, terrorism appears to have its roots in religion—specifically, obscure religious sects, the names of which have entered into our vernacular.[5]

The Thugs, a Hindu sect that was finally destroyed in the nineteenth century after having operated for many centuries in India, were highway ambushers who secretly killed thousands of other Hindus, apparently out of a perverse sense of religious duty. An extremist Jewish group known as the Zealots killed outsiders and helped provoke rebellion against pagan Rome in 66–73 CE. Beginning in the eleventh century, a Shi'ite Muslim sect, the Assassins, murdered outsiders in a campaign to "purify" Islam. Toward the end of the Middle Ages and later during the Reformation, violent sects arose within Christianity as well.[6]

Modern-day revolutionary terror is usually traced to more secular roots, often to the French Revolution or the writings and deeds of nineteenth-century Russian anarchists.[7] Some experts contend the type of contemporary terrorism we see on the nightly news sprouted from seeds planted in the late 1960s; a few even cite 1968 as the year of its inception. The confluence of turbulent and unsettling events in the late 1960s included racial strife in the United States, an escalating conflict in Vietnam, and the Arab-Israeli Six Days' War of 1967. The year 1968 brought these portents:

- Three Palestinian terrorists seized an Israeli El Al airliner and forced its crew to fly the plane to Algeria, one of the first of many acts of air piracy.
- The Baader-Meinhof gang announced its presence in West Germany by torching a Frankfurt department store.

---

*The distinction between religion and ideology breaks down completely when adherents pursue patently political ends and use religion to justify the means. Islamic extremists, for example, frequently call for jihad (holy war) against Israel and the "Crusaders" (to use Osama bin Laden's epithet). But every Muslim knows that the Koran (Islam's holy scripture) strictly forbids the taking of innocent life and makes no exceptions. Terrorism certainly has no more of a place in Islam than it has in Christianity.

- Yasir Arafat, an advocate of armed struggle against Israel, became the leader of the PLO.
- The assassination of Martin Luther King Jr. precipitated an outbreak of domestic violence in the United States by such groups as the Black Panthers and the Weathermen.[8]

At least three longer-term historical forces helped create a climate conducive to terrorism. First, direct military confrontations and conflicts became infinitely more dangerous in the Nuclear Age; what starts as a conventional war between, say, India and Pakistan might escalate out of control. Therefore, nations whose interests coincided with certain terrorist objectives sometimes provided moral, financial, or military support to these groups. In this manner, terrorism became a kind of proxy for violence between nations. Second, European colonialism had drawn to a close, leaving many newly formed nations to work out a host of unresolved territorial, national, and religious disputes. The result was a variety of low-intensity wars, many punctuated by terrorist activity, within and between these nations. Third, reverence for life and concern for the individual, common to democratic societies, combined with dramatic "up close and personal" world-wide television news coverage to make terrorist incidents major media events. Consequently, the impact of such incidents—the publicity "payoff" from the terrorist's point of view—has been greatly magnified since the 1960s.

counterterrorism
Methods used to combat terrorism.

But it was in the 1970s that terrorism and **counterterrorism**, or opposing terrorism, became major growth industries. According to one estimate, the number of terrorist incidents multiplied tenfold between 1971 and 1985.[9] The level of terrorism remained high throughout the 1980s. Precise figures vary widely, however, reflecting, among other things, differences in how terrorism is defined. Risks International, for example, put the total number of terrorist incidents in 1985 at slightly more than 3,000, whereas the U.S. government conservatively counted fewer than one-fourth that number.[10]

The international terrorist threat to the U.S. homeland culminated in the 9/11 attacks. Both before and after 2001, terrorism plagued Europe, the Middle East, and Latin America far more than it did the United States. Surprisingly, at the end of the 1990s, terrorism was less common in the Middle East than in any other region of the world *except* North America. However, that changed dramatically after the U.S.-led invasion of Iraq in 2003. The National Counter-Terrorism Center (NCTC) reported no fewer than 62,805 worldwide terrorist attacks during the years 2005–2009, of which roughly one-third occurred in a single country—Iraq. Given these numbers, it is clear that the war on terror, far from solving the problem, has coincided with a steep rise in terrorism across the globe.

The Logic of Terrorism

Why do terrorists act as they do? Terrorist acts are often designed to undermine support and confidence in the existing government by creating a climate of fear and uncertainty. Terrorists use violence as a form of psychological warfare on behalf of an "overvalued idea" or cause. Terrorists are fiercely anti–status quo and despair of peaceful methods; they seek to bring about change or chaos, the latter either as an end in itself or as a prelude to change. They often aim not so much to spark an immediate revolution as to provoke the government into acts of repression, to make it look weak or inept, and to prepare the way for revolution.

Terrorism strikes at vulnerable societies, not necessarily unjust ones. Indeed, one expert on terrorism noted, "Societies with the least political participation and the most injustice have been the most free from terrorism in our time."[11] By logical extension, democratic societies such as the United States and the United Kingdom, with long traditions of respect for civil rights and the rule of law, have both been potential and actual targets of terrorist attacks.

Terrorist Tactics

Terrorism has often been described as the weapon of the weak against the strong. Typically, individuals or tiny groups lacking resources act against defenseless targets. Terrorism requires little money and can be funded by actions normally associated with common crime, such as armed robbery and drug trafficking.

Terrorists' weapons of choice are often crude and cheap (small arms and dynamite). However, as we now know, they can also be highly sophisticated (passenger airplanes used as guided missiles or a particularly lethal form of anthrax). Even before 9/11, terrorism had become a worldwide phenomenon, as news stories of attacks in airports and crowded train terminals, kidnappings of wealthy business executives, and hijacked airliners grew all too familiar.

Although terrorism is usually directed at innocents, it has been blamed for many assassinations of world leaders, including Italy's former prime minister Aldo Moro (1978); Queen Elizabeth's cousin, Lord Louis Mountbatten (1979); Egyptian president Anwar al-Sadat (1981); Indian prime minister Indira Gandhi (1984) and her son the former prime minister Rajiv Gandhi (1991); and Pakistan's former prime minister Benazir Bhutto (December 27, 2007). Terrorists have also attempted to assassinate Pope John Paul II (1981); former British Prime Minister Margaret Thatcher (1984); and her successor, John Major (1991). It is possible the White House was one of the intended targets of the September 11 attacks. If so, the conspirators probably hoped to kill the U.S. president.

The relationship between terrorist tactics and objectives is revealed in the Brazilian terrorist Carlos Marighella's chilling but incisive *Mini-Manual of the Urban Guerrilla*, a 48-page do-it-yourself handbook for aspiring terrorists and revolutionaries. It spells out how to blow up bridges, raise money through kidnappings and bank robberies, and plan the "physical liquidation" of enemies. The book offers a range of practical advice: learn to drive a car, pilot a plane, sail a boat; be a mechanic or radio technician; keep physically fit; learn photography and chemistry; acquire "a perfect knowledge of calligraphy"; study pharmacology, nursing, or medicine. It also stresses the need to "shoot first" and aim straight. In general, terrorists champion violence above all other forms of political activity. Furthermore, revolutionaries such as Marighella glorify violence, not as a necessary evil but as a positive form of liberation and creativity.[12] According to Marighella, terrorism succeeds when strategies and tactics come together:

> The government has little or no alternative except to intensify repression. The police roundups, house searches, arrests of innocent people, make life in the city unbearable. [The government appears] unjust, incapable of solving

problems....The political situation is transformed into a military situation, in which the militarists appear more and more responsible for errors and violence....Pacifists and right-wing opportunists...join hands and beg the hangmen for elections.[13]

Rejecting the "so-called political solution," the urban guerrilla must become more aggressive and violent, resorting without mercy to sabotage, terrorism, expropriations, assaults, kidnappings, and executions, heightening the disastrous situation in which the government must act.[14] An urban guerrilla group called the Tupamaros terrorized Uruguay from 1963 to 1972, seeking to overthrow the government. The Tupamaros became the very embodiment of Marighella's revolutionary principles and have since served as an inspiration for terrorists and extremists throughout the world. Significantly, the insurgency in Uruguay ended only after most of the guerrillas were murdered in a brutal government crackdown. Today, Uruguay is a peaceful, democratic country.

Acts of Terrorism versus Acts of War

The al Qaeda operatives who hijacked four commercial airliners on September 11, 2001, were carrying out a terrorist act *by definition* and an act of war *only by inference or interpretation*. When Japanese kamikaze pilots flew fighter planes into U.S. warships anchored in Pearl Harbor on December 7, 1941, and sank most of the Pacific fleet, it was an act of war first and an act of terror only incidentally, if at all. In war-fighting jargon, this attack was a classic example of the preemptive strike. However heinous and treacherous it appeared to U.S. citizens at the time (and still does), it was extremely successful as a single strategic event.[*]

The 9/11 attacks and Pearl Harbor are often compared, but the comparison is inapt. Pearl Harbor was the result of a decision made by the government and military high command of an established state with which the United States had diplomatic relations at the time. It was without question an act of war. Moreover, it was directed exclusively against *military* targets—the kamikaze pilots could have hit civilian targets in Hawaii but did not. Finally, the attacks were designed not to overthrow or destabilize the U.S. government or any other government, but rather to cripple U.S. naval power in the Pacific and thus forestall U.S. interference with Japan's imperialist designs in Asia.

The 9/11 attacks contrast sharply on all three points. They were not undertaken by an established state (although Afghanistan harbored al Qaeda network's top leaders and many of its fighters); they were directed mainly at civilians who had nothing to do with making U.S. foreign policy or with the armed forces; and they were clearly aimed at exposing the vulnerability of the United States, embarrassing the government, and undermining U.S. economic might, while tarnishing the Pentagon's image both at home and abroad. Even more to the point,

---

[*]Of course, in the perspective of the entire war, it takes on a very different aspect in that it galvanized the American people, who were up until then resolutely opposed to entering the war, and gave President Roosevelt the green light to ask Congress for a declaration of war on Japan and Germany.

these attacks were designed to rally support for bin Laden's extreme brand of Islamism and lead to the eventual toppling of "apostate" governments in the Arab world (including bin Laden's native Saudi Arabia).

Illegal Enemy Combatants

The very ambiguity of the status of terrorists in domestic and international law raises questions about how captured suspected terrorists ought to be treated. Are they prisoners of war, criminals, or neither? If they are neither, it means they exist in a legal limbo and can be denied even the most basic rights. In theory, they can be tortured or killed in captivity and the world would never know. They can be imprisoned for months or even years without being charged or having legal counsel or contact with family members—this is, in fact, the status of an unknown number of suspected terrorists taken captive by U.S. military forces in Afghanistan, Iraq, and elsewhere after 9/11.[15]

The Bush administration declared these captives were neither common criminals nor prisoners of war (POWs), but rather "illegal combatants"—a category tailor-made for the war on terror but widely rejected by other governments, as well as by experts on international law. Many suspected al Qaeda terrorists rounded up in Afghanistan (about 650 according to published reports) were taken to the U.S. naval base at Guantánamo Bay (also known as "Gitmo") in Cuba, where they were to be kept indefinitely in a maximum-security facility off limits to the press and the public.

The constitutionality of indefinite detention without trial was finally challenged in June 2007 in the case of Ali al-Marri, a student at Bradley University who was initially arrested and jailed on charges having nothing to do with terrorism. Al-Marri was eventually classified as an illegal combatant and transferred to the Naval Consolidated Brig in Charleston, South Carolina. In June 2007, a federal appeals court ruled that U.S. residents cannot be incarcerated indefinitely as enemy combatants without being charged. "Put simply, the Constitution does not allow the President to order the military to seize civilians residing within the United States and then detain them indefinitely without criminal process, and this is so even if he calls them 'enemy combatants,'" the court said. The same federal appeals court held a rehearing of the ruling and reversed itself 5 to 4. But in March 2009, the Supreme Court erased that ruling after al-Marri was indicted on federal criminal charges in Illinois, thus belatedly granting his constitutional right to a trial by jury in a civilian court. Al-Marri entered a guilty plea to one count of conspiracy involving a foreign terrorist organization.[16]

The concept of "illegal combatants" does not exist in international law and did not exist in U.S. public policy or jurisprudence before 9/11. Presidents George W. Bush and Barack Obama have both viewed it as a necessary tool in the war on terror. Critics, including the American Bar Association, have questioned the constitutionality of capturing prisoners outside the jurisdiction of the United States, holding them incommunicado, and denying them access to counsel.

Characteristics of Terrorist Groups

Most terrorist groups are short-lived, operate locally, and get very little publicity. Although our national news media covers only a few, hundreds of identifiable terrorist groups exist worldwide.[17] They tend to be small and tight-knit, seldom numbering more than 100 members and usually fewer than several dozen. Many of the most notorious are found in the Middle East and associated with Islamic fundamentalism—the Abu Nidal Organization, al Qaeda, Islamic Jihad, Hamas, and Hezbollah (Party of God) are five contemporary examples. Because they are often ethnically and politically homogeneous, with members who are close friends or even relatives, terrorist cells are extremely difficult to penetrate or monitor, frequently confounding the best efforts of intelligence agencies.

Illustration of Abbottabad Compound

7 feet high (privacy wall)
11 feet high
Opaque windows (located on north side of building)
12 feet high
Gate
Trash burning location
10 feet high
13 feet high
Gate
18 feet high
12 feet high
N
Pakistan

Osama bin Laden was the wealthy Saudi mastermind behind a series of terrorist attacks on U.S. targets that culminated in the destruction of the World Trade Center. On May 2, 2011, U.S. Navy Seals killed bin Laden in a night raid on his walled compound near Abbottabad, Pakistan. Bringing down the architect of the 9/11 attacks on the United States and the supreme leader of the al Qaeda terrorist organization was a major victory for the Obama administration, but the hunt for bin Laden and the decade-old war in Afghanistan it occasioned ultimately came at a high cost in blood and treasure. The unilateral U.S. military action that ended bin Laden's life deepened the distrust between the U.S. and Pakistan, both because it violated Pakistan's sovereignty and because of U.S. suspicions that Pakistan's Inter-Service Intelligence (ISI), as well as elements in the military, were protecting bin Laden. When the smoke cleared, the war itself was still far from over.

As the world learned after the release of the fourth post-9/11 bin Laden videotape in mid-December 2001, al Qaeda operates on a need-to-know basis, closely guarding and compartmentalizing information within its own ranks, much like official intelligence services do. This emphasis on secrecy is essential for the success and survival of terrorist groups and networks, especially under greatly heightened security in the United States, Europe, the Arab world, and elsewhere.

Even so, the life span of most terrorist groups is only about five to ten years. By the same token, the leaders of terrorist groups tend to come and go. However, there are exceptions—two of the most notorious being Abu Nidal, who masterminded countless terrorist acts (including airport massacres in Rome and Vienna) for three decades until he was murdered in Baghdad in 2002, reportedly on direct orders from Saddam Hussein; and Osama bin Laden, founder of al Qaeda and the prime mover behind the 9/11 attacks. Finally, terrorist groups seldom operate from a fixed location. Although the perpetrators of the 9/11 attacks were exceptions, terrorists often have relatively little training, use unsophisticated equipment, and acquire the "tools of the trade"—some of which could be purchased at any hardware store—by theft.

Algeria in the 1990s: Nightmare and Prelude

In Algeria, the line between Islamic fundamentalism and terrorism—or between revolution and civil war—was difficult to discern in the 1990s. Algeria can be seen as a preview of the political crises that have swept across the Arab world in recent years and destabilized Libya, Egypt, and Syria, among others, where popular anger has become dry tinder for extremists bent on the overthrow of established secular governments in the region. Few stories about Algeria's horrific internecine war appeared in the U.S. press, and even today, few in the United States are aware of what happened there.

Algeria gained its independence from France in 1962 after a long, violent revolutionary struggle. For most of the next thirty years, pro-Marxist military strongmen ruled. Eventually, however, a core of Muslim fundamentalists became dangerously discontented. From this disquiet emerged the political organization Islamic Salvation Front (FIS). Later, when Algeria's first multiparty elections were held in 1991, the FIS gained a dazzling first-round victory. However, in 1992, the military simply canceled the second round of elections and installed a new president. This cynical act radicalized the FIS and prompted it to go underground. Even worse, it split the armed Islamist movement in Algeria and gave the most extreme jihadist elements—advocates of all-out terrorism—the upper hand. At the end of 1992, the Armed Islamic Group (GIA) emerged as a murderous alternative to the somewhat less violent and uncompromising FIS.

Algeria's terrorist nightmare began with GIA attacks primarily on the police, security forces, and government officials. Soon the terrorists began targeting other groups as well. In 1993 and 1994, there were dozens of attacks on opposition groups, foreigners, intellectuals, journalists, and other civilians. Between 1995 and 1998, only about 25% of the attacks were directed against security forces and government officials; the rest struck at civilians. Schools and school employees were among the favorite targets.

As the strategy changed to targeting mainly civilians, the insurgents' tactics changed as well. In 1996, there were more bombings than assassinations, violent clashes with security forces, and organized armed attacks. After the mid-1990s, the bombings increasingly targeted markets, cinemas, and restaurants, as well as schools. According to one Middle East authority on the Algerian Islamist movement:

> Violence reached its ultimate level of cruelty in a series of massacres that began at the end of 1996. At least 67 massacres took place between November 1996 and July 1999, but most…took place in 1997 (42 massacres)…These massacres involved militants armed with guns, crude bombs, knives, and axes descending on villages at night to kill their inhabitants, often by hacking them to death and slitting their throats. Other atrocities involved fake security checkpoints set up by militants to identify specific targets—e.g., state employees and men with conscription papers.[18]

The government countered with lethal force. In November 1996, constitutional amendments that appeared to move Algeria toward a limited democracy were popularly ratified. The main aim, however, was to curtail radical Islamic groups and ban all political parties based on language or religion, while retaining preponderate power in the executive branch. Thus, during the June 1997 elections, the FIS and similar groups could not run candidates and could only urge citizens not to vote.

The FIS condemned the new constitution and continued to struggle against the regime until September 1997, when its armed wing, the Islamic Salvation Army (AIS), declared a cease-fire. But it was the vicious bands of zealots and thugs that comprised the GIA, not the AIS, that had carried out most of the bloody massacres. Not surprisingly, the hard-line "eradicators" in the government favored finding and killing the terrorists rather than trying to negotiate with them. This stance was not unreasonable given the fact that the GIA had shown no proclivity toward compromise.

The election of a new president in 1999 broke the ice. The government released some political prisoners and pushed through the Law of Civil Reconciliation, extending amnesty to rebels who had not committed atrocities. The AIS, which benefited from a general amnesty due to its 1997 cease-fire, began disbanding its militia under state supervision at the end of 1999. Thousands of AIS rebels took advantage of the general amnesty granted by the regime; at the beginning of 2000, even some GIA militias began declaring they would abide by the cease-fire.

Amnesty International called Algeria the most violent country in the Middle East at the end of the 1990s. The proximate cause of the violence was the military's illegal cancellation of a national election in 1992, but the roots of Algeria's nightmare run deep in social and economic failure. Despite its extensive oil and natural gas reserves, its people are overwhelmingly poor. Unemployment hovers around 25%. Nearly one-third of the population is under 15 years of age. High unemployment hits youth the hardest, which may, in part, explain why terrorists and revolutionaries are disproportionately young. Meanwhile, tensions based on ethnic and linguistic divisions persist. Most notably, Berbers are a sizable minority who feel alienated and powerless, a feeling intensified when Algeria moved to make Arabic its sole official language.

Nevertheless, terrorism still plagues Algeria. One of various terrorist groups operating in Algeria today calls itself al Qaeda in the Islamic Maghreb (AQIM). In 2008 dozens of suicide bombings and other attacks against police, foreigners, government employees, and civilians threatened to plunge the country into anarchy, but Algerian security forces reportedly killed, wounded, or arrested hundreds of terrorists.

The number of terrorist incidents dropped sharply for several years after a bloody 2008, but in August 2011 a suicide attack on a military academy left 18 people dead, including 16 soldiers, and 20 wounded. In December 2013 a terrorist attack on a BP gas facility in eastern Algeria left 37 hostages and at least 32 militants dead. The attack, carried out by anti-Western Islamist elements, "fanned fears of a new terror front" (CNN, 1/23/2013)—not least because in 2012 Islamist insurgents seized control of a large swath of territory in neighboring Mali. France sent troops into Mali in early 2013; in February, French and Malian forces succeeded in regaining control of the strategic northern city of Gao, as well as the legendary town of Timbuktu.

Terrorists in Algeria, Mali, and the Maghreb (northwest Africa) continue to find fertile ground for fresh recruits. In retrospect, Algeria in the 1990s was a prelude to the upheavals today tearing apart the Arab societies of North Africa and the Middle East—from Libya to Syria.

TERRORIST OR FREEDOM FIGHTER?

The terrorism that ravaged Algerian society in the 1990s is hard for people living normal lives to comprehend. Who are the perpetrators of these despicable acts? How do they differ from common criminals, guerrilla fighters, and revolutionaries? Why is terrorism any different from other forms of violence?

Official U.S. policy treats terrorism as an illegal *political* phenomenon. This approach stresses the illegitimacy of terrorism and advocates combating it with swift punishment and due vigilance. Critics (including some European countries and NATO allies) focus on the *socioeconomic* causes of the problem. These divergent views point to quite different policy responses, including targeted programs of trade, aid, and investment designed to alleviate misery, hunger, and disease in poverty-stricken, violence-prone countries and regions, as well as diplomacy that does not exclude talking to regimes and dictators we despise.

Policy differences aside, terrorists are criminals, though by no means ordinary ones. Killing and kidnapping, robbing banks, and hijacking airplanes are heinous crimes, no matter who perpetrates them or why; they become terrorist acts when the *motive* is political. When a serial killer is on the loose in a community, the victims are typically innocent people, but psychopaths are not motivated by religion or ideology. Sometimes the line is blurred, as in the case of narcoterrorists—armed rebels in Colombia associated with powerful drug lords or drug traffickers in Mexico who use terrorist tactics to intimidate the public, press, and police. In 2008 alone, some 5,700 Mexicans were killed in drug-related violence. In January 2009, drug traffickers staged a grenade attack on Mexico's top TV network, Televisa, during the nightly news broadcast.[19] By May 2011, the death toll from Mexico's drug war had claimed a staggering 34,000 victims, and the cost to Mexico's sluggish economy in human resources and lost tourism revenues was inestimable.

If terrorists are not ordinary criminals, neither are they ordinary guerrillas or freedom fighters. Guerrillas often constitute the armed wing of a revolutionary movement or party—Mao's Red Army is one well-known historical example. Guerrilla forces sometimes commit atrocities against civilians (as do soldiers in uniform), but most insurgent violence is directed at the security forces and government. By contrast, terrorists target civilians and noncombatants, as well as police and security forces—a strategy designed to sow the seeds of fear and doubt so people will not cooperate with the police and military, and to show people the government cannot protect them.

Certainly, many revolutionaries in the twentieth century have resorted to terror—both before and after taking power. But, unlike terrorists, revolutionaries seek to overthrow the government *in existing circumstances*, rather than trying to precipitate a political and social crisis by *changing* the circumstances. To that end, revolutionaries attempt to build a subversive party; infiltrate the government, the police, and the military; spread propaganda; agitate among trade unions; recruit and indoctrinate the young; and incite strikes, riots, and street demonstrations. Terrorism in the hands of revolutionaries is a tactic, not a strategy; in the hands of terrorists, terror is both a tactic *and* a strategy. Terrorists often appear to share the view of Émile Henry, a French anarchist who, when charged with throwing a bomb in a Paris café in 1894, replied, "No one is innocent."

TERRORISM AND SOCIETY

Europeans abhor terrorism as much as Americans do, but they tend to sympathize with the social classes or ethnic communities from which terrorists often arise. In sharp contrast to the United States' pro-Israeli stance, most European governments are openly critical of Israeli policy toward the Palestinians. The best way to defeat terrorism, in their view, is to ameliorate its underlying causes—injustice, despair, and hopelessness. To European critics, Israeli policy exacerbates these conditions and plays into the hands of extremists.

Even where Middle Eastern governments suppress extreme Islamist groups, many people secretly sympathize with them. In Palestine, sympathy with groups like Hamas and Hezbollah is widespread and hardly a secret. Many Arabs admit that throughout the Arab world people expressed admiration for Osama bin Laden. Indeed, in some Arab countries, Osama has reportedly become one of the most popular names for baby boys.

To be sure, any comprehensive theory of terrorism in today's world must take account of its social context, including the dehumanizing effects of life in refugee camps or ghettos, youth unemployment, and Western intrusion—first colonization and now globalization. People unable to cope with these stresses react in different ways. Some turn to crime, others to alcohol or drugs, and some drop out. A few become terrorists. Of course, not all terrorists are products of poverty. Many are well educated and come from relatively privileged backgrounds; Osama bin Laden was born into a fabulously wealthy family in Saudi Arabia.

Why youths decide to become martyrs is unclear. Perhaps it is from a sense of hopelessness (nothing to lose) or religious zeal, perhaps from idealism, or because they want to be a hero in the eyes of friends and family.

Youthful Recruits

Occasionally young females become suicide bombers, especially in the Middle East. The Shi'ite suicide bomber who drove her explosives-packed Peugeot into an Israeli Army convoy in southern Lebanon in 1985 was 16 years old. But most terrorists are male, single, and young.[20] The Jordanian who tried to assassinate a United Arab Emirates diplomat in Rome in 1984 was 22. The oldest of the four Palestinian terrorists who hijacked a Mediterranean cruise ship (the *Achille Lauro*) carrying 400 passengers in October 1985 was 23; the youngest, 19.

Research puts the median age of terrorists between 22 and 23 years. Twelve- and 14-year-old terrorists have been arrested in Northern Ireland; 14- and 15-year-old children are recruited by Arab and Iranian groups, sometimes for particularly dangerous missions.[21] A German psychologist who interviewed captured members of the Red Army Faction noted elements of an "adolescent crisis" among terrorists, and an expert on the Provisional Irish Republican Army (IRA) observed a "terrorist tradition" at work in some countries where "whole families pass on to their children that [terrorism] is the way you struggle for your rights."[22]

Eric Hoffer touched on the susceptibility of certain youths to fanatical causes in *The True Believer*. He placed them in a group he called "misfits," a category he further broke down into temporary and permanent. Hoffer wrote:

> Adolescent youth, unemployed college graduates, veterans, new immigrants, and the like are of this category. They are dissatisfied and haunted by the fear that their best years will be wasted before they reach their goal.[23]

At the same time, although they tend to be "receptive to the preaching of a proselytizing movement," Hoffer argued that they "do not always make staunch converts."

If the grievances that give rise to terrorism were removed, would there be no terrorists? Possibly, and yet there are many societies where abject poverty and injustice have not given rise to terrorism. The logical conclusion: Oppression is a necessary condition of terrorism but not a sufficient one.

The Psychology of Terrorism

According to one expert on the psychology of terrorism, "terrorists with a cause" are the most dangerous to democratic society.[24] Who are these rebels? What motivates them? Not surprisingly, many of the most common traits exhibited by members of terrorist groups are associated with adolescence, including the following:[25]

- *Oversimplification of issues.* Terrorists see complex issues in black-and-white terms; they have no interest in debate; they often live out a "fantasy war," imagining the people overwhelmingly support their cause.
- *Frustration.* Terrorists feel society has cheated them, life is unfair, and they deserve far more; they are unwilling to wait or work for something better and believe the only way to get is to take.
- *Orientation toward risk-taking.* Many terrorists seek situations offering adventure and are easily bored.
- *Self-righteousness.* Terrorists display belligerent assertiveness, dogmatism, and intolerance of opposing views.
- *Utopianism.* They harbor an unexamined belief that heaven on earth is just over the horizon; the only thing standing in the way is the corrupt and oppressive existing order.
- *Social isolation.* Terrorists, one expert noted, are often "people who are really lonely." For some, a terrorist cell may be the only "family" they have.
- *A need to be noticed.* Terrorists share a need to feel important, a desire to make a personal imprint by getting media attention.
- *A taste for blood.* Interviews with captured terrorists, testimony of relatives and acquaintances, and eyewitness accounts by former hostages point to a final, startling characteristic: Some terrorists kill without an ounce of remorse.

Terrorists often oversimplify reality; thus they may see victims as mere objects—a habit of mind observed among Nazi guards at extermination camps during the Holocaust.[26] In a similar vein, Paul R. McHugh, a distinguished Johns Hopkins School of Medicine psychiatrist, argued that terrorists, like other actors with a "ferocious passion," have an "overvalued idea," defined as "a thought shared with others in a society or culture but in the patient held with an intense emotional commitment capable of provoking dominant behaviors in its service."[27] One clinical disorder prompted by an overvalued idea is anorexia nervosa. Adolf Hitler (anti-Semitism), Carry Nation (temperance), and John Brown (abolitionism) are three examples of historical figures with overvalued ideas.

Those who suffer personality or emotional disorders associated with overvalued ideas are commonly called fanatics. Once again, Hoffer's discussion of fanatics in *The True Believer* proves appropriate. Fanaticism—excessive, blind devotion—whether political or religious, is almost always based on hatred, according to Hoffer; the fanatic places hatred in the service of a cause or a vision. Hatred is, in turn, a unifying force for like-minded fanatics, whereas love is divisive. Thus, hatred provides a reason for living, often appealing to individuals who are insecure, have little sense of self-worth, or lack meaning in their lives. Finally, Hoffer noted:

> The fanatic is perpetually incomplete and insecure. He cannot generate self-assurance out of his individual resources—out of his rejected self—but finds it only by clinging passionately to [some cause]. This passionate attachment is the essence of his blind devotion and religiosity....And he is ready to sacrifice his life to demonstrate to himself and others that such indeed is his role. He sacrifices his life—for example, in a suicide bombing—to prove his worth.[28]

Nor are fanatics necessarily motivated by a good cause. They embrace a cause not primarily because it is just or holy, but because they have a desperate need for something to hold on to. It is this need for passionate attachment that turns a cause into *the* cause. From there it can be a short step to jihad or a terrorist campaign.[29] But for normal people fortunate enough to be living normal lives in normal times, it remains a mystery how anyone can commit barbarous acts out of idealism or religious fervor.

Terrorism and the Media

Terrorists seek publicity. As they see it, the more attention they can get, the better. Why? Because media coverage—above all, the dramatic images that flash across our television and computer screens—draws worldwide attention to the act itself and the overvalued idea embraced by those who perpetrated it. This coverage is not only politically prized, but it is personally gratifying—it makes otherwise obscure individuals feel important. The prime-time exposure terrorists frequently get on CNN and other network news all over the world is also free. And, of course, the most daring, deadly, or otherwise sensational terrorist acts receive the most extensive media attention. Without question, the two fatal blows struck against the World Trade Center are the most widely and repeatedly televised terrorist acts in history.

In light of terrorists' need for publicity, many political analysts outside the profession of journalism blame the rapid rise of terrorism in part on the media—on television, in particular. After all, bad news makes for better headlines and better copy, and bad news that is also sensational and shocking garners the most attention and the highest Nielsen ratings, which in turn translates into higher advertising revenues for the networks. In this sense, at least, terrorism is tailor-made for television.

In a market economy, simply reporting the news is not enough; the news industry must also sell the news. The audience share that chooses to watch television news determines how much companies will pay to advertise their products on a particular network. Thus, producers of news shows are loath to pass up a good story, even if it means playing into the hands of terrorists. Of course, an airplane hijacking involving hundreds of innocent people is newsworthy by any standard. The media do, after all, have a responsibility to keep people informed. And even if one network decided not to cover a particular terrorist incident or to pay only slight attention to it, the others would not ignore it.

Media self-restraint is the only practical solution. Realistically, the news industry is not likely to cut back significantly on its reporting of terrorism until public opinion turns against such reports. As consumers of news, we often get what we demand and, in that sense, deserve what we get.

COUNTERING TERRORISM

The question facing democratic societies is how terrorism can be curtailed without jeopardizing democratic rights and liberties. The rise of international and state-sponsored terrorism, the danger of nuclear weapons falling into the hands of terrorists, and use of the Internet to plot and coordinate terrorist attacks—these developments all underscore the need for governments to coordinate global counterterrorist efforts.

Domestic Legislation

Authoritarian and totalitarian states are free to deal quickly and harshly with terrorists and accused terrorists. Democratic states, however, are committed to following the rule of law whenever and wherever possible. Over the past two decades, many democracies have enacted new laws or adapted old laws to deal more effectively with terrorists and terrorism.

Skyjacking and committing an act of violence against an airline passenger were made crimes in the United States way back in 1961, four decades before 9/11. In the wake of the first World Trade Center bombing in 1993 and the Oklahoma City bombing two years later, Congress passed an antiterrorism act in April 1996, which provided more resources for federal law enforcement to fight terrorism, tightened immigration, and loosened deportation procedures for aliens suspected of being terrorists.

But in 2001, on that fateful day in September, the second assault on the World Trade Center revealed the inadequacy of existing counterterrorist policies. President Bush quickly set up a new cabinet-level Office of Homeland

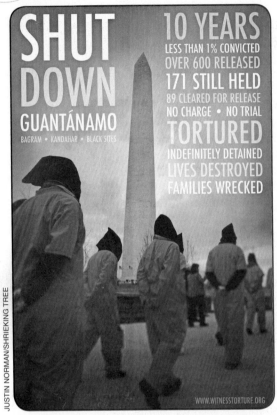

SHUT DOWN GUANTÁNAMO
BAGRAM • KANDAHAR • BLACK SITES

10 YEARS
LESS THAN 1% CONVICTED
OVER 600 RELEASED
171 STILL HELD
89 CLEARED FOR RELEASE
NO CHARGE • NO TRIAL
TORTURED
INDEFINITELY DETAINED
LIVES DESTROYED
FAMILIES WRECKED

WWW.WITNESSTORTURE.ORG

JUSTIN NORMAN/SHRIEKING TREE

In the war on terror, the United States used waterboarding as an interrogation technique. Human rights advocates argue that waterboarding is a form of torture and violates the 1949 Geneva Conventions on the treatment of prisoners of war.

Security, designed to coordinate the work of all federal departments and agencies engaged in any aspect of counterterrorism, and also issued a controversial directive creating military tribunals for suspected terrorists.[30]

The major changes in the government's power over legal aliens in the United States are contained in a law passed by Congress after the 9/11 attacks. The cumbersome name of this law—necessary to produce the desired acronym—is the Uniting and Strengthening America by Providing Appropriate Tools Required to Intercept and Obstruct Terrorism Act of 2001, more commonly known as the USA PATRIOT Act. In addition to greatly expanding the FBI's wiretapping authority, this act broadens the notion of who is considered a terrorist suspect and gives the U.S. attorney general sweeping authority to detain Arabs and Muslims, as well as other foreigners; it permits the government to deny entry into the United States to any foreigner who publicly endorses terrorism or belongs to a terrorist group; it expands the definition of *terrorist activity* to include any foreigner who uses "dangerous devices" or raises money for a terrorist group, *wittingly or unwittingly;* finally, it allows the government to detain any foreigner the attorney general considers a menace.

Taken together, the antiterrorist measures growing out of executive orders and the Patriot Act give the U.S. federal government powers of surveillance and infiltration unprecedented in modern times. At first supportive, public opinion is now deeply divided on the wisdom and necessity of warrantless wiretaps and other forms of government spying on civilians. In 2005, a CBS poll found respondents split (49% approved; 45% disapproved); in 2008, the candidate who opposed intrusive government measures—Barack Obama—won the election. As commander in chief, however, President Obama backed extension of the Patriot Act.

The Bush administration's counterterrorist methods and policies were controversial and, according to critics, illegal. (One of the most divisive was the use of waterboarding to extract information from prisoners suspected of belonging to Iraqi terrorist groups.) These method also appeared to be counterproductive (see "Maps that Matter"). Only in 2007 after President Bush ordered a troop surge in Iraq did the insurgency and violence there finally subside, although the level of violence rose again in 2009. Today, after more than a decade of turmoil, Iraq's prospects for social peace and governmental stability are dim.

The availability of special counterterrorist units such as the British SAS is not enough; governments must also demonstrate a willingness to use them in order "to establish an unmistakable pattern of failure and retribution."[35] There is always the risk of failure (for example, the 1980 U.S. attempt to free hostages in Iran), and the immediate consequences can be tragic. But the long-term consequences of acting indecisively can be even more tragic.

Other steps governments can take include controlling arms and explosives and, perhaps most important (though most difficult), developing better domestic and foreign intelligence-gathering capabilities. Modern technology using satellites, electronic surveillance, advanced search technologies, explosives detection, scanners, robotic vehicles, and drones have greatly enhanced existing counterterrorist capabilities, for only by obtaining information about terrorists' hideouts, movements, and plans can governments prevent attacks. There is also ongoing research in the promising new field of network analysis, using social science techniques to better understand the workings of terrorist networks.

Time is a crucial factor in fighting both insurgencies and terrorism (which often go hand in hand in today's world). The conventional wisdom long held that time was on the side of the insurgents—they are more highly motivated, closer to the people, and so on. There is reason to doubt the truth of this axiom. Consider the case of the Tamil minority in Sri Lanka.

The defeat of the Tamil Tigers, modern Asia's longest-lasting insurgency, in the spring of 2009 demonstrates that a patient strategy, allowing time for terrorists' acts to work against them, can succeed. At one point, the Tamil insurgents controlled a third of Sri Lanka; they used terrorist tactics—child soldiers and suicide bombers—and fought a conventional war, with outside aid from China, Pakistan, and high-earning Tamils abroad. But in the end, the Tamil Tigers' brutality and the Sinhalese-majority government's refusal to negotiate in the face of terrorist blackmail drained the lifeblood from the insurgency.[36]

Obviously, the nature of democratic societies and the constitutional framework in which governments operate present obstacles to police and investigative agencies charged with thwarting terrorism. Citizens are unaccustomed to acting as informants, and intelligence gathering is divided among several agencies, in part to prevent any one of them from gaining too much power. In the United States, for example, intelligence and counterintelligence have traditionally been separated; the CIA is responsible for foreign intelligence and is forbidden to engage in domestic spy operations against U.S. citizens or groups, and counterintelligence is the function of the FBI. Coordinating the work of these two agencies after 9/11 was the prime reason behind President Bush's decision to create the new Office of Homeland Security.

Private Measures

Finally, private citizens and firms have developed strategies to protect themselves.[37] Just as many governments were "hardening" their embassies and other overseas facilities in the 1980s and 1990s, private companies were spending billions of dollars annually on security services and hardware in the United States and elsewhere.[38]

Most citizens cannot afford to hire private security guards, but an alert public can make the terrorist's job more difficult. In Israel, for example, where everyone is acutely aware of the terrorist threat, officials claim 80% of bombs in public places are disarmed because suspicious objects are usually noticed and reported in time.[39] Most security experts agree that success in countering terrorism depends on vigilant citizens, as well as police and security forces.

THE TERRORISTS AMONG US

Multiple killings such as the massacres in Aurora, Colorado, and Newtown, Connecticut, in 2012 raise serious moral and political issues. Who cares how such heinous acts are labeled? And yet it matters. To understand why, consider the problem of "dirty hands" in politics. We all face moral dilemmas in life, but politicians have to make choices that have far-reaching effects on the whole society—plus, they want to get reelected. So it's no surprise when they clamber to show how tough they are on terrorism.

But the problem of dirty hands becomes a problem of bloody hands when politicians in the U.S. Congress climb into bed with the gun lobby and the National Rifle Association (NRA) because they care more about not getting targeted for defeat in the next election than about the safety of school-children. Arguably, the most dangerous "terrorists" are not the ones we tend to fear the most—imagined "foreigners" who infiltrate our society with malicious intent. Perhaps we have the most to fear from individuals who are "natural-born citizens" and who may even live next door. And, in stark contrast to virtually all other Western societies (with the exception of Switzerland), adult citizens in the United States can legally possess a veritable arsenal of deadly weapons.

CAN TERRORISM BE DEFEATED?

Terrorism poses a continuing threat that shows few signs of abating, despite the ongoing post-9/11 war on terror. Is a "war on terror" winnable? If not, why not? If so, how?

There is no single or totally effective solution to terrorism. Even one terrorist can be too many. One terrorist with a small support system—a few friends, safe houses, and supplies—can inflict enormous damage. Still, as we have seen, there are ways of limiting the opportunities available to terrorists and of deterring, punishing, or simply eradicating terrorism before it becomes an epidemic as it did in Italy in the 1970s and early 1980s, Peru in the 1980s, Algeria in the 1990s, and Pakistan in the late 2000s.

Meanwhile, doomsday scenarios involving terrorist plots to use weapons of mass destruction (WMD)—from anthrax to a "dirty" radiation bomb—cannot be dismissed lightly. No single state can meet this threat alone. Unfortunately, declaring "war on terror" is better theater than public policy, and fear of terrorist attacks can be exploited by governments to silence opposition or erode constitutional rights.

Words matter in politics. *War* is one of the words that matters most. The word, like the phenomenon itself, has a definite meaning and a long history. It is a word we often use loosely—too loosely. Terrorism cannot be defeated the way Germany and Japan were defeated in World War II. Terrorism does not have a territory or a seat of government. It can be contained but not occupied the way Germany and Japan were occupied (and Iraq and Afghanistan are today).

Terrorism is war by other means. War is politics by other means—and the focus of the next chapter.

SUMMARY

Terrorism, a political effort to oppose the status quo by inducing fear in the civilian population through the widespread and publicized use of violence, has become an everyday occurrence in the contemporary world. Although it has ancient roots in religious conflict, contemporary terrorism can be traced to the 1960s.

Terrorists seek to create a climate of chaos and confusion in the belief that political instability will hasten the downfall of a government. They form groups that are close-knit, homogeneous, small, and (often) short-lived. Terrorists can pose great challenges to countries facing political and economic problems; Muslim fundamentalism in Algeria provides such an example.

Although terrorists violate the law, they are not *criminals* in the everyday sense of the term. Nor are they guerrillas or ordinary revolutionaries. All terrorists are revolutionaries, but not all revolutionaries are terrorists. A terrorist is a kind of revolutionary who does not seek to obtain political power, but whose primary objective is to protest and combat the perceived injustice of the existing political order through random acts of violence. Terrorists tend to be young, single males who share a variety of key psychological characteristics, including fanaticism and hatred.

Democracy and terrorism are implacable enemies. Democracy depends for its existence on compromise, tolerance, and mutual trust; whereas terrorists are zealots who seek to radicalize society and destabilize the political system. Furthermore, democratic societies are, by nature, open and vulnerable to terrorist attacks. This vulnerability is both physical and psychological.

The problems democracies face in countering terrorism are complicated by the need to preserve individual freedoms while also protecting national security. Still, various singular and cooperative measures that democracies have undertaken show promise of containing—though not eliminating—terrorism.

KEY TERMS

terrorism   448
state terrorism   449
international
   terrorism   449

state-sponsored
   terrorism   449
domestic
   terrorism   450

transnational
   terrorism   450
counterterrorism   452

REVIEW QUESTIONS

1. How is terrorism different from common crime? From guerrilla warfare?
2. What tactics do terrorists typically employ, and how are their ends and means related?
3. What are the psychological roots of terrorism and the characteristics of the typical terrorist?
4. Why are democracies vulnerable to terrorism? Assess the terrorist threat to constitutional democracies.
5. What obstacles stand in the way of an effective counterterrorist policy?
6. What steps did the United States take to protect itself against terrorism after 9/11? Comment on U.S. successes and failures in the fight against terrorism.
7. Cite several examples of successful counterterrorist efforts in other countries, then identify several failures. What have we learned about how to fight terrorism?
8. Is technology on the side of governments or terrorists? Explain.

Politics without Government

CHAPTER 17

World Politics
The Struggle for Power

THINK ABOUT IT

What can Machiavelli and Morgenthau teach us about the principles of international politics?

How did the classical balance of power system differ from the Cold War system that emerged after World War II?

How did the balance of power change after the Cold War ended, and what is the role of the United States in the new world order?

What is the "national interest," and how is this concept instrumental in making foreign policy?

How can statecraft be used to reconcile power and morality, to achieve an optimal blend of hard and soft power, and to distinguish between humanitarian intervention and armed aggression?

In 416 BCE, Athens sent ships and troops against the island of Melos, a colony of Sparta that had remained neutral and wanted no part of the war between Sparta and Athens.[1] Negotiating from a position of overwhelming strength, the Athenians insisted on unconditional surrender, telling the Melians, "You know as well as we do that right, as the world goes, is only in question between equals in power—the strong do what they can, and the weak suffer what they must." The Melians responded, "And how, pray, could it turn out as good for us to serve as for you to rule?" "Because," the Athenians answered, "you would have the advantage of submitting before suffering the worst, and we should gain by not destroying you."

Undaunted, the Melians insisted the interest of all would be enhanced by peaceful relations between the two states. The Athenians would have no part of this logic. With ruthless disregard for justice, they reasoned that if the Melians were permitted to remain independent, they and others would take it as a sign of Athenian weakness. "[By] extending our empire," the Athenians pointed out, "we should gain in security by your subjection; the fact that you are islanders and weaker than others rendering all the more important that you should not succeed in baffling the masters of the sea." Thus, the cold calculus of power politics doomed the Melian state:

> Reinforcements afterwards arriving from Athens in consequence, under the command of Philocrates, son of Demeas, the siege was now pressed vigorously; and some treachery taking place inside, the Melians surrendered at discretion to the Athenians, who put to death all the grown men whom they took, and sold the women and children for slaves, and subsequently sent out five hundred colonists and inhabited the place themselves.

Melos was a real place, and the tragedy depicted in the story really happened. The context was the Peloponnesian War (431–404 BCE), and we know the Melians' cruel fate because the Greek historian Thucydides wrote about it.

GET REAL! MACHIAVELLI AND MORGENTHAU

The greatest political thinker of the Italian Renaissance, Niccolò Machiavelli, taught that the wise ruler must always play to win, for "how we live is so far removed from how we ought to live, that he who abandons what is done for what ought to be done, will rather learn to bring about his own ruin than his preservation."[2] Prudent rulers, he argued, recognize what must be done to preserve and enlarge their dominions and do not allow moral qualms to cloud their judgment. Rulers should keep their promises only when it suits their purposes to do so:

> A prudent ruler ought not to keep faith when by doing so it would be against his interest, and when the reasons which made him bind himself no longer exist.... If men were all good, this precept would not be a good one; but as they are bad, and would not observe their faith with you, so you are not bound to keep faith with them.[3]

The teachings of Machiavelli, and the fate of the Melians, suggest morality plays a less significant role in politics *among* nations than *within* nations. As long as international politics resembles the state of nature, tensions between nations will persist, talking will fail, reason will take a holiday, and the only question left will be who lives and who dies. When survival is at stake, necessity is often a tyrant.

Machiavelli's intellectual honesty and relentless realism were the basis for perhaps the most successful and influential political philosophy in the modern world—and evidence for its validity has continually mounted. The theory that nations act on the basis of interests, rather than ideals, is known as **political realism**. Today, this theory is most closely identified with the writings of Hans Morgenthau (1904–1980).

Following Machiavelli's rationale, political realists pay little heed to the way nations *ought* to act. Rather, they focus on how nations actually *do* act and why they act as they do. Survival is the basic goal of national policy, and the best way to ensure survival is to enhance the nation's power. In international politics, Morgenthau argued, whatever the ultimate aim, the immediate aim is *always* power. Thus, interest is defined as power; indeed, for Morgenthau, these two concepts merge into one—it is in the best interest of every nation to seek power first and other objectives second, and then only as they enhance national power, prestige, and the like.

Political realists stress that success in international politics, even without confrontation, ultimately depends on power. According to Morgenthau, power is "man's control over the minds and actions of other men."[4] Military force is important but is not the only aspect of political power. Geopolitical, economic, and social concerns also contribute. Even the personal charisma or competence of a nation's leader or the effectiveness of its political institutions gives it an edge.[5]

According to Morgenthau, "Realism considers prudence—the weighing of the consequences of political action—to be the supreme virtue in politics."[6] A foreign policy based on realism will avoid "the blindness of crusading frenzy [that] destroys nations and civilizations—in the name of moral principle, ideal, or God himself."[7]

To the political realist, the successful statesman is one who balances national interests and objectives against national capabilities (or power). Prudence demands that a statesman distinguish between what is necessary and what is merely desirable. The essence of statecraft lies in bringing the expectations and desires of a nation into line with its capabilities and correctly differentiating between vital and expendable interests. Political realism places a premium on flexibility, objectivity, and lack of sentimentality in the conduct of foreign policy. Thus, the political realist would say there are no permanent allies, only permanent interests.

In the perilous world of international politics, morality is different than in our *domestic* lives. Because other nations act on the basis of their perceived interests, rather than lofty ideals, one's own nation must do likewise; all try to gain an advantage at the expense of others. Therefore, Morgenthau asserted, political realism not only explains *why* nations act the way they do, but in the true spirit of science, it can also predict *how* they will act.

THE CLASSICAL MULTIPOLAR SYSTEM: 1648–1945

Machiavelli and Morgenthau were both products of tumultuous but very different times. Machiavelli was influenced by the fierce rivalries, intrigue, and conflict among Italian city-states of the fifteenth and sixteenth centuries.

---

political realism
The philosophy that power is the key variable in all political relationships and should be used pragmatically and prudently to advance the national interest; policies are judged good or bad on the basis of their effect on national interests, not on their level of morality.

FIGURE 17.1   Adjusting the Balance of Power. Equilibrium (A) is upset by adding a new participant (B); it is restored (C) by the transfer of one state from one alliance to another.

SOURCE: Edward V. Gulick, *Europe's Classical Balance of Power* (New York: Norton, 1967).

(A)   david Long (B)   (C)

equilibrium
A synonym for the word *balance*; also often used interchangeably with *stability* in the literature on international relations.

balance of power system
A classic theory of international relations that holds that nations of approximately equal strength will seek to maintain the status quo by preventing any one nation from gaining superiority over the others. Participating nations form alliances and frequently resort to war as a means of resolving disputes, seizing territory, gaining prestige, or seeking glory.

The modern nation-state system was in its infancy; the classical European system was launched with the signing of the Treaty of Westphalia in 1648 (see "Landmarks in History" in Chapter 1), more than a century after his death. Morgenthau was born in Germany shortly before World War I. The European system was one of the casualties of that war, along with its conscious effort to maintain **equilibrium** (or balance) among the participating states. Although this collective balancing act was based on nations' individual interests, it depended on a common definition of *interest* that emphasized self-preservation of each through a system that depended on the survival of all.

Europe's famed **balance of power system** operated for almost three centuries (Figure 17.1), beginning with the Treaty of Westphalia and ending with the outbreak of World War I. Although Napoleonic France came perilously close at the start of the nineteenth century, no state was able to establish hegemony on the Continent during this 266-year period—a remarkable achievement for any era.

At the Straits of Dover, a narrow channel (less than the distance between Washington, D.C. and Annapolis, Maryland) separates the British Isles from Europe's mainland. Today, Britain and France are connected by a rail tunnel that runs underneath the channel. The geographic distance is slight; not so the political distance the channel has meant in the modern history of Europe.

The Balance of Power: Essential Elements

The international system functioned effectively because one nation, the **keeper of the balance**, repeatedly threw its political and military weight behind the weaker alliance in crisis and conflict. Great Britain was ideally suited to this role because of its geographic detachment and military (especially naval) prowess. A major British concern was which power controlled the Lowlands (modern-day Belgium and Holland) just across the English Channel, a mere twenty-two miles wide at its narrowest point. But Britain was an impregnable fortress as long as no single power succeeded in conquering the Continent. Finally, its unchallenged naval supremacy and economic vitality made it a powerful ally or a formidable foe, while its lack of a large standing army removed any threat of British domination on the Continent.

Another important factor underpinning the traditional European system was a basic moral consensus—a common outlook held by nations sharing a single civilization. Historians Edward Gibbon and Arnold Toynbee, as well as philosophers Emmerich de Vattel and Jean-Jacques Rousseau, stressed the power of cultural and religious traditions that pervaded European society and transcended national boundaries during the heyday of the balance of power system.[8]

Under these extraordinary conditions, "international politics became indeed an aristocratic pastime, a sport for princes, all recognizing the same rules of the game and playing for the same limited stakes."[9] Even when war broke out, the belligerents did not seek to annihilate each other. Adopting the rationalistic outlook of the eighteenth-century Enlightenment, rulers mostly adopted a pragmatic approach to governing and viewed fanaticism as absurd and dangerous. Economic and military capabilities were limited too: Few countries could afford to squander their national wealth on high-risk adventures, and military action was constrained by the absence of modern technology. Ideology was also absent in this pan-European culture. Realignments occurred as circumstances changed, adding to the smooth functioning of the system.

The Sunset of the Old European Order

What happened to upset the relatively stable international order? First, Napoléon's nearly successful attempt in the early nineteenth century to conquer Europe—creating the first mass-conscription, popular army in modern history—heralded the rise of modern nationalism (see Chapter 15). Although France's bid ultimately failed, it was a harbinger of things to come, and it demonstrated the power of a nation united by a common cause. The cause itself was rooted in the explosive idea of human equality, enshrined in both the American and French revolutions (see Chapter 14). Between the Napoleonic Wars and World War I, ideas such as national self-determination and universal rights changed fundamental assumptions about politics and undermined the old aristocratic order.

In the nineteenth century, the Industrial Revolution's economic and technological changes transformed the art of warfare. Prussia used railroads to move troops in victorious military campaigns against Austria (1866) and France (1870). New instruments of war were not far off—military applications of the internal combustion engine included self-propelled field artillery and, by World War I, combat aircraft.

A final factor that helped undermine the European system was the rigidity of military alliances. Toward the end of the nineteenth century, coalitions were becoming fixed, while nations were steadily accumulating military power. Unprecedented peacetime outlays for military research and development, the creation of relatively large standing armies, and a spiraling arms race reinforced the increasing division of Europe into two opposing alliances. This development set the stage for World War I, which signaled the beginning of the end of the classical balance of power system. It would take another world war to finish the job.

THE COLD WAR BIPOLAR SYSTEM: 1945–1991

World War II produced a new configuration, one that continues to shape world politics today. Replacing the European system was a *global* system dominated by two preeminent powers.

The Dawn of Bipolarity

World War II greatly accelerated the transformation that had already begun. Instead of the seven former **Great Powers** at the outbreak of the war, there were now two **superpowers**—the United States and the Soviet Union. To qualify as a superpower, a state has to have a full range of power capabilities, including not only military muscle but also economic, political, diplomatic, and even moral clout. Second, it must have global reach, the capacity to project power to all parts of the world. Third, it must be willing to assert its leadership role in the international arena.

During the Cold War, the United States formed a kind of protectorate over the western half of war-torn Europe. By the same token, the Soviet Union created a "satellite" empire in the eastern half, and a **bipolar system** was born. According to the three-part test outlined here, the United States was the sole superpower after the Soviet Union self-destructed in 1991.

After World War II, the United States, first to develop and use the atomic bomb, enjoyed a short-lived nuclear monopoly. The Soviet Union, to Western observers' surprise and dismay, successfully tested an atomic device in 1949—serving notice that it, too, had become a full-fledged superpower. In military might, global reach, and economic resources, the United States and the Soviet Union dwarfed all other nations in the 1950s. But the ideological chasm dividing them precluded collaboration of any kind.

The Primacy of Ideology

Because one superpower was capitalist and democratic and the other was communist and dictatorial, the rivalry between them turned especially acrimonious and dangerous. After World War II, Allied mistrust of Joseph Stalin, the Soviet dictator, was greatly heightened by his nation's permanent occupation of Eastern Europe, which the Red Army had liberated from the Germans, and his attempt to force Western powers to abandon West Berlin. No less alarming was the prospect of a totalitarian Soviet state with nuclear weapons.

superpower
A term that evolved in the context of the Cold War to denote the unprecedented destructive capabilities and global reach of the United States and the Soviet Union and to differentiate these two nuclear behemoths from the Great Powers that existed prior to the advent of the Nuclear Age.

bipolar system
Following World War II, the traditional European balance of power system gave way to two rival power blocs, one headed by the United States and the other by the former Soviet Union, each with overwhelming economic and military superiority and each unalterably opposed to the politics and ideology of the other.

containment
The global status quo strategic policy followed by the United States after World War II; the term stems from the U.S. policy of containing attempts by the Soviet Union to extend its sphere of control to other states as it had done in Eastern Europe. NATO, the Marshall Plan, and the Korean and Vietnam wars grew out of this policy.

The Soviets, meanwhile, charged that U.S. foreign policy actions (the cutoff of lend-lease aid, the refusal to grant large loans, and the launching of massive U.S. foreign aid for Europe under the Marshall Plan) proved "American imperialism" was plotting the destruction of the "world socialist system." Stalin's chief ideologue, Andrei Zhdanov, declared the world had been divided into two camps, an idea whose counterpart in the West was the notion of a "world Communist conspiracy," a secret Soviet blueprint to subvert all democratic societies. Although these beliefs seem exaggerated in retrospect, extreme rhetoric on both sides lent them credibility.

U.S.-led efforts at **containment** were epitomized in Western Europe by the creation of a powerful military alliance, the North Atlantic Treaty Organization (NATO). The Soviet Union countered with a military pact of its own, the Warsaw Treaty Organization, known as the **Warsaw Pact,** linking Moscow and Eastern Europe (Figure 17.2). The aura of confrontation that permeated the two

FIGURE 17.2   NATO and the Warsaw Pact. During the Cold War (1947–1991), Europe was divided between East (the Soviet Union and the Warsaw Pact "satellite states") and West (the United States and its NATO allies). Only a handful of European states (Ireland, Sweden, Finland, Austria, Switzerland, and Yugoslavia) managed to remain outside of these two alliance systems.

SOURCE: http://astro.temple.edu/~barbday/Europe66/resources/coldwardivisionmap1.htm.

alliance systems left little room for compromise or conciliation. (See Chapter 18 for a more detailed discussion of the NATO alliance today.)

At its inception, the Cold War was waged by two extraordinarily powerful nations whose aims, interests, and values seemed incompatible. At the least, each sought to block the other's ambitions; at worst, each sought the other's collapse, in sharp contrast to the traditional European system they had replaced.

The Danger of Nuclear War

When the European balance of power held sway, observed rules and available technology both limited war aims. Two technological breakthroughs in the twentieth century, however, greatly expanded the destructive potential of military weaponry—the development of airborne bombers and missile delivery systems and the invention of fission (atomic) and fusion (hydrogen) bombs capable of leveling entire cities. From these advances grew the formidable U.S. and Soviet arsenals of increasingly accurate land- and sea-based missiles armed with multiple nuclear warheads.

The two nations commanded a vast overkill capacity—each held enough nuclear weapons to destroy the other many times over. All-out war would have amounted to mutual suicide. This realization, as we shall see, played a major role in promoting a new international security scheme intended to ensure human survival in a world threatened with almost instantaneous destruction.

Mutual Deterrence: A Lasting Legacy

The unprecedented power of nuclear weapons made the concept of deterrence paramount during the heyday of the Soviet–American rivalry. The Cold War is over now, but the legacy—and the awesome destructive capability it represents—will live on so long as the nuclear weapons amassed by the two superpowers remain in existence.

The United States lost its nuclear monopoly shortly after World War II but retained a measure of nuclear superiority for more than two decades thereafter. In 1957, however, the Soviet Union put the first artificial satellite (*Sputnik*) into orbit, demonstrating to the world that it had the technology to build long-range rockets and launch offensive weapons from Soviet soil directly at U.S. targets.

By the late 1960s, the era of U.S. invulnerability was over. The Soviets had built a land-based missile force against which there was no adequate defense. Both sides stared into the nuclear abyss. **Deterrence** became the new watchword in a great debate over military strategy and an integral part of the post–World War II balance of power.

According to **deterrence theory**, nations acquire nuclear weapons not to use them, but to deter other nations' use of them. Public expenditure for such weapons is thus markedly different from appropriation of money for such projects as schools, libraries, and parks. If these public facilities are *not* used, it represents a serious domestic policy failure. By contrast, if nuclear weapons ever *were* used, this far more serious foreign policy failure could jeopardize the very survival of humanity.

Deterrence is fundamentally psychological and incorporates some of the elements of a high-stakes poker game; players must minimize risks, and bluffing is part of the process. It depends not only on the realities of power, but also on the perceptions

Warsaw Pact
A military alliance between the former Soviet Union and its satellite states, created in 1955, which established a unified military command and allowed the Soviet army to maintain large garrisons within the satellite states, ostensibly to defend them from outside attack.

deterrence
In international relations, the theory that aggressive wars can be prevented if potential victims maintain a military force sufficient to inflict unacceptable punishment on any possible aggressor.

deterrence theory
Holds that states acquire nuclear weapons mainly to deter the use of such weapons by other states; this idea spawned a whole new literature on war in the Nuclear Age in the second half of the twentieth century.

each side has of the other's will, intentions, and resolve in the face of grave danger. If Country A uses military power to keep Country B from pursuing its foreign policy objective, Country B's prestige is damaged and Country A gains a psychological edge.

A number of assumptions underlie nuclear deterrence theory. First, nations have communicated to potential adversaries a clear will to use weapons of mass destruction if attacked. Second, decision makers on both sides are rational, and neither side will launch a nuclear strike unless it can protect itself from a counterattack. Third, each side possesses a second-strike capability, meaning enough of the attacked nation's nuclear capabilities would survive a surprise attack (first strike) to make possible a retaliatory blow (second strike) adequate to inflict unacceptable damage on the attacker.

To ensure the survivability of its nuclear forces, the United States built three separate but interrelated nuclear weapon delivery systems after World War II. This so-called triad consisted of land-based intercontinental ballistic missiles (ICBMs), submarine-launched ballistic missiles (SLBMs), and manned bombers (known as the Strategic Air Command, or SAC), some of which were always aloft. The Soviet Union also had a three-pronged deterrence system that depended heavily on land-based missiles and warheads, which it possessed in larger numbers than the United States. The United States' sea-based deterrent was more powerful than the Soviet Union's.

Deterrence and the arms race went hand in hand for decades. Each nation had specific goals and priorities that governed its expenditures for armaments. Each was also swayed by its perception of what the other was doing; an accelerated Soviet weapons buildup in the 1970s prompted the United States to launch a major rearmament program. A stable balance was thus impossible when one nation, particularly one with an expansionistic foreign policy, possessed a clear advantage in number and strength of weapons. Finally, technology exerted its own influence. On one hand, because technological knowledge cannot be unlearned, both nations were wary of disarmament; on the other hand, the possibility that one nation might achieve a technological breakthrough provided an incentive to continue high levels of weapons research and development.

POST–COLD WAR: RETURN TO MULTIPOLARITY?

Political realism emphasizes national self-interest as the principle guiding foreign policy. Some contemporary critics, however, say self-centered national interest is outmoded. They argue for "a new diplomacy and for new institutions and regulatory regimes to cope with the world's growing environmental interdependence" because "our accepted definition of the limits of national sovereignty as coinciding with national borders is obsolete."[10] Perhaps, but there is still little concrete evidence that state behavior has changed fundamentally.

New World, Old Ideas

The dissolution of the Soviet Union marked the end of the post–World War II balance of power. As countries redefine their relationships with one another, some observers say a new world order is emerging. What are the characteristics of this brave new world, and how does it differ from the old one?

International politics currently does *not* exhibit a clear balance of power configuration whereby participants with incompatible aims, conflicting interests, and roughly equal power interact in predictable ways to maintain stability and peace. The emerging international order is instead marked by contradictory trends—in Europe, for example, the movement toward integration in the European Union, which transcends traditional state boundaries, and the simultaneous rise of religious and ethnic particularism *within* nations, which caused the breakup of three multinational states: the Soviet Union, Yugoslavia, and Czechoslovakia. The shape of the world to come is still not clear, but it will not be dominated by a single superpower.

Today's profound environmental challenges of global warming, air pollution, oil spills, disappearing rainforests, and the like, as well as reckless depletion of nonrenewable natural resources, overpopulation, and world poverty, are global in scope and require global solutions.[11] "Think globally, act locally" expresses the idea that nations have a moral obligation not to pursue narrow self-interests at the expense of solutions to pressing global problems. Global interests replace national interests. The best (and only) way for any nation to ensure its prosperity and security is to look outward, not inward.

This approach requires a drastic change in the way we think and states behave and a far broader definition of *self-interest* than some political realists embrace. To old-school realists, talk of a "global community" sounds like soft-boiled idealism. But the new realists advocate policies rooted in enlightened self-interest and argue that global security and self-preservation require a radical rethinking of world politics. In today's world, they contend, yesterday's realism is not only obsolete, but also dangerous.

Globalization

With the reduction of military competition and political conflicts among the world's most powerful nations, two contradictory economic trends came to the fore—one toward increased interdependence, the other toward intensified competition.

Interdependence is a companion of **globalization**. Globalization is another name for the transformation of the world economy, from one in which interactions across national borders are restricted by a fragmented political structure, to one in which far more interactions occur as national borders remain in place but recede in importance.[12] Globalization is driven, in part, by multinational corporations (MNCs) seeking to maximize profits and revolutionary advances in transport, communications, and information technology, all of which transcend national boundaries. By the same token, many problems in today's world—trade liberalization, global warming, and arms control, to name a few—are not susceptible of national solutions.

Recent crises in the global economy occurred in 1997 and in 2008. In 1997, several Asian economies suffered a sudden, sharp downturn that threatened to disrupt global trade and finance. In response, a rescue package amounting to some $40 billion in loans was made available to South Korea, Indonesia, and

globalization
The process by which values, attitudes, preferences, and products associated with the most technologically advanced democracies are spread around the world via mass media and trade.

Thailand (where the crisis started) through the **International Monetary Fund** (IMF), a specialized agency of the United Nations designed to promote worldwide economic stability. The IMF made acceptance of tough economic reforms a precondition for the emergency loans.

In 2008–2010, a deep global recession followed a financial meltdown that started on Wall Street. At the beginning of 2009, the new Obama administration called for a massive $775 billion stimulus program to kick-start the sinking U.S. economy and asked the leaders of the other G-20 countries to follow suit. (G-20 stands for "Group of 20" and comprises the world's major economies.) Europe refused to follow the U.S. lead, preferring to emphasize tighter regulation of business (especially finance). At the G-20 economic summit in London in 2009, President Obama declared U.S. interests were "tied up with the larger world," and leaders agreed to provide $1.1 trillion in new funds to recapitalize the IMF.

But competition in the global economy has intensified in the second decade of the twenty-first century, one of the lingering effects of a worldwide recession. Protectionist practices inhibit free trade and lead to international tensions, even among friends and allies. The EU, for example, has accused Brazil of protectionism in the past, but in bilateral trade talks in early 2013, neither side dared to raise this issue. Why not? Two obvious reasons: (1) "protectionism" is a dirty word in diplomacy, one not conducive to settling differences; and (2) everybody does it—as the saying goes, people who live in glass houses shouldn't throw stones. A third reason is mutual self-interest: the EU is a *bona fide* economic superpower, and Brazil is fast becoming one.

Governments continue to subsidize domestic industries and agriculture, levy tariffs on imports, and erect ingenious non–trade barriers. Relations between the United States and Japan have at times been strained over Japanese protectionism, and trade between the United States and its European allies has been marred by wrangling over agricultural subsidies. The United States and other countries accuse Beijing of keeping the value of the renminbi (RMB) or yuan (China's currency) artificially low to boost its exports. Not surprisingly, China rejects such accusations; ironically, the United States must tread lightly because China is America's major source of foreign capital. Even so, China reduced its U.S. bond holdings from $1.314 trillion in mid-2011 to $1.169 trillion in mid-2012.

Competition and rivalry remain prominent features of the new world order. At the same time, globalization has greatly reduced America's economic footprint, and will continue to do so in the coming years.

The IT Revolution

How is the revolution in information technology (IT) changing the landscape of world politics? The carrying capacity of the global communications network of computers, telephone, and television has grown by leaps and bounds. According to Moore's Law (named for Gordon Moore, cofounder of Intel), computing power per dollar doubles every eighteen months. A $1,500 laptop computer today is far more powerful than a $10 million mainframe was in the mid-1970s. In the 1970s, there were only about 50,000 computers in the world; by the turn

TABLE 17.1   Surfing the Web: Two Billion and Counting

Top 15 Countries by Internet Population 2010

1. China: 420,000,000
2. United States: 310,232,000
3. Japan: 99,000,000
4. Germany: 65,123,000
5. United Kingdom: 51,422,000
6. France: 44,625,000
7. India: 81,000,000
8. Russia: 59,700,000
9. Brazil: 75,943,000
10. South Korea: 19,040,000
11. Canada: 26,225,000
12. Italy: 30,026,000
13. Spain: 29,094,000
14. Mexico: 30,600,000
15. Netherlands: 14,872,000

Worldwide Internet Audience

- Asia Pacific: 825,094,000 (42%)
- Europe: 475,069,000 (24.2%)
- North America: 262,224,000 (13.5%)
- Latin America: 204,689,000 (10.4%)
- Africa: 110,931,000 (5.6%)
- Middle East 3,284,000 (3.2%)

SOURCE: Internet World Stats at http://www.internetworldstats.com/stats3.htm#asia; see also Erick Schonfeld, "ComScore: Internet Population Passes One Billion; Top 15 Countries," TechCrunch.com, January 23, 2009 at http://www.techcrunch.com/2009/01/23/.

of the twenty-first century, there were more than 140 million. A transatlantic telephone cable could carry only 138 conversations simultaneously in 1960, a fiber-optic cable now carries 1.5 million. The number of Internet users stood at about 361 million at the end of 2000; a decade later estimates put the number at nearly 2 billion (Table 17.1).

One profound political consequence of the IT revolution is to weaken individual governments' hold over citizens. Citizens worldwide now have access to independent sources of information. Everything from criticism of government to pornography to a "build your own nuclear bomb" Web page can be accessed from most any country, usually despite the efforts of government. The Internet even threatens to undermine traditional cultures and civilizations that do not share Western values. Many Arab states, for example, censor Internet content, shut down some blogs, arrest hackers, and generally treat those who break the rules harshly.

The Internet also poses a threat to dictatorial regimes, which is why the People's Republic of China and Iran routinely block certain websites and jam radio broadcasts of the BBC, Voice of America, and Radio Free Europe/Radio Liberty. The latter broadcasts daily in Farsi (the Persian language) from Prague and Washington as Radio Farda. But these efforts do not prevent all international contacts via Twitter, Facebook, and the like, nor do they prevent all international exchanges of cell phone text messages.

Paradoxically, computers and the Internet also greatly magnify the potential for government intrusion into the private lives of citizens. High-tech sensors, meters, cameras, and the like give the modern state the means to monitor most anything and everything it chooses.[13] In George Orwell's classic novel, *Nineteen Eighty-Four*, new eavesdropping technology—including a poster of Big Brother with moving eyes and two-way "telescreens" that watched the watcher—enhanced the ruthless grip of tyrannical rulers. The kind of technology Orwell imagined is no longer confined to the realm of science fiction.

Some political consequences of the IT revolution we can only dimly perceive at present. However, we can say for certain that computers and the Internet make it more difficult for the state to control what people know and how they know it—and vice versa.

The Rise of Regionalism

When the European Coal and Steel Community (ECSC) was launched about 1950, it was a modest effort to integrate two industrial sectors among six countries (France, Germany, Italy, and the Benelux countries). From its seeds grew the world's largest single economy, the twenty-seven-nation European Union (EU). Until the EU's recent troubles following the 2008 global banking crisis, the impressive gains achieved by Europe's integrated "single economy" inspired efforts to form geography-based trading blocs in other regions of the globe. (The European Union is explored in greater depth in Chapter 18.)

European integration has evolved through decades of economic and military cooperation in the West. Its results, however, are revolutionary. Despite the "euro crisis" of 2010–2012, the EU symbolizes the success of Europe's post–WWII resolve to settle centuries of rivalry, especially between France and Germany, once and for all. (By the same token, France and the United Kingdom signed a defense treaty in November 2010 pledging the two former Great Power rivals to set up a joint *military* force, as well as to share equipment and nuclear missile research.)

Then, too, the end of the Cold War witnessed the geopolitical transformation of Europe—three new countries were admitted to the EU in 1995 (Austria,

Finland, and Sweden), ten in 2004 (Cyprus, the Czech Republic, Estonia, Hungary, Latvia, Lithuania, Malta, Poland, Slovakia, and Slovenia), and Bulgaria and Romania joined in 2007. Serbia and Croatia are knocking on the door, as is Turkey. Ukraine also wants to join the West (NATO and the EU), but Russia remains adamantly opposed.

Elsewhere, the United States, Mexico, and Canada launched the North American Free Trade Association (NAFTA) in January 1994. Today, NAFTA is the world's largest free trade area, but two decades after its inception it remains highly controversial. Economists say NAFTA has greatly spurred trade and created millions of jobs, but U.S. unions and consumer groups complain that outsourcing and lower wages have hurt U.S. workers and the U.S. economy. Viewed from a distance, the pact has benefited all three members. The U.S.'s two-way trade with Canada and Mexico in 2010, for example, totaled $918 million.

Latin America launched Mercosur in 1991; today, it is a fledgling common market encompassing https://netbanking.netpnb.com/web/L001/images/home-logo.png Argentina, Brazil, Paraguay, Uruguay, and Venezuela, plus five associate members. Mercosur's combined population totals more than 260 million, covers an area four times larger than the EU, and accounts for more than 75% of South America's GDP. It is the world's fourth-largest trading bloc ($1.1 trillion a year), after the EU, NAFTA, and the Association of South East Asian Nations (ASEAN). Mercosur aims to create a free-trade area for all of South America in the long run, but trade disputes among members have impeded progress toward closer economic ties. In 2013, Cuba was poised to join, and Mercosur was pushing a free-trade deal with Canada.

Indonesia, Malaysia, Philippines, Singapore, and Thailand formed ASEAN in 1967. Brunei, Cambodia, Laos, Myanmar (Burma), and Vietnam have since been admitted as full members. Today, ASEAN encompasses a population of some 560 million, a total area of 4.5 million square kilometers, a combined gross domestic product of more than $1 trillion, and total trade of $1.4 trillion. In an agreement called ASEAN Vision 2020, the member states pledged "to create a stable, prosperous and highly competitive ASEAN economic region in which there is a free flow of goods, services, investment and a freer flow of capital, equitable economic development and reduced poverty and socioeconomic disparities."[14] The ASEAN free-trade area has been in place since the early 1990s. Also, both China and Japan have strong economic partnerships with ASEAN and other Pacific Basin nations.

What will emerge from these new regional economic blocs? Some say the nation-state as we know it is being eclipsed by regionalism and globalization. Will regional blocs coexist happily and harmoniously? Competition is inevitable (and desirable), but there are also strong incentives for interregional cooperation. Or will regional groupings become obstacles rather than stepping stones to a truly global economy? Rising shipping costs, concerns over energy security, and the current global recession could cause globalization to give way to a greater emphasis on local production and consumption. What that would mean for the future of regional trading blocs, which fall between global and local, is anybody's guess. What do you think?

Preventing Nuclear Proliferation

As symbols and instruments of national power, weapons of mass destruction (WMDs)—nuclear, biological, and chemical—are in a class by themselves. The states that possess these weapons and the means to deliver them want to prevent other states, notably Iran and North Korea, from acquiring them.

Although various arms limitation treaties covering WMDs do exist (see Chapter 18), many states refuse to sign or be constrained by them. As Table 17.2 indicates, the number of nuclear "haves" is still quite small, yet it has grown from only five in the 1960s to as many as nine at present. In the past, some developing countries that possess valuable natural resources, such as oil-rich Libya, Iran, and Iraq, sought to acquire WMDs. After 2003, however, Iraq was forced out of this "club," and Libya renounced WMDs to avoid a similar fate. Nonetheless, these facts only hint at the true dangers of nuclear proliferation.

The world got a wake-up call in February 2004, when Pakistan's top nuclear scientist, Abdul Qadeer Khan ("the father of Pakistan's bomb"), publicly confessed to having shared Pakistan's nuclear secrets with Libya, Iran, and North Korea—both Iran and North Korea are on the U.S. list of "rogue" states. Unauthorized nuclear transfers are strictly forbidden under the Nuclear Nonproliferation Treaty (NPT), but Pakistan has never signed the NPT and is therefore not bound by it. The same, of course, is true of Iran and North Korea (see "Ideas and Politics: Weapons of Mass Destruction and Pariah States").

Argentina, Brazil, Egypt, Saudi Arabia, Syria, Iran, Turkey, Japan, both Koreas, and Taiwan are all "nuclear threshold" states. (A threshold state is

TABLE 17.2   Proliferation of Nuclear Weapons

Have Nuclear Weapons	Have Pledged Not to Build Nuclear Weapons	Have Given Up Nuclear Weapons	Have an Active R & D Program in Progress
China	Algeria	Belarus	Iran
France	Argentina	Kazakhstan	North Korea*
Great Britain	Brazil	Ukraine	
Israel	Germany		
India	Japan		
Pakistan	South Africa		
Russia			
United States			

© CENGAGE LEARNING

*Under pressure from the United States, China, and the UN, North Korea in February 2007 pledged to disable a plutonium reactor at Yongbyon and eventually to dismantle all its nuclear facilities; but in 2008 and 2009, North Korea conducted nuclear and missile tests, proving right the skeptics who predicted dictator Kim Jong II would not keep his word.

WEAPONS OF MASS DESTRUCTION AND PARIAH STATES: WHO'S WHO?

FIGURE 17.3   In addition to the five declared nuclear powers (the United States, Russia, China, France, and the United Kingdom), three other countries (India, Pakistan, and Israel) are known to possess nuclear weapons, and North Korea is thought to have successfully tested such weapons. Iran probably does not possess nuclear weapons yet, but the country is widely believed to have a nuclear weapons program in an advanced stage of development. The five declared nuclear powers have all signed the Nuclear Nonproliferation Treaty (NPT). India, Pakistan, and Israel have not signed the NPT, but these countries are generally considered responsible members of the international community. North Korea and Iran reject the established rules of conduct, which most other sovereign states embrace as the basis for a stable world order.

(Continued)

(CONTINUED)

In 2003, the Bush administration justified the invasion of Iraq on the grounds that Saddam Hussein possessed a secret WMD arsenal. As we now know, these allegations were false. Nonetheless, the Iraq War was the first in the Nuclear Age fought for the ostensible purpose of preventing nuclear proliferation.

Having ousted Saddam and setting up an interim government in Iraq, the United States confronted two other pariah states, North Korea and Iran, calling them the "axis of evil" and demanding they discontinue all WMD research and development and submit to international inspections.

A defiant North Korea conducted its first-ever atomic test in October 2006, prompting alarm in Japan and the United States, as well as in the wider international community. Veiled U.S. military threats, combined with diplomatic pressure from China, induced President Kim Jong Il to accept a six-nation accord in February 2007, which committed North Korea to shutting down its nuclear weapons program in return for certain trade and aid concessions. But the Pyongyang regime broke the agreement in 2008–2009 when it conducted nuclear tests, ran six short-range missile tests, and twice attempted to test-launch long-range missiles.

In 2007, the United States turned the spotlight on Iran's nuclear weapons program (Figure 17.3). When President Bush assumed a confrontational stance, the Iranian government responded in kind. For a time, the long-standing diplomatic stalemate appeared to be escalating toward war. President Obama vowed to seek a negotiated solution, but relations between the United States and Iran have remained icy and adversarial.

one with the technological know-how to manufacture nuclear weapons.) The Republic of South Africa had a small nuclear arsenal, which it dismantled in the early 1990s.

Iran and North Korea top the list of "wannabe" nuclear powers. If and when a pariah state like Iran or North Korea goes nuclear, other threshold states in the region are likely to follow suit.[15] As the number of states with WMDs grows, the likelihood that such weapons will fall into the wrong hands—those of terrorists or drug traffickers—also goes up.

Following the midterm elections in November 2010, Republican leaders in the U.S. Senate moved to block a vote on a new nuclear arms reduction treaty with Russia, saying the matter was too important to be decided by a lame duck Congress.* But supporters contended that failure to approve the treaty would send the wrong message and jeopardize Russian support for U.S. efforts to stop Iran from acquiring nuclear weapons. In the end, the supporters won and the treaty was approved—a victory for Obama and perhaps a modest step toward deeper nuclear arms cuts in the future.

---

*Under the treaty, each side within seven years is barred from deploying more than 1,550 strategic warheads or 700 launchers. Because of counting rules and past reductions, however, neither side has to scrap large numbers of weapons to comply with the new limits. Even so, the treaty reestablished an inspection regime that lapsed in December 2010.

The End of the World as We Know It

Environmental dangers remained largely unrecognized in the United States until the early 1960s, when Rachel Carson's best-selling book, *Silent Spring*, first appeared.[16] Since then, protecting the environment has become more and more political, fueled by declining biodiversity, evidence of global warming, and other signs of climate change. Acid rain, global warming, receding water tables, declining forests and fisheries, and the rapid depletion of the earth's fossil fuels all have contributed to a new sense of urgency. Today, green parties exist in virtually every major democracy except the United States, where organizations such as the Sierra Club, the Audubon Society, Save the Whales, and the National Wildlife Federation nonetheless exert considerable political clout. In addition, many research institutes and public policy "think tanks" monitor the state of the environment and advocate ecology-conscious public policies.

The signing of the Kyoto Protocol in 1997 represented a major step toward a global action plan to combat climate change. Kyoto called for the 37 industrialized countries and the European Union to reduce GHG emissions—carbon dioxide, nitrous oxide, methane, and fluorocarbons; by 2012, the Protocol had been endorsed by 192 countries. The United States, Canada, and Afghanistan are the only holdouts now.* (See Chapter 13 for a fuller discussion of environmental policy.)

In 2001, then President George W. Bush announced the United States was withdrawing from the Kyoto accord on the grounds that complying with its provisions would hurt the U.S. economy. In 2004, Russia announced it would ratify the treaty, further isolating the United States on this issue. In June 2007, the Bush administration reversed itself and pledged U.S. support for global efforts to combat climate change at a G-8 summit meeting in Europe. And in 2009, President Obama created a new post of White House energy czar, tasked with developing and directing federal efforts to reduce greenhouse gas (GHG) emissions. Environmentalists lament what they see as a continuing lack of leadership from Washington on this issue.

---

*Canada ratified it but withdrew in 2011.

Shrinking Superpower, More Level Playing Field

The crumbling of the Soviet empire, the demonstration of U.S. military prowess in two wars against Iraq (1990–1991 and 2003), and the war on terror (1991 to the present) all served to reinforce the idea that the United States continued to be the world's sole remaining superpower. But the world has changed dramatically since the Cold War era, and the changes have highlighted the danger of defining power too narrowly in the new Age of Globalization.

The emergence of China as a major global economic force, however, also points to the changing international power structure and the rapid eclipse of the **unipolar system** that saw the United States as the sole dominant actor on the world stage. In the eyes of many critics, the squandering of U.S. economic, diplomatic, and military resources in two unwinnable wars, the recession of 2008–2009, the bankruptcy of two former world-class U.S. automakers (GM and Chrysler)—and the resulting loss of U.S. standing in the world—badly eroded the foundations of the unipolar system in the first decade of the twenty-first century.

At present, China is the world's second largest economy after the United States ($8.77 trillion in 2009). By far the world's fastest-growing major economy, China has achieved average growth rates of 10% for the past thirty years. China is already the world's largest exporter and the second largest trading nation. Projections based on current trends predict that China will catch up with the United States in GDP by 2025 and surpass it by 2030, if not sooner.

India and Brazil are two other emerging global giants. If current trends hold, India will soon become the third largest economy, moving ahead of Japan and Germany, and Brazil's economy is catching up to France's in size. Brazil's GDP was estimated at $2.45 trillion in 2011 compared to France's $2.7 trillion. The discovery of major underwater oil reserves in 2008, one of the two largest finds in the world in a decade, boosted Brazil's prospects for the future.

Although it remains the number-one military power in the world, the United States no longer boasts the world's largest single market, a distinction the European Union now holds. And while the combined share of China, India, and Brazil in the global economy is rapidly rising, that of the United States is falling—from 32% of global GDP in 2000 to 24% in 2009. China exports far more to the United States than it imports every year, a chronic imbalance sustained only by heavy U.S. borrowing—from China. As a result, China is mounting a big challenge to U.S. global leadership—arguably bigger even than that of the Soviet Union during the Cold War.

Comparing the United States with the thirty-two other developed countries belonging to the Organization for Economic Co-operation and Development (OECD) reveals some startling facts. In 2008, the United States ranked third in the percent of the total population in poverty; Turkey and Mexico are the only OECD nations with higher poverty levels. For those living below the poverty line, only Chile had a lower level of income than the United States. Yet, in per capita gross national income, the United States was 7.4% above the OECD average and 18.8% above the average for the European Union.

Of the fourteen high-income OECD countries, the United States had by far the highest cost of health care, the largest portion of the population without health coverage, second from the lowest life expectancy, and the highest rate of infant mortality.

unipolar system
In international relations theory, the existence of a single invincible superpower; the international system said to have existed after the collapse of the Soviet Union left the United States as the sole remaining (and thus unrivalled) military and economic superpower on the world stage.

As of 2010, approximately 46.5 million (15%) U.S. residents fell below the poverty line, and more than 50 million (16–17%) were without health insurance coverage.[17]

Whether the world was ever truly unipolar is debatable. The rapid rise of new global actors and the relative decline in the U.S. share of total global GDP mean the playing field is now more level than it has been at any time since the end of World War II, rendering old notions of what it means to be a superpower obsolete.

U.S. FOREIGN POLICY: CONTINUITY AMID CHANGE

The ends in foreign policy are goals; the means are the strategies and policies nations adopt in pursuit of predetermined goals and objectives. Goals are by nature long range, deeply rooted, and slow to change. Strategies and policies, in turn, can be pragmatic and flexible. They can vary over time and be global or regional.

Power and the National Interest

One key to understanding international politics is the concept of the **national interest**, defined in terms of power. A primary purpose of the state is to protect and defend its citizens from acts of aggression by other states. Fears of attack or invasion are often the motivation behind the buildup of powerful military machines and arms races. Paradoxically, the universal desire for security creates conditions that make war more likely—thus making everyone less secure.

Without power, states cannot deter or resist aggression by other states. But what is power? Does power "grow out of the barrel of a gun," as Mao Zedong famously said? Is it synonymous with brute force—the capability to conquer and coerce? There is no denying the role of military power and prowess in international politics. But powerful military states are not always long-lived or successful. Nazi Germany, for example, lasted little more than a decade and was defeated, occupied, and partitioned. The Soviet Union lasted longer, but it eventually collapsed and broke up into many separate states.

The examples of Nazi Germany and Stalinist Russia suggest that military power alone is not enough for a nation to thrive and prosper in a competitive and perilous world—or even to survive. Clearly, **hard power** in the form of military might is not the whole story. Nations need other forms of power to be viable and sustainable. A robust economy, for example, is vital, as is the power that derives from scientific research, technological advances, industrial innovation, and entrepreneurship—in other words, the kinds of **derivative power** that accompany modernization and are often associated with vibrant market economies. Then, too, a whole host of intangibles—sometimes called **soft power**—are also extremely important. Such things include political stability, social harmony, national character, and the congruence between a nation's self-image and its reputation in the outside world. In the "global village" that is now the arena of international politics, the ability of one country to get other countries to see the world the way it does—and to want what it does—is a major, often woefully underrated, dimension of power.

Nations seeking to change existing power relationships are typically opposed by nations wishing to freeze them. Dissatisfaction with the status quo is often the motivation for behavior designed to provoke wars, initiate arms races, promote revolutions abroad, and generally destabilize the international system.

national interest
A term often invoked but seldom defined, it is usually associated with power enhancement; shorthand for whatever enhances the power and best serves the supreme purposes of the nation, including prosperity, prestige, security, and, above all, survival.

hard power
In international politics, the use of military force or the threat to use force or other coercive measures such as freezing foreign assets or imposing strict economic sanctions.

derivative power
Political power that arises indirectly as a result of achievements in other areas (art, science, technological prowess, and the like); derivative power is often a product of the heightened prestige or respect that results from such achievements.

soft power
The ability to get others to want what you want by example and moral suasion, as well as respect and admiration earned through the success of your ideas, institutions, and actions in the world.

MORAL AMBIGUITY IN INTERNATIONAL POLITICS: The Case of the Middle East

After World War II, Jewish nationalists, or Zionists, waged a successful war against the British and the Arabs for a homeland in Palestine. In their defense, they cited historical, biblical, and legal authority and argued that in the aftermath of the Holocaust, Jews could live in security only in a Jewish homeland. But Palestinian Arab refugees, who had fled in droves rather than live in a Jewish state, regarded the Israelis as imperialists. Neighboring Arab states declared a holy war against **Zionism** and vowed to destroy Israel.

Subsequently, radical Palestinian groups directed acts of terrorism against the Israeli population with the complicity of several Arab governments, notably Egypt. In 1956, Egypt seized the Suez Canal from Great Britain and France, which then actively backed Israel in a war with Egypt over which nation would control access to the canal. This episode only strengthened the Arab belief that Zionism and Western imperialism were conspiring to dominate the Muslim nations of the Middle East.

After more than a decade of smoldering hostilities, another war erupted. In 1967, reacting to Egyptian threats and intelligence reports suggesting it was about to attack, Israel launched a preemptive military operation that resulted in the so-called Six Days' War. After less than a week of fighting, the Israelis had routed their enemies and occupied large tracts of Arab territory, including the Sinai Peninsula and Gaza Strip in Egypt, the Golan Heights in Syria, and the West Bank of the Jordan River in Jordan. Jerusalem, until then partitioned, fell under complete Israeli control.

Humiliated by defeat, Egypt and Syria prepared for yet another round of fighting. In 1973, they attempted to revise the post-1967 status quo by attacking Israeli-held territories. The Israelis were again equal to the challenge, but this time they suffered a setback early on. With the United States acting as a mediator, the Egyptians eventually regained the Sinai desert by agreeing to a peace treaty with Israel in 1979 (the Camp David Accords). The other Arab nations charged Egypt with selling out to Zionism and "imperialism."

In the decades that followed, peace has remained elusive. In December 2008, Israel launched air strikes against targets in the Gaza Strip, killing civilians and destroying homes, and then invaded Gaza in an effort to hunt down Hamas militants. Israel claims Hamas is responsible for launching rocket attacks against southern Israel. Meanwhile, about 1.4 million impoverished Palestinians living in Gaza were cut off from the world by an Israeli embargo.

Who is right, and who is wrong? The Arab states, along with the Palestine Liberation Organization, refused to recognize Israel's right to exist. But Israel has also, at times, been part of the problem, such as when it permitted the establishment of Jewish settlements on land seized from the Arabs. Both sides believe they are absolutely right, and the other side is absolutely wrong.

Similar ambiguities crop up frequently in international politics. Competing claims do not preclude judgments about right and wrong; they merely make them more difficult to reach.

Zionism
The national movement for the return of the Jewish people to the land of Abraham and the resumption of Jewish sovereignty in what is now known as Israel.

Although the distinction between aggressive and defensive states is clear in theory, it blurs in practice (see "Ideas and Politics: Moral Ambiguity"). Thus, if no rival nation is engaging in an arms buildup, status quo states are content with existing levels of military readiness. But if a dissatisfied rival state is adding new weapons to its arsenal, even the most satisfied status quo state(s) will typically follow suit, thus raising the level of tension and fueling the arms race. American foreign policy after World War II provides a vivid illustration of this ambiguity. The United States refused to recognize the existence of the People's Republic of China for more than two decades after the Communist takeover in 1949 on the grounds

MANIFEST DESTINY

The United States has always pretended to pursue a status quo policy, even when it was, in fact, expanding. The story of how the United States grew from thirteen states huddled along the Atlantic seaboard (the original colonies) into a vast empire stretching across an entire continent is known to every U.S. schoolchild, but teachers rarely present it as a story about imperialism or expansionism—unless, perhaps, the children and the teacher are Native Americans. Spaniards and Mexicans would have reason to differ over this point as well, as people living in Texas, Arizona, California, or Florida (among other states) ought to know. Having ventured into Alaska before the United States existed, even Russians might object. Expansionists in the U.S. Congress called it Manifest Destiny, but, as Shakespeare said, a rose by any other name is still a rose.

that China was not a democracy and therefore lacked legitimacy. At the same time, the United States often intervened militarily on the side of friendly dictatorships faced with popular insurrection. But the Reagan administration (1980–1988) aided a variety of anticommunist insurgents around the world in the 1980s, including groups in Central America (the Contras in Nicaragua), in Asia (mujahedeen rebels in Afghanistan), and in Africa (UNITA guerrillas in Angola). The fact that President Reagan called the guerrilla forces he liked "freedom fighters" did not fool anybody (except perhaps in the United States). And in the more recent cases of Iraq and Afghanistan, the United States led invasions that overthrew existing governments.

These examples demonstrate the importance (and difficulty) of maintaining moral objectivity in foreign policy analysis. A strategy aimed at preventing change in the existing distribution of power and wealth is not proof of moral superiority; rather, it is evidence that realism has swayed policy makers, rightly or wrongly, to take a certain course of action.

Few states consistently follow status quo strategies, as the diplomatic history of the United States illustrates. On one hand, the United States pursued a policy of expansionism in the nineteenth century (see "Landmarks in History: Manifest Destiny"). On the other hand, the United States fought to preserve the status quo for much of the twentieth century. Two examples are the **Monroe Doctrine** and the post–World War II policy of containment, mentioned earlier in the chapter.

The Monroe Doctrine President James Monroe promulgated the Monroe Doctrine in his annual message to Congress on December 2, 1823, pledging the United States would strictly respect the existing political configurations in the Western Hemisphere. "With the existing colonies or dependencies of any European power we have not interfered and shall not interfere," Monroe observed. But, he continued,

> [as for] the governments who have declared their Independence, and maintain it…we could not view any interposition for the purpose of oppressing them, or controlling in any other manner their destiny, by any European power, in any other light than as the manifestation of an unfriendly disposition towards the United States.[18]

Monroe Doctrine
A status quo international policy laid down by U.S. President James Monroe, who pledged the United States would resist any attempts by outside powers to alter the balance of power in the American hemisphere.

With this declaration, the United States served notice that henceforth it would resist any attempt by an outside power to upset the hemispheric balance of power. In effect, the Monroe Doctrine asserted the right of the United States of America to maintain a preeminent position in roughly half the world—the half it believed vital to its national security.

Containment   Another example of U.S. status quo policy, containment, operated from the late 1940s until 1991, when the Soviet Union disintegrated. World War II had drastically altered the European and thus the global balance of power. In its aftermath, the United States was thrust for the first time into the role of paramount world leader—a role challenged by a formidable adversary under Stalin's leadership. It seemed as if Tocqueville's century-old prophecy that the United States and Russia had each been "marked out by the will of Heaven to sway the destinies of half the globe"[19] was about to be fulfilled.

The containment idea was unveiled in a celebrated article in the journal *Foreign Affairs* in July 1947. The anonymous author, "X," turned out to be George F. Kennan (1904–2005), then the director of the State Department's Policy Planning Staff and later an ambassador to the USSR. "It is clear," Kennan wrote:

> that the main element of any United States policy toward the Soviet Union must be that of a long-term, patient but firm and vigilant containment of Russian expansive tendencies....Soviet pressure against the free institutions of the Western world is something that can be contained by the adroit and vigilant application of counter-force at a series of constantly shifting geographical and political points.[20]

Kennan went on to predict that if a policy of containment were applied consistently for a decade or so, the Soviet challenge would diminish significantly. He also suggested (prophetically) that if containment proved successful, the totalitarian Soviet state would ultimately fall victim to severe internal pressures.

At bottom, containment was a remodeled status quo policy adapted to a new set of circumstances. Its first major test came in 1947, when Greece appeared about to fall to a communist insurgency. In an urgent message to Congress requesting authority to provide aid to Greece and Turkey, President Harry Truman enunciated what came to be known as the **Truman Doctrine**: "I believe that it must be the policy of the United States to support free peoples who are resisting attempted subjugation by armed minorities or by outside pressures."[21] When Congress approved the president's request, containment became the official policy of the U.S. government.

After a communist government gained power in Czechoslovakia in February 1948, the United States countered with the **Marshall Plan**, a $16.5 billion program aimed at reconstructing the war-torn economies of Western Europe. At the time, it was feared that communism might come in "through the back door"—meaning the powerful communist parties of France and Italy might be able to capitalize on the demoralization of the general populace and, with Moscow's covert backing, seize power in Paris and Rome as they had done in Prague. The Marshall Plan formed an integral part of the overall U.S. effort to preserve the status quo after World War II. In 1949, the United States established NATO, thus militarizing containment.

The "loss" of China to the Communists in 1949 provoked another great wave of anxiety throughout the United States. When the Korean War broke out in 1950, the United States stretched containment to cover Asia, as well as Europe. During the

Truman Doctrine
President Harry Truman's pledge of U.S. support for any free people threatened with revolution by an internal armed minority or an outside aggressor.

Marshall Plan
A post–World War II program of massive economic assistance to Western Europe, inspired by the fear that those war-devastated countries were ripe for communist-backed revolutions.

1960s, the policy was stretched again—this time to cover the entire Third World. The Cold War strategy of intervention against Communism reached its high-water mark in the 1960s, when hundreds of thousands of U.S. troops were sent to Vietnam in what ultimately proved to be an ill-fated attempt to prevent Communist-ruled North Vietnam from vanquishing the U.S.-backed regime in South Vietnam.

The collapse of the Soviet Union and the end of the Cold War undercut the whole rationale for containment and caused many critics to question whether the NATO alliance, aimed at deterring a Soviet attack on Western Europe, was still necessary. A decade later, in the aftermath of 9/11, the "war on terror" replaced the "Red menace" as a rationale for reverting to a Cold War crisis mode in foreign policy—and military spending levels to match.

Blowback: The Curse of Unintended Consequences

The concept of *blowback* has been at the center of a debate over U.S. foreign policy since the end of the Cold War. Chalmers Johnson, an expert on Asia who wrote the best-selling book *Blowback*, popularized the term.[22] According to Johnson:

> [Blowback] refers to the unintended consequences of policies that were kept secret from the American people. What the daily press reports as the malign acts of "terrorists" or "drug lords" or "rogue states" or "illegal arms merchants" often turn out to be blowback from earlier operations.[23]

As examples, Johnson cited the 1988 bombing of Pan Am Flight 103 over Lockerbie, Scotland, which, he asserted, "was retaliation for a 1986 Reagan administration aerial raid on Libya that killed President Muammar Qaddafi's stepdaughter."[24] He also suggested that drug trafficking in the United States is, in part, the result of past U.S. support for dictators and anticommunist insurgents in Latin America and that terrorist attacks against U.S. targets are blowback, citing a 1997 Pentagon report: "Historical data shows a strong correlation between U.S. involvement in international situations and an increase in terrorist attacks against the United States."[25] The picture Johnson painted is nothing short of alarming:

> The most direct and obvious form of blowback often occurs when the victims fight back after a secret American bombing, or a U.S.-sponsored campaign of state terrorism, or a CIA-engineered overthrow of a foreign political leader. All around the world today, it is possible to see the groundwork being laid for future forms of blowback.[26]

These words of gloom and doom, written in 1999, looked prophetic in the days after terrorists leveled the World Trade Center. In this same passage, Johnson wrote about the 1990–1991 Gulf War and its aftermath and the suffering caused by the U.S.-imposed economic blockade on Iraq, charging "it helped contribute to the deaths of an estimated half million Iraqi civilians due to disease, malnutrition, and inadequate medical care." Osama bin Laden and the al Qaeda high command "justified" the 9/11 attacks on the grounds that the United States (1) defiled the sacred soil of Saudi Arabia by stationing military forces in the country, (2) supported Israel's repression of Palestinians' rights, and (3) waged economic war against Iraqi civilians.

Washington blamed bin Laden for the terrorist attacks on U.S. embassies in 1998 in Nairobi (the capital of Kenya) and Dar es Salaam (the capital of

Tanzania). President Clinton retaliated by bombing a pharmaceutical plant in Khartoum (the capital of Sudan) and an al Qaeda training camp in Afghanistan. Neither of these air strikes accomplished its intended purpose, but the attack against Sudan was particularly embarrassing to the United States when it turned out the pharmaceutical plant was not manufacturing chemical weapons of mass destruction, as the United States had alleged. However:

> Government spokesmen continue to justify these attacks as "deterring" terrorism, even if the targets proved to be irrelevant to any damage done to facilities of the United States. In this way, future blowback possibilities are seeded into the world.[27]

Johnson cites many examples of incidents likely, in his estimation, to produce future blowback in our relationships with Japan (Okinawa), South Korea (the 1980 Kwangju massacre), China, Indonesia, and others. Although his critique is incisive and thought-provoking, his views are controversial and by no means shared by all academic or government experts. Indeed, in the wake of 9/11, many in the United States tended to be suspicious of *any* criticism of U.S. foreign policy, viewing it as unpatriotic.

The Bush Doctrine

After the 9/11 attacks, President Bush lost little time in declaring a war against terror. He also made it clear the United States would retaliate against terrorists and those who harbor them. When the fundamentalist Taliban regime ignored Bush's ultimatum to hand over Osama bin Laden and shut down al Qaeda operations in Afghanistan, the United States orchestrated a large-scale military invasion with the intention of bringing about regime change and hunting down bin Laden and his al Qaeda confederates. The UN Security Council gave the United States a green light, and world public opinion overwhelmingly supported military action against the repressive Taliban.

But for Bush, overthrowing the Taliban and destroying the al Qaeda training camps in Afghanistan were only the first step. There still existed an "axis of evil" that included Iraq, Iran, and North Korea. Bush argued that the universal right of self-defense justifies the use of preemptive action when an "imminent danger of attack" exists. In this context, he enunciated what has come to be called the **Bush Doctrine**:

Bush Doctrine
Asserts the right of the U.S. government to act pre-emptively to forestall or prevent hostile acts against the United States.

> The United States has long maintained the option of preemptive actions to counter a sufficient threat to our national security. The greater the threat, the greater is the risk of inaction—and the more compelling the case for taking anticipatory action to defend ourselves, even if uncertainty remains as to the time and place of the enemy's attack. To forestall or prevent such hostile acts by our adversaries, the United States will, if necessary, act preemptively.[28]

The logic of this foreign policy stance was invoked to justify the invasion of Iraq.

On May 1, 2003, after the U.S. military had invaded Iraq, ousted Saddam Hussein, and replaced his brutal regime with a Coalition Provisional Authority (occupation government), Bush declared "mission accomplished"—the end of the major fighting in Iraq. It was a triumphant moment for the president, but premature. Over the next twelve months, the death toll mounted steadily as Iraqi insurgents planted bombs, launched missile attacks, and staged ambushes. By June 2009,

When the Arab uprisings of 2011 spread to Libya and Muammar Qaddafi ordered mass arrests and brutal attacks on unarmed protestors, President Obama came under heavy pressure to intervene militarily in support of rebel forces seeking to oust the Libyan dictator. As reports of indiscriminate bombing and shelling that claimed the lives of many civilians, as well as rebel fighters, mounted, Obama announced that the United States would undertake to establish a "no fly zone" in Libya. In so doing, he reversed the prescription for intervention set forth by then Secretary of State Colin Powell when the United States invaded Iraq in 2003. In Powell's formulation, the United States should not get involved militarily unless vital national interests were threatened, there was a clear exit strategy, and overwhelming force could be used to ensure success.

In Libya, Obama stood the Powell doctrine on its head. He did not argue that the United States has a vital interest in overthrowing Qaddafi. He made it clear that the United States would not intervene unilaterally except in cases of self-defense or to prevent an imminent attack. And he was at pains to point out that the use of force against Qaddafi met the following stringent tests: "an international mandate for action, a broad coalition prepared to join us, the support of Arab countries, and a plea for help from the Libyan people themselves." Obama added, "We also had the ability to stop Qaddafi's forces in their tracks without putting American troops on the ground."

Does that amount to a new "doctrine"? Maybe and maybe not. But clearly if it were to become established as the basis for the use of force in years to come, it would be a turning point in the history of postwar U.S. foreign policy.

more than 4,160 U.S. soldiers had died in Iraq *after* the "mission accomplished" pronouncement. Other casualties included 1,306 contract workers, 138 journalists, and 308 coalition troops—and an estimated 1.3 million Iraqis.[29]

President Bush ordered a troop surge in 2008 in a desperate attempt to defeat the urban guerrilla war of attrition in Iraq. He saw his approval ratings fall as a rising chorus of criticism continued to take its toll and cast a shadow over his administration. The Bush Doctrine looked destined to be yet another example of blowback in postwar-U.S. foreign policy.

President Obama, who had campaigned on a promise to withdraw U.S. forces from Iraq, did not depart from the foreign policy of his predecessor. On the contrary, upon taking office, when the war in Afghanistan was going from bad to worse, Obama ordered a troop surge, imitating what George Bush did when the war was going badly in Iraq. And given the tumult in Tunisia, Egypt, Libya, and throughout much of the Arab World in 2011, Obama's decision to intervene militarily in Libya was a little like wandering blindfolded in uncharted territory and wading into quicksand (see "Ideas and Politics: Intervention in Libya").

STATECRAFT: BEYOND REALISM

Some international theorists contend that not much has changed in the post–Cold War era. They contend the United States "must anchor its security and prosperity in a less-than-utopian set of objectives [and] think in terms not of the whole world's well-being but...of purely national interest."[30]

SHANE T. MCCOY/U.S. NAVY/MCT /LANDOV

Prisoners at the U.S. "Gitmo" detention facility at Guantanamo Bay, Cuba. The methods and policies associated with the Bush Doctrine in the conduct of the war on terror caused a "blowback" effect that damaged President Bush's popularity at home and his credibility abroad. But Barack Obama, who as a candidate had pledged to close Guantanamo if elected, changed his mind when he landed in the White House as the nation's commander in chief.

Some foreign policy experts argue that the United States has strayed from primary reliance on diplomacy to an overemphasis on military solutions. These critics argue for multilateralism over unilateralism and the use of **statecraft** over force and the threat of force whenever and wherever possible.

What is statecraft? According to Dennis Ross, chief Middle East peace negotiator under Presidents George H. W. Bush and Bill Clinton:

> It is the use of the assets or the resources and tools (economic, military, intelligence, media) that a state has to pursue its interest and to affect the behavior of others, whether friendly or hostile. It involves making sound assessments and understanding where and on what issues the state is being challenged and can counter a threat or create a potential opportunity or take advantage of one. Statecraft requires good judgment in the definition of one's interests and a recognition of how to exercise hard military or soft economic power to provide security and promote the well-being of one's citizens. It is as old as conflict between communities and the desire to avoid or prevent it. Plato wrote about statecraft. Machiavelli theorized about it. And Bismarck practiced it, never losing sight of his objectives and recognizing that a nation's ambitions should never exceed its capabilities.[31]

Ideals and Self-Interest: The Power of Morality

In sharp contrast to political realism, **idealism** places great emphasis on the role of values, ideals, and moral principles. It not only helps explain why nations act, but it also furnishes guidelines for how nations ought to act. Idealists tend to view war as irrational—a manifestation of misguided ideology or fervent nationalism. They see trade, aid, diplomacy, and international law and organizations (see Chapter 18) as antidotes—and alternatives—to war. Idealists often regard realists as cynics; realists say idealists are naive. Who is right?

Even the arch-realist, Hans Morgenthau, did not deny morality's role in international relations. Some actors on the world stage clearly give moral principle more weight than others. President Woodrow Wilson emphasized national self-determination and collective security, Hitler obsessed over territorial expansion

statecraft
The art of achieving political or strategic aims and objectives by force of example, persuasion, and the use of incentives rather than by coercion and threats; synonymous with *statesmanship* and *far-sighted diplomacy*.

idealism
A political philosophy that considers values, ideals, and moral principles as the keys to comprehending, and possibly changing, the behavior of nation-states.

(*Lebensraum*), British Prime Minister Neville Chamberlain sought peace through appeasement, and President Jimmy Carter actively promoted global human rights. Nations *do* sometimes act altruistically—for example, by offering asylum to refugees who flee political persecution, economic disaster, or civil war. Between the two world wars, British leaders sought to alleviate harsh conditions imposed on Germany by the Treaty of Versailles, a stand hailed as "a noble idea, rooted in Christianity, courage, and common sense."[32]

The U.S. military action in Somalia from 1992 to 1994 was undertaken to alleviate mass starvation. That humanitarian intervention, which cost U.S. lives and offered no political or economic advantage, cannot be explained by self-interest alone.[33] Sadly, however, in the end it accomplished little but to alienate Islamic extremists who saw it as another example of U.S. interference in the internal affairs of a Muslim society.

Still, it is easier by far to cite instances when leaders and states do *not* act altruistically. President Bill Clinton did not intervene against the genocide in Rwanda, and President George W. Bush did not send troops to stop the savagery in Darfur. The major European nations, too, stayed on the sidelines in both instances.

Most foreign policy contains elements of both ideals and self-interest. The Marshall Plan was magnanimous by any reasonable measure. Even Winston Churchill, who measured his words carefully, called it the "most unsordid act in history."[34] But the Marshall Plan was also consistent with the United States' post–World War II status quo strategic policy of reestablishing a stable Western European community, able to resist armed aggression from without and organized subversion from within. Germany sent massive amounts of aid to Russia in the winter of 1991–1992, partly for humanitarian reasons and partly out of fear a failed Russia would destabilize Western Europe and unleash a horde of refugees in Germany's direction.

Nations have occasionally sacrificed concrete national interests for the sake of moral principle. Although an occupied country during World War II, Denmark was granted much political autonomy by the Nazi government. The Danish people and their government openly defied German edicts and protected Jewish citizens and other refugees, thereby putting themselves at risk. Through acts of uncommon moral courage, the Danes created "an extraordinary obstacle which arose in the path of the German destruction machine: an uncooperative Danish administration and a local population unanimous in its resolve to save its Jews."[35] Denmark, "too weak to seek self-preservation through power," limited its foreign policy "largely to humanitarian causes, and…in the end survived Hitler's conquest."[36]

A true understanding of the national interest takes into account both power and morality. Power without morality is mere expedience and, as history shows, can be self-defeating, whereas morality without power rarely goes beyond good intentions.[37]

Aggression: In the Eyes of the Beholder?

Aggression is strictly condemned in international law and diplomacy. Not every state with a territorial claim against another or a desire to change the global distribution of power and wealth is guilty of aggression, however. A border

Here boys are playing at "ethnic cleansing" in Kosovo in the former Yugoslavia where genocide happened in the 1990s. Is aggression inherent in human nature, a necessity in a dangerous world, or a form of learned behavior?

dispute, for example, does not in itself mean either contending country has an appetite for empire. Neither does the demand by many developing countries for a "new international economic order" (a redistribution of global wealth). Challenging the status quo in this way is hardly proof of aggression, both because the objectives are limited and reasonable and because the methods are political and diplomatic rather than military or economic.

Historically, when one nation's army invaded and occupied the territory of another nation, it was an act of aggression—a violation of international law. Invaders are seldom welcomed by the native inhabitants, and aggressors are seldom embraced by the international community. But, as suggested above, the United States since World War II has intervened militarily in some countries and invaded others without *intending* to plunder or seize territory, without intending to take over the country's government, and without intending to stay. Unfortunately, "good" intentions are often misunderstood, misinterpreted, or, in the eyes of others, not good at all. When that happens—and it almost always does—a danger of unintended consequences arises.

Aggression is often in the eyes of the beholder. It is something others do. When we do it, it is self-defense. Thus, in the crisis presented by the 9/11 terrorist attacks, President George W. Bush called for punitive measures against any state(s) that harbored international terrorists.[38] The methods the United States subsequently used were violent—bombing and inserting special operations combat teams in order to (1) overthrow the Taliban regime in Afghanistan and (2) kill or capture Osama bin Laden and his al Qaeda terrorist network. Later, the United States led the invasion of Iraq, the ouster of dictator Saddam Hussein followed and then his capture and execution. By any reasonable definition, these acts were certainly aggressive, but did they constitute aggression? What do you think?

Hard Facts about Soft Power

Scholar Joseph Nye argues that power in contemporary world politics is "distributed among countries in a pattern that resembles a complex three-dimensional chess game." Imagine three chess games on as many chessboards taking place on three levels simultaneously. On the top board, military power is concentrated in the United States; the world looks unipolar. On the middle chessboard, however, economic power is distributed more evenly among the United States, Europe, Japan, and China; and the world appears multipolar. Finally, there "is the realm of transnational relations that cross borders outside government control" on the bottom of the chessboard:

> This realm includes actors as diverse as bankers electronically transferring sums larger than most national budgets at one extreme, and terrorists transferring weapons or hackers disrupting Internet operations at the other. On this bottom board, power is widely dispersed, and it makes no sense to speak of unipolarity, multipolarity or hegemony.[39]

In a three-dimensional game, Nye argues, you will lose if you focus only on the top board and fail to notice the other boards and the vertical connections among them. Nye draws an even more fundamental distinction between "hard coercive power" and "soft or attractive power," which he defines as "the important ability to get others to want what you want." He concludes: "The paradox of American power in the 21st century is that the largest power since Rome cannot achieve its objectives unilaterally in a global information age."[40]

THE MORE THINGS CHANGE . . .

What does the future hold? During the Cold War, many feared that the world as we know it would be incinerated in a nuclear holocaust. When the Cold War ended, one famous scholar, the late Samuel Huntington, warned that the old clash of ideologies was being replaced by a "clash of civilizations."[41] In his words, "The breaking apart and remaking of the atlas is only now beginning."[42] Then came 9/11, which was widely viewed as a vindication of Huntington's thesis, supposedly pitting the Judeo-Christian West against the Islamic world (an oversimplification that nonetheless has some basis in reality).

About the same time, another scholar, Robert Kaplan, saw a different danger on the horizon—what he called "the coming anarchy." The nation-state as we know it, he argued, is obsolete and destined to be replaced not by larger regional groupings or a world-state (as idealists predicted after World War II), but by a formless force field of political whirlpools energized by the teeming, chaotic, crime-infested cities or "city-states" of the future. The picture Kaplan painted was bleak in the extreme.[43] West Africa in the 1990s presented a glimpse of this grim future, as did the Balkans war after the breakup of Yugoslavia.

There is a famous French adage that goes, *plus ça change, plus c'est la même chose* (the more things change, the more it's the same thing). Apocalyptic visions of the future are titillating and thought-provoking, but they typically take a real danger facing the world and exaggerate it. Conflict is not confined to any era in history or to any one society or region of the world. Success in containing conflict and minimizing war will depend, in part, on the effectiveness of the international institutions created after World War II for those purposes. These institutions, especially the United Nations and the European Union, are our focus in Chapter 18.

SUMMARY

The character of international politics differs significantly from that of domestic politics due to the absence of a world government capable of maintaining law and order. The struggle for power, inherent in the international system, is designed to advance national interests. Sovereign states choose a variety of ends, almost always overshadowed by one ultimate aim, to maximize power.

Modern European history saw the rise of the nation-state and the emergence of a multipolar world order sustained by a balance of power characterized by a relatively equal distribution of resources and capabilities among several major states. The traditional balance of power system that came into being in Europe in 1648 was limited in size and scope. All members shared certain common values and beliefs; Great Britain acted as keeper of the balance. The system worked because means and ends were limited, alliances were flexible, and crusading zeal was absent.

The demise of the old Eurocentric order following the two world wars fought in the first half of the twentieth century ushered in a bipolar system in the second half of the twentieth century in which two rival "superpowers" were preeminent. In the Cold War, the United States adopted a status quo policy of containment, aimed at preventing the Soviet Union from expanding or upsetting the global balance of power. A bipolar system replaced the old multipolar European system, with ideological differences and the specter of nuclear holocaust characterizing the bitter rivalry between the two superpowers. By the late 1960s, a strategic stalemate based on mutual deterrence made war between these two titans equally irrational for both.

With the disintegration of the Soviet Union and the end of the Cold War, a new international order emerged. Following a brief "unipolar moment" during which time the United States was unrivalled as the sole remaining superpower, a new era of multipolarity rapidly emerged characterized by ever-greater interdependence in a dynamic global economy driven by the revolution in information technology; a growing concentration of economic power in three regions, namely, Europe (the twenty-seven-member EU), northwest Asia (China, Japan, and South Korea), and North America; a deteriorating global economy; the unmitigated danger of nuclear proliferation; climate change and a threatened global environment; and a leveling of the playing field as the share of U.S. GNP in the world economy shrinks.

The world has changed dramatically since the Cold War ended, but U.S. foreign policy has remained basically unchanged. In the Western Hemisphere, the Monroe Doctrine was designed to perpetuate the status quo; after World War II, containment in effect applied the same logic to the entire globe. On many occasions the United States intervened militarily to prevent leftist takeovers in Africa, Asia, and Latin America. Sometimes these interventions caused "blowback"— self-induced policy problems arising from imprudent past actions—as happened in Vietnam. The Bush Doctrine asserting a U.S. right to take preemptive measures whenever and wherever it deems necessary provided the rationale for the U.S.-led invasions of Afghanistan and Iraq.

Political realists run the risk of underestimating the power of moral principles. Aggression is universally denounced in international politics but difficult to define. Neorealists stress the value of "soft power"—power derived from good-will and good works rather than from threats and the use of force. Critics of recent U.S. foreign policy urge a greater reliance on statecraft, or the skillful and prudent practice of diplomacy, as an alternative to an overreliance on military force (or "hard power").

Conflict is endemic in the world, always has been and always will be. Apocalyptic visions of the future tend toward alarmism, exaggerating dangers and seeing more disorder in the world than actually exists.

KEY TERMS

political realism 476
equilibrium 477
balance of power
   system 477
keeper of the
   balance 478
Great Powers 479
superpower 479
bipolar system 479
containment 480

Warsaw Pact 480
deterrence 481
deterrence theory 481
globalization 483
International Monetary
   Fund (IMF) 484
unipolar system 492
national interest 493
hard power 493
derivative power 493

soft power 493
Zionism 494
Monroe Doctrine 495
Truman Doctrine 496
Marshall Plan 496
Bush Doctrine 498
statecraft 500
idealism 500

REVIEW QUESTIONS

1. What does Thucydides' account of the confrontation between the Melians and the Athenians reveal about the nature of international politics?
2. What does a Machiavellian approach to politics entail? What sort of world-view does it embrace?
3. What is the meaning of the term *national interest?* How do political realists use this term?
4. What two basic foreign policy goals are available to nation-states?
5. What foreign policy strategies are open to nation-states? Do nation-states usually pursue one strategy at a time? Explain.
6. Explain the difference between "hard power" and "soft power."
7. What is the Bush Doctrine? When and how was it applied? Critique the doctrine and its application.
8. World War II changed the shape and form of the international system. When and how did the present international system come into being? Contrast the new world order with the old one.

CHAPTER (18)

International Organization(s)
Globalization and the Quest for Order

Nonstate Actors
The European Union
The United Nations

Unconventional Nonstate Actors
International Law
The Quest for a Perpetual Peace

What are the main types of nonstate actors, and why are they increasingly important in the Age of Globalization?

Why is the European Union a unique international organization? When and why did it come into being, and what are its main achievements?

When and why was the United Nations established? How does it work, and why does it continue to exist despite its obvious limitations?

What are two types of unconventional nonstate actors?

What is the role of international law in world politics? Why is it least likely to be enforceable when it is most needed, and if it cannot be enforced, what good is it?

If you want peace, "prepare for war." This famous dictum, penned by a Roman military writer named Vegetius in 390 CE, suggests what history shows: Conflict is part of the human condition, one we can at best prevent or deter with vigilance and military readiness. On the other hand, in a "hyperconnected" world where, as the saying goes, everything is connected to everything else, we also need new ideas and ways of thinking.[1]

After World War II some writers imagined an age of global interdependence based on new forms of confidence-building cooperation and organization. One school of thought, called **functionalism**, argued cogently that the practical benefits of global commerce would in time give rise to conditions for perpetual peace.

Functionalism has taken a back seat to the transformational magic of computers and digital communications, otherwise known as globalization. In the words of syndicated columnist Thomas Friedman, "No matter what your profession—doctor, lawyer, architect, accountant—if you are an American, you better be good at the touchy-feely service stuff, because anything that can be digitized can be outsourced to either the smartest or the cheapest producer, or both."[2]

The steady growth of the world economy since World War II has resulted in no small part from multilateral efforts to remove or reduce artificial trade barriers such as tariffs, quotas, and subsidies. Trade expansion arguably reduces local and regional conflicts and the risks of general war.

Strengthening regional trade ties and economic integration underlie the European Union's decision to create a single economy, as well as its subsequent moves to establish a common currency, the euro, and grow to twenty-seven member-states (adding ten in 2004, two more in 2007). The emergence of regional trading blocs such as the North American Free Trade Association (NAFTA), the Caribbean Community and Common Market (CARICOM), Mercosur in South America, the Association of Southeast Asian Nations (ASEAN), the Asia-Pacific Economic Cooperation (APEC), and the South Asian Association for Regional Cooperation (SAARC) reflects nations' growing interest in expanding regional cooperation outside Europe as well.

In theory, more jobs and higher living standards will reduce discord and increase collaboration among nations and governments. But has the rise of regional economic pacts really advanced world peace? Has the United Nations made the world a more peaceful place? Has the World Court fostered greater respect for international law?

To answer these questions, we first examine the types of nonstate organizations in today's world, as well as the professionals who serve them and who run the gamut from MBAs, petroleum engineers, and peace activists to terrorists and mercenaries.

NONSTATE ACTORS

The role of **nonstate actors** in international relations has grown steadily since World War II. Examples include multinational corporations, international organizations like Amnesty International, and privatized military firms (PMFs). International terrorist groups such as al Qaeda and Hezbollah (see Chapter 15) are also nonstate actors.

functionalism
According to functionalist theory, the gradual transfer of economic and social functions to international cooperative agencies (for example, specialized UN agencies, such as UNESCO) will eventually lead to a transfer of actual authority and integration of political activities on the international level.

nonstate actor
An entity other than a nation-state, including multinational corporations, nongovernmental organizations, and international nongovernmental organizations, that plays a role in international politics.

Multinational Corporations

Businesses "with foreign subsidiaries which extend the production and marketing of the firm beyond the boundaries of any one country" are **multinational corporations** (MNCs). These entities are "best viewed as a global network of subsidiaries."[3]

In the Age of Globalization, the landscape of the world economy is constantly changing. The top ten U.S.-based MNCs in 2012, according to *Fortune* magazine's annual ranking, are Exxon Mobil (1), Walmart (2), Chevron (3), ConocoPhillips (4), General Motors (5), General Electric (6), Berkshire Hathaway (7), Fannie Mae (8), Ford Motor (9), and Hewlett-Packard (10). On a worldwide basis, three of the four top ten global corporations—Royal Dutch, Shell, and BP—are headquartered in Europe; one—the Sinopec Group—is China's biggest oil producer and refiner. Fewer than one-third of the Fortune Global 500 companies were headquartered in the United States at the end of 2008; Europe was home to the largest number (Table 18.1). By 2012 there were more Global 500 companies headquartered in Asia than in either Europe or the United States, signaling a major regional shift in wealth and power under way in the 21st century.

Between 1980 and 2000, the number of MNCs increased eightfold to roughly 60,000, with some 800,000 foreign affiliates. Today, these giant companies control huge assets, generate trillions of dollars in worldwide sales, and employ tens of millions of people.[4] In democratic countries, they are also key players in a variety of policy areas from taxation, energy, and the environment to international trade, defense, and foreign affairs. Annual sales of the wealthiest MNCs exceed the GDP of many nations. In the words of one analyst:

> Multinational corporations—once made vulnerable to the expropriation of property or blockage of funds and forbidden to trade with hostile countries and to buy and sell freely the latest high technology and scarce commodities—are now more likely to guide foreign policy than follow it.[5]

Technological advancements, market reforms in many countries, and relatively stable political conditions in Europe and Asia have contributed to the rapid growth of MNCs, creating new opportunities for corporate expansion, foreign investment, and personal mobility. The process has accelerated as more and more companies seek cheaper labor and ease of access to expanding consumer markets abroad.[6]

TABLE 18.1   Don't Look Back, Somebody Might Be Gaining on You...Top Fortune 500 Corporate Headquarters by Region of the World in 2008 and 2012

2008		2012	
EU	184	Asia	166
United States	153	EU	135
Asia	124	United States	132

SOURCE: Global 500 at http://money.cnn.com/magazines/fortune/global500/2012/countries/Australia.html. Data distilled from "Pick a country."

Big multinational banks with trillions of dollars in assets play a key role in this process. Many of the largest are located in the United States, Europe, and Japan. The People's Republic of China (PRC) has also become a major lender to the world, especially the United States.

Commercial banks have at times acted to stabilize the world's financial system during unsettled times. In 1973–1974, for example, when the **Organization of Petroleum Exporting Countries** (OPEC) launched an oil embargo, causing the price of oil to soar fourfold, the international banking system stepped in, lending money from oil-rich OPEC nations to countries hardest hit by the high oil prices. But banks—especially ones "too big to fail"—can also destabilize economies, both national and global, as the banking crisis of 2008 and ensuing Great Recession painfully demonstrated.

The 2008 crisis was associated with a bubble in the housing market caused by (a) reckless banking policies (for example, "no doc" home loans); (b) a runaway derivatives market in which securities with obscure and mystifying acronyms—CDOs (collateralized debt obligations), CDSs (credit default swaps), and MBSs (mortgage-backed securities)—created trillions of dollars in dodgy assets; and (c) a failure of federal regulatory agencies, especially the Securities and Exchange Commission (SEC) and the Federal Trade Commission FTC), to hold Wall Street and the wider financial industry accountable. In the wake of the banking crisis, Washington made no moves to reregulate TBTF (too big to fail) banks, and the Federal Bureau of Investigation (FBI) declined to prosecute Wall Street bankers and financiers despite mounting evidence of criminal activity (in particular, an "epidemic" of control fraud). William Black, Matt Taiibi, Joseph Stiglitz, Paul Krugman, and Neil Barofsky are among the many prominent experts—economists, lawyers, and journalists—who have tried to focus public attention on this issue in recent years, but official Washington has turned a deaf ear.

Clearly, multinational corporations are major actors in today's interdependent world. Most economists applaud MNCs, saying they enhance worldwide competition, improve economic efficiency, and promote technology. Critics counter that MNCs often lack a social conscience and point to the 1984 Union Carbide gas leak in Bhopal, India, called "the world's worst industrial catastrophe," in which as many as 15,000 people died. Critics also point to the alleged role of ITT Corporation in the overthrow of the Chilean government in the early 1970s.

But it is not necessary to reach back that far for an example of how nonstate actors can destabilize world order and the global economy, not to mention domestic economies and national governments (in Europe, for example, Greece, Spain, Italy, Portugal, and Ireland). Arguably, the existence of banks too big to fail—and bankers too big to prosecute—in the United States puts the global economy and America's closest allies at risk. Because MNCs operate outside the legal control of any one national government, they arguably pose a special challenge to state sovereignty.

Whatever the validity of these specific criticisms, MNCs collectively represent a potent force that has changed the face of world politics. In the words of one academic expert:

> Multinational firms...put into question the value of models of world politics that proceed from the assumptions of national self-sufficiency.... According

Organization of Petroleum Exporting Countries (OPEC) An international cartel established in 1961 that, since 1973, has successfully manipulated the worldwide supply of and price for oil, with far-reaching consequences for the world economy and political structure.

to one view, they are the international counterpart of the nineteenth-century industrial revolution; according to another, they may be the skeleton of the world economy of the future.[7]

International Organizations: INGOs and IGOs

international nongovernmental organization (INGO)
Comprised of private individuals and groups, an INGO transcends borders in pursuit of common causes.

international governmental organization (IGO)
A grouping of established states; IGOs are based on treaties, have formal structures, and meet at regular intervals.

International organizations made up of private individuals and affiliated groups are called **international nongovernmental organizations** (INGOs). The International Committee of the Red Cross (ICRC) is a well-known example of an INGO. Others include Greenpeace, the World Council of Churches (WCC), the Salvation Army, Save the Children, Amnesty International, and the International Olympic Committee (IOC), to name but a few.

International governmental organizations (IGOs) such as the Organization of American States (OAS), the Organization of African Unity (OAU), and the Association of Southeast Asian Nations (ASEAN) are regional groupings of states. Some IGOs are based on a specific purpose; for example, the World Trade Organization (WTO) is dedicated to trade liberalization. As we shall see, the United Nations (UN) is in a class by itself—a multipurpose IGO with a universal membership.

IGOs first rose to prominence between the two world wars (1919–1939) under the aegis of the League of Nations, the first universal IGO. By 1940, more than 80 IGOs and nearly 500 INGOs existed; following World War II, the number of both types climbed. A half century later there were nearly 5,000 INGOs and more than 350 IGOs.

Typically IGOs have restricted membership based on territory and function, and they exist to advance a single goal.[8] The OAU, for example, restricts its membership regionally but has an ambitious charter that cuts across economic, political, and social lines. The World Health Organization (WHO), on the other hand, serves a single purpose but is open to worldwide membership. The most important IGO in the world today is the United Nations, which both promotes a global membership and advances a multipurpose agenda.

By the late 1970s, the vast array of IGOs and INGOs had created what one scholar described as "networks of **interdependence**,"[9] a process that has since greatly accelerated. We examine two particularly important types of IGOs: economic pacts and military alliances. The

The International Committee of the Red Cross (ICRC) provides vital humanitarian aid around the world. Here an ICRC worker distributes essential household items to refugees in the Central African Republic.

BJORGVINSSON, JON/ICRC

European Union (EU) is a leading example of the former, and the **North Atlantic Treaty Organization** (NATO)—more than two decades after the end of the Cold War that spawned it—remains *the* leading example of the latter.

Military Alliances Although rarely described as IGOs, military alliances are, in fact, the first major form of intergovernmental organization to grow out of the modern state system and are a prominent feature of international politics.

The purpose of military alliances is simply to deter or fight enemies, potential and immediate. Not surprisingly, such alliances often have been part of arms races, which usually precede major wars. This observation led a number of political scientists and world leaders to conclude that alliances were a form of international organization that, paradoxically, were at odds with world peace and order. President Woodrow Wilson, for example, believed military alliances were one of the main causes of World War I, and, as we will see, he tried to forge the League of Nations, a new international organization based on the principle of "open covenants, openly arrived at." Such an organization, he believed, would erase the need for military alliances, which, for many centuries, had been arranged behind the scenes and were at times maintained in secret.

But alliances did not disappear. After World War II, the United States sought to counter the perceived Soviet threat to Western Europe by creating the North Atlantic Treaty Organization (NATO). For the United States, it was the first peacetime military pact since George Washington, in his famous Farewell Address, warned a young American nation against involvement in "entangling alliances." NATO came into being in 1949; in 1955, the Soviet Union countered by creating the Warsaw Pact (formally named the Warsaw Treaty Organization).

interdependence
In international politics, a condition in which national economies become inextricably entwined in the global economy, as political and business elites design strategies for continued growth and prosperity around access to foreign markets, labor, and capital.

North Atlantic Treaty Organization (NATO)
A permanent peacetime military alliance created by the United States in 1949 to deter Soviet aggression in Europe; today, NATO has twenty-eight members, including twelve Central and East European countries.

COURTESY OF NATO

NATO is a remnant of the Cold War, but the international system has changed dramatically since late 1989 and 1991 and so has the alliance. During the popular uprising in Libya in 2011, for example, the United States did not undertake airstrikes against the Qaddafi regime until NATO allies France and the UK agreed to take an active role.

The Warsaw Pact was disbanded when the communist regimes in Eastern Europe toppled in 1989, only two years before the Soviet Union disintegrated. Thus, NATO fulfilled its original mission, but rather than disband, it did something remarkable: It redefined its reason for being and, led by the United States, sought to play a peacekeeper role in Europe. Its first new test was an effort to limit the conflict in Bosnia by sending troops and conducting airstrikes.

NATO has expanded eastward. Ten of its twelve original members were in Western Europe (the United States and Canada were the other two). Four more West European countries joined later: Greece (1952), Turkey (1952), West Germany (1955), and Spain (1982). Between 1999 and 2004, ten former members of the Warsaw Pact were admitted: Poland, Hungary, the Czech Republic, the three Baltic States (Latvia, Lithuania, and Estonia), Slovakia, Slovenia, Bulgaria, and Romania. In 2009, Croatia and Albania joined the alliance, bringing the total to twenty-eight. Moscow stayed on the sidelines but accused the United States of using NATO to pursue an aggressive policy aimed at isolating Russia from Europe.

NATO's role in the new world order of the twenty-first century is controversial. Some even question whether NATO's existence is justified now that the Cold War is over, and many Europeans fear a U.S.-led NATO will provoke Russia and rekindle an East-West conflict in Europe. For example, in the 1990s, Russia backed Serbia in the Balkans wars, whereas NATO and the United States viewed Serbia as the aggressor. NATO and the European Union, in turn, denounced Putin's brutal military response to the secessionist movement in Chechnya, his ruthless methods of dealing with critics (particularly journalists) and political opponents, the lurch toward authoritarian rule under Putin's leadership, and Russia's decision to invade Georgia in 2008 in a dispute over South Ossetia and Abkhazia. In U.S.-led invasions and interventions from Iraq and Afghanistan after 9/11 to Libya in 2011–2012, NATO partners have lent moral, diplomatic, and military assistance vital to these costly, open-ended commitments.

In the United States, critics of NATO's expansion contended it would unnecessarily divide Europe, leaving important countries such as Estonia, Latvia, Lithuania, and Ukraine on the other side. Worse still, they argued, any policy that poisons relations between the United States and Russia threatens European stability.[10] But periodic tensions between Russia and Europe lend credence to the view that NATO remains necessary. Russia's brief war with Georgia in 2008 underscored this point, as did an incident between Russia and Estonia involving a disputed World War II monument in the spring of 2007.

COURTESY OF NATO

NATO headquarters near Brussels, Belgium. Under the terms of the treaty, the Supreme Allied Commander Europe (SACEUR) must always be an American.

For millions of Eastern Europeans, NATO is the key to security and liberty. The difference between the crisis outcomes in Estonia, which is a member of NATO, and Georgia, which is not, is instructive: Russia did not invade Estonia; Georgia was not so fortunate.

Economic Pacts Many significant international agreements of the post–World War II period are trade treaties, the great majority bilateral treaties (between two countries). In addition, five forms of multilateral economic pacts have played varying roles in creating noteworthy IGOs and promoting economic integration among their member-states. These are:

1. *Preferential trade arrangements.* Several states agree to grant one another exclusive trade preferences, including tariff reductions. One example is the Commonwealth of Nations, made up of Great Britain and many of its former colonies.
2. *Nondiscriminatory trade organizations.* These pacts promote closer trade relations on a global or regional scale. The World Trade Organization (WTO) is the most important.
3. *Free-trade areas.* These arrangements completely eliminate trade barriers among members, who surrender their sovereign right to determine trade policy with other member-states while remaining free to set trade policies with nonmember states. The most important is the North American Free Trade Agreement (NAFTA) between the United States, Canada, and Mexico. Another is the European Free Trade Association (EFTA), which has lost members to the European Union and is now almost eclipsed by it.
4. *Customs unions.* One step above free-trade areas on the ladder of economic integration, customs unions promote free trade among members and a common external tariff for all trade with nonmembers. The Southern Cone Common Market (or Mercosur) has four full members (Argentina, Paraguay, Brazil, and Uruguay) and two associate members (Bolivia and Chile) who trade freely among themselves while moving toward a common external tariff of 14% on capital goods.
5. *Economic unions.* Less than a federation but more than a customs union, an economic union countenances the free flow of capital and labor, as

EUROPEAN FEDERALIST PARTY

The European Union started out as a six-member common market for coal and steel in the early 1950s and has grown into a highly integrated single market with twenty-seven member-states, a common currency (the euro), and no internal border controls among twenty-six European countries that have implemented the Schengen agreement signed in 1985. The EU has the world's biggest economy and is the USA's largest trading partner.

well as goods and services. It requires a high level of economic integration and policy coordination among member-states, as well as a limitation of sovereignty. There is one sterling example in today's world, the European Union.

THE EUROPEAN UNION

The **European Union** (EU) is by far the most dynamic example of this type of supranational organization. By 2009, the EU encompassed twenty-seven countries; sixteen member-states had adopted the euro; and it was possible to travel freely and cross borders in most of Europe without a passport.

Origins and Evolution

The EU traces its origins to 1952, when Belgium, France, West Germany, Italy, Luxembourg, and the Netherlands founded the European Coal and Steel Community (ECSC). In 1957, these six countries met in Rome and agreed to launch the European Economic Community (EEC), and the European Atomic Energy Community (Euratom) the following year. The ECSC, EEC, and Euratom were merged into a single entity—the European Community (EC) or Common Market in 1967. Nine more states were admitted: Denmark, Ireland, and the United Kingdom in 1973; Greece in 1981; Portugal and Spain in 1986; and Austria, Finland, and Sweden in 1995. In 2004, the EU admitted eight former communist states in Eastern Europe, including the Czech Republic, Estonia, Hungary, Latvia, Lithuania, Poland, Slovakia, and Slovenia, plus Cyprus and Malta. In 2007, Romania and Bulgaria joined, bringing the total to twenty-seven. Talks are currently under way to admit Turkey, Serbia, and the Republic of Macedonia. Turkey (population 73 million) is the largest candidate for membership in EU history; if admitted, it will be second only to Germany and the only Muslim majority country in the EU.

Major Institutions

The EU's political institutions fulfill many functions of a supranational government. They include the European Council and Council of Ministers, the Commission, the European Parliament, and the Court of Justice. The European Council, Council of Ministers, and the Commission exercise executive powers; the European Council and Council of Ministers are intergovernmental, and the Commission is supranational. The Councils directly represent the interests of the national governments; the Commission represents the EU as a whole. On crucial issues, the two Councils vote on the basis of unanimity—everyone at the table has a veto. Increasingly, issues are decided by **qualified majority vote** (QMV), reflecting a shift from intergovernmental to supranational decision making.

The European Parliament (EP) is a deliberative body that shares **co-decision** legislative powers with the Council of Ministers but remains the junior partner. Since 1979, its members have been elected by direct universal suffrage. The European Court of Justice (ECJ) interprets and applies EU treaties and adjudicates disputes between member-states and the EU bodies.

European Union (EU)
The successor to the Common Market or European Economic Community; the governing body that presides over the world's largest single economy.

qualified majority vote (QMV)
In the European Union, a form of voting in the European Council and Council of Ministers in which no member state has a veto, but passage of a measure requires a triple majority, including more than 70% of the votes cast.

co-decision
In the European Union, a method of legislation and rule-making that involves both the European Council (heads of government) and the European Parliament.

The 1993 Treaty on the European Union (TEU) created three pillars: the European Community (EC), the Common Foreign and Security Policy (CFSP), and Justice and Home Affairs (JHA). Decisions on the economy (Pillar One) are made by supranational method (qualified majority voting). Decisions on foreign and security policy (Pillar Two) and justice and home affairs (Pillar Three) are made by the intergovernmental method (unanimity); however, some policy matters—for example, the internal open-border system, immigration, and asylum—formerly under Pillar Three (intergovernmental) have been shifted to Pillar One (supranational).

EU member-states agree to place the *acquis communautaire*—the total body of EU community law—over national law. The *acquis* comprises a billion words and has been translated into twenty-two official EU languages.

The **Common Agricultural Policy** (CAP) has been an EU fixture since the inception of the original common market in 1958. The CAP sets and collects tariffs on agricultural products coming into the EU and provides subsidies to EU farmers. In the past, agricultural expenditures (mainly subsidies) accounted for nearly 50% of the EU budget. The CAP's share was projected to drop below one-third in 2013, but agriculture's share remained closer to 40% because France has resisted any reductions in subsidies to French farmers. Brussels also faces growing pressure from new member-states to reallocate EU resources to regional development programs and projects (called "structural" and " cohesion" funds) aimed at helping lagging areas—many in Central and Eastern Europe—catch up.

By far the gravest challenge to the EU in recent years, however, has been the sovereign debt crisis (aka the "euro crisis") triggered by Greece's threat to default—to declare bankruptcy and leave creditors out in the cold. The danger of a panic in capital markets on the heels of the 2008 global financial crisis posed a policy dilemma for the EU Council: whether to evict Greece from the EU (the so-called Grexit option) or put together a financial rescue package (the bailout option). The problem with bailing out Greece was that Spain, Portugal, and Ireland were also sinking into insolvency. Eventually, the richer EU member-states agreed to bailouts for all four countries. But the bailouts came with strings attached: the givers (mainly Germany) made the recipients agree to tough and unpopular austerity programs. Nobody can say how this story will end; let's take a look at how it began.

The Single Market Economy

A landmark in the history of European integration, the Single European Act (SEA) of 1986 aimed to create a single market in the EU by 1992. It thus made several key institutional reforms, including a cooperative procedure giving the European Parliament a greater voice in legislation and extending qualified majority voting to new policy areas.

The SEA allowed wider and deeper integration of all the national economies, including establishment of a European Monetary Union (EMU) and new unit of currency (the euro). A treaty signed at the Maastricht summit in 1991 transformed the European Community (EC) into the European Union (EU) and paved the way for creating a European Central Bank (ECB) in 1998 and

Common Agricultural Policy (CAP) An EU fixture since the inception of the original common market in 1958. Sets and collects tariffs on agricultural products coming into the EU and provides subsidies to EU farmers.

Schengen area
The visa-free zone within the EU, encompassing twenty-six countries and more than 400 million people who can now travel freely about Europe without being stopped at border-crossings.

Emissions Trading Scheme (ETS)
In the European Union, part of an antipollution drive aimed at significantly reducing Europe's carbon footprint by 2020 by assigning carbon-emission allowances to industries and factories and creating a carbon exchange, or a market where "clean" companies (ones that do not use their full allowances) can sell the credits they accumulate by not polluting to "dirty" companies (ones that exceed their allowances).

launching the euro in 1999. The euro went into circulation in twelve EU countries in 2002 and has now been adopted by a total of seventeen; the twelve countries that joined the EU from 2004 to 2007 are treaty-bound to join the euro area as soon as they meet the criteria for membership (see "Landmarks in History: The Euro Crisis"). Five of the seventeen EU countries in the euro zone joined between 2007 and 2011: Slovenia, Cyprus, Malta, Slovakia, and Estonia.

The **Schengen area** grew out of a 1985 agreement among five countries (France, Germany, and the Benelux countries of Belgium, Luxembourg, and the Netherlands) to create a passport-free zone. The Amsterdam Treaty incorporated the Schengen system into the EU *acquis* in 1997. Today twenty-six countries, including several not in the EU (Iceland, Norway, and Switzerland), belong to Schengen; and it is possible to travel from Finland to Greece by car, train, or bus without a passport, much like traveling within the United States.

The **Emissions Trading Scheme** (ETS) is Europe's major climate change project, a cap-and-trade system that sets limits on the volume of pollutants the five dirtiest industries in any given country can spew into the atmosphere each year. Companies that exceed allowances can buy pollution permits from other entities that have "credits" or unused permits. At first, the system did not work as intended, as national governments bowed to domestic fears and gave away (rather than sold) permits and set the allowances too high. The EU has made adjustments aimed at tightening regulations and significantly reducing carbon emissions in the coming decades, but the cap-and-trade idea has yet to prove itself in practice. The global recession in 2008–2009 raised further questions about how vigorously national governments would push already stressed key industries to invest in cleaner technologies, as has the euro crisis since 2010.

The EU on the World Stage

The Atlantic Community forged after World War II was dominated by the United States, with Western Europe as a junior partner, but the distribution of power today is quite different. Asia and Europe—especially the European Union and China—play a larger role; the former superpowers play a smaller role (in the case of Russia, much smaller). The question is not *whether* the power picture will continue to change, but rather by how much.

Individually, the European countries cannot compete with the United States, China, Japan, and even India. Together, however, they most definitely can, as Europe's single market amply demonstrates. In 2010, only a decade after the euro was launched, the EU accounted for 28–29% of total global GDP, a larger share than either the United States or China. But there remains a huge disparity between Europe's economic power and its political clout on the world stage. To translate its combined economic power into political power, Europe has to speak with one voice in its dealings with the rest of world.

Achieving a Common Foreign and Security Policy (CFSP) has been a declared aim since the early 1990s, but so far the EU has rarely succeeded in presenting a united front to the world. One of the principal goals of the new

THE EURO CRISIS

In December 2009, Greece's credit rating was downgraded by a leading rating agency, plunging the government into a financial crisis. In January 2010, Prime Minister George Papandreou ordered a second round of austerity measures, including public sector pay cuts, fuel increases, and a crackdown on tax evasion. EU leaders promised to help Greece meet its debt obligations but made no concrete pledges. General strikes and protests prompted by the unpopular austerity program continued into March, when Papandreou likened the budget crisis to a "wartime situation" and announced a third round of tax hikes and spending cuts. As the Greek government balanced precariously on the brink of default, the key euro-zone countries stepped up with a $145 billion (€110 billion) rescue package for the country; for its part, the Greek government agreed to still more stringent austerity measures. Trade unions called a general strike in protest.

In August 2010, Greece qualified for the second tranche of the EU/IMF bailout loan, and in October, the Greek government unveiled an even tougher austerity budget for 2010 with new taxes and a higher value-added tax (VAT) rate. Finally, in November the EU and IMF approved the third tranche of rescue funding for Greece.

Greece's financial crisis deepened in 2011 and 2012 as mass protests destabilized the government. Worse, the crisis spread like a contagion to Ireland, Portugal, Spain, and Italy. In 2012, Spain's economy tanked, raising new doubts about the EU's political viability and dire predictions of the euro's impending demise. Mark Twain's fabled quip—"Reports of my death have been greatly exaggerated"—can be aptly applied to the euro. Despite Europe's turbulent economic trials and tribulations of recent years, the euro's value continues to hold up remarkably well, in large part because of Germany's reflexive fear of inflation. (Critics maintain that what the EU's single-market economy needed to recover from the post-2008 global recession was strong stimulus, not austerity.) The fate of the euro (and the global economy) hangs in the balance.

Lisbon Treaty (also known as the Reform Treaty) that came into force in 2009 is to create a strengthened foreign policy post, as well as a more efficacious presidency. The EU has embraced the idea of a European Rapid Reaction Force (ERRF) to intervene where NATO is unable or unwilling to act. Since 2007, some 60,000 soldiers have been committed to a rapid reaction force potentially deployable for one year.

Economic integration has succeeded in Europe because it works. Europe's ever-expanding market creates a space conducive to competition and commerce to flourish. The result is an unprecedented era of peace and prosperity in a part of the world where for many centuries war was endemic. But the impetus for European integration is not solely economic; politics has also played a vital role.

The Politics of Economic Integration

Historically, Europe was a battleground on which autocratic rulers and sadistic tyrants sought power and grandeur through conquest. No longer. Since the advent of the first modest experiment in integration (the ECSC) nearly six

The euro crisis of 2010–2012 highlighted the importance of the European Central Bank (ECB) in restoring the fiscal solvency of dangerously indebted EU governments and, going forward, monitoring the public finances of EU member-states to ensure that the euro remains a viable common currency.

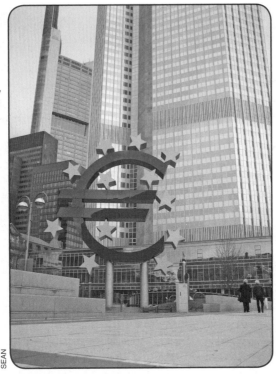

SEAN

decades ago, the ever-wider integrated area of Europe has been a success story, notwithstanding the destabilizing effects and discontents arising from the sovereign debt crisis in recent years.

Nothing succeeds like success. Until the euro crisis cast a shadow over the Single Market Economy, the spotlight was almost always on the EU as an engine of growth and material progress. As such, the EU as the progenitor of the New Europe—a historically war-prone continent at peace most of the time for nearly seven decades now—has often been overlooked. Countries cannot join the EU unless or until they demonstrate a firm commitment to constitutional rule, free elections, and human rights. All member countries are liberal democracies today—a remarkable achievement. No less remarkable is that within the twenty-seven-nation EU, war is now unthinkable. The logic of integration is about perpetuating peace and promoting freedom in Europe, as well as achieving prosperity.

THE UNITED NATIONS

The quest for peace in response to two catastrophic world wars in the first half of the twentieth century led to the birth of the United Nations. But to understand the United Nations, it is necessary to place it in a larger historical context.

Historical Background

Beginning in the nineteenth century, several international peacekeeping federations were founded, usually in the aftermath of increasingly destructive wars. The Holy Alliance, formed in 1815 in the wake of the Napoleonic Wars, represented an attempt by Europe's major powers to control international events by means of meetings and conferences. A more elaborate organization was the League of Nations, set up in 1919 after World War I.

When the Covenant of the League of Nations was sealed in 1919, Wilsonians (followers of Woodrow Wilson) hailed it as the advent of a new age. The League's Assembly was a deliberative body of representatives from each member-state, and all votes carried equal weight. Motions required unanimous approval for passage, so no matter how tiny, every member enjoyed veto power over nearly every decision. The much-smaller Council was made up of four permanent and four non-permanent members who investigated and reported on threats to the peace and proposed or recommended appropriate action to the Assembly. The two bodies were supervised by the Permanent Secretariat, the League's administrative arm.

After defeating Germany in World War I, leaders from the United States, Britain, France, and Italy met at the Paris Peace Conference in 1919 and drafted the Treaty of Versailles. Council of Four at the WWI Paris peace conference, May 27, 1919 (L–R): Prime Minister David Lloyd George, Great Britain; Premier Vittorio Orlando, Italy; French Premier Georges Clemenceau; and President Woodrow Wilson. The treaty imposed harsh terms on Germany and established a League of Nations to prevent future wars.

The League's ambitious aims included, above all, the maintenance of international peace through the promise of swift and certain retribution against aggressor nations—peace and punishment were two sides of the same coin. War, like crime, would not pay. In this respect, the League became the institutional embodiment of President Wilson's desire to replace the traditional balance of power with "a single overwhelming, powerful group of nations who shall be trustees of the peace of the world."[11] The key was to create a system of **collective security** with the combined military forces of all law-abiding nations so formidable that no single challenger would stand a chance against it. The very existence of such a potential force was itself the deterrent.

Despite Wilson's inspired advocacy of the League of Nations, the United States was sidelined because Republicans in the Senate opposed the Treaty of Versailles. The U.S. failure to join the League foreshadowed the organization's future misfortunes. By the early 1930s, conflicting interests and bitter rivalries had resurfaced with a vengeance.

The League was doomed to failure due to several fatal flaws. First, it was supposedly a world organization, but it lacked universal acceptance—both the United States and the upstart Soviet Union were absent, for different reasons. Second, it was procedurally flawed—the requirement for unanimity guaranteed paralysis in a crisis. Third, the collective security measures were triggered by acts of aggression, yet the Charter failed to define *aggression*. Nor would the League's members ever agree on a definition when, for example, Hitler's Germany remilitarized the Rhineland, Italy invaded Ethiopia, Germany threatened (and ultimately invaded) Poland and Czechoslovakia, or Japan embarked on conquest in Asia.

collective security
In international relations, a system designed to prevent war by combining the armed forces of law-abiding and peace-loving nations in a powerful league capable of deterring or defeating any would-be aggressor.

EDWARD N. JACKSON/FOTER.COM

Finally, the success of the League depended, above all, on the United States. World War I had transformed the balance of power from one based in Western Europe to one that was truly global and moved the United States front and center on the world stage.

The Founding of the United Nations

The shocking death toll and terrifying new weapons of World War II sparked renewed efforts to ensure world peace through a powerful international organization. The founders of the United Nations recognized the need for an organizational improvement over the League of Nations. Critics of the League argued the lesser powers had too much clout, the Great Powers too little. And the absence of several Great Powers—particularly the United States—meant the League's mandate was universal in theory but circumscribed in practice.

The founders of the United Nations in 1945 made a major effort to ensure that no potential member would be excluded. The General Assembly was designed as a deliberative body in which all would have an equal voice and an equal vote. More important, the UN Charter created a Security Council entrusted with "primary responsibility for the maintenance of international peace and security" and made up of five permanent members—the United States, the Soviet Union (recently replaced by the Russian Republic), the United Kingdom, France, and China—and ten nonpermanent members. In contrast to the League, the so-called Big Five alone were given the right to veto certain matters, such as the selection of the secretary-general and proposed peacekeeping measures. In the United Nations, the most powerful countries would have responsibilities commensurate with their capabilities.

These responsibilities are spelled out in Chapter 7 of the UN Charter, titled "Action with Respect to Threats to the Peace, Breaches of the Peace, and Acts of Aggression." Article 39 specifies that "the Security Council shall determine the existence of any threat to the peace, breach of the peace, or act of aggression and shall make recommendations, or decide what measure shall be taken in accordance with Articles 40 and 42, to maintain or restore international peace and security." Subsequent articles spell out how the Security Council is expected to discharge its obligations.

Article 41 deals with economic sanctions, including "complete or partial interruption of economic relations and of rail, sea, air, postal, telegraphic, radio, and other means of communication, and the severance of diplomatic relations." Article 42 contemplates situations in which economic sanctions may be inadequate; in such cases, the Security Council "may take action by air, sea, or land forces as may be necessary to maintain or restore international peace and security. Such action may include demonstrations, blockades, and other operations by air, sea, or land forces of Members of the United Nations." Other articles in Chapter 7 of the Charter deal with organizing the military components of a fullfledged collective security system, including the establishment of the Military Staff Committee (Article 47).

The machinery of international peacekeeping outlined by these articles far surpassed that of the League of Nations. Moreover, through its specialized agencies, the United Nations plays an important role in worldwide disaster relief, resettlement of refugees, technical assistance in food and agriculture, health concerns, and many other areas. It actively promotes a higher world standard of living through the Economic and Social Council (ECOSOC) and the United Nations International Children's Emergency Fund (UNICEF). Finally, financial and developmental assistance has been extended to economically troubled states through the World Bank, the International Monetary Fund, and the United Nations Conference on Trade and Development (UNCTAD). The variety of specialized agencies makes clear that the United Nations was committed from the outset to promoting world welfare, as well as preventing world war.

However, the UN Charter was not designed as a blueprint for a world government. Article 2, paragraph 7, of the Charter puts matters "essentially within the domestic jurisdiction of any state" beyond the purview of UN authority. Article 2 states unequivocally that the United Nations "is based on the principle of sovereign equality of all its members."

Nevertheless, other provisions of the Charter give greater weight to the most powerful or most prominent member-states. The most obvious reason is the need to guarantee their participation. But there was another, subtler reason: Some of the United Nation's original supporters viewed the new international organization as the forerunner of a world government in which the larger states would have to play a greater role than the smaller. Thus, the contradictions in the Charter mirror the mix of realism and idealism present at the UN's creation; for the "one-world" idealists, they also represented the compromises of the past necessary to pave the way for the future.

The United Nations during the Cold War

The United Nations faced problems not unlike those that destroyed the League of Nations. A world government capable of keeping the peace implied nothing less than a wholesale forfeiture of state sovereignty. Anything short of a world government would leave the UN unable to punish an aggressor or preserve the peace unless all the Great Powers—at a minimum the five permanent Security Council members—were in complete accord.

On one hand, the Charter obligates member-states to act in accordance with the rule of law and empowers the Security Council to punish states when they do not; on the other hand, it provides a number of loopholes and escape clauses for states that wish to evade or ignore their obligations. Article 51, for example, states, "Nothing in the present Charter shall impair the inherent right of individual or collective self-defense." Such a provision invites aggression as long as "self-defense" is a lawful justification to resort to force and individual states are free to define as self-defense any action they deem in their national interest. The dilemma is obvious: without escape clauses such as Article 51, the UN Charter would not have been acceptable; with them, it may not be enforceable.

Another problem plaguing the world body until recently was the persistent state of tension between the United States and the Soviet Union, which seriously hampered the workings of the United Nations during the Cold War. Because each superpower maintained a coalition of allies, followers, and admirers that at one time or another held the majority in the General Assembly, deadlock became the hallmark of most UN deliberations. The consensus necessary to promote peace through collective security was also absent at many critical junctures; when the Soviet Union did not veto a controversial measure, the United States often did. Despite these difficulties, the United Nations has contributed valuable, if limited, efforts toward peace by sending mediators, truce supervision teams, and quasi-military forces to various parts of the world, including the Congo, Cyprus, the Middle East, and the Balkans.

The United Nations after the Cold War

The mid- to late 1980s saw an unprecedented period of cooperation among the five permanent members of the Security Council, particularly between the United States and the Soviet Union. The catalyst was the Soviet Union's new conciliatory foreign policy, initiated by Mikhail Gorbachev. This era of increased cooperation produced two significant results. First, the United Nations embraced a particularly vigorous approach to international peacekeeping, sometimes bordering on peacemaking (see "Maps That Matter: UN Peacekeeping Operations").[12] Second, it sanctioned collective military action against Iraq after it invaded Kuwait.

Peacekeeping Operations Recent UN peacekeeping efforts have encompassed a wide array of tasks, some unprecedented. A mere fifty observers helped facilitate the Soviet Union's withdrawal from Afghanistan in 1988, whereas peacekeeping forces from 109 nations helped secure peace and independence for Namibia in 1989 by creating the conditions for elections and securing the repeal of discriminatory and restrictive legislation, the release of prisoners, and the return of exiles.

Starting in 1991, the UN fielded major peacekeeping operations in El Salvador and Cambodia. In Cambodia, for example, the UN demobilized the various armies, repatriated 350,000 refugees, and organized elections. In 1993, the UN dispatched nearly 40,000 peacekeepers to the former Yugoslavia. The presence of this force, combined with NATO military support and UN-sponsored sanctions, induced Serbian President Slobodan Milosevic to negotiate in good faith and helped bring about the U.S.-brokered peace settlement known as the Dayton Accords in 1995. Later Milosevic was defeated in national elections and a popular groundswell developed when he tried to cancel the results; the United Nations was instrumental in bringing the brutal former president and other accused war criminals in Yugoslavia to justice.

During the 1990s, the United Nations launched peacekeeping operations in Kosovo (Yugoslavia), Sierra Leone (West Africa), East Timor (formerly part of Indonesia), the Congo (central Africa), and Ethiopia and Eritrea (the horn of Africa). Such missions are never risk free, and they come with no guarantee of success. UN troops sent to Somalia in 1992 to facilitate the safe distribution of food to starving people were attacked by rebels who viewed the UN as a cat's paw for the West.

UN peacekeepers generally try to avoid combat but have suffered many casualties over the years, including some 2,591 fatalities (as of mid-2009)

UN PEACEKEEPING OPERATIONS

The presence of peacekeeping forces around the globe testifies to the United Nations' enhanced post–Cold War role. A total of sixty-seven such operations were launched between 1948 and 2012, more than three-fourths of them since the end of the Cold War.

At the end of 2012, more than 96,300 UN uniformed personnel from 115 countries were engaged in sixteen peacekeeping operations on four continents. The United Nations does not have its own military forces but relies on contributions from member-states.

FIGURE 18.1   UN Map.

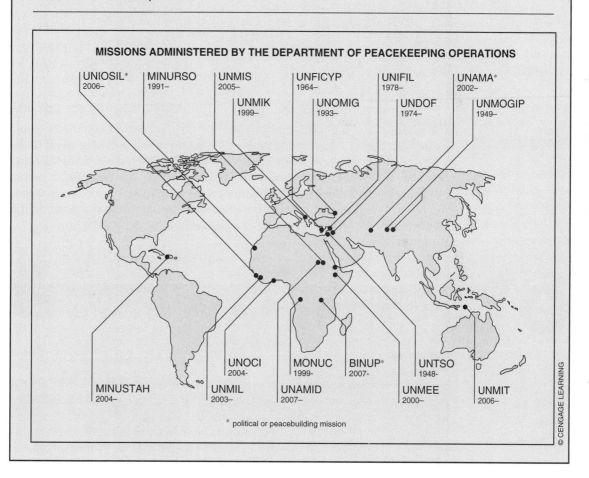

since 1948. Peacekeeping in Lebanon (244 fatalities) and Cyprus (170 fatalities) has been particularly hazardous, and the UN presence has become a permanent fixture. Of the ten peacekeeping operations launched in the 1990s, most incurred fewer than 15 fatalities; however, 46 members of the UN mission in Sierra Leone (UNAMSIL) were killed there; and in August 2003, terrorists destroyed the UN headquarters in Baghdad, killing 17 people, including Sergio Vieira de Mello, the head of the UN mission in Iraq (see Chapter 15). The worst year for UN peacekeeping fatalities was 2010 the place was Haiti. The cause was not conflict but rather a devastating earthquake that took the lives of more than 222,000 (including 100 UN peacekeepers), injured more than 300,000, and displaced 1.3 million people. In the half-century between 1948 and 1999, just over 1,600 UN military personnel were killed in action, compared to nearly 1,400 between 1999 and 2012.

UN peacekeeping actions come with no guarantees. In the former Yugoslavia, the UN's best efforts to promote a cease-fire were overwhelmed by fighting and became effective only after NATO airstrikes and ground support were brought to bear. In the end, the Serbian army was defeated and President Milosevic was forced to negotiate. One of the lessons of Bosnia and Kosovo is that UN peacekeeping efforts are unlikely to succeed without the military backing of major member-states and regional military alliances such as NATO. Experience makes a strong case for the creation of new regional military groups to act as the law-enforcement apparatus of the United Nations.

Some UN peacekeeping operations have become permanent fixtures without leading to a final settlement—Kashmir, Cyprus, and Lebanon are prime examples. These missions stretch the UN budget to the breaking point. Even so, the cost of UN peacekeeping is tiny measured against national defense budgets or the cost of a major war. The war in Iraq, for example, has cost the United States more than $3 trillion, according to one authoritative estimate.[13] By comparison, the cost of a peacekeeping operation is a real bargain (see "Ideas and Politics: Peace on the Cheap").

IDEAS AND POLITICS

PEACE ON THE CHEAP: Too Good to Be True?

According to the United Nations, UN peace operations are less expensive than other forms of international interventions, and costs are shared more equitably among UN member-states:

- A survey by Oxford University economists found that international military intervention under Chapter VII of the UN Charter is the most cost-effective means of reducing the risk of conflict in post-conflict societies.
- The approved peacekeeping budget for the period July 1, 2012, to June 30, 2013, was approximately US$7.23 billion. This represents about 0.5% of global military spending (estimated at US$1.6 trillion for 2010).
- A study by the U.S. Government Accounting Office estimated that it would cost the United States about twice as much as the UN to conduct a peacekeeping operation similar to the UN Stabilization Mission in Haiti (MINUSTAH)—$876 million compared to the UN budgeted $428 million for the first fourteen months of the mission.

SOURCE: United Nations, "Peacekeeping Fact Sheet," http://www.un.org/en/peacekeeping/resources/statistics/factsheet.shtml.

Collective Military Action In August 1990, when Iraq invaded Kuwait, the United Nations responded by authorizing collective military action. This use of force recalled Woodrow Wilson's failed dream of collective security under the League of Nations flag and an early attempt at collective military action under the auspices of the UN.

In June 1950, when North Korea invaded South Korea, the United Nations at the urging of the United States responded with military force. As a permanent member of the Security Council, the Soviet Union was in a position to block this action. But the United States avoided a Soviet veto by taking the matter to the General Assembly (in the form of the "Uniting for Peace" resolution) where it enjoyed an automatic majority. Although the UN flag was raised, the Korean conflict was in truth a war fought by the United States against North Korea and, later, the People's Republic of China. The supreme commander, General Douglas MacArthur, was responsible to the president of the United States, not to the secretary-general of the United Nations.

It would be four decades before the United Nations was again used in building an international coalition against an aggressor, for during the Cold War each superpower vetoed enforcement actions proposed by the other. In 1990–1991, when the United States (backed by the British) launched Operation Desert Storm against Iraq, the Security Council became a forum for the major powers to consult on how to respond to Iraqi aggression. The Council backed resolutions condemning Iraq, establishing tough economic sanctions, and ultimately approving the use of force to expel the Iraqi army from Kuwait. After the Gulf War's end, UN inspectors were allowed access to sites in Iraq suspected of hiding biological, chemical, or nuclear weapons. Iraq later would dispute the terms of these inspections, leading the United States to threaten to bomb (an action at least temporarily avoided by the successful diplomatic efforts of then Secretary-General Kofi Annan).

What the United Nations did *not* do before and during the 1990–1991 Gulf War is equally important, however. The United Nations did not provide any forces of its own, and the secretary-general had no control over how the coalition forces were deployed or employed. There was no UN general staff, nor did the United Nations coordinate the military or diplomatic operations undertaken by coalition members (principally the United States and Great Britain). Nor did the United Nations provide any funding. The war was financed in large part by contributions from the United States' richest allies, including Japan, Germany, Kuwait, and Saudi Arabia.

The 1990–1991 Gulf War was a broad-based coalition forged by the United States with the imprimatur of the United Nations. In 2003, however, the exact opposite was true: the United States invaded Iraq without the authorization of the Security Council and in the face of overwhelming opposition in the General Assembly.

The United Nations and the Iraq War In the fall of 2002, the UN Security Council passed Resolution 1441 requiring Iraq to disarm and allow weapons inspections or face "serious consequences." Though Iraq's ruler, Saddam Hussein, had evicted UN weapons inspectors in 1998, he acquiesced under heavy international pressure and a massive U.S. military buildup in the Persian Gulf.

UN weapons inspectors visited 300 sites in December 2002 and January 2003. They found no weapons of mass destruction or weapons laboratories, but the Bush administration claimed to have evidence to the contrary.

The UN Security Council was strongly against an immediate invasion. In opposing a rush to war, France and Germany, the United States' longtime NATO allies, took the lead. Russia and China, both permanent members of the Security Council (like France), also demurred. U.S. polls showed that the public was ambivalent and self-contradictory: a majority favored U.S. action to oust Saddam from power, but an even larger majority agreed the UN Security Council "should make the final decision regarding the disarmament of Iraq." If the United Nations did not approve the action, the United States should stay out.[14]

Secretary of State Colin Powell presented the Security Council with what he claimed was clear proof—secret intelligence—that Iraq had WMDs. But the Security Council was not swayed. President Bush decided to act without UN approval, asserting that postponing military action would only play into Saddam's hands. In the months that followed, relations between the United States and the United Nations plunged to their lowest (as did transatlantic relations). Hawks suggested the United Nations was irrelevant or worse and that the United States was wise to ignore it.

The outcome of the invasion was never in doubt: The United States had overwhelming military superiority and was banking on a quick war with a happy ending—one that would rid the Iraqi people of a sadistic ruler and lead directly to a flourishing democracy. The outcome of the occupation, however, was a different matter.

Urban guerrilla warfare plagued the occupation forces, kept Iraqi society in a constant state of turmoil, and proved an albatross for the United States. Those who remembered the lessons of Vietnam fed a rising tide of doubts about the war. In the 2004 and 2008 presidential elections, foreign policy—in particular, the growing human and financial cost of the war—was a major issue. In the 2008 Democratic primary, it pitted Hillary Clinton, who had supported the decision to invade Iraq, against Barack Obama, who had opposed it and campaigned on a promise to end U.S. military involvement there.

Is the United Nations Irrelevant? It has been said that if the United Nations did not exist, it would have to be invented. One thing is clear: In many conflict-ridden parts of the world, the United Nations is *not* irrelevant. Ironically, although the United States played the leading role in creating it, it has had to rediscover this truth repeatedly in the past half-century—occasionally in a maelstrom of its own making.

The Limits of International Organization

Despite its successes, the United Nations has not lived up to all the expectations of its founders, and some problems resemble those of the League that the UN sought to overcome. Procedural difficulties, however, are often rooted in deep-seated political differences.

jurisdiction in advance, as Article 36 invites them to do, or they may simply choose to submit certain cases on an ad hoc basis.

In the first twenty years of the World Court's existence, forty-two governments declared their intent to accept its compulsory jurisdiction. But declarations are not deeds, especially when they involve sovereign states, and appearances can be deceiving. The U.S. "acceptance" of Article 36 in 1946 is a case in point. It was, in fact, a diplomatic sleight of hand. It states, in part:

> This declaration shall not apply to: a. disputes the solution of which the parties shall entrust to other tribunals by virtue of agreements already in existence or which may be concluded in the future; or b. disputes with regard to matters which are essentially within the domestic jurisdiction of the United States of America as determined by the United States of America; or c. disputes arising under a multinational treaty, unless (1) all parties to the treaty affected by the decision are also parties to the case before the Court, or (2) the United States of America especially agrees to jurisdiction.

Together, these qualifications meant the U.S. government agreed to compulsory jurisdiction only on the condition that the agreement did not compel it to accept the Court's jurisdiction. But the United States' qualified acceptance was not unique. No government in the contemporary world has agreed unconditionally to commit itself to abide by the rulings of the World Court.

The United States and the World Court What would prevent the United States and, say, Great Britain from setting a positive example by promising to submit all future disputes between them to the compulsory jurisdiction of the World Court? At least on the surface, nothing. But even if it were possible, why would it be necessary? For more than a century, the United States and Great Britain have had very few disputes requiring protracted negotiations. Any they might have in the foreseeable future are likely to be minor—close allies seldom face differences that require adjudication. Obviously, we cannot judge the effects of compulsory jurisdiction accurately when two governments are on such amicable terms and *voluntarily* turn minor differences over to the jurisdiction of an international tribunal anyway.

The World Court's utility was tested in the 1980s in the confrontation between Nicaragua's former Marxist (Sandinista) regime and the Reagan administration. In early 1985, Nicaragua filed suit against the United States in the World Court, charging Washington with aggression for mining the harbor at Corinto and supporting the Contra rebels. The United States promptly boycotted the proceedings and suspended bilateral talks on the grounds Nicaragua was using the Court for political and propaganda purposes.

In June 1986, the World Court ruled decisively against the United States in the case. At Nicaragua's initiative, the Security Council voted 11 to 1 to support the World Court's decision (with the United Kingdom, France, and Thailand abstaining.) Unfortunately, as this controversial case illustrates, the problem with compulsory jurisdiction, as with international law in general, is that it is least effective when it is most necessary.

In February 1998, the World Court again ruled against the United States in a high-profile dispute that stemmed from the 1988 terrorist bombing of Pan Am

Flight 103 over Lockerbie, Scotland, in which 270 people died (including 11 on the ground). In 1992, the United States and Great Britain led a successful fight for UN sanctions against Libya when its government refused to extradite two Libyan nationals suspected of perpetrating this attack. The Libyan government took the dispute to the World Court for relief, but the United States argued, unsuccessfully, that the Court lacked jurisdiction. The case is now moot, as the United States and the international community officially rehabilitated Libya after its leader, Muammar Qaddafi, surrendered two suspects in the 1988 Pan Am bombing and denounced terrorism in the late 1990s.

International Law: Who Cares?

Some nations infrequently break the precepts of international law; others obey them only as a matter of expedience. In either case, that nations *can* refuse to be bound means international law will be uniformly followed only when it is in the national interest of all governments to do so. In other words, respect for international law ultimately depends on national self-interest.

Are principles of justice unimportant in international politics? Not exactly. They are of great value in understanding and evaluating the actions of governments and rulers. At times, governments can be punished (for example, through sanctions, as Iraq, Iran, Libya, and North Korea have discovered). Rogue rulers can also be punished, as the trial of former Yugoslav President Slobodan Milosevic in 2003–2004 illustrates.

The first principle of international political life is national self-preservation. International law is most effective when it serves the interests of rich and powerful nations. At such times, the machinery of international peace and justice is likely to spring into action. However, the major powers still prefer to seek traditional political and military solutions (where they have greater control over the outcomes) rather than judicial remedies (where they relinquish control to judges whose allegiances are unknown and unknowable).

THE QUEST FOR A PERPETUAL PEACE

In 2001, the United Nations and Secretary-General Kofi Annan were awarded the Nobel Peace Prize for working toward a more peaceful world. It was a fitting tribute to the individual and the organization he served so well.

Wherever there was conflict or a humanitarian crisis, the UN was called upon. President Bill Clinton renounced unilateralism and made it a rule to seek UN approval before resorting to military force. The prestige of the UN was at an all-time high.

After the Cold War, with the superpower rivalry a thing of the past, the United Nations momentarily blossomed. Although balance of power politics and nuclear deterrence forged a relatively stable system of order after 1945, the end of the Cold War gave rise not only to new opportunities for order building, but also to new dangers and sources of instability.

In the wake of 9/11, the Bush administration sought UN support in the fight against terrorism. The U.S.-led military action against Afghanistan's Taliban regime was undertaken with the United Nation's blessing and the full cooperation of the international community. But subsequently, when the United Nations did not share Washington's enthusiasm for invading Iraq, U.S. foreign policy veered toward unilateralism, ignoring the wishes of the United States' NATO allies and the United Nations.

Exhibit at Disneyland in Hong Kong.

IRENE CHU HAMPSON

International law and organizations are not likely to replace diplomacy and war (or the threat of war) as the usual means by which nation-states resolve most disputes. Nor is respect for international law or the sanctity of treaties likely to increase enough so that countervailing force is no longer our chief means of preventing or limiting war.

International organizations can play a vital role in conflict management, but there is no silver bullet that will resolve the problem of conflict once and for all. No amount of goodwill or enlightened statesmanship can usher in a world without war. Ending the ideological rivalry between the world's most powerful states was a significant step toward a safer and saner world, but as the rise of international terrorism shows, it did not guarantee perpetual peace.

Politics has been called the art of the possible. Ending conflict is not possible. But reducing the tensions, prejudices, and injustices that often lead to it is a goal worth pursuing.

SUMMARY

To what extent have international organizations and international law contributed to a more peaceful world? The removal of national barriers to trade, travel, and transfers of all kinds is reflected by the great increase in nonstate actors in the modern world, including multinational corporations, international governmental organizations, and international nongovernmental organizations. Multinational economic pacts and military alliances have also enhanced regional or worldwide interdependence.

This impressive network of international organizations and international pacts has not been free of national rivalries, however. And comprehensive international organizations have proved no more successful in bringing long-lasting peace and stability to the international arena. In the twentieth century, the League of Nations was torn apart by conflicting national interests. During the Cold War that lasted from the early post–World War II period until the collapse of the Soviet Union in 1991, the United Nations encountered many obstacles, although it had modest success as a peacekeeping institution. Peacekeeping activity expanded in the post–Cold War era, when the United Nations authorized collective military action in the Persian Gulf (Iraq), the Horn of Africa (Somalia), the Balkans (Bosnia and Kosovo), West Africa (Sierra Leone and Liberia), and Central Asia (Afghanistan), among others. However, the United Nations refused to back the U.S.-led invasion of Iraq in 2003.

International law facilitates and regulates relations among sovereign and independent states whose interactions might otherwise be chaotic. In general, it has had a checkered history. Modern-day examples of international law include the Geneva and Hague Conventions, which set rules for warfare, and the multilateral arms limitations treaties. International environmental agreements, such as the 1997 Kyoto Protocol, are becoming an increasingly important part of international law.

The limitations of international law are starkly apparent in the difficulties encountered by the World Court. The United Nations is similarly constrained by its inability to act against the wishes of the major powers, especially the five permanent members of the Security Council.

KEY TERMS

functionalism   507
nonstate actor   507
multinational corporation (MNC)   508
Organization of Petroleum Exporting Countries (OPEC)   509
international nongovernmental organization (INGO)   510
international governmental organization (IGO)   510

interdependence   510
North Atlantic Treaty Organization (NATO)   511
European Union (EU)   514
qualified majority voting   514
co-decision   514
Common Agricultural Policy (CAP)   515
Schengen area   516
Emissions Trading Scheme (ETS)   516
collective security   519
international law   530

Geneva Convention   531
Hague Convention   531
Strategic Arms Reduction Treaty II (START II)   534
Antarctic Treaty   534
Outer Space Treaty   534
Nonproliferation Treaty   534
Seabed Treaty   534
Biological Weapons Convention   534
Chemical Weapons Convention   534
World Court   536

REVIEW QUESTIONS

1. Who are the most important nonstate actors in international politics? What impact have they had on the international system?
2. What prompted the founding of the United Nations? How successful are its peacekeeping operations?
3. Does international law serve a useful purpose in contemporary international relations? If not, why? If so, in what ways?
4. What are the limitations of international law? How effectively has the World Court functioned? What suggestions for improvement present themselves?

Chapter 1

1. See Joseph Nye, *The Paradox of American Power: Why the World's Only Superpower Can't Go It Alone* (London: Oxford University Press, 2002). This quote is from Nye's article, "The New Rome Meets the New Barbarians," *The Economist,* March 23, 2002, p. 24.

2. Baron de Montesquieu's classification of political governments in Book II of *The Spirit of the Laws* has proved most influential. Montesquieu distinguished among republics, monarchies, and despotic governments, further subdividing democratic republics, ruled by the whole people, from aristocratic republics, ruled by part of the people (specifically, by the wealthy class). Republics also have been historically distinguished from direct democracies. Thus, James Madison (perhaps the leading U.S. Founder) called governments in which the people directly participated in their own governing and did not rely on representation *direct democracies*. Because the U.S. government provides for representation, it is called a *republic*.

3. See, for example, Arthur Schlesinger Jr., *The Disuniting of America* (New York: Norton, 1993).

4. Aristotle, *The Politics,* trans. and ed. Ernest Barker (New York: Oxford University Press, 1962), p. 4.

5. Irving Kristol, "The Nature of Nazism," in *The Commentary Reader,* ed. Norman Podhoretz (New York: Atheneum, 1965), p. 16.

6. Hannah Arendt, *Eichmann in Jerusalem: A Report on the Banality of Evil* (New York: Penguin Books, 1964). Compare Gideon Hausner, *Justice in Jerusalem* (New York: Schocken Books, 1968), p. 465.

7. As opposed to Plato, who is sometimes classified as the first political philosopher.

8. Jack H. Nagel and John E. McNulty, "Partisan Effects of Voter Turnout in Senatorial and Gubernatorial Elections," *American Political Science Review* 90 (December 1996): 780–793.

9. See Leo Strauss, *What Is Political Philosophy? and Other Studies* (New York: Free Press, 1959), pp. 10–12.

10. There are variations to this approach; for instance, traditional realist theory has been updated (but not without controversy) by political scientists referred to as neorealists or *structural realists*. A leading work here is Kenneth Waltz, *Theory of International Politics* (Reading, MA: Addison-Wesley, 1979). Also see his "Realist Thought and Neo-Realist Theory," *Journal of International Affairs* 44 (Spring/Summer 1990): 21–37.

11. For a scholarly attempt to reconcile the two approaches, see Robert O. Keohane, *International Institutions and State Power* (Boulder, CO: Westview Press, 1989). Keohane's theory is sometimes referred to as *neoliberal institutionalism*.

12. See Robert Guest, "The few" [A special report on global leaders], *The Economist,* January 22, 2011, pp. 3–20.

Chapter 2

1. Aristotle, *The Politics,* trans. and ed. Ernest Barker (New York: Oxford University Press, 1962), 1279a, p. 112.

2. This discussion builds on Andrew Heywood, *Political Ideologies: An Introduction* (New York: St. Martin's Press, 1992), pp. 6–8. Heywood's (and our) discussion, in turn, builds on a definition offered in May Selinger, *Politics and Ideology* (London: Allen & Unwin, 1976).

3. The Anti-Defamation League of B'nai B'rith, *Hate Groups in America: A Record of Bigotry and Violence* (New York, n.d.), p. 11.

4. See, for example, Diana B. Henriques, "As Exemptions Grow, Religion Outweighs Regulation," *New York Times,* October 6, 2006 (electronic edition).

5. Jack C. Plano and Roy Olton, *The International Relations Dictionary* (Santa Barbara, CA: ABC, 1982), p. 81.
6. Bertrand Russell, *A History of Western Philosophy* (New York: Simon & Schuster, 1965), p. 364.
7. Martin Diamond, Winston Fisk, and Herbert Garfinkel, *The Democratic Republic: An Introduction to American Government* (Skokie, IL: Rand McNally, 1971), pp. 4–5.
8. Baron de Montesquieu, *The Spirit of the Laws,* trans. Thomas Nugent (New York: Hafner Press, 1949), bk. 5, chap. 6, p. 46.
9. Adam Smith, *An Inquiry into the Nature and Causes of the Wealth of Nations* (New York: Modern Library, 1965), p. 14.
10. As is pointed out in Robert Heilbroner, *The Worldly Philosophers: The Lives, Times, and Ideas of the Great Economic Thinkers* (New York: Modern Library, 1965), p. 14.
11. See "A Heavyweight Champ, at Five Foot Two," *The Economist,* November 25, 2006, p. 29.
12. John Stuart Mill, *On Liberty* (Lake Bluff, IL: Regnery/Gateway, 1955), p. 85.
13. Fareed Zakaria, "How Today's Conservatives Lost Touch with Reality," *Time,* June 16, 2011, accessed online at http://www.time.com/time/nation/article/0,8599,2077943,00.html.
14. James Davison Hunter, *Culture Wars: The Struggle to Define America* (New York: Basic Books, 1991). The discussion here generally follows, but does not duplicate, Hunter's. See also John Kenneth White, *The Values Divide: American Politics and Culture in Transition* (New York: Chatham House, 2003).
15. Ibid. As Hunter makes clear, members of the same faith often strongly disagree on these issues.
16. See, for example, Marc Ambinder, "A Nation of Free Agents," *Washington Post,* September 3, 2006 (electronic edition): "Independent voters comprise about 10 percent of the electorate, but the percentage of persuadable independents has shot up to about 30 percent. In the 27 states that register voters by party, self-declared independents grew from 8 percent of the registered electorate in 1987 to 24 percent in 2004, according to political analyst Rhodes Cook. Consistently, about 30 percent of U.S. voters tell pollsters they don't belong to a party."

Chapter 3

1. See Leo Strauss, *What Is Political Philosophy? and Other Studies* (New York: Free Press, 1959), p. 10.
2. From Robert Dale Owen's personal account titled "My Experience of Community Life," *The Atlantic Monthly,* September, 1873, vol. 32, p. 343.
3. Allan Bloom, "Interpretive Essay," in *The Republic of Plato,* trans. Allan Bloom (New York: Basic Books, 1968), pp. 308–310.
4. Plato's ideal political order is most accurately translated as "city." The Greek word *polis* implies a small, self-sufficient community that provides for all human relationships. Modern distinctions between, for example, society and government or church and state are quite foreign to this concept.
5. Bloom, *The Republic of Plato,* p. 410.
6. Ibid.
7. Howard White, *Peace Among the Willows: The Political Philosophy of Francis Bacon* (The Hague: Martinus Nijhoff, 1968), pp. 97, 102.
8. Karl Marx, "Capital: Selections," in *The Marx-Engels Reader,* ed. Robert C. Tucker (New York: Norton, 1972), p. 259.
9. Karl Marx and Friedrich Engels, "Manifesto of the Communist Party," in *The Marx-Engels Reader,* p. 352.
10. Friedrich Engels, "Socialism: Utopian and Scientific," in *The Marx-Engels Reader,* p. 635.
11. Karl Marx, "Outlines of a Future Society, from 'The Germany Ideology,'" in *Capital, Communist Manifesto, and Other Writings,* ed. Max Eastman (New York: Modern Library, 1932), p. 1.
12. Ibid.

13. Joseph Cropsey, "Karl Marx," in *History of Political Philosophy*, eds. Leo Strauss and Joseph Cropsey (Skokie, IL: Rand McNally, 1969), p. 717.

14. Jerome Gilison, *The Soviet Image of Utopia* (Baltimore, MD: Johns Hopkins University Press, 1975), p. 110.

15. Roy Macrides, *Contemporary Political Ideologies* (Cambridge, MA: Winthrop, 1980), p. 180.

16. B. F. Skinner, *Walden Two* (New York: Macmillan, 1962), p. 159.

17. Ibid., p. 161.

18. Ibid., pp. 104–105.

19. Ibid., p. 262.

20. Ibid., p. 193.

21. Ibid., p. 272.

22. Ibid., p. 295.

23. Josiah Warren, The Quarterly Letter: Devoted to Showing the Practical Applications and Progress of Equity.... Vol. 1, No. 1 (dated October, 1867) at http://www.crispinsartwell.com/warrennarrative.htm.

24. Anthony Burgess, "The Clockwork Condition," *The New Yorker*, June 4 & 11, 2012, p. 70. The quote at the beginning of this section can be found on p. 74.

25. Ibid., pp. 69–76. The quotes in this paragraph and the next are on p. 71.

26. Ibid., p. 73.

27. Paul Berman, "Terror and Liberalism," *The American Prospect*, October 22, 2001.

28. See, for example, the writings of Daniel Pipes, especially *The Hidden Hand: Middle East Theories of Conspiracy* (New York: Free Press, 1997) and *Conspiracy: How the Paranoid Style Flourishes and Where It Comes From* (New York: Free Press, 1998); see also Fouad Ajami, *The Dream Palace of the Arabs: A Generation's Odyssey* (New York: Pantheon, 1998).

Chapter 4

1. See David Held, *Models of Democracy* (Stanford, CA: Polity and Stanford University Press, 1996) and David Held, *Democracy and the Global Order: From the Modern State to Cosmopolitan Governance* (Stanford, CA: Polity and Stanford University Press, 1995).

2. Richard S. Katz, "Models of Democracy: Elite Attitudes and the Democratic Deficit in the European Union." Unpublished paper presented at a meeting of the European Consortium of Political Research, Copenhagen, April 2000.

3. Alexander Hamilton, John Jay, and James Madison, *The Federalist* no. 31 (New York: Modern Library, 1964), p. 190.

4. Ibid., no. 31, pp. 226–227.

5. Ibid., no. 49, p. 329.

6. Martin Diamond, Winston Fisk, and Herbert Garfinkel, *The Democratic Republic: An Introduction to American National Government* (Skokie, IL: Rand McNally, 1970), p. 136.

7. Stephen Cahn, *Education and the Democratic Ideal* (Chicago: Nelson-Hall, 1979), p. 3.

8. Alexis de Tocqueville, *Democracy in America*, vol. 1 (New York: Schocken Books, 1961), pp. 299–300.

9. Ibid., p. 301.

10. Jay Hamilton and James Madison, *The Federalist*, no. 9, pp. 48–49.

11. Ibid., no. 10, p. 57.

12. Ibid., no. 51, p. 337.

13. Ibid.

14. Ibid.

15. Ibid., no. 6, p. 27.

16. Ibid., no. 51, p. 37.

17. G. Ross Stephens, "Federal Malignancies," unpublished paper, March 15, 2009; see also Malcolm M. Freeley and Edward Rubin, *Federalism: Political Identity and Tragic Compromise* (Ann Arbor, MI: University of Michigan Press, 2008); and David Cay Johnston, *Free Lunch* (New York, NY: Portfolio, Penguin Books, Ltd., 2007).

18. However, federalism does not protect individuals from abuse by state or local government, which the African American experience in various southern states well illustrates.
19. Diamond, Fisk, and Garfinkel, *The Democratic Republic,* p. 136.
20. Tocqueville, *Democracy in America,* pp. 304–398.
21. Aristotle, *The Politics,* trans. and ed. Ernest Barker (New York: Oxford University Press, 1962), 1287a, p. 146.
22. John Locke, *Second Treatise on Civil Government* (New York: New American Library, 1965), sec. 202, p. 448.
23. 8 Co. Rep. 114a (1610).
24. See *Youngstown Sheet and Tube Company v. Sawyer,* 343 U.S. 579 (1952), especially the concurring opinion of Justice Jackson.
25. William E. Hudson, *American Democracy in Peril: Eight Challenges to America's Future,* 4th ed. (Chatham, NJ: Chatham House, 2003).
26. Ibid., pp. 10–12.
27. David Held, *Democracy and the Global Order* (Stanford, CA: Stanford University Press, 1996).
28. See, for example, George Ross, "The European Union and the Future of European Politics," in Mark Kesselman and Joel Krieger, et. al., *European Politics in Transition,* 4th ed. (New York: Houghton-Mifflin Company, 2002).

Chapter 5

1. Bernard Crick, *Basic Forms of Government: A Sketch and a Model* (London: Macmillan, 1980), p. 53.
2. See Robert Kaplan, *The Coming Anarchy: Shattering the Dreams of the Post Cold War* (New York: Vintage Books, 2000), pp. 3–7. The article was later bundled with several other articles by the same author and reprinted in this highly readable little volume.
3. Aristotle, *The Politics,* trans. and ed. Ernest Barker (New York: Oxford University Press, 1962), 1279a, p. 112.
4. China's success prompted India to try setting up its own version of SEZs. See Bruce Einhorn, "India Struggles to Copy China's SEZs," Eye on Asia blog, *BusinessWeek,* posted on October 9, 2006, at http://www.businessweek.com/globalbiz/blog/eyeonasia/archives/2006/10/india_struggles.html. India announced its intent to create SEZs in 2000. For more information on SEZs in India go to http://www.sezindia.nic.in/index.asp.
5. A. Doak Barnett, "Ten Years After Mao," *Foreign Affairs* (Summer 1986), p. 38.
6. China's military spending grew from $30 billion in 2000 to $120 billion in 2010 according to SIPRI (a Stockholm-based research institute). Beijing announced a big double-digit increase for 2012. See, for example, Edward Carr, "Brushwood and Gall" (A special report on China's place in the world), *The Economist,* December 4, 2010; see also, "The Dragon's Teeth: A Rare Look inside the World's Biggest Military Expansion," *The Economist,* April 7, 2012, pp. 27–32.
7. "Deng's China," *The Economist,* February 22, 1997, p. 21.
8. "Privatization in China," *The Economist,* September 23, 2011, online edition at http://www.economist.com/node/21528262.
9. "Suddenly Vulnerable," *The Economist,* December 13, 2008, p. 15.
10. "China Learns the World's Rule," *The World in 2001* (London: The Economist Newspaper Limited, 2000), pp. 85–86.
11. P. Ferdinand, "Social Change and the Chinese Communist Party: Domestic Problems of Rule," *Journal of International Affairs,* 49 (2) (Winter 1996); pp. 478–483.
12. See, for example, "The Dragon's Teeth: A Rare Look inside the World's Biggest Military Expansion," *The Economist,* April 7, 2012, pp. 27–32.
13. Speech by Secretary of Defense Robert Gates at the Air Force Association Convention, September 16, 2009. Gates repeated this warning in mid-January 2011 during an official visit to Japan. The speech was widely reported in the press. Online at http://www.defense.gov/speeches/speech.aspx?speechid=1379.

14. Jane Perlez, "As Dispute over Islands Escalates, Japan and China Send Fighter Jets to Scene," *New York Times*, January 18, 2013. Accessed online at http://www.nytimes.com/2013/01/19/world/asia/china-japan-island-dispute-escalates-to-air.html?pagewanted=1.

15. "That's right Iceman, I am dangerous," *The Economist*, November 14, 2011, p. 53.

16. Aristotle, *The Politics*, 1313b, p. 245; see also, John Dunn, *Democracy: A History* (New York: Atlantic Monthly Press, 2006).

17. Maurice Latey, *Patterns of Tyranny* (New York: Atheneum, 1969), p. 115.

18. Fyodor Dostoyevsky, *The Brothers Karamazov*, ed. Ernest Rhys (London: Dent, 1927), p. 259.

19. Crick, *Basic Forms of Government*, p. 35.

20. See Karl Wittfogel, *Oriental Despotism: A Comparative Study of Total Power* (New York: Random House, 1981).

21. Crick, *Basic Forms of Government*, p. 36.

22. Samuel P. Huntington, "How Countries Democratize," *Political Science Quarterly* 106, no. 4 (1991–1992): 579.

23. Robert M. Press, "Africa's Struggle for Democracy," *Christian Science Monitor*, March 21, 1991, p. 4.

24. "Russia Deserves Pity as Well as Fear," *The Economist*, December 2, 2006, p. 15.

25. Huntington, "How Countries Democratize," p. 579.

26. Juan Forero, "Latin America Is Growing Impatient with Democracy," *New York Times*, June 24, 2004.

27. See, for example, Steven W. Hook and John Spanier, *American Foreign Policy since World War II* (Washington, DC: CQ Press, 2004), especially Chapter 4 ("Developing Countries in the Crossfire"), pp. 81–111; Chalmers Johnson, *Blowback* (New York: Henry Holt, 2000), especially Chapters 3 and 4, pp. 65–118; Thomas M. Magstadt, *An Empire If You Can Keep It: Power and Principle in American Foreign Policy* (Washington, DC: CQ Press, 2004), especially Chapter 6.

28. Kaplan, *The Coming Anarchy*, p. 65.

29. Ibid., pp. 65–66.

30. Ibid., p. 66.

Chapter 6

1. William Kornhauser, *The Politics of Mass Society* (New York: Free Press, 1959), p. 123.

2. C. W. Cassinelli, *Total Revolution: A Comparative Study of Germany under Hitler, the Soviet Union under Stalin, and China under Mao* (Santa Barbara, CA: Clio Books, 1976), p. 225.

3. Leonard Shapiro, *Totalitarianism* (New York: Praeger, 1972), p. 104. Shapiro quotes scholar Hans Buchheim on this point.

4. Carl Friedrich and Zbigniew Brzezinski, *Totalitarian Dictatorship and Autocracy*, 2nd ed. (New York: Praeger, 1966).

5. Eric Hoffer, *The True Believer: Thoughts on the Nature of Mass Movements* (New York: Harper & Row, 1951), pp. 104–105.

6. Friedrich and Brzezinski, *Totalitarian Dictatorship*, pp. 279–339.

7. Eric Hoffer, *The True Believer*, p. 86.

8. Raul Hilberg, *The Destruction of the European Jews* (New York: Harper & Row, 1961), p. 12.

9. Cited in Cassinelli, *Total Revolution*, p. 16.

10. Adolph Hitler, speech in Munich, Germany, March 13, 1936.

11. Karl Dietrich Bracher, *The German Dictatorship* (New York: Holt, 1972), p. 181.

12. Adolf Hitler, *Mein Kampf*, trans. R. Manheim (Boston: Houghton-Mifflin, 1971), pp. 179–180.

13. Ibid., p. 182.

14. Eugene Hadamovsky, *Propaganda und nationale Macht, 1933*, p. 22. Quoted in Hannah Arendt, *The Origins of Totalitarianism* (Cleveland: Meridian Books, 1961 edition), p. 341 (see note 1).

15. See Leo Strauss, *Thoughts on Machiavelli* (Seattle: University of Washington Press, 1968), p. 9.

16. Maurice Latey, *Patterns of Tyranny* (New York: Atheneum, 1969), p. 100.

17. Cassinelli, *Total Revolution*, p. 103.

18. Ibid., p. 186. Cassinelli's observation that Mao "never hesitated to destroy his enemies [including] rival communists, Kuomintang activists, and 'landlords'" can be applied to all successful totalitarian rulers.

19. Quoted in Bracher, *German Dictatorship*, p. 257.

20. Ibid., p. 272.

21. W. S. Allen, *The Nazi Seizure of Power: The Experience of a Single German Town, 1930–1935* (Chicago: Quadrangle Books, 1965).

22. Peter Drucker, "The Monster and the Lamb," *Atlantic*, December 1978, p. 84.

23. Friedrich and Brzezinski, *Totalitarian Dictatorship*, p. 374.

24. Ibid., pp. 9–10.

25. Hannah Arendt, *The Origins of Totalitarianism* (Boston: Houghton-Mifflin, 1973), Preface to Part III: Totalitarianism. Online at http://www.barnesandnoble.com/w/origins-of-totalitarianism-hannah-arendt/1100278208?ean=9780547543154.

26. See Stalin, *Mastering Bolshevism*, p. 10; cited in Merle Fainsod, *How Russia Is Ruled*, rev. ed. (Cambridge, MA: Harvard University Press, 1964), p. 435.

27. Aleksandr Solzhenitsyn, *The Gulag Archipelago, 1918–1956* (New York: Harper & Row, 1974), p. 595.

28. Bracher, *German Dictatorship*, p. 258.

29. Ibid., pp. 259–260.

30. Ibid., p. 262.

31. Ibid.

32. Hilberg, *Destruction of the European Jews*, p. 31.

33. Mao Zedong, *Selected Works* (Beijing: Foreign Languages Press, 1960–1965), p. 224.

34. Franz Michaels and George Taylor, *The Far East in the Modern World* (New York: Holt, 1964), p. 479.

35. John King Fairbank, *The United States and China*, 4th ed. (Cambridge, MA: Harvard University Press, 1979), p. 409.

36. Ibid., p. 413.

37. Ibid.

38. Cassinelli, *Total Revolution*, p. 195.

39. Ibid., p. 243. Of course, figures vary widely. For example, Rummel, using somewhat different criteria, postulated significantly different individual figures for Hitler, Lenin–Stalin, and Mao. Yet, his total of almost 105.5 million people killed is remarkably close to Cassinelli's estimate. See R. J. Rummel, *Death by Government* (New Brunswick, NJ: Transaction, 1996), p. 8.

40. For instance, almost 1.5 million pages of formerly classified documents (German messages intercepted by Britain during World War II as well as newly released Russian documents) revealed that Hitler probably murdered closer to 7 million Jews (as opposed to the 5 or 6 million, as Cassinelli and others had estimated). Also see comment in note 42.

41. Cassinelli, *Total Revolution*, p. 46.

42. Ibid., p. 186. Since Cassinelli published his book, new evidence indicates that these figures vastly understated the actual number of deaths during this period. According to one authority, a three-year famine between 1959 and 1962 *alone* caused at least 30 million Chinese deaths. The immediate cause of the famine was Mao's policy of taking property from Chinese peasants and relocating those peasants in communes. See Jasper Becker, *Hungry Ghosts: Mao's Secret Famine* (New York: Free Press, 1997).

43. Ibid., p. 187.

44. See Thomas M. Magstadt, "Bleeding Cambodia: The Great Leap Downward," *Reason*, July 1982, pp. 45–50; and "Marxism, Moral Responsibility, and the Cambodian Revolution," *National Review*, July 24, 1981, pp. 831–836.

45. See Thomas M. Magstadt, "Ethiopia's Great Terror," *Worldview*, April 1982, pp. 5–6.

46. "Iran to offer West nuke package soon," *China Daily*. Online at http://www.chinadaily.net/cndy/2009-04/16/content_7681807.htm.

47. Laqueur applied this concept to the Soviet Union, particularly in his chapter on totalitarianism. See Walter Laqueur, *The Dream That Failed, Reflections on the Soviet Union* (New York: Oxford University Press, 1994), pp. 77–95, 84.

Chapter 7

1. Aristotle, *The Politics*, Book 4, trans. and ed. Ernest Barker (New York: Oxford University Press, 1962, 1276b, pp. 101–102; see also, Benjamin Jowett's translation online at http://www.constitution.org/ari/polit_00.htm (especially the first three paragraphs in Book 40).

2. The Life Peerage Act of 1958 enables the monarch, upon the advice of the prime minister, to confer nontransferable titles for life on commoners. The rationale for the legislation was to ensure party balance and to increase the number of working members in the House of Lords. Approximately one-quarter of all Lords (and a higher percentage of working members of the House of Lords) are appointed in this way.

3. "Lording it: Britain's Parliament is deadlocked over House of Lords reform. Let the people decide," *The Economist*," July 14, 2012, pp. 10–11.

4. Sydney Bailey, *British Parliamentary Democracy*, 3rd ed. (Westport, CT: Greenwood, 1978), pp. 130–131.

5. Suzanne Berger, *The French Political System*, 3rd ed. (New York: Random House, 1974), p. 368. Berger quotes then Prime Minister (later President) Georges Pompidou in 1964 commenting on the Fifth Republic's institutional balancing act: "France has now chosen a system midway between the American presidential regime and the British parliamentary regime, where the chief of state, who formulates general policy, has the basis of authority in universal suffrage but can only exercise his functions with a government that he may have chosen and named, but which in order to survive, must maintain the confidence of the Assembly."

6. "Left Bankers: A Socialist Landslide, but Trouble Looms Ahead," *The Economist*, June 23, 2012, pp. 56–57.

7. Roy Macridis, ed., *Modern Political Systems: Europe*, 6th ed. (Englewood Cliffs, NJ: Prentice-Hall, 1986), p. 120.

8. See Thomas M. Magstadt, "Ethics and Emigration: The East German Exodus, 1989," *Carnegie Council on Ethics and International Affairs—Case Studies in Ethics and International Affairs*, no. 6, 1990.

9. Guido Goldman, *The German Political System* (New York: Random House, 1974), p. 56.

10. See John W. Dower, *Embracing Defeat: Japan in the Wake of World War II* (New York: Norton, 2000).

11. See Herbert P. Bix, *Hirohito and the Making of Modern Japan* (New York: HarperCollins, 2000).

12. Franz Michael and George Taylor, *The Far East in the Modern World* (New York: Holt, 1964), p. 263.

13. Ibid., p. 607.

14. Nobutaki Ike, *Japanese Politics: Patron-Client Democracy*, 2nd ed. (New York: Knopf, 1972), p. 17.

15. Michael and Taylor, *Far East in the Modern World*, p. 603.

16. "India Overheats," *The Economist*, February 3, 2007, p. 11.

17. "Good News: Don't Waste," *The Economist*, May 23, 2009, p. 13.

18. Jodi Rudoren, "Tepid Vote for Netanyahu in Israel Is Seen as a Rebuke," *New York Times*, January 22, 2013.

19. Bailey, *British Parliamentary Democracy*, p. 130.
20. *Marbury v. Madison*, 5 U.S. (1 Cranch) 137 (1803).
21. Edward Courtier, *Principles of Politics and Government* (Boston: Allyn & Bacon, 1981), p. 84.
22. See, for example, Norman J. Ornstein and Thomas E. Mann, "When Congress Checks Out," *Foreign Affairs*, November/December 2006, pp. 67–82; see also Norman Ornstein and Thomas Mann, *The Broken Branch: How Congress Is Failing America and How to Get It Back on Track* (New York: Oxford University Press, 2006). The authors take Congress to task for failing to exercise oversight from 2000 to 2006—that is, during most of George W. Bush's tenure in the White House. In the 2006 mid elections, the Democrats regained control of both the House of Representatives and Senate but failed to win a large enough majority in the Senate to break a filibuster. (It takes sixty votes to pass a cloture motion to end debate.)

Chapter 8

1. Thomas M. Magstadt, *Nations and Governments: Comparative Politics in Regional Perspective,* 5th ed. (Belmont, CA: Wadsworth/Thomson, 2005), pp. 226–238.
2. Susan Dentzer, Jeff Trimble, and Bruce Auster, "The Soviet Economy in Shambles," *US News & World Report,* November 20, 1989, pp. 25–26.
3. Hedrick Smith, *The Russians* (New York: Times Books, 1983), p. 83.
4. Dentzer et al., "The Soviet Economy in Shambles," pp. 25–29, 32, 35–37, 39.
5. Walter Laqueur, *The Dream That Failed* (New York: Oxford University Press, 1994), pp. 71–73.
6. See Milovan Djilas, *The New Class* (New York: Praeger, 1957); and Smith, *The Russians,* pp. 30–67.
7. START stands for Strategic Arms Reduction Treaty; the United States and Russia signed START II in 1993.
8. "Russia," *World Factbook* (Washington, DC: Central Intelligence Agency, 1996), p. 6 (electronic edition).
9. "Emerging Market Indicators," *The Economist,* March 15, 1997, p. 108.
10. Ibid., February 10, 2007, p. 105.
11. See Marshall Goldman, *Petrostate: Putin, Power, and the New Russia* (New York: Oxford University Press, 2008). See also Jason Bush, "Is Russia Blowing Its Oil Bonanza?" *Business Week Online,* October 5, 2005, http://www.businessweek.com/bwdaily/dnflash/oct2005/nf2005105_1326_db089.htm.
12. Vera Tolz, "Thorny Road Toward Federalism in Russia," *Radio Free Europe/Radio Liberty Research Report* 48 (December 1993), p. 1.
13. Claire Sterling, "Redfellas: The Growing Power of Russia's Mob," *The New Republic,* April 11, 1994, p. 19.
14. Xan Smiley, "Russia Wobbles Ahead," *The World in 1997* (an annual publication of *The Economist),* p. 39.
15. See, for example, Masha Lipman, "The Third Wave of Russian De-Stalinization," *Foreign Policy* (electronic edition), December 16, 2010. The author asks: "Is the Kremlin finally coming to terms with its dark history?"
16. Ibid. In 1940 on the eve of World War II, Stalin ordered the massacre of 22,000 Poles, including 4,500 Polish officers, by the Soviet secret police in the Katyn Forest near the Russian city of Smolensk. The official Soviet history blamed the atrocity on Germany under Nazi rule. Finally, in 2010, almost two decades after the collapse of the Soviet Union, the Russian government admitted the shattering truth about a horrific crime that happened eighty years ago. The admission came in the form of a formal statement issued by the Russian parliament: *"The Katyn crime was committed on direct order by Stalin and other Soviet leaders."*
17. See, Luke Harding, *Mafia State: How One Reporter Became the Enemy of the Brutal New Russia* (United Kingdom: Guardian Press, 2012). The book received mixed reviews, but the author's account of the systematic harassment and obstructionism he encountered in

his job as Moscow correspondent for a British newspaper (*The Guardian*) is a tale that in its broad outlines rings true.

18. Peter Savodnik, "Skolkovo, Russia's Would-Be Silicon Valley," *Businessweek*, September 1, 2011 (online edition); see also, "Can Russia Create a New Silicon Valley?" *The Economist*, July 14, 2012, p. 58.

19. See Matthew Valencia, "Limping towards Normality: A Survey of Poland," *The Economist*, October 27, 2001, pp. 3–16.

20. Dilma Rousseff, "The Brazilian Model," *The World in 2012* (an annual publication of *The Economist*), 2011, p. 60.

21. The term is taken from the title of Alan Riding's much-acclaimed book, *Distant Neighbors: A Portrait of the Mexicans* (New York: Alfred A. Knopf, 1984).

22. "Putting the Brakes on Change," *The Economist*, July 12, 2003, p. 32.

Chapter 9

1. Michael Perry, "Malaria and dengue: The sting in climate change," Reuters, November 20, 2008. At http://www.reuters.com/article/environmentNews/idUSTRE4AJ2RQ20081120.

2. John Allen, *Student Atlas of World Politics* (Guilford, CT: Dushkin, 1994), p. 16. Thailand was then called Siam, and Iran was named Persia.

3. Ibid., p. 17. However, given the fluidity of contemporary politics, especially in the former Yugoslavia, this number is highly unstable.

4. As pointed out by Robert Clark, *Power and Policy in the Third World*, 4th ed. (New York: Macmillan, 1991), p. 26.

5. See Jared Diamond, *Guns, Germs, and Steel: The Fate of Human Societies* (New York: Norton, 1997).

6. Robert D. Kaplan, *The Coming Anarchy* (New York: Vintage Books, 2001), pp. 3–59.

7. These points are generally emphasized in the literature. See James A. Bill and Robert L. Hardgrave Jr., *Comparative Politics: The Quest for Theory* (Websterville, OH: Merrill, 1973), pp. 70–71.

8. For instance, see Seymour Lipset, *Political Man: The Social Bases of Democracy* (Garden City, NY: Doubleday, 1983); Tatu Vanhanen, *The Process of Democratization: A Comparative Study of 147 States, 1980–1988* (Bristol, UK: Taylor & Francis, 1990); and Samuel P. Huntington, "Will More Countries Become Democratic?" *Political Science Quarterly* 99 (1984), pp. 193–218. See also Thomas Scanton, "Democracy's Fragile Flower Spreads Its Roots," *Time*, July 13, 1987, pp. 10–11. An optimistic outlook for democracy, based on such correlates, is offered by Carl Gershman, "Democracy as the Wave of the Future: A World Revolution," *Current* (May 1989), pp. 18–23.

9. Gershman, "Democracy as the Wave of the Future," p. 23.

10. Vanhanen, *Process of Democratization*, pp. 51–65.

11. See, for example, Justin Yifu Lin, Fang Cai, and Zhou Li, *The China Miracle: Development Strategy and Economic Reform* (Hong Kong: The Chinese University Press, 2003); see also Gregory Chow, *China's Economic Transformation*, 2nd ed. (Malden, MA: Blackwell, 2007).

12. Kaplan, *Coming Anarchy*, pp. 59–98.

13. Samuel Huntington, "How Countries Democratize," *Political Science Quarterly* 106 (1991–1992), p. 579.

14. See, for example, Robert M. Press, "Africa's Struggle for Democracy," *Christian Science Monitor*, March 21, 1991, p. 4; and Kenneth B. Noble, "Despots Dwindle as Reform Alters Face of Africa," *New York Times*, April 13, 1991, p. 1.

15. Thomas R. Lansner, "Out of Africa," *Wall Street Journal*, December 10, 1996, p. A18.

16. Huntington, "How Countries Democratize," p. 12.

17. Jean Herskovits, "Nigeria: Power and Democracy in Africa," *Headline Series* 527 (January–February 1982), p. 8.

18. "Transparency International, Berlin." Reprinted from the *Wall Street Journal*, January 2, 1997, sec. 1, 5.
19. Lydia Polgreen, "As Nigeria Tries to Fight Graft, a New Sordid Tale," *New York Times*, November 29, 2005 (electronic edition).
20. See, for example, "Big Men, Big Fraud, and Big Trouble," *The Economist*, April 28, 2007, pp. 55–58.
21. "Please Hurry Up," *The Economist*, October 25, 2008, p. 60.
22. Simon Long, "India's Shining Hopes (A Survey of India)," *The Economist*, February 21, 2004, p. 3.
23. "Suddenly Vulnerable," *The Economist*, December 13, 2008, p. 15.
24. Vyvyan Tenorio, "Sri Lanka Peace Process at Delicate Point," *Christian Science Monitor*, September 2, 1986, p. 11.
25. Robert E. Gamer, *Developing Nations: A Comparative Perspective*, 2nd ed. (Dubuque, IA: William C. Brown, 1982), pp. 312–314.
26. See, for example, Daniel Pepper, "The Toxic Consequences of the Green Revolution," *US News and World Report*, July 7, 2008. At http://www.usnews.com/articles/news/world/2008/07/07/the-toxic-consequences-of-the-green-revolution.html.
27. Samuel Huntington, *Political Order in Changing Societies* (New Haven, CT: Yale University Press, 1968), p. 35.
28. See P. W. Singer, *Children at War* (Berkeley: University of California Press, 2006); see also Michael Wessells, *Child Soldiers: From Violence to Protection* (Cambridge, MA: Harvard University Press, 2006). On the use of girls as sex slaves, see, for example, Hannah Strange, "Wounds of sex slaves in Sierra Leone's civil war are a long time healing," *Times Online*, April 30, 2008, at http://www.timesonline.co.uk/tol/news/world/africa/article3848621.ece.
29. Jean-Jacques Rousseau, "The First Discourse," in *The First and Second Discourses*, ed. Roger D. Masters (New York: St. Martin's Press, 1964), p. 39.

Chapter 10

1. Aristotle, *The Politics*, trans. and ed. Ernest Barker (New York: Oxford University Press, 1962), 1276b, pp. 101–102.
2. Scott Shane, "Waterboarding Used 266 Times on Two Suspects," *New York Times*, April 19, 2009 (electronic edition).
3. Aristotle, *The Politics*, 1274b, p. 93.
4. Immanuel Kant, *The Science of Right*, vol. 42 (Chicago: Encyclopaedia Britannica, 1952), p. 436.
5. Daniel J. Elazar, *American Federalism: A View from the States*, 3rd ed. (New York: Crowell, 1984). Elazar, a noted expert on U.S. federalism and intergovernmental relations, argued that there are three distinct political cultures in the United States—individualistic, moralistic, and traditionalistic. It is debatable, however, whether these are separate political cultures or merely different aspects of one political culture.
6. John Stuart Mill, *A System of Logic, Ratiocinative and Deductive*, vol. 2 (London: Longmans, Green, 1879), p. 518.
7. The modern study of political socialization is closely tied to the Greek concern for character formation. One key difference between the two is that behavioral political science focuses primarily on the process by which political opinions are formed whereas the Greeks emphasized the traits of character that all good citizens should display.
8. Barbara Defoe Whitehead provided persuasive evidence in "Dan Quayle Was Right," *Atlantic* (April 1993), p. 41. However, single-parent families are only one reason some families fail. Note James Q. Wilson's comment that one way "the family has become weaker is that more and more children are being raised in one-parent families, and often that one parent is a teenage girl. Another way is that parents, whether in one- or two-parent families, are spending less time with their children and are providing poorer discipline." For a thoughtful review of two-parent families, in light of the academic

debate on the subject, see James Q. Wilson, "The Family-Values Debate," *Commentary* 95 (April 1993), pp. 24–31. The quotation is from page 24.

9. See James Q. Wilson, *The Moral Sense* (New York: Free Press, 1995), pp. 141–163.

10. Herbert Winter and Thomas Bellows, *People and Politics* (New York: Wiley, 1977), p. 120.

11. Harry Holloway and John George, *Public Opinion*, 2nd ed. (New York: St. Martin's Press, 1985), pp. 73–77.

12. Dean Jaros, *Socialization to Politics* (New York: Praeger, 1973), pp. 87–88.

13. See M. Margaret Conway and Frank Fergert, *Political Analysis: An Introduction* (Boston: Allyn & Bacon, 1972), p. 106.

14. Holloway and George, *Public Opinion*, p. 79.

15. See M. Kent Jennings, "Preface"; Henry Kenst, "The Gender Factor in a Changing Electorate"; and Arthur Miller, "Gender and the Vote," in *The Politics of the Gender Gap: The Social Construction of Political Influence*, ed. Carol Mueller (Newbury Park, CA: Sage, 1987). Much of the political literature advocating natural differences between the sexes presumes the existence of scholarship in the field of developmental psychology; see Carol Gilligan, *In a Different Voice* (Cambridge, MA: Harvard University Press, 1982); and M. Belenky, B. Clinchy, W. Goldberger, and J. Tarule, *Women's Ways of Knowing: The Development of Self, Voice, and Mind* (New York: Basic Books, 1986).

16. Michael Barone and Grant Ujifusa, *The Almanac of American Politics* (Washington, DC: National Journal, 1994), p. xxvii.

17. Ralph Buultjens, "India: Religion, Political Legitimacy, and the Secular State," *Annals of Political and Social Sciences* 483 (January 1986), p. 107.

18. James Billington, "The Case for Orthodoxy," *New Republic*, May 30, 1994, p. 26.

19. A. James Reichley, *Religion in American Public Life* (Washington, DC: Brookings Institution, 1985), p. 2.

20. See, for example, Laurie Goodstein, "More Atheists Shout It From the Rooftops," *New York Times*, April 26, 2009 (electronic edition).

21. This is not to deny, of course, that unscrupulous leaders can exploit religion for ignoble purposes.

22. This discussion builds on William Flanigan and Nancy Zingale, *Political Behavior of the American Electorate* (Boston: Allyn & Bacon, 1979), pp. 184–187.

23. Kenneth Langton and M. Kent Jennings, "Political Socialization and the High School Civics Curriculum," *American Political Science Review* (September 1968), p. 851.

24. Conway and Fergert, *Political Analysis*, p. 110. Also see Judith Torney-Purta, "From Attitudes and Knowledge to Schemata: Expanding the Outcomes at Political Socialization Research," in *Political Socialization, Citizenship Education, and Democracy*, ed. Orit Ichilov (New York: Teachers College Press, 1990), p. 99.

25. Or so it would seem. But it is important to determine not only what is studied but also how it is studied. See Albert Speer's comments on German education in Albert Speer, *Inside the Third Reich*, trans. R. Winston and C. Winston (New York: Avon, 1971), p. 35.

26. Robert Erikson, Norman Luttbeg, and Kent Tedin, *American Public Opinion* (New York: Macmillan, 1991), p. 113.

27. Ibid., p. 7.

28. This is commonly recognized. See James MacGregor Burns, J. W. Peltason, Thomas E. Cronin, and David B. Magleby, *Government by the People*, 17th ed. (Upper Saddle River, NJ: Prentice Hall, 1998), p. 293.

29. Ibid., pp. 49–50.

30. James Q. Wilson and Richard Hernstein, *Crime and Human Nature* (New York: Simon & Schuster, 1985), p. 293.

31. See "Radio's Future II: The 2010 American Youth Study," Edison Research, at http://www.edisonresearch.com/Edison_Research_American_Youth_Study_Radios_Future.pdf.

32. Donna Abu-Nasr, "The Beauty Isn't Skin Deep," *Kansas City Star*, Thursday, May 7, 2009, p. A18.

33. This section builds on the analysis offered in Montague Kern, *Thirty-Second Politics: Political Advertising in the Eighties* (New York: Praeger, 1989).

34. Thomas E. Patterson, *Out of Order* (New York: Vintage, 1994), p. 25.
35. Daniel Hallin's study is cited as part of a wider discussion of the issue in Samuel Popkin, *The Reasoning Voter: Communication and Persuasion in Presidential Campaigns* (Chicago: University of Chicago Press, 1991), pp. 228–229.
36. University Wisconsin news release, November 21, 2006. Online at http://www.news. wisc.edu/releases/13213.
37. See, for example, Al Franken, *Lies and the Lying Liars Who Tell Them: A Fair and Balanced Look at the Right* (New York: Dutton, 2003). Franken, now a United States Senator, is an unabashed liberal who gained fame as a comic writer on *Saturday Night Live* but has since turned to political satire and is endeavoring to create a new liberal radio network to combat what he believes to be a strong right-wing slant in the corporate-controlled mass media. In 2008, he ran for the United States Senate in Minnesota, won by a few hundred votes, but found himself in a legal battle with the incumbent, Norm Colman, who contested the results in the courts in a failing effort to win in court what he had lost in the political arena.
38. M. Margaret Conway, *Political Participation in the United States* (Washington, DC: CQ Press, 1987), pp. 52–53.
39. Hence, the author of one classic behavioral study long ago concluded, "The principles of freedom and democracy are less widely and enthusiastically favored when they are confronted in their specific or applied forms." See Herbert McCloskey, "Consensus and Ideology in American Democracy," *American Political Science Review* 58 (June 1964), pp. 361–384.
40. Donald Devine, *The Political Culture of the United States* (Boston: Little, Brown, 1972), pp. 187–230. Also see Seymour Martin Lipset, *American Exceptionalism: A Double-Edged Sword* (New York: Norton, 1996) for an extensive discussion of the values that make up the American creed.

Chapter 11

1. Howard Schuman and Stanley Presser, *Questions and Answers in Attitude Surveys* (Orlando, FL: Academic Press, 1981), pp. 70–71. This study is illustrated in James Q. Wilson, *American Government*, 4th ed. (Lexington, MA: Heath, 1989), p. 99.
2. See, for example, John L. Fund, "The Perils of Polling," *Wall Street Journal,* August 13, 1996, p. A12; for a commentary on the polls in the 1996 presidential election (Clinton versus Dole), see Everett Carl Ladd, Jr., "The Pollsters' Waterloo," *Wall Street Journal,* November 19, 1997, p. A22.
3. Costas Panagopolous, "Poll Accuracy in the 2008 Presidential Election," November 5, 2008, accessed electronically on May 2, 2009 at http://www.fordham.edu/images/academics/graduate_schools/gsas/elections_and_campaign_/poll%20accuracy%20in%20 the%202008%20presidential%20election.pdf.
4. One study found that almost two-thirds of the promises made in major-party platforms were kept; see Gerald M. Pomper with Susan Lederman, *Elections in America: Control and Influence in Democratic Politics*, 2nd ed. (New York: Dodd, Mead, 1980), p. 161.
5. See Thomas Cronin, *Direct Democracy: The Politics of Initiative, Referendum, and Recall* (Cambridge, MA: Harvard University Press, 1990).
6. Ibid., p. 87.
7. The fact that voters in many democracies do not need to register is often cited as a reason their participation rate is higher. In several democracies (including Australia and Belgium), citizens who do not vote are subject to a fine.
8. Harry Holloway and John George, *Public Opinion: Coalitions, Elites, and Masses,* 2nd ed. (New York: St. Martin's Press, 1986), p. 161.
9. Ibid., pp. 162–163.
10. See Julian L. Woodward and Elmo Roper, "Political Activity of American Citizens," *American Political Science Review* 44 (1950), pp. 822–885.
11. Sidney Verba and Norman Nie, *Participation in America* (New York: Harper & Row, 1972), pp. 79–80.

12. Mark Hugo Lopez, "*Dissecting the 2008 Electorate: Most Diverse in U.S. History*," Pew Research Center, April 30, 2009. Online at http://pewresearch.org/pubs/1209/racial-ethnic-voters-presidential-election.

13. Scott Keeter, Juliana Horowitz, and Alex Tyson, *Young Voters in the 2008 Election*, Pew Research Center, November 12, 2008. Online at http://pewresearch.org/pubs/1031/young-voters-in-the-2008-election.

14. Students interested in learning more about the changing patterns of wealth and income distribution in the United States are encouraged to read Daniel Cay Johnston, *Perfectly Legal: The Secret Campaign to Rig Our Tax System to Benefit the Super Rich—And Cheat Everybody Else* (New York: Portfolio, 2003); Joseph E. Stiglitz, *The Roaring Nineties: A New History of the World's Most Prosperous Decade* (New York: Norton, 2003); and Paul Krugman, *The Great Unraveling: Losing Our Way in the New Century* (New York: Norton, 2003), among other recent books on this topic.

15. Alexis de Tocqueville, *Democracy in America*, vol. 2 (New York: Schocken Books, 1961), p. 18.

16. Ibid., pp. 153, 159.

17. Robert D. Putnam, "Bowling Alone: America's Declining Social Capital," *Journal of Democracy* (January 1995), pp. 65–78.

18. Richard Morin, "Who's in Control? Many Don't Know or Care," *Washington Post,* January 29, 1996, p. A6. The article cited a Harvard University-Washington, DC poll.

19. Ibid.

20. Wilson, *American Government*, p. 100.

21. Richard Niemi and Herbert Weisberg, *Controversies in Voting Behavior,* 3rd ed. (Washington, DC: CQ Press, 1992), p. 103.

22. Samuel Popkin, *The Reasoning Voter and Persuasion in Presidential Campaigns* (Chicago: University of Chicago Press, 1991), pp. 212–216.

23. C. Wright Mills, *The Power Elite* (New York: Oxford University Press, 1956).

24. Thomas Dye and L. Harmon Ziegler, *The Irony of Democracy: An Uncommon Introduction to American Government,* 4th ed. (North Scituate, MA: Duxbury Press, 1978), p. 374.

25. Andrew Greeley, "Power Is Diffused Throughout Society," in *Taking Sides: Clashing Views on Controversial Political Issues,* eds. George McKenna and Stanley Feingad (Guilford, CT: Dushkin, 1983), p. 23. Also see Arnold Rose, *The Power Structure: Political Process in American Society* (London: Oxford University Press, 1967), pp. 483–493.

26. Thomas Jefferson to Francis Hopkinson, March 13, 1789, in *The Political Writings of Thomas Jefferson,* ed. Edward Dumbauld (Indianapolis: Bobbs-Merrill, 1955), p. 46.

27. Ibid.

28. See, for example, Thomas Magstadt, "This Corrupt(ed) Republic," *Reader Supported News*, September 13, 2012. Online at http://readersupportednews.org/pm-section/78-78/13459-this-corrupted-republic. This article also appeared in *Nation of Change*, August 31, 2012. Online at http://www.nationofchange.org/world-s-most-corrupted-republic-1346419376.

29. This paragraph is based on figures and analysis in G. Ross Stephens, "Our Corrupt, Constitutionally Constipated Government," *Reader Supported News*, January 13, 2013. Online at http://readersupportednews.org/pm-section/26-26/15528-our-corrupt-constitutionally-constituted-government.

30. Paul Best, Kul Rai, and David Walsh, *Politics in Three Worlds: An Introduction to Political Science* (New York: Wiley, 1986), pp. 271–272.

31. Gabriel Almond and G. Bingham Powell, *Comparative Politics: A Developmental Approach* (Boston: Little, Brown, 1966), chap. 4.

32. Ibid.

33. This discussion is indebted to William Keefe and Morris Ogul, *The American Legislative Process: Congress and the States,* 8th ed. (Englewood Cliffs, NJ: Prentice-Hall, 1992), p. 334.

34. Thomas DiLorenzo, "Who Really Speaks for the Elderly?" *Consumers' Research* 79 (September 1996), p. 15; and Charles Morris, *The AARP: America's Most Powerful Lobby and the Clash of Generations* (New York: Times Books, 1996), pp. 4, 10–11.

35. Jeffrey H. Birnbaum, "Overhaul of Lobbying Laws Unlikely to Succeed Thanks to Opposition of Lobbyists Themselves," *Wall Street Journal,* May 30, 1991, p. A20.

36. Jeffrey H. Birnbaum, "The Road to Riches," *Washington Post,* June 22, 2005 (online edition); see also Jonathan Rauch, "The Hyperpluralism Trap," *New Republic,* June 6, 1994, p. 22.

37. Birnbaum, "Overhaul of Lobbying," 1991.

38. John Harwood, "Political Treadmill: For California Senator, Fundraising Becomes Overwhelming Burden," *Wall Street Journal,* March 2, 1994, p. A1. Feinstein's concerted effort to raise money was spurred by the fact that her 1992 election victory was for only a two-year term. Harwood estimated that her 1992 race and her failed 1990 gubernatorial race together cost about $30 million. Another example of spiraling election costs was the 1996 Virginia senatorial election, in which the loser, Mark Warner, spent $11 million (an expenditure of $3.30 per voter, compared with Huffington's $2.03 per voter).

39. Figures obtained from CQ MoneyLine (formerly PoliticalMoneyLine), at http://www.fecinfo.com.

40. See http://www.opensecrets.org/bigpicture/stats.asp.

41. See "Campaign Finance Reform" at the Pew Charitable Trusts website, http://www.pewtrusts.com/ideas.

42. Claire Cain Miller, "How Obama's Campaign Changed Politics," *New York Times,* November 7, 2008 (electronic edition) at http://bits.blogs.nytimes.com/2008/11/07/how-obamas-internet-campaign-changed-politics/.

43. Ibid.

44. See, for example, Johnston, *Perfectly Legal,* or Krugman, *Great Unraveling.*

Chapter 12

1. Robert C. Tucker, *Politics as Leadership* (Columbia: University of Missouri Press, 1995), p. iii.

2. Walter Lippmann, *A Preface to Morals* (Boston: Beacon Press, 1960), p. 280. The quotations that follow are from pp. 279–283.

3. See Harry Jaffa, "The Emancipation Proclamation," in *100 Years of Emancipation,* ed. Robert Goldwin (Skokie, IL: Rand McNally, 1964), pp. 1–24.

4. Douglass Adair, "Fame and the Founding Fathers," in *Fame and the Founding Fathers: Essays by Douglass Adair* (New York: Norton, 1974), p. 10.

5. Ibid., p. 8.

6. Alexander Hamilton, John Jay, and James Madison, *The Federalist* (New York: Modern Library, n.d.), p. 470.

7. Robert J. Alexander, *Rómulo Betancourt and the Transformation of Venezuela* (New Brunswick, NJ: Transaction Books, 1982), p. 435.

8. Ibid., p. 436.

9. Ibid.

10. John Edwin Fagg, *Latin America: A General History,* 2nd ed. (New York: Macmillan, 1969), p. 627.

11. Aaron Wildavsky, *The Nursing Father: Moses as a Political Leader* (Tuscaloosa: University of Alabama Press, 1984). The author makes the point that the mark of a model leader, like a model parent, is to make himself or herself dispensable. Children growing up need to learn how to get along without their parents; likewise, viable nation-states need to be able to survive a change of leadership.

12. Martin Gilbert, *Churchill* (Garden City, NY: Doubleday, 1980), pp. 100–126.

13. Ibid., p. 172.

14. U.S. Department of State, *Selected Documents,* April 1979.

15. Alexis de Tocqueville, *Democracy in America,* vol. 2 (New York: Schocken Books, 1961), pp. 102–106.
16. Morton Frisch and Richard Stevens, "Introduction," in *American Political Thought: The Philosophic Dimension of American Statesmanship,* ed. Morton Frisch and Richard Stevens (Dubuque, IA: Kendall/Hunt, 1976), p. 5.
17. Quoted in Roman J. Zorn, "Theodore G. Bilbo: Shibboleths for Statesmanship," reprinted in *A Treasury of Southern Folklore: Stories, Ballads, Traditions, and Folkways of the People of the South,* ed. B. A. Brotkin (New York: Crown, 1949), p. 304.
18. James W. Silver, *Mississippi: The Closed Society* (Orlando, FL: Harcourt, 1964), p. 19.
19. Ibid.
20. Hodding Carter, "Huey Long: American Dictator," in *The Aspirin Age: 1919–1941,* ed. Isabel Leighton (New York: Simon & Schuster, 1949), p. 347.
21. Ibid., p. 361.
22. See, for example, Silla Brush, "A Vote of No-Confidence," *U.S. News and World Report,* October 22, 2006 (online edition).
23. Joseph Tussman, as quoted in Marie Collins Swaley, "A Quantitative View," in *Representation,* ed. Hannah Pitkin (New York: Atherton Press, 1969), p. 83.
24. Hannah Pitkin, "The Concept of Representation," in *Representation,* ed. Hannah Pitkin (New York: Atherton Press, 1969), p. 21.
25. Quoted in Harvey Mansfield Jr., *Statesmanship and Party Government: A Study of Burke and Bolingbroke* (Chicago: University of Chicago Press, 1965), p. 23.
26. Edmund Burke, "The English Constitutional System," in *Representation,* ed. Hannah Pitkin (New York: Atherton Press, 1969), p. 175.
27. Ibid.
28. Martin Luther King Jr., "Letter from Birmingham City Jail," in *Civil Disobedience: Theory and Practice* (New York: Pegasus, 1969), pp. 78–79.
29. Ibid., p. 75.
30. David J. Garrow, *Bearing the Cross: Martin Luther King, Jr., and the Southern Christian Leadership Conference, 1955–1968* (New York: Random House, 1988), p. 11.
31. Ibid., p. 12.
32. "Mandela's Life and Times," BBC News, February 25, 2012, accessed online at http://www.bbc.co.uk/news/world-africa-12305154.
33. Margaret Coker, Nour Malas, and Marc Champion, "Google Executive Emerges as Key Figure in Revolt," *Wall Street Journal,* February 7, 2011 (online edition).

Chapter 13

1. Aristotle, *The Politics,* trans. and ed. Ernest Barker (New York: Oxford University Press, 1962), 1252b, p. 5.
2. The complete text of this speech can be found at http://www.yale.edu/ lawweb/avalon/presiden/speeches/eisenhower001.htm.
3. James Madison, "Political Observations," 1795. From *The Letters and Other Writings of James Madison.* http://www.informationclearinghouse.info/article18562.htm.
4. For a well-documented account of this little-noticed policy change, see P. W. Singer, *Corporate Warriors: The Rise of the Privatized Military Industry* (Ithaca, NY: Cornell University Press, 2003).
5. See, for example, Dean Baquet and Bill Keller, "When Do We Publish a Secret?" *New York Times,* July 1, 2006 (electronic edition) on the Bush administration's secret program to monitor international bank transactions; Peter Dale Scott, "Homeland Security Contracts for Vast New Detention Camps," *New America Media,* February 8, 2006, online at http://news.newaniericamedia.org/news/; and Laurie Kellman, "Powell Endorses Efforts to Block Bush Terrorist Plan," Associated Press, September 14, 2006, online at http://www.signonsandiego.com/news/politics/20060914-0755-bush-congress.html.
6. Daniel Patrick Moynihan, "Defining Deviance Down," *American Scholar* 62 (Winter 1993), p. 1.

7. Drug Policy Clearing House, Office of National Drug Control Policy (ONDCP), http://www.whitehousedrugpolicy.gov/publications/factsht/crime/index.html.

8. Robert Pear, "Recession Drains Social Security and Medicare," *New York Times,* May 12, 2009 (electronic edition).

9. David M. Walker, "The Debt No One Wants to Talk About," *New York Times,* February 4, 2004 (online edition).

10. Dennis Cauchon, "What Is the Real Federal Deficit?" *USA Today,* August 2, 2006 (updated August 4, 2006), http://www.usatoday.com/news/ washington/2006-08-02-deficit-usat_x.htm.

11. David Cay Johnston, *Perfectly Legal: The Covert Campaign to Rig Our Tax System to Benefit the Super Rich—And Cheat Everybody Else* (New York: Portfolio, 2003), p. 18.

12. Government Accounting Office, "Climate Change: Trends in Greenhouse Gas Emissions," submitted to the Senate Committee on Commerce, Science, and Transportation by John B. Stephenson, director, Natural Resources and Environment, October 28, 2003, http://www.gao.gov/new.items/d04146r.pdf.

13. Felicity Barringer, "Nations Ranked as Protectors of the Environment," *New York Times,* January 24, 2005 (electronic edition).

14. The author is indebted to the late Martin Diamond for this observation.

15. Johnston, *Perfectly Legal,* p. 16.

16. Ibid., pp. 169–170.

17. Ibid., p. 11.

18. Dawn Kawamoto, "Members of Congress Getting Richer Despite Market Meltdown," *Daily Finance,* November 17, 2010 at http://www.dailyfinance.com.

19. Associated Press, "Don't Feel Alone If Tax Is Confusing: 50 Experts Differ Over Family Returns," *Lincoln Star,* February 18, 1989, p. 2.

20. National Center for Education Statistics at http://nces.ed.gov/FastFacts/display.asp?id=1.

21. If you want to know more about the bogus theory behind your own experience in the public schools, you can't do better than to read Gail Collins's delightful, tongue-in-cheek, *As Texas Goes....How the Lone Star State Highjacked the American Agenda* (New York: Norton, 2012).

22. "Viva la différence!" *The Economist,* May 9, 2009, p. 28.

23. Associated Press, "Wal-Mart, Unions Back Universal Health Care," *Star Tribune,* February 7, 2007, http://www.startribune.com/535/story/986879.html.

24. See Ruy Teixeira, Center for American Progress, March 23, 2007 online at http://www.americanprogress.org/issues/2007/03/opinion_health_care.html.

25. I am indebted to my colleague, G. Ross Stephens, for the statistical analysis used here. The raw data are from the 1962, 1979, and 2006 Statistical Abstract, online at http://www.census.gov/compendia/statab/.

26. Steven Rattner, "The Rich Get Even Richer," *New York Times*, March 16, 2012; see also, Ezra Klein, "In 2010, 93 percent...," *Washington Post*, March 5, 2012. http://www.washingtonpost.com/blogs/wonkblog/post/in-2010-93-percent-of-income-gains-went-to-the-top-1-percent/2011/08/25/gIQA0qxhsR_blog.html.

27. Johnston, *Perfectly Legal,* pp. 15–16.

28. Ibid., pp. 31–37.

29. Paul Krugman, *The Great Unraveling: Losing Our Way in the New Century* (New York: Norton, 2003), p. 221. Krugman is also a distinguished economist who teaches at Princeton University.

30. *Civil Rights Cases,* 109 U.S. 3 (1883).

31. *Plessy v. Ferguson,* 163 U.S. 537 (1896).

32. *Shelley v. Kraemer,* 334 U.S. 1 (1948).

33. *Sweatt v. Painter,* 339 U.S. 629 (1950).

34. *Brown et al. v. Board of Education of Topeka et al.,* 347 U.S. 483 (1954).

35. And it was upheld as a legitimate exercise of the government's commerce power; see *Heart of Atlanta Motel v. United States,* 379 U.S. 241 (1964), and *Katzenbach v. McClung,* 379 U.S. 294 (1964).

36. *Milliken v. Bradley,* 418 U.S. 717 (1974).

37. *Regents of the University of California v. Bakke,* 438 U.S. 265 (1978).

38. In fact, the Supreme Court may have gone beyond *Bakke* by letting stand a federal court's decision that race cannot be a factor for purposes of law school admission. See *Texas v. Hopwood,* 116 S. Ct. 2581, cert denied (1996), 84 Fed. 3d 720 (1996).

39. *Wygant v. Jackson Board of Education,* 476 U.S. 267 (1986).

40. *Johnson v. Transportation Agency, Santa Clara County,* 480 U.S. 616 (1979).

41. *Adarand Construction, Inc. v. Pena,* 515 U.S. 200 (1995).

42. See, for instance, *United States v. Paradise,* 480 U.S. 149 (1987); *City of Richmond v. J. A. Croson Co.,* 488 U.S. 469 (1989); and *Metro Broadcasting, Inc. v. Federal Communications Commission,* 497 U.S. 547 (1990).

43. Elaine Cassels, "Why Citizens Should Be Concerned When Their Government Mistreats Aliens," Findlaw's Book Reviews, http://writ.news.fmdlaw. com/books/ reviews/20031031_cassel.html. This article is a review of David Cole's *Enemy Aliens: Double Standards and Constitutional Freedoms in the War on Terrorism* (New York: New Press, 2003).

44. *Romer v. Evans,* 116 S. Ct. 1620 (1996).

45. The FBI memo mentioned here was reported in the *New York Times,* November 13, 2003; cited in Noah Leavitt, "Ashcroft's Subpoena Blitz: Targeting Lawyers, Universities, Peaceful Demonstrators, Hospitals, and Patients, All with No Connection to Terrorism," FindLaw's Writ, February 18, 2004, http://writ.news.findlaw.com/commentary/20040–218.1eavitt.htm.

46. Ibid.

47. Ibid.

48. *Texas v. Johnson,* 491 U.S. 397 (1989).

49. *Brandenberg v. Ohio,* 395 U.S. 444 (1969).

50. This issue was resolved in *R.A.V. v. City of St. Paul,* 505 U.S. 112 (1992). A white 18-year-old male burned a cross on the lawn of the only black family living in a St. Paul, Minnesota, neighborhood. Although he might have been arrested for trespassing or disturbing the peace, he was charged under a local hate crime ordinance that made it illegal to place "on private or public property, a symbol, object, or graffiti, including but not limited to a burning cross or Nazi swastika, which one knows or has reasonable grounds to know arouses anger, alarm, or resentment in others on the basis of race, color, creed, religion, or gender." The Supreme Court decreed in 1992 that the ordinance, on its face, violated the First Amendment.

51. The Hays Press Enterprise Lecture, Riverside, California, May 7, 2004, accessed online at http://www.ap.org/pages/about/whatsnew/hayspress.html.

52. See *New York Times Co. v. United States,* 403 U.S. 713 (1971); and *Nebraska Press Association v. Stuart,* 427 U.S. 539 (1976).

53. *Reynolds v. United States,* 98 U.S. 145 (1879).

54. Most notably in *Abington School District v. Schempp,* 374 U.S. 203 (1963); and *Engle v. Vitale,* 370 U.S. 421 (1963).

55. *Lee v. Wiesman,* 505 U.S. 577 (1992).

56. *Wallace v. Jaffree,* 472 U.S. 38 (1985).

57. Andrew J. Coulson, "Obama's Compromise on D.C.'s School Vouchers Program," *Washington Post,* May 10, 2009 (electronic edition).

58. The original case upholding a woman's right to an abortion is *Roe v. Wade,* 410 U.S. 113 (1973). Other important cases include *Harris v. McRae,* 448 U.S. 297 (1980); *Webster v. Reproductive Health Services,* 492 U.S. 490 (1989); and *Rust v. Sullivan,* 500 U.S. 173 (1991). Also see *Planned Parenthood of Southeast Pennsylvania v. Casey,* 505 U.S. 833 (1992).

59. *N.O. W. v. Scheidler,* 510 U.S. 249 (1994).

60. *Schenck v. Pro Choice Network of Western New York,* 117 S. Ct. 855 (1997).

61. Leavitt, "Ashcroft's Subpoena Blitz."

62. Robert Pear and Eric Lichtblau, "Administration Sets Forth a Limited View on Privacy," *New York Times,* March 6, 2004 (online edition).

63. *Stenberg v. Carhart,* (99–830), 530 U.S. 914 (2000).

64. Pear and Lichtblau, "Administration Sets Forth a Limited View on Privacy."

65. *Planned Parenthood of Southeast Pennsylvania v. Casey.*

66. *Washington v. Glucksberg*, 117 S. Ct. 82258 (1997).

67. Burton Leiser, *Liberty, Justice, and Morals: Contemporary Value Conflicts* (New York: Macmillan, 1973), p. 192.

68. The answer provided by the Supreme Court is that the state must provide effective assistance of counsel through the first appeal. See *Douglas v. California*, 372 U.S. 353 (1963), and *Ross v. Moffitt*, 471 U.S. 600 (1974).

69. *Mapp v. Ohio*, 367 U.S. 643 (1961).

70. See, for instance, Chief Justice Burger's dissent in *Bivens v. Six Unknown Agents of the Federal Bureau of Narcotics*, 403 U.S. 897 (1970).

71. *United States v. Leon*, 468 U.S. 897 (1984).

72. National Association of Criminal Defense Lawyers, http://www.nacdl.org/public.nsf/legislation/ ci_01_005?opendocument; Laurie Aucoin, "Righting Wrongful Convictions," Northwestern (Spring 1999), http://www. northwestern.edu/ magazine/northwestern/spring99/convictions.htm.

73. See, for example, "The Battle in Congress," *The Economist*, October 20, 2001, pp. 31, 34.

Chapter 14

1. Jack A. Goldstone, "An Analytical Framework," in *Revolutions of the Late Twentieth Century*, ed. Jack A. Goldstone, Ted Robert Gurr, and Farroyh Moshiri (Boulder, CO: Westview Press, 1991), p. 325.

2. Goldstone, "Revolutions in World History," in *Revolutions: Theoretical, Comparative, and Historical Studies*, 2nd ed., ed. Jack A. Goldstone (San Diego: Harcourt, 1993), p. 320.

3. Quoted in Thomas Greene, *Comparative Revolutionary Movements* (Englewood Cliffs, NJ: Prentice-Hall, 1989), p. 5.

4. Ibid., p. 5.

5. Ibid., p. 6.

6. Ted Robert Gurr and Jack Goldstone, "Comparisons and Policy Implications," in *Revolutions of the Late Twentieth Century*, p. 324. The linguistic distinction between *revolution* (a modern term) and *rebellion* is also noteworthy. The distinction is not uniformly made in the literature, however.

7. Barrington Moore Jr., *Reflections on the Causes of Human Misery and upon Certain Proposals to Eliminate Them* (Boston: Beacon Press, 1972), p. 170.

8. James Dougherty and Robert Pfaltzgraff Jr., *Contending Theories of International Relations*, 3rd ed. (New York: Harper & Row, 1990), p. 321. The authors cite the scholarly works of Hannah Arendt, among others.

9. Irving Kristol, "The American Revolution as a Successful Revolution," in *Readings in American Democracy*, ed. Paul Peterson (Dubuque, IA: Kendall Hunt, 1979), pp. 52–53.

10. Cecilia Kenyon, "Republicanism and Radicalism in the American Revolution: An Old-Fashioned Interpretation," in *The Reinterpretation of the American Revolution, 1763–1789*, ed. J. Greene (New York: Harper & Row, 1968), p. 291.

11. See, for instance, Bernard Bailyn, "Political Experience and Enlightenment in Eighteenth-Century America," in *The Reinterpretation of the American Revolution*, ed. J. Greene (New York: Harper & Row, 1968), pp. 282–283.

12. Martin Diamond, "The Revolution of Sober Expectations," in *Readings in American Democracy*, ed. Paul Peterson (Dubuque, IA: Kendall Hunt, 1979), p. 66.

13. Thomas Jefferson to Roger C. Weightman, June 24, 1826, in *The Political Writings of Thomas Jefferson: Representative Samples*, ed. Edward Dumbauld (Indianapolis: Bobbs-Merrill, 1965), p. 9.

14. Benjamin Wright, *Consensus and Continuity, 1776–1787* (New York: Norton, 1967), p. 3. Here Wright relies on the work of J. Franklin Jameson.

15. Ibid., p. 1.

16. Ibid.
17. Kristol, "American Revolution," p. 53.
18. Diamond, "Revolution of Sober Expectations," p. 3.
19. Ibid., p. 65.
20. Crane Brinton, *The Anatomy of Revolution* (Magnolia, MA: Peter Smith, 1990), pp. 122–123.
21. Hannah Arendt, *On Revolution* (New York: Penguin, 1976), p. 60.
22. Kristol, "The American Revolution," p. 6.
23. Ibid., p. 61.
24. Edmund Burke, *Reflections on the Revolution in France* (Indianapolis: Library of Liberal Arts, 1955), p. 197.
25. Thomas Paine, "The Rights of Man," in *Thomas Paine: Representative Selections*, ed. H. Clark (New York: Hill and Wang, 1967), p. 159.
26. Ibid., pp. 184–185.
27. Ibid., p. 162.
28. Ibid., p. 61.
29. Ibid., p. 70.
30. Nonetheless, Burke became something of a supporter of the American cause in the Revolutionary War, urging his nation to recognize the legitimacy of the Americans' grievances.
31. John Locke, "An Essay Concerning the True Original Extent and End of Civil Government," in *Two Treatises on Government* (New York: New American Library, 1963), p. 466.
32. Ibid., p. 463.
33. Ibid., pp. 452–453.
34. See Joseph Cropsey, *Political Philosophy and the Issues of Politics* (Chicago: University of Chicago Press, 1977), pp. 157–162.
35. Goldstone, "Analytical Framework," p. 50.
36. Alexis de Tocqueville, *The Old Regime and the French Revolution* (Garden City, NY: Doubleday, 1955), p. 176.
37. James C. Davies, "Toward a Theory of Revolution," *American Sociological Review*, February 1962, p. 6.
38. Raymond Tanter and Manus Midlarsky, "A Theory of Revolution," *Journal of Conflict Resolution* 11 (1967), p. 272, table 6.
39. Ted Gurr, *Why Men Rebel* (Princeton, NJ: Princeton University Press, 1970), pp. 3–21.
40. As pointed out by Jack A. Goldstone in "Theories of Revolution: The Third Revolution," *World Politics* (April 1980), pp. 425–453.
41. This discussion builds heavily on Gurr and Goldstone, "Comparisons and Policy Implications," pp. 324–352.
42. Barry Schutz and Robert Slater, "A Framework for Analysis," in *Revolution and Political Change in the Third World*, ed. Barry Schutz and Robert Slater (Boulder, CO: Lynne Rienner, 1990), pp. 7–9. Also see Gurr and Goldstone, "Comparisons and Policy Implications," p. 331.
43. Since the publication of his *Thinking about Crime* in 1975, James Q. Wilson's writings on crime in America have emphasized that socializing young males is the greatest challenge for a law-abiding society; there are now suggestions in the literature that this demographic fact also has implications for revolution. Compare Gurr and Goldstone, "Comparisons and Policy Implications," p. 335 (who emphasize age, not gender), and Wilson, *Thinking about Crime* (New York: Basic Books, 1975).
44. Walter Lacqueur, "Revolution," in *International Encyclopedia of the Social Sciences* (New York: Macmillan/Free Press, 1968), p. 501. See also Robert Hunter, *Revolution: Why? How? When?* (New York: Harper & Row, 1940), p. 126.
45. Theda Skocpol, *States and Social Revolutions: A Comparative Analysis of France, Russia, and China* (Cambridge: Cambridge University Press, 1979), p. 249.
46. Tocqueville, *The Old Regime*, p. 176.
47. Ibid.

48. Ibid., p. 187.
49. D. E. H. Russell, *Rebellion, Revolution, and Armed Forces: A Comparative Study of Fifteen Countries with Special Emphasis on Cuba and South Africa* (Orlando, FL: Academic Press, 1974).
50. Charismatic leadership is a particularly important element in totalitarian revolution. See Chapter 6.
51. Gurr and Goldstone, "Comparisons and Policy Implications," pp. 353–354.
52. Ibid., p. 334.
53. José Ortega y Gasset, *The Revolt of the Masses* (New York: Norton, 1993). Originally published in 1930.
54. This quote is taken from an excerpt published at http://www.historyguide.org/europe/gasset.html.
55. Ibid.

Chapter 15

1. Paul Seabury and Angelo M. Codevilla, *War: Ends and Means* (New York: Basic Books, 1990), p. 6.
2. G. W. F. Hegel, *Philosophy of Right*, trans. T. M. Knox, in *Great Books of the Western World*, vol. 46, ed. R. Hutchins (Chicago: Encyclopaedia Britannica, 1952), p. 149.
3. Friedrich Nietzsche, *Human, All Too Human*, trans. Marion Farber (Lincoln: University of Nebraska Press, 1984), pp. 230–231, aphorism #477.
4. Benito Mussolini, "The Doctrine of Fascism," trans. M. Oakeshott, in *Great Political Thinkers*, ed. William Ebenstein (New York: Holt, 1965), p. 621.
5. John Vasquez, "Introduction: Studying War Scientifically," in *The Scientific Study of Peace and War: A Text Reader*, ed. John Vasquez and Marie Henehan (New York: Lexington, 1992), p. xix.
6. Ibid., p. xxii.
7. For an excellent introduction to the statistical methodology associated with quantitative war studies, see Stuart Bremer et al. (adapted by Marie Henehan), "The Scientific Study of War: A Learning Package," in *Scientific Study of Peace*, pp. 373–437.
8. James Dougherty and Robert Pfaltzgraff Jr., *Contending Theories of International Relations: A Comprehensive Study*, 3rd ed. (New York: HarperCollins, 1990), p. 356.
9. Greg Cashman, *What Causes War? An Introduction to Theories of International Conflict* (New York: Lexington, 1993), p. 279.
10. This discussion comprises a variation of the classification scheme presented by Kenneth N. Waltz, *Man, the State, and War: A Theoretical Analysis* (New York: Columbia University Press, 1965). We acknowledge our debt to his scholarship.
11. The quotation is from Sir Norman Angell's "Neutrality and Collective Security," cited in Edward Hallett Carr, *The Twenty Years' Crisis, 1919–1939* (New York: Harper & Row, 1964), p. 39.
12. Thomas Hobbes, *The Leviathan* (London: Everyman's Library, 1965), p. 64.
13. Hans J. Morgenthau, *Politics among Nations: The Struggle for Power and Peace*, 5th ed. (New York: McGraw-Hill, 1992), pp. 3–4.
14. Ibid., p. 29.
15. Jean-Jacques Rousseau, *First and Second Discourses*, trans. Roger Masters and Judith Masters, ed. Roger Masters (New York: St. Martin's Press, 1964), p. 197. The quotation is from Rousseau's Notes, *Second Discourse*.
16. Ibid., pp. 195–196.
17. Ibid., *Second Discourse*, pp. 141–142.
18. Ibid., p. 161.
19. Frederick Hartmann, *The Relations of Nations* (New York: Macmillan, 1978), p. 32.
20. William Galston, *Kant and the Problem of History* (Chicago: University of Chicago Press, 1975), pp. 26–27.
21. Immanuel Kant, "Eternal Peace," in *Immanuel Kant's Moral and Political Writings*, ed. Carl Friedrich (New York: Modern Library, 1949), p. 438.

22. V. I. Lenin, *Imperialism: The Highest Stage of Capitalism* (New York: International Publishers, 1939), p. 124.

23. Robert Goldwin, "John Locke," in *History of Political Philosophy,* ed. L. Strauss and J. Cropsey (Skokie, IL: Rand McNally, 1963), p. 442.

24. Richard Falk, *This Endangered Planet: Prospects and Proposals for Human Survival* (New York: Vintage Books, 1972), pp. 106–107.

25. Ibid., p. 107.

26. Ibid., p. 113.

27. Ibid., p. 155.

28. Cashman, *What Causes War?* p. 157.

29. Aristotle, *The Politics,* trans. and ed. Ernest Barker (New York: Oxford University Press, 1962), 1313b, p. 245.

30. Hannah Arendt, *Totalitarianism* (New York: Harcourt, 1951), pp. 113–114.

31. William Dixon, "Democracy and the Peaceful Settlement of International Conflict," *American Political Science Review* 88 (March 1994), p. 14.

32. On democracies' proclivity to join wars more often than other forms of government, see Stuart Bremer, "Are Democracies Less Likely to Join Wars?" (paper presented at the annual meeting of the American Political Science Association, Chicago, September 3–6, 1992).

33. For an extended discussion, see Bruce Russett, *Grasping the Democratic Peace* (Princeton, NJ: Princeton University Press, 1993).

34. As pointed out by Cashman, *What Causes War?* p. 129.

35. Ibid.

36. Ibid., pp. 137–139.

37. Rudolph Rummel, "Some Empirical Findings," *World Politics* 21 (1969), pp. 238–239.

38. This discussion selectively follows Cashman, *What Causes War?* pp. 132–134.

39. Morgenthau, *Politics among Nations,* pp. 51–57.

40. Ibid., p. 133.

41. Michael Haas, "Societal Approaches to the Study of War," in *The War System,* ed. Richard Falk and Samuel Kim (Boulder, CO: Westview Press, 1980), pp. 355–356, 365.

42. See John Vasquez, "The Steps to War," in *The Scientific Study of Peace and War: A Text Reader,* ed. John Vasquez and Marie Henehan (New York: Lexington, 1992), pp. 343–370.

43. Jack Levy, "Alliance Formation and War Behavior: An Analysis of the Great Powers, 1495–1975," in *Scientific Study of Peace and War,* pp. 3–36.

44. Vasquez, "Steps to War," p. 370.

45. Cashman, *What Causes War?* p. 137.

46. Ibid.

47. Dougherty and Pfaltzgraff, *Contending Theories,* pp. 354–355.

48. Ibid., pp. 145–152; however, as Cashman notes, the evidence is not unanimous.

49. The studies are summarized in ibid., pp. 142–145. See also Paul Diehl, "Arms Races to War: Testing Some Empirical Linkages," *Sociological Quarterly* 26 (Fall 1985), pp. 331–349; and his "Continuity and Military Escalation in Major Power Rivalries, 1816–1980," *Journal of Politics* 47 (November 1985), pp. 1203–1211.

50. Nazli Chourci and Robert North, "Lateral Pressure in International Relations: Concept and Theory," in *Handbook of War Studies,* ed. Manus Midlarsky (Boston: Unwin Hyman, 1989), pp. 310–311.

51. Waltz, *Man, the State, and War,* p. 233.

52. Quoted in Lee McDonald, *Western Political Theory: From Its Origins to the Present* (Orlando, FL: Harcourt, 1968), p. 127.

53. Cited in Dougherty and Pfaltzgraff, *Contending Theories,* pp. 354–355. For an in-depth discussion of St. Ambrose's teachings on ethics and the use of force, see Louis J. Swift, "St. Ambrose on Violence and War," *Transactions and Proceedings of the American Philological Association,* Vol. 101, (1970), pp. 533–543.

54. Michael Walzer, *Just and Unjust Wars* (New York: Basic Books, 1968), p. 1.

55. http://www.netwarcom.navy.mil;http://www.wvec.com/news/military/stories/wvec_military_080106_cyper_ops_change.4fc6405.html.

56. Tony Halpin, "Putin Accused of Launching Cyber War," *The Times Online* (London), May 18, 2007. http://www.timesonline.co.uk/tol/news/world/europe/article1805636.ece.

57. Thom Shanker and David E. Sanger, "Privacy May Be a Victim in Cyberdefense Plan," *New York Times*, June 13, 2009. http://www.nytimes.com/2009/06/13/us/politics/13cyber.html.

Chapter 16

1. This story was widely reported in the world press. The UN promptly shut down all of its World Population food aid centers in Pakistan.

2. "Nihilism and Terror," *New Republic*, September 29, 1986, p. 11.

3. See also Martha Crenshaw, "The Causes of Terrorism," in *International Terrorism: Characteristics, Causes, Controls*, ed. Charles W. Kegley Jr. (New York: St. Martin's Press, 1990), p. 113.

4. See, for example, Ekaterina Stepanova, *Terrorism in Asymmetrical Conflict*, SIPRI Research Report No. 23, Oxford University Press, 2008, especially Chapters 2 and 3, pp. 28–99.

5. For a more complete discussion, see David Rapoport, "Religion and Terror: Thugs, Assassins, and Zealots," in *International Terrorism*, ed. Kegley, pp. 146–157. Also see Leonard Weinberg and Paul Davis, *Introduction to Political Terrorism* (New York: McGraw-Hill, 1989), pp. 19–23.

6. Weinberg and Davis, *Introduction to Political Terrorism*, p. 22.

7. Compare Rapoport, "Religion and Terror," p. 146, and Weinberg and Davis, *Introduction to Political Terrorism*, pp. 24–26.

8. Rushworth M. Kidder, "Unmasking Terrorism," *Christian Science Monitor*, May 13, 1986, p. 19.

9. Ibid., p. 20.

10. Ibid.

11. Walter Laqueur, *Terrorism* (Boston: Little, Brown, 1979), p. 220.

12. Paul Johnson, "The Seven Deadly Sins of Terrorism," in *International Terrorism*, ed. Kegley, p. 65.

13. Carlos Marighella, *Mini-Manual for Urban Guerrillas*, trans. Gene Hanrahan (Chapel Hill, NC: Documentary Publication, 1984). Originally published in Spanish in 1970.

14. Claire Sterling, *The Terror Network: The Secret War of International Terrorism* (New York: Holt, 1981), pp. 21–22.

15. Neil A. Lewis and Eric Schmitt, "Cuba Detentions May Last for Years," *New York Times*, February 13, 2004 (online edition).

16. See Adam Liptak, "Justices Erase Ruling That Allowed Detention," *New York Times*, March 6, 2009; see also http://www.cnn.com/2007/LAW/06/11/terror.ruling.ap/index.html.

17. In the 1990s, estimates ranged as high as 600. See, for example, David E. Long, *The Anatomy of Terrorism* (New York: Free Press, 1990), p. 165.

18. Mohammad M. Hafez, *Middle East Journal* 4 (Fall 2000), pp. 584–585.

19. Sara Miller Llana, "Narcotraffickers Attack Televisa, Mexico's Top TV Network," *Christian Science Monitor*, January 8, 2009 (online edition).

20. Long, *The Anatomy of Terrorism*, p. 17.

21. Cynthia C. Combs, *Terrorism in the Twenty-first Century* (Upper Saddle River, NJ: Pearson, 2012), p. 68.

22. Kidder, "Unmasking Terrorism," p. 18.

23. Eric Hoffer, *The True Believer* (New York: Harper & Row, 1951), p. 49.

24. See Frederick J. Hacker, *Crusaders, Criminals, Crazies: Terror and Terrorism in Our Time* (New York: Norton, 1977).

25. Kidder, "Unmasking Terrorism," p. 19.

26. Regarding the lack of remorse, see Long, *Anatomy of Terrorism*, p. 19.

27. See Paul McHugh, *The Weekly Standard*, December 10, 2001.

28. Hoffer, *True Believer*, p. 80.

29. Ibid., p. 81.

30. Matthew Purdy, "Bush's New Rules to Fight Terror Transform the Legal Landscape," *New York Times*, December 16, 2001 (electronic edition). According to Purdy, President Bush was also "considering the possibility of trials on ships at sea or on United States installations, like the naval base at Guantánamo Bay, Cuba. The proceedings promise to be swift and largely secret…[and] the release of information might be limited to the barest facts, like the defendant's name and sentence. Transcripts of the proceedings…could be kept from public view for years, perhaps decades."

31. Tim Heffernan, "Who the Hell is Stanley McChrsystal," *Esquire*, May 19, 2009, online at http://www.esquire.com/the-side/feature/who-is-stanley-mcchrystal-051909.

32. Weinberg and Davis, *Introduction to Political Terrorism*, pp. 168–170.

33. See Kristin Archick, "U.S.-EU Cooperation against Terrorism," CRS Report for Congress, October 16, 2006 online at http://www.fas.org/sgp/crs/terror/RS22030.pdf.

34. Gayle Rivers, *The Specialist: Revelations of a Counterterrorist* (New York: Charter Books, 1985), p. 40. Examples Rivers cites: "The daring July 1976 raid by Israeli commandos at Uganda's Entebbe Airport proved that terrorists are not invincible even after they have taken hostages and dug in, as did the successful commando assault on Túpac Amaru (MRTA) guerrillas holding hostages in the Japanese Embassy in Lima, Peru, in December 1996. Success in hostage rescue operations necessitates highly skilled, quick-hitting commando units, such as Germany's GSG-9, which freed hostages from a Lufthansa airliner hijacked to Mogadishu, Somalia, in 1977; Britain's Special Air Services (SAS); and the U.S. Delta Force. Local police agencies are typically not equipped or trained to deal with terrorism." According to Rivers, "When you are operating with the SAS on the ground in an area like Armagh [in Northern Ireland], you very quickly realize that you are fighting a war, not taking part in a police operation. Night after night,… IRA active-service units [infiltrate] from the safety of the South [move] about freely in areas they made safe for themselves by murder, torture, kneecappings and other intimidation. They are using sophisticated weapons, [including] heavy machine-guns, rocket launchers, landmines and massive quantities of explosives. Through audio surveillance, you listen to the planning sessions at which the orders are given for acts of sabotage that will involve indiscriminate civilian casualties. Civilian police procedures cannot deal with this kind of threat. If you locate a team…in the process of organizing an attack on a shopping center with milk churns packed with high explosives and nails, you send a fighting patrol to attack it; you don't call the local bobby."

35. Richard Clutterbuck, *Protest and the Urban Guerrilla* (New York: Abelard-Shuman, 1974), p. 287.

36. See, Christopher Hitchens, "The End of the Tamil Tigers: Insurgencies Don't Always Have History on their Side," *Slate* (online daily news magazine), May 25, 2009.

37. See, generally, Brian Jenkins, ed., *Terrorism and Personal Protection* (Boston: Butterworth, 1985).

38. Kidder, "Unmasking Terrorism," p. 16.

39. Ibid., p. 17.

Chapter 17

1. The quotations in this discussion are from Thucydides, "The Melian Conference," from *Readings in World Politics*, 2nd ed., ed. Robert Goldwin and Tony Pearce (New York: Oxford University Press, 1970), pp. 472–478.

2. Niccolò Machiavelli, *The Prince*, in *The Prince and the Discourses* (New York: Modern Library, 1952), p. 56.

3. Ibid., p. 64.

4. Hans J. Morgenthau, *Politics among Nations: The Struggle for Power and Peace*, 5th ed. (New York: McGraw-Hill, 1992), p. 11.

5. Ibid., pp. 22–23.

6. Ibid., p. 11.

7. Ibid.

8. Ibid., pp. 221–223.

7.

Tuchman Mathews, "The Environment and International Security," in *World* [...]ty: *Challenges for a New Century,* 2nd ed., ed. Michael Klare and Daniel Thomas [...] York: St. Martin's Press, 1994), p. 286.

[...] for example, Lester R. Brown, *Plan B 3.0: Mobilizing to Save Civilization* 3rd ed. [...]w York: Norton and the Earth Policy Institute, 2008).

[...] the "globalization" entry in the *Stanford Encyclopedia of Philosophy* (SEP) at http://[...]to.stanford.edu/entries/globalization/.

[...]iving in a see-through world," *The Economist,* November 6, 2010, pp. 21–22.

[...]ASEAN Vision 2020" at http://www.aseansec.org/1814.htm.

[...]ee, especially, Kurt M. Campbell, Robert Einhorn, and Mitchell Reiss, *The Nuclear Tipping Point: Why States Reconsider Their Nuclear Options* (Washington, DC: Brookings Institution, 2005).

16. Rachel Carson, *Silent Spring* (Boston: Houghton-Mifflin, 2002). This is the 40th-anniversary edition of the book, originally published in 1962.

17. Eric Eckholm, "Recession Raises Poverty Rate to a 15-Year High," *New York Times,* September 16, 2010.

18. Quoted in Alexander de Conde, *A History of American Foreign Policy: Growth to World Power,* vol. 1, 3rd ed. (New York: Scribner's, 1978), p. 130.

19. Alexis de Tocqueville, *Democracy in America,* vol. 1 (New York: Schocken Books, 1961), p. 522.

20. George F. Kennan, "Sources of Soviet Conduct," in *Caging the Bear: Containment and the Cold War,* ed. Charles Gati (Indianapolis: Bobbs-Merrill, 1974), p. 18.

21. *Congressional Record,* 80 Cong., 1st sess. (March 1947), 1981.

22. See Chalmers Johnson, *Blowback: The Costs and Consequences of American Empire* (New York: Holt, 2000).

23. Ibid., p. 8.

24. Ibid.

25. Ibid., p. 9.

26. Ibid.

27. Ibid., p. 11.

28. Speech by George W. Bush at West Point, New York, June 1, 2002, published as part of a larger document under the title "National Security Strategy of the United States," released by the White House on September 17, 2002. (The quote here is found on p. 15.)

29. Statistics cited at http://www.antiwar.com/casualties/. This website has a link to a list of U.S. service members killed since May 1, 2008.

30. See, for example, Alan Tonelson, "What Is the National Interest?" in *America's National Interest in a Post–Cold War World,* ed. Alvin Z. Rubinstein (New York: McGraw-Hill, 1994), p. 56; also see Thomas M. Magstadt, *An Empire If You Can Keep It: Power and Principle in American Foreign Policy* (Washington, DC: CQ Press, 2004), especially pp. 220–242.

31. Dennis Ross, *Statecraft: And How to Restore America's Standing in the World* (New York: Farrar, Straus and Giroux, 2007), p. x.

32. Martin Gilbert, *The Roots of Appeasement* (New York: New American Library, 1966), p. xi.

33. Although a few commentators suggested that President Bill Clinton's policy helped solidify political alliances with key African American leaders in Congress, this was not likely his main purpose. A different example of altruism took place in 1920–1921, when a terrible famine occurred in the Soviet Union. Despite the Soviet government's avowed support of anticapitalist revolutions in the West, the U.S. government created a relief organization (known as the Hoover Commission). Millions of dollars in food supplies were sent, and many lives were saved in the severely stricken Volga region. At the time, an official Soviet journal observed, "Of all the capitalist countries, only America showed us major and real help." Quoted in Adam Ulam, *Expansionism and Coexistence: Soviet Foreign Policy, 1917–1973,* 2nd ed. (New York: Praeger, 1974), p. 148. Also see John Lewis Gaddis, *Russia, the Soviet Union, and the United States: An Interpretive History* (New York: Wiley, 1978), pp. 99–101.

34. Quoted in Joseph Marion Jones, *The Fifteen Weeks* (New York: Harbinger, 1955), p. 256.
35. Raul Hilberg, *The Destruction of the European Jews* (New York: Harper & Row, 1961), pp. 358–359.
36. Arnold Wolfers, *Discord and Collaboration: Essays on International Politics* (Baltimore, MD: Johns Hopkins University Press, 1965), p. 93.
37. See, for example, Nathan Tarcov, "Principle and Prudence in Foreign Policy: The Founders' Perspective," *The Public Interest* 76 (Summer 1984), pp. 45–60.
38. See Magstadt, *An Empire If You Can Keep It*, pp. 202–219.
39. Joseph Nye, "The New Rome Meets the New Barbarians," *The Economist*, March 23, 2002, pp. 23–24.
40. Ibid., p. 25.
41. Samuel Huntington, "The Clash of Civilizations?" *Foreign Affairs* 72 (Summer 1993), pp. 22–43; and Samuel Huntington, "If Not Civilizations, What? Paradigms of the Post-Cold War Era," *Foreign Affairs* 72 (December 1993), pp. 24–39; Huntington has since published his view on this subject in *The Clash of Civilizations and the Remaking of World Order* (New York: Simon & Schuster, 1996).
42. Huntington, "Clash of Civilizations," p. 40.
43. Robert D. Kaplan, *The Coming Anarchy* (New York: Vintage Books, 2001). This best-selling book is a collection of previously published articles. Kaplan wrote, "Imagine cartography in three dimensions, as if in hologram. In this hologram would be the overlapping sediments of group and other identities atop the merely two-dimensional color markings of city-states and the remaining nations, themselves confused in places by shadowy tentacles, hovering overhead, indicating the power of drug cartels, mafias, and private security agencies. Instead of borders, there would be moving 'centers' of power, as in the Middle Ages. Many of these layers would be in motion. Replacing fixed and abrupt lines on a flat space would be a shifting pattern of buffer entities….To this protean cartographic hologram one must add other factors, such as migrations of populations, explosions of birth rates, vectors of disease. Henceforward the map of the world will never be static. This future map—in a sense, the Last Map—will be an ever-mutating representation of chaos" (pp. 50–51).

Chapter 18

1. Charles W. Kegley Jr. and Eugene Wittkopf, *American Foreign Policy: Pattern and Process*, 2nd ed. (New York: St. Martin's Press, 1987), pp. 149–150; see also, Thomas Friedman, *The World Is Flat: A Brief History of the Twenty-first Century* (New York: Farrar, Straus and Giroux, 2006) and *Lexus and the Olive Tree: Understanding Globalization* (New York: Knopf, 2000).
2. Friedman, *The World Is Flat*, p. 15.
3. The first quote is in Joan Edelman Spero, *The Politics of Economic Relations*, 4th ed. (New York: St. Martin's Press, 1991), p. 104; the second is in Bruce Kogut, "International Business: The New Bottom Line," *Foreign Policy* (Spring 1998), pp. 152-166.
4. U.S. Bureau of Economic Analysis, "Globalization and Multinational Corporations: What Are the Questions and How Well Are We Doing in Answering Them?" United Nations Economic and Social Council, May 26, 2003, p. 2, http://www.unece.org/stats/documents/ces/2003/9.e.pdf. See also, *UN World Investment Report*. For a summary, see Francis Williams, "Global Business: A Fact of Life—UNCTAD's World Investment Report Assesses Role of Multinationals," *Financial Times*, August 31, 1994, p. 4.
5. Kogut, "International Business," p. 152. This article can be accessed online at http://pre.docdat.com/docs/index-119268.html.
6. Spero, *Politics of Economic Relations*, pp. 112–113.
7. George Modelski, ed., *Transnational Corporations and World Order* (New York: Freeman, 1979), p. 3.
8. See Charles W. Kegley Jr. and Eugene Wittkopf, *World Politics: Trend and Transformation*, 6th ed. (New York: St. Martin's Press, 1997), pp. 144–148. The authors quite sensibly classify IGOs by breadth of membership and number of goals.

ocused (though now somewhat dated) study of this phenomenon, see Harold K.
on, *Networks of Interdependence: International Organizations and the Global*
al System (New York: Knopf, 1979).

Cato Institute, a libertarian think tank, has been one of the leading voices on this
within the Washington policy community. See Ted Galen Carpenter, ed., *NATO at*
Confronting a Changing World (Lexington, MA: D.C. Heath, 1990); see also Ted
en Carpenter and Barbara Conry, eds., *NATO Enlargement: Illusions and Reality*
ashington, DC: Cato Institute, 1998).

s L. Claude Jr., *Power and International Relations* (New York: Random House,
)62), p. 97.

ee Margaret Karns, "Maintaining International Peace and Security: UN Peacekeeping
and Peacemaking," in *World Security: Challenges for a New Century,* 2nd ed., ed.
Michael Klare and Daniel Thomas (New York: St. Martin's Press, 1994), p. 199.

13. Joseph E. Stiglitz and Linda J. Bilmes, "The True Cost of the Iraq War: $3 Trillion and
beyond," *Washington Post,* September 5, 2010 (electronic edition).

14. Karen Tumulty, "The Doubts of War," *Time,* March 3, 2003, pp. 40–43.

15. P. W. Singer, *Corporate Warriors: The Rise of the Privatized Military Industry* (Ithaca,
NY: Cornell University Press), 2003, p. 5.

16. Ibid.

17. David Halberstam, *War in a Time of Peace* (New York: Scribners, 2001), pp. 335–336.

18. Hans J. Morgenthau, *Politics among Nations: The Struggle for Power and Peace,* 5th ed.
(New York, Knopf, 1978), p. 281.

19. Lassa Francis Oppenheim, *International Law: A Treatise,* vol. 1, 2nd ed. (London: Longman,
1912), p. 93.

20. Kegley and Wittkopf, *World Politics,* p. 472.

ABC war A general term for war involving weapons of mass destruction (WMD), especially atomic (nuclear), biological, and chemical weapons.

accidental war In the modern age, the unintentional launching of a nuclear attack because of a mistake or miscalculation.

affirmative action Giving preferential treatment to a socially or economically disadvantaged group in compensation for opportunities denied by past discrimination.

American Revolution Also called the War of Independence and the Revolutionary War (1775–1783), this epoch-making event led to the end of British rule over the thirteen American colonies and to the formation of the United States of America in 1787–1789; usually dated from the Declaration of Independence in 1776.

anarchism A system that opposes in principle the existence of any form of government, often through violence and lawlessness.

Antarctic Treaty An international agreement that prohibits all military activity on the Antarctic continent and allows for inspection of all nations' facilities there. It also nullifies all territorial claims to Antarctic land and pledges the signatories to peaceful cooperation in exploration and research.

apartheid system The South African system designed to perpetuate racial domination by whites prior to the advent of black majority rule there in the early 1990s.

arms race Reciprocal military buildups between rival states; a process that tends to accelerate research, technology, and development in weapons systems and, according to some experts, is a potential cause of war.

ascriptive status An individual's status and position in society are ascribed on the basis of religion, gender, age, or some other attribute.

Asian flu A term used to describe the widespread financial turmoil in Asian stock markets, financial institutions, and economies in 1997.

authoritarian state Wherever supreme political power is concentrated in one person (dictatorship) or a small group of persons (oligarchy), individual rights are subordinate to the wishes of the state, and all means necessary are used to repress dissent and crush opposition.

authority Command of the obedience of society's members by a government.

autocracy Unchecked political power exercised by a single ruler.

Balanced Budget Act of 1997 Passed by Congress in 1997, this historic measure mandated a balanced federal budget by 2001 but was ironically undone in that very year by the events of 9/11.

balance of power system A classic theory of international relations that holds that nations of approximately equal strength will seek to maintain the status quo by preventing any one nation from gaining superiority over the others. Participating nations form alliances and frequently resort to war as a means of resolving disputes, seizing territory, gaining prestige, or seeking glory.

Balfour Declaration Named for the British foreign secretary who, in 1947, declared that the United Kingdom favored "the establishment in Palestine of a national home for the Jewish people" and pledged to "facilitate the achievement of this object, it being clearly understood that nothing shall be done which may prejudice the civil and religious rights of the existing non-Jewish communities in Palestine or the rights and political status enjoyed by Jews in any other country."

Bastille At the time of the French Revolution (1789), the Bastille was the infamous royal prison in Paris; the mass storming of the Bastille on July 14, 1789, and the freeing of the prisoners constituted a direct attack against the monarchy and symbolized the end of an era in French history; the revolutionaries then used the guillotine against none other than the reigning Bourbon monarch, King Louis XVI, and his extravagant wife, Queen Marie Antoinette.

behavioral engineering The carefully programmed use of rewards and punishments to instill desired patterns of behavior in an individual or an animal.

behavioral psychology A school of psychological thought that holds that the way people (and animals) act is determined by the stimuli they receive from the environment and from other persons and that human or animal behavior can be manipulated by carefully structuring the environment to provide positive stimuli for desired behavior and negative stimuli for unwanted behavior.

behaviorism An approach to the study of politics that emphasizes fact-based evaluations of action.

bicameralism Division of the legislature into two houses.

Biological Weapons Convention A 1972 international arms control treaty that pledged the destruction of biological weapons stockpiles and outlawed the production and storage of such weapons.

bipolar system Following World War II, the traditional European balance of power system gave way to two rival power blocs, one headed by the United States and the other by the former Soviet Union, each with overwhelming economic and military superiority and each unalterably opposed to the politics and ideology of the other.

bourgeoisie In Marxist ideology, the capitalist class.

brinkmanship In diplomacy, the deliberate use of military threats to create a crisis atmosphere; the calculated effort to take a tense bilateral relationship to the brink of war to achieve a political objective (for example, deterring a common enemy from carrying out an act of aggression against an ally).

British Raj British colonial rule on the Asian subcontinent from the eighteenth century to 1947, when India and Pakistan became independent.

brokered democracy This theory holds that the interests of major groups cannot be steamrolled by the majority without jeopardizing democracy and that legislators and decision makers should act as brokers in writing laws and devising policies that are acceptable to all major groups in society.

Bundesrat The upper house in the German federal system; its members, who are appointed directly by the *Länder* (states), exercise mostly informal influence in the legislative process (see also *Bundestag*).

Bundestag The lower house in the German federal system; most legislative activity occurs in this house (see also *Bundesrat*).

Camp David Accords A 1979 agreement by which Israel gave the Sinai back to Egypt in return for Egypt's recognition of Israel's right to exist; the two former enemies established full diplomatic relations and pledged to remain at peace with each other.

capitalism An economic system in which individuals own the means of production and can legally amass unlimited personal wealth. Capitalist theory holds that governments should not impose any unnecessary restrictions on economic activity and that the laws of supply and demand can best regulate the economy. In a capitalist system, the private sector (mainly business and consumers), rather than government, makes most of the key decisions about production, employment, savings, investment, and the like; the opposite of a centrally planned economy such as existed in the Soviet Union under Stalin and Stalin's successors.

catalytic war A conflict that begins as a localized and limited encounter but grows into a general war after other parties are drawn into the conflict through the activation of military alliances.

cells Small, tightly knit organizational units at the grassroots level of V. I. Lenin's Bolshevik Party.

charismatic leader A political leader who gains legitimacy largely through the adoration of the populace deriving from past heroic feats (real or imagined), personality traits, oratorical skills, and the like.

checks and balances Constitutional tools that enable branches of government to resist any illegitimate expansion of power by other branches.

Chemical Weapons Convention A 1993 international arms control treaty to eliminate chemical weapons within ten years. It calls for the destruction of chemical weapons stockpiles and monitoring companies making compounds that can be used to produce nerve agents in order to end production of chemical weapons.

citizen-leader An individual who influences government decisively even though he or she holds no official government position.

citizenship The right and the obligation to participate constructively in the ongoing enterprise of self-government.

Citizens United Landmark 2010 Supreme Court decision against campaign finance reform equating money donated to support or oppose political candidates or causes with free speech protected under the First Amendment: the upshot of this ruling is to allow unlimited amounts of money to be poured into political action committees called Super PACs.

civic education The process of inculcating in potential citizens the fundamental values and beliefs of the established order.

civil liberties Basic constitutional rights guaranteed to all citizens, including the right to life and freedom of speech, religion, and association, as well as freedom from arbitrary arrest and incarceration, torture, and slavery. But there is no universally accepted definition or list.

civil war A war between geographical sections or rival groups within a nation.

classless society In Marxist political theory, the ideal society in which wealth is equally distributed according to the principle "from each according to his ability, to each according to his needs."

coalition government In a multiparty parliamentary system, the political situation in which no single party has a majority and the largest party allies itself loosely with other, smaller parties to control a majority of the legislative seats.

co-decision In the European Union, a method of legislation and rule-making that involves both the European Council (heads of government) and the European Parliament.

collective memory The history we learn about in grade school; what we come to know about our leaders, about crises we have survived as a nation, and about wars we have fought.

collective security In international relations, a system designed to prevent war by combining the armed forces of law-abiding and peace-loving nations in a powerful league capable of deterring or defeating any would-be aggressor.

collectivization The belief that the public good is best served by common (as opposed to individual) ownership of a political community's means of production and distribution; derived from "collective," denoting a form of community or commune in Marxist ideology.

colonialism The policy of seeking to dominate the economic or political affairs of underdeveloped areas or weaker countries (see also *imperialism*).

commercial republic This concept, found in the Federalist Papers, is most closely identified with Alexander Hamilton, who championed the idea of a democracy based on economic vitality, capitalistic principles, and private enterprise free of undue state regulation.

Common Agricultural Policy (CAP) An EU fixture since the inception of the original common market in 1958. Sets and collects tariffs on agricultural products coming into the EU and provides subsidies to EU farmers.

common law In Great Britain, laws derived from consistent precedents found in judges' rulings and decisions, as opposed to those enacted by Parliament. In the United States, the part of the common law that was in force at the time of the Revolution and not nullified by the Constitution or any subsequent statute.

Commonwealth of Independent States (CIS) A loose federation of newly sovereign nations created after the collapse of the Soviet Union; it consisted of almost all the republics that previously had made up the USSR.

communism An ideology based on radical equality; the antithesis of capitalism.

concurrent majority John Calhoun's theory of democracy, which holds that the main function of government is to mediate between and among the different economic, social, and sectional interests in U.S. society.

conservative A political philosophy that emphasizes prosperity, security, and tradition above other values (see also *liberal*).

constitutional democracy A system of limited government, based on majority rule, in which political power is scattered among many factions and interest groups and governmental actions and institutions must conform to rules defined by a constitution.

constitutionalism The concept that the power and discretion of government and its officials ought to be restrained by a supreme set of neutral rules that prevent arbitrary and unfair action by government; also called the *rule of law*.

containment The global status quo strategic policy followed by the United States after World War II; the term stems from the U.S. policy of containing attempts by the Soviet Union to extend its sphere of control to other states as it had done in Eastern Europe. NATO, the Marshall Plan, and the Korean and Vietnam wars grew out of this policy.

cosmopolitan democracy A model of democracy that sees the individual as part of a world order, not merely (or even primarily) as a citizen of a particular nation-state; often summarized in the slogan, "Think globally, act locally."

counterterrorism Methods used to combat terrorism.

country As a political term, it refers loosely to a sovereign state and is roughly equivalent to "nation" or "nation-state"; *country* is often used as a term of endearment—for example, in the phrase "my country 'tis of thee, sweet land of liberty" in the patriotic song every U.S. child learns in elementary school; *country* has an emotional dimension not present in the word *state*.

coup d'état The attempted seizure of government power by an alternate power group (often the military) that seeks to gain control of vital government institutions without any fundamental alteration in the form of government or society.

crimes against humanity A category of war crimes, first introduced at the Nuremberg trials of Nazi war criminals, covering the wanton, brutal extermination of millions of innocent civilians.

crimes against peace A Nuremberg war crimes trials category, covering the violation of international peace by waging an unjustified, aggressive war.

Declaration of the Rights of Man Enacted by the French National Assembly in August 1789, this brief manifesto was intended as the preamble to a liberal-democratic constitution to be written later; it affirmed the sovereign authority of the nation but limited that authority by recognizing individual rights to life, property, and security.

delegate theory of representation The theory that elected officials should reflect the views of the voters back home, rather than following their own conscience or substituting their own judgment for that of their constituents; in other words, elected representatives should be followers rather than leaders.

demagogue Someone who uses his or her leadership skills to gain public office through appeals to popular fears and prejudices and then abuses that power for personal gain.

Democracy Wall A wall located near the Forbidden City in the heart of Beijing; on this wall thousands of people wrote criticisms and complaints against the regime in the winter of 1978–1979. It was a rare opportunity for public dissent that ended in a government crackdown.

democratic correlate A condition or correlate thought to relate positively to the creation and maintenance of democracy within a nation.

Democratic Socialism A form of government based on popular elections, public ownership and control of the main sectors of the economy, and broad welfare programs in health and education to benefit citizens.

democratization Mikhail Gorbachev's policy of encouraging democratic reforms within the former Soviet Union, including increased electoral competition within the Communist Party.

derivative power Political power that arises indirectly as a result of achievements in other areas (art, science, technological prowess, and the like); derivative power is often a product of the heightened prestige or respect that results from such achievements.

deterrence In criminal justice theory, punishing a criminal for the purpose of discouraging others from committing a similar crime. In international relations, the theory that aggressive wars can be prevented if potential victims maintain a military force sufficient to inflict unacceptable punishment on any possible aggressor.

deterrence theory Holds that states acquire nuclear weapons mainly to deter the use of such weapons by other states; this idea spawned a whole new literature on war in the Nuclear Age in the second half of the twentieth century.

developing country Term long used in the West to denote any country that had not achieved levels of economic prosperity and political stability found in North America, Western Europe, Australia, New Zealand, and parts of Asia (particularly Japan, South Korea, Taiwan, and Singapore) during roughly the Cold War era (1945–1989); in general, a country where the ratio of population to land, jobs, and other factors (private capital, infrastructure, education, etc.) is unfavorable and where political stability, public services, and individual safety are lacking. High levels of unemployment, widespread poverty and malnutrition, highly restricted access to education and medical care, official corruption, and social inequality are among the problems often associated with the early stages of economic development.

developmental democracy A model of democracy that emphasizes the development of virtuous citizens: postulates that one essential role of representative government is to serve as a school for civic education to create a politically literate electorate.

dialectical materialism Karl Marx's theory of historical progression, according to which economic classes struggle with one another, producing an evolving series of economic systems that will lead, ultimately, to a classless society.

dictatorship of the proletariat In Marxist theory, the political stage immediately following the workers' revolution, during which the Communist Party controls the state and defends it against a capitalist resurgence or counterrevolution; the dictatorship of the proletariat leads into pure communism and the classless society.

direct democracy A form of government in which political decisions are made directly by citizens, rather than by their representatives.

divided executive Situation in French government in which the president and the prime minister differ in political party or outlook.

domestic terrorism A form of terrorism practiced within a country by people with no ties to any government.

dual executive In a parliamentary system, the division of the functions of head of state and chief executive officer between two persons; the prime minister serves as chief executive, and some other elected (or royal) figure serves as ceremonial head of state.

dual federalism Under this system, which prevailed in the United States between 1835 and 1860, the power of the national government was limited to enumerated powers; during this period, the southern states claimed sovereign powers.

due process A guarantee of fair legal procedure; it is found in the Fifth and Fourteenth Amendments of the U.S. Constitution.

due process of law The established legal and court procedures aimed at ensuring that arrests, interrogations, jury selection, the rules of evidences, verdicts, and sentencing are fair, uniform, and bent toward a common result: justice.

Duma Officially called the State Duma, it is the lower house of the Federal Assembly, Russia's national legislature, reestablished in the 1993 constitution, after having been abolished in 1917. It comprises 450 members, half of whom are elected from nationwide party lists, with the other half elected from single-member constituencies.

dystopia A society whose creators set out to build the perfect political order only to discover that they cannot remain in power except through coercion and by maintaining a ruthless monopoly over the means of communication.

economic stimulus A fiscal tool of government designed to bolster a weak economy and create jobs via public works projects and deficit spending.

elitist theory of democracy In political thought, the theory that a small clique of individuals (a "power elite") at the highest levels of government, industry, and other institutions exercise political power for their own interests; according to elitist theories, ordinary citizens have almost no real influence on governmental policy.

Emissions Trading Scheme (ETS) In the European Union, part of an antipollution drive aimed at significantly reducing Europe's carbon footprint by 2020 by assigning carbon-emission allowances to industries and factories and creating a carbon exchange, or a market where "clean" companies (ones that do not use their full allowances) can sell the credits they accumulate by not polluting to "dirty" companies (ones that exceed their allowances).

entitlements Federal- and state-provided benefits in the United States such as Social Security and Medicare funded by mandatory tax contributions; such benefits become a right, rather than a privilege, in the public mind because recipients typically pay into the system for many years before they are eligible to take anything out.

equal protection The doctrine enshrined in the Fourteenth Amendment that holds that the prohibitions placed on the federal government and the protections afforded American citizens under the Bill of Rights also apply to the states.

equilibrium A synonym for the word *balance*; also often used interchangeably with *stability* in the literature on international relations.

Estates-General Prior to the French Revolution, a quasi-legislative body in France in which each of the three estates (clergy, nobility, and commoners) was represented; it convened in 1789 for the first time since 1614.

ethnic cleansing The practice of clearing all Muslims out of towns and villages in Bosnia by violent means; the term has also been used to characterize genocidal assaults on minority populations in other parts of the world, including the Darfur region of Sudan.

ethnocentric bias The common tendency of human beings to see the world through a cultural lens that distorts reality and exaggerates the good in one's own society and the evil in others.

eugenics The science of controlling the hereditary traits in a species, usually by selective mating, in an attempt to improve the species.

euro area In the European Union, the euro zone refers to the twelve member states that have adopted the euro, including Germany, France, and Italy, but not the United Kingdom.

European Union (EU) The successor to the Common Market or European Economic Community; the governing body that presides over the world's largest single economy.

exclusionary rule In judicial proceedings, the rule that evidence obtained in violation of constitutional guidelines cannot be used in court against the accused.

exit polling Voters leaving the polling place are asked how they voted; designed to provide a snapshot of the likely outcome of an election before the actual votes can be tallied.

fascism A totalitarian political system that is headed by a popular charismatic leader and in which a single political party and carefully controlled violence form the bases of complete social and political control. Fascism differs from communism in that the economic structure, although controlled by the state, is privately owned.

Federal Assembly Russia's national legislature, a bicameral parliament, established under the 1993 constitution, comprising a lower chamber (State Duma) and an upper chamber (Federation Council).

federal budget deficit In the United States, the difference between federal revenues and federal expenditures in a given year; the national debt is the cumulative sum of budget deficits over many years.

federalism A system of limited government based on the division of authority between the central government and smaller regional governments.

first past the post An electoral method used in the United States and United Kingdom whereby candidates run in single-member districts and the winner is decided by plurality vote; favors broad-based, entrenched political parties and tends toward a two-party configuration.

French Revolution This 1789 war brought down the Bourbon monarchy in France in the name of "*liberté, egalité, et fraternité*" (liberty, equality, and fraternity); introduced the contagion of liberalism in a Europe still ruled by conservative, aristocratic, and royalist institutions; and ushered in the rule of Napoléon Bonaparte. Prelude to the First Republic in France and to the Napoleonic Wars.

functionalism According to functionalist theory, the gradual transfer of economic and social functions to international cooperative agencies (for example, specialized UN agencies, such as UNESCO) will eventually lead to a transfer of actual authority and integration of political activities on the international level.

gender gap Differences in voting between men and women in the United States; this disparity is most obvious in political issues and elections that raise the issue of appropriateness of governmental force.

Geneva Convention A body of international law dealing with the treatment of the wounded, prisoners of war, and civilians in a war zone.

Gestapo In Nazi Germany, the secret state police, Hitler's instrument for spreading mass terror among Jews and political opponents.

glasnost Literally "openness"; this term refers to Mikhail Gorbachev's curtailment of censorship and encouragement of political discussion and dissent within the former Soviet Union.

Gleichschaltung Hitler's technique of using Nazi-controlled associations, clubs, and organizations to coordinate his revolutionary activities.

globalization The process by which values, attitudes, preferences, and products associated with the most technologically advanced democracies are spread around the world via mass media and trade.

government The persons and institutions that make and enforce rules or laws for the larger community.

gradualism The belief that major changes in society should take place slowly, through reform, rather than suddenly, through revolution.

Great Leap Forward Mao Zedong's attempt, in the late 1950s and early 1960s, to transform and modernize China's economic structure through mass mobilization of the entire population into self-sufficient communes in which everything was done in groups.

Great Power During the era of the classical balance of power in Europe from the mid-seventeenth century to the outbreak of World War II in 1939, the states big enough to challenge or pose a threat to the status quo or to lead a coalition in defense of the status quo against acts of armed aggression or territorial expansion were called Great Powers, at one time or another to include Great Britain, France, Russia, Prussia (later Germany), Austria-Hungary, Spain, and Sweden, as well as the United States from the 1890s on.

Great Proletarian Cultural Revolution A chaotic period beginning in 1966, when the youth of China (the Red Guards), at Mao Zedong's direction, attacked all bureaucratic and military officials on the pretext that a reemergence of capitalist and materialist tendencies was taking place. The offending officials were sent to forced-labor camps to be "reeducated."

Green Revolution A dramatic rise in agricultural output, resulting from modern irrigation systems and synthetic fertilizers, characteristic of modern India, Mexico, Taiwan, and the Philippines.

guerrilla warfare The tactics used by loosely organized military forces grouped into small, mobile squads that carry out acts of terrorism and sabotage, then melt back into the civilian population.

gulag archipelago Metaphorical name for the network of slave labor camps established in the former Soviet Union by Joseph Stalin and maintained by his secret police to which nonconformists and politically undesirable persons were sent.

Hague Convention A widely accepted set of rules governing conduct in land wars, the use of new weapons, and the rights and duties of both neutral and warring parties.

hard power In international politics, the use of military force or the threat to use force or other coercive measures such as freezing foreign assets or imposing strict economic sanctions.

Hare plan In parliamentary democracies, an electoral procedure whereby candidates compete for a set number of seats, and those who receive a certain quota of votes are elected. Voters vote only once and indicate both a first and a second choice.

Hundred Flowers campaign A brief period in China (1956) when Mao Zedong directed that freedom of expression and individualism be allowed; it was quashed when violent criticism of the regime erupted.

idealism A political philosophy that considers values, ideals, and moral principles as the keys to comprehending, and possibly changing, the behavior of nation-states.

ideology Any set of fixed, predictable ideas held by politicians and citizens on how to serve the public good.

imperialism A policy of territorial expansion (empire building), often by means of military conquest; derived from the word *empire*.

inadvertent war A war resulting from misperception, misinformation, or miscalculation; an unnecessary war.

incarceration The isolation of criminals in an effort to protect society and to prevent lawbreakers from committing more crimes.

individualism According to Alexis de Tocqueville, the direction of one's feelings toward oneself and one's immediate situation; a self-centered detachment from the broader concerns of society as a whole. According to John Stuart Mill, the qualities of human character that separate humans from animals and give them uniqueness and dignity.

initiative A mechanism by which voters act as legislators, placing a measure on the ballot by petition and directly deciding whether or not to make it a law on election day.

Institutional Revolutionary Party (PRI) The dominant political party in Mexico from 1929 to the present. The PRI had never lost an election until 2000, when Vicente Fox of the National Action Party won the presidency.

intercontinental ballistic missile (ICBM) A long-range missile armed with multiple nuclear warheads capable of striking targets anywhere in the world; both the United States and Russia possess large arsenals of these ultimate strategic weapons.

interdependence In international politics, a condition in which national economies become inextricably entwined in the global economy, as political and business elites design strategies for continued growth and prosperity around access to foreign markets, labor, and capital.

interest aggregation How the interests, concerns, and demands of various individuals and groups in society are translated into policies and programs; in constitutional democracies, a major function of political parties.

interest group An association of individuals that attempts to influence policy and legislation in a confined area of special interest, often through lobbying, campaign contributions, and bloc voting.

international governmental organization (IGO) A grouping of established states; IGOs are based on treaties, have formal structures, and meet at regular intervals.

internationalist Theorist favoring peace and cooperation among nations through the active participation of all governments in some sort of world organization.

international law The body of customs, treaties, and generally accepted rules that define the rights and obligations of nations when dealing with one another.

International Monetary Fund (IMF) A specialized agency of the United Nations designed to promote worldwide monetary cooperation, international trade, and economic stability. It also helps equalize balance of payments by allowing member countries to borrow from its fund.

international nongovernmental organization (INGO) Comprised of private individuals and groups, an INGO transcends borders in pursuit of common causes.

international terrorism Headline-grabbing, politically motivated acts of violence having consequences and ramifications not confined to a single country; terrorism that spills over into the international arena for whatever reason, whether state-sponsored or not.

interstate war Armed conflict between sovereign states.

intifada An Arabic word meaning "uprising"; the name given to the prolonged Palestinian uprising against Israeli occupation in the West Bank and Gaza in 1987–1993 and again in 2001–2002.

iron law of oligarchy According to this theory, the administrative necessities involved in managing any large organization, access to and control of information and communication, inevitably become concentrated in the hands of a few bureaucrats, who then wield true power in the organization.

judicial review The power of a court to declare acts by the government unconstitutional and hence void.

junta A ruling oligarchy, especially one made up of military officers.

justice Fairness; the distribution of rewards and burdens in society in accordance with what is deserved.

just war A war fought in self-defense or because it is the only way a nation can do what is right.

keeper of the balance In a balance of power system, the nation-state that functions as an arbiter in disputes, taking sides to preserve the political equilibrium.

Knesset The unicameral Israeli parliament.

kulaks A class of well-to-do landowners in Russian society that was purged by Joseph Stalin because it resisted his drive to establish huge collective farms under state control.

Kuomintang The Chinese Nationalist Party, led by Chiang Kai-shek, defeated by Mao Zedong in 1949.

Kyoto Protocol Countries that ratify this treaty, which went into effect in 2005, agree to cut emissions of carbon dioxide and five other greenhouse gases or to engage in emissions trading if they exceed a certain cap; the United States signed it under President Bill Clinton, but President George W. Bush renounced it shortly after taking office in 2001 and President Barack Obama, who was sympathetic to the Kyoto pact as a candidate, in office has shown little inclination to push for a new global climate-change treaty.

law of capitalist accumulation According to Karl Marx, the invariable rule that stronger capitalists, motivated solely by greed, will gradually eliminate weaker competitors and gain increasing control of the market.

law of pauperization In Karl Marx's view, the rule that capitalism has a built-in tendency toward recession and unemployment, and thus workers inevitably become surplus labor.

laissez faire capitalism An ideology that views the marketplace, unfettered by state interference, as the best regulator of the economic life of a society.

least developed countries (LDCs) Countries where the ratio of population to land and jobs is unfavorable, where the economy is not highly diversified, and where literacy rates are low; three criteria used to classify LDCs also indicate the challenges they face: (1) low income; (2) human resource weakness (nutrition, health, education, adult literacy); and (3) economic vulnerability.

legislative referendum A vote through which citizens may directly repeal a law.

legitimacy The exercise of political power in a community in a way that is voluntarily accepted by the members of that community.

legitimate authority The legal and moral right of a government to rule over a specific population and control a specific territory; the term *legitimacy* usually implies a widely recognized claim of governmental authority and voluntary acceptance on the part of the population(s) directly affected.

liberal A political philosophy that emphasizes individualism, equality, and civil rights above other values (see also *conservative*).

liberal education A type of education often associated with private colleges in the United States; stresses the development of critical thinking skills through the study of literature, philosophy, history, and science.

libertarianism The belief that the state is a necessary evil best kept small and weak relative to society; libertarians typically value individual liberty above social services and security.

limited war The opposite of all-out war, particularly an all-out nuclear war, in which adversaries choose not to use the most potent weapons available to them.

list system Method of proportional representation by which candidates are ranked on the ballot by their party and are chosen according to rank.

lobby An interest group that operates in Washington, D.C., or in a state capital, and attempts to influence legislators, decision makers, and regulators to bend laws, policies, and rules in ways that benefit its membership or constituency.

Lok Sabha The lower house of India's Federal Parliament; the directly elected House of the People. In India, as in the United Kingdom and other parliamentary systems, governments are formed by the majority party (or a coalition of parties) in the lower house following national elections (see also *Rajya Sabha*).

low-information rationality The idea that voters can make sensible choices in elections even though they lack knowledge and sophistication about public policy, candidates, and current events.

low-intensity conflict Internal warfare that is sporadic and carried out on a small scale but often prolonged and debilitating to the state and society in which it occurs.

Loyal Opposition The belief, which originated in England, that the out-of-power party has a responsibility to formulate alternative policies and programs; such a party is sometimes called the Loyal Opposition.

Magna Carta A list of political concessions granted in 1215 by King John to his barons that became the basis for the rule of law in England.

majority rule The principle that any candidate or program that receives at least half of all votes plus one prevails.

Marshall Plan A post–World War II program of massive economic assistance to Western Europe, inspired by the fear that those war-devastated countries were ripe for communist-backed revolutions.

Marxism An ideology based on the writings of Karl Marx (1818–1883), who theorized that the future belonged to a rising underclass of urban-industrial workers he called "the proletariat."

Marxism-Leninism In the history of the Russian Revolution, Lenin's anticapitalist rationale for the overthrow of the czar (absolute monarch) and the establishment of a new political order based on communist principles set forth in the writings of Karl Marx.

massive retaliation Strategic military doctrine based on a plausible standing threat of nuclear reprisal employed by the United States in the 1950s during the short-lived era of the U.S. nuclear monopoly. According to this doctrine, if the Soviet Union attacked U.S. allies with conventional military forces, the United States would retaliate with nuclear weapons.

mass media The vehicles of mass communication, such as television, radio, the Internet, film, books, magazines, and newspapers.

Meiji Restoration The end of Japan's feudal era, in 1868, when a small group of powerful individuals crowned a symbolic emperor, embarked on an economic modernization program, and established a modern governmental bureaucracy.

methodology The way scientists and scholars set about exploring, explaining, proving, or disproving propositions in different academic disciplines. The precise methods vary according to the discipline and the object, event, process, or phenomenon under investigation.

mixed regime A nation in which the various branches of government represent social classes.

Moghuls Muslim invaders who created a dynastic empire on the Asian subcontinent; the greatest Moghul rulers were Babur (1526–1530), Akbar (1556–1605), Shah Jahan (1628–1658), and Aurangzeb (1658–1707); Shah Jahan was the architect of the Taj Mahal.

monarchism A system based on the belief that political power should be concentrated in one person (for example, a king) who rules by decree.

monopoly capitalism The last stage before the downfall of the whole capitalist system.

Monroe Doctrine A status quo international policy laid down by U.S. President James Monroe, who pledged the United States would resist any attempts by outside powers to alter the balance of power in the American hemisphere.

moral relativism The idea that all moral judgments are conditional and only "true" in a certain religious, cultural, or social context; the belief that there is no such thing as universal truth in the realm of ethics or morality.

motor voter law A statute that allows residents of a given locality to register to vote at convenient places, such as welfare offices and drivers' license bureaus; the idea behind laws of this kind is to remove technical obstacles to voting and thus promote better turnouts in elections.

multinational corporation (MNC) A company that conducts business in more than one country; major MNCs operate on a global scale.

multiple independently targeted reentry vehicle (MIRV) Intercontinental missiles containing many nuclear warheads that can be individually programmed to split off from the nose cone of the rocket upon reentry into the earth's atmosphere and hit different specific targets with a high degree of accuracy.

mutual assured destruction (MAD) A nuclear stalemate in which both sides in an adversarial relationship know that if either one initiates a war, the other will retain enough retaliatory ("second strike") capability to administer unacceptable damage even after absorbing the full impact of a nuclear surprise attack; during the Cold War, a stable strategic relationship between the two superpowers.

mutual deterrence The theory that aggressive wars can be prevented if potential victims maintain a military force sufficient to inflict unacceptable damage on any possible aggressor.

nation Often interchangeable with *state* or *country*; in common usage, denotes a specific people with a distinct language and culture or a major ethnic group—for example, the French, Dutch, Chinese, and Japanese people each constitute a nation as well as a state, hence the term *nation-state*. Not all nations are fortunate enough to have a state of their own; modern examples include the Kurds (Turkey, Iraq, and Iran), Palestinians (West Bank and

Gaza, Lebanon, Jordan), Pashtuns (Afghanistan), and Uighurs and Tibetans (China).

nation-building The process of forming a common identity based on the notion of belonging to a political community separate and distinct from all others; often the concept of "nation" is based on common ethnolinguistic roots.

nation-state A geographically defined community administered by a government.

National Action Party (PAN) The main opposition party in Mexico; the PAN's candidate, Vicente Fox, was elected president in 2000.

National Assembly Focal point of France's bicameral legislative branch that must approve all laws.

national interest A term often invoked but seldom defined, it is usually associated with power enhancement; shorthand for whatever enhances the power and best serves the supreme purposes of the nation, including prosperity, prestige, security, and, above all, survival.

national security Protection of a country from external and internal enemies.

national self-determination The right of a nation to choose its own government.

nationalism Devotion to one's nation; closely akin to patriotism.

nationalistic universalism A messianic foreign policy that seeks to spread the ideas and institutions of one nation to other nations.

natural harmony of interests According to Adam Smith, what is good for the happiness of the individual is also good for society, and vice versa, because people will unintentionally serve society's needs as they pursue their own self-interests without government intervention.

Nazism Officially called National Socialism, Nazism is a form of fascism based on extreme nationalism, militarism, and racism; the ideology associated with Adolf Hitler and the Holocaust.

neocolonialism A theory holding that unequal and exploitative economic arrangements created by former colonial powers continued to be used to maintain control of former colonies and dependencies long after they gained formal independence in the 1950s and 1960s.

neoconservative In the United States, a term associated with the ideology of top advisors and Cabinet members during the presidency of George W. Bush; neoconservatives advocate a strong national defense, decisive military action in the face of threats or provocations, pro-Israeli policy in the Middle East, and a minimum of government interference in the economy. In general, neoconservatives are opposed to federal regulation of business and banking.

nihilism A philosophy that holds that the total destruction of all existing social and political institutions is a desirable end in itself.

no-confidence vote In parliamentary governments, a legislative vote that the sitting government must win to remain in power.

nomenklatura The former Soviet Communist Party's system of controlling all important administrative appointments, thereby ensuring the support and loyalty of those who managed day-to-day affairs.

Nonproliferation Treaty An international agreement, drafted in 1968, not to aid nonnuclear nations in acquiring nuclear weapons; it was not signed by France, China, and other nations actively seeking to build these weapons.

nonstate actor An entity other than a nation-state, including multinational corporations, nongovernmental organizations, and international nongovernmental organizations, that plays a role in international politics.

nonviolent resistance A passive form of confrontation and protest; also called civil disobedience at times.

normativism An approach to the study of politics that is based on examining fundamental and enduring questions.

North American Free Trade Agreement (NAFTA) An agreement signed in 1994 by the United States, Mexico, and Canada that established a compact to allow free trade or trade with reduced tariffs among the three nations.

North Atlantic Treaty Organization (NATO) A permanent peacetime military alliance created by the United States in 1949 to deter Soviet aggression in Europe; today, NATO has twenty-eight members, including twelve Central and East European countries.

North-South conflict A shorthand term for the tensions and disputes that arose between the rich industrialized countries and the former colonies during the Cold War era.

nuclear monopoly When only one side in an adversarial relationship possesses a credible nuclear capability; the United States enjoyed a nuclear monopoly for roughly a decade after World War II.

nullification According to this controversial idea, a state can nullify acts of the U.S. Congress within its own borders; John Calhoun and other states' rights advocates put forward this doctrine prior to the Civil War.

oligarchy A form of authoritarian government in which a small group of powerful individuals wields absolute power.

one-party dominant One-party dominant systems are different from authoritarian one-party systems in that they hold regular elections, allow open criticism of the government, and do not outlaw other parties. Until recently, Japan operated as a one-party dominant system, as did Mexico; South Africa is one current example.

order In a political context, an existing or desired arrangement of institutions based on certain principles such as liberty, equality, prosperity, and security. Also often associated with the rule of law (as in the phrase "law and order") and with conservative values such as stability, obedience, and respect for legitimate authority.

Organization of Petroleum Exporting Countries (OPEC) An international cartel established in 1961 that, since 1973, has successfully manipulated the worldwide supply of and price for oil, with far-reaching consequences for the world economy and political structure.

Outer Space Treaty An international agreement, signed by the United States and the former Soviet Union, that banned the introduction of military weapons into outer space, prohibited the extension of national sovereignty in space, and encouraged cooperation and sharing of information about space research.

overkill Amassing a much larger nuclear arsenal than is (or would be) needed to annihilate any adversary.

paradox of democratic peace Democratic states are often militarily powerful, fight other states, engage in armed intervention, and sometimes commit acts of aggression, but they rarely fight one another.

parliamentary sovereignty In the United Kingdom, the unwritten constitutional principle that makes the British Parliament the supreme law-making body; laws passed by Parliament are not subject to judicial review and cannot be rejected by the Crown.

parliamentary system In contrast to the U.S. presidential model based on the separation of powers, parliamentary systems feature a fusion of powers in which Parliament chooses the prime minister who then forms a government; Parliament can in turn force the government to resign at any time by a simple majority no-confidence vote.

participatory democracy A model of democracy that seeks to expand citizen participation in government to the maximum possible degree; emphasizes universal suffrage, transparency in government, and opportunities for direct action; includes elements of direct democracy.

partiinost The spirit of sacrifice, enthusiasm, and unquestioning devotion required of Communist Party members.

party discipline In a parliamentary system, the tendency of legislators to vote consistently as a bloc with fellow party members in support of the party's platform.

peer group A group of people similar in age and characteristics—for example, college students.

perestroika Term given to Mikhail Gorbachev's various attempts to restructure the Soviet economy while not completely sacrificing its socialist character.

philosopher-king Wise philosopher who governs Plato's ideal city in *The Republic*.

plebiscite A vote by an entire community on some specific issue of public policy.

pluralist democracy A model of democracy that stresses vigorous competition among various interests in a free society; akin to the idea of market forces and the role of free enterprise in classic economic theory.

plurality Something less than an absolute majority. Where the plurality vote principle applies, the candidate or party receiving the largest number of votes wins; where there are multiple parties or candidates, winners typically receive fewer than half the total votes cast.

plurality vote system A system in which candidates who get the largest number of votes win, whether or not they garner a majority of the votes cast; in a majority vote system, if no candidate gets more than half the votes cast, a runoff election is held to determine the winner.

Politburo A small clique that formed the supreme decision-making body in the former Soviet Union. Some Politburo members also belonged to the Secretariat and were ministers of key government departments.

political action committee (PAC) Group organized to raise campaign funds in support of or in opposition to specific candidates.

political apathy Lack of interest in politics resulting from complacency, ignorance, or the conviction that "my vote doesn't really count" or "nobody cares what I think anyway."

political culture The moral values, beliefs, and myths by which people live and for which they are willing to die.

political development A government's ability to exert power effectively, to provide for public order and services, and to withstand eventual changes in leadership.

political efficacy The ability to participate meaningfully in political activities; relevant factors include education, social background, and sense of self-esteem.

political literacy The ability to think and speak intelligently about politics.

political party An organization whose adherents share a political philosophy and common interests and whose primary reason for existing is to win control of government.

political realism The philosophy that power is the key variable in all political relationships and should be used pragmatically and prudently to advance the national interest; policies are judged good or bad on the basis of their effect on national interests, not on their level of morality.

political socialization The process by which members of a community are taught the basic values of their society and are thus prepared for the duties of citizenship.

politician A public officeholder who is prepared to sacrifice previously held principles or shelve unpopular policies to get reelected.

politics The process by which a community selects rulers and empowers them to make decisions, take action to attain common goals, and reconcile conflicts within the community.

popular referendum A device which allows citizens to approve or repeal a legislative act; the measure is placed on the ballot via a petition signed by voters.

positivism A philosophy of science, originated by Auguste Comte, that stresses observable, scientific facts as the sole basis of proof and truth; a skeptical view of ideas or beliefs based on religion or metaphysics.

power The capacity to influence or control the behavior of persons and institutions, whether by persuasion or coercion.

power of the purse Under the U.S. Constitution, the provision that gives the Congress the exclusive right to impose taxes and the final word on government spending.

prior restraint The legal doctrine that the government does not have the power to censor the press, except in cases of dire national emergency.

proletariat In Marxist theory, a member of the working class.

propaganda The use of mass media to create whatever impression is desired among the general population and to influence thoughts and activities toward desired ends.

proportional representation (PR) Any political structure under which seats in the legislature are allocated to each party based on the percentage of the popular vote each receives.

protective democracy A self-contradictory governing model put in place in the United States after the 9/11 terrorist attacks; a government that places national security above liberty and justifies curtailment of constitutional rights in times of crisis or war; an oxymoron.

proxy war A war in which two adversaries back opposing parties to a conflict by supplying money, weapons, and military advisors, while avoiding direct combat operations against each other.

public good The shared beliefs of a political community as to what goals government ought to attain (for example, to achieve the fullest possible measure of security, prosperity, equality, liberty, or justice for all citizens).

public interest The pursuit of policies aimed at the general good or the betterment of society as a whole; in contrast to special interests that pursue laws or policies more narrowly favoring individuals or groups.

public opinion In general, the ideas and views expressed by taxpayers and voters. When a majority of the people hold strong opinions one way or the other on a given issue or policy question, it tends to sway legislators and decision makers who know they will be held accountable at the next election.

purges The elimination of all rivals to power through mass arrests, imprisonment, exile, and murder, often directed at former associates and their followers who have (or are imagined to have) enough influence to be a threat to the ruling elite.

qualified majority vote (QMV) In the European Union, a form of voting in the European Council and Council of Ministers in which no member state has a veto, but passage of a measure requires a triple majority, including more than 70% of the votes cast.

Question Time In the United Kingdom, the times set aside Monday through Thursday every week for Her Majesty's Loyal Opposition (the party out of power) to criticize and scrutinize the actions and decisions of the government (the party in power); twice each week, the prime minister must answer hostile questions fired at him or her by the opposition or backbenchers.

Rajya Sabha The upper house of India's Federal Parliament; the indirectly elected Council of States (see also *Lok Sabha*).

random sampling A polling method that involves canvassing people at random from the population; the opposite of stratified sampling.

rational choice The role of reason over emotion in human behavior. Political behavior, in this view, follows logical and even predictable patterns so long as we understand the key role of self-interest.

reasons of state The pragmatic basis for foreign policy that places the national interest above moral considerations or idealistic motives; also *raison d'état*.

recall Direct voting to remove an elected official from office.

rectification In Maoist China, the elimination of all purported capitalist traits, such as materialism and individualism.

referendum A vote through which citizens may directly repeal a law.

rehabilitation Education, training, and social conditioning aimed at encouraging imprisoned criminals to become normal, productive members of society when they are released.

Reign of Terror During the French Revolution, Robespierre and his Committee of Public Safety arrested and mass executed thousands of French citizens for the "crime" of opposing the revolution or daring to dissent.

republic A form of government in which sovereignty resides in the people of that country, rather than with the rulers. The vast majority of republics today are democratic or representative republics, meaning that sovereign power is exercised by elected representatives who are responsible to the citizenry.

reserved powers The reserved powers arise from the Tenth Amendment, which provides that powers not delegated to the federal government, "nor prohibited by it to the States, are reserved to the States respectively, or to the people."

retribution The punishment of criminals on the ground that they have done wrong and deserve to suffer as a consequence.

reverse discrimination In effect, going overboard in giving preferences to racial minorities and victims of gender discrimination in hiring, housing, and education; the U.S. Supreme Court has ruled that in some cases, affirmative action quotas are unconstitutional.

revolution A fundamental change in the rules and institutions that govern a society, often involving violent conflict in the form of mass action, insurrection, secession, or civil war.

Revolutionary War The American War of Independence (1775–1783).

right to revolution John Locke's theory that the end of government is the good of society and that when government deprives people of natural rights to life, liberty, and property, it is asking for trouble. If government fails to mend its ways, it deserves to be overthrown.

rule of law The concept that the power and discretion of government and its officials ought to be restrained by a supreme set of neutral rules that prevent arbitrary and unfair action by government; also called constitutionalism.

salami tactics The methods used by Vladimir Lenin to divide his opponents into small groups that could be turned against one another and easily overwhelmed.

Schengen area The visa-free zone within the EU, encompassing twenty-six countries and more than 400 million people who can now travel freely about Europe without being stopped at border-crossings.

Seabed Treaty An international agreement that forbids the establishment of nuclear weapons on the ocean floor beyond the twelve-mile territorial limit.

second strike Retaliation in kind against a nuclear attack(er); this capability paradoxically minimizes the likelihood that a nuclear confrontation will lead to a nuclear exchange.

Selective Service System The means by which the United States keeps a list of all individuals eligible for the draft; upon turning 18, male citizens between the ages of 18 and 25 are required by law to register within thirty days.

separation of powers The organization of government into distinct areas of legislative, executive, and judicial functions, each responsible to different constituencies and possessing its own powers and responsibilities; the system of dividing the governmental powers among three branches and giving each branch a unique role to play while making all three interdependent.

social contract A concept in political theory most often associated with Thomas Hobbes, Jean-Jacques Rousseau, and John Locke. The social contract is an implicit agreement among individuals to form a civil society and to accept certain moral and political obligations essential to its preservation.

socialism A public philosophy favoring social welfare and general prosperity over individual self-reliance and private wealth.

society An aggregation of individuals who share a common identity. Usually that identity is at least partially defined by geography because people who live in close proximity often know one another, enjoy shared experiences, speak the same language, and have similar values and interests.

soft money Campaign contributions to U.S. national party committees that do not have to be reported to the Federal Election Commission as long as the funds are not used to benefit a particular candidate; the national committees funnel the funds to state parties, which generally operate under less stringent reporting requirements. Critics argue that soft money is a massive loophole in the existing system of campaign finance regulation and that it amounts to a form of legalized corruption.

soft power The ability to get others to want what you want by example and moral suasion, as well as respect and admiration earned through the success of your ideas, institutions, and actions in the world.

sovereignty A government's capacity to assert supreme power successfully in a political state.

sovereign wealth funds A state-owned investment fund made up of financial assets such as stocks, bonds, precious metals, and property; such funds invest globally. China, for example, has invested huge sums in the United States via its sovereign wealth fund.

Special Economic Zones (SEZs) In the People's Republic of China SEZs are designed to attract foreign investment and facilitate trade with other countries by relaxing state-controls; enclaves where market forces are allowed to operate relatively free of state interference; taking a page out of China's playbook, India has also created SEZs in recent years, as have several other countries, including Egypt and Ethiopia.

special interests An organization or association that exists to further private interests in the political arena; examples in the United States are the U.S. Chamber of Commerce or the National Association of Manufacturers (business), the AFL-CIO (labor), and the National Farmers Organization (NFO).

state In its sovereign form, an independent political-administrative unit that successfully claims the allegiance of a given population, exercises a monopoly on the legitimate use of coercive force, and controls the territory inhabited by its citizens or subjects; in its other common form, a state is the major political-administrative subdivision of a federal system and, as such, is not sovereign but rather depends on the central authority (sometimes called the "national government") for resource allocations (tax transfers and grants), defense (military protection and emergency relief), and regulation of economic relations with other federal subdivisions (nonsovereign states) and external entities (sovereign states).

state-building The creation of political institutions capable of exercising authority and allocating resources effectively within a nation.

state capitalism An economy falling somewhere between a Soviet-style command economy and a Western-style market economy. The economy in Communist China after Mao is one contemporary example.

statecraft The art of leading in difficult times, promoting the common good, and protecting vital national interests while avoiding unnecessary conflict. The art of achieving political or strategic aims and objectives by force of example, persuasion, and the use of incentives rather than by coercion and threats; synonymous with *statesmanship* and *far-sighted diplomacy*.

stateless nation People (or nations) scattered over the territory of several states or dispersed widely and who have no autonomous, independent, or sovereign governing body of their own; examples of stateless nations include the Kurds, Palestinians, and Tibetans (see also *nation*).

state of nature The human condition before the creation of a social code of behavior and collective techniques to control normal human impulses.

statesman A political architect who creates new states, a peacemaker who resolves conflicts, or an orator who inspires the popular masses in times of national crisis. He or she is yesterday's founder, today's pathfinder, and tomorrow's legend.

state-sponsored terrorism International terrorism that is aided and abetted by an established state; for example, Libya was linked to many terrorist acts against Western countries until Muammar el-Qaddafi made peace overtures in December 2003 and before he became an international pariah all over again in 2011 in the face of a popular rebellion against his autocratic rule during the so-called Arab Revolution.

state terrorism Usually violent methods used by a government's security forces to intimidate and coerce its own people.

status quo strategy A national policy of maintaining the existing balance of power through collective security agreements, diplomacy, and negotiation, as well as through "legitimizing instruments," such as international law and international organizations.

Strategic Arms Reduction Treaty II (START II) A post–Cold War confidence-building treaty aimed at curbing strategic nuclear weapons negotiated between the United States and the former Soviet Union in 1993.

stratified sampling A manner of polling in which participants are chosen on the basis of age, income, socioeconomic background, and the like, so that the sample mirrors the larger population; the opposite of random sampling.

straw poll Unscientific survey; simple, inexpensive poll open to all sorts of manipulation and misuse.

submarine-launched ballistic missile (SLBM) Strategic missiles with multiple nuclear warheads launched from submarines that prowl the ocean depths and that cannot be easily detected or destroyed by a preemptive attack.

superpower A term that evolved in the context of the Cold War to denote the unprecedented destructive capabilities and global reach of the United States and the Soviet Union and to differentiate these two nuclear behemoths from the Great Powers that existed prior to the advent of the Nuclear Age.

Supremacy Clause Article VI, Section 2, of the Constitution, which declares that acts of Congress are "the Supreme law of the Land…binding on the Judges in every State."

surplus value Excessive profits created through workers' labor and pocketed by the capitalist or owning class.

sustainable growth A concept popular among environmentalists and liberal economists that emphasizes the need for economic strategies that take account of the high-cost and long-term impact on the environment (including global warming) of economic policies aimed at profit-maximization, current consumption, and the like.

symbolic speech Forms of expression other than words: for example, flag-burning, provocative gestures, black armbands, and the like.

terms of trade In international economics, the valuation (or price) of the products (commodities, manufactures, services) that countries buy on the world market relative to the valuation of the products they sell; for example, if manufactured goods are generally priced high relative to minerals and agricultural products, then the terms of trade are unfavorable for countries that produce only farm commodities or raw materials.

terrorism Politically or ideologically motivated violence aimed at public officials, business elites, and civilian populations designed to sow fear and dissension, destabilize societies, undermine established authority, induce policy changes, or even overthrow the existing government.

theocracy A state like present-day Iran in which religious leaders monopolize political power, legitimate authority derives from a common belief in one god, and there is no separation of church and state.

Third World Collectively, the developing nations of Asia, Africa, and Latin America, most of which were once European colonies; Third World nations tend to be poor and densely populated.

Tiananmen Square massacre In 1989, unarmed civilian workers and students marched in Tiananmen Square in Beijing to demand democratic freedom and government reforms. Army troops responded with force, killing 1,500 demonstrators and wounding another 10,000.

totalitarianism A political system in which every facet of the society, the economy, and the government is tightly controlled by the ruling elite. Secret police terrorism and a radical ideology implemented through mass mobilization and propaganda are hallmarks of the totalitarian state's methods and goals.

tracking poll Repeated sampling of voters to assess shifts in attitudes or behavior over time.

traditional societies A common term for often resource-poor societies that continue to observe pre-modern ways of life, work, and worship; often associated with high infant mortality rates, low life expectancy, poverty, illiteracy, hunger, and lack of the most basic medical services.

transnational terrorism Terrorist groups in different countries who cooperate with one another, or a group that crosses national boundaries to commit acts of terror.

Truman Doctrine President Harry Truman's pledge of U.S. support for any free people threatened with revolution by an internal armed minority or an outside aggressor.

trustee theory of representation The theory that elected officials should be leaders, making informed choices in the interest of their constituencies.

tyranny of the majority The condition arising when a dominant group uses its control of the government to abuse the rights of minority groups.

ultranationalism Extreme nationalism often associated with fascism; a radical right-wing orientation typically characterized by militarism, racial bigotry, and xenophobia.

unconditional surrender Giving an enemy on the verge of defeat a stark choice between surrendering immediately (placing itself entirely at the mercy of the victor) or being utterly destroyed.

unipolar system In international relations theory, the existence of a single invincible superpower; the international system said to have existed after the collapse of the Soviet Union left the United States as the sole remaining (and thus unrivaled) military and economic superpower on the world stage.

unitary system A form of government in which most or all power to make and enforce laws resides in the central government; opposite of a federal system.

USA Patriot Act A post-9/11 expansion of federal law-enforcement powers that greatly enlarged the powers of the executive branch to conduct domestic surveillance including warrantless wiretaps against U.S. citizens.

utopia Any visionary system embodying perfect political and social order.

war Organized violence, often on a large scale, involving sovereign states or geographic parts of the same state or distinct ethnic or social groups within a given state (civil war).

war by misperception Armed conflict that results when two nations fail to read each other's intentions accurately.

war crimes Violation of generally accepted rules of war as established in the Geneva Conventions on the conduct of war. The Geneva Conventions call for the humanitarian treatment of civilians and prisoners of war, and respect for human life and dignity; crimes against humanity, such as genocide and ethnic cleansing, are also war crimes.

war on terror After 9/11, President George W. Bush declared a worldwide "war on terrorism" aimed at defeating international terrorist organizations, destroying terrorist training camps, and bringing terrorists themselves to justice.

war powers The U.S. Constitution gives the Congress the power to raise and support armies, to provide and maintain a navy, to make rules regulating the armed forces, and to declare war; it makes the president the commander in chief of the armed forces.

Warsaw Pact A military alliance between the former Soviet Union and its satellite states, created in 1955, which established a unified military command and allowed the Soviet army to maintain large garrisons within the satellite states, ostensibly to defend them from outside attack.

Weimar Republic The constitutional democracy founded in Germany at the end of World War I by a constitutional convention convened in 1919 at the city of Weimar; associated with a period of political and economic turmoil, it ended when Hitler came to power in 1933.

welfare state A state whose government is concerned with providing for the social welfare of its citizens and does so usually with specific public policies, such as health insurance, minimum wages, and housing subsidies.

winner-takes-all system Electoral system in which the candidate receiving the most votes wins.

withering away of the state A Marxist category of analysis describing what happens after capitalism is overthrown, private property and social classes are abolished, and the need for coercive state power supposedly disappears.

World Court Also known as the International Court of Justice, the principal judicial organ of the United Nations; the Court hears any case brought before it by parties who voluntarily accept its jurisdiction.

Zionism The movement whose genesis was in the reestablishment, and now the support, of the Jewish national state of Israel. The national movement for the return of the Jewish people to the land of Abraham and the resumption of Jewish sovereignty in what is now known as Israel.

INDEX

NOTE: Locators in bold refer to definitions; page numbers followed by *f* and *t* indicate figures and tables, respectively.